Payroll Accounting 2020

Sixth Edition

Jeanette M. Landin, Ed.D., M.B.A.
Landmark College

Paulette Schirmer, D.B.A., M.B.A.
University of Alaska Southeast

PAYROLL ACCOUNTING 2020

This book is printed on acid-free paper.

1 2 3 4 5 6 7 8 9 LWI 21 20 19

ISBN 978-1-260-24796-1 (bound edition)
MHID 1-260-24796-1 (bound edition)
ISBN 978-1-260-48108-2 (loose-leaf edition)
MHID 1-260-48108-5 (loose-leaf edition)
ISSN 2373-2644

Executive Portfolio Manager: *Steve Schuetz*
Product Developers: *Alexandra Kukla, Sarah Sacco*
Marketing Manager: *Claire McLemore*
Lead Content Project Managers: *Jill Eccher, Brian Nacik*
Senior Buyer: *Sandy Ludovissy*
Design: *Jessica Cuevas*
Content Licensing Specialists: *Melissa Homer, Lorraine Buczek*
Content Licensing Specialist: *Beth Cray*
Cover Image: *Shutterstock/Venomous Vector*
Compositor: *SPi Global*

mheducation.com/highered

About the Authors

©Tom Raffelt

Jeanette Landin

Landmark College

Jeanette Landin is an Associate Professor of business and accounting at Landmark College in Putney, Vermont, where she teaches undergraduate accounting and business courses to an at-risk student population. She is a baccalaureate student advisor and directs a short-term program to help students develop their study skills. Dr. Landin earned her BA degree from the University of California at Irvine before receiving her MBA and EdD from the University of Phoenix, where she conducted research into college success strategies for at-risk students. She has earned master's certificates in accounting and in autism spectrum disorders.

Dr. Landin is an active member of the Institute for Management Accountants (IMA), Teachers of Accounting Curriculum at Two-Year Colleges (TACTYC), the Association of Certified Fraud Examiners (ACFE), and Vermont Women in Higher Education (VWHE), and she previously served as an active member of the California Business Educators Association and the Western Business Educators Association. Dr. Landin served as the Chair of the IMA's Committee for Academic Relations and as a peer reviewer for the American Accounting Association. She is a peer reviewer for the *Transnational Journal of Business* and a member of the Business Editorial Board with the Multimedia Educational Resource for Learning and Online Teaching (MERLOT).

©Ryan Kauzlarich

Paulette Schirmer

University of Alaska Southwest

Paulette Schirmer is an accountant with the Division of Finance for the State of Alaska, where she works as the statewide training coordinator and assists with the development and troubleshooting of the reporting system for the accounting program. Dr. Schirmer is active in the preparation of Alaska's Comprehensive Annual Financial Report and assists as needed with the budgetary and departmental accounting and structure training.

Dr. Schirmer also works with the University of Alaska Southeast as an online instructor for its accounting courses. She received her BS in accounting from Metropolitan State College of Denver (now Metropolitan State University of Denver), her MBA from Regis University, and her DBA from University of Phoenix, where she conducted research on globalization strategies for small businesses.

Dedications

The authors dedicate this book to the following individuals:

For Chris, Kierstan, and Meaghan, who are the center of my universe, and for Dad, who believed in me until the very end.

—Jeanette Landin

For Royce and Elizabeth, who kept me grounded and reminded me to have fun. For Christina, who remind me to stop and breathe.

—Paulette Schirmer

A Note from the Authors

We are excited to share the new edition of *Payroll Accounting 2020* with you. Payroll accounting is detailed, deadline driven, and of utmost importance for the successful functioning of a business. The changing, detailed nature of payroll accounting involves legal challenges, economic changes, technological advances, and—above all—governmental obligations. Our text takes a modern approach to payroll accounting, incorporating coverage of real-world issues that students will face in their careers, such as cybersecurity, payroll fraud, labor planning, and labor costs. We believe that this information contributes to a comprehensive understanding of payroll accounting in the 21st century and that it will make accounting students more valuable to the organizations they work for in their careers.

But as educators, we understand that providing the content is not enough, so we provide multiple opportunities for students to practice in Connect. Whether you are teaching face-to-face, hybrid, or online, *Payroll Accounting 2020* is flexible enough to be used in courses as short as 3 weeks and as long as 15 weeks. We are proud of what we have accomplished with this text, and we thank the faculty and students who have provided feedback to help shape the content in this edition. We strongly believe that we have taken payroll accounting education to a higher level of rigor.

Our approach to payroll accounting is different from other existing texts because of our perspective about payroll's role in business. To us, payroll is more than pressing buttons, writing checks, and submitting forms—payroll is the story of **people**. These people include the ones within the business who make decisions about the company's directions and the people who work for the business and depend on their paychecks to support their livelihoods. We wrote this text because we wanted students to develop a sense of how business directly affects employees' lives.

To foster the connection between business and people, each chapter's introductory story contains recent events involving payroll accounting that highlight the connections among payroll, legislation, business decisions, and people affected by all the decisions made. In Chapter 1 and Chapter 2, we highlighted specific challenges to the Affordable Care Act and to the treatment of independent contractors under the Personal Responsibility and Work Opportunity Act. In Chapter 3, we explored the challenge of paying long-distance truck drivers a minimum wage and recognition if their actual hours worked. The Chapter 4 introduction highlights what is becoming the hottest fringe benefit for employees: employer contributions toward payment of student loans that have been authorized by the IRS. Chapter 5 contains a comparison of employee pay increases and employee health insurance premium costs over time, which reveals a disturbing fact that net pay simply has not kept pace with employee health insurance costs. In Chapter 6, we explore the effect of climate change on payroll costs, adding another dimension to the climate change debate. Finally, our Chapter 7 introduction highlights a large-scale accounting fraud that occurred in a small town and that affected everything from town projects to payroll.

What makes this text a modern approach is that we believe that payroll is the connection between financial and managerial accounting and that it has everyday connections to businesses, people, and the greater economy in a myriad of ways. Our approach is to encourage students to know the **how** of computing payroll as well as the **why** because we believe strongly that the future of the accounting profession involves knowledge of both the process and the purpose within the broader scheme of business. We have included materials to demonstrate the integration of payroll in other aspects of both managerial and financial accounting as well as business operations. Within Appendixes D and E, we have provided information that allows readers to connect their learning about payroll within the context of their own state's legal framework and links to each state's revenue department to facilitate specific learning. We are passionate about college education because we are both accounting faculty, and we bring a wealth of experience in accounting, education, industry, and governmental settings that informs our writing.

Our text features many interesting real-world connections. We've drawn examples from many different disciplines to help make payroll accounting come alive for teachers and students alike. We want to call specific attention to two discussions that are unique to our text: (1) the content in Chapter 6 that explores labor planning (Learning Objectives 6-5 and 6-6) and (2) the discussion in Chapter 7 about the function of labor costs in business and employee benefit reports as strategic tools (Learning Objectives 7-5 and 7-6). We believe that this information contributes to a comprehensive understanding of payroll accounting in the 21st century and that it will make accounting students more valuable as emerging accountants embarking upon their careers.

We strongly believe that payroll accounting needs to be applied, so we provide both a continuing problem, located at the end of each chapter, and a comprehensive problem, located in Appendix A, that may be presented in either three-month or one-month versions. Technological integration of the continuing problem and Appendix A within Connect provides an excellent tool for student learning and faculty assessment of course learning objectives. SmartBook 2.0, LearnSmart, and guided example videos of tax-form completion lead to reinforcement of both concepts and key terminology. We are excited to produce this work through McGraw-Hill because of its top-quality teaching and learning resources available through Connect. Teaching traditional payroll accounting and Internet-based financial accounting via McGraw-Hill's Connect platform for several years has been a wonderful experience for both our students and ourselves.

The AACSB guidelines encourage achievement of the highest possible standards in business education. We believe that students should understand both how payroll should be completed as well as how it can be manipulated for personal gain. Payroll fraud continues to be a major source of loss for companies, and it is surprising to find how common it is. We've included examples of the frauds that employees have perpetrated in recent years. According to the Government Accounting Office, payroll fraud of all types, including misclassification of workers, costs the federal government $16 billion annually. We hope that these stories enliven and enrich class discussion. We've also updated our ethical framework in Chapter 1 to reflect an accurate representation of the ethical issues that payroll accountants face (Learning Objective 1-3) and in Chapter 2 about internal controls (Learning Objective 2-5) to teach students how to prevent payroll fraud and to identify potential data breaches. We believe that this information about internal controls will become increasingly important as sensitive personnel information becomes more readily accessible with the increased use of cloud-based payroll systems.

Another new piece in this edition is a discussion of how cryptocurrency is starting to affect payroll (Learning Objective 5-6) and how one state is already accepting Bitcoin as method for remitting taxes. It is important to understand that cryptocurrency as a means of paying employees, while being considered, is a complicated issue because of its connection to the stock market, as opposed to a central bank, as a basis for its value. This topic is evolving and we are certain that we will witness the evolution of pay methods that will involve some sort of cryptocurrency in the future.

We continue to rely on the guidance of our colleagues, instructor feedback, and student suggestions to keep us grounded and to push us to deliver the best possible content. We hope you enjoy reading this book as much as we enjoy writing it!

Jeanette Landin
Paulette Schirmer

Changes to the Sixth Edition

Based on feedback from our reviewers and users, we have included additional content in this sixth edition of *Payroll Accounting*. During the process of updating the content for the sixth edition, we expanded our coverage of fringe benefits as an employer issue, which is the sole focus of Chapter 4. We explored pre-tax deductions and qualified Section 125 cafeteria plans, and we discussed excluded fringe benefits and valuation rules with a specific focus on the effects of the Tax Cuts and Jobs Act, which we covered in Chapter 1. Employee net pay and pay methods have now been moved to a separate chapter (Chapter 5). We added video links to the end-of-chapter materials to help students learn the concepts presented in each chapter in multiple formats.

We have maintained our content about payroll certification exams available. A correlation guide is included in Appendix F that aligns the learning objectives in the text with the topics included on payroll certification examinations offered by the National Association of Certified Professional Bookkeepers (NACPB), the American Institute of Professional Bookkeepers (AIPB), and the American Payroll Association (APA).

We appreciate all feedback and user recommendations we have received because they have helped us create a stronger, more complete text. The changes we have made have added clarity, updated information, and given additional opportunities for students to demonstrate their understanding of the concepts presented.

The following are specific changes to each chapter.

Chapter 1

In Chapter 1, we updated payroll-related legislation to reflect as many changes as possible prior to publication. We addressed the repeal of the Affordable Care Act by a federal judge in Texas and related appeals in process at the time of print, as well as 2018-specific changes to the ACA. We have expanded the explanation of disabilities and accommodations provided by the Americans with Disabilities Act. We refined our ethics code and expanded it to include concepts from the IMA and the ACCA in their respective codes of ethics. We added a discussion of online banks and online-based payroll and banking services. We expanded our explanation of Certified Payroll requirements to offer more depth to the section.

Chapter 2

Chapter 2 now contains an explanation of the purpose of H-1B visas. We updated the graph depicting the trend of average hours worked per week. We expanded the explanation of leased employees and explained the connection of leased employees to the Tax Cuts and Jobs Act. We included a link to the Massachusetts Institute of Technology's living wage calculator to help explain the difference between minimum wage and living wage. We clarified the purpose of cross-training employees within the accounting department to offer breadth of understanding and to help prevent fraud. We included a proposed action plan in the event of payroll data breaches. We clarified state termination guidelines to include resignation guidelines as they pertain to payroll and final paycheck regulations.

Chapter 3

Chapter 3 opens with updated minimum wage and tipped minimum wage information. We discussed the change to the tipped minimum wage in the District of Columbia, which has different guidelines from other parts of the United States. We included information about changes to the Department of Labor rules regarding sleep time for household employees. We addressed situations in which FLSA violations have occurred in terms of overtime compensation and mandatory breaks. We presented information about mandatory paid breaks for emergency personnel and about the effects of retroactive pay for faculty.

Chapter 4

We have expanded the discussion of fringe benefits in Chapter 4. Since fringe benefits are an increasingly important deciding factor for prospective employees, especially because such benefits affect employee morale, it is important to note that those seemingly "free" fringe benefits are actually subject to income taxes. We discussed that certain states consider paid time of such as sick and vacation time as fringe benefits and include that time in taxable income computations, regardless of the employee's use of the time. We addressed the *de minimis* doctrine and how certain employers have attempted to apply the *de minimis* doctrine to requests for employees work while not "on the clock."

We presented a side-by-side comparison of FSA and HSA plans to facilitate student understanding. We discussed that many IRS audits of employers stem from their reporting—and often the underreporting—of fringe benefits

Chapter 5

Chapter 5 contains expanded information about the thresholds for the Additional Medicare Tax related to the Affordable Care Act. We included a discussion of monies withheld for Social Security tax and compared it to the average payout in Social Security benefits. We explored the reduction of payroll-related state income taxes in certain areas that were designed to inject state revenues through other means, such as housing. We explained electronic income withholding orders (e-IWOs) as a means of communicating required employee garnishments to employers. We concluded the chapter with a discussion of cryptocurrency's involvement in payroll and one state's use of cryptocurrency as a means of remitting employer payroll taxes.

Chapter 6

In Chapter 6, we updated employer payroll tax information and all tax forms with the current year's editions. We expanded our presentation of state and local tax remittances and included examples of completed state and local tax return forms to prepare students for real-world situations. We included a discussion of employer hiring costs per employee and the training costs for new employees. We discussed the penalty for willfully not depositing employee-share payroll taxes, as mandated by IRS code. We concluded the chapter with a discussion of the purpose of completing benefit analysis reports within the context of industry partners and company strategy.

Chapter 7

Chapter 7 explores the need for payroll accountants during a time when artificial intelligence (AI) is increasing its role in the accounting process. We highlighted the shift in the payroll accountant's duties to involve less data entry and more data and trend analysis. We discussed the effect of payroll issues, such as those experienced during the partial government shutdown of 2019, on both the employees and the other entities that are affected by payroll. We expanded our explanation of the basic financial statements to connect them more explicitly to payroll accounting. We concluded the chapter with a discussion of how the Internet of Things (IoT) affects payroll, especially as it relates to report generation and accurate financial reports. We have streamlined the overall view of the payroll process from beginning to end to provide students with a concise guide to completing payroll.

Appendix A: Comprehensive Payroll Project

In Appendix A, we continued the emphasis on completion of the payroll register and the transfer of data to both employees' earnings records and accounting entries. Students have all of the federal and state forms required for year-end and ACA compliance reporting.

Appendix C: Federal Income Tax Tables

We updated both the percentage and the wage-bracket methods of determining federal income tax withholding to reflect the most current tax rates available.

Appendix D: State Income Tax Information

We updated the tax rates for each state in Appendix D.

Appendix F: Payroll Certification Information

We continued correlating the learning objectives in this text with the topics included on payroll certification examinations offered by the National Association of Certified Professional Bookkeepers (NACPB), the American Institute of Professional Bookkeepers (AIPB), and the American Payroll Association (APA). We included the certification exam requirements and contact information for each certification organization.

Text Features

Chapter Opener

Each chapter opens by focusing on a payroll accounting topic related to a real-world company to set the stage for the topic of the chapter.

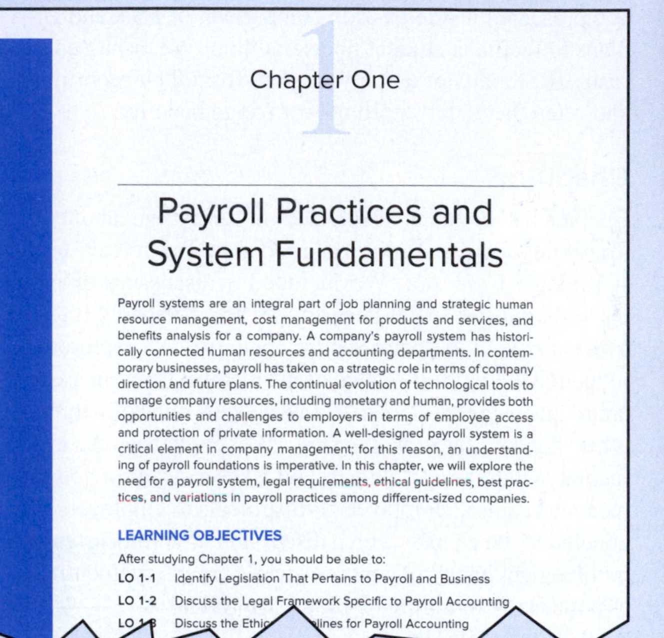

Chapter One

1

Payroll Practices and System Fundamentals

Payroll systems are an integral part of job planning and strategic human resource management, cost management for products and services, and benefits analysis for a company. A company's payroll system has historically connected human resources and accounting departments. In contemporary businesses, payroll has taken on a strategic role in terms of company direction and future plans. The continual evolution of technological tools to manage company resources, including monetary and human, provides both opportunities and challenges to employers in terms of employee access and protection of private information. A well-designed payroll system is a critical element in company management; for this reason, an understanding of payroll foundations is imperative. In this chapter, we will explore the need for a payroll system, legal requirements, ethical guidelines, best practices, and variations in payroll practices among different-sized companies.

LEARNING OBJECTIVES

After studying Chapter 1, you should be able to:

LO 1-1 Identify Legislation That Pertains to Payroll and Business

LO 1-2 Discuss the Legal Framework Specific to Payroll Accounting

LO 1-3 Discuss the Ethic[illegible]lines for Payroll Accounting

Stop & Check

The Stop & Check feature allows students to review their understanding of the content just read. It also enables instructors to conduct formative assessments at multiple points throughout each chapter, testing the students' understanding informally as well as offering opportunities to expand on the material.

Which Law?

Stop & Check

1. Requires employers to verify the employee's legal right to work in the United States?
2. Protects the rights of disabled workers?
3. Governs the management of retirement plans?
4. Protects discrimination of workers older than age 40?
5. Creates safe work environments for employees?
6. Mandates equal pay for equal work?
7. Extends medical benefits for terminated employees?
8. Ensures that child support obligations will be paid?
9. Protects workers and families with preexisting medical conditions?
10. Enforces payment of monetary damages because of discrimination?
11. Requires internal controls on payroll practices of public companies?

a. COBRA
b. ERISA
c. Civil Rights Act of 1991
d. PRWOR
e. SOX
f. ADEA
g. HIPAA
h. ADA
i. OSHA
j. Equal Pay Act of 1963
k. IRCA

Trends to Watch

Each chapter contains a feature box that connects payroll-related recent events with industry trends that shape the future of the profession. These trends offer instructors more opportunities to expand upon chapter topics, fostering discussion and application.

Trends to Watch

LEGAL ENVIRONMENT

To say that the legal environment of payroll is continually evolving is an understatement. Since 2016, we have witnessed the following legal challenges:

- Increasing numbers of private employers and localities raising the minimum wage significantly to close the gap between the minimum wage and the living wage.
- Changes to fringe benefits and state taxation of transportation benefits.
- Supplemental wage rate changes for payments of bonuses.
- State enforcement of predictive scheduling, fair/flexible scheduling laws on changing employee's schedules.
- Reframing the federal income tax structure, treatment for nonresident aliens, supplemental wage withholding rates, and inflation adjustments.

Some trends to watch include the following:

- Changes to the Affordable Care Act, up to and possibly including repeal.
- The expansion of artificial intelligence (AI) into the payroll process.
- Continued increase of data privacy initiatives at the company, state, and federal levels.
- Federally mandated paid leave provisions for both sick and bereavement time that would affect all companies in the nation.
- Acceleration in businesses moving to a completely cloud-based operations management and payroll process.

End-of-Chapter Assessments

Students can demonstrate their understanding through assessments designed to complement the chapter's learning objectives. Each chapter has review questions, exercises, and problems, with the exercises and problems having two sets each chapter (Set A and Set B). Each type of assessment is designed to measure student learning as follows:

- Questions for review are designed to check for students' remembrance of concepts.
- Exercises check for understanding and application of chapter concepts.
- Problems allow students to apply and analyze payroll accounting principles.

Exercises Set A

E1-1A. LO 1-1, 1-2 Lupore Fabrics obtained a contract in Watts Mills, South Carolina that involves the production of materials for military uniforms, a project contracted with the federal government for $2,800,000. What laws govern the wages Lupore Fabrics pays to its workers for this project? (Select all that may apply.)
1. Davis–Bacon Act
2. Sarbanes–Oxley Act
3. Walsh–Healey Act
4. FLSA

E1-2A. LO 1-1, 1-2 Martine Piccirillo works as the payroll clerk for Centinix, a security company that hires many part-time and temporary workers who are paid on an hourly basis. What law governs the hiring or documenting of these workers?
1. ADEA
2. FLSA
3. IRCA
4. USERR

Critical Thinking Exercises

Want to challenge your students further? The Critical Thinking Exercises require students to consider complex real-world situations that build confidence and turn learning into mastery. These exercises offer possibilities for team presentations or class debate.

Critical Thinking

CT1-1. You have been hired as a consultant for Dynozz Medical Software, whi an IRS audit of its accounting records. During your review, you notice in the payroll system involving overpayments of labor and paymen nated employees. What should you do?

CT1-2. Liliya Milic is the accountant for Syiva, a local nonprofit organization. Sh tasked with managing the costs of the payroll so that staffing levels r the same even if funding levels change. She considers outsourcing th a payroll processing company. What are some factors that Liliya shou in her decision? Why are these factors important?

In the Real World: Scenarios for Discussion

Each chapter contains a discussion scenario that is drawn from real-world events. These scenarios encourage the expansion of chapter content and allow students to apply their learning to real situations.

In the Real World: Scenario for Discussion

Domino's Pizza franchises in New York were sued by the state of New York in 201 wage theft at 10 stores. Under New York law, a corporation and a franchiser are employers if they meet certain criteria regarding employee control. The state found Domino's met the criteria for being a joint employer because it mandates a signif number of policies with which franchisers must comply. The problem arose when Dom

Internet Activities

The Internet Activities at the end of each chapter offer students the chance to use their web navigation skills to expand on their learning. These exercises attract tech-savvy learners, allowing them to form their own understanding of payroll concepts on their own terms.

Internet Activities

1-1. Using the website www.jstor.org, search for articles about payroll-related laws or relevant employment legislation. Once you find an article, summarize the article, and explain how the legislation influenced contemporary payroll practices.

1-2. Visit the website of the American Payroll Association at www.americanpayroll.org. On the right side of the Home page, you will find articles about recent developments in payroll practices and legislation. Choose an article and create a presentation to your class about how its content affects payroll practice.

1-3. Want to know more about the specifics of some of the concepts in this chapter? Check out these websites:

Continuing Payroll Project: Prevosti Farms and Sugarhouse

slanc/Shutterstock

Toni Prevosti is opening a new business, Prevosti Farms ar Sugarhouse, which is a small company that will harvest, refine, and se maple syrup products. In subsequent chapters, students will have th opportunity to establish payroll records and complete payroll inform tion for Prevosti Farms and Sugarhouse.

Toni has decided that she needs to hire employees for the business to grow. Complete th application for Prevosti Farms and Sugarhouse's Employer Identification Number (Form ss- with the following information:

Prevosti Farms and Sugarhouse is located at 820 Westminster Road, Bridgewater, Vermor 05520 (which is also Ms. Prevosti's home address), phone number 802-555-345 Bridgewater is in Windsor County. Toni, the responsible party for a Limited Liability Corporatio

Continuing Payroll Project: Prevosti Farms and Sugarhouse

Starting with Chapter 1, each chapter has an integrated, continuing payroll project—about a fictional company Prevosti Farms and Sugarhouse—that matches the chapter content and affords students a macro-level understanding of how each piece of payroll fits together.

Comprehensive Payroll Project: Wayland Custom Woodworking

The Comprehensive Payroll Project (Appendix A) allows students to track a quarter's worth of payroll transactions for a company. This Comprehensive Payroll Project offers instructors increased flexibility in teaching and assessment by offering a simulation equivalent to a full quarter of a fictitious company's payroll activities, including payroll transactions, pay processing, and tax form completion. The Comprehensive Payroll Project may be presented in different lengths—as short as one month or in its three-month entirety—to meet curricular needs. Instructors may assign this in connection with many chapters of the book or use it as a final project for their courses.

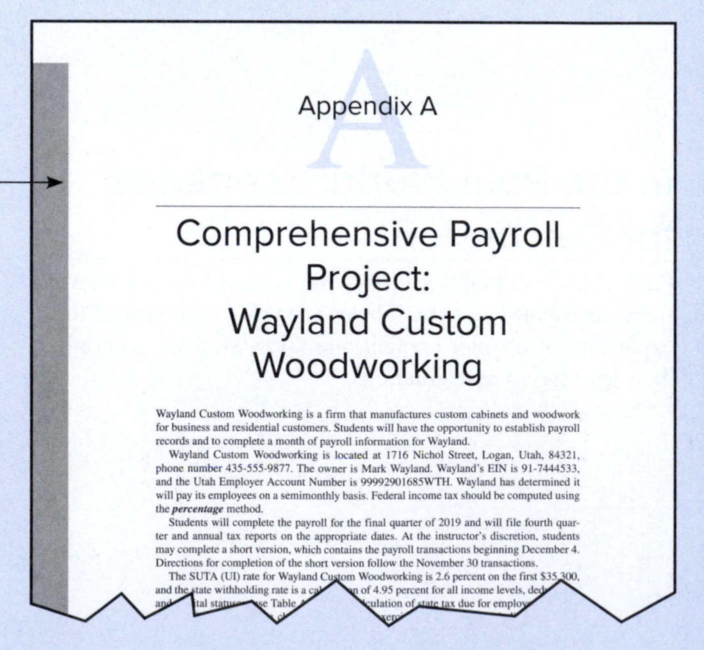

Appendix A

Comprehensive Payroll Project: Wayland Custom Woodworking

Wayland Custom Woodworking is a firm that manufactures custom cabinets and woodwork for business and residential customers. Students will have the opportunity to establish payroll records and to complete a month of payroll information for Wayland.

Wayland Custom Woodworking is located at 1716 Nichol Street, Logan, Utah, 84321, phone number 435-555-9877. The owner is Mark Wayland. Wayland's EIN is 91-7444533, and the Utah Employer Account Number is 99992901685WTH. Wayland has determined it will pay its employees on a semimonthly basis. Federal income tax should be computed using the *percentage* method.

Students will complete the payroll for the final quarter of 2019 and will file fourth quarter and annual tax reports on the appropriate dates. At the instructor's discretion, students may complete a short version, which contains the payroll transactions beginning December 4. Directions for completion of the short version follow the November 30 transactions.

The SUTA (UI) rate for Wayland Custom Woodworking is 2.6 percent on the first $35,300, and the state withholding rate is a ca... of 4.95 percent for all income levels, de...

Connect for *Payroll Accounting 2020*

- **SmartBook 2.0®** A personalized and adaptive learning tool used to maximize the learning experience by helping students study more efficiently and effectively. Smartbook 2.0 highlights where in the chapter to focus, asks review questions on the materials covered and tracks the most challenging content for later review recharge. Smartbook 2.0 is available both online and offline.
- **End-of-Chapter** Content is a robust offering of review and question material designed to aid and assess the student's retention of chapter content. The end-of-chapter content is composed of both static and algorithmic exercises, problems, critical thinking exercises, and continuing payroll projects, which are designed to challenge students using McGraw-Hill Education's state-of-the-art online homework technology. Guided example videos are also provided with select end-of-chapter problems, which help walk students through complex payroll processes. Instructors can also assign test bank questions to students in both static and algorithmic versions.
- **Auto-Graded Payroll and Tax Forms** are integrated into Connect and are assignable. Students can complete the forms in these problems to gain a better understanding of how payroll forms are prepared in today's digital world.
- **Guided example videos** are also provided with select end-of-chapter problems, which help walk students through complex payroll processes. Instructors can also assign test bank questions to students in both static and algorithmic versions.
- The **Comprehensive Payroll Project** from Appendix A is available on Connect in an auto-graded format. Students will apply skills, such as preparing tax forms and payroll registers, to complete the payroll process for a company from start to finish. Instructors can choose from the full three-month version or the shorter one-month version for their Connect assignment.
- **The Test Bank** for each chapter has been updated for the sixth edition to stay current with new and revised chapter material, with all questions available for assignment through Connect. Newly available within Connect, Test Builder is a cloud-based tool that enables instructors to format tests that can be printed or administered within a LMS. Test Builder offers a modern, streamlined interface for easy content configuration that matches course needs, without requiring a download. Test Builder provides a secure interface for better protection of content and allows for just-in-time updates to flow directly into assessments.

Auto-Graded Forms

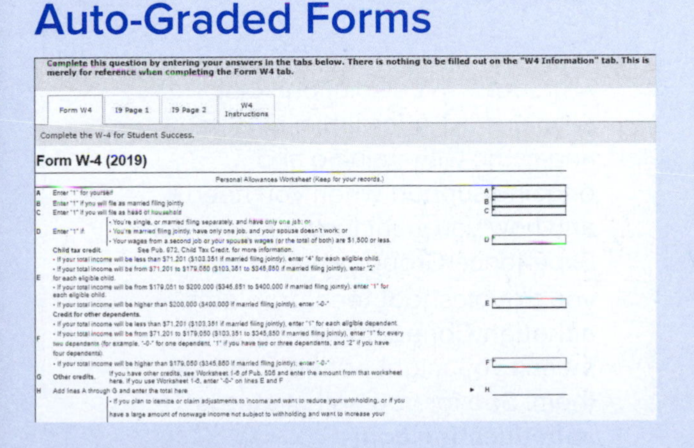

Complete this question by entering your answers in the tabs below. There is nothing to be filled out on the "W4 Information" tab. This is merely for reference when completing the Form W4 tab.

Form W4 | I9 Page 1 | I9 Page 2 | W4 Instructions

Complete the W-4 for Student Success.

Form W-4 (2019)

Personal Allowances Worksheet (Keep for your records.)

A Enter "1" for yourself — A
B Enter "1" if you will file as married filing jointly — B
C Enter "1" if you will file as head of household — C
D Enter "1" if: • You're single, or married filing separately, and have only one job; or • You're married filing jointly, have only one job, and your spouse doesn't work; or • Your wages from a second job or your spouse's wages (or the total of both) are $1,500 or less. — D
E Child tax credit. See Pub. 972, Child Tax Credit, for more information.
• If your total income will be less than $71,201 ($103,351 if married filing jointly), enter "4" for each eligible child.
• If your total income will be from $71,201 to $179,050 ($103,351 to $345,850 if married filing jointly), enter "2" for each eligible child.
• If your total income will be from $179,051 to $200,000 ($345,851 to $400,000 if married filing jointly), enter "1" for each eligible child.
• If your total income will be higher than $200,000 ($400,000 if married filing jointly), enter "-0-" — E
F Credit for other dependents.
• If your total income will be less than $71,201 ($103,351 if married filing jointly), enter "1" for each eligible dependent.
• If your total income will be from $71,201 to $179,050 ($103,351 to $345,850 if married filing jointly), enter "1" for every two dependents (for example, "-0-" for one dependent, "1" if you have two or three dependents, and "2" if you have four dependents).
• If your total income will be higher than $179,050 ($345,850 if married filing jointly), enter "-0-" — F
G Other credits. If you have other credits, see Worksheet 1-6 of Pub. 505 and enter the amount from that worksheet here. If you use Worksheet 1-6, enter "-0-" on lines E and F
H Add lines A through G and enter the total here ► H
• If you plan to itemize or claim adjustments to income and want to reduce your withholding, or if you have a large amount of nonwage income not subject to withholding and want to increase your

Comprehensive Payroll Project

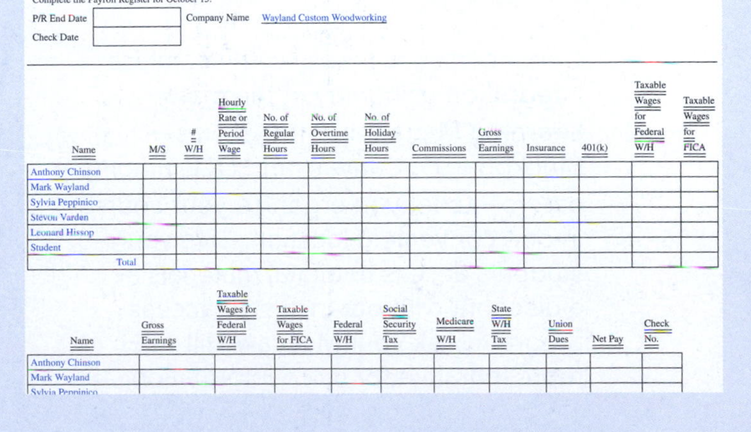

Complete the Payroll Register for October 15.

P/R End Date
Check Date
Company Name Wayland Custom Woodworking

Name	M/S	# W/H	Hourly Rate or Period Wage	No. of Regular Hours	No. of Overtime Hours	No. of Holiday Hours	Commissions	Gross Earnings	Insurance	401(k)	Taxable Wages for Federal W/H	Taxable Wages for FICA
Anthony Chinson												
Mark Wayland												
Sylvia Peppinico												
Stevon Varden												
Leonard Hissop												
Student												
Total												

Name	Gross Earnings	Taxable Wages for Federal W/H	Taxable Wages for FICA	Federal W/H	Social Security Tax	Medicare W/H	State W/H Tax	Union Dues	Net Pay	Check No.
Anthony Chinson										
Mark Wayland										
Sylvia Peppinico										

FOR INSTRUCTORS

You're in the driver's seat.

Want to build your own course? No problem. Prefer to use our turnkey, prebuilt course? Easy. Want to make changes throughout the semester? Sure. And you'll save time with Connect's auto-grading too.

65%
Less Time Grading

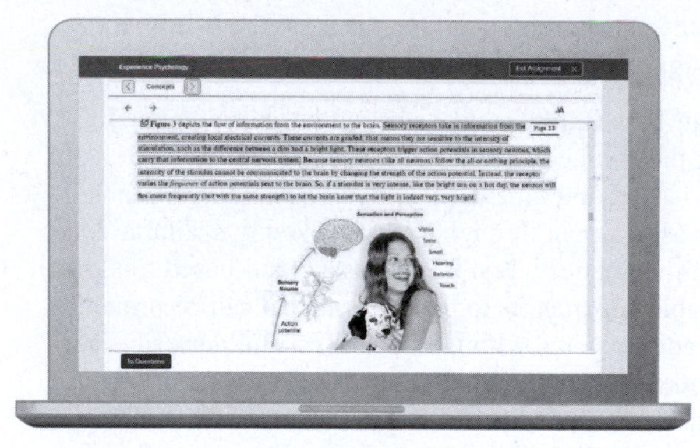

Laptop: McGraw-Hill Education

They'll thank you for it.

Adaptive study resources like SmartBook® 2.0 help your students be better prepared in less time. You can transform your class time from dull definitions to dynamic debates. Find out more about the powerful personalized learning experience available in SmartBook 2.0 at **www.mheducation.com/highered/connect/smartbook**

Make it simple, make it affordable.

Connect makes it easy with seamless integration using any of the major Learning Management Systems—Blackboard®, Canvas, and D2L, among others—to let you organize your course in one convenient location. Give your students access to digital materials at a discount with our inclusive access program. Ask your McGraw-Hill representative for more information.

Padlock: Jobalou/Getty Images

Solutions for your challenges.

A product isn't a solution. Real solutions are affordable, reliable, and come with training and ongoing support when you need it and how you want it. Our Customer Experience Group can also help you troubleshoot tech problems—although Connect's 99% uptime means you might not need to call them. See for yourself at **status.mheducation.com**

Checkmark: Jobalou/Getty Images

FOR STUDENTS

Effective, efficient studying.

Connect helps you be more productive with your study time and get better grades using tools like SmartBook 2.0, which highlights key concepts and creates a personalized study plan. Connect sets you up for success, so you walk into class with confidence and walk out with better grades.

Study anytime, anywhere.

Download the free ReadAnywhere app and access your online eBook or SmartBook 2.0 assignments when it's convenient, even if you're offline. And since the app automatically syncs with your eBook and SmartBook 2.0 assignments in Connect, all of your work is available every time you open it. Find out more at **www.mheducation.com/readanywhere**

"I really liked this app—it made it easy to study when you don't have your text-book in front of you."

— Jordan Cunningham,
Eastern Washington University

Calendar: owattaphotos/Getty Images

No surprises.

The Connect Calendar and Reports tools keep you on track with the work you need to get done and your assignment scores. Life gets busy; Connect tools help you keep learning through it all.

Learning for everyone.

McGraw-Hill works directly with Accessibility Services Departments and faculty to meet the learning needs of all students. Please contact your Accessibility Services office and ask them to email **accessibility@mheducation.com**, or visit **www.mheducation.com/about/accessibility** for more information.

Top: Jenner Images/Getty Images, Left: Hero Images/Getty Images, Right: Hero Images/Getty Images

Acknowledgments

This sixth edition of *Payroll Accounting* would not have been possible without the patience, guidance, and encouragement of Steve Schuetz, executive portfolio manager; the diligence and commitment of Allie Kukla and Sarah Sacco, product developers; the support and leadership of Jill Eccher and Brian Nacik, content project managers; the incredible form templates designed by Kitty O'Donnell; and the amazing artwork of Jessica Cuevas, designer. We further want to thank Claire McLemore, marketing manager; Beth Cray, content licensing specialist; Kevin Moran, director of digital content; Xin Lin, lead product manager; and the composition team at SPi Global. Thanks go to our project development team who handled every formatting request with professionalism. Special thanks to Danica Olson, Milwaukee Area Technical College, for her contributions to verify the accuracy of our content.

Countless other colleagues have offered their feedback, insights, and inspiration during various stages of this project. We want to extend sincere thanks to the reviewers who helped us shape the sixth edition:

Annette Frank
Mott Community College

April Mohr
Jefferson Community and Technical College

Cameron Lee
Cape Fear Community College

Carmela Gordon
Trident Technical College

Carol Rogers
Central New Mexico Community College

Carolyn Strauch
Crowder College

Corey Frad
Muscatine Community College

Erica Beam
Modesto Junior College

Gay Lynn Brown
Northwest Florida State College

Ira Hickam
Kaskaskia College

Ivan Lowe
York Technical College

James Murray
Western Technical College

Jana Hosmer
Blue Ridge Community College

Janice Akao
Butler County Community College

Jeanine Metzler
North Hampton Community College

Jennifer Stauffer
Minneapolis Community & Technical College

Jerrilyn Eisenhauer
Tulsa Community College

John Livingston
Rhodes State College

Joseph Nicassio
Westmoreland County Community College

Kathy Adams McIntosh
Antonelli College

Kim Gatzke
Delgado Community College

Kimberley Hurt
Central Community College

Kirk Lynch
Sand Hills Community College

Kou Yang
Northcentral Technical College

Larry Ardner
Stark State College

Lina Fedynyshyn
Emily Griffith Technical College

M. Jeff Quinlan
Madison College

Marilyn Ciolino
Delgado Community College

Marina Grau
Houston Community College

Mellissa Youngman
National Institute for the Deaf

Merrily Hoffman
San Jacinto College

Molly McFadden-May
Tulsa Community College

Paige Paulsen
Salt Lake Community College

Rick Street
Spokane Community College

Rosemarie Le Coz
Cerritos College

Susan Davis
Green River College

Susan L. Pallas-Duncan
Southeast Community College

William Lyle
Georgia Piedmont Technical College

Our heartfelt thanks to all who have helped us continue to improve this text.

Jeanette Landin

Paulette Schirmer

Brief Contents

1 Payroll Practices and System Fundamentals 2

2 Payroll System Procedures 40

3 Gross Pay Computation 104

4 Fringe Benefits and Voluntary Deductions 156

5 Employee Net Pay and Pay Methods 194

6 Employer Payroll Taxes and Labor Planning 244

7 The Payroll Register, Employees' Earnings Records, and Accounting System Entries 316

APPENDIXES

A Comprehensive Payroll Project: Wayland Custom Woodworking 360

B Special Classes of Federal Tax Withholding 396

C Federal Income Tax Tables 403

D State Income Tax Information 426

E State Revenue Department Information 432

F Payroll Certification Information 441

GLOSSARY 446

INDEX 450

Contents

About the Authors iii

Chapter 1
Payroll Practices and System Fundamentals 2

1-1 Identify Legislation That Pertains to Payroll and Business 4
1-2 Discuss the Legal Framework Specific to Payroll Accounting 9
1-3 Discuss the Ethical Guidelines for Payroll Accounting 16
Confidentiality 16
Professionalism 16
Integrity 17
Objectivity and Independence 17
Professional Competence and Due Care 17
1-4 Identify Contemporary Payroll Practices 18
Payroll Preparation Options 19
Privacy Protection 21
1-5 Compare Payroll Processing Options for Different Businesses 24
Large Businesses 24
Small Businesses 25
Computer-Based Systems 26
Internet-Based Systems 26
Manual Systems 27
Outsourced Payroll Systems 28
Certified Payroll 28
Summary of Payroll Practices and System Fundamentals 29
Trends to Watch: *Legal Environment* 30
Key Points 30
Vocabulary 31
Review Questions 31
Exercises Set A 32
Problems Set A 33
Exercises Set B 34
Problems Set B 35
Critical Thinking 36
In the Real World: Scenario for Discussion 36
Internet Activities 37
Continuing Payroll Project: Prevosti Farms and Sugarhouse 37
Answers to Stop & Check Exercises 39

Chapter 2
Payroll System Procedures 40

2-1 Identify Important Payroll Procedures and Pay Cycles 42
Pay Cycles 43
2-2 Prepare Required Employee Documentation 45
Employees versus Independent Contractors 45
Reporting New Employees 47
Entering New Employees into the Database 54
2-3 Differentiate Between Exempt and Nonexempt Workers 55
Leased and Temporary Employees 57
2-4 Explain Pay Records and Employee File Maintenance 58
2-5 Describe Internal Controls and Record Retention for a Payroll System 62
Review of Time Collected 64
Overtime Approval 64
Approval for Leave of Absence or Other Unpaid Time Off 64
File Security 65
Alternating Duties and Cross-Training 65
Best Practices Involved in Employee File Maintenance 66
Electronic Records 66
Payroll as a Non-Solo Effort 67
Document Retention Requirements 68
2-6 Discuss Employee Termination and Document Destruction Procedures 70
Employee Termination 70
Document Destruction 72
Electronic Records 73
Trends to Watch: *Payroll Procedures* 74
Summary of Payroll System Procedures 74
Key Points 75
Vocabulary 75
Review Questions 75
Exercises Set A 76
Problems Set A 77
Exercises Set B 83
Problems Set B 84
Critical Thinking 92
In the Real World: Scenario for Discussion 92
Internet Activities 92
Continuing Payroll Project: Prevosti Farms and Sugarhouse 92
Answers to Stop & Check Exercises 102

Chapter 3
Gross Pay Computation 104

3-1 Analyze Minimum Wage Pay for Nonexempt Workers 106
Minimum Wage 106
Tipped Employees 108
3-2 Compute Gross Pay for Different Pay Bases 112
Salaried Workers 112
Hourly Workers 115
Hourly Workers in More Than One Job Classification 115
Commission Work 115
Piece-Rate Work 118
3-3 Calculate Pay Based on Hours and Fractions of Hours 120
Hourly Calculations 121
Quarter-Hour System 121
Hundredth-Hour System 122
3-4 Calculate Overtime in Various Situations 123
Standard Overtime Pay 124
Overtime for Employees of Hospitals and Residential Care Facilities 125
Tipped Employee Overtime 126
Piece-Rate Employee Overtime 127
Salaried Nonexempt Overtime 127
Overtime for Employees Who Work in Two or More Separate Functions 128
3-5 Create a Payroll Register 129
Payroll Register Data 129
Track Employee Compensation Using a Payroll Register 130
3-6 Apply Combination Pay Methods 132
Base Salary Plus Commission 132
Payroll Draw 133
Salary Plus Commission and Draw 134
Incentive Stock Options (ISOs) 135
3-7 Explain Special Pay Situations 136
Compensatory Time 136
On-Call Time 136
Sleep Time, Travel Time, and Wait Time 137
Jury Duty 138
Sub-Minimum Wage Situations 138
Nonqualified Deferred Compensation 139
Pension Payments 140
Retroactive Pay 140
Wages for Deceased Employees 140
Trends to Watch: *Employee Compensation* 141
Summary of Gross Pay Computation 141
Key Points 141
Vocabulary 142
Review Questions 142
Exercises Set A 143
Problems Set A 144
Exercises Set B 147
Problems Set B 149
Critical Thinking 152
In the Real World: Scenario for Discussion 152
Internet Activities 152
Continuing Payroll Project: Prevosti Farms and Sugarhouse 153
Answers to Stop & Check Exercises 154

Chapter 4
Fringe Benefits and Voluntary Deductions 156

4-1 Define Fringe Benefits within the Context of Payroll 158
Purpose of Fringe Benefits 158
Including Benefits in Pay 159
Fringe Benefits and Payroll Taxes 159
4-2 Interpret Cafeteria Plan Types 162
Premium Only Plan (POP) 162
Flexible Spending Arrangement (FSA) 163
Health Savings Account (HSA) 163
4-3 Describe Fringe Benefit Exclusion Rules 165
Prizes and Awards 166
Gym Memberships 166
Personal Use of Company Vehicle 166
Gift Cards 167
Employer-Provided Snacks and Meals 167
4-4 Explain Fringe Benefit Valuation Rules 168
General Valuation Rule 168
Unsafe Conditions 171
Other Transportation Benefits 171
4-5 Differentiate Between Pre-Tax and Post-Tax Deductions 172
Insurance 172
Supplemental Health and Disability Insurance 174
Retirement Plans 174
Post-Tax Deductions 175
4-6 Apply Rules for Withholding, Depositing, and Reporting Benefits 177
Rules for Withholding Amounts Related to Benefits 177
Treatment of Taxable Benefit Withholdings 178
Rules for Depositing Amounts Related to Benefits 178
Rules for Reporting Benefits 179
Trends to Watch: *Employee Benefits* 180
Summary of Fringe Benefits and Voluntary Deductions 180
Key Points 181
Vocabulary 181
Review Questions 181
Exercises Set A 182

Problems Set A 183
Exercises Set B 185
Problems Set B 186
Critical Thinking 188
In the Real World: Scenario for Discussion 189
Internet Activities 189
Continuing Payroll Project: Prevosti Farms and Sugarhouse 189
Answers to Stop & Check Exercises 193

Chapter 5
Employee Net Pay and Pay Methods 194

5-1 Compute Employee Net Pay 196
Pay Computation Steps 196
5-2 Determine Federal Income Tax Withholding Amounts 198
Federal Income Taxes 198
Federal Income Tax Computation Examples 199
Wage-Bracket Method 199
Percentage Method 203
5-3 Compute Social Security and Medicare Tax Withholding 207
Social Security Tax 208
Examples of Social Security Tax Computations 208
Medicare Tax 208
Examples of Medicare Tax Computations 209
5-4 Calculate State and Local Income Taxes 212
State-Specific Taxes 212
Local Income Taxes 213
5-5 Apply Post-Tax Deductions 214
Charitable Conributions 214
Garnishments 215
Consumer Credit 216
Union Dues 217
Employee Advances and Overpayments 218
5-6 Discuss Employee Pay Methods 218
Cash 219
Check 219
Direct Deposit 221
Paycards 221
Cryptocurrency 222
Trends to Watch: *Taxes and Payment Methods* 223
Summary of Employee Net Pay and Pay Methods 224
Key Points 224
Vocabulary 224
Review Questions 224
Exercises Set A 225
Problems Set A 226
Exercises Set B 230
Problems Set B 231
Critical Thinking 235
In the Real World: Scenario for Discussion 235
Internet Activities 236
Continuing Payroll Project: Prevosti Farms and Sugarhouse 236
Answers to Stop & Check Exercises 242

Chapter 6
Employer Payroll Taxes and Labor Planning 244

6-1 List Employer-Paid and Employee-Paid Obligations 246
Social Security and Medicare Taxes 246
Federal and State Unemployment Taxes 248
FUTA Credit Reduction 250
State Unemployment Taxes 251
Other State and Local Employer-Only Payroll Taxes 253
Workers' Compensation Insurance 253
6-2 Discuss Reporting Periods and Requirements for Employer Tax Deposits 255
Lookback Period 255
Deposit Frequencies 256
6-3 Prepare Mid-Year and Year-End Employer Tax Reporting and Deposits 258
Form 941 258
Schedule B 258
State Tax Remittance 263
Form 944 263
Unemployment Tax Reporting 263
Matching Final Annual Pay to Form W-2 269
6-4 Describe Payroll within the Context of Business Expenses 278
Employees and Company Framework 279
6-5 Relate Labor Expenses to Company Profitability 280
The Labor Distribution Report 281
6-6 Complete Benefit Analysis as a Function of Payroll 282
Annual Total Compensation Report 284
Trends to Watch: *Employer Taxes and Benefit Analysis* 286
Summary of Employer Payroll Taxes and Labor Planning 286
Key Points 286
Vocabulary 287
Review Questions 287
Exercises Set A 288
Problems Set A 289
Exercises Set B 299
Problems Set B 300
Critical Thinking 311
In the Real World: Scenario for Discussion 312
Internet Activities 312
Continuing Payroll Project: Prevosti Farms and Sugarhouse 312
Answers to Stop & Check Exercises 315

Chapter 7
The Payroll Register, Employees' Earnings Records, and Accounting System Entries 316

7-1 Connect the Payroll Register to the Employees' Earnings Records 318
The Employees' Earnings Records and Periodic Tax Reports 320
7-2 Describe Financial Accounting Concepts 320
Debits and Credits 321
The General Journal 322
The General Ledger 322
7-3 Complete Payroll-Related General Journal Entries 323
Employee Pay-Related Journal Entries 324
Employer Payroll-Related Journal Entries 325
Other Payroll-Related Journal Entries 325
Payroll Accruals and Reversals 326
7-4 Generate Payroll-Related General Ledger Entries 328
General Ledger Posting Practices 328
7-5 Describe Payroll Effects on the Accounting System 331
Payroll-Related Business Expenses 331
Payroll-Related Liabilities 332
7-6 Explain Payroll Entries in Accounting Reports 332
Labor Reports 335
Trends to Watch: *Economic Effects of Payroll* 336
Summary of the Payroll Register, Employees' Earnings Records, and Accounting System Entries 336
Key Points 337
Vocabulary 338
Review Questions 338
Exercises Set A 339
Problems Set A 340
Exercises Set B 346
Problems Set B 347
Critical Thinking 353
In the Real World: Scenario for Discussion 353
Internet Activities 354
Continuing Payroll Project: Prevosti Farms and Sugarhouse 354
Answers to Stop & Check Exercises 358

Appendixes

Appendix A: Comprehensive Payroll Project: Wayland Custom Woodworking 360

Appendix B: Special Classes of Federal Tax Withholding 396

Appendix C: Federal Income Tax Tables 403

Appendix D: State Income Tax Information 426

Appendix E: State Revenue Department Information 432

Appendix F: Payroll Certification Information 441

Glossary 446

Index 450

Payroll Accounting 2020

1

Chapter One

Payroll Practices and System Fundamentals

Payroll systems are an integral part of job planning and strategic human resource management, cost management for products and services, and benefits analysis for a company. A company's payroll system has historically connected human resources and accounting departments. In contemporary businesses, payroll has taken on a strategic role in terms of company direction and future plans. The continual evolution of technological tools to manage company resources, including monetary and human, provides both opportunities and challenges to employers in terms of employee access and protection of private information. A well-designed payroll system is a critical element in company management; for this reason, an understanding of payroll foundations is imperative. In this chapter, we will explore the need for a payroll system, legal requirements, ethical guidelines, best practices, and variations in payroll practices among different-sized companies.

LEARNING OBJECTIVES

After studying Chapter 1, you should be able to:

LO 1-1 Identify Legislation That Pertains to Payroll and Business

LO 1-2 Discuss the Legal Framework Specific to Payroll Accounting

LO 1-3 Discuss the Ethical Guidelines for Payroll Accounting

LO 1-4 Identify Contemporary Payroll Practices

LO 1-5 Compare Payroll Processing Options for Different Businesses

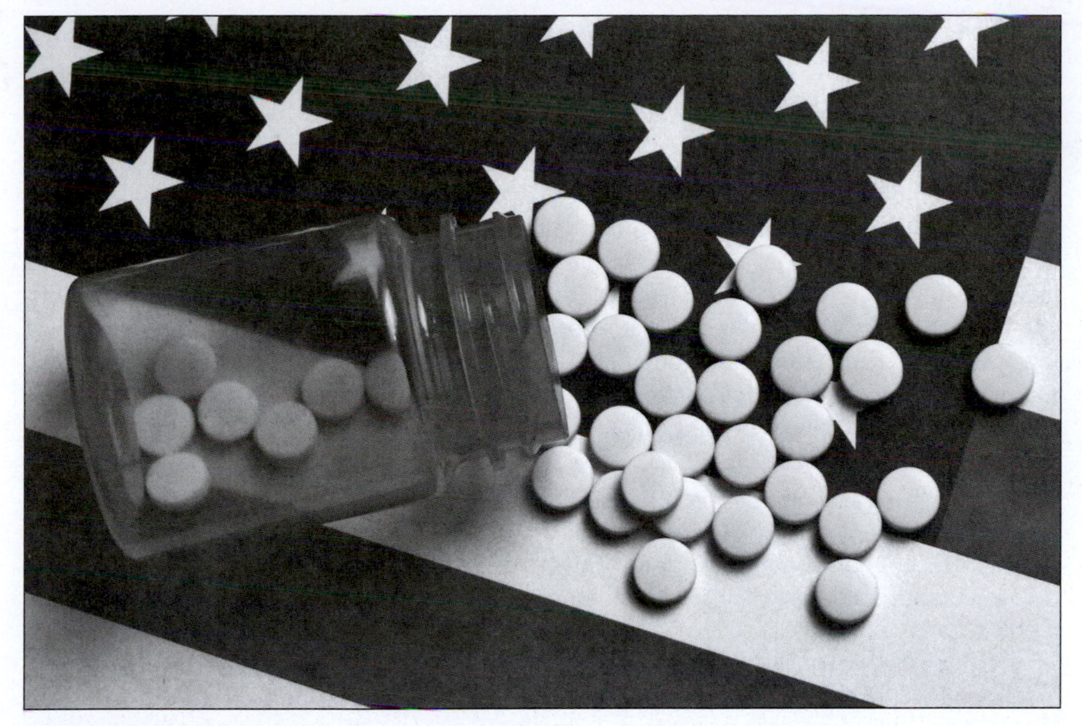

Douglas Sacha/Getty Images

Now Contested: The Affordable Care Act

The Affordable Care Act (ACA), often called "Obamacare," had a major lawsuit brought against it in late 2018. The problem arose following passage of the Tax Cuts and Job Act of 2017, in which the penalty associated with the individual mandate for people to have health care was lowered to $0, formally nullifying that provision of the law. A group of governors filed a lawsuit because they felt the removal of the individual mandate, which made health care coverage compulsory, had rendered the Affordable Care Act unconstitutional because it acted as a tax only on certain groups of people, specifically people with pre-existing conditions. A federal district judge in Texas agreed and upheld the governors' legal filing. Since that decision, a group of states' attorneys general have appealed the decision, Although the case is in a pending status, the Affordable Care Act remains the law in the United States and all provisions and reporting requirements still apply. This case may go to the federal Supreme Court, so payroll accountants should be conscious of the status as they work.

Corporate human resources and payroll personnel undertake a critical function in their companies. They must ensure that payroll is not only disbursed in a timely and accurate manner, they must also abide by an ever-changing legal landscape. Under the Affordable Care Act, employers must both provide access to health coverage and file the required forms at the necessary intervals. Additionally, employers must provide access to insurance that includes all required medical coverage mandated by the ACA and disclosures about any costs shared by the employer and employee.

(Source: American Payroll Association)

Employment legislation is highly complex and dynamic. Large or small, employers must abide by the law and be aware when it changes. In Chapter 1, we will explore the basics of payroll systems, including legal and ethical issues involved with employee pay.

LO 1-1 Identify Legislation That Pertains to Payroll and Business

Unlike many other types of accounting, payroll affects most (if not all) members of an organization. Payroll errors can lead to serious internal and external problems. Internal errors may cause a company to pay excessive wages for unneeded overtime, underpay employees, forego profits, or employ the wrong number or type of workers during seasonal or other workflow changes. Managers use internal reports about labor usage, staffing levels, and employee compensation trends to ensure operational effectiveness. Organizational decision makers use these reports to control labor costs, hire additional employees to meet surge demands, and manage the cost of goods sold. Payroll errors can result in governmental fines, taxes, or legal charges related to the violation of labor laws. Employers provide external reports to the Internal Revenue Service (IRS), state government tax departments, and many more agencies, depending upon the nature of the company.

> The Louisiana Department of Revenue took action in 2018 against three companies for underreporting employee tax liabilities. The Government Against Misclassified Employees Operational Network (GAME ON) Task Force found that these three companies had deliberately misclassified workers as independent contractors instead of employees to avoid employee income tax liability. During the three years investigated, the total of tax liabilities, penalties, and interest due for the three companies was approximately $250,000. (Source: Louisiana Department of Revenue)

According to the United States Bureau of Labor Statistics in 2016, employment in accounting jobs is expected to increase 10 percent through 2026, which is faster than the average growth for business professions. Salaries average $43,845 for payroll clerks and $85,650 for payroll managers and supervisors, according to the 2019 salary guides available via www.salary.com and Financial Executives International.

The legislative framework governing employers' payroll systems is complex. Although several fundamental laws still exist, payroll and human resource laws tend to reflect societal evolution over time. Note how some of these laws have been challenged or changed since their inception.

The Equal Pay Act of 1963 mandated that males and females be paid equally for equal work. As of 2019, 48 states have enacted legislation that clarifies and/or extends the original 1963 Act. Any employees who feel they have been paid unequally based upon gender have legal options to rectify the situation.

- First, they should gather documentation regarding the differential and determine if other employees in question are willing to substantiate the difference.
- Second, they should speak with their supervisor to question the pay differential.
- Should the supervisor be unwilling to discuss or adjust the pay discrepancy, an attorney may become a necessary third step.

This Act was modified by the ***Lilly Ledbetter Fair Pay Act of 2009***, which removed the 180-day statute of limitations on claims of unequal treatment.

> In 1979, Lilly Ledbetter, an employee of Goodyear Tire and Rubber Company, started at the same rate of pay as males in the same position. Over time, she was declined raises by management, which based its decisions on negative reviews that Ms. Ledbetter later claimed were discriminatory. Under the provisions of the 1963 Equal Pay Act, the claimant had 180 days to file a complaint. Although the U.S. Supreme Court agreed with her discrimination claims, it ruled in favor of Goodyear because of the lack of timeliness of Ms. Ledbetter's filing. This ruling ultimately led to the Lilly Ledbetter Fair Pay Act of 2009. (Source: US. EEOC)

Library of Congress Prints and Photographs Division [LC-DIG-ppmsca-05542]

The Civil Rights Act of 1964 prohibited discrimination based on race, creed, color, gender, and national origin. Since 1964, this act has been extended by Executive Order 11478 to protect people with AIDS, pregnant workers, people with different sexual orientations, and people with disabilities. In June 2015, the U.S. Supreme Court ruled in *Obergefell v. Hodges* (U.S. Supreme Court No. 14-556) that same-sex marriage was legal and could not be banned in any state. This extension of the 1964 Civil Rights Act represented another step toward the legal protection of worker dignity.

The Age Discrimination in Employment Act of 1967 (ADEA) prevents mandatory retirement of older employees (older than age 40) and prohibits age-based discrimination in hiring.

> Several landmark cases have followed ADEA's enactment. As of 2018, IBM has been accused of targeted age discrimination among its older employees. Among the complaints filed, IBM has denied employees information for them to determine the presence of age bias, targeted older workers for layoff, and then offered the same workers re-employment at significantly reduced wages. (Source: ProPublica)

The Occupational Safety and Health Act of 1970 (OSHA) defined and enforced healthy and safe working environments for employees. Employee safety programs and personal protective equipment represent an additional cost to the employer, but fines for noncompliance and payments made following workplace injuries are often far more costly: fines range from $13,260 per serious violation to $132,598 (2019 figures) for willful or repeated violations.

DnDavis/Shutterstock

The Employee Retirement Income Security Act of 1974 (ERISA) regulates the management of retirement and pension plans. ERISA has been extended by the ***Consolidated Omnibus Budget Reformation Act of 1985 (COBRA)***. During the recession of 2007–2009, the value of some employee retirement funds decreased, causing employees to postpone retirement. The Internal Revenue Service imposes limitations on retirement plan contributions, and those limits have shifted to reflect the need for employees to recoup losses sustained during the recession. Since that time, employee retirement benefits have shifted from being a financial burden to becoming an employee hiring and retention strategy, and retirement researchers are contemplating proposing a mandatory retirement savings law.

States have enacted legislation about employers' contributions to retirement income. For example, California enacted the Secure Choice Retirement Savings Program (SB-1234) and implemented it in 2017. This program requires eligible employers to offer employees the opportunity to use direct deposit to contribute to their retirement savings account. Unless employees choose not to participate in the program, the employee must contribute 3 percent to a retirement account.

> A development in 2019 involved the IRS approval of an employer connecting employee 401(k) contributions toward payment of their student loans. In one instance, the guidelines for employer contribution to the employee's student loan was that the employee was paying at least 2 percent of their salary toward their student loans during a given period. Other companies, such as Abbott, offer an expanded 401(k) employer match for employees who meet similar guidelines as far as their student loan repayment. (Source: Employee Benefit News)

COBRA extended medical benefits for terminated employees at the employee's expense. The federal government, in response to the high unemployment rates at the start of 2010, briefly subsidized COBRA insurance. The temporary reduction in COBRA remains available, but only for employees who were terminated between September 1, 2008, and March 31, 2010. The repeal of the Defense of Marriage Act (DOMA) in 2013 forced employers to offer COBRA coverage to same-sex spouses.

COBRA benefits currently extend to beneficiaries including employees, dependent spouses, and children. Benefits are paid to beneficiaries in the event of reduced hours or separation of employment for any reason excluding gross misconduct, and upon death of the employee. In the event that the company offers retiree benefits, COBRA coverage also extends to beneficiaries in the event of Chapter 11 bankruptcy.

The Immigration Reform and Control Act of 1986 (IRCA) requires employers to verify that employees are legally able to work in the United States. Form I-9 is the most common payroll-related application of this law. Immigration and citizenship laws require the collection of information within an I-9, and retention is three years from date of hire or one year from date of termination (whichever is longer).

> Information collected on Form I-9 is monitored closely to ensure that the employee is legally authorized to work in the United States. The E-verify system does not replace the completion of the I-9 but does offer employers the opportunity to check legal employment eligibility rapidly via the Internet.

The Americans with Disabilities Act of 1990 (ADA) extended the provisions of the Civil Rights Act of 1964 by ensuring that people with disabilities have the same opportunities as those without mental or physical impairment. This law applies to employers with 15 or more employees on the payroll, including full-time and part-time workers. The enactment of the ***Americans with Disabilities Act Amendments Act (ADAAA)*** in 2008 extended the definition of disability to include a greater number of disabilities. Final Regulations on the ADAAA in 2011 clarified the definitions of disability and the required accommodations to include the following:

- Expansion of the definition of disability includes a lower standard of the definition of impairment.
- The determination of impairments require the employee to be assessed individually.
- With the exception of corrective lenses, determination of disability does not include devices that provide relief or mitigation of the condition, such as hearing aids.
- Impairments that occur periodically or episodically or that are in remission are still considered impairments.
- Any disability determination must not require analysis that is extensive,

The Civil Rights Act of 1991 granted employees who have been discriminated against the chance to be paid monetary damages through legal proceedings. This act applies to American employers and American-controlled employers with internationally based operations.

> Workplace diversity cases have plagued Google in the wake of reports that hiring practices had resulted in significantly skewed gender and ethnicity ratios. The class-action suit followed the previous year's lawsuit over equal pay for male and female employees and was filed after an employee was fired for circulating a memo stating that women were biologically unsuited for tech careers. As of the time of writing, the lawsuit is scheduled to be settled out of court. (Source: *The New York Times*, Dhillion Law Group)

The Family and Medical Leave Act of 1993 (FMLA) granted employees the right to take medical leave under reasonable circumstances without fear of job loss. The employee may have to take unpaid leave, but medical benefits must continue under FMLA provisions. Upon

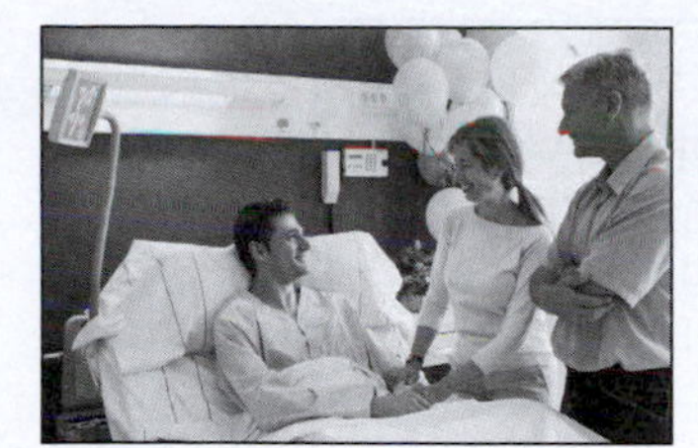
Pixtal/AGE Fotostock

return from family leave, the employer must provide an equivalent position with equivalent pay, benefits, and terms of employment. The employer has many responsibilities under the FMLA that involve employee notification of benefits and processes while on leave. The repeal of DOMA provoked the need to clarify the term "family member." Following the U.S. Supreme Court decision in *Obergefell v. Hodges (2015),* the U.S. Department of Labor updated the definition of spouse to include same-sex marriages, regardless of where they live.

At the end of 2017, the ***Tax Cuts and Jobs Act*** (Public Law 115-97) was passed by legislators in Washington. This provided a tax credit to employers who offer their employees paid leave under the FMLA. Employers may receive from 12.5 percent to 25 percent, whereas the rate of payment to the employee is 50 percent or more of what the employee would normally be paid during the normal course of work for the company. Eligibility limits of the type of the employer and employee exist under the regulations (see Sec. §13403).

> In 2017, the Society for Human Resource Management (SHRM) commented on a rise in the number of weeks being taken for FMLA-related leave. Under FMLA, up to 12 weeks of leave are authorized per employee; however, employees have been requesting additional time over and above FMLA provisions. The Equal Employment Opportunity Commission (EEOC) commented that disability provisions under the Americans with Disabilities Act (ADA) may be appropriate in certain situations. Employers faced with these situations should verify the legality of this application when employees need extended FMLA leave. (Source: SHRM)

The Uniformed Services Employment and Reemployment Rights Act of 1994 (USERRA) governs the rights of military service members in terms of length of military service, return to work, and accommodations for injured veterans. USERRA was amended as to service members' rights in 2005. In 2011, USERRA was further amended by the Veterans Opportunity to Work Act, which allowed USERRA to recognize claims of a hostile work environment resulting from an individual's military status.

> The U.S. Department of Labor investigates many cases involving service members' rights. Army veteran Lisa Slater returned to her job as a security officer, in which she had 13 years with her company, after deployment on active duty. However, upon her return to her employment, she found that she was classified as a new employee, which was found to be a violation of USERRA. She received approximately $20,000 in back wages, and her seniority was restored following arbitration. (Source: US DOL)

The Personal Responsibility and Work Opportunity Reconciliation Act of 1996 (PRWOR) mandated that employers file a new hire reporting form within 20 days after an employee initially commences work. This act protects children and needy families by enforcing child support obligations. The child support provisions of PRWOR were strengthened by the passage of the ***Personal Responsibility, Work and Family Promotion Act of 2002***, which reauthorized PRWOR when it expired.

The Health Insurance Portability and Accountability Act of 1996 (HIPAA) protects workers and their families who have preexisting medical conditions from discrimination based on those conditions. The Ebola outbreak in 2014 led to additional guidance about HIPAA rights and notifications to interested parties, including employers, during emergency situations.

The Defense of Marriage Act of 1996 (DOMA) restricted payroll-related taxes and benefits to include only traditionally married couples, denying married status to people in same-sex unions. The U.S. Supreme Court overturned DOMA in its ruling in *U.S. v. Windsor* on

HIPAA protections continue even after a business ceases operations. Filefax Inc. of Illinois was ordered to pay approximately $100,000 in fines because of HIPAA violations, although the company is no longer in business. The issue leading to the fines involved a lack of secure storage of employee health records following investigation by the Office of Civil Rights. (Source: US HHS)

September 6, 2013; the Internal Revenue Service subsequently mandated that all married same-sex couples must be treated as married for all tax purposes. The repeal of DOMA had a ripple effect throughout all phases of payroll because of the need to amend business and personal tax return filings back to 2011, owing to the three-year amendment rule. The effects of DOMA's repeal also have had a ripple effect on employee rights, highlighting the need for additional legislative clarification.

Maskot/Getty Images

In *U.S. v. Windsor,* Ms. Windsor and her wife were recognized as a married couple by the state of New York, and her compensation was taxed accordingly. However, the IRS sued Windsor for unpaid taxes because her same-sex marriage violated DOMA. The U.S. Supreme Court found that DOMA violated Windsor's Fifth Amendment right to liberty and overturned DOMA. The IRS subsequently dropped its lawsuit. (Source: U.S. Supreme Court)

The Sarbanes–Oxley Act of 2002 (SOX) provided criminal penalties for violations of ERISA. SOX provides protections for whistle-blowers and mandates the rotation of auditors among publicly owned companies. An additional consideration for public companies of SOX regarding payroll is that the internal controls of a payroll system must be reported under the guidelines set out in Section 404. Costs of SOX compliance have sparked discussion about the Act's effectiveness, especially following the 2008 financial crisis.

An employee of Countrywide Mortgage, a Bank of America subsidiary, alerted governmental officials to fraud in the company's financial records. This employee led internal investigations that revealed significant fraud in monetary transactions, as well as a history of retaliation against other whistle-blowers. In 2011, the U.S. Department of Labor found Bank of America to be in violation of the Sarbanes–Oxley Act's whistle-blower provision and awarded $930,000 to the employee. (Source: The Center for Public Integrity)

The American Recovery and Reinvestment Act of 2009 (ARRA) provided tax credits for employers and employees through the Making Work Pay provisions. Although ARRA's provisions have expired, parts of it were reinstated through the **American Taxpayer Relief Act of 2012 (*ATRA*)**. Many of the ATRA provisions were extended through 2015 by the extension of the Work Opportunity Tax Credit and extended through 2019 by the ***Protecting Americans from Tax Hikes (PATH) Act*** of 2015.

As times change, new legislation will be enacted, and existing laws are sometimes repealed and amended. An example of evolving legislation includes new local laws regarding fairness in scheduling employees' shift work schedules. Right-to-work laws are another example of employment-related legislation. As of 2019, 26 U.S. states and territories have enacted right-to-work legislation that promotes an employee's right to opt out of union membership.

The payroll accountant's job is one of consistent and continual learning and research to ensure that the company is complying with all current regulations and reporting requirements. Many states, but not all, have additional payroll tax laws. Federally mandated payroll laws will be addressed in the next section.

See www.americanpayroll.org/weblink/statelocal-wider/ for more information about state-specific legislation.

Stop & Check

Which Law?

1. Requires employers to verify the employee's legal right to work in the United States?
2. Protects the rights of disabled workers?
3. Governs the management of retirement plans?
4. Protects discrimination of workers older than age 40?
5. Creates safe work environments for employees?
6. Mandates equal pay for equal work?
7. Extends medical benefits for terminated employees?
8. Ensures that child support obligations will be paid?
9. Protects workers and families with preexisting medical conditions?
10. Enforces payment of monetary damages because of discrimination?
11. Requires internal controls on payroll practices of public companies?

a. COBRA
b. ERISA
c. Civil Rights Act of 1991
d. PRWOR
e. SOX
f. ADEA
g. HIPAA
h. ADA
i. OSHA
j. Equal Pay Act of 1963
k. IRCA

Vintage Tone/Shutterstock

LO 1-2 Discuss the Legal Framework Specific to Payroll Accounting

Why did businesses start withholding taxes from people's paychecks? Federal income tax withholding was temporarily instituted in 1861 as a way to recover from the high costs of the Civil War; however, this tax was repealed in 1872. Throughout the 19th century, cities were growing in the wake of the Industrial Revolution, as factories and companies increased automation and institutionalized mass production. People were moving from rural to urban areas in unprecedented numbers, and the need for infrastructure and civil services grew. Roads needed to be built, law enforcement personnel needed to be increased, and outbreaks of disease prompted a need for sanitation systems. Therefore, the U.S. Congress formalized the permanent continuation of the federal income tax instituted during the Civil War as a means to fund the infrastructure improvements of the booming cities. After many failed attempts to reinstate a federal income tax, Congress passed the ***Sixteenth Amendment to the U.S. Constitution***, in 1909, which was ratified by states in 1913. This version incorporated a tiered income tax, including exemptions and deductions to limit the tax imposed on wages earned; it was the harbinger of many employment-related laws (see Figure 1-1).

During the Great Depression of the 1930s, the stock market collapsed, financial institutions went bankrupt, and companies released workers or ceased business operations. The government needed money to fund programs that would stimulate economic recovery. Additionally, the need for a social welfare system emerged as the number of displaced workers increased. The 1930s became a decade of landmark employment legislation that defined the legal environment for employers and employees, most of which remains enforced in 2018.

In 1931, Congress passed the ***Davis–Bacon Act***, creating a standard of wages for governmental contracts totaling more than $2,000. The increased standard wages created under the Davis–Bacon Act brought additional revenue to small businesses and the communities where the contract workers lived, bought groceries, and purchased other services or goods. The Davis–Bacon Act comprised more than 60 different federal statutes, providing a prevailing wage and wage classification strategy to guide employers and contractors. As of 2019, the minimum wage for all employees affected by the Davis-Bacon Act is $10.60 per hour, unless the local prevailing minimum wage rate is higher.

FIGURE 1-1
Timeline of Payroll Legislation

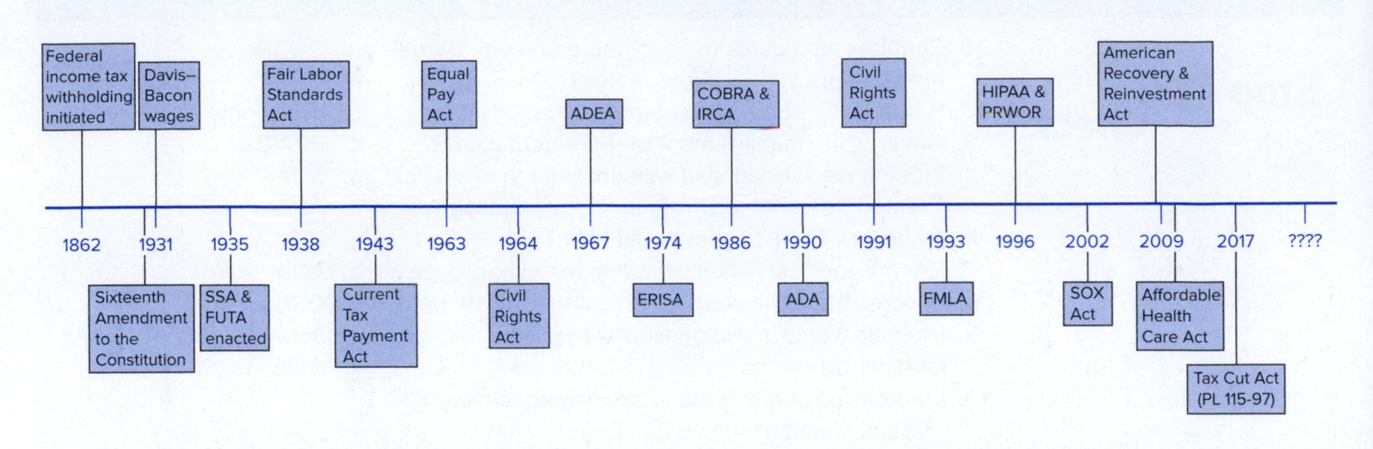

> The determination of wages to be paid to workers affected by the Davis-Bacon Act varies by geographic area, contract, and type of work performed. To facilitate wage determination, the US Department of Labor maintains a website (https://www.wdol.gov/dba.aspx) in which employers may access their specific contract in question and research the provisions of the contract to ensure that employees are paid appropriately. (Source: US Department of Labor)

The ***Walsh–Healey Public Contracts Act*** of 1936 affected governmental contractors providing goods or services exceeding $10,000. The act required companies to pay workers a minimum wage for all hours worked under 40 per week and time and a half (regular pay times 1.5) per hour for any hours over 40 per week. The Walsh–Healey Public Contracts Act also prohibited the employment of individuals younger than 16 years of age. Compliance with this act is enforced through the Employment Standards Administration Wage and Hour Division of the Department of Labor. These standards also apply to workers within the District of Columbia.

In 1935, the ***Social Security Act (SSA)***, also known as the ***Federal Insurance Contributions Act (FICA)***, established a contribution-driven fund that would help the average U.S. worker in response to the social and financial distress caused by the Great Depression. Originally, the Social Security tax was designed such that younger workers supported retired, disabled workers and surviving families of deceased workers. It is important to note that the worker does not need to die or become disabled to receive Social Security benefits; the truth is that age and disability are components in the decision but are not the only factors considered when awarding Social Security benefits. A contribution-driven fund's employees and employers pay a percentage of gross earnings into the Social Security fund. Originally, the fund was designed to be earmarked for a specific individual upon retirement, but the fund currently provides assistance for families who experience diminished wages and working situations because of infirmity of the worker or a family member, as well as monetary benefits to dependents of retired or deceased workers. Social Security is synonymous with ***Old-Age, Survivors, and Disability Insurance*** (***OASDI***). ***Medicare***, a government-mandated health insurance program for individuals was also included in the SSA legislation. As of 2018, the age at which individuals may receive full retirement benefits is 66 years and four months. The full retirement age will increase two months each year until it reaches a full retirement age of 67. However, individuals may begin receiving permanently reduced benefits as early as age 62, but their Social Security payments will be reduced by 25–30 percent.

As another part of its social welfare legislation, the U.S. Congress passed the ***Federal Unemployment Tax Act*** (***FUTA***) as a way to help displaced workers, individuals from the workforce who find themselves unemployed and meet certain state or federal qualifications. FUTA and its state counterpart, ***SUTA***, are based upon the wages earned by the employees. Unlike

As of 2019, Social Security paid Americans over $1 trillion dollars in benefits. This figure represented a milestone for the Social Security Agency because that number was the highest that had ever been paid. Furthermore, the Social Security agency estimated that approximately 62 percent of American retirees depended on their Social Security checks for basic needs such as food and shelter. and reduces the poverty rate among senior citizens. (Source: Motley Fool)

Angela Waye/Alamy

Social Security taxes, only employers pay FUTA. Some states require both employers and employees to contribute to SUTA. For example, Alaskan employees contribute up to an annual amount of $199.50 (2019 figure) to SUTA, which is collected at a rate of 0.50 percent of wages; employers contribute up to 1.78 percent of employee wages until they reach $39,900 in annual gross earnings (2019 figure). Should an employee have more than one employer, the employee is allowed to request a return for the amounts over the annual earnings maximum in the following year.

The enactment of the ***Fair Labor Standards Act (FLSA)*** of 1938 required more detailed record keeping and worker protection. This act regulates the minimum wage, a topic with which most workers are familiar, stated as the lowest an individual under certain classifications can be paid. Less commonly known, minimum wage applies only to workers at businesses that meet certain conditions. For example, small businesses that conduct no interstate commerce, such as a restaurant that serves only locally obtained food from one state, are not subject to the minimum wage provisions of FLSA. Additionally, tipped employees, such as restaurant servers, are exempt from minimum wage standards under FLSA. In the contemporary business world, a business that does not conduct interstate commerce is rare, but the provision in FLSA remains in effect.

An important fact about FLSA wage guidelines is that no maximum wage cap exists. Securities and Exchanges Commission (SEC) regulations stipulate that the compensation packages of high-ranking employees of public companies must be published with the company's mandatory annual report.

The minimum wage may differ from a "living wage," which is an amount needed to meet basic subsistence needs. As of 2019, 44 cities and/or counties have enacted living wage ordinances to rise in relation to the Consumer Price Index. The following cities are examples of places with living wage ordinances:

- San Leandro, California
- Pine Bluff, Arkansas
- Asheville, North Carolina
- Pittsburgh, Pennsylvania
- Albuquerque, New Mexico
- Portland, Maine
- Prince George's County, Maryland

(Source: UC Berkeley Center for Labor Research and Education)

FLSA guidelines define maximum hours, minimum age, pay rates, and mandatory break times. This part of the FLSA is an outgrowth of the industrial environment of the early 20th century, when no such guidelines existed. Horror stories about working conditions and children working 12- to 14-hour days abounded during the 1930s. The FLSA created the classifications of exempt and nonexempt workers. Exempt workers are salaried workers who are not subject to certain wage and overtime provisions of FLSA. Nonexempt workers are protected by the provisions of the FLSA and are therefore subject to wage and overtime provisions.

Additionally, under FLSA, pay periods are not regulated, nor is the amount of paid time off given to employees. Those two items are at the discretion of the employer. Paid time off has become a topic of discussion since 2010, and companies such as McDonald's began offering it to nonexempt employees in 2015 as a regular part of employee benefit packages in response to pressure from labor leaders. Eleven states, including Massachusetts, Oregon, Connecticut, California, Washington, Arizona, and Vermont, have instituted paid sick leave for employees as of early 2019.

A third class of workers, independent contractors, is not subject to the pay provisions of the FLSA. ***Independent contractors*** are typically treated as vendors of a business. Independent contractors are not employees of the business and are not reflected on payroll records. In July 2015, the Department of Labor ruled that improper classification of workers diminished workers' legal protections under the FLSA and declared that the following items must be considered when classifying a worker as an employee or an independent contractor:

1. The extent to which a worker is an integral element of the employer's business.
2. Whether the worker's managerial skills affect his or her opportunity for profit or loss.
3. Relative investments in facilities and equipment by *both* the employee and the employer.
4. The extent to which the worker exercises independent business judgment.
5. The permanent nature of the working relationship between the employer and employee.
6. The type and extent of the control that the employer has over the employee.

(Source: U.S. Department of Labor)

Penalties for misclassification of employees as independent contractors can be high. If the misclassification is found to be intentional on the part of the employer, the monetary amount of the penalty is higher. In the case of *Fair v. Communications Unlimited Inc.*, the U.S. District in Missouri found that the employer had deliberately miscategorized workers in 10 states as independent contractors to avoid paying the overtime wages required under the FLSA. The employer was ordered to provide the names and other contact information to the court in order to determine appropriate overtime compensation awards. (Source: Google Scholar)

To obtain the remittance of employers' withholding taxes, the federal government needed a way to standardize the collection of taxes from employers. Before the ***Current Tax Payment Act (CTPA) of 1943***, no formalized guidelines for remittance of taxes existed. During the time before the CTPA, the remittance of taxes from employers was inconsistent and unreliable as a funding source for governmental projects. The CTPA was passed during World War II as a means of guaranteeing a source of funds to support the country's involvement in the war. The CTPA created the requirement for the submission of estimated taxes on wages earned during the year of earning instead of after the end of the year as previously required.

Another employer obligation is ***workers' compensation***, commonly known as *workers' comp.* Unlike other payroll-specific laws, state laws govern workers' compensation laws. Employer requirements for providing workers' comp coverage vary from state to state and are not required in certain states if the employer has fewer than a certain minimum number of employees. Because workers' compensation is an insurance program, it is not considered a 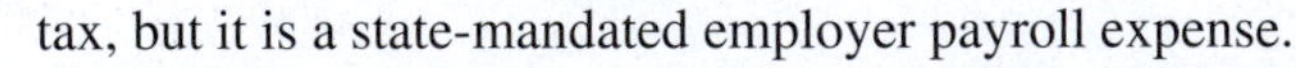 tax, but it is a state-mandated employer payroll expense.

Holly Hildreth/McGraw-Hill Education

Workers' compensation is an insurance policy carried by employers to provide wage continuation and to pay for medical services for workers injured in the course of doing business. The amounts assigned to the policy vary by type of work being performed and associated risks for various professions. For example, heavy equipment operators would have a higher workers' comp rate than office workers because their exposure to injury is deemed higher by the insurance industry.

Workers' compensation plans are subject to annual audits and are based upon payroll wages less any employees exempted from the coverage, typically working owners. Employers must report all wages earned by the employee; however, only one-third of overtime hours are reported to the workers' compensation auditor. Each state has different requirements for coverage and eligibility. The number of employees over which workers' compensation insurance is required varies per state, as shown in Table 1-1.

TABLE 1-1
Workers' Compensation Laws by State

STATE	MINIMUM NUMBER OF EMPLOYEES
Alaska	1 (may be self-insured)
Alabama	5
Arizona	1
Arkansas	3
California	1
Colorado	1
Connecticut	1 (including uninsured subcontractors)
Delaware	1
D.C.	1
Florida	1 (construction), 6 (agricultural)
Georgia	3
Hawaii	1
Idaho	1
Illinois	1
Indiana	1
Iowa	1
Kansas	1 (exempt if annual gross payroll is less than $20,000 or agricultural employer. Sole proprietors and LLC members are exempt from coverage)
Kentucky	1
Louisiana	1
Maine	1 (subcontractors must also be covered)
Maryland	1 (agricultural employers must have at least 3 employees or a payroll of less than $15,000 annually)
Massachusetts	1 (domestic workers must be covered if they work more than 16 hours per week)
Michigan	1 (certain family members who are employees may be exempt)
Minnesota	1
Mississippi	5 (certain subcontractors' employees are covered)
Missouri	5 (construction employers must have at least 1 employee)
Montana	1
Nebraska	1
Nevada	1
New Hampshire	1
New Jersey	1
New Mexico	3 (construction employers, any employees)
New York	1
North Carolina	3 (only 1 employee for businesses that involve radiation exposure)
North Dakota	1
Ohio	1
Oklahoma	1 (when a business has 5 or fewer family members as employers, the family member are exempt from coverage)
Oregon	1
Pennsylvania	1
Rhode Island	4
South Carolina	4 (some occupations exempt if <$3,000 in annual payroll)
South Dakota	1
Tennessee	5 (construction and coal businesses must always have it)
Texas	No mandatory coverage except government contractors
Utah	1
Vermont	1 (agricultural/farming employers with annual payroll <$10,000 are exempt)
Virginia	2
Washington	1
West Virginia	1
Wisconsin	3
Wyoming	1

Source: NFIB.

The ***Affordable Care Act (ACA)*** of 2010 was one of the most significant changes in payroll accounting in recent years. Although the primary focus of the act was to ensure health care coverage for all Americans, employers have several reporting responsibilities related to the act. One of the responsibilities included in Section 1003 is the disclosure and justification for rates of plans and any increases in premiums. Another reporting requirement is the number of full-time equivalent (FTE) employees, the cost of insurance coverage provided to employees, and the elimination of a waiting period for health insurance coverage. The legislation of the Affordable Care Act is 974 pages containing many provisions and contingencies, including a requirement for continuing premium review. In 2017, a mandate of the Affordable Care Act that levied a financial penalty on individuals who elected not to have medical insurance was overturned by Executive Order 13765. In 2018, a judge in Texas ruled that Executive Order 13765 caused the ACA to be unconstitutional. As of the release of this edition, the future of the ACA in light of the Texas judge's ruling has been appealed, so the future of this act is in question. However, the provisions and requirements of the ACA are still in force and employers must comply with the existing requirements.

According to the Internal Revenue Service, employers must report whether they provide Minimum Essential Coverage that is part of their company-sponsored benefits including any group health plans, COBRA plans, or preexisting insurance coverage. Health insurance coverage is reported on IRS Form 1095 A, B, or C as follows:

- Form 1095-A is for individuals who have purchased insurance from the Healthcare Marketplace, not through an employer. This form is issued by the Marketplace.
- Form 1095-B is to report information to the IRS for individuals who have minimum essential coverage through group insurance plans provided by governmental employers and qualified private-sector employers. This form is issued by health insurers and plan sponsors for self-insured employers.
- Form 1095-C is for large employers who provide health insurance where the employer is responsible for the shared responsibility provision of the Act. This form is issued by employers who offer coverage but are not self-insured, and who have 50 or more full-time and/or full-time equivalent employees.

The employer must file IRS form 1095-B or 1095-C and furnish a copy to the insured if the insured received medical insurance benefits for as few as one day of one month during a calendar year.* (Source: IRS)

*It should be noted that the parts of the Affordable Care Act have been changed and others are being debated as of the time of publication.

Legislative provisions and reporting requirements remain in effect until formal repeal of the legislation. Changes in 2018 include the following:

- Reduced affordability standard: The percentage of an employee's monthly household income that would be used to obtain affordable coverage has been reduced from 9.69 percent to 9.56 percent.
- Certain preventive care items are included, such as aspirin for adults over 50 who are at risk for cardiovascular issues.
- IRS assessments of employers for legal compliance, including penalties for employee misclassification or intentional disregard of the law.

(Source: HRDive)

Public Law 115-97, the ***Tax Cuts and Jobs Act***, was enacted in December 2017 and represented sweeping changes to the tax code. This law had a profound effect on payroll taxes, especially employee federal income tax liability, and required a comprehensive reframing of employee income tax computation. Specific changes to payroll included a change to the Social Security wage base, adjustments to nonresident alien withholding, adjustments for inflation, and decreases in supplemental wage withholding rates. The Internal Revenue Service issued new mid-year tax withholding tables and forms in response to the changes mandated in this act.

In March 2018, President Trump signed the ***Consolidated Appropriations Act of 2018***. One part of this act increased the funding for the E-Verify program, which is an Internet-based system that offers employers instant verification of an employee's eligibility to work in the United States. It is important to note that the E-Verify program does not replace the need for the completion of Form I-9 upon employee hire because it is a voluntary service. The following table from the USCIS compares the E-Verify program against the I-9 requirement.

Form I-9	E-Verify
Mandatory	Voluntary for most businesses
Requires a Social Security number	Requires a Social Security number
No photo required on identity documents	Photo is required on identity documents
MUST be used to re-verify expired employment authorization	MAY NOT be used to re-verify expired employment authorization

(Source: USCIS)

Another important part of the Consolidated Appropriations Act included monetary penalties of $1,000 per instance (plus damages) for employers who withhold employee tip earnings inappropriately. This section of the act repealed a 2017 Department of Labor regulation that prevented employers from requiring that all tips be placed into a pool for tipped and non-tipped employees. Although the act did not remove the use of tip pools, it prevented managers and supervisors from participating in the tip pools.

Which Payroll Law?

Stop & Check

1. Established requirements for employer record keeping?
2. Provided government assistance for workers who are too old or infirm to work?
3. Established protection for displaced workers?
4. Required employers to file taxes collected in a timely manner?
5. Set aside funds for health insurance?
6. Regulated wages for employees whose employer engaged in governmental contracts?
7. Is governed on a state-to-state basis and protects employees injured during the course of work activities?
8. Is responsible for reporting requirements of essential health coverage for full-time equivalent employees?
9. Restructured payroll tax calculations, supplemental withholdings, and the Social Security wage base?
10. Funded E-Verify programs for employee eligibility to work?

a. Social Security Act
b. Workers' compensation
c. Current Tax Payment Act
d. Fair Labor Standards Act
e. Tax Act (PL 115-97)
f. Federal Unemployment Tax Act
g. Medicare
h. Consolidated Appropriations Act
i. Affordable Care Act
j. Davis–Bacon Act

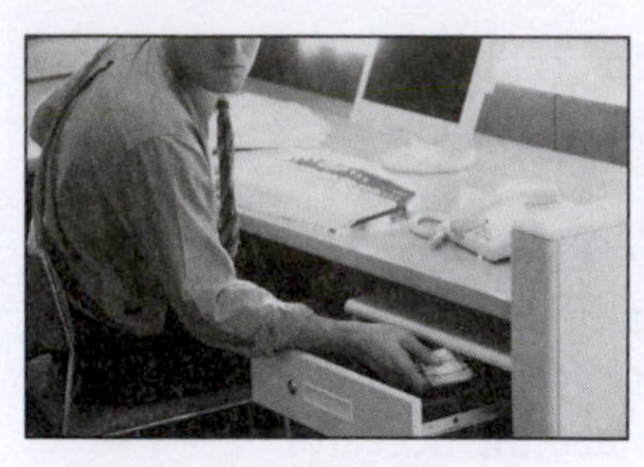
Digital Vision/Getty Images

LO 1-3 Discuss the Ethical Guidelines for Payroll Accounting

Professional ***ethics*** is critical in any accounting context, and especially so in payroll accounting. After the Enron accounting scandal and the passage of the Sarbanes–Oxley Act of 2002 (SOX), ethics became a focus of the accounting profession as a whole. Even with the SOX framework, the payroll industry is rife with ethical violations including fraud and theft. The payroll accountant is entrusted to handle money belonging to the firm and rightfully owed to the government and company employees. Payment of these monies becomes a moral contract between the company and the recipients; therefore, ethics are a vital element in payroll accounting. Several accounting organizations, including the American Institute of Certified Public Accountants (AICPA), Institute of Management Accountants (IMA) and International Federation of Accountants (IFAC) have delineated codes of ethics that are applied in the accounting profession. The basic guidelines of an ethics code include the following tenets, shown in Figure 1-2.

FIGURE 1-2
Basic Guidelines of a Code of Ethics

Confidentiality
Professionalism
Integrity
Objectivity and Independence
Professional Competence and Due Care

Ethisphere maintains an annual list of the most ethical companies in the world. In 2019, the list included many companies based in the United States, such as AFLAC, Hasbro, Paychex®, and several others. Although the companies on the list are in a variety of industries, certain ethical principles are common to all: integrity, social responsibility, care for all stakeholders, and honesty and transparency in all business dealings. (Source: Ethisphere)

Confidentiality

An accountant is responsible for maintaining confidences and exercising moral judgment in all actions. A payroll accountant deals with sensitive personnel information that must remain confidential. Social Security numbers, employee legal obligations, and an employer's tax liabilities are a few examples of information that a payroll accountant must protect.

The state of New Jersey enacted the Diane B. Allen Equal Pay Act, which strengthened existing antidiscrimination laws by preventing pay differences based on traits protected under other civil rights laws. It also protected employees who discussed pay with other employees. However, it should be noted that the payroll accountant is still responsible for maintaining the confidentiality of employee records in order for this law to function in the way it was intended. (Source: State of New Jersey 2018 Legislature)

GaudiLab/Shutterstock

Professionalism

Accountants must uphold ***professionalism*** by maintaining confidentiality, maintaining the public's trust, and upholding professionalism in their practice. In terms of payroll accounting, professionalism includes honoring the needs of the firm, its employees, and associated governmental entities. A payroll accountant must complete all tasks and adhere to deadlines, despite any personal issues. Personal honesty and transparency of transactions are the core of acting professionally.

Brinker International, the parent entity for restaurants such as Maggiano's Little Italy and Chili's, outlines its ethical policy and expectations for employee compliance, especially as they pertain to the Brinker International Payroll Company, L.P., in its Ethical Business Policy. An emphasis on transparency, integrity, and action in the public interest are key components of the policy. (Source: Brinker International)

Integrity

In the workplace, integrity is the most important asset a professional can possess. ***Integrity*** involves doing the right thing despite any external pressure, personal temptations, or conflicts of interest. The main question when weighing the integrity of a decision is, Am I doing what is right and just for everyone concerned? Any course of action that lacks integrity potentially restricts the rights of interested parties and compromises the best interests of the company. The AICPA code of ethics includes express direction about not covering up mistakes as part of an accountant's integrity.

Payroll fraud can happen anywhere that pressures, opportunities, and rationalizations exist. A payroll specialist for a District of Columbia consulting firm was indicted on embezzlement charges involving fictitious employees. The payroll specialist stole over $250,000, including amounts deposited for payroll taxes, by changing the pay disbursement details of terminated employees. Instead of leaving the employees' files in a "terminated" status, the altered detail allowed automatic salary payments to continue—but to be deposited to the payroll specialist's personal account. The payroll specialist, who plead guilty to wire fraud, was ordered to repay the employer $250,000 and was sentenced to 21 months in prison. (Source: U.S. Department of Justice)

Objectivity and Independence

Accountants must take care to be independent of any pressures that would compromise the integrity of their work. These pressures can come from business or personal relationships that may affect a payroll accountant's judgment concerning the best interests of all concerned in a given situation. ***Objectivity*** in accounting means that the accountant considers only facts relevant to the task at hand, independent of all other pressures. The Public Company Accounting Oversight Board (PCAOB) specifies that ***independence*** may be compromised if any of the following situations occur:

- Commitment to a future purchase of financial interest in a client's business.
- Personal or family ownership in excess of 5 percent of a client's business.
- Professional engagement with a client's firm in which the payroll professional had a personal interest such as partial ownership..

Social obligations may compromise a payroll accountant's objectivity. The AICPA Code of Ethics section 17 specifically addresses social club membership as a factor in the loss of an accountant's independence or objectivity. Such club membership could create a social debt that may cause an accountant to commit payroll fraud. (Source: AICPA)

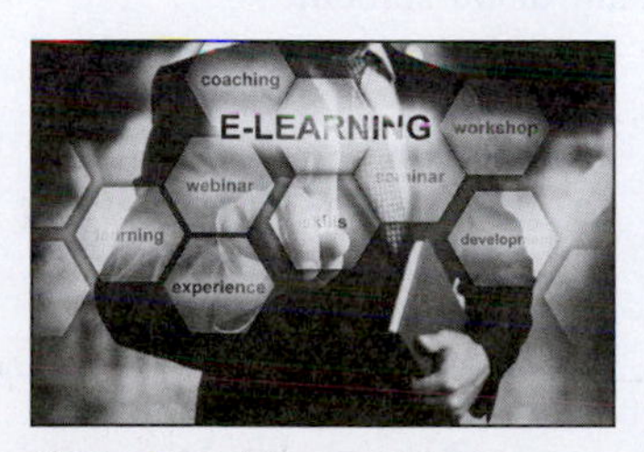

Wright Studio/Shutterstock

Professional Competence and Due Care

Professional competence and ***due care*** revolves around an accountant's competence and assumes that the accounting professional is equally competent as other people in a similar role. In payroll accounting, due care is an ongoing process that involves education, training, and experience. According to the AICPA, an accountant must remain current with accounting practices and legal developments to comply with due care requirements. Payroll laws and tax guidelines change regularly. As a payroll accountant, it is extremely important to remain aware of annual changes that the IRS and other accounting bodies publish through participation in professional accounting organizations, subscriptions to accounting industry publications, and participation in discussions at accounting conferences.

Staying current with payroll changes is an ongoing task. Some of the sources for this information include

- IRS (www.irs.gov).
- AICPA (www.aicpa.org).
- Financial Accounting Standards Board (FASB) (www.fasb.org).
- American Payroll Association (www.americanpayroll.org).
- U.S. Department of Labor (www.dol.gov).
- Compliance Tools for HR Professionals (www.hr.blr.com).

What's Ethical?

Stop & Check

1. Giles Montragon is the payroll accountant for his company. His boss informs him that the company is considering switching payroll systems and asks for his input. What are some ethical concerns involved in changing accounting software?
2. Liza Beals, the payroll manager, is in a sorority. At a social event, she discovers that one of her sorority sisters works for the same company. Her sorority sister asks Liza for confidential information about one of the employees in her department, claiming that the sorority oath requires Liza's compliance. What should Liza do?

LO 1-4 Identify Contemporary Payroll Practices

Andrey_Popov/Shutterstock

Contemporary accounting practices reflect the effects of technology and electronic communications on business. Payroll practices have adapted to include modern tools that facilitate data transmission, and new challenges have emerged. Examples include the following:

- Direct deposit regulations for employee pay and tax remittances.
- Electronic filing requirements.
- New timekeeping methods.
- The availability of paycards as a method of wage and salary disbursement.
- Government contract influences on payroll.
- International employees.
- Simultaneous in-house and outsourced payroll personnel.
- Integration of payroll into other company functions.
- Security of confidential, electronic personnel information.

Payroll is no longer a stand-alone department. Integrated software packages offered by mainstream accounting software providers, such as QuickBooks and Sage 100 Standard, allow business owners to view data across departments and synthesize the information to make large-scale decisions. Contemporary payroll systems serve as a tool for strategic planning, performance measurement, and customer/vendor relations. Payroll accountants are a key element in the decision-making process and must remain educated about legal and compliance issues.

The payroll accountant plays a vital role in a company's structure, no matter how large or small. Payroll and other employee benefits often represent the largest category of a company's expenses. McDonald's Corporation reported more than $3.5 billion in payroll expense in its company-owned stores during fiscal year 2017, which decreased to just under $3 billion in 2018. The McDonald's Corporation has shifted its model in recent years and 90 percent of its restaurants are franchises, which represents a shift away from company-owned stores and explains the decreasing trend in company-store payrolls.

OPERATING COSTS AND EXPENSES (in millions)			
Company-Operated Restaurant Expenses	**2018**	**2017**	**2016**
Food & Paper	**3,153.8**	4,033.5	4,896.9
Payroll & Employee Benefits	**2,937.9**	3,528.5	4,134.2
Occupancy & Other Operating Expenses	**2,174.2**	2,847.6	3,667.7
Franchised Restaurants—Occupancy Expenses	**1,973.3**	1,790.0	1,718.4
Selling, General, & Administrative Expenses	**2,200.2**	2,231.3	2,384.5
Other Operating (income) Expense, Net	**(236.8)**	(1,163.2)	75.7
Total Operating Costs	**12,202.6**	13,267.7	16,877.4
Operating Income	**8,822.6**	5,192.3	4,686.5

Source: McDonald's 10-k Filing, 2019

Payroll Preparation Options

Several options exist for payroll preparation. The most frequently used method for contemporary payroll preparation is electronic accounting programs. Other options available are manual calculation of payroll using spreadsheets and charts prepared by the Internal Revenue Service and payroll preparation by outsourcing the process to a third party such as ADP, Paychex®, and myPay Solutions. A hybrid solution that allows the company to outsource certain payroll functions to an external provider exists with online accounting software provided by companies such as Intuit and Sage, creators of QuickBooks and Sage 100cloud, respectively.

Online banks are starting to enter the payroll industry as a means to facilitate payroll access via smartphones. Chime Bank advertises access to directly deposited funds up to two days prior to the employer's pay date, based on the employer's funds availability. Another option targeted for small employers includes Amboy Bank, which offers payroll processing, reporting, and banking services that simplify the payroll process for both employers and their employees.

Regardless of the payroll preparation method, it is important for the payroll accountant to understand how the process should work. In the event of hardware failure, legislative actions, or tax changes, the accountant must ensure accurate payroll preparation. Companies can lose credibility as the result of flawed payroll, as well as be subject to substantial fines, IRS audits, and civil litigation. Cases in which companies have paid fines for improper payroll practices abound.

> Shield Packaging of Massachusetts was fined $1 million as a settlement with its employees for minimum wage and overtime violations. The company had paid its employees at a rate lower than the state's minimum wage from 2014 to 2016, which caused the company's computations of overtime wages to be inaccurate. In addition, two company employees deliberately misled government investigators. Since they had disobeyed the state's minimum wage law and obstructed the investigation, the company was ordered to pay 480 employees and to improve its payroll record-keeping practices. (Source: *Worcester Business Journal*)

Some companies have seriously shortchanged employees' paychecks, paying fines in addition to the standard payroll expenditures. Other tales of employee overpayment highlight problems in payroll systems, such as computer glitches that have delayed payment of the company's wages. Because the computer glitches are ultimately the responsibility of a company's president or CEO and represent a potential for ethical breaches, the volume of legislation and stories of problems involving payroll administration point to the need for a well-established payroll system. Despite the numerous federal and state legislative actions concerning payroll practices, none delineate the format and design of a payroll system.

The information contained in the personnel records is highly sensitive and must be protected against intrusion from unnecessary parties. The ***Privacy Act of 1974*** guarantees the safeguarding of information contained in private personnel records and mandates information safekeeping as well as due process rights to individuals. Consider the implications of the legal requirements of information safekeeping:

- Personnel records contain information about an individual's marital status, children, other dependents, and legal residence—sensitive information that must be protected under the Privacy Act of 1974.
- Payroll records generally have information about the hourly rate and salary information for each employee. Access to these records is protected by provisions of the ***Equal Employment Opportunity Commission (EEOC)*** and could provoke or inhibit discrimination lawsuits.
- The information contained in payroll records influences the accuracy and integrity of a company's accounting records. The recording of payroll expenses and liabilities affect the profitability of a company, which influences investor and customer relations.
- Companies engaging in business with the federal government must comply with the Davis–Bacon Act (for federal contracts) and potentially the ***Copeland Anti-Kickback Act*** of 1934 (or construction projects, protecting taxpayers from unethical pay practices).
- The number of hours worked by an employee must comply with the provisions of the Fair Labor Standards Act.
- Deductions for payroll, especially for retirement plans, must be documented and verified in accordance with the Sarbanes–Oxley Act of 2002.

Employers are required to file tax deposits for employee withholding, Social Security, Medicare, FUTA, and SUTA taxes according to an identified timeline depending upon the size of the company's payroll. Taxes may be remitted via telephone, Internet, mail, or the company's payroll software program. Additional reports are required from the employer on either a quarterly or an annual basis. A company has many responsibilities within its payroll system:

- Tax withholding must be done consistently, reflecting the requirements of federal, state, and local authorities.
- Employers must match amounts withheld from employee paychecks for certain payroll taxes.

- Withholding of deductions that the employee voluntarily elects, such as health care, insurance, and investments, must be correctly recorded and reported.
- Timely and accurate payment must be made to the employee, government agencies, and companies for which the employee has designated the voluntary deductions.
- Tax and other liabilities must be reported to governmental agencies in accordance with established deadlines.

An accurate payroll system allows managers to focus on the firm's business, not payroll administration. As such, a well-designed system benefits the employees and governmental agencies, and thus the firm. The timely forwarding of any monies withheld from employees, either by governmental regulation or voluntary election, is critical to a firm's success. If the establishment and implementation of a payroll system sounds complex, it is!

Besides administrating employee pay, a well-designed and accurately maintained payroll system is necessary during inevitable governmental audits. An audit is a process by which a third-party organization, either a public accounting firm or a government agency, inspects the accounting records of a firm for accuracy, integrity, and compliance with federal rules and regulations. During a payroll audit, the auditor inspects the company's records of employee pay, tax remittance, and voluntary deduction maintenance. The thought of audits instills fear into the hearts of even the most seasoned accounting professionals. Their salvation, however, is to establish and maintain an accurate payroll system.

Consider the growth of selected companies:

Tom's of Maine started in 1968 as a local organic personal care product company and is now a nationally recognized leader in environmental stewardship and sustainability. (Source: www.tomsofmaine.com)

Aaron Roeth Photography

Ben and Jerry's, which started with a $5 correspondence course in ice-cream making and a $12,000 investment in 1978, has become an icon of premium ice cream and environmental causes. Ben and Jerry's has since been purchased by the Unilever Corporation and maintains an independent board of directors. (Source: www.benjerry.com)

McDonald's Corporation was started in 1955 by the McDonald brothers when they sold their hamburger business to Ray Kroc. The brand is now an international icon for fast food, serving approximately 68 million customers in 120 countries each day.

These two companies share similar beginnings: one location, a few employees, and a relatively simple payroll. As each company has grown, so has the payroll complexity, including multiple departments and facilities in many states and countries. At the heart of each company is a well-run business model and a sound payroll system that has evolved with it.

Tracking and monitoring employee hours, locations, and applicable governmental requirements within various nations requires a knowledgeable payroll staff, willing to remain current with accounting trends and international regulations. Sophisticated payroll systems enable companies to create, populate, and file a multitude of documents using current software and Internet technology.

Privacy Protection

A company must make every reasonable effort to protect personnel information contained in payroll records. This is a critical part of any payroll accountant's job. Several federal privacy acts exist to protect the information contained in payroll and personnel records. Additionally, 13 states have enacted specific data privacy legislation. Each state's privacy law refers to "reasonable" steps that companies must take to protect customer's information.

Rawpixel.com/Shutterstock

The privacy acts include (but are certainly not limited to)

- U.S. Department of Labor OCFO-1, which pertains to the privacy of information in payroll files.

- U.S. Department of Health and Human Services Privacy Act 09-40-0006, which pertains to eligibility of public employees for pay, entitlements, raises, and benefits.
- Common Law Privacy Act, which pertains to freedom from misuse or abuse of one's private affairs.
- Privacy Act of 1974, pertaining to the use of information about private citizens.
- Computer Fraud and Abuse Act (CFAA) of 1986, which addresses cyber crime, an issue that has grown in importance in recent years.

The General Accounting Office of the federal government has been working to revise guidelines about records privacy and release of information as the Internet and e-business evolve. The United States Congress has sought ways to address contemporary computer-based cyber threats, but as yet has not passed legislation at the federal level. States have enacted privacy laws, especially as they pertain to social media, to protect employees against cyber hacks.

> Online privacy is a growing concern, and it affects the security of payroll data. Data breaches occur each month in businesses around the world. For example, in February 2018, Entergy notified its employees that their 2016 form W-2 information was stolen by criminals who hacked the Equifax subsidiary, TALX. (Source: Databreaches.net)

Benoit Daoust/Shutterstock

The common element among these laws is the protection of sensitive employee information such as addresses, dependents, compensation amounts, and payroll deductions. The payroll accountant is also responsible for discretion in discussing pay rates, bonuses, or other compensation-related topics with employees and management. Sensitive topics should never be discussed with anyone other than the employee or appropriate managers. All employment-related items may be viewed during an audit of payroll records, and auditors must treat the information with absolute confidentiality.

One way that the federal government keeps track of employers is with Employer Identification Numbers (EINs). The EIN allows the IRS to know which companies may have employees, therefore generating employment tax revenue for the government and creating tax liabilities for employers. Form SS-4 (see Figure 1-3) is used to apply for a EIN by providing the personal Social Security number, type of business, and existence of any prior EINs for a business owner. The EIN is required for all tax deposits, tax returns, and informational returns. It will appear on the company's Form W-2s, 940s, 941s, any state tax forms, and the annual tax return for the company. Form SS-4 may be completed either on paper or through an online request portal processed by the IRS that contains the same information as the paper form.

Confidential Records

Stop & Check

You are the payroll clerk of a company. A group of students approaches you to work on a class project and asks to see confidential personnel and payroll records. What would you do? What are the laws regarding the situation?

FIGURE 1-3
Example of Form SS-4

Form **SS-4** (Rev. December 2017) Department of the Treasury Internal Revenue Service

Application for Employer Identification Number
(For use by employers, corporations, partnerships, trusts, estates, churches, government agencies, Indian tribal entities, certain individuals, and others.)
▶ Go to *www.irs.gov/FormSS4* for instructions and the latest information.
▶ See separate instructions for each line. ▶ Keep a copy for your records.

OMB No. 1545-0003
EIN

Type or print clearly.

1 Legal name of entity (or individual) for whom the EIN is being requested
Thomas Braden

2 Trade name of business (if different from name on line 1)
Braden Fisheries

3 Executor, administrator, trustee, "care of" name

4a Mailing address (room, apt., suite no. and street, or P.O. box)
1234 Coastal Highway

5a Street address (if different) (Do not enter a P.O. box.)

4b City, state, and ZIP code (if foreign, see instructions)
Anchorage, AK 99509

5b City, state, and ZIP code (if foreign, see instructions)

6 County and state where principal business is located

7a Name of responsible party
Thomas Braden

7b SSN, ITIN, or EIN
445-54-4554

8a Is this application for a limited liability company (LLC) (or a foreign equivalent)? . . . . ☑ Yes ☐ No

8b If 8a is "Yes," enter the number of LLC members . . . . . . ▶ 3

8c If 8a is "Yes," was the LLC organized in the United States? . . . . ☑ Yes ☐ No

9a **Type of entity** (check only one box). **Caution.** If 8a is "Yes," see the instructions for the correct box to check.
☐ Sole proprietor (SSN)
☐ Partnership
☑ Corporation (enter form number to be filed) ▶ 2553
☐ Personal service corporation
☐ Church or church-controlled organization
☐ Other nonprofit organization (specify) ▶
☐ Other (specify) ▶
☐ Estate (SSN of decedent)
☐ Plan administrator (TIN)
☐ Trust (TIN of grantor)
☐ Military/National Guard
☐ State/local government
☐ Farmers' cooperative
☐ Federal government
☐ REMIC
☐ Indian tribal governments/enterprises
Group Exemption Number (GEN) if any ▶

9b If a corporation, name the state or foreign country (if applicable) where incorporated
State: Alaska
Foreign country:

10 **Reason for applying** (check only one box)
☑ Started new business (specify type) ▶ Commercial Fishing
☐ Hired employees (Check the box and see line 13.)
☐ Compliance with IRS withholding regulations
☐ Other (specify) ▶
☐ Banking purpose (specify purpose) ▶
☐ Changed type of organization (specify new type) ▶
☐ Purchased going business
☐ Created a trust (specify type) ▶
☐ Created a pension plan (specify type) ▶

11 Date business started or acquired (month, day, year). See instructions.
05/01/2019

12 Closing month of accounting year December

13 Highest number of employees expected in the next 12 months (enter -0- if none). If no employees expected, skip line 14.

Agricultural	Household	Other
15		

14 If you expect your employment tax liability to be $1,000 or less in a full calendar year **and** want to file Form 944 annually instead of Forms 941 quarterly, check here. (Your employment tax liability generally will be $1,000 or less if you expect to pay $4,000 or less in total wages.) If you do not check this box, you must file Form 941 for every quarter. ☐

15 First date wages or annuities were paid (month, day, year). **Note:** If applicant is a withholding agent, enter date income will first be paid to nonresident alien (month, day, year) . . . . ▶ 05/15/2019

16 Check **one** box that best describes the principal activity of your business.
☐ Construction ☐ Rental & leasing ☐ Transportation & warehousing ☐ Health care & social assistance ☐ Wholesale-agent/broker
☐ Real estate ☐ Manufacturing ☐ Finance & insurance ☐ Accommodation & food service ☐ Wholesale-other ☐ Retail
☑ Other (specify) ▶ Commercial Fishing

17 Indicate principal line of merchandise sold, specific construction work done, products produced, or services provided.
Fish and seafood

18 Has the applicant entity shown on line 1 ever applied for and received an EIN? ☐ Yes ☑ No
If "Yes," write previous EIN here ▶

Third Party Designee
Complete this section **only** if you want to authorize the named individual to receive the entity's EIN and answer questions about the completion of this form.
Designee's name
Designee's telephone number (include area code)
Address and ZIP code
Designee's fax number (include area code)

Under penalties of perjury, I declare that I have examined this application, and to the best of my knowledge and belief, it is true, correct, and complete.
Applicant's telephone number (include area code) 907-555-8915
Name and title (type or print clearly) ▶ Thomas Braden
Applicant's fax number (include area code) 907-555-8916
Signature ▶ Thomas Braden Date ▶ 05/03/2019

For Privacy Act and Paperwork Reduction Act Notice, see separate instructions. Cat. No. 16055N Form **SS-4** (Rev. 12-2017)

Source: Internal Revenue Service.

LO 1-5 Compare Payroll Processing Options for Different Businesses

Companies have several options for payroll processing. The option a company chooses depends on the size of the business, the complexity of the business in terms of geographic placement and business model, the capital available for payroll processing, and the availability of trained personnel.

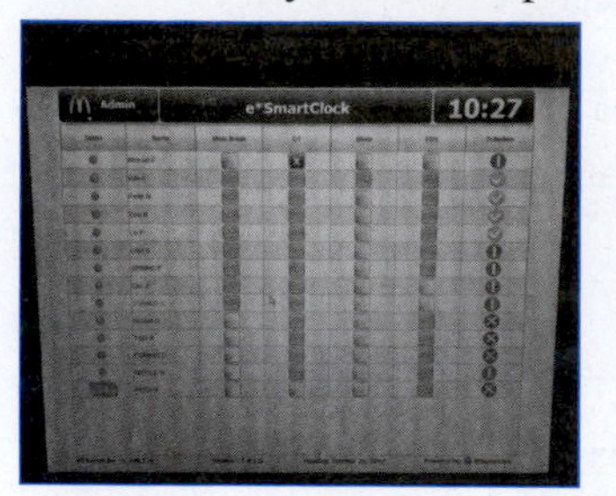

Jeanette Landin

During the middle of the 20th century, worker time was measured by using punch clocks and handwritten time sheets. Contemporary time collection devices serve as more than simple time clocks. Although the old-fashioned punch clocks still exist, companies have integrated different time-collection systems as part of their office security and computer access procedures. Time clocks are used as part of a security system to log in people as they enter a building for work, which can yield analysis of simple on-site versus working-hour time.

Many companies now use biometric devices such as fingerprint readers to collect time for their hourly employees. Systems such as Kronos offer biometric badges and time-collection devices that connect with office telephones. Using computer access as another type of collection device serves a similar function and can offer the additional functionality of specific task tracking and precise timekeeping. With the growth of mobile connectivity, companies now have a large number of smartphone apps, such as WhenIWork and ExacTime, to track employee attendance and productivity. Practices relating to time collection are a vital element in payroll accuracy.

The basic elements of a payroll system are similar for all companies, but this is a case when size does matter. However, it is not only the size of the company but also the complexity of the laws that affect payroll procedures. Let's look at the differences between large and small company payrolls and then explore certified payroll issues.

Large Businesses

Large companies present intricate problems for payroll accountants. Companies such as Apple, Alphabet (Google), and Microsoft have multiple divisions, many of which exist in different geographical locations. General Electric (GE) has different companies that operate as separate entities within GE's framework. Payroll procedures reflect the intricacy of the company's structure and may take many forms.

Rawpixel.com/Shutterstock

One of the major challenges in larger organizations is the existence of multiple departments in which an individual employee may work on any given day. Some companies can have shared employees, who will have allocable time to more than one department; for example, one employee may work for both the marketing and the production departments. When this occurs, the payroll accountant will have to record the time worked for each department, and pay rates may differ based on the tasks that the employee performs for each department.

A common payroll procedure with large companies involves employee portals on company websites. On the company's payroll website, employees may enter vacation time, overtime, and other issues that pertain to the employee's payroll data. Through the same website, employees may change withholding allowances and voluntary deductions and maintain certain other aspects of their employee files. Such web-based portals contain highly sensitive information, and security of the information is an obvious concern for the companies who use them. Multiple identity checks and security measures are in place to ensure privacy of employee data, such as SSL (secure sockets layer) encryption, ***VPN*** (virtual private network), and CAPTCHA programs that are designed to differentiate between humans and other computer programs.

To overcome some of the issues with payroll processing, large companies may rely heavily on payroll service vendors to assist with payroll preparation and human resources integration. Providers such as myPay Solutions and ADP work with the security needs of the company

Providing employees with Internet-based access to their personnel files is a challenging issue. Federal laws do not grant employees the right to access their personnel files, and companies must be aware of state laws before providing access. Questions of assigning access to other parties (such as union representatives), access to file artifacts, and the right of the employee to challenge items contained in their file are issues that a firm should address when creating a web portal through which employees may access payroll records. In addition, issues of cyber security and online privacy must be addressed. (Source: SHRM)

to offer websites that are secure and integrate multiple personnel functions seamlessly. Some larger firms will work with software engineers to develop independent systems specifically meeting unique company needs.

Large companies face other issues related to accurate timekeeping, such as the volume of employee records. Companies with computerized time-measurement systems may link employees' computer logins, telephone logins, or building access with the payroll system. Companies working with radio frequency time cards and electronic payroll monitoring can properly allocate employee time to specific machines or production lines. With the computer software and services currently available, large companies have many options to maintain the accuracy and integrity of their payroll systems.

Small Businesses

One apparent difference between large and small businesses is the volume and handling of payroll records. A small number of employees generally leads to fewer payroll-related transactions. Manual payroll systems may be maintained in very small businesses, including the use of handwritten time cards. Outsourcing of payroll activities may not be as prominent. With a small company, the amount of time to complete payroll-related tasks may be less than in a large company. For a small company, the task can be performed without disrupting the revenue-producing tasks of the business.

Small companies have the option of processing payroll in-house with a minimum of difficulty. However, small companies may lack specifically trained payroll personnel, which may place the responsibility for employee pay and benefits on other personnel and may increase the risk of pay or tax inaccuracies. The human resource director, office manager, and payroll professional may frequently be the same person. Using payroll software and a properly designed payroll system, the task of payroll for a small company is generally manageable by minimal company staff. Small companies may choose to explore outsourcing as the company grows. Outsourcing payroll may be a viable option if the task becomes unwieldy or legal obligations become unmanageable.

Sigrid Gombert/Image Source

Small companies have an option to use hosting services as a way to access cloud-storage, subscription-based services that possess security comparable to on-site accounting software. Hosted payroll accounting software can change in scale without the need for additional software licensing, update issues, or specific hardware.

For more information about hosted payroll, check out these top-rated services:

- Intuit Payroll
- Gusto
- OnPay
- SurePayroll

Depending on the size of the company, number of employees, and complexity of the payroll process, the company may choose to purchase a computer-based accounting system, it may continue to prepare worksheets and manual payroll checks, or it can decide to outsource the payroll preparation and associated tasks. Whichever decisions the company makes as it grows, the importance of understanding the mechanics of the payroll process is paramount. The next section provides an overview of the various computer-based systems available.

> Common payroll mistakes made by small firms include
>
> - Misclassifying employees as independent contractors.
> - Paying payroll late.
> - Omitting the value of gift cards awarded to employees as part of their taxable income.
> - Failure to make timely and/or accurate payroll tax deposits.
> - Improper treatment of expense reimbursements made to employees.
> - Incorrect treatment of taxable fringe benefits.
>
> (Source: *Accounting Today*)

Large vs. Small

Stop & Check

1. What are three payroll processing issues faced by large companies?
2. How does payroll processing differ between large and small companies?

Computer-Based Systems

Various accounting software packages exist to facilitate payroll-related accounting tasks, including QuickBooks, Sage 100 Standard, and Microsoft Dynamics GP. The use of computerized payroll systems eliminates approximately 80 percent of payroll processing time and errors. Computerized accounting systems foster the integration of payroll data with other company financial functions through Enterprise Resource Planning (ERP), which allows decision makers to develop a comprehensive understanding of the operational needs of the company. Although payroll professionals must verify employee data and update the software at regular intervals, computerized systems reduce the burdens of manual pay calculations, pay disbursement, and report compilation from the payroll accountant.

When used properly, small companies may benefit from a computerized payroll system. Although concerns about confidentiality of personnel records exist, electronic access to records may streamline certain tasks, such as employee information updates and overtime reporting. Additionally, as year-end approaches, companies can deliver the employees' W-2 (see Figure 1-4) tax forms electronically, ensuring employees rapid access to their tax documents.

A trend in payroll processing involves the issuance of electronic paycards, much like pre-loaded credit cards, as opposed to paper checks. Paycards offer the employees the flexibility of not having to wait for their paycheck to be deposited at a bank. Companies that offer direct deposit as a pay option must offer paycards as an option to employees who do not have bank accounts. However, a paycard can be lost or stolen, and with it, the employee's paycheck. Additionally, employers may be charged fees for loading a paycard. When companies consider paycards as an option, it is important to communicate to employees an understanding that there may be costs assessed by the card issuer.

Internet-Based Systems

Internet-based accounting software is an option for a company that does not have the need for or the resources to purchase a computer-based accounting system. Computer-based accounting systems such as QuickBooks, Microsoft Dynamics GP, and Sage 100 Standard offer both

FIGURE 1-4

Form W-2 Wage and Tax Statement

22222

a Employee's social security number: 444-44-4444

OMB No. 1545-0008

b Employer identification number (EIN): 12-1234567

c Employer's name, address, and ZIP code:
Some company name
1111 Fifth Avenue
Some City, OK 73217

d Control number

e Employee's first name and initial / Last name / Suff.:
Connie Barnes
PO BOX 11211
Some City, OK 73217

f Employee's address and ZIP code

Box	Amount	Box	Amount
1 Wages, tips, other compensation	21689.20	2 Federal income tax withheld	1858.00
3 Social security wages	22396.20	4 Social security tax withheld	1388.56
5 Medicare wages and tips	22396.20	6 Medicare tax withheld	324.74
7 Social security tips		8 Allocated tips	
9		10 Dependent care benefits	
11 Nonqualified plans		12a Code	DD 707.00
13 Statutory employee / Retirement plan / Third-party sick pay		12b Code	
14 Other		12c Code	
		12d Code	

15 State	Employer's state ID number	16 State wages, tips, etc.	17 State income tax	18 Local wages, tips, etc.	19 Local income tax	20 Locality name
OK	1866748	21689.20	976.01			

Form **W-2** Wage and Tax Statement 2019

Department of the Treasury—Internal Revenue Service

Source: Internal Revenue Service.

desktop and Internet-based services for businesses. In addition, companies such as Xero and Wave have developed Internet-only accounting packages that are accessible for a monthly fee. Advantages of using Internet-based services include the ease of access for accounting personnel and managers and automatic software updates. A potential disadvantage of relying on Internet-based software for a company's accounting is information security issues.

Accounting Today conducted case studies with firms that had used Internet-based accounting software and highlighted the following:

Positive Aspects	Challenges
Timely identification of financial issues because of the ease of access to company records	Users cannot usually customize certain information layouts to suit specific company needs
Low price for software access and "real time" knowledge of business information	Not suitable for highly complex businesses such as large manufacturing operations
Increased opportunity for collaboration in the business planning and monitoring process	Employee resistance to learning about new software and company accounting process
Continual software updates for changes in tax rates or other related practices	More options available than company personnel knew how to use

It is estimated that advances in predictive software and Artificial Intelligence-based systems will make accounting software more useful for small businesses, enabling companies to engage in real-time business analysis that had been previously out of their reach. Additionally, software advances will enable business owners to be more flexible in the way they conduct business as far as work location, information demands, and data transmittal. (Source: *Accounting Today*)

Manual Systems

With manual payroll systems, the payroll employee relies on deduction percentages that come presented in publications from the Internal Revenue Service. ***Publication 15*** (also known as ***Circular E***) is the manual payroll accountant's best friend, along with periodic updates and supplemental publications.

Rawpixel.com/Shutterstock

The largest challenges the manual payroll preparer faces are time constraints and updated tax tables. Companies can determine the length of time between the end of the payroll period and the employee payments with some degree of latitude. However, employers must make every reasonable effort to pay their employees in a timely and accurate manner to avoid ethical breaches and potentially costly litigation.

Manual payroll accountants may use spreadsheet programs, such as Excel, in which the accountant can create lookup formulas or other connecting formulas to facilitate the accurate completion of the payroll process. Spreadsheets with formulas or macros should be used only if the accountant understands the formulas and can verify the linkage prior to finalizing payroll to ensure that calculations are correct.

According to the IRS, approximately one-third of all small businesses make payroll errors. The amount of money involved in errors ranged between $963 in the business's favor to $3,180 in the IRS's favor. (Source: *Journal of Accountancy*)

Outsourced Payroll Systems

Outsourced payroll processing has become rather popular as a way to ensure compliance with the changing legal structure and withholding requirements. When a company chooses to use an outsourcing firm for the completion of the payroll processes, there are several considerations: records retention, confidentiality, compliance, timeliness, and thoroughness. Managers should review the cost/benefits of outsourcing a firm's payroll processes prior to making the commitment.

External payroll providers offer flexibility and advanced data analysis that might be challenging for smaller internal departments. During a survey of more than 2,000 accounting professionals, an overwhelming margin stated they would prefer to outsource payroll functions because of the time involved in the process. External payroll management providers such as ADP and Paychex® assist company owners and managers with strategic planning and related human resources issues. However, outsourcing is not a wise decision for all companies. For a small company, outsourcing may not be cost-effective. For large or international companies, outsourcing may be the only option to manage the payroll complexity.

A recent trend in payroll accounting involves cloud-based computing, meaning that the data is housed on a server external to the firm and accessible via an Internet connection. Companies such as ADP offer cloud-based payroll and human resource functions for businesses. These services reduce costs by allowing a company to avoid hardware and software costs associated with payroll. However, issues have arisen with payroll vendor stability and information security. Before turning to a cloud-based external payroll provider, a company needs to determine its needs to ensure that it makes the appropriate choice.

Certified Payroll

Companies who do business with the federal government under the Davis–Bacon Act are required to file a report (see Figure 1-5 for Form WH-347) delineating the payroll paid as part of the government contract with each payroll. ***Certified payroll*** is a way that the federal government keeps track of the money spent as part of government contracts. Davis–Bacon Act–related wages and the state versions of those regulations require special handling and knowledge. Certified payroll facilitates governmental internal accountability and verifies that Davis–Bacon Act requirements are met.

Information needed to complete a Certified Payroll report includes the following:

✓ Company-specific identifying information
✓ The job being worked on and its duration
✓ Employee information that includes social security number and address
✓ Hours worked on each job and the pay rate associated with it

✓ Gross pay earned for the week
✓ Taxes, withholdings, and fringe benefits
✓ Net pay earned per employee

FIGURE 1-5
Form WH-347 Certified Payroll

U.S. Department of Labor
Wage and Hour Division

PAYROLL
(For Contractor's Optional Use; See Instructions at www.dol.gov/whd/forms/wh347instr.htm)
Persons are not required to respond to the collection of information unless it displays a currently valid OMB control number.

WHD
U.S. Wage and Hour Division
Rev. Dec. 2008

NAME OF CONTRACTOR ☐ OR SUBCONTRACTOR ☐		ADDRESS		OMB No.:1235-0008 Expires: 04/30/2021
PAYROLL NO.	FOR WEEK ENDING	PROJECT AND LOCATION	PROJECT OR CONTRACT NO.	

(1) NAME AND INDIVIDUAL IDENTIFYING NUMBER (e.g. LAST FOUR DIGITS OF SOCIAL SECURITY NUMBER) OF WORKER	(2) NO. OF WITHHOLDING EXEMPTIONS	(3) WORK CLASSIFICATION	OT OR ST	(4) DAY AND DATE / HOURS WORKED EACH DAY							(5) TOTAL HOURS	(6) RATE OF PAY	(7) GROSS AMOUNT EARNED	(8) DEDUCTIONS FICA	WITH-HOLDING TAX			OTHER	TOTAL DEDUCTIONS	(9) NET WAGES PAID FOR WEEK
			O																	
			S																	
			O																	
			S																	

Source: U.S. Department of Labor.

What Is the Difference?

Stop & Check

In a few words, compare the following:

a. Manual payroll systems
b. Computerized payroll systems
c. Outsourced payroll systems
d. Certified payroll

Summary of Payroll Practices and System Fundamentals

Accounting practices have existed for centuries, and a need continually exists for employers to compensate employees for the work they have performed. Once the United States began taxing personal income, payroll processing became increasingly complex. During the 20th century, payroll practices evolved to include provisions for withholding taxes from employees, remitting payroll taxes to government agencies, maintaining accurate and confidential records, and incorporating civil rights–related legislation. Payroll accounting is a field that, due to its changing nature, requires precision and attention to minute details. Additionally, because of the nature of their work, payroll accountants must adhere to ethical guidelines including due care, objectivity and independence, integrity, and the public interest.

The establishment of a 21st-century payroll system involves careful, deliberate planning. The framework used for the payroll system must have ample room for company growth, structure to ensure system stability, and trained payroll personnel to ensure that company and government deadlines are met. Using the best practices outlined in this chapter may help a company implement a robust payroll system, whether the system is maintained by company personnel, outsourced, completed manually, or accomplished through the use of specifically designed software. Robust payroll system design may reduce or prevent problems with employees and governmental entities.

LEGAL ENVIRONMENT

To say that the legal environment of payroll is continually evolving is an understatement. Since 2016, we have witnessed the following legal challenges:

- Increasing numbers of private employers and localities raising the minimum wage significantly to close the gap between the minimum wage and the living wage.
- Changes to fringe benefits and state taxation of transportation benefits.
- Supplemental wage rate changes for payments of bonuses.
- State enforcement of predictive scheduling, fair/flexible scheduling laws on changing employee's schedules.
- Reframing the federal income tax structure, treatment for nonresident aliens, supplemental wage withholding rates, and inflation adjustments.

Some trends to watch include the following:

- Changes to the Affordable Care Act, up to and possibly including repeal.
- The expansion of artificial intelligence (AI) into the payroll process.
- Continued increase of data privacy initiatives at the company, state, and federal levels.
- Federally mandated paid leave provisions for both sick and bereavement time that would affect all companies in the nation.
- Acceleration in businesses moving to a completely cloud-based operations management and payroll process.

Key Points

- Legislation that has affected employees' working conditions has mandated many aspects of the workplace, including civil rights, retirement and health benefits, and reinvestment in American workers.
- Payroll-specific legislation has influenced working hours and employee wages.
- Employer and employee tax laws have been enacted, and the remittance of tax obligations has been mandated.
- Payroll accountants must adhere to ethical guidelines because of the nature of the work performed.
- The ethical principles of confidentiality, the public interest, integrity, objectivity and independence, and professional competence and due care guide the payroll accounting profession.
- Payroll practices include the electronic transmission of employee pay and tax obligations.
- Security of employee information is an ongoing concern for companies, especially with electronic transmission of sensitive data.
- Payroll may be processed at a central corporate site or through an outsourced payroll processing company.
- Many companies use payroll accounting software such as QuickBooks and Sage 100 Standard.
- Cloud-based payroll processing has offered many resources for companies, including partial or total payroll preparation services.

Vocabulary

ACA
ADA
ADAAA
ADEA
ARRA
ATRA
Certified payroll
Circular E
Civil Rights Act of 1964
Civil Rights Act of 1991
COBRA
Consolidated Appropriations Act of 2018
Copeland Anti-Kickback Act
Current Tax Payment Act of 1943
Davis–Bacon Act of 1931
DOMA
Due care
EEOC
Equal Pay Act of 1963
ERISA
Ethics
FICA
FLSA
FMLA
FUTA
HIPAA
Independence
Independent contractor
Integrity
IRCA
Lilly Ledbetter Fair Pay Act of 2009
Medicare
OASDI
Objectivity
OSHA
Personal Responsibility, Work and Family Promotion Act of 2002
Privacy Act of 1974
Protecting Americans from Tax Hikes (PATH) Act
Professional competence
PRWOR
Professionalism
Publication 15
Sixteenth Amendment to the U.S. Constitution
Social Security Act (SSA)
SOX
SUTA
Tax Cuts and Jobs Act
USERRA
VPN
Walsh–Healey Public Contracts Act
Workers' compensation

Review Questions

1. What is the purpose of a payroll system?
2. What are two differences between large- and small-company payroll practices?
3. What is certified payroll? Which companies must use it?
4. Why might it be a good idea to let employees manage their pay records? What are some of the pitfalls?
5. What are two ways that a payroll system may protect a company in the event of a visit from a government auditor?
6. What is payroll outsourcing? When might a company consider outsourcing its payroll?
7. What are three examples of federal laws that are essential to ensure legal, fair hiring practices?
8. What are the major types of payroll processing methods?
9. What are two laws governing the taxes that employers must withhold from employees?
10. What are the guidelines for FLSA in terms of overtime and pay rate?
11. Why was the Social Security Act of 1935 created? What were its provisions?
12. What are two advantages of a computerized payroll system over a manual system?
13. Which act created the term "Full-Time Equivalents"?
14. How has cloud-based payroll processing affected contemporary payroll practices?
15. What are two differences between the completion of the I-9 and the use of E-Verify systems?

Exercises Set A

E1-1A. LO 1-1, 1-2

Lupore Fabrics obtained a contract in Watts Mills, South Carolina that involves the production of materials for military uniforms, a project contracted with the federal government for $2,800,000. What laws govern the wages Lupore Fabrics pays to its workers for this project? (Select all that may apply.)

1. Davis–Bacon Act
2. Sarbanes–Oxley Act
3. Walsh–Healey Act
4. FLSA

E1-2A. LO 1-1, 1-2

Martine Piccirillo works as the payroll clerk for Centinix, a security company that hires many part-time and temporary workers who are paid on an hourly basis. What law governs the hiring or documenting of these workers?

1. ADEA
2. FLSA
3. IRCA
4. USERRA

E1-3A. LO 1-1, 1-2

Benson Rake is a member of the hiring board for Quambo Dynamics, a software firm. As the board reviews candidates for a position, one of the other board members wants to exclude Nicholas Mathers, a man in his 50s, because his age might mean that he would be retiring within the next 10 years. What law protects Nicholas against this practice?

1. FLSA
2. ADEA
3. ADA
4. Civil Rights Act of 1991

E1-4A. LO 1-1, 1-2

Ovenet Inc. is a qualified private-sector company that provides health insurance to its employees. The company is self-insured. Which of the following forms should the company provide its employees to comply with the Affordable Care Act?

1. 1095-A
2. 1095-B
3. 1095-C

E1-5A. LO 1-3

Julia Chaudhari is the new payroll accountant for Insulose Chemicals. She is a member of a local young professional networking organization. At a social gathering of the organization, her brother-in-law, Osher Nicastro, approached her about reviewing the company's payroll records to help her make sure they were correct. What ethical guidelines should Julia consider before agreeing to meet? (Select all that apply.)

1. Confidentiality
2. Objectivity and independence
3. Professional competence and due care
4. Integrity

E1-6A. LO 1-4, LO 1-5

Merlin Anson owns Uninix Computers, a company with five employees. As a small business owner, he has several options for payroll processing. What factors should he consider when deciding on which payroll processing option is best for Uninix Computers? (Select all that apply.)

1. The number of independent contractors.
2. The physical size of the office facility.
3. The amount of money he has to spend on payroll processing.
4. The computer technology used by the business.

Match the following terms with their definitions:

E1-7A. Manual payroll
E1-8A. Time card
E1-9A. Paycard
E1-10A. Employee Internet portal
E1-11A. Certified payroll
E1-12A. Outsourced payroll
E1-13A. Auditor
E1-14A. ADP and Paychex®
E1-15A. Time collection
E1-16A. Davis–Bacon Act
E1-17A. Consolidated Appropriations Act

a. A preloaded credit card used to pay employees.
b. The process of gathering information about hours worked for one or more employees.
c. A web-based application wherein employees can modify certain payroll-related information.
d. Governs accounting for firms with federal government contracts in excess of $2,000.
e. A record of the time worked during a period for an individual employee.
f. Examples of companies used for outsourcing payroll processing.
g. Provided funding for the E-Verify program.
h. Payroll administration using a paper payroll register.
i. The use of an external company to track time and benefits and pay employees.
j. A person or group who examines a company's accounting records for accuracy.
k. A way for governmental agencies to track the payroll associated with a government contract.

Problems Set A

P1-1A. LO 1-2
Hayim Accardi is the accounting manager for a small, local firm that has full- and part-time staff. How do FLSA guidelines regarding working hours apply to Hayim's employees?

P1-2A. LO 1-4, 1-5
Jessalyn Poulsen is an accountant for her firm, a medium-sized company with 125 employees. The firm has traditionally maintained the administration of its payroll. Her co-worker, the only other accountant in the firm, retires. Because of budget concerns, the firm chooses not to refill the position. What options does Jessalyn have regarding administration of the payroll?

P1-3A. LO 1-1, 1-2
Elias Motta is the office manager and payroll clerk for his company, which is composed of 12 employees. An employee, Sylvia Gladwin, stops by Elias's office and wants to view her payroll record. What privacy regulations must Elias consider before granting his co-worker access?

P1-4A. LO 1-3
A group of employees, who read on a website that income tax collection is illegal, approach Hawa Furst, the controller for a large company. They request that he stop withholding income taxes from their pay unless he can explain what laws govern income tax collection. What should Hawa tell them?

P1-5A. LO 1-1, 1-2
Kalea Germain is a warehouse worker for a small grocery market. As she was moving some merchandise, the loading dock door unexpectedly fell and injured her. How does OSHA apply to Kalea for this type of injury?

P1-6A. LO 1-4
Ennis Locatelli is a new payroll accountant at Avata Electronics. In his review of previous manual payroll records, he noted several errors that required the issuance of additional checks to employees for unpaid payroll amounts. What are Ennis's options to avoid similar problems in the future?

P1-7A. LO 1-3
Libbi Alberighi and Flavia van Peij are friends who work for the same company. Libbi manages a manufacturing department and Flavia supervises the payroll clerks. Which ethical guidelines or rules would these friends need to remember when discussing work?

P1-8A. LO 1-1, 1-2 — At Denniston Industries, employees have the option of choosing employer-sponsored health insurance. What responsibilities does the employer have according to COBRA upon termination of an employee?

P1-9A. LO 1-3 — Katelijn Preston is a new manager at Resterra Inc. She is looking at using the E-Verify process for new hires. What recommendations can you give her about the differences between having an employee complete the I-9 and the E-Verify process?

P1-10A. LO 1-4 — Cahya Russell is a new employee in the payroll department for Winhook Industries. She has had several employees approach her with questions but is unsure how privacy regulations could affect her response. What advice would you give her about privacy laws and payroll?

Exercises Set B

E1-1B. LO 1-1, 1-2 — Emmett Colquhoun is a military veteran who requires many absences for medical reasons. His boss at Betri Farms has demanded that he reduce the number of sick days unless he provides his medical history. Which law(s) protect Emmett? (Select all that apply.)

1. ADA
2. FLSA
3. USERRA
4. HIPAA

E1-2B. LO 1-1, 1-2 — Gale Rana is a production worker at Gexo Manufacturing, which produces air conditioning systems. After working there for 10 years, she discovers through conversations with a colleague with the same title and similar seniority that her wage is 20 percent lower than his wage. She feels that she has been a victim of discrimination. Which law(s) govern her situation?

1. FLSA
2. Civil Rights Act of 1964
3. ADEA
4. Equal Pay Act

E1-3B. LO 1-4, 1-5 — Mathias Acker is the new bookkeeper for Meganyx Enterprises, a small business consulting firm, and was hired to replace a long-time employee who retired. Upon starting the position, Mathias notices that the prior bookkeeper used a purely manual system. The company owner has said that Mathias may update the payroll system. What options are available?

E1-4B. LO 1-2 — Paula Aggio is the accounting manager for Sugent Communications. The company has a staff that includes five full-time employees and eight on-call workers who independently determine the number of hours and their work location. The on-call consultants claim that they should be classified as employees. What criteria should Paula use to determine the workers' employment status? (Select all that apply.)

1. The extent to which the on-call workers control their hours and working locations.
2. The number of hours worked by the on-call workers.
3. The number and types of job-specific tools that the employer provides.
4. How the workers are compensated for their work, by the job or by hours.

E1-5B.
LO 1-3

Erkan Dioli is the payroll accountant for Prosario Imports. His most recent experience with accounting was when he was in college, which was eight years ago. Which ethical guideline addresses his need to remain current with accounting practice?

1. Integrity
2. Professionalism
3. Professional competence and due care
4. Confidentiality

E1-6B.
LO 1-5

Khaled Watson is the payroll accountant for Antizio Electronics, a company that engages in work on federal contracts. He wants to ensure that the company is compliant with the provisions of the Davis–Bacon Act. What is the name of the process used to monitor payroll compliance in this situation?

1. Contracted payroll
2. Davis–Bacon verification
3. Certified payroll
4. Outsourced payroll

Match the following items with their definitions:

E1-7B. USERRA
E1-8B. *U.S. v. Windsor*
E1-9B. Internal controls documentation
E1-10B. HIPAA
E1-11B. Lilly Ledbetter Fair Pay Act
E1-12B. Sixteenth Amendment
E1-13B. Walsh–Healey Public Contracts Act
E1-14B. Independent contractor
E1-15B. Personal Responsibility, Work and Family Promotion Act of 2002
E1-16B. IRCA
E1-17B. Tax Cuts and Jobs Act

a. A provision of the Sarbanes–Oxley Act.
b. Instituted a tiered income tax on workers.
c. Prohibited employment of individuals younger than 16 years of age.
d. Strengthened the child support provisions of PRWOR.
e. Legislation that governs the treatment of military service personnel.
f. A worker who is not subject to a company's direction or its payroll laws.
g. Repealed the 180-day statute of limitations on equal pay complaints.
h. Re-framing federal employee income tax computations.
i. The case responsible for the U.S. Supreme Court's repeal of DOMA
j. Protects the confidentiality of employee medical records.
k. Mandates completion of Form I-9.

Problems Set B

P1-1B.
LO 1-4, 1-5

Albina Kravitz is the payroll administrator for Exity Enterprises. Because of economic conditions, her boss has assigned her the additional duties of office management, and Albina is considering outsourcing her payroll duties. What are the pros and cons of outsourcing the company's payroll?

P1-2B.
LO 1-1, 1-2

Jolana Thomas is the payroll clerk for Telemba Communications. One of the company's employees, Darijo Boon, informs Jolana that he feels that he was the victim of unequal pay three years prior. What law(s) provide guidance about Darijo's complaint?

P1-3B. LO 1-3
Clara Hudnall is Conosis Incorporated's payroll accountant. During a casual conversation with co-workers, she learns that Thorben Vinkovic, a co-worker, is deliberately overstating the number of hours worked during each pay period because of a personal economic situation. Which ethical guidelines pertain to this situation? What should Clara do with this knowledge?

P1-4B. LO 1-4
Perpetua Holguin is a payroll accountant for Marore Industries. She is asked to explain the differences between manual and computerized accounting practices. What differences should she highlight in her explanation?

P1-5B. LO 1-1, 1-2, 1-3
During a review of payroll records, Osvaldo Morena notices that a female employee in Department A is receiving a significantly lower salary than similarly skilled male employees in the same department. What actions should Osvaldo take in this situation?

P1-6B. LO 1-3
Samuel Alescio is an accountant for Diado, a large, multinational firm. During payroll processing, he notices that the new state payroll tax updates have not been installed in the firm's software. What ethical guidelines govern his behavior in this situation?

P1-7B. LO 1-2
Nitza Croce is an employee of Autonder, a contractor that provides governmental construction services in Washington, DC. The current contract is for $250,000. Nitza is 22 and is paid $9.50 per hour. How does the Walsh–Healey Public Contracts Act affect her?

P1-8B. LO 1-4
Eugene Robertson works as a payroll clerk at Hyperend Inc. He shares an office with three other co-workers and must examine documents containing personal information as a regular part of his duties. Based on the provisions of the Privacy Act of 1974, what responsibilities does Eugene have regarding the payroll records he handles?

P1-9B. LO 1-5
Larissa Abiodun is a senior payroll administrator for Falcive Landscape Design. The company has 15 employees and annual revenues of $10 million. She has been using and maintaining manual payroll records for the last 20 years of her career, and the president of Falcive Landscape Design wants to explore options for computerized payroll processing. Which payroll option is the most suitable for both Larissa and Falcive Landscape Design? Why?

P1-10B. LO 1-2
Alfredo Bellini is the payroll accountant for Pyrondo Fireworks and he has been asked for information about employees and independent contractors. What are three key differences between employees and independent contractors?

Critical Thinking

CT1-1. You have been hired as a consultant for Dynozz Medical Software, which is facing an IRS audit of its accounting records. During your review, you notice anomalies in the payroll system involving overpayments of labor and payments to terminated employees. What should you do?

CT1-2. Liliya Milic is the accountant for Syiva, a local nonprofit organization. She has been tasked with managing the costs of the payroll so that staffing levels may remain the same even if funding levels change. She considers outsourcing the payroll to a payroll processing company. What are some factors that Liliya should consider in her decision? Why are these factors important?

In the Real World: Scenario for Discussion

Domino's Pizza franchises in New York were sued by the state of New York in 2016 for wage theft at 10 stores. Under New York law, a corporation and a franchiser are joint employers if they meet certain criteria regarding employee control. The state found that Domino's met the criteria for being a joint employer because it mandates a significant number of policies with which franchisers must comply. The problem arose when Domino's mandated the use of PULSE payroll software, which the pizza company knew to be flawed and did not attempt to remedy. The flawed software led to employees being paid at rates below the legal minimum wage, failed to pay overtime, did not reimburse employees for vehicle use, and abused tip credit guidelines.

Food for thought:

1. Should the franchisers be held liable as joint employers with Domino's? Why or why not?
2. Which laws pertain to employee wages? How would they apply in this situation?
3. What could be done to ensure future legal compliance?

Internet Activities

1-1. Using the website www.jstor.org, search for articles about payroll-related laws or relevant employment legislation. Once you find an article, summarize the article, and explain how the legislation influenced contemporary payroll practices.

1-2. Visit the website of the American Payroll Association at www.americanpayroll.org. On the right side of the Home page, you will find articles about recent developments in payroll practices and legislation. Choose an article and create a presentation to your class about how its content affects payroll practice.

1-3. Want to know more about the specifics of some of the concepts in this chapter? Check out these websites:

www.dol.gov/whd/

www.taxhistory.com/1943.html

www.workerscompensationinsurance.com

www.Kronos.com

www.adp.com

www.paychex.com

1-4. Would it help to see a video explanation of FLSA coverage? Go to the link below and select Topic 1: Coverage.

https://www.dol.gov/whd/flsa/videos.htm

1-5. Check out www.employer.gov to see the Department of Labor's Office of Compliance site. This site contains guidelines for employers about their specific responsibilities to employees, compliance deadlines, posters, and other resources. Its employee-focused website, www.worker.gov, contains worker-focused resources geared to foster understanding of employee rights under the law.

sianc/Shutterstock

Continuing Payroll Project: Prevosti Farms and Sugarhouse

Toni Prevosti is opening a new business, Prevosti Farms and Sugarhouse, which is a small company that will harvest, refine, and sell maple syrup products. In subsequent chapters, students will have the opportunity to establish payroll records and complete payroll information for Prevosti Farms and Sugarhouse.

Toni has decided that she needs to hire employees for the business to grow. Complete the application for Prevosti Farms and Sugarhouse's Employer Identification Number (Form ss-4) with the following information:

Prevosti Farms and Sugarhouse is located at 820 Westminster Road, Bridgewater, Vermont, 05520 (which is also Ms. Prevosti's home address), phone number 802-555-3456. Bridgewater is in Windsor County. Toni, the responsible party for a Limited Liability Corporation with one member, has decided that Prevosti Farms and Sugarhouse, will pay its employees on a biweekly basis. Toni's Social Security number is 055-22-0443. The beginning date of the business is February 1, 20XX. Prevosti Farms and Sugarhouse will use a calendar year as its accounting year. Toni anticipates that she will need to hire six employees initially for the business, three of whom will be agricultural and three who will be office workers. The first date of wage disbursement will be February 13, 20XX. Toni has not had a prior EIN.

Form **SS-4** (Rev. December 2017) Department of the Treasury Internal Revenue Service

Application for Employer Identification Number
(For use by employers, corporations, partnerships, trusts, estates, churches, government agencies, Indian tribal entities, certain individuals, and others.)
▶ Go to *www.irs.gov/FormSS4* for instructions and the latest information.
▶ See separate instructions for each line. ▶ Keep a copy for your records.

OMB No. 1545-0003
EIN

Type or print clearly.

1 Legal name of entity (or individual) for whom the EIN is being requested

2 Trade name of business (if different from name on line 1) | 3 Executor, administrator, trustee, "care of" name

4a Mailing address (room, apt., suite no. and street, or P.O. box) | 5a Street address (if different) (Do not enter a P.O. box.)

4b City, state, and ZIP code (if foreign, see instructions) | 5b City, state, and ZIP code (if foreign, see instructions)

6 County and state where principal business is located

7a Name of responsible party | 7b SSN, ITIN, or EIN

8a Is this application for a limited liability company (LLC) (or a foreign equivalent)? . . . . ☐ Yes ☐ No
8b If 8a is "Yes," enter the number of LLC members . . . . . ▶

8c If 8a is "Yes," was the LLC organized in the United States? . . . . ☐ Yes ☐ No

9a **Type of entity** (check only one box). **Caution.** If 8a is "Yes," see the instructions for the correct box to check.
- ☐ Sole proprietor (SSN) ____________
- ☐ Partnership
- ☐ Corporation (enter form number to be filed) ▶ ____________
- ☐ Personal service corporation
- ☐ Church or church-controlled organization
- ☐ Other nonprofit organization (specify) ▶ ____________
- ☐ Other (specify) ▶
- ☐ Estate (SSN of decedent) ____________
- ☐ Plan administrator (TIN) ____________
- ☐ Trust (TIN of grantor) ____________
- ☐ Military/National Guard ☐ State/local government
- ☐ Farmers' cooperative ☐ Federal government
- ☐ REMIC ☐ Indian tribal governments/enterprises

Group Exemption Number (GEN) if any ▶

9b If a corporation, name the state or foreign country (if applicable) where incorporated | State | Foreign country

10 **Reason for applying** (check only one box)
- ☐ Started new business (specify type) ▶ ____________
- ☐ Hired employees (Check the box and see line 13.)
- ☐ Compliance with IRS withholding regulations
- ☐ Other (specify) ▶
- ☐ Banking purpose (specify purpose) ▶ ____________
- ☐ Changed type of organization (specify new type) ▶ ____________
- ☐ Purchased going business
- ☐ Created a trust (specify type) ▶ ____________
- ☐ Created a pension plan (specify type) ▶ ____________

11 Date business started or acquired (month, day, year). See instructions. | 12 Closing month of accounting year

13 Highest number of employees expected in the next 12 months (enter -0- if none). If no employees expected, skip line 14.

Agricultural	Household	Other

14 If you expect your employment tax liability to be $1,000 or less in a full calendar year **and** want to file Form 944 annually instead of Forms 941 quarterly, check here. (Your employment tax liability generally will be $1,000 or less if you expect to pay $4,000 or less in total wages.) If you do not check this box, you must file Form 941 for every quarter. ☐

15 First date wages or annuities were paid (month, day, year). **Note:** If applicant is a withholding agent, enter date income will first be paid to nonresident alien (month, day, year) . . . . ▶

16 Check **one** box that best describes the principal activity of your business.
☐ Health care & social assistance ☐ Wholesale-agent/broker
☐ Construction ☐ Rental & leasing ☐ Transportation & warehousing ☐ Accommodation & food service ☐ Wholesale-other ☐ Retail
☐ Real estate ☐ Manufacturing ☐ Finance & insurance ☐ Other (specify) ▶

17 Indicate principal line of merchandise sold, specific construction work done, products produced, or services provided.

18 Has the applicant entity shown on line 1 ever applied for and received an EIN? ☐ Yes ☐ No
If "Yes," write previous EIN here ▶

Third Party Designee
Complete this section **only** if you want to authorize the named individual to receive the entity's EIN and answer questions about the completion of this form.
Designee's name | Designee's telephone number (include area code)
Address and ZIP code | Designee's fax number (include area code)

Under penalties of perjury, I declare that I have examined this application, and to the best of my knowledge and belief, it is true, correct, and complete. | Applicant's telephone number (include area code)
Name and title (type or print clearly) ▶
Applicant's fax number (include area code)
Signature ▶ Date ▶

For Privacy Act and Paperwork Reduction Act Notice, see separate instructions. Cat. No. 16055N Form **SS-4** (Rev. 12-2017)

Source: Internal Revenue Service.

Answers to Stop & Check Exercises

Which Law?

1. k
2. h
3. b
4. f
5. i
6. j
7. a
8. d
9. g
10. c
11. e

Which Payroll Law?

1. d
2. a
3. f
4. c
5. g
6. j
7. b
8. i
9. e
10. h

What's Ethical?

1. Answers will vary. Some concerns include data privacy and integrity in the software switchover, tax and employee pay integrity on the new software, and employee pay methods.
2. Answers will vary. Liza could choose to ignore her sorority sister's request, claiming confidentiality. She could also discontinue active participation in the sorority. In any case, Liza must not consent to her sorority sister's request for confidential information.

Confidential Records

As a payroll clerk, your task is to protect the privacy and confidentiality of the information you maintain for the company. If a student group—or any personnel aside from the company's payroll employees and officers—wishes to review confidential records, you should deny their request. If needed, you should refer the group to your department's manager to discuss the matter in more depth. The laws that apply to this situation are the Privacy Act of 1974, U.S. Department of Labor OCFO-1, and potentially HIPAA.

Large vs. Small

1. Large companies have computer-based accounting packages like QuickBooks, Sage 100 Standard, and Microsoft Dynamics GP available. Additionally, they may consider outsourcing their payroll functions to companies like ADP and Paychex, which provide companies with comprehensive payroll services and tax reporting.
2. For small companies, the cost of outsourcing the payroll function needs to be considered. On one hand, a small company may not have personnel who are proficient with payroll regulations and tax reporting requirements, which leaves a company vulnerable to legal actions and stringent fines. However, engaging a payroll service company may be cost prohibitive. The decision to outsource the payroll for a small company should take into account the number of personnel, locations, and types of operations in which the company engages.

What Is the Difference?

a. Manual payroll systems involve the use of paper-and-pencil record keeping or a spreadsheet program, such as Microsoft Excel. This is most appropriate for very small firms.
b. Computerized payroll systems can be used by any company, regardless of size. Examples of computerized systems include QuickBooks, Sage 100 Standard, and Microsoft Dynamics GP. These computer packages range in price, depending on the company size and operational scope.
c. Outsourced payroll involves the engagement of a third party to manage a company's payroll data, issue employee compensation, and prepare tax forms.
d. Certified payroll pertains to companies with employees who work on federal government contracts. Certified payroll ensures that a company reports payroll expenditures of contractually allocated money.

Chapter Two

Payroll System Procedures

Payroll procedures have a dual focus: (1) governmental rules and (2) the company's needs. The company must abide by the applicable governmental and industrial regulations or face potential fines, sanctions, or closure. To comply with regulations, a company must make several decisions: pay frequency, pay types (e.g., direct deposit, paycards, or paper checks), employee benefits, and handling of pay advances. The payroll accountant must prepare for the integration of new hires, transfer of employees among departments, and terminations that occur during the normal course of business. Employee benefits and government-required payroll deductions complicate the pay process.

Accountants handle documents that have varying levels of confidentiality. Some items include receipts for expenses, invoices from vendors, and other business-related documents that are not confidential. Employee-related documents that payroll accountants handle are usually private and often contain highly sensitive personal information. Various regulations regarding the length of retention and storage procedures apply to payroll documents. An important note about financial or personnel documentation is this: Any documents connected with fraudulent activity have no time limit for retention purposes. In the event of suspected fraud, investigators may request relevant fraud-related documents at any time.

LEARNING OBJECTIVES

After studying Chapter 2, you should be able to:

LO 2-1 Identify Important Payroll Procedures and Pay Cycles

LO 2-2 Prepare Required Employee Documentation

LO 2-3 Differentiate Between Exempt and Nonexempt Workers

LO 2-4 Explain Pay Records and Employee File Maintenance

LO 2-5 Describe Internal Controls and Record Retention for a Payroll System

LO 2-6 Discuss Employee Termination and Document Destruction Procedures

Kristy-Anne Glubish/Design Pics

New-Hire Reporting: Employees, Independent Contractors, and the Government

An element of the PRWOR Act of 1996 is the employer's mandatory reporting of new hires within 20 days. After more than 20 years since enactment, this law has encountered a challenge with the growing gig (i.e., independent contractor based) economy. Reporting of new employees. The treatment of independent contractors is important because cases in which independent contractors have been reclassified as employees have occurred and do contribute to fraud and potential tax avoidance by employers.

Classification of workers as employees or independent contractors can pose ethical challenges for employers. One one hand, the Department of Labor and the IRS have published clear guidelines about the difference between employees and independent contractors. One the other hand, the cost of employee-related taxes and benefits can be avoided if the worker is truly an independent contractor. Another issue involves new-hire reporting: Independent contractors are not employees of a business and are not included in a business's employee reports to governmental authorities when they commence work in most states. Since independent contractors are not reported as employees, any income withholding orders, such as child-support payments, are not communicated to the employer. This leads to gaps in child-support payments and problems with enforcement of state and federal laws. As of 2019, only 15 states mandate the reporting of independent contractors during the new hire process.

(Source: American Payroll Association)

Personnel and payroll files are closely related. In Chapter 2, we will explore payroll system procedures, including information about file security, legally required documents, and internal controls.

LO 2-1 Identify Important Payroll Procedures and Pay Cycles

Roberto Westbrook/Blend Images

The documentation required for paying employees starts before the first employee is hired. The Employer Identification Number (EIN), obtained online from the IRS, is the first step in employer documentation, closely followed by the employee information files. Under the Fair Labor Standards Act (FLSA), certain information is required in every employee file. According to the U.S. Department of Labor, the list of required information to be maintained in the employee file includes:

1. Employee's full name as used for Social Security purposes, and the employee's identifying symbol or number, if such is used in place of the employee's name on any time, work, or payroll records.
2. Address, including zip code.
3. Birth date, if younger than 19.
4. Sex and occupation.
5. Time and day of week when employee's workweek begins.
6. Hours worked each day and total hours worked each workweek.
7. Basis on which employee's wages are paid.
8. Regular hourly pay rate.
9. Total daily or weekly straight-time earnings.
10. Total overtime earnings for the workweek.
11. All additions to or deductions from the employee's wages.
12. Total wages paid each ***pay period***.
13. Date of payment and the pay period covered by the payment.

Payroll documentation regulations protect employees by ensuring that they receive accurate paychecks. These regulations also keep employers in compliance with tax regulations and provide an audit trail for government bodies. ***New hire reporting*** requirements ensure that employees pay legal obligations such as child support and garnishments. Figure 2-1 shows a sample Employee Information Form, which contains elements of the information from the employee file. Note that the employee file is maintained by the firm's human resources department, and the employee information form shown in Figure 2-1 is maintained by the payroll department, so some FLSA elements may not appear on the form.

FIGURE 2-1

Sample Employee Information Form

NAME	Jonathan A. Doe	Hire Date	1/1/2019	
ADDRESS	100 Main Street	Date of Birth	4/16/1983	
CITY/STATE/ZIP	Anytown, MD 21220	Position	Sales	PT / (FT)
TELEPHONE	202-555-4009	No. of Exemptions	4	M / (S)
SOCIAL SECURITY NUMBER	987-65-4321	Pay Rate	$15.00	(Hr) / Wk / Mo

Period Ended	Hrs Worked	Reg Pay	OT Pay	Gross Pay	Social Sec Tax	Medicare	Fed Inc Tax	State Inc Tax	401(k)	Total Deduc	Net Pay	YTD
1/7/2019	40	600.00	-	600.00	37.20	8.70	-	12.00	25.00	82.90	517.10	517.10

The Equal Employment Opportunity Commission's protection of employee rights, especially when it leads to a lawsuit, involves the firm's personnel documentation. Accurate and correctly maintained payroll records are especially important because they reflect the firm's treatment of its employees. In certain states, such as Illinois, employees have the right to inspect their personnel files and to issue rebuttals for incorrect items.

When a company develops or reviews its payroll system, the payroll accountant faces a multifaceted task. The employer must answer several questions:

- How will the company handle new hires?
- What information will be maintained in employee personnel files?
- Where will files be stored and who is responsible for file security?
- What will the procedure be when an employee transfers from one department to another?
- What is the procedure to follow upon employee termination?
- What processes should the company establish to ensure government compliance?
- How will employee time and attendance be tracked?
- How long do employee files need to be retained after an employee leaves the company?
- Do employees have the legal right to inspect their files, and what procedures should be in place when employees request to see their files?
- Where will the mandatory FLSA Minimum Wage Poster (Figure 2-2) be displayed?

Pay Cycles

Let's start with a basic question: How often should the company pay its employees? Regardless of which accounting system the company is using, the determination of pay cycle, or pay periods, is the first thing a new company needs to establish. Options for payroll cycles include the following:

Daily payroll is typically paid at the end of the day or by the end of the next business day. This method of payroll processing is typical in day labor situations; however, it should be noted that day labor could be treated as independent contractor work and thus not be subject to payroll, payroll taxes, or a W-2. Daily payroll could potentially have 365 or 366 pay periods.

Weekly payroll is typically used in a five-day workweek. The employees receive their paychecks the following Friday. Several types of companies use a weekly payroll system, including grocery stores, construction, and professional offices. This pay frequency may lead to 52 pay periods per year.

Biweekly payroll is typically processed based on a two-week period, and employees receive their paychecks approximately a week after the end of the pay period. Pay dates may be any weekday. This pay frequency generally has 26 pay periods per year. On rare occasions there may be 27 pay periods in a biweekly payroll; however, this is rare, and typical calculations will use 26.

Semimonthly payroll is paid twice a month. Examples of semimonthly payroll pay dates include (1) the 1st and 15th of the month and (2) the 15th and last day of the month. This is not the same as biweekly payroll, and taxation and hours paid are different. Employees receive 24 pay disbursements per year when using a semimonthly payroll system.

Monthly payroll is less frequently used than other methods. Some companies process payroll once per month and may allow a semimonthly draw to the employees. When employees are allowed to draw their wages at mid-month, the employer may or may not take payroll taxes out of the draw. If the mid-month draw does not have payroll taxes withheld, the month-end payroll will need to recover all taxes and withholdings for the month from the employee.

FIGURE 2-2
FLSA Minimum Wage Poster

EMPLOYEE RIGHTS

UNDER THE FAIR LABOR STANDARDS ACT

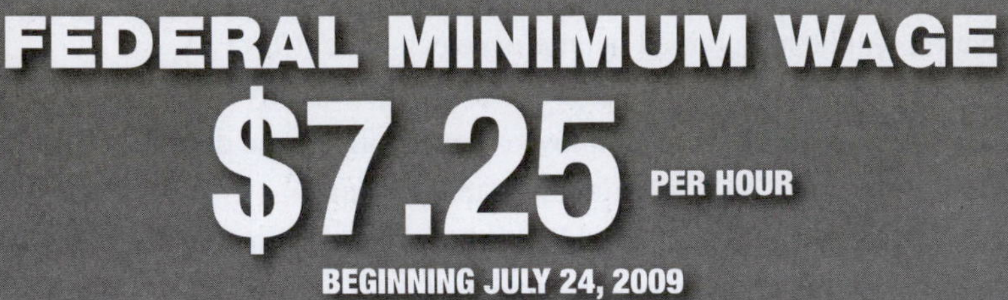

The law requires employers to display this poster where employees can readily see it.

OVERTIME PAY At least 1½ times the regular rate of pay for all hours worked over 40 in a workweek.

CHILD LABOR An employee must be at least 16 years old to work in most non-farm jobs and at least 18 to work in non-farm jobs declared hazardous by the Secretary of Labor. Youths 14 and 15 years old may work outside school hours in various non-manufacturing, non-mining, non-hazardous jobs with certain work hours restrictions. Different rules apply in agricultural employment.

TIP CREDIT Employers of "tipped employees" who meet certain conditions may claim a partial wage credit based on tips received by their employees. Employers must pay tipped employees a cash wage of at least $2.13 per hour if they claim a tip credit against their minimum wage obligation. If an employee's tips combined with the employer's cash wage of at least $2.13 per hour do not equal the minimum hourly wage, the employer must make up the difference.

NURSING MOTHERS The FLSA requires employers to provide reasonable break time for a nursing mother employee who is subject to the FLSA's overtime requirements in order for the employee to express breast milk for her nursing child for one year after the child's birth each time such employee has a need to express breast milk. Employers are also required to provide a place, other than a bathroom, that is shielded from view and free from intrusion from coworkers and the public, which may be used by the employee to express breast milk.

ENFORCEMENT The Department has authority to recover back wages and an equal amount in liquidated damages in instances of minimum wage, overtime, and other violations. The Department may litigate and/or recommend criminal prosecution. Employers may be assessed civil money penalties for each willful or repeated violation of the minimum wage or overtime pay provisions of the law. Civil money penalties may also be assessed for violations of the FLSA's child labor provisions. Heightened civil money penalties may be assessed for each child labor violation that results in the death or serious injury of any minor employee, and such assessments may be doubled when the violations are determined to be willful or repeated. The law also prohibits retaliating against or discharging workers who file a complaint or participate in any proceeding under the FLSA.

ADDITIONAL INFORMATION

- Certain occupations and establishments are exempt from the minimum wage, and/or overtime pay provisions.
- Special provisions apply to workers in American Samoa, the Commonwealth of the Northern Mariana Islands, and the Commonwealth of Puerto Rico.
- Some state laws provide greater employee protections; employers must comply with both.
- Some employers incorrectly classify workers as "independent contractors" when they are actually employees under the FLSA. It is important to know the difference between the two because employees (unless exempt) are entitled to the FLSA's minimum wage and overtime pay protections and correctly classified independent contractors are not.
- Certain full-time students, student learners, apprentices, and workers with disabilities may be paid less than the minimum wage under special certificates issued by the Department of Labor.

DEPARTMENT OF LABOR · UNITED STATES OF AMERICA

WHD WAGE AND HOUR DIVISION
UNITED STATES DEPARTMENT OF LABOR

1-866-487-9243
TTY: 1-877-889-5627
www.dol.gov/whd

WH1088 REV 07/16

Source: U.S. Department of Labor.

FIGURE 2-3
Pay Periods

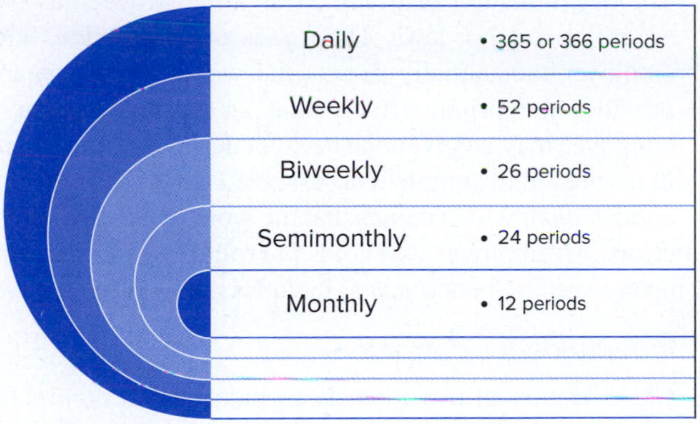

Pay frequency	Number of periods
Daily	• 365 or 366 periods
Weekly	• 52 periods
Biweekly	• 26 periods
Semimonthly	• 24 periods
Monthly	• 12 periods

Figure 2-3 shows the different types of pay cycles a company can offer their employees.

Stop & Check: What's in the File?

1. Which of the following artifacts must be included in the employee file?
   a. Full name and address.
   b. Occupation.
   c. Mother's maiden name.
   d. Pay rate.
   e. Date of payment.
   f. Spouse's name.

Match the pay frequencies:	Number of pay periods:
2. Monthly	a. 26
3. Semimonthly	b. 12
4. Biweekly	c. 52
5. Weekly	d. 24

LO 2-2 Prepare Required Employee Documentation

Employees versus Independent Contractors

People who work for a company may be classified as either employees or independent contractors depending on the nature of the work and the withholding of payroll-related taxes from the worker's compensation. According to the Internal Revenue Service (IRS), millions of workers have been misclassified, which has led to employers not depositing the full amount of taxes due and employees missing out on benefits. IRS Form SS-8, the Determination of Worker Status for Purposes of Employment Taxes and Income Tax Withholding, is a way that employers may receive official guidance about worker classification. This form is available from the IRS and elicits information about the behavioral control, financial control, and the relationship of the worker to the firm as ways to determine the correct status of the worker as an employee or an independent contractor. When the employer submits this form, the IRS makes the final determination of employee status.

Mike Kemp/Blend Images

Employees

The determination of a worker as an employee has two primary criteria according to labor laws. The first is *work direction,* which means that the employer substantially directs the worker's performance. The employer provides the primary tools that an employee uses; for example, the employee may be given the use of a desk, computer, company car, or other items needed to complete the assigned work. The other criterion is *material contribution,* which means that the work that the employee completes must involve substantial effort. An employer withholds payroll taxes from an employee's compensation, provides company-specific benefits, and includes the worker on governmental reports.

Photographee.eu/Shutterstock

Independent Contractors

Classification of a worker as an independent contractor (IC) means that the employer does not direct the worker's specific actions and does not provide the tools needed to complete the work. For example, if a worker performed accounting services for a company but used a privately owned computer and printer, as well as determined the number and timing of the hours worked for the company, the worker could be classified as an independent contractor. An independent contractor may or may not perform work that constitutes material contribution for the employer.

Another identifier of an independent contractor is in the duration of the relationship with the employer. Independent contractors tend of have shorter-term relationships with the business than employees do. Furthermore, an independent contractor will not share in profits or losses of the company in the same manner as employees. Finally, independent contractors are not subject to FLSA provisions for minimum wage and overtime pay.

> A contemporary issue in worker classification is the gig economy, in which people choose to work multiple short-term contracts or freelance jobs. In 2018, a driver sued GrubHub, claiming that he should be classified as an employee because of the signage on his car and the level of direction given by the company. The judge assigned to the case found that the worker was indeed an independent contractor because he provided his own car and retained control over his contributions to the company. This particular case revealed a "gray area" in employment law because of the factors involved in determining the levels of employer control and worker contribution. As of the end of 2018, approximately 35 percent of workers in the United States participated in the gig economy as secondary or tertiary work. (Source: *Forbes*; Independent Contractor Misclassification and Compliance)

Payment records for ICs, although maintained separately from payroll records, are an instance in which payroll accountants must be aware of employee classification and recordkeeping requirements to avoid fraudulent activity. The independent contractor generally workers for specified fees that they bill to the company, which typically pay them through their accounts payable department, not payroll. Independent contractors are also responsible for their own payroll taxes. The topic of worker classification as employee or independent contractor has become increasingly important in the past decade as many employers have sought to reduce governmental fines and other liabilities stemming from the incorrect classification of workers.

The IRS uses three common-law tests to clarify whether a worker is an employee or an independent contractor:

1. **Behavioral Control:** To what extent does the employer have the right to control and direct the worker's actions?
2. **Financial Control:** This guideline pertains to the worker's unreimbursed expenses, investment in job-related tools, availability of worker's services to other entities outside the company, and how the worker is paid.

3. **Relationship of the Parties:** This includes details related to any work-related contracts between the employer and the worker, benefits offered, permanency of the relationship, and relationship between the worker's services and the firm's normal business operations.

Further clarification about determining employment status may be located in IRS Publication 1779. Upon request, the firm may request official guidance from the IRS by submitting Form SS-8. Penalties are levied on employers who deliberately misclassify employees in an effort to cut payroll costs; in addition to penalties, the employers may have to provide unpaid wages to misclassified employees. As of 2018, the Wage and Hour Division of the Department of Labor has recovered in excess of $1.3 billion in back wages due to misclassified workers over the past five years.

In the case of *Douglas O'Connor, et al. v. Uber Technologies, Inc.* (2016), plaintiffs brought a class-action lawsuit against the company demanding that they be classified as employees instead of independent contractors. The case was settled out of court for $100 million. The drivers for Uber remain classified as independent contractors. (Source: Uberlitigation.com)

Reporting New Employees

Reporting newly hired employees is considered important by governmental bodies. Why is this so?

- First, reporting employees creates a registry to monitor people who owe child or other court-ordered garnishments.
- Second, it helps immigration agencies track immigrants to ensure that they are still legally able to work in the United States.
- Third, for certain professions such as teaching, the new hire reporting system can be used to communicate issues such as ethical violations for which the professional has been censured by governmental or accrediting bodies.
- Finally, the new hire reporting system assists with the administration of COBRA medical benefits.

All newly hired employees must have certain specific documentation. For legal purposes, the minimum amount of documentation allowed is the ***W-4*** (see Figure 2-4) and ***I-9*** forms (see Figure 2-5). The W-4 is a publication of the Internal Revenue Service. The main purpose behind the W-4 is to help the employer determine the correct amount of federal income taxes to withhold from the employee's payroll. It is worth nothing that the higher the number of withholding allowances entered on line 5 leads to less federal income tax being withheld from an employee's pay, which can cause problems with tax liability when the annual tax return is filed. Employees may make changes to the information on Form W-4 at any time during the year. A best practice with regard to Form W-4 is to request that employees file a new form each January. States may have similar withholding forms, which should similarly be completed.

Additional Withholding

If an employee has more than one job or a spouse who works, an option to avoid having to owe taxes at the end of the year is to withhold additional federal income taxes out of each check. Additional withholdings are requested within the employee's Form W-4. This can be either a straight dollar value or an additional percentage. These amounts are withheld from the employee and submitted with the normal federal payroll tax deposits by the employer. Additional withholdings reduce the employee's tax liability, the same as standard federal income taxes.

Employees may elect to include backup withholding amounts on line 6 of Form W-4, which directs the employer to withhold additional tax amounts. Backup withholding may occur in situations where the employee received additional, nontaxable income (such as dividends, royalties, or interest payments) or in situations when the IRS notified the employee of underreported income issues.

FIGURE 2-4

Form W-4 Employee Withholding Allowance Certificate

Form W-4 (2019)

Future developments. For the latest information about any future developments related to Form W-4, such as legislation enacted after it was published, go to *www.irs.gov/FormW4*.

Purpose. Complete Form W-4 so that your employer can withhold the correct federal income tax from your pay. Consider completing a new Form W-4 each year and when your personal or financial situation changes.

Exemption from withholding. You may claim exemption from withholding for 2019 if **both** of the following apply.

- For 2018 you had a right to a refund of **all** federal income tax withheld because you had **no** tax liability, **and**
- For 2019 you expect a refund of **all** federal income tax withheld because you expect to have **no** tax liability.

If you're exempt, complete **only** lines 1, 2, 3, 4, and 7 and sign the form to validate it. Your exemption for 2019 expires February 17, 2020. See Pub. 505, Tax Withholding and Estimated Tax, to learn more about whether you qualify for exemption from withholding.

General Instructions

If you aren't exempt, follow the rest of these instructions to determine the number of withholding allowances you should claim for withholding for 2019 and any additional amount of tax to have withheld. For regular wages, withholding must be based on allowances you claimed and may not be a flat amount or percentage of wages.

You can also use the calculator at ***www.irs.gov/W4App*** to determine your tax withholding more accurately. Consider using this calculator if you have a more complicated tax situation, such as if you have a working spouse, more than one job, or a large amount of nonwage income not subject to withholding outside of your job. After your Form W-4 takes effect, you can also use this calculator to see how the amount of tax you're having withheld compares to your projected total tax for 2019. If you use the calculator, you don't need to complete any of the worksheets for Form W-4.

Note that if you have too much tax withheld, you will receive a refund when you file your tax return. If you have too little tax withheld, you will owe tax when you file your tax return, and you might owe a penalty.

Filers with multiple jobs or working spouses. If you have more than one job at a time, or if you're married filing jointly and your spouse is also working, read all of the instructions including the instructions for the Two-Earners/Multiple Jobs Worksheet before beginning.

Nonwage income. If you have a large amount of nonwage income not subject to withholding, such as interest or dividends, consider making estimated tax payments using Form 1040-ES, Estimated Tax for Individuals. Otherwise, you might owe additional tax. Or, you can use the Deductions, Adjustments, and Additional Income Worksheet on page 3 or the calculator at *www.irs.gov/W4App* to make sure you have enough tax withheld from your paycheck. If you have pension or annuity income, see Pub. 505 or use the calculator at *www.irs.gov/W4App* to find out if you should adjust your withholding on Form W-4 or W-4P.

Nonresident alien. If you're a nonresident alien, see Notice 1392, Supplemental Form W-4 Instructions for Nonresident Aliens, before completing this form.

Specific Instructions

Personal Allowances Worksheet

Complete this worksheet on page 3 first to determine the number of withholding allowances to claim.

Line C. *Head of household please note:* Generally, you may claim head of household filing status on your tax return only if you're unmarried and pay more than 50% of the costs of keeping up a home for yourself and a qualifying individual. See Pub. 501 for more information about filing status.

Line E. Child tax credit. When you file your tax return, you may be eligible to claim a child tax credit for each of your eligible children. To qualify, the child must be under age 17 as of December 31, must be your dependent who lives with you for more than half the year, and must have a valid social security number. To learn more about this credit, see Pub. 972, Child Tax Credit. To reduce the tax withheld from your pay by taking this credit into account, follow the instructions on line E of the worksheet. On the worksheet you will be asked about your total income. For this purpose, total income includes all of your wages and other income, including income earned by a spouse if you are filing a joint return.

Line F. Credit for other dependents. When you file your tax return, you may be eligible to claim a credit for other dependents for whom a child tax credit can't be claimed, such as a qualifying child who doesn't meet the age or social security number requirement for the child tax credit, or a qualifying relative. To learn more about this credit, see Pub. 972. To reduce the tax withheld from your pay by taking this credit into account, follow the instructions on line F of the worksheet. On the worksheet, you will be asked about your total income. For this purpose, total

Separate here and give Form W-4 to your employer. Keep the worksheet(s) for your records.

Form **W-4** | Department of the Treasury | Internal Revenue Service

Employee's Withholding Allowance Certificate

▶ **Whether you're entitled to claim a certain number of allowances or exemption from withholding is subject to review by the IRS. Your employer may be required to send a copy of this form to the IRS.**

OMB No. 1545-0074 | **2019**

1 Your first name and middle initial	Last name	2 Your social security number
Jonathan A.	Doe	987-65-4321

Home address (number and street or rural route)	3 ☑ Single ☐ Married ☐ Married, but withhold at higher Single rate.
123 Main Street	**Note:** If married filing separately, check "Married, but withhold at higher Single rate."
City or town, state, and ZIP code	4 **If your last name differs from that shown on your social security card, check here. You must call 800-772-1213 for a replacement card.** ▶ ☐
Anytown, KS 54932	

5 Total number of allowances you're claiming (from the applicable worksheet on the following pages) . . . . | 5 | 1

6 Additional amount, if any, you want withheld from each paycheck . . . . | 6 | $

7 I claim exemption from withholding for 2019, and I certify that I meet **both** of the following conditions for exemption.

- Last year I had a right to a refund of **all** federal income tax withheld because I had **no** tax liability, **and**
- This year I expect a refund of **all** federal income tax withheld because I expect to have **no** tax liability.

If you meet both conditions, write "Exempt" here . . . . ▶ | 7 |

Under penalties of perjury, I declare that I have examined this certificate and, to the best of my knowledge and belief, it is true, correct, and complete.

Employee's signature
(This form is not valid unless you sign it.) ▶ **Date** ▶

8 Employer's name and address (**Employer:** Complete boxes 8 and 10 if sending to IRS and complete boxes 8, 9, and 10 if sending to State Directory of New Hires.)	9 First date of employment	10 Employer identification number (EIN)
Homestead Retreat, 9010 Old Manhattan Highway, Olathe, KS 59384	1/3/2019	92-1117654

For Privacy Act and Paperwork Reduction Act Notice, see page 4. Cat. No. 10220Q Form **W-4** (2019)

(Source: Internal Revenue Service.)

FIGURE 2-5

I-9 Employment Eligibility Verification Form

Employment Eligibility Verification
Department of Homeland Security
U.S. Citizenship and Immigration Services

USCIS
Form I-9
OMB No. 1615-0047
Expires 08/31/2019

▶**START HERE: Read instructions carefully before completing this form. The instructions must be available, either in paper or electronically, during completion of this form. Employers are liable for errors in the completion of this form.**

ANTI-DISCRIMINATION NOTICE: It is illegal to discriminate against work-authorized individuals. Employers **CANNOT** specify which document(s) an employee may present to establish employment authorization and identity. The refusal to hire or continue to employ an individual because the documentation presented has a future expiration date may also constitute illegal discrimination.

Section 1. Employee Information and Attestation *(Employees must complete and sign Section 1 of Form I-9 no later than the **first day of employment**, but not before accepting a job offer.)*

Last Name *(Family Name)*	First Name *(Given Name)*	Middle Initial	Other Last Names Used *(if any)*
Doe	Jonathan	A	

Address *(Street Number and Name)*	Apt. Number	City or Town	State	ZIP Code
123 Main Street		Anytown	KS	54932

Date of Birth *(mm/dd/yyyy)*	U.S. Social Security Number	Employee's E-mail Address	Employee's Telephone Number
05/17/1991	987-65-4321	jonathandoe@anymail.com	(620) 552-2299

I am aware that federal law provides for imprisonment and/or fines for false statements or use of false documents in connection with the completion of this form.

I attest, under penalty of perjury, that I am (check one of the following boxes):

- [X] 1. A citizen of the United States
- [ ] 2. A noncitizen national of the United States *(See instructions)*
- [ ] 3. A lawful permanent resident (Alien Registration Number/USCIS Number): ____________
- [ ] 4. An alien authorized to work until (expiration date, if applicable, mm/dd/yyyy): ____________
  Some aliens may write "N/A" in the expiration date field. *(See instructions)*

Aliens authorized to work must provide only one of the following document numbers to complete Form I-9:
An Alien Registration Number/USCIS Number OR Form I-94 Admission Number OR Foreign Passport Number.

1. Alien Registration Number/USCIS Number: ____________
   OR
2. Form I-94 Admission Number: ____________
   OR
3. Foreign Passport Number: ____________
   Country of Issuance: ____________

QR Code - Section 1
Do Not Write In This Space

Signature of Employee	Today's Date *(mm/dd/yyyy)*
Jonathan Doe Type text here	01/03/2019

Preparer and/or Translator Certification (check one):

[X] I did not use a preparer or translator. [ ] A preparer(s) and/or translator(s) assisted the employee in completing Section 1.

(Fields below must be completed and signed when preparers and/or translators assist an employee in completing Section 1.)

I attest, under penalty of perjury, that I have assisted in the completion of Section 1 of this form and that to the best of my knowledge the information is true and correct.

Signature of Preparer or Translator	Today's Date *(mm/dd/yyyy)*

Last Name *(Family Name)*	First Name *(Given Name)*

Address *(Street Number and Name)*	City or Town	State	ZIP Code

STOP *Employer Completes Next Page* STOP

Form I-9 07/17/17 N

Page 1 of 3

Employment Eligibility Verification
Department of Homeland Security
U.S. Citizenship and Immigration Services

USCIS
Form I-9
OMB No. 1615-0047
Expires 08/31/2019

Section 2. Employer or Authorized Representative Review and Verification

(Employers or their authorized representative must complete and sign Section 2 within 3 business days of the employee's first day of employment. You must physically examine one document from List A OR a combination of one document from List B and one document from List C as listed on the "Lists of Acceptable Documents.")

Employee Info from Section 1	Last Name *(Family Name)*	First Name *(Given Name)*	M.I.	Citizenship/Immigration Status
	Doe	Jonathan	A	1

List A Identity and Employment Authorization	OR	List B Identity	AND	List C Employment Authorization
Document Title		Document Title Driver's license issued by state/territory		Document Title Social Security Card (Unrestricted)
Issuing Authority		Issuing Authority Kansas		Issuing Authority Social Security Administration
Document Number		Document Number G93847562		Document Number 987-65-4321
Expiration Date *(if any)(mm/dd/yyyy)*		Expiration Date *(if any)(mm/dd/yyyy)* 05/17/2022		Expiration Date *(if any)(mm/dd/yyyy)* N/A
Document Title		Additional Information		QR Code - Sections 2 & 3 Do Not Write In This Space
Issuing Authority				
Document Number				
Expiration Date *(if any)(mm/dd/yyyy)*				
Document Title				
Issuing Authority				
Document Number				
Expiration Date *(if any)(mm/dd/yyyy)*				

Certification: I attest, under penalty of perjury, that (1) I have examined the document(s) presented by the above-named employee, (2) the above-listed document(s) appear to be genuine and to relate to the employee named, and (3) to the best of my knowledge the employee is authorized to work in the United States.

The employee's first day of employment *(mm/dd/yyyy)*: 01/03/2019 ***(See instructions for exemptions)***

Signature of Employer or Authorized Representative	Today's Date *(mm/dd/yyyy)*	Title of Employer or Authorized Representative
Jessica Stolpp	01/03/2019	Human Resources

Last Name of Employer or Authorized Representative	First Name of Employer or Authorized Representative	Employer's Business or Organization Name
Stolpp	Jessica	Homestead Retreat

Employer's Business or Organization Address (Street Number and Name)	City or Town	State	ZIP Code
9010 Old Manhattan Highway	Olathe	KS	59384

Section 3. Reverification and Rehires *(To be completed and signed by employer or authorized representative.)*

A. New Name *(if applicable)*			B. Date of Rehire *(if applicable)*
Last Name *(Family Name)*	First Name *(Given Name)*	Middle Initial	Date *(mm/dd/yyyy)*

C. If the employee's previous grant of employment authorization has expired, provide the information for the document or receipt that establishes continuing employment authorization in the space provided below.

Document Title	Document Number	Expiration Date *(if any) (mm/dd/yyyy)*

I attest, under penalty of perjury, that to the best of my knowledge, this employee is authorized to work in the United States, and if the employee presented document(s), the document(s) I have examined appear to be genuine and to relate to the individual.

Signature of Employer or Authorized Representative	Today's Date *(mm/dd/yyyy)*	Name of Employer or Authorized Representative

LISTS OF ACCEPTABLE DOCUMENTS
All documents must be UNEXPIRED

Employees may present one selection from List A
or a combination of one selection from List B and one selection from List C.

LIST A **Documents that Establish Both Identity and Employment Authorization**	OR	**LIST B** **Documents that Establish Identity**	AND	**LIST C** **Documents that Establish Employment Authorization**
1. U.S. Passport or U.S. Passport Card		1. Driver's license or ID card issued by a State or outlying possession of the United States provided it contains a photograph or information such as name, date of birth, gender, height, eye color, and address		1. A Social Security Account Number card, unless the card includes one of the following restrictions: (1) NOT VALID FOR EMPLOYMENT (2) VALID FOR WORK ONLY WITH INS AUTHORIZATION (3) VALID FOR WORK ONLY WITH DHS AUTHORIZATION
2. Permanent Resident Card or Alien Registration Receipt Card (Form I-551)		2. ID card issued by federal, state or local government agencies or entities, provided it contains a photograph or information such as name, date of birth, gender, height, eye color, and address		2. Certification of report of birth issued by the Department of State (Forms DS-1350, FS-545, FS-240)
3. Foreign passport that contains a temporary I-551 stamp or temporary I-551 printed notation on a machine-readable immigrant visa		3. School ID card with a photograph		3. Original or certified copy of birth certificate issued by a State, county, municipal authority, or territory of the United States bearing an official seal
4. Employment Authorization Document that contains a photograph (Form I-766)		4. Voter's registration card		4. Native American tribal document
5. For a nonimmigrant alien authorized to work for a specific employer because of his or her status: a. Foreign passport; and b. Form I-94 or Form I-94A that has the following: (1) The same name as the passport; and (2) An endorsement of the alien's nonimmigrant status as long as that period of endorsement has not yet expired and the proposed employment is not in conflict with any restrictions or limitations identified on the form.		5. U.S. Military card or draft record		5. U.S. Citizen ID Card (Form I-197)
6. Passport from the Federated States of Micronesia (FSM) or the Republic of the Marshall Islands (RMI) with Form I-94 or Form I-94A indicating nonimmigrant admission under the Compact of Free Association Between the United States and the FSM or RMI		6. Military dependent's ID card		6. Identification Card for Use of Resident Citizen in the United States (Form I-179)
		7. U.S. Coast Guard Merchant Mariner Card		7. Employment authorization document issued by the Department of Homeland Security
		8. Native American tribal document		
		9. Driver's license issued by a Canadian government authority		
		For persons under age 18 who are unable to present a document listed above:		
		10. School record or report card		
		11. Clinic, doctor, or hospital record		
		12. Day-care or nursery school record		

Examples of many of these documents appear in Part 13 of the Handbook for Employers (M-274).

Refer to the instructions for more information about acceptable receipts.

Form I-9 07/17/17 N Page 3 of 3

(Source: USCIS.)

The I-9 form is published by the Department of Homeland Security, which stipulates that all new hires be reported within 20 days of their start date. Registration of employees by using the I-9 form minimizes negative implications associated with monitoring legally authorized workers in the United States and tracking people with legal obligations such as child support and other garnishments.

As of the most recent U.S. Census Bureau report, the estimated amount of child support supposed to be transferred between custodial and noncustodial parents for children younger than the age of 21 in the United States exceeded $67.4 billion. (Source: U.S. Census Bureau)

Please refer to the following information for the Form W-4 shown in Figure 2-4 and the I-9 shown in Figure 2-5. The final page of the I-9 form contains the employee-provided documents needed to verify identity and eligibility to work in the United States. Employees must provide either one item from List A *or* one item from both List B *and* List C.

Jonathan A. Doe was born on 5/17/1981 and lives at 123 Main Street, Anytown, Kansas 54932. He is single and claims one withholding allowance. His Social Security number is 987-65-4321. His employer is Homestead Retreat at 9010 Old Manhattan Highway, Olathe, Kansas 59384, with an Employer Identification Number of 92-1117654. His email address is jonathandoe@anymail.com, and his phone number is (620) 552-2299. When he filled out his new hire paperwork on January 3, 2019, Jessica Stolpp in Human Resources for Homestead Retreat verified his identity with both his Social Security card and his driver's license (G93847562), which expires on his birthday in 2022.

The US Citizen and Immigration Service (USCIS) implemented new changes in 2017:

- A fillable PDF version of the form with drop-downs for dates and prefilled lists.
- A new citizenship/immigration status section.
- Form availability in Spanish.

The E-Verify system was implemented in 2017 to provide employers with a fast, free way to verify an employee's legal eligibility to work in the United States. It should be noted that participation in E-Verify is *voluntary* and that completion of the I-9 is *mandatory.* (Source: USCIS)

The payroll accountant should retain a copy of the Employment Eligibility Verification Form (I-9) and a current Employee Withholding Allowance Certificate (W-4) in every employee's permanent file. The employer should request a new W-4 from employees annually in January to ensure that all addresses, life situations, and other information remain current. Because of the timing constraints on the release of annual tax documents such as the W-2 and W-3, employers should verify employees' W-4 information as close to January 1 as possible each year.

Hiring Packet Contents

The ***hiring packet*** maintained by many companies may be as basic as a simple W-4 and I-9 form or may be incredibly complex if foreign workers and multiple types of voluntary deductions are involved. Common items in a hiring packet are the federal forms mentioned earlier, state and local withholding allowance forms, elections for voluntary deductions, insurance paperwork, and the offer letter that specifies the pay rate and start date. Not all companies have the same items in the hiring packet, and no legislative guidelines exist. The firm's management, after reviewing the needs of the company and the legal requirements for the position, determines the hiring packet contents. Many companies also are including diversity self-declaration papers to ensure compliance with equal opportunity legislation, requirements under federal contracts, and other special requirements.

fizkes/Shutterstock

Notification of New Hires to State Offices

The Immigration Reform and Control Act mandates that employers notify state offices within 20 days of an employee's start date. State forms for fulfilling this requirement vary, and states offer online registration for new hires. One purpose of registering new hires with states is to maintain databases for child support enforcement. Fines for nonreporting of new hires vary, both on the number of nonreported new hires and for incomplete information. The penalty for noncompliance is strictly enforced and ranges from $25 per unreported employee to $500 for intentional nonreporting.

Reporting of new hires is a complex task with high potential for errors for companies with employees in multiple states. The Office of Management and Budget (OMB) has designed a form (see excerpt in Figure 2-6) for multistate employers to register and designate one state as the primary place to which they will send new hire reports. They can designate on the form the other states in which they have employees. The use of the multistate registry helps employers ensure they remain in compliance with the law.

Jensen Walker/DreamPictures/Blend Images

Foreign Workers

Employers who hire non–U.S. citizens face additional challenges. The employer must verify that the employee is legally allowed to work in the United States. Generally, the I-9 form serves this purpose, but there may be occasions when the prospective employee does not have an appropriate government-issued visa for working in the United States. If no visa exists, the employer may file a petition with the U.S. Citizenship and Immigration Services office to gain permission for the foreign employee to work in the United States. Some exceptions exist to the rules for the visa. The fees for permanent workers not in the protected classes can range from $500 to $5,000, depending on the classification of the worker's preference, the size of the employer, and the employee's nonimmigrant status. In the case of foreign workers, the employer must file Form 1042 for any payments made. For information about the Permanent Worker Visa Preference Categories, please visit the U.S. Citizenship and Immigration Services website (www.uscis.gov).

FIGURE 2-6

Multistate Employer Notification Form

OMB Control No: 0970-0166
Expiration Date: 07-31-2019

MULTISTATE EMPLOYER NOTIFICATION FORM FOR NEW HIRE REPORTING

Employers who have employees working in two or more states may use this form to register to submit their new hire reports to one state or make changes to a previous registration. Multistate employers may also visit https://ocsp.acf.hhs.gov/OCSE/ to register or make changes electronically.

Federal law (42 USC 653A(b)(1)(A)) requires employers to supply the following information about newly hired employees to the State Directory of New Hires in the state where the employee works:

- Employee's name, address, Social Security number, and the date of hire (the date services for remuneration were first performed by the employee)
- Employer's name, address, and Federal Employer Identification Number (FEIN)

If you are an employer with employees working in two or more states AND you will transmit the required information or reports magnetically or electronically, you may use this form to designate one state where any employee works to transmit ALL new hire reports to the State Directory of New Hires.

Source: United States Department of Health and Human Services.

> The purpose of H-1B visas is to facilitate the employment of foreign workers who possess specialty skills, as defined by U.S. statute 20 CFR § 655.700. "Specialty occupation" is defined as possessing specialized knowledge, with the minimum educational requirement being a bachelor's degree or commensurate experience, or a distinguished fashion model. (Source: Cornell Law School)

mapodile/Getty Images

Statutory Employees

Some personnel who would normally be classified as independent contractors must be treated as employees for tax purposes. The IRS classifies ***statutory employees*** as personnel who meet any of the following guidelines:

- A driver who distributes beverages (other than milk) or meat, vegetable, fruit, or bakery products or who picks up and delivers laundry or dry cleaning, if the driver is a single company's agent or is paid on commission.
- A full-time life insurance sales agent whose principal business activity is selling life insurance or annuity contracts, or both, primarily for one life insurance company.
- An individual who works at home on materials or goods that a company supplies and that must be returned to that company or a designated agent in accordance with furnished specifications for the work to be done.
- A full-time traveling or city salesperson who works on a single company's behalf and turns in orders from wholesalers, retailers, contractors, or operators of hotels, restaurants, or other similar establishments. The goods sold must be merchandise for resale or supplies for use in the buyer's business operation. The work performed for that single company must be the salesperson's principal business activity.

Recall that the primary differences between an employee and an independent contractor are that the independent contractor sets his or her own hours and provides the tools necessary to complete the task. Statutory employees are a hybrid of employee and independent contractor. To ensure proper and timely remittance of employment taxes, the IRS has mandated that the employer withhold FICA taxes from statutory employees in the same manner as other company personnel; however, federal income taxes are not withheld from statutory employees' pay.

> The term *statutory employee* may be applied to other types of workers on occasions. In 2014, the National Labor Relations Board (NLRB) ruled that Northwestern University athletes who receive scholarships from the university are statutory employees. The employment tax implications of this ruling are that the university would be responsible for withholding and remitting FICA taxes from student scholarships. This ruling was overturned in 2015 and re-affirmed in 2017 based on the idea that the players were statutory employees of the university. (Source: *Inside Higher Ed*)

U.S. Workers in Foreign Subsidiaries

Many companies have foreign subsidiaries and divisions that employ U.S. expatriate workers. The ***Foreign Account Tax Compliance Act (FATCA)*** of 2010 requires employers to report to the IRS the wages of employees who are permanent U.S. citizens working in foreign locations in order to facilitate appropriate taxation of such workers. Under the IRS Foreign Earned Income Exclusion, expatriate workers must file Form 673 with their employer to exclude the first $105,900 of annual wages (2019 figure) from U.S. taxation but must pay income tax on income in excess of that amount.

Entering New Employees into the Database

The method of entering a new employee into the payroll system depends upon the system that the employer chooses to utilize. A manual system would require tasks such as adding the employee to the federal, state, and local lists for taxes withheld as well as adding the new hire to the list of employees to pay. Manual systems should have a checklist of all employees to ensure that no one is missed in the process.

FIGURE 2-7
Employee Database Information Sample

Personal Information
Salary
Vacation
Tax Details
Benefits & Deductions
Employee Files
Direct Deposit
Employee History

$14.59/hour

Salary History

Amount	Effective on
$14.59/hour	04/04/2016
$13.75/hour	01/01/2015

Setting up a new employee in an automated system involves many more steps. The payroll employee enters in the pertinent data (see Figure 2-7). Employee number, name, address, Social Security number, wage, pay frequency, withholding information from W-4, department, and contact information are typically included. The payroll employee must designate a worker's compensation classification, state of employment, and local jurisdiction (when local taxes are applicable). Depending on state requirements and employer preferences, additional location codes, job classification codes, and other identifying characteristics may also be required.

Who Are You?

Stop & Check

1. Go to the website for the U.S. Citizenship and Immigration Services, located at www.uscis.gov, and type I-9 into the search box on the website. Click on the link for the PDF version of the I-9 form to obtain a digital copy. What are two different ways that you would be able to prove your eligibility for work in the United States?
2. Go to the IRS website, located at www.irs.gov, and type W-4 into the search box on the website. Click on the link for the PDF version of the W-4 to obtain a digital copy. Before you start, ask yourself how many exemptions you think you should claim. Complete the Personal Allowances Worksheet. How did the number of allowable exemptions compare with your estimate? Explain.
3. What are three examples of statutory employees?

LO 2-3 Differentiate Between Exempt and Nonexempt Workers

Company employees may be classified as either exempt or nonexempt workers. The distinction between the two terms is how the wage and hour provisions of FLSA apply to the worker. Exempt workers are not subject to (i.e., are exempt from) the FLSA wage and hour provisions; wage and hour laws usually apply to nonexempt workers. The details of the worker's classification as exempt or nonexempt are always maintained in payroll records, but inclusion of this information in other personnel records is at the employer's discretion.

Gajus/Shutterstock

Many different types of employees are classified as exempt from FLSA provisions, including certain computer professionals and outside salespersons.

Companies will typically classify highly skilled workers such as accountants, general managers, human resource managers, and upper management as exempt, salaried employees. Because job titles alone are not a basis for classification of employees as exempt from FLSA provisions, the U.S. Department of Labor has issued guidelines for the most common types of employees. Note that for workers to be classified as exempt, they must meet ***all*** elements in the following tests to achieve exempt status.

- Executive Exemption
  - Salary compensation must be no less than $455 per week.
  - Managing the firm must be a primary duty of the employee.
  - The employee must supervise and otherwise direct the work of at least two other full-time employees (or an equivalent).
  - The employee must have the authority to hire and fire other employees.
- Administrative Exemption
  - Salary compensation must be no less than $455 per week.
  - The primary duty must include the performance of office or other nonmanual labor that relates directly to the management of the firm's operations.
  - The employee must exercise independent judgment in the performance of normal duties.
- Professional Exemption
  - Learned Professional
    - Salary compensation must be no less than $455 per week.
    - This employee must perform work that is characterized by advanced learning or that is primarily academic in nature and requires consistent discretion and judgment.
    - The employee's advanced knowledge must be in a field that involves science or learning.
    - The employee must have acquired that knowledge through specialized intellectual education.
  - Creative Professional
    - Salary compensation must be no less than $455 per week.
    - This employee's primary work duty must involve invention, imagination, or originality that requires judgment and discretion.

(Source: DOL)

2016 marked the first time in several years that the minimum salary for exempt workers was addressed legislatively. The previous minimum salary of $455 per week represented an average wage of $11.38 per hour. This weekly amount was raised to $913 and placed the minimum salary for exempt workers at $47,476 annually in May 2016. However, on November 22, 2016, U.S. District Court Judge Amos Mazzant placed an injunction on the implementation of the law. Additionally, presidential memorandum M-17-16 placed the implementation of this rule on hold for further review.

As of January 2018, the Department of Labor was revising rules governing exempt workers from the provisions of the FLSA wage and hour requirements. Until these requirements are revised, the DOL will enforce the existing wage and hour requirements. The estimated completion date as of publication is mid-2019. (Sources: DOL, US White House)

When workers are employed on a salary basis, they are paid to perform a specific job regardless of the number of hours worked to accomplish that job. A 2017 Gallup Work and Education poll (see Figure 2-8) reflected that more than half of American workers surveyed worked in excess of 40 hours per week; however, it should be noted the law currently provides that if salaried employees show up or are called by their employer for even an hour, the company may be required to pay them for the full eight-hour day.

FIGURE 2-8
Gallup Hours Worked per Week Poll

In a typical week, how many hours do you work?

Based on adults employed full or part time

	<30	30 to 34	35 to 44	45 to 59	60+	No opinion	Mean
	%	%	%	%	%	%	
2017 Aug 2-6	8	4	43	29	16	*	44.5
2016 Aug 3-7	10	7	36	29	17	*	44
2015 Aug 5-9	12	3	42	25	17	--	44
2014 Aug 7-10	10	4	45	24	16	1	43.4
2013 Aug 7-11	12	5	43	25	15	1	43.1

Source: Based on Gallup's Work and Workplace poll, conducted August 7–10, 2014.

A primary difference is that nonexempt salaried individuals receive overtime pay for any hours exceeding 40 per week. The difference between salaried and hourly workers in reference to overtime calculation is that salaried workers will receive their normal shift hours of pay, even when not working the full shift, and do not receive overtime when they work more than 40 hours per week.

Hourly (nonexempt) employees receive a predetermined amount per hour of work performed (or fraction thereof). Some employers may make an election that permits four 10-hour shifts; should the election be made, the employee would be subject to overtime rates only after the 40 hours have been performed. It should be noted that some employers have a company policy stating that they pay overtime for employees who work in excess of of 8 hours per day (or 10 hours, if that is the normal work shift); however, paid overtime is only mandated by the FLSA on a weekly basis. According to the Bureau of Labor Statistics (see Figure 2-9), the average number of hours worked per week in the United States is less than 40 hours.

FIGURE 2-9
Average Working Hours of All Employees

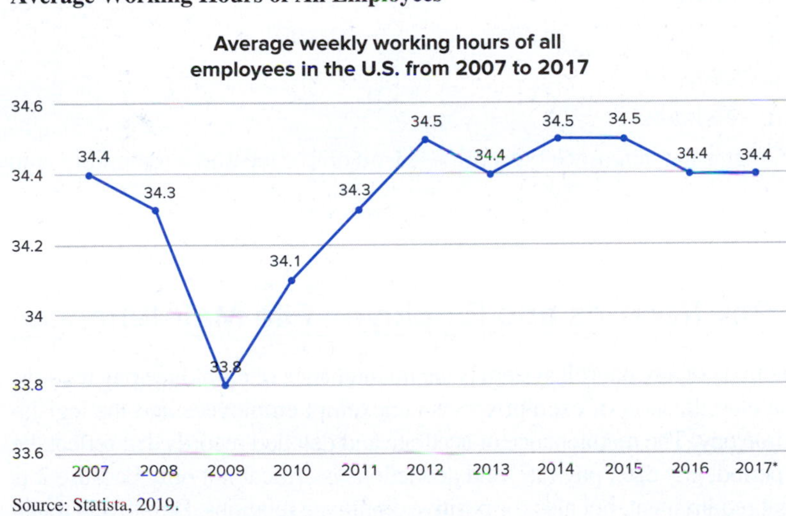

Source: Statista, 2019.

Leased and Temporary Employees

Employers occasionally experience a need to have an additional employee but do not have the time to use a traditional hiring process. In this event, employers may opt either to lease an employee or to contact a temporary employment agency. Although these terms may sound similar, the difference between the leased and temporary employees involves the determination of employer intent and liability for worker injuries and errors.

Under IRS code section 414(n), an employee is classified as a ***leased employee*** if all the following conditions exist:

1. A formal agreement exists between the employer and the employee leasing organization.
2. The employee works on a full-time basis.
3. Employee actions are directed by the recipient company (i.e., the lessee).

Leased employees are considered common-law employees and are eligible for the same benefits as regular employees, including compensation practices, employer contributions, and so forth. The IRS stipulates that no more than 20 percent of a company's employees may be leased employees.

> The Tax Cuts and Jobs Act of 2017 included a provision in which employers who leased employees from Professional Employer Organizations (PEOs) could qualify for a 20 percent profit deduction under section 199A of the Act. PEOs serve companies by acting as the hiring body and human resource managers for workers. in January 2019, the IRS clarified under §1.199A-2(b)(2)(ii) that employers who use third-party employees through a PEO could consider those leased employees as common-law employees and would qualify for the profit deduction and subsequent decrease in tax liability. (Source: JDSupra)

A temporary employee differs from a leased employee in the direction of the employee's actions. The ***temporary employee*** is an employee of the employment agency, which directs them to fill specific short-term needs of a variety of employers. Temporary employees may work either full-time or part-time, depending on the needs of the employer, and are only eligible for the benefits made available by the temporary agency.

Exempt vs. Nonexempt

Stop & Check

1. What is the difference between exempt and nonexempt workers?
2. What is the threshold after which an employee must be paid overtime, according to FLSA?
   a. 30 hours
   b. 35 hours
   c. 40 hours
   d. 45 hours
3. What is the difference between a leased employee and a temporary employee?

LO 2-4 Explain Pay Records and Employee File Maintenance

One of the most important parts of any payroll system is the maintenance of employee pay records, especially considering the classification of exempt versus nonexempt employees and the legislation that pertains to overtime pay. The maintenance of accurate and detailed records that reflect the pay period, pay date, pay rate, and deductions is critical not only because it is a legal requirement, but also for positive employee relations. Employers retain physical copies of employees' time records, pay advice, and any other documentation processed with the paycheck. Other types of documentation include

Dean Drobot/Shutterstock

- Request for a day off.
- Reports of tardiness or absenteeism.
- Detailed records of work completed during that day's shift.
- Records of overtime worked.

Technological advances allow employers to scan and save this information digitally, such as using an Adobe Acrobat file within the payroll accounting system. The availability of digital copies facilitates managerial, auditor, or authorized executives' review, approval, or commentary on the documentation attached to payroll documents. Digital copies also permit transparency of records between the employer and employee, reducing miscommunication and payroll discrepancies, and facilitating the use of Internet employee record portals.

Pay Records

Employee wages involve far more than simple hourly rates or periodic salary payments. The first payroll decision a company should make is the company's pay frequency (daily, weekly, biweekly, semimonthly, monthly). Choice of pay frequency affects the applicable amounts for employee income tax withholding. Separate schedules for federal income taxes are provided in IRS Publication 15 (available at www.irs.gov), which is released in November for the following year (i.e., 2020 tax information is released during November 2019). Once the employer determines the pay frequency, the payroll accountant can establish the payroll record submission and pay disbursement schedule for company employees.

Pay Rate

Pay rate is the amount per hour per pay period the company determines the employee should be compensated. The determination of pay rate depends upon many employee variables: experience, education, certifications, governmental regulations (minimum wage, Davis–Bacon wages, etc.), hours worked, or a combination of all of the above. Employers may also pay specific rates for jobs performed. For example, employees working in a manufacturing environment may be subject to a different pay scale when cross-trained and working in a sales capacity. Minimum wage rates vary per state, and different parts of the same state may have different wages and may increase minimum wage amounts at various times during the year.

The idea of paying a living wage continues to be a prominent issue. A living wage is defined as the amount of money needed to sustain a desired lifestyle. In Virginia, the Richmond Living Wage Program is a certificate program co-sponsored by state and local leaders to encourage businesses to focus more on the needs of employees than on the business's profitability. This program encourages consumers to patronize businesses that have demonstrated their dedication to delivering a living wage to their employees.

The Massachusetts Institute of Technology (MIT) created a living wage calculator to facilitate awareness of the cost of living in different communities in the United States. This calculator is located at http://livingwage.mit.edu/ (Source: Virginia Business)

Classifying employee wages as to salary versus hourly is a basic determination, linked to the type of work performed and the position within the company. Salaried ***exempt*** employees are not subject to overtime, are paid to do a specific job, and fulfill the FLSA requirement

EXAMPLE: PAY PERIOD COMPUTATION, BIWEEKLY EMPLOYEE

Juan de la Cruz is a manager for a textiles firm. He earns $52,000 per year, is classified as an exempt employee and is paid biweekly. He normally works 40 hours per week.

During June, the following occurred:

Pay period ending June 15: Juan worked 85 hours.

Pay period ending June 29: Juan worked 78 hours.

Salary for the June 15 pay period = $52,000/26 periods per year = $2,000

Salary for the June 29 pay period = $52,000/26 periods per year = $2,000

Juan's salary for each pay period would be the fixed amount no matter how many hours he worked because he is classified as an exempt employee.

of self-direction; however, not all salaried employees are classified as exempt. Certain jobs such as nurses, police officers, and upper-level administrators may earn a fixed salary but are classified as ***nonexempt*** because of the nature of management direction in their function. Nonexempt workers do not generally supervise other employees and generally work under the direction of a supervisor.

Hourly employees are protected by the FLSA and eligible for overtime pay. When overtime pay is applied, hourly employees may earn more than their salaried counterparts. Overtime rules and rates are determined by FLSA; however, some states may have additional requirements for overtime pay. Overtime is calculated at one-and-a-half times the employee's hourly rate. For FLSA, overtime applies only to hours worked exceeding 40 in a week (with some exceptions). Some states, such as California, may also require that employees receive overtime pay for any hours worked exceeding 8 per day in addition to the 40 hours per week, making it possible for an hourly employee to earn overtime pay without reaching the 40 hours in the week. In this textbook, nonexempt employees receive overtime pay for hours worked in excess of 40 hours per week, unless otherwise noted.

> The concept of a fluctuating workweek for salaried nonexempt employees has been a source of confusion for employers. Some salaried nonexempt employees work in industries that require them to be available at different times based on company needs. If an employee is nonexempt and salaried but has hours that are changeable due to the nature of their job, then they may receive overtime during periods when they work more than 40 hours in a given week.

Commissions and piece rate compensation offer employees incentives for specific jobs. A ***commission*** is a percentage of sales or services performed by an individual. An example of a commission would be a sales representative receiving 1 percent of all sales he or she initiates. ***Piece rate*** connects employee compensation with the production of a good or service. Piece rate compensation was widely used in the United States prior to industrialization and automated manufacturing. For example, when a shoe was being made, the person preparing the sole would receive a set rate per item.

> The California state legislature passed Assembly Bill (AB) 1513, which established guidelines about productive time and rest time for piece rate employees. This bill also established a specified time period for employers to pay employees back pay because of the legal change. AB 1513 affected employees in a variety of industries, including spas and salons in which workers' compensation was connected to the number of treatments completed. (Source: California DIR)

Compensation structures can become complex if the employee is compensated using multiple pay types. A sales representative may receive a salary and commissions while working on the sales floor but receive hourly and piece rate if filling in on the manufacturing floor. Proper classification of the various aspects of the employee's workday becomes exceptionally important for the correct processing of the payroll.

Entering Hours

When it is time to prepare the payroll, an automated system will provide the payroll employee with a simple form to complete, typically including wage type and number of hours worked. In complex organizations, an additional classification of job location may be required if the employee works in multiple departments or locations. The automated systems will complete the mathematics to obtain gross pay, and most automated systems will calculate overtime and shift differentials (i.e., higher pay for working during times not considered "normal business hours").

Andrey_Popov/Shutterstock

Many web-based applications exist to track employee attendance and calculate pay. TimeStation, ClockShark, and TimeDock use Quick-Read (QR) codes, employee PINs, and GPS location tagging to verify employee work. These apps may be useful tools for companies with employees at remote locations. Apps such as CalculateHours allow employees to calculate their hours worked and to email the time sheet to a supervisor. Other apps, such as the iTookOff paid leave tracker, allow employees to manage their paid time off through a synchronized app.

Calculations of Weekly Regular Time and Overtime

Even with the use of automated systems, the payroll accountant must determine the breakdown of each employee's regular and overtime hours. Recall the discussion regarding the FLSA standard of 40 hours in a week. This is where the calculation of overtime becomes important. The employee's hours are added up, the total for the pay period is computed to determine if the employee worked more than 40 hours total for any given week, and overtime is separated from regular hours worked for wage calculations. If the employee did not work more than 40 hours, the total regular hours are noted on the time card. If the employee did work more than 40 hours, hours worked will be divided between the 40 regular hours and the overtime pay computation.

Depending upon company policy, the existence of paid holidays or sick days may alter payroll calculations. However, holiday hours, sick time taken, and vacation days are not usually included in the worked hours to determine overtime. Figure 2-10 shows a few examples of states and locations that offer mandatory paid sick leave.

According to the FLSA, employers are not required to pay for employee sick time; however, many states have either passed legislation or have pending bills that would mandate employer-paid sick time. Since 2008, more than 30 separate locations, including cities and entire states, have passed paid sick time legislation. This is a partial list of areas that have legislated paid sick leave.

FIGURE 2-10
Locations with Mandatory Paid Sick Leave

States/Districts	Counties	Cities
Washington, DC	Orange County, FL	Pittsburgh, PA
Arizona	Montgomery County, MD	Milwaukee, WI
California	Cook County, IL	Seattle, WA
Connecticut	Westchester County, NY	Plainfield, NJ
Massachusetts		Elizabeth, NJ
Maryland		New Brunswick, NJ
Michigan		Jersey City, NJ
New Jersey		Tacoma, WA
Oregon		Newark, NJ
Rhode Island		New York City, NY
Vermont		Passaic, NJ
Washington		East Orange, NJ
		Paterson, NJ
		Irvington, NJ
		Montclair, NJ
		Trenton, NJ
		Minneapolis, MN
		Philadelphia, PA
		Bloomfield, NJ
		Chicago, IL

Source: ABetterBalance.org
Note: States that have passed mandatory sick-time laws may have cities whose sick-time laws differ.

Worker Facts

Stop & Check

1. Which classification of workers is subject to the wage and hour provisions for overtime in the Fair Labor Standards Act?
2. What is the difference between exempt and nonexempt employees in overtime pay requirements?
3. What is the difference between commission and piece rate pay as far as the basis for the compensation?
4. What is the difference between minimum wage and "living wage"?

LO 2-5 Describe Internal Controls and Record Retention for a Payroll System

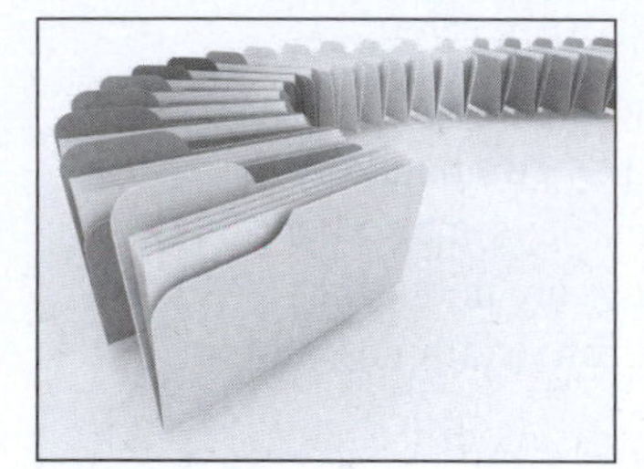

koya979/Shutterstock

Internal controls are critical to ensure the integrity of a payroll system. Confidentiality of payroll information is one of the most important controls in establishing a payroll system. Pay records such as time records are considered confidential documents, and personnel who handle or maintain such records must ensure the privacy of the information they contain. Small firms may be able to maintain the confidentiality of handwritten time sheets; however, multifacility companies may need to use more secure time-collection methods to ensure information privacy.

Strategic planning of the payroll system prior to its inception can prevent data errors and losses related to inadequate ***internal controls***. Most importantly, the payroll system design should be reviewed at regular intervals to determine its effectiveness and appropriateness for the company size and to correct errors before they become magnified.

> Internal controls are a necessity, especially for small companies. The median loss to companies where fraud has occurred is $108,000. Examples of easily implemented internal controls include
>
> - Transparency in the flow of money in and out of the organization.
> - Involvement in cost management and expense disbursal.
> - Engagement of multiple employees in the record-keeping process.
> - Attentiveness to employee behavior.
> - Recognition that any organization may become a fraud victim.
>
> The need for internal controls increases as a company engages more fully with internet portals such as time tracking and payroll processing sites. Technological changes introduce a new level of vulnerability into a company's data, so robust internal control practices are vital. (Source: *Strategic Finance*)

A company with many departments and many employees will generally have a more complex ***review process*** than a small company will. In an organization that has one office and a dozen or fewer employees, certain steps of the verification process may be omitted and fewer people are required to conduct it. Conversely, a large organization with several departments and many employees could have several levels of verification in the ***payroll review*** process. Even outsourced payroll requires levels of the review process. The payroll executed by an external company is only as accurate as the data provided. For instance, a company could have a payroll review process such as the one shown in Figure 2-11.

FIGURE 2-11
Payroll Review Process: Steps to Ensure Accurate Payroll

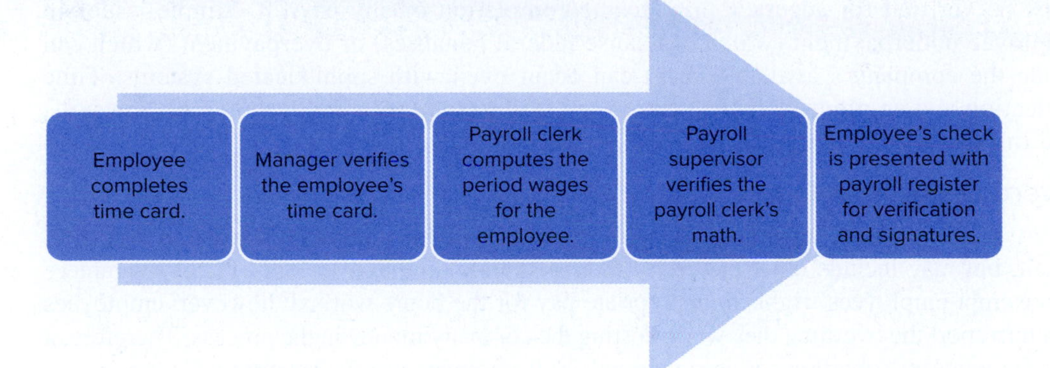

An extremely important issue within internal controls is the determination of authorized signers. A common (and good!) practice in a company is to have more than one designated signatory for payroll checks. Often, these signers are different people than those involved in the review process. In many companies, more than one person signs the payroll checks as another level of review of the accuracy. Remember that the most important part of payroll is *accuracy*. The extra time it takes to review and obtain the necessary signatures is time well spent, as long as it prevents costly errors.

Documentation of the payroll process is vital. As should be clear by now, execution of payroll is not merely writing checks to employees. Proper documentation of payroll entails a well-delineated procedure and properly trained personnel. Table 2-1 contains examples of different documentation controls, the activities involved in each, and the personnel who may be required.

TABLE 2-1
Documentation Controls

Procedure	Example of Internal Control Activities	Could Be Performed by
Review and approval of time data from time cards or other time collection devices	Completion of the time collection procedure Review of time collection for accuracy and approval	Employee's supervisor
Overtime approval	Approve the amount and type of overtime to be paid	Employee's supervisor
Approval for leave of absence or other unpaid time off	Obtain all prior approvals for unpaid time away due to FMLA or other reasons	Employee's supervisor
Timely entering of payroll data	Enter the payroll data into the payroll system in a timely manner, and check for data integrity and accuracy	Payroll clerk
Payroll system security	Make sure that only designated employees or payroll vendors have access to payroll data	Payroll supervisor
Approval of the payroll prior to issuance	Obtain the approval from signatory prior to issuing checks	Authorized signer(s)
Maintenance of paid time off (e.g., vacation, sick, etc.)	Ensure that employees receive the exact amount agreed upon	Payroll clerk; employee; supervisor; other designee
Access to payroll data	Ensure that payroll data is confidential and secure	Payroll supervisor
Separation of duties	Make sure that different people verify data, enter data, verify checks	Payroll supervisor
Training of payroll staff	Ensure that payroll department employees and other department supervisors are aware of and follow company payroll policies	Payroll supervisor

Review of Time Collected

All workers hours reported manually on time cards or electronically through other methods must be verified for accuracy prior to the completion of any payroll. Simple issues in employee underpayment (which can cause federal penalties) or overpayment (which can erode the company's available cash) can occur even with sophisticated systems. Time collection and employee payment errors can lead to reduced employee morale, lawsuits, and fines.

Overtime Approval

Hourly employees are subject to federal overtime provisions, commonly known as time-and-a-half, but may include other pay bases such as double-time and so forth. FLSA guarantees nonexempt employees' rights to appropriate pay for the hours worked; however, employees can misreport the overtime they work, costing the company money in the process. Therefore, a good practice is to obtain supervisor approval on all employee-reported overtime.Computerized systems can also affect the reported overtime. The data is only as accurate as the person who entered it. One of the authors worked at a company that once paid her for 75 hours of overtime in one pay period—when she should have had only 7.5! This kind of error can cause chaos for both the employee, who must return the money, and the employer, who should not have paid it in the first place. Once again, improper pay can erode the morale of the employees. Overpayment on hours can create many other overpayments; federal withholding taxes, Medicare, Social Security taxes, and pension or 401(k) contributions that are driven by gross wages are just a few examples.

Digital Vision/2007 Getty Images, Inc.

A significant percentage of corporate fraud involves payroll tampering or embezzlement. A payroll and accounting manager in Atlanta, Georgia, plead guilty to wire fraud after investigators discovered that she had embezzled $1.5 million over a six-year period through improper payroll deposits. The employee had created a fake employee and instructed the outsourced payroll company to direct deposit that employee's pay into her own personal bank account. The employee had a file for the fictitious worker. A multiperson payroll verification process could have shortened the duration and reduced the amount of the embezzlement. (Source: *Accounting Today*)

Approval for Leave of Absence or Other Unpaid Time Off

The employee's supervisor is one level of oversight to ensure that the payroll data reaches the payroll department accurately and in a timely fashion. Supervisors work closely with their employees and should approve overtime and paid time off. Supervisors review individual time sheets for accuracy prior to delivery to the payroll department. Control of time away from work is the responsibility of the employee's supervisor, at the very minimum. The department supervisor should approve the time off. This approval needs to be tracked and maintained by the payroll department to ensure integrity in the payroll records. A suggested best practice is to keep requests for time away attached to the payroll stub for the affected pay period. The use of leave forms provides companies with a paper trail used to clarify perceived discrepancies in pay.

Web-based services facilitate requests, approvals, and tracking for paid time off. Apps such as Zenefits allow managers to adjust paid time off, approve and track employee requests, synchronize calendars, and download reports detailing employee time away from work. (Source: Zenefits)

Ingram Publishing

File Security

Based on the amount of legislation regarding the privacy and security of personnel information, it is important to understand that all files pertaining to payroll, whether paper or electronic, must be kept secure from tampering. Another reason for ***file security***, or restriction of personnel file access, is the firm's governmental payroll obligations. The tax information contained in the payroll records is required to prepare timely and accurate payment of payroll taxes, a factor that is nearly as important as paying the employees. Examples of methods to secure payroll records include multiple passwords for system access, locking of file cabinets with controlled key disbursement, and encryption programs.

Because payroll data contains highly personal and private information, security of the information is important. To maintain file security, access to payroll records is restricted to a relatively small number of people. Paper-based payroll data is stored in a secure location; similarly, electronic payroll data is securely backed up and encrypted.

Data privacy and fund protection are a high priority for companies and legislators. Preventing breaches of payroll record security is a high priority and an evolving issue. The Electronic Fund Transfer Act of 1978, created to prevent problems with newly created ATM cards, has been expanded to address fraud and theft issues with ***paycards***, a preloaded credit card that allows an employee to access funds without needing a bank account. Paycard use for payroll disbursement was estimated to be nearly $57 billion in 2015 and continues to be the fastest-growing payroll method in the United States, with 5.9 million active paycards being used as of 2017. With the growth of the gig economy and the number of unbanked employees, paycards are a relatively secure method of disbursing immediately accessible pay.

In *Jessie Chavez v. PVH Corporation* (2013) , the defendant had to pay $1.85 million to Chavez because of fees deducted from the plaintiff's payroll card, which meant that the full amount of the wages was reduced; additionally, the plaintiff had not agreed to paycard use in advance. The Consumer Financial Protection Bureau (CFPB) proposed legislation in 2014 that would include specific language on paycards, informing employees of their right to request another form of pay disbursement. As of October 2016, the CFPB issued a rule that regulated the posting of accounting, disclosures, and overdraft credit that became effective as of October 2017. (Source: Law360)

Alternating Duties and Cross-Training

The cross-training of payroll professionals can act as a safeguard of payroll information. One of the goals of the Sarbanes–Oxley Act of 2002 was to protect the integrity of accounting data by legislating document retention requirements and the rotation of duties by auditors. The same principle applies to payroll system workers. Cross-training and alternating the duties of the

Cross-training employees has more benefits than fraud deterrence. Offering employees the chance to learn other duties empowers them in their professional development, which fosters a sense of fulfillment among employees. Cross-training also grants employees the opportunity to consider differing perspectives and to gain a broader understanding of the company's operations. Finally, cross-training is linked to better problem-solving ability because employees understand diverse tasks. (Source: *Forbes*)

people in the payroll process may avoid or minimize errors and potential issues stemming from corruption. Furthermore, cross-training and rotation of duties foster professional development and proficiency with multiple tasks. This rotation of payroll duties refers only to personnel within the payroll department, not opening the payroll processing to non-accounting departments.

Who Does Which Job?

Stop & Check

Imagine that you have been approached to assist a business owner who is concerned about the security of his or her company's payroll. In a team of three or four people, decide how you would distribute payroll responsibilities to implement excellent internal control procedures. How did you divide the responsibilities? Explain.

Best Practices Involved in Employee File Maintenance

Maintenance of employee files is as important as the protection of employee information. IRS Regulation 26 CFR 1.6001 clearly states that the method of ***file maintenance*** is the responsibility of the employer. The Internal Revenue Code recommends record labeling, creation of backup copies, and secure record storage. An important note is that despite the choice of record maintenance, the employer retains all liability for auditor access to the information upon demand. Items such as time and work records, including time cards and electronic work records, must be maintained to be available for auditors because these items are vital components of a payroll system audit.

26 CFR 1.6001–1 Records.
(a) *In general.* Except as provided in paragraph (b) of this section, any person subject to tax under subtitle A of the Code (including a qualified State individual income tax which is treated pursuant to section 6361(a) as if it were imposed by chapter 1 of subtitle A), or any person required to file a return of information with respect to income, shall keep such permanent books of account or records, including inventories, as are sufficient to establish the amount of gross income, deductions, credits, or other matters required to be shown by such person in any return of such tax or information. (Source: GPO)

ninun/123RF

Payroll record maintenance is important for employees at all levels of the organization. IRS Revenue Procedure 98-25, 1998-1 CB 689, was enacted in 1998 to govern the maintenance procedures and duration of record keeping for companies with employees. Provisions of the law include payroll transaction details such as time worked, pay dates, employee status, record reconciliation, and correlation of IRS reports and employee records. With regard to executive-level pay, the company must keep records of how the executive's pay was derived, including benchmarks from similar companies, payout period, and scheduled increases. All pay disbursed must be justified according to the amount and type of work performed, regardless of employee level or classification. A company's payroll and legal department should work closely to determine and implement a maintenance and record destruction program that complies with IRS requirements but avoids the inaccessibility of data that occurs with information overload.

Electronic Records

Many companies have moved to electronic scanned copies of payroll records that allow immediate access to employee files from a password-protected format. In remote locations, payroll accountants can send the managers and employees Adobe Acrobat files requiring a password to access pay records. Several data encryption programs are currently on the market,

Andrey_Popov/Shutterstock

allowing payroll managers to select the best fit for their individual company. All hard copies (i.e., paper versions) of payroll information must be in a locked file cabinet with limited access.

Computers have become a necessary part of business and offer significant benefits to the accounting department. Most accounting software for the preparation of payroll includes password requirements that the company can control, limiting access to electronic information about employees, pay, and personal information. Many regulatory agencies have addressed the issue of record security and safeguarding procedures; for example, the Food and Drug Administration enacted 21 CFR Part 11 that delineates electronic record security and safeguarding procedures.

Payroll accounting, according to the definition by the Internal Revenue Code, is a closed system because only certain employees are granted access to the information contained in the electronic records. All aspects of information security are the employer's responsibility, including access to, creation of, and maintenance of electronic personnel and pay records. Record identifiers would log who had accessed an electronic file, when, and from what location. Record logging provides an additional measure of security and protection against unauthorized access (also called "hacking") as well as tracking whether unauthorized changes occur on records.

According to the FBI, more than $1 billion per year has been lost to hackers using ransomware. Ransomware is malicious code placed into a computer system by hackers, aimed at obtaining a monetary fee to release access to a company's computerized information. The city of Atlanta, Georgia, encountered ransomware that was downloaded onto the city's computer system during a city-related Internet search. As a result of the attack, the city's daily operations were halted because workers could not access their computers. (Source: ArsTechnica, TrendMicro)

Like other payroll records, electronic records, especially those accessible over the Internet, must be safeguarded to prevent fraudulent activity and data corruption. Employers can provide access to information via a company's intranet (inside the organization) or via the Internet using encryption programs, passwords, and secured website locations. It is important to note that once a company has allowed Internet access to its payroll files, the company is opening itself up to additional risks from hacking or wrongful use of the payroll information. It is the payroll accountant's responsibility to report any suspicious activity to company managers or the information security department of the company.

Payroll as a Non-Solo Effort

One best practice is to have more than one person involved in the generation and maintenance of payroll records. Many errors can occur when the total payroll responsibility rests with

- Nonexistent or "ghost" employees could be created and paid via the payroll system. The person committing the fraud could circumvent the payroll system and divert the funds to himself or an accomplice.
- Terminated employees could continue to be paid via the payroll system, or the funds could be subverted to someone else perpetrating the fraud.
- Sales commission plans, employee bonus plans, incentive programs, and other arrangements intended to induce particular behaviors are subject to the employee's and management's manipulation.
- The payroll checks distributed to employees could be stolen individually or en masse prior to their distribution. In addition, check fraud could be perpetrated using actual checks or just the account information.
- The company's payroll system or payroll service provider could suffer a breach of the security protocols protecting the computer systems, which could allow any combination of fraud or theft to be perpetrated.

one person. Errors that occur may be the result of a complex hacking effort or a simple failure to remove the system access from a former employee.

Other instances of payroll fraud could have been avoided with a ***separation of duties***, which involves the division of related tasks to prevent fraud. Internal controls promote improved accuracy when more than one person is involved in payroll preparation and disbursement. A division of record maintenance, employee verification, and the spread of pay disbursement responsibilities among different employees, depending upon the size of the company, would prevent many of the preceding problems. This not only protects the employer from complaints and potential legal issues stemming from payroll anomalies, but also provides a level of protection and verification to employees. Auditors look for well-defined internal controls within organizations to ensure legal compliance and file integrity.

- A payroll worker, disgruntled with his job, stole almost $300,000 from different companies by transferring the organizations' money into different bank accounts that he owned.
- A former bookkeeper forged $80,000 in payroll checks before the company owner discovered the discrepancy.
- In the Los Angeles Unified School District, internal inspectors found that the pay system was issuing paychecks to deceased employees.
- In an audit of Department of Transportation records in Florida, the auditors found that the paper files supporting the payroll system had been discarded to make room in the office. The audit revealed overpayments to employees caused by an incorrect calculation and a lack of payroll verification. Of the employees who were overpaid, only one returned the money.

In the event of a data breach, the company must act quickly to contain the damage and prevent additional issues. The American Payroll Association offered the following action steps that companies should take when they experience a breach in their accounting data software:

Step 1 Prevent the spread of the data breach by taking payroll systems to an offline state and restrict access to records.

Step 2 Determine the scale of the threat or breach. Gather all related data and facts involving the breach and assess any vulnerabilities in the system.

Step 3 Contact the appropriate law enforcement officials to notify them of the crime and to open an investigation. Notify the Federation of Tax Administrators at www.taxadmin.org to engage their service in the investigation.

Step 4 Review the company's data storage, retention, and authorization policies to identify ways to prevent future occurrences.

Document Retention Requirements

According to IRS Regulation 26 CFR 1.6001, records pertaining to any financial transaction must remain available for ***payroll audit***, the inspection by regulating bodies, at all times. The purpose of the tax code is to maintain records for legal purposes in the event of the suspicion of fraudulent activity. IRS Regulation 26 CFR 1.6001 pertains to both manual and computerized records, including payroll records prepared by third-party sources. Both manual and electronic documents must be maintained in such a way that they maintain accessibility for the duration similar to tax record retention.

When a company institutes a retention schedule, the requirements of legislation and the IRS must be considered. The retention period does not begin until the disbursement of pay occurs or the employee terminates employment, whichever occurs last. Remember: In the event of fraudulent activity, retention requirements no longer apply, and all company records can be requested by the courts.

Companies must abide by both state and federal law regarding document retention. Employee payroll records, consisting of all forms and payroll compensation statements, must be retained following ***termination*** or separation. Although no regulations exist for the retention and archiving of internal payroll documents (e.g., a ***payroll register***), a general guideline is that the internal documents should be stored with the other payroll accounting records and destroyed in accordance with accounting record guidelines.

When an employee is terminated, records for the employee and reason for termination must be retained for a period of one year. If an employee qualifies under ADEA, all payroll records must be retained for a period of three years. The Lilly Ledbetter Fair Pay Act created a record retention requirement of an additional three years for primary records (pay records or bargaining agreements) and two years for supplementary data (time cards, wage rate tables, piece rate records). As a good practice to meet the various requirements, many businesses will set document retention at three years for all files.

In 2018, the state of Massachusetts discovered that the state comptroller's website had not listed the Massachusetts State Police salaries in its reports since 2010. Because most of the State Police earn more than $150,000 annually, the omitted amount was substantial. The governor requested an overtime audit to detect potential abuses that could leave the state vulnerable to legal proceedings. (Source: WBUR News)

Agencies that have the right to audit payroll records include

- The Internal Revenue Service (IRS).
- Federal and state Departments of Labor.
- Department of Homeland Security.
- Other state and local agencies.
- Labor unions.

The following is a chart that explains federal record retention requirements, including relevant laws and types of documents.

Record Type	Requirements
Payroll Records (time sheets, electronic records, etc.)	• 3-year retention period • An additional 5-year post-termination retention is recommended due to Lilly Ledbetter Act • Includes employee data, any pay records, and all compensation, financial and nonfinancial
Employee Federal, State, and Local Tax Records	• 4 years from date the tax is due or paid • Includes all W-4s, state and local tax withholding forms, requests for additional tax withholding, and tax remittances
Form I-9 and Accompanying Employment Eligibility Documents	• 3 years after hire OR • 1 year after termination, whichever is longer
Employee Benefits and Contributions	• 6 years • All retirement plan contributions, plan changes, records pertaining to any other employee voluntary deductions
Health Plan Documentation	• No written guidelines, but a minimum of 6 years is recommended • All written notices about changes in health coverage, especially for health coverage after termination of employment

Even if your company outsources payroll activities, it is still accountable for all records and the information transmitted to the payroll service companies. The third-party payroll service provider attends only to the processing of company payroll but is not responsible for payroll tax payments. Tax remittance remains the liability of the company. Instances in which companies have diverted payroll tax liabilities for personal purposes have resulted in sizable fines and sanctions for companies.

> In 2017, the IRS levied a $1 million lien against the property of CCH Oncology of Buffalo, New York. The company failed to remit or file returns for income, Social Security, and Medicare taxes for both the employees' and the employer's shares starting approximately July 2016. The lien amount included failure to pay and failure to file penalties as well as interest. (Source: *The Buffalo News*)

Internal Controls and Audits

Stop & Check

1. Which of these is *not* a payroll internal control procedure?
   a. Overtime approval.
   b. Removal of payroll oversight.
   c. Cross-training.
   d. File security.
2. Which of these records should be retained in the event of a payroll audit?
   a. Employee medical records.
   b. Employee reviews.
   c. Employee time and work records.
   d. Employee nonpayroll correspondence.

LO 2-6 Discuss Employee Termination and Document Destruction Procedures

When employees are terminated, either voluntarily or involuntarily, the employer has payroll issues unique to the situation. The common element to each termination is the paperwork needed. When an employer terminates a worker's employment involuntarily, the burden of proof for the termination is on the employer, should the case ever require legal scrutiny.

> In *Graziadio v. Culinary Institute of America* (2016), the plaintiff was terminated involuntarily after taking two consecutive three-week leaves to care for her children because the Culinary Institute of America claimed that Graziadio had not filed the required paperwork for leave under the FMLA. At first, the court ruled in favor of the Culinary Institute of America because the proper paperwork was not on file. However, further investigation found that the human resources director of the Culinary Institute of America, who refused to allow Graziadio to return to work, had not responded to Graziadio's numerous email requests for FMLA paperwork to justify her absence and to return to work. (Source: FindLaw)

Employee Termination

There are two different methods of separation of an employee from the company: ***termination*** and ***resignation***. When an employee leaves a company, the payroll accountant must

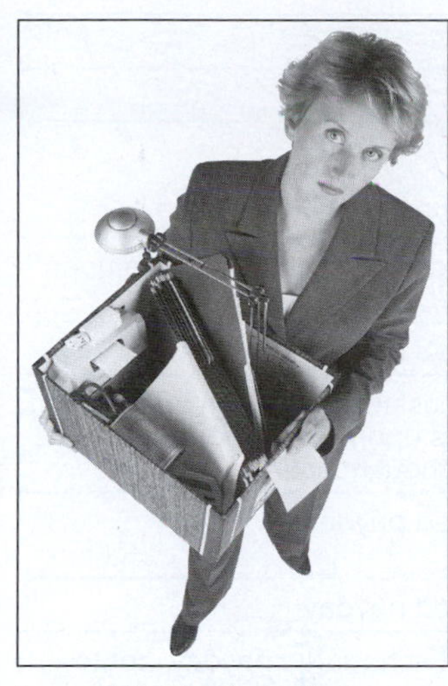

Ingram Publishing/SuperStock

complete several steps with regard to the employee's and the firm's records. The employee's final paycheck will reflect a culmination of hours worked, and possibly, depending on the company policies, vacation earned and not taken and sick time earned and not taken. Depending on the company's policies, if the employee's compensation is commission based, there should be an agreement between management and the employee regarding sales and timing of the final paycheck to ensure payment of all earned commissions.

Final hours are calculated the same as for any normal pay period. The employee's daily hours are calculated to determine regular and overtime, and the worked hours are added together to determine weekly hours and weekly overtime. If the employee earned any vacation or sick time, then those hours may also need to be paid out on the final paycheck. Vacation and sick time are not included in the worked hours for the determination of overtime.

A limited amount of legislation exists about the payment of a severance package upon termination. In general, two situations exist in which severance packages may be required by legislation: the closure of a company facility and a large number of employee layoffs. In the event that a large number of employees are laid off, a severance package may be required if any promise, written or oral, of a severance package exists or if the company has a history of paying severance packages to laid-off employees. For specific guidelines, the state's employment department would be the primary resource for official guidance (see Appendix E for state contact information).

In terms of payroll accounting, a major difference between the termination and the resignation of an employee, besides the circumstances surrounding the employee's separation from the company (layoff, termination for cause, resignation, etc.), is the timing of the delivery of the final pay disbursement. When an employee quits, any compensation due will be processed and disbursed on the company's next scheduled pay date. However, when the employee is terminated, the company may be mandated to issue the final paycheck immediately or within a short time frame to comply with state labor laws. There is no federal regulation for the immediate issuance of the employee's final pay, although the Department of Labor explicitly mandates back pay owed to former employees. Table 2-2 contains information about states' employee termination pay guidelines.

TABLE 2-2
States' Termination Pay Guidelines

State	Guideline	State	Guideline
AL	No termination pay guidelines	**MO**	Immediately upon termination; no law for resignation
AK	Within three working days upon termination; at the next regular pay date upon resignation	**MT**	Immediately upon termination unless employer's written policy extends the time to the next regular payday; next regular pay date or 15 days, whichever is earlier, for resignation
AZ	Within seven working days or the end of the next pay period, whichever is sooner	**NE**	Next regular payday or within two weeks, whichever is sooner
AR	Within seven days of discharge	**NV**	Immediately upon termination; next scheduled pay date or seven days, whichever is sooner upon resignation
CA	Immediately upon discharge	**NH**	Within 72 hours upon termination; next pay date in the event of a layoff
CO	Immediately upon discharge (i.e., within 6 hours of the next business day or 24 hours if payroll is processed off site) for termination; next scheduled pay date upon resignation	**NJ**	Next regularly scheduled payday
CT	No later than the next business day upon termination; next scheduled pay date upon resignation	**NM**	Within five days upon termination; next scheduled pay date upon resignation

(continued)

State	Guideline	State	Guideline
DE	Next regularly scheduled payday	NY	Next regularly scheduled payday
DC	No later than the next business day following termination; next scheduled pay date or within 7 days upon resignation	NC	Next regularly scheduled payday
FL	No termination pay guidelines	OH	No termination pay guidelines; within 15 days upon resignation
GA	No termination pay guidelines	OK	Next regularly scheduled payday
HI	At time of termination unless conditions render pay impossible, next business day in that case; next business day if resignation with notice	OR	By the end of the next business day upon termination; within five business days upon resignation with notice or next business day without notice
ID	Next regular payday or within 10 days, excluding weekends and holidays, whichever occurs first	PA	Next regularly scheduled payday
IL	Next regularly scheduled payday	RI	Next regularly scheduled payday
IN	Next regularly scheduled payday	SC	Within 48 hours or next scheduled payday, not to exceed 30 days
IA	Next regularly scheduled payday	SD	Next regularly scheduled payday or whenever the terminated employee returns all the employer's property
KS	Next regularly scheduled payday	TN	Next regularly scheduled payday or 21 days, whichever comes later
KY	Next regular payday or 14 days, whichever is later	TX	No later than six days after termination; by the next scheduled pay date upon resignation
LA	Next regular payday or 15 days, whichever is sooner	UT	Within 24 hours upon termination; next scheduled pay date upon resignation
ME	Next scheduled payday or within two weeks after demand from the employee, whichever is sooner	VT	Within 72 hours upon termination; next scheduled pay date or the following Friday (if not pay date) upon resignation
MD	Next regularly scheduled payday	VA	Next regularly scheduled payday
MA	Immediately upon termination; next scheduled pay date or the following Saturday upon resignation	WA	Next regularly scheduled payday
MI	Next regularly scheduled payday	WV	Within 72 hours upon termination; next scheduled pay date upon resignation
MN	Immediately upon termination; next regular pay date upon resignation	WI	Next regularly scheduled payday or within one month, whichever is sooner upon termination; within 24 hour if layoff; next scheduled pay date upon resignation
MS	No termination pay guidelines	WY	Within five business days

Source: FindLaw.

Ingram Publishing/SuperStock

Document Destruction

Although many state and federal laws delineate the time requirement for document retention, there are also several methods for regulated ***document destruction*** of sensitive payroll data. How must confidential payroll-related documents be destroyed? It is not as simple as throwing old payroll documents in the trash. Preferred destruction methods of confidential payroll documents include incineration, confidential shredding services, or pulping of the paper records. Electronic records must be purged from the server. Although specific destruction procedures and regulations vary among states and localities, the basic guidelines of confidential destruction after the required retention period are common to most areas. From small-scale record destruction using in-office paper shredders to large-scale operations such as ProShred, Iron Mountain, and many other companies, destruction of confidential business documents is a serious concern because of the federal privacy laws governing payroll documents.

A best practice in terms of document destruction is to create a policy regarding document retention and destruction schedules. An employee in charge of these schedules would be tasked with ensuring that all paper records are stored appropriately and retained for the proper legal time. Another best practice is to separate payroll-related documentation into the following categories:

- Personnel information such as Forms W-4 and I-9, garnishments, wage information, and direct deposit instructions.
- Employee benefits paperwork including benefit elections, FMLA documentation, workers' compensation evidence, and flexible spending account information.
- Any investigative information, maintained separately because of the absence of a statute of limitations on employee fraud.

By separating the employee paper files into these categories, document retention and destruction guidelines may be observed more efficiently.

deepadesigns/Shutterstock

Electronic Records

As the use of electronic payroll records has grown, the need to define appropriate destruction procedures has become increasingly apparent. Simply deleting a website or a portion of the data does not guarantee the security of confidential information. Details of the website's design and system change documentation must be maintained to facilitate record disposal. Guidelines for electronic records disposition include

- Data disposition instructions including dates and authorized administrators.
- Record destruction schedules involving security encryption.
- Technical documentation for each record system.
- Identifying information for file indexes and unique records.
- If a website is involved, technical documentation of the site architecture should be maintained.

The proliferation of electronic accounting records, especially payroll-related data, has led to the adoption of the Department of Defense Data Wipe Method, commonly referred to as DoD 5220.22-M, which sanitizes electronic records. Various data wiping tools have this software tool, including DBAN, CBL Data Shredder, and ErAse. (Source: Lifewire)

Destroy and Terminate

Stop & Check

1 How should paper payroll records be destroyed? How about electronic records?

2. Charlie, a resident of Hawaii, is terminated without cause from his job on October 11. He is terminated at the end of the day after the payroll manager has left. When must he receive his final pay? Is the employer required to pay him a severance package? Explain.

Trends to Watch

PAYROLL PROCEDURES

As we move further into the digital age, payroll procedures are changing to meet employer needs, technological availability, and employee accessibility. Some procedures that have changed since 2014 include the following:

- Affordable Care Act employer reporting requirement clarification.
- An increase in the use of Internet-based employee files, which requires increasingly sophisticated security software and company protocols.
- Changes to limitations on the number of and fees related to visas for foreign workers.
- Increased "job swapping" that requires employees to be cross-trained and employers to consider compensation needs of different positions.
- An increase in the "virtual marketplace," in which employers and employees will telecommute or otherwise perform work from geographically dispersed locations.

Some trends to watch include the following:

- Tighter security protocols regarding electronic data and restricting access to electronic records to prevent cyber hacking and fraud.
- Revision to the Department of Labor proposed Final Rule regarding a minimum salary for exempt employees.
- Increased transparency and outreach on the part of the U.S. Department of Labor to promote worker education about work-related rights and legislation.
- Financial stress and wellness related to cost sharing of ACA and pay.
- Expanded integration of cloud-based apps to capture employee personnel and payroll information to promote accuracy in employee tracking and clarity for audits.

Summary of Payroll System Procedures

The establishment of a payroll system involves careful planning and deliberation. The framework used for the payroll system needs to have enough room for company growth and enough structure to make sure that company and governmental deadlines are met. Using the best practices outlined in this chapter can help a company implement a robust payroll system, whether the system is maintained by company personnel or outsourced, completed manually or electronically with the use of specifically designed software. Adequate payroll system design can save a company from problems with employees and governmental entities and may prevent data breaches and fraud.

Although pay processes and methods vary among companies, the framework of internal review and the necessity for accuracy remain the fundamental aspects of any payroll system. Documentation of an employee's eligibility to work in the United States as well as compensation method, rates, tax liabilities, and voluntary withholdings are critical elements of employee files that the payroll accountant must maintain. The process of entering items into a payroll system varies depending on the type of work done and the compensation rates, for which the payroll accountant must have documentation. Depending on the company's preferences, anything from manual records to computerized records to external payroll vendors may be used to track the payroll. At employee termination, final pay must be issued, but the timing of that final pay depends on state legislation.

Payroll record-keeping and maintenance are complex issues and subject to several federal and state regulations. Employee personal information must be safeguarded at all times, and information privacy is paramount. Now that many companies are resorting to electronic pay records, information safeguarding is especially important, and encryption efforts are multidimensional, involving the accounting, legal, and information systems departments of an organization. Destruction of payroll-related documents after the required retention period is a serious concern, and an entire industry focuses on document retention and destruction.

Key Points

- Communication protocol varies among companies and departments within companies.
- Ethical payroll practices require protection of information and dissemination only to the employee or specifically relevant supervisory staff.
- Employees are classified as either exempt or nonexempt from FLSA provisions.
- To be classified as an exempt employee requires an examination of job duties.
- Control of the payroll system involves regular system design review and delineation of specific tasks.
- Payroll, whether completed internally or by an ***outsourced vendor*** (a payroll service external to the company), is only as accurate as the information provided.
- Pay periods are at the discretion of the company. The IRS has developed ***tax tables*** (i.e., tax withholding amounts) for each pay interval that are contained in Publication 15, an annual IRS guide to payroll.
- File security is of utmost importance, especially when files are stored electronically and accessed via an Internet portal.
- Documentation for payroll exceptions such as time away from work should be maintained separately from regular work time documentation.
- Calculations of pay can involve many variables and require review of each employee prior to pay issuance.
- Final pay needs to reflect all earned compensation, paid time off, and deductions up to the date of termination.
- The timing of final pay disbursement when an employee is terminated depends on state law.
- Document retention and destruction are important for legal compliance and data security purposes.

Vocabulary

Biweekly payroll
Commission
Daily payroll
Document destruction
Exempt
File maintenance
File security
Foreign Account Tax Compliance Act (FATCA)
Hiring packet
I-9
Internal control
Leased employee
Monthly payroll
New hire reporting
Nonexempt
Outsourced vendor
Pay period
Paycard
Payroll audit
Payroll register
Payroll review
Piece rate
Resignation
Review process
Semimonthly payroll
Separation of duties
Statutory employee
Tax table
Temporary employee
Termination
W-4
Weekly payroll

Review Questions

1. What are necessary elements of internal control for a payroll department?
2. Why should more than one person prepare/verify payroll processing?
3. What documents should be included in all new-hire packets?
4. Why are new hires required to be reported to the state's employment department?
5. For the state in which you live, when must a terminated employee be paid his or her final paycheck?
6. What are the five main payroll frequencies?
7. What are two of the best practices in establishing a payroll system?
8. What are the important considerations in setting up a payroll system?
9. What are two different tasks involved in payroll accounting?
10. What agencies or organizations can audit a company's payroll records?
11. How long should employee records be retained?

12. Why are independent contractors not paid through a company's payroll system?
13. What is the difference between termination and resignation?
14. What are the differences among daily, weekly, biweekly, semimonthly, and monthly pay periods?
15. What differentiates exempt and nonexempt employees?
16. What categories exist for the purposes of document retention?

Exercises Set A

E2-1A. LO 2-1, 2-4

Krystal Valdez, a nonexempt employee at Misor Investments, works a standard 8:00–5:00 schedule with an hour for lunch each day. Krystal received overtime pay for hours in excess of 40 per week. During the week, she worked the following schedule:

- Monday: 7.5 hours
- Tuesday: 8.25 hours
- Wednesday: 8 hours
- Thursday: 8.5 hours
- Friday: 10 hours

How many hours of overtime did Krystal work this week?

1. 0 hours
2. 1.5 hours
3. 2 hours
4. 2.25 hours

E2-2A. LO 2-1

Roger Ortega receives his pay twice per month working for Megaveo Enterprises. Which of the following choices describes his pay frequency?

1. Biweekly
2. Semimonthly
3. Weekly
4. Monthly

E2-3A. LO 2-2

Lila Rivera is a new employee for Divera Glass. Which federal forms must she complete as part of the hiring process?

1. W-4
2. W-2
3. SS-8
4. I-9

E2-4A. LO 2-5, 2-6

Wilbur Matthews, a resident of Wisconsin, ended his employment with Bovill Farms on December 6, 2019. The next pay date for the company is December 20. By what date should he receive his final pay?

1. December 9
2. December 13
3. December 20
4. December 31

E2-5A. LO 2-5

Charlene Kelley is a new nonexempt sales clerk for Oyondo Retail Stores. She completes her time card for the pay period. To ensure proper internal control, what is the next step in the payroll review process?

1. Submit the time card to the payroll clerk
2. Have a friend check her math for accuracy
3. Submit the time card to her manager for review
4. Enter the time card data directly into the payroll system

E2-6A. LO 2-6

Alfonso Silva needs additional filing space at the end of the year in the company's off-site, secured storage. He sees several boxes of payroll records marked for the current year's destruction. What methods can Alfonso use to dispose of the payroll records? (Select all that apply.)

1. Contact an off-site record destruction service
2. Place the boxes containing the records in the company trash disposal
3. Shred the records, and then dispose of the shredded paper
4. Incinerate the payroll records marked for destruction

E2-7A. LO 2-1 Ed Myers is verifying the accuracy and amount of information contained in the employee records for his employer, Genible Industries. Which of the following items should be present in the employee information? (Select all that apply.)
1. Job title
2. Social Security number
3. Birth date
4. Employee address

E2-8A. LO 2-2 Ginger Klein is the payroll clerk for Neolane Transportation. A colleague who is classified as an independent contractor requests to be classified as an employee. What factors should Ginger consider? (Select all that apply.)
1. Relationship of the parties
2. Behavioral control
3. Method of compensation
4. Financial control

E2-9A. LO 2-2 What are the forms of identification that establish *identity* for the I-9? (Select all that apply.)
1. Driver's license
2. Native American tribal document
3. Voter registration card
4. Social Security account card

E2-10A. LO 2-2 What are the forms of identification that establish *employment authorization* for the I-9? (Select all that apply.)
1. U.S. Citizen I.D. Card
2. U.S. Passport
3. School record
4. Certified copy of the birth certificate

E2-11A. LO 2-3 Jamie Patil is a candidate for the position of sales manager with Retrozz Furniture. She is going to be required to supervise several employees and can determine the direction in which she will complete the assignments given to her. What guidelines should she follow when classifying workers as exempt or nonexempt? (Select all that apply.)
1. OSHA
2. FLSA
3. Department of Labor
4. IRS

E2-12A. LO 2-3 Susana Robledo is the office manager for Wardley and Sons Auto Detailing. Because it is a small office, she is required to keep track of all employee records and pay both employees and contractors. Which of the following are legal factors that will differentiate exempt from nonexempt employees? (Select all that apply.)
1. Number of hours worked
2. Type of work performed
3. Employee age and education
4. Amount of supervisor-given direction

Problems Set A

P2-1A. LO 2-1 Henrietta Morales is a salaried employee earning $75,000 per year. What is Henrietta's period pay for each of the following pay frequencies?
1. Biweekly
2. Semimonthly
3. Weekly
4. Monthly

P2-2A. LO 2-2, 2-3 Beth Caldwell is in the payroll accounting department of Acerill Films. An independent contractor of the company requests that Social Security and Medicare taxes be withheld from future compensation. What advice should Beth offer?

P2-3A. LO 2-5
You are the new payroll supervisor for your company. Which payroll documentation control procedures are now your responsibility?

P2-4A. LO 2-2
Leona Figueroa is a new employee in the payroll department of Octolium Computers. After working at the company for one week, she asks you why it is so important to submit new hire documentation. What guidance will you offer her?

P2-5A. LO 2-4
You are the payroll accounting clerk for your company, Conose Advertising, which has 50 employees. The controller has recently switched the firm from an in-house payroll system to an outsourced payroll provider. What are your responsibilities within the company for payroll records and employee file issues?

P2-6A. LO 2-2
Aaron Tallchief is a citizen of the Northern Pomo Indian Nation. In completing his I-9, he provides an official Northern Pomo Indian Nation birth certificate to establish identification and employment eligibility. Is this sufficient documentation? Why or why not?

P2-7A. LO 2-3
Ian Burns is the new payroll accountant for ECG Marketing. Certain employees have been requesting changes in classification from nonexempt to exempt. How do the U.S. Department of Labor guidelines help him answer the employees' questions?

P2-8A. LO 2-6
Twinte Cars, a California corporation, has internal corporate requirements that stipulate a three-year payroll document retention period. It enters into a contract with an international company that mandates a six-year payroll document retention requirement. How should Twinte Cars balance these requirements?

P2-9A. LO 2-2
Ted McCormick is a full-time life insurance agent with Centixo Insurance, a small insurance company. The company has classified him as an employee, and he feels that he should be classified as an independent contractor because he receives no company benefits and sets his own office hours. Should he be reclassified as an independent contractor? Why or why not?

P2-10A. LO 2-2
Evelyn Hardy is an employee of Polyent Plastics, a company with headquarters in Rock Island, Illinois. She lives and works in Doha, Qatar, and earns an annual salary of $97,300. The company has been withholding U.S. federal income taxes from her pay, but Evelyn believes that she should be exempt because she is an expatriate. What course of action should Evelyn take?

P2-11A. LO 2-2, 2-4
Complete the W-4 for employment at Superore Wheels starting 3/15/2019, the employer's EIN is 91-1701225.
Erma Jane Grant
441 West Hill Road
Montrose, Colorado 81401
SSN: 432-55-6792
Single with no withholding allowances
Does not require any additional amount to be withheld

P2-12A. LO 2-2, 2-4
Complete the I-9 for employment at Superore Wheels at 5421 Woodbridge Road, Montrose, Colorado 81401. Erma is starting 2/15/2019. Be sure to complete Section 2 of Form I-9.
Erma Jane Grant
441 West Hill Road
Montrose, Colorado 81401
SSN: 432-55-6792
Maiden name: Grant
Single with no withholding allowances claimed
Date of Birth: June 12, 1986
U.S. Citizen
Erma presented her passport for her employer to review.
Passport number 389049392, issued by the United States Department of State, expires April 1, 2026
Administrative assistant Samantha Cook verified the information for the company.

Form W-4 (2019)

Future developments. For the latest information about any future developments related to Form W-4, such as legislation enacted after it was published, go to *www.irs.gov/FormW4*.

Purpose. Complete Form W-4 so that your employer can withhold the correct federal income tax from your pay. Consider completing a new Form W-4 each year and when your personal or financial situation changes.

Exemption from withholding. You may claim exemption from withholding for 2019 if **both** of the following apply.

• For 2018 you had a right to a refund of **all** federal income tax withheld because you had **no** tax liability, **and**

• For 2019 you expect a refund of **all** federal income tax withheld because you expect to have **no** tax liability.

If you're exempt, complete **only** lines 1, 2, 3, 4, and 7 and sign the form to validate it. Your exemption for 2019 expires February 17, 2020. See Pub. 505, Tax Withholding and Estimated Tax, to learn more about whether you qualify for exemption from withholding.

General Instructions

If you aren't exempt, follow the rest of these instructions to determine the number of withholding allowances you should claim for withholding for 2019 and any additional amount of tax to have withheld. For regular wages, withholding must be based on allowances you claimed and may not be a flat amount or percentage of wages.

You can also use the calculator at ***www.irs.gov/W4App*** to determine your tax withholding more accurately. Consider using this calculator if you have a more complicated tax situation, such as if you have a working spouse, more than one job, or a large amount of nonwage income not subject to withholding outside of your job. After your Form W-4 takes effect, you can also use this calculator to see how the amount of tax you're having withheld compares to your projected total tax for 2019. If you use the calculator, you don't need to complete any of the worksheets for Form W-4.

Note that if you have too much tax withheld, you will receive a refund when you file your tax return. If you have too little tax withheld, you will owe tax when you file your tax return, and you might owe a penalty.

Filers with multiple jobs or working spouses. If you have more than one job at a time, or if you're married filing jointly and your spouse is also working, read all of the instructions including the instructions for the Two-Earners/Multiple Jobs Worksheet before beginning.

Nonwage income. If you have a large amount of nonwage income not subject to withholding, such as interest or dividends, consider making estimated tax payments using Form 1040-ES, Estimated Tax for Individuals. Otherwise, you might owe additional tax. Or, you can use the Deductions, Adjustments, and Additional Income Worksheet on page 3 or the calculator at *www.irs.gov/W4App* to make sure you have enough tax withheld from your paycheck. If you have pension or annuity income, see Pub. 505 or use the calculator at *www.irs.gov/W4App* to find out if you should adjust your withholding on Form W-4 or W-4P.

Nonresident alien. If you're a nonresident alien, see Notice 1392, Supplemental Form W-4 Instructions for Nonresident Aliens, before completing this form.

Specific Instructions

Personal Allowances Worksheet

Complete this worksheet on page 3 first to determine the number of withholding allowances to claim.

Line C. *Head of household please note:* Generally, you may claim head of household filing status on your tax return only if you're unmarried and pay more than 50% of the costs of keeping up a home for yourself and a qualifying individual. See Pub. 501 for more information about filing status.

Line E. Child tax credit. When you file your tax return, you may be eligible to claim a child tax credit for each of your eligible children. To qualify, the child must be under age 17 as of December 31, must be your dependent who lives with you for more than half the year, and must have a valid social security number. To learn more about this credit, see Pub. 972, Child Tax Credit. To reduce the tax withheld from your pay by taking this credit into account, follow the instructions on line E of the worksheet. On the worksheet you will be asked about your total income. For this purpose, total income includes all of your wages and other income, including income earned by a spouse if you are filing a joint return.

Line F. Credit for other dependents. When you file your tax return, you may be eligible to claim a credit for other dependents for whom a child tax credit can't be claimed, such as a qualifying child who doesn't meet the age or social security number requirement for the child tax credit, or a qualifying relative. To learn more about this credit, see Pub. 972. To reduce the tax withheld from your pay by taking this credit into account, follow the instructions on line F of the worksheet. On the worksheet, you will be asked about your total income. For this purpose, total

Separate here and give Form W-4 to your employer. Keep the worksheet(s) for your records.

Form **W-4**
Department of the Treasury
Internal Revenue Service

Employee's Withholding Allowance Certificate

▶ **Whether you're entitled to claim a certain number of allowances or exemption from withholding is subject to review by the IRS. Your employer may be required to send a copy of this form to the IRS.**

OMB No. 1545-0074
2019

1 Your first name and middle initial	Last name	2 **Your social security number**
Home address (number and street or rural route)	3 ☐ Single ☐ Married ☐ Married, but withhold at higher Single rate. **Note:** If married filing separately, check "Married, but withhold at higher Single rate."	
City or town, state, and ZIP code	4 **If your last name differs from that shown on your social security card, check here. You must call 800-772-1213 for a replacement card.** ▶ ☐	

5 Total number of allowances you're claiming (from the applicable worksheet on the following pages) 5

6 Additional amount, if any, you want withheld from each paycheck . . . . 6 $

7 I claim exemption from withholding for 2019, and I certify that I meet **both** of the following conditions for exemption.

• Last year I had a right to a refund of **all** federal income tax withheld because I had **no** tax liability, **and**

• This year I expect a refund of **all** federal income tax withheld because I expect to have **no** tax liability.

If you meet both conditions, write "Exempt" here . . . . ▶ 7

Under penalties of perjury, I declare that I have examined this certificate and, to the best of my knowledge and belief, it is true, correct, and complete.

Employee's signature
(This form is not valid unless you sign it.) ▶ **Date** ▶

8 Employer's name and address (**Employer:** Complete boxes 8 and 10 if sending to IRS and complete boxes 8, 9, and 10 if sending to State Directory of New Hires.)	9 First date of employment	10 Employer identification number (EIN)

For Privacy Act and Paperwork Reduction Act Notice, see page 4. Cat. No. 10220Q Form **W-4** (2019)

Source: Internal Revenue Service.

Employment Eligibility Verification
Department of Homeland Security
U.S. Citizenship and Immigration Services

USCIS
Form I-9
OMB No. 1615-0047
Expires 08/31/2019

►START HERE: Read instructions carefully before completing this form. The instructions must be available, either in paper or electronically, during completion of this form. Employers are liable for errors in the completion of this form.

ANTI-DISCRIMINATION NOTICE: It is illegal to discriminate against work-authorized individuals. Employers **CANNOT** specify which document(s) an employee may present to establish employment authorization and identity. The refusal to hire or continue to employ an individual because the documentation presented has a future expiration date may also constitute illegal discrimination.

Section 1. Employee Information and Attestation *(Employees must complete and sign Section 1 of Form I-9 no later than the* ***first day of employment****, but not before accepting a job offer.)*

Last Name *(Family Name)*	First Name *(Given Name)*	Middle Initial	Other Last Names Used *(if any)*

Address *(Street Number and Name)*	Apt. Number	City or Town	State	ZIP Code

Date of Birth *(mm/dd/yyyy)*	U.S. Social Security Number	Employee's E-mail Address	Employee's Telephone Number
	☐☐☐ - ☐☐ - ☐☐☐☐		

I am aware that federal law provides for imprisonment and/or fines for false statements or use of false documents in connection with the completion of this form.

I attest, under penalty of perjury, that I am (check one of the following boxes):

☐ 1. A citizen of the United States

☐ 2. A noncitizen national of the United States *(See instructions)*

☐ 3. A lawful permanent resident (Alien Registration Number/USCIS Number): ____________________

☐ 4. An alien authorized to work until (expiration date, if applicable, mm/dd/yyyy): ____________
Some aliens may write "N/A" in the expiration date field. *(See instructions)*

Aliens authorized to work must provide only one of the following document numbers to complete Form I-9:
An Alien Registration Number/USCIS Number OR Form I-94 Admission Number OR Foreign Passport Number.

1. Alien Registration Number/USCIS Number: ____________________

OR

2. Form I-94 Admission Number: ____________________

OR

3. Foreign Passport Number: ____________________

Country of Issuance: ____________________

QR Code - Section 1
Do Not Write In This Space

Signature of Employee	Today's Date *(mm/dd/yyyy)*

Preparer and/or Translator Certification (check one):

☐ I did not use a preparer or translator. ☐ A preparer(s) and/or translator(s) assisted the employee in completing Section 1.

(Fields below must be completed and signed when preparers and/or translators assist an employee in completing Section 1.)

I attest, under penalty of perjury, that I have assisted in the completion of Section 1 of this form and that to the best of my knowledge the information is true and correct.

Signature of Preparer or Translator	Today's Date *(mm/dd/yyyy)*

Last Name *(Family Name)*	First Name *(Given Name)*

Address *(Street Number and Name)*	City or Town	State	ZIP Code

STOP *Employer Completes Next Page* STOP

Employment Eligibility Verification
Department of Homeland Security
U.S. Citizenship and Immigration Services

USCIS
Form I-9
OMB No. 1615-0047
Expires 08/31/2019

Section 2. Employer or Authorized Representative Review and Verification

(Employers or their authorized representative must complete and sign Section 2 within 3 business days of the employee's first day of employment. You must physically examine one document from List A OR a combination of one document from List B and one document from List C as listed on the "Lists of Acceptable Documents.")

Employee Info from Section 1	Last Name *(Family Name)*	First Name *(Given Name)*	M.I.	Citizenship/Immigration Status

List A Identity and Employment Authorization	**OR**	**List B** Identity	**AND**	**List C** Employment Authorization
Document Title		Document Title		Document Title
Issuing Authority		Issuing Authority		Issuing Authority
Document Number		Document Number		Document Number
Expiration Date *(if any)(mm/dd/yyyy)*		Expiration Date *(if any)(mm/dd/yyyy)*		Expiration Date *(if any)(mm/dd/yyyy)*
Document Title		Additional Information		QR Code - Sections 2 & 3 Do Not Write In This Space
Issuing Authority				
Document Number				
Expiration Date *(if any)(mm/dd/yyyy)*				
Document Title				
Issuing Authority				
Document Number				
Expiration Date *(if any)(mm/dd/yyyy)*				

Certification: I attest, under penalty of perjury, that (1) I have examined the document(s) presented by the above-named employee, (2) the above-listed document(s) appear to be genuine and to relate to the employee named, and (3) to the best of my knowledge the employee is authorized to work in the United States.

The employee's first day of employment *(mm/dd/yyyy)*: ______________ ***(See instructions for exemptions)***

Signature of Employer or Authorized Representative	Today's Date *(mm/dd/yyyy)*	Title of Employer or Authorized Representative

Last Name of Employer or Authorized Representative	First Name of Employer or Authorized Representative	Employer's Business or Organization Name

Employer's Business or Organization Address (Street Number and Name)	City or Town	State	ZIP Code

Section 3. Reverification and Rehires *(To be completed and signed by employer or authorized representative.)*

A. New Name *(if applicable)*			**B.** Date of Rehire *(if applicable)*
Last Name *(Family Name)*	First Name *(Given Name)*	Middle Initial	Date *(mm/dd/yyyy)*

C. If the employee's previous grant of employment authorization has expired, provide the information for the document or receipt that establishes continuing employment authorization in the space provided below.

Document Title	Document Number	Expiration Date *(if any) (mm/dd/yyyy)*

I attest, under penalty of perjury, that to the best of my knowledge, this employee is authorized to work in the United States, and if the employee presented document(s), the document(s) I have examined appear to be genuine and to relate to the individual.

Signature of Employer or Authorized Representative	Today's Date *(mm/dd/yyyy)*	Name of Employer or Authorized Representative

LISTS OF ACCEPTABLE DOCUMENTS
All documents must be UNEXPIRED

Employees may present one selection from List A
or a combination of one selection from List B and one selection from List C.

LIST A **Documents that Establish Both Identity and Employment Authorization**	OR	LIST B **Documents that Establish Identity**	AND	LIST C **Documents that Establish Employment Authorization**
1. U.S. Passport or U.S. Passport Card		**1.** Driver's license or ID card issued by a State or outlying possession of the United States provided it contains a photograph or information such as name, date of birth, gender, height, eye color, and address		**1.** A Social Security Account Number card, unless the card includes one of the following restrictions: (1) NOT VALID FOR EMPLOYMENT (2) VALID FOR WORK ONLY WITH INS AUTHORIZATION (3) VALID FOR WORK ONLY WITH DHS AUTHORIZATION
2. Permanent Resident Card or Alien Registration Receipt Card (Form I-551)		**2.** ID card issued by federal, state or local government agencies or entities, provided it contains a photograph or information such as name, date of birth, gender, height, eye color, and address		**2.** Certification of report of birth issued by the Department of State (Forms DS-1350, FS-545, FS-240)
3. Foreign passport that contains a temporary I-551 stamp or temporary I-551 printed notation on a machine-readable immigrant visa		**3.** School ID card with a photograph		**3.** Original or certified copy of birth certificate issued by a State, county, municipal authority, or territory of the United States bearing an official seal
4. Employment Authorization Document that contains a photograph (Form I-766)		**4.** Voter's registration card		**4.** Native American tribal document
5. For a nonimmigrant alien authorized to work for a specific employer because of his or her status: **a.** Foreign passport; and **b.** Form I-94 or Form I-94A that has the following: (1) The same name as the passport; and (2) An endorsement of the alien's nonimmigrant status as long as that period of endorsement has not yet expired and the proposed employment is not in conflict with any restrictions or limitations identified on the form.		**5.** U.S. Military card or draft record		**5.** U.S. Citizen ID Card (Form I-197)
6. Passport from the Federated States of Micronesia (FSM) or the Republic of the Marshall Islands (RMI) with Form I-94 or Form I-94A indicating nonimmigrant admission under the Compact of Free Association Between the United States and the FSM or RMI		**6.** Military dependent's ID card		**6.** Identification Card for Use of Resident Citizen in the United States (Form I-179)
		7. U.S. Coast Guard Merchant Mariner Card		**7.** Employment authorization document issued by the Department of Homeland Security
		8. Native American tribal document		
		9. Driver's license issued by a Canadian government authority		
		For persons under age 18 who are unable to present a document listed above:		
		10. School record or report card		
		11. Clinic, doctor, or hospital record		
		12. Day-care or nursery school record		

Examples of many of these documents appear in Part 13 of the Handbook for Employers (M-274).

Refer to the instructions for more information about acceptable receipts.

Form I-9 07/17/17 N Page 3 of 3

Source: United States Citizenship and Immigration Services.

Exercises Set B

E2-1B. LO 2-1, 2-4

Stacy Romero, a nonexempt employee of Prosaria Publishers, works a standard 6:00 a.m. to 3:00 p.m. schedule with an hour for lunch. Stacy works in California, a state that requires overtime pay for hours exceeding 8 per day and for those exceeding 40 in a week. During the week, she worked the following schedule:

- Monday: 8.25 hours
- Tuesday: 8 hours
- Wednesday: 8.75 hours
- Thursday: 7 hours
- Friday: 9 hours

Based on the requirements above, how much overtime has Stacy worked during the period?

1. 2 hours
2. 0.5 hour
3. 1 hour
4. 3 hours

E2-2B. LO 2-1

Grant Saunders is a salaried employee earning $84,000 per year. He receives his payroll twice a month. Which of the following best describes the pay frequency?

1. Biweekly
2. Semimonthly
3. Weekly
4. Monthly

E2-3B. LO 2-4, 2-6

On October 31, 2019, Dolores Goodman quit her job after 10 years with Omnivue Optics in Utah. Omnivue Optics pays employees weekly on Fridays. Upon quitting, Dolores had 38.5 hours of vacation accrued that she had not used, and she had worked 45 hours, 5 hours of which was subject to overtime. When must she receive her final paycheck?

1. On the next pay date
2. Within seven days
3. Immediately upon discharge
4. Within 24 hours

E2-4B. LO 2-4, 2-6

Adrienne Norman terminated her employment with Univee Inc. on December 16, 2019. When is the earliest that Univee Inc. may destroy her payroll records?

1. December 16, 2020
2. December 16, 2021
3. December 16, 2022
4. December 16, 2023

E2-5B. LO 2-5

Elijah Brown is a new payroll clerk at Zata Imports, a company with 250 employees. He has completed entering all time card data for the pay period. What should Elijah's next step in the payroll review process be?

1. Ask employees to verify that the time Elijah entered is accurate
2. Generate pay checks and prepare them for signature
3. Ask his supervisor to verify the accuracy of the payroll data
4. Have another payroll clerk verify the data accuracy

E2-6B. LO 2-6

Elaine Wheeler needs additional filing space at the end of the year in the company's office and chooses to use off-site, secured storage. Upon arriving at the storage facility, she discovers that the unit is nearly full and sees several boxes marked for destruction at the end of the calendar year. What are Elaine's options regarding the destruction of the payroll records marked for destruction? (Select all that apply.)

1. She should take the oldest year's boxes to the closest recycling facility
2. She should make arrangements to pulp or burn the paper payroll records marked for destruction
3. She should arrange to have a document destruction service pick up the boxes marked for destruction
4. She should bring a shredding machine to the storage facility and prepare to shred the records marked for destruction

E2-7B. LO 2-1
Gerardo Rogers is conducting a review of the payroll files for each employee at Meejo Games. Which of the following items must be present in the file? (Select all that apply.)
1. Basis upon which compensation is paid
2. Overtime pay earned during each pay period
3. Hours worked during each pay period
4. Break times taken each day

E2-8B. LO 2-2
Jane McCarthy is preparing to compute employee pay and needs to determine the amount of employee federal income taxes to be withheld. Which of the following should she consult?
1. USCIS I-9
2. IRS Publication 15
3. DHS Schedule F
4. SSA Schedule 8

E2-9B. LO 2-2
John Franklin is a new employee of Camidel Clothiers. Which of the following will provide proof of *identity* for the completion of the I-9? (Select all that apply.)
1. U.S. Passport
2. U.S. Military Identification Card
3. U.S. Citizen Identification Card
4. New York driver's license

E2-10B. LO 2-2
Sheri Jennings is completing the I-9 for her new employment at Insulend Tours. Which of the following provides proof of her *employment authorization*? (Select all that apply.)
1. Social Security card
2. Certificate of birth abroad, issued by the U.S. Department of State
3. Louisiana driver's license
4. U.S. Passport

E2-11B. LO 2-3
Laverne Watkins is a candidate for the position of marketing clerk with the promotions department of Paramba Productions, earning $10.25 per hour. She will work occasional overtime in her new position and will not have managerial or supervisory duties as a regular part of her job description. Why should Laverne be classified as a nonexempt employee? (Select all that apply.)
1. Her annual wages are lower than the minimum exempt salary
2. She has no supervisory or managerial duties
3. She has the term *clerk* in her job title
4. She will work occasional overtime

E2-12B. LO 2-3
Rex Marshall manages a ski resort with year-round and seasonal employees. Assuming that the ski resort engages in interstate commerce, which are the FLSA requirement(s) that Rex should consider?
1. Hourly wages paid to employees
2. Safety of the working conditions
3. Number of hours worked per week
4. Employee age and weekly work schedule

Problems Set B

P2-1B. LO 2-2
Tasha Webb is an independent contractor for Antimbu Exports, where you are the payroll accountant. She feels that she should receive employee benefits because of the number of hours that she dedicates to the company. What guidance could you offer Tasha?

P2-2B. LO 2-6
Joseph Lyons was terminated for cause from Telecy Industries in Hawaii on August 21, 2019. As of the date of his termination, he had worked 22 hours of regular time. Employees at Telecy Industries are paid semimonthly on the 15th and last day of the month. Joseph would like to know when he will be paid for the accrued hours. What will you tell him?

P2-3B. LO 2-2
Sara Northman is a member of the Algonquin Indian Nation and is a new employee at Predeo Game Designs. During the process of completing her I-9, she claims that the only way to prove her identity is the Algonquin Indian Nation official birth certificate. Is this document sufficient to prove identity for the purposes of the I-9? Why or why not?

P2-4B. LO 2-2
Abraham Manning is a new employee of Symity Batteries. He is curious about the purpose of the requirements for new hire documentation to be forwarded to government agencies. What should you tell him?

P2-5B. LO 2-1
Frances Perez wants to start her own company. As a seasoned payroll professional, she approaches you for guidance about the differences among weekly, biweekly, and semimonthly pay periods. What would you tell her?

P2-6B. LO 2-5
Katrina Wilkins is a new payroll clerk for Remm Plumbing. She is curious about the purpose of the different steps in the payroll review process and asks you, her supervisor, for guidance. What would you tell her?

P2-7B. LO 2-4
George Andrews started as a payroll accountant at Portose Herbals, a company with 70 employees. He soon notices that the former payroll accountant had been processing payroll manually and suggests that the company immediately switch to Cloud-based payroll. Although the company is switching to an electronic payroll processing system, what types of paper documentation must be maintained in employee records?

P2-8B. LO 2-5
Tara Morris, a payroll clerk, has received a promotion and is now the payroll supervisor for Fligen Enterprises. What document control items could now become her responsibility?

P2-9B. LO 2-2
Herman Watkins is in the payroll department of Neombee Plastics, a multistate company. The company has historically been filing employee information with each state. What alternative exists for multistate employers?

P2-10B. LO 2-1
Derek Allen is the payroll supervisor for Caposis Freight. His company is preparing to merge with another distribution company that has a different pay cycle. The president of the company wants to know the difference between biweekly and semimonthly pay cycles as far as pay dates and pay amounts are concerned. What should Derek tell him?

P2-11B. LO 2-2, 2-4
Complete the W-4 for employment at Equtri Farms effective 6/17/2019:
Linda Ellen Marshall
8924 County Line Road
Taylorville, Illinois 62555
SSN: 129-53-2309
Married filing jointly
Three dependents and does not wish to withhold additional amounts.
Linda earns $32,000 at her primary job. She has a second job as a delivery driver for Tazio Labs, where she earns $12,000/year.

P2-12B. LO 2-2, 2-4
Complete the I-9 for employment effective 7/23/2019 at Ecovee Energy located at 244 Winston Drive, Gretna, Virginia 24557. Be sure to complete Section 2 of Form I-9.
Lloyd Gregory Flowers
SSN: 382-10-0392
Date of Birth: 11-20-1993
1298 Chatham Road
Gretna, Virginia 24557
U.S. Citizen
Lloyd presented his driver's license and Social Security card to the Human Resources Manager, Amanda Weeble, to review.
Virginia Driver's License #293034293, Expires 11/20/2021

Form W-4 (2019)

Future developments. For the latest information about any future developments related to Form W-4, such as legislation enacted after it was published, go to *www.irs.gov/FormW4*.

Purpose. Complete Form W-4 so that your employer can withhold the correct federal income tax from your pay. Consider completing a new Form W-4 each year and when your personal or financial situation changes.

Exemption from withholding. You may claim exemption from withholding for 2019 if **both** of the following apply.

- For 2018 you had a right to a refund of **all** federal income tax withheld because you had **no** tax liability, **and**
- For 2019 you expect a refund of **all** federal income tax withheld because you expect to have **no** tax liability.

If you're exempt, complete **only** lines 1, 2, 3, 4, and 7 and sign the form to validate it. Your exemption for 2019 expires February 17, 2020. See Pub. 505, Tax Withholding and Estimated Tax, to learn more about whether you qualify for exemption from withholding.

General Instructions

If you aren't exempt, follow the rest of these instructions to determine the number of withholding allowances you should claim for withholding for 2019 and any additional amount of tax to have withheld. For regular wages, withholding must be based on allowances you claimed and may not be a flat amount or percentage of wages.

You can also use the calculator at ***www.irs.gov/W4App*** to determine your tax withholding more accurately. Consider using this calculator if you have a more complicated tax situation, such as if you have a working spouse, more than one job, or a large amount of nonwage income not subject to withholding outside of your job. After your Form W-4 takes effect, you can also use this calculator to see how the amount of tax you're having withheld compares to your projected total tax for 2019. If you use the calculator, you don't need to complete any of the worksheets for Form W-4.

Note that if you have too much tax withheld, you will receive a refund when you file your tax return. If you have too little tax withheld, you will owe tax when you file your tax return, and you might owe a penalty.

Filers with multiple jobs or working spouses. If you have more than one job at a time, or if you're married filing jointly and your spouse is also working, read all of the instructions including the instructions for the Two-Earners/Multiple Jobs Worksheet before beginning.

Nonwage income. If you have a large amount of nonwage income not subject to withholding, such as interest or dividends, consider making estimated tax payments using Form 1040-ES, Estimated Tax for Individuals. Otherwise, you might owe additional tax. Or, you can use the Deductions, Adjustments, and Additional Income Worksheet on page 3 or the calculator at *www.irs.gov/W4App* to make sure you have enough tax withheld from your paycheck. If you have pension or annuity income, see Pub. 505 or use the calculator at *www.irs.gov/W4App* to find out if you should adjust your withholding on Form W-4 or W-4P.

Nonresident alien. If you're a nonresident alien, see Notice 1392, Supplemental Form W-4 Instructions for Nonresident Aliens, before completing this form.

Specific Instructions

Personal Allowances Worksheet

Complete this worksheet on page 3 first to determine the number of withholding allowances to claim.

Line C. *Head of household please note:* Generally, you may claim head of household filing status on your tax return only if you're unmarried and pay more than 50% of the costs of keeping up a home for yourself and a qualifying individual. See Pub. 501 for more information about filing status.

Line E. Child tax credit. When you file your tax return, you may be eligible to claim a child tax credit for each of your eligible children. To qualify, the child must be under age 17 as of December 31, must be your dependent who lives with you for more than half the year, and must have a valid social security number. To learn more about this credit, see Pub. 972, Child Tax Credit. To reduce the tax withheld from your pay by taking this credit into account, follow the instructions on line E of the worksheet. On the worksheet you will be asked about your total income. For this purpose, total income includes all of your wages and other income, including income earned by a spouse if you are filing a joint return.

Line F. Credit for other dependents. When you file your tax return, you may be eligible to claim a credit for other dependents for whom a child tax credit can't be claimed, such as a qualifying child who doesn't meet the age or social security number requirement for the child tax credit, or a qualifying relative. To learn more about this credit, see Pub. 972. To reduce the tax withheld from your pay by taking this credit into account, follow the instructions on line F of the worksheet. On the worksheet, you will be asked about your total income. For this purpose, total

---

Separate here and give Form W-4 to your employer. Keep the worksheet(s) for your records.

Form **W-4**
Department of the Treasury
Internal Revenue Service

Employee's Withholding Allowance Certificate

▶ **Whether you're entitled to claim a certain number of allowances or exemption from withholding is subject to review by the IRS. Your employer may be required to send a copy of this form to the IRS.**

OMB No. 1545-0074

2019

1 Your first name and middle initial	Last name	**2 Your social security number**
Home address (number and street or rural route)		3 ☐ Single ☐ Married ☐ Married, but withhold at higher Single rate. **Note:** If married filing separately, check "Married, but withhold at higher Single rate."
City or town, state, and ZIP code		**4 If your last name differs from that shown on your social security card, check here. You must call 800-772-1213 for a replacement card.** ▶ ☐

5	Total number of allowances you're claiming (from the applicable worksheet on the following pages)	5	
6	Additional amount, if any, you want withheld from each paycheck	6	$
7	I claim exemption from withholding for 2019, and I certify that I meet **both** of the following conditions for exemption. • Last year I had a right to a refund of **all** federal income tax withheld because I had **no** tax liability, **and** • This year I expect a refund of **all** federal income tax withheld because I expect to have **no** tax liability. If you meet both conditions, write "Exempt" here . . . ▶ 7		

Under penalties of perjury, I declare that I have examined this certificate and, to the best of my knowledge and belief, it is true, correct, and complete.

Employee's signature
(This form is not valid unless you sign it.) ▶ **Date ▶**

8 Employer's name and address (**Employer:** Complete boxes 8 and 10 if sending to IRS and complete boxes 8, 9, and 10 if sending to State Directory of New Hires.)	9 First date of employment	10 Employer identification number (EIN)

For Privacy Act and Paperwork Reduction Act Notice, see page 4. Cat. No. 10220Q Form **W-4** (2019)

Form W-4 (2019) Page **3**

Personal Allowances Worksheet (Keep for your records.)

A	Enter "1" for yourself	**A**	______
B	Enter "1" if you will file as married filing jointly	**B**	______
C	Enter "1" if you will file as head of household	**C**	______
D	Enter "1" if: • You're single, or married filing separately, and have only one job; or • You're married filing jointly, have only one job, and your spouse doesn't work; or • Your wages from a second job or your spouse's wages (or the total of both) are $1,500 or less.	**D**	______
E	**Child tax credit.** See Pub. 972, Child Tax Credit, for more information. • If your total income will be less than $71,201 ($103,351 if married filing jointly), enter "4" for each eligible child. • If your total income will be from $71,201 to $179,050 ($103,351 to $345,850 if married filing jointly), enter "2" for each eligible child. • If your total income will be from $179,051 to $200,000 ($345,851 to $400,000 if married filing jointly), enter "1" for each eligible child. • If your total income will be higher than $200,000 ($400,000 if married filing jointly), enter "-0-"	**E**	______
F	**Credit for other dependents.** See Pub. 972, Child Tax Credit, for more information. • If your total income will be less than $71,201 ($103,351 if married filing jointly), enter "1" for each eligible dependent. • If your total income will be from $71,201 to $179,050 ($103,351 to $345,850 if married filing jointly), enter "1" for every two dependents (for example, "-0-" for one dependent, "1" if you have two or three dependents, and "2" if you have four dependents). • If your total income will be higher than $179,050 ($345,850 if married filing jointly), enter "-0-"	**F**	______
G	**Other credits.** If you have other credits, see Worksheet 1-6 of Pub. 505 and enter the amount from that worksheet here. If you use Worksheet 1-6, enter "-0-" on lines E and F	**G**	______
H	Add lines A through G and enter the total here	▶ **H**	______

For accuracy, **complete all worksheets that apply.**

- If you plan to **itemize** or **claim adjustments to income** and want to reduce your withholding, or if you have a large amount of nonwage income not subject to withholding and want to increase your withholding, see the **Deductions, Adjustments, and Additional Income Worksheet** below.
- If you **have more than one job at a time** or are **married filing jointly and you and your spouse both work,** and the combined earnings from all jobs exceed $53,000 ($24,450 if married filing jointly), see the **Two-Earners/Multiple Jobs Worksheet** on page 4 to avoid having too little tax withheld.
- If **neither** of the above situations applies, **stop here** and enter the number from line H on line 5 of Form W-4 above.

Deductions, Adjustments, and Additional Income Worksheet

Note: Use this worksheet *only* if you plan to itemize deductions, claim certain adjustments to income, or have a large amount of nonwage income not subject to withholding.

1	Enter an estimate of your 2019 itemized deductions. These include qualifying home mortgage interest, charitable contributions, state and local taxes (up to $10,000), and medical expenses in excess of 10% of your income. See Pub. 505 for details	**1**	$ ______
2	Enter: $24,400 if you're married filing jointly or qualifying widow(er); $18,350 if you're head of household; $12,200 if you're single or married filing separately	**2**	$ ______
3	**Subtract** line 2 from line 1. If zero or less, enter "-0-"	**3**	$ ______
4	Enter an estimate of your 2019 adjustments to income, qualified business income deduction, and any additional standard deduction for age or blindness (see Pub. 505 for information about these items)	**4**	$ ______
5	**Add** lines 3 and 4 and enter the total	**5**	$ ______
6	Enter an estimate of your 2019 nonwage income not subject to withholding (such as dividends or interest)	**6**	$ ______
7	**Subtract** line 6 from line 5. If zero, enter "-0-". If less than zero, enter the amount in parentheses	**7**	$ ______
8	**Divide** the amount on line 7 by $4,200 and enter the result here. If a negative amount, enter in parentheses. Drop any fraction	**8**	______
9	Enter the number from the **Personal Allowances Worksheet,** line H, above	**9**	______
10	**Add** lines 8 and 9 and enter the total here. If zero or less, enter "-0-". If you plan to use the **Two-Earners/ Multiple Jobs Worksheet,** also enter this total on line 1 of that worksheet on page 4. Otherwise, **stop here** and enter this total on Form W-4, line 5, page 1	**10**	______

Form W-4 (2019) Page **4**

Two-Earners/Multiple Jobs Worksheet

Note: Use this worksheet *only* if the instructions under line H from the **Personal Allowances Worksheet** direct you here.

1. Enter the number from the **Personal Allowances Worksheet,** line H, page 3 (or, if you used the **Deductions, Adjustments, and Additional Income Worksheet** on page 3, the number from line 10 of that worksheet) . . . . . 1 ______
2. Find the number in **Table 1** below that applies to the **LOWEST** paying job and enter it here. **However,** if you're married filing jointly and wages from the highest paying job are $75,000 or less and the combined wages for you and your spouse are $107,000 or less, don't enter more than "3" . . . . . 2 ______
3. If line 1 is **more than or equal to** line 2, subtract line 2 from line 1. Enter the result here (if zero, enter "-0-") and on Form W-4, line 5, page 1. **Do not** use the rest of this worksheet . . . . . 3 ______

Note: If line 1 is **less than** line 2, enter "-0-" on Form W-4, line 5, page 1. Complete lines 4 through 9 below to figure the additional withholding amount necessary to avoid a year-end tax bill.

4. Enter the number from line 2 of this worksheet . . . . . 4 ______
5. Enter the number from line 1 of this worksheet . . . . . 5 ______
6. **Subtract** line 5 from line 4 . . . . . 6 ______
7. Find the amount in **Table 2** below that applies to the **HIGHEST** paying job and enter it here . . . . . 7 $ ______
8. **Multiply** line 7 by line 6 and enter the result here. This is the additional annual withholding needed . . . 8 $ ______
9. **Divide** line 8 by the number of pay periods remaining in 2019. For example, divide by 18 if you're paid every 2 weeks and you complete this form on a date in late April when there are 18 pay periods remaining in 2019. Enter the result here and on Form W-4, line 6, page 1. This is the additional amount to be withheld from each paycheck . . . . . 9 $ ______

Table 1

Married Filing Jointly		All Others	
If wages from **LOWEST** paying job are—	Enter on line 2 above	If wages from **LOWEST** paying job are—	Enter on line 2 above
$0 - $5,000	0	$0 - $7,000	0
5,001 - 9,500	1	7,001 - 13,000	1
9,501 - 19,500	2	13,001 - 27,500	2
19,501 - 35,000	3	27,501 - 32,000	3
35,001 - 40,000	4	32,001 - 40,000	4
40,001 - 46,000	5	40,001 - 60,000	5
46,001 - 55,000	6	60,001 - 75,000	6
55,001 - 60,000	7	75,001 - 85,000	7
60,001 - 70,000	8	85,001 - 95,000	8
70,001 - 75,000	9	95,001 - 100,000	9
75,001 - 85,000	10	100,001 - 110,000	10
85,001 - 95,000	11	110,001 - 115,000	11
95,001 - 125,000	12	115,001 - 125,000	12
125,001 - 155,000	13	125,001 - 135,000	13
155,001 - 165,000	14	135,001 - 145,000	14
165,001 - 175,000	15	145,001 - 160,000	15
175,001 - 180,000	16	160,001 - 180,000	16
180,001 - 195,000	17	180,001 and over	17
195,001 - 205,000	18		
205,001 and over	19		

Table 2

Married Filing Jointly		All Others	
If wages from **HIGHEST** paying job are—	Enter on line 7 above	If wages from **HIGHEST** paying job are—	Enter on line 7 above
$0 - $24,900	$420	$0 - $7,200	$420
24,901 - 84,450	500	7,201 - 36,975	500
84,451 - 173,900	910	36,976 - 81,700	910
173,901 - 326,950	1,000	81,701 - 158,225	1,000
326,951 - 413,700	1,330	158,226 - 201,600	1,330
413,701 - 617,850	1,450	201,601 - 507,800	1,450
617,851 and over	1,540	507,801 and over	1,540

Privacy Act and Paperwork Reduction Act Notice. We ask for the information on this form to carry out the Internal Revenue laws of the United States. Internal Revenue Code sections 3402(f)(2) and 6109 and their regulations require you to provide this information; your employer uses it to determine your federal income tax withholding. Failure to provide a properly completed form will result in your being treated as a single person who claims no withholding allowances; providing fraudulent information may subject you to penalties. Routine uses of this information include giving it to the Department of Justice for civil and criminal litigation; to cities, states, the District of Columbia, and U.S. commonwealths and possessions for use in administering their tax laws; and to the Department of Health and Human Services for use in the National Directory of New Hires. We may also disclose this information to other countries under a tax treaty, to federal and state agencies to enforce federal nontax criminal laws, or to federal law enforcement and intelligence agencies to combat terrorism.

You aren't required to provide the information requested on a form that's subject to the Paperwork Reduction Act unless the form displays a valid OMB control number. Books or records relating to a form or its instructions must be retained as long as their contents may become material in the administration of any Internal Revenue law. Generally, tax returns and return information are confidential, as required by Code section 6103.

The average time and expenses required to complete and file this form will vary depending on individual circumstances. For estimated averages, see the instructions for your income tax return.

If you have suggestions for making this form simpler, we would be happy to hear from you. See the instructions for your income tax return.

Source: Internal Revenue Service.

Employment Eligibility Verification
Department of Homeland Security
U.S. Citizenship and Immigration Services

USCIS
Form I-9
OMB No. 1615-0047
Expires 08/31/2019

▶ START HERE: Read instructions carefully before completing this form. The instructions must be available, either in paper or electronically, during completion of this form. Employers are liable for errors in the completion of this form.

ANTI-DISCRIMINATION NOTICE: It is illegal to discriminate against work-authorized individuals. Employers **CANNOT** specify which document(s) an employee may present to establish employment authorization and identity. The refusal to hire or continue to employ an individual because the documentation presented has a future expiration date may also constitute illegal discrimination.

Section 1. Employee Information and Attestation *(Employees must complete and sign Section 1 of Form I-9 no later than the* ***first day of employment****, but not before accepting a job offer.)*

Last Name *(Family Name)*	First Name *(Given Name)*	Middle Initial	Other Last Names Used *(if any)*

Address *(Street Number and Name)*	Apt. Number	City or Town	State	ZIP Code

Date of Birth *(mm/dd/yyyy)*	U.S. Social Security Number	Employee's E-mail Address	Employee's Telephone Number
	☐☐☐ - ☐☐ - ☐☐☐☐		

I am aware that federal law provides for imprisonment and/or fines for false statements or use of false documents in connection with the completion of this form.

I attest, under penalty of perjury, that I am (check one of the following boxes):

☐ 1. A citizen of the United States

☐ 2. A noncitizen national of the United States *(See instructions)*

☐ 3. A lawful permanent resident (Alien Registration Number/USCIS Number): ____________

☐ 4. An alien authorized to work until (expiration date, if applicable, mm/dd/yyyy): ____________
Some aliens may write "N/A" in the expiration date field. *(See instructions)*

Aliens authorized to work must provide only one of the following document numbers to complete Form I-9:
An Alien Registration Number/USCIS Number OR Form I-94 Admission Number OR Foreign Passport Number.

1. Alien Registration Number/USCIS Number: ____________
OR
2. Form I-94 Admission Number: ____________
OR
3. Foreign Passport Number: ____________
Country of Issuance: ____________

QR Code - Section 1
Do Not Write In This Space

Signature of Employee	Today's Date *(mm/dd/yyyy)*

Preparer and/or Translator Certification (check one):

☐ I did not use a preparer or translator. ☐ A preparer(s) and/or translator(s) assisted the employee in completing Section 1.

(Fields below must be completed and signed when preparers and/or translators assist an employee in completing Section 1.)

I attest, under penalty of perjury, that I have assisted in the completion of Section 1 of this form and that to the best of my knowledge the information is true and correct.

Signature of Preparer or Translator	Today's Date *(mm/dd/yyyy)*

Last Name *(Family Name)*	First Name *(Given Name)*

Address *(Street Number and Name)*	City or Town	State	ZIP Code

STOP *Employer Completes Next Page* STOP

Form I-9 07/17/17 N

Page 1 of 3

Employment Eligibility Verification
Department of Homeland Security
U.S. Citizenship and Immigration Services

USCIS
Form I-9
OMB No. 1615-0047
Expires 08/31/2019

Section 2. Employer or Authorized Representative Review and Verification

(Employers or their authorized representative must complete and sign Section 2 within 3 business days of the employee's first day of employment. You must physically examine one document from List A OR a combination of one document from List B and one document from List C as listed on the "Lists of Acceptable Documents.")

Employee Info from Section 1	Last Name *(Family Name)*	First Name *(Given Name)*	M.I.	Citizenship/Immigration Status

List A Identity and Employment Authorization	**OR**	**List B** Identity	**AND**	**List C** Employment Authorization
Document Title		Document Title		Document Title
Issuing Authority		Issuing Authority		Issuing Authority
Document Number		Document Number		Document Number
Expiration Date *(if any)(mm/dd/yyyy)*		Expiration Date *(if any)(mm/dd/yyyy)*		Expiration Date *(if any)(mm/dd/yyyy)*
Document Title		Additional Information		QR Code - Sections 2 & 3 Do Not Write In This Space
Issuing Authority				
Document Number				
Expiration Date *(if any)(mm/dd/yyyy)*				
Document Title				
Issuing Authority				
Document Number				
Expiration Date *(if any)(mm/dd/yyyy)*				

Certification: I attest, under penalty of perjury, that (1) I have examined the document(s) presented by the above-named employee, (2) the above-listed document(s) appear to be genuine and to relate to the employee named, and (3) to the best of my knowledge the employee is authorized to work in the United States.

The employee's first day of employment *(mm/dd/yyyy)*: ______________ ***(See instructions for exemptions)***

Signature of Employer or Authorized Representative	Today's Date *(mm/dd/yyyy)*	Title of Employer or Authorized Representative

Last Name of Employer or Authorized Representative	First Name of Employer or Authorized Representative	Employer's Business or Organization Name

Employer's Business or Organization Address (Street Number and Name)	City or Town	State	ZIP Code

Section 3. Reverification and Rehires *(To be completed and signed by employer or authorized representative.)*

A. New Name *(if applicable)*			**B.** Date of Rehire *(if applicable)*
Last Name *(Family Name)*	First Name *(Given Name)*	Middle Initial	Date *(mm/dd/yyyy)*

C. If the employee's previous grant of employment authorization has expired, provide the information for the document or receipt that establishes continuing employment authorization in the space provided below.

Document Title	Document Number	Expiration Date *(if any) (mm/dd/yyyy)*

I attest, under penalty of perjury, that to the best of my knowledge, this employee is authorized to work in the United States, and if the employee presented document(s), the document(s) I have examined appear to be genuine and to relate to the individual.

Signature of Employer or Authorized Representative	Today's Date *(mm/dd/yyyy)*	Name of Employer or Authorized Representative

LISTS OF ACCEPTABLE DOCUMENTS
All documents must be UNEXPIRED

Employees may present one selection from List A
or a combination of one selection from List B and one selection from List C.

LIST A **Documents that Establish Both Identity and Employment Authorization**	**OR**	**LIST B** **Documents that Establish Identity**	**AND**	**LIST C** **Documents that Establish Employment Authorization**
1. U.S. Passport or U.S. Passport Card		**1.** Driver's license or ID card issued by a State or outlying possession of the United States provided it contains a photograph or information such as name, date of birth, gender, height, eye color, and address		**1.** A Social Security Account Number card, unless the card includes one of the following restrictions: (1) NOT VALID FOR EMPLOYMENT (2) VALID FOR WORK ONLY WITH INS AUTHORIZATION (3) VALID FOR WORK ONLY WITH DHS AUTHORIZATION
2. Permanent Resident Card or Alien Registration Receipt Card (Form I-551)		**2.** ID card issued by federal, state or local government agencies or entities, provided it contains a photograph or information such as name, date of birth, gender, height, eye color, and address		**2.** Certification of report of birth issued by the Department of State (Forms DS-1350, FS-545, FS-240)
3. Foreign passport that contains a temporary I-551 stamp or temporary I-551 printed notation on a machine-readable immigrant visa		**3.** School ID card with a photograph		**3.** Original or certified copy of birth certificate issued by a State, county, municipal authority, or territory of the United States bearing an official seal
4. Employment Authorization Document that contains a photograph (Form I-766)		**4.** Voter's registration card		**4.** Native American tribal document
5. For a nonimmigrant alien authorized to work for a specific employer because of his or her status: **a.** Foreign passport; and **b.** Form I-94 or Form I-94A that has the following: (1) The same name as the passport; and (2) An endorsement of the alien's nonimmigrant status as long as that period of endorsement has not yet expired and the proposed employment is not in conflict with any restrictions or limitations identified on the form.		**5.** U.S. Military card or draft record		**5.** U.S. Citizen ID Card (Form I-197)
6. Passport from the Federated States of Micronesia (FSM) or the Republic of the Marshall Islands (RMI) with Form I-94 or Form I-94A indicating nonimmigrant admission under the Compact of Free Association Between the United States and the FSM or RMI		**6.** Military dependent's ID card		**6.** Identification Card for Use of Resident Citizen in the United States (Form I-179)
		7. U.S. Coast Guard Merchant Mariner Card		**7.** Employment authorization document issued by the Department of Homeland Security
		8. Native American tribal document		
		9. Driver's license issued by a Canadian government authority		
		For persons under age 18 who are unable to present a document listed above:		
		10. School record or report card		
		11. Clinic, doctor, or hospital record		
		12. Day-care or nursery school record		

Examples of many of these documents appear in Part 13 of the Handbook for Employers (M-274).

Refer to the instructions for more information about acceptable receipts.

Form I-9 07/17/17 N

Page 3 of 3

Source: United States Citizenship and Immigration Services.

Critical Thinking

2-1. When Omnimia Graphics was looking to implement a payroll accounting system, the manufacturing firm had several options. With only 40 employees, the manual preparation of payroll through spreadsheets and handwritten time cards was a comfortable option for the firm. Another option was to convince the senior management of Omnimia Graphics to implement a software program for payroll processing. How should the company handle maintenance of the current payroll records? What internal control issues should be addressed?

2-2. You have been hired as a consultant for Semiva Productions, a company facing an IRS audit of its accounting records. During your review, you notice anomalies in the payroll system involving overpayments of labor and payments to terminated employees. What would you do?

In the Real World: Scenario for Discussion

The Lilly Ledbetter Fair Pay Act of 2009 centered on a case in which Ms. Ledbetter discovered documents that revealed discrimination against her that resulted in unequal pay practices. The company argued that the documents were confidential and scheduled for destruction and that Ms. Ledbetter should not have had access to the information. What are the issues in this case in terms of document privacy and retention? How could the situation have been prevented in the first place?

Internet Activities

2-1. Using a search engine such as Google, Yahoo, or Bing, search the Internet for the term "new hire packet contents." Compile a list of the different new hire packet items that you find in at least three companies. What are some unique items that you found on the companies' lists? Check out the IRS's video about determining the correct amount of withholding allowances for your Form W-4, www.youtube.com/watch?v=6FSOvxkhxdM.

2-2. Go to www.irs.gov and search for IRS e-file security. List the facts that the IRS cites about why e-filing is secure. What about these practices makes the customer's information secure? How could the IRS improve e-filing security?

2-3. Want to know more about some of the concepts discussed in this chapter? Check out

www.uscis.gov

www.irs.gov/businesses

www.archives.gov/federal-register/cfr/subject-title-26.html

www.proshred.com

www.ironmountain.com

2-4. The Massachusetts Institute of Technology (MIT) has created a website with a living wage calculator. This tool is designed to help people compute the wages they need to earn in order to achieve their desired lifestyle. Check it out at Living Wage Calculator, http://livingwage.mit.edu.

Continuing Payroll Project: Prevosti Farms and Sugarhouse

Prevosti Farms and Sugarhouse pays its employees according to their job classification. The following employees make up Sugarhouse's staff:

Employee Number	Name and Address	Payroll information
A-Mille	Thomas Millen 1022 Forest School Rd Woodstock, VT 05001 802-478-5055 SSN: 031-11-3456 401(k) deduction: 3%	Hire Date: 2-1-2019 DOB: 12-16-1982 Position: Production Manager PT/FT: FT, exempt No. of Exemptions: 4 M/S: M Pay Rate: $35,000/year

Employee Number	Name and Address	Payroll information
A-Towle	Avery Towle 4011 Route 100 Plymouth, VT 05102 802-967-5873 SSN: 089-74-0974 401(k) deduction: 5%	Hire Date: 2-1-2019 DOB: 7-14-1991 Position: Production Worker PT/FT: FT, nonexempt No. of Exemptions: 1 M/S: S Pay Rate: $12.00/hour
A-Long	Charlie Long 242 Benedict Road S. Woodstock, VT 05002 802-429-3846 SSN: 056-23-4593 401(k) deduction: 2%	Hire Date: 2-1-2019 DOB: 3-16-1987 Position: Production Worker PT/FT: FT, nonexempt No. of Exemptions: 2 M/S: M Pay Rate: $12.50/hour
B-Shang	Mary Shangraw 1901 Main Street #2 Bridgewater, VT 05520 802-575-5423 SSN: 075-28-8945 401(k) deduction: 3%	Hire Date: 2-1-2019 DOB: 8-20-1994 Position: Administrative Assistant PT/FT: PT, nonexempt No. of Exemptions: 1 M/S: S Pay Rate: $11.00/hour
B-Lewis	Kristen Lewis 840 Daily Hollow Road Bridgewater, VT 05523 802-390-5572 SSN: 076-39-5673 401(k) deduction: 4%	Hire Date: 2-1-2019 DOB: 4-6-1960 Position: Office Manager PT/FT: FT, exempt No. of Exemptions: 3 M/S: M Pay Rate: $32,000/year
B-Schwa	Joel Schwartz 55 Maple Farm Way Woodstock, VT 05534 802-463-9985 SSN: 021-34-9876 401(k) deduction: 5%	Hire Date: 2-1-2019 DOB: 5-23-1985 Position: Sales PT/FT: FT, exempt No. of Exemptions: 2 M/S: M Pay Rate: $24,000/year base plus 3% commission per case sold
B-Prevo	Toni Prevosti 10520 Cox Hill Road Bridgewater, VT 05521 802-673-2636 SSN: 055-22-0443 401(k) deduction: 6%	Hire Date: 2-1-2019 DOB: 9-18-1967 Position: Owner/President PT/FT: FT, exempt No. of Exemptions: 5 M/S: M Pay Rate: $45,000/year

The departments are as follows:

Department A: Agricultural Workers

Department B: Office Workers

1. You have been hired to start on February 1, 2019, as the new accounting clerk. Your employee number is B-XXXXX, where "B" denotes that you are an office worker and "XXXXX" is the first five letters of your last name. If your last name is fewer than five letters, use the first few letters of your first name to complete the employee number. Your Social Security number is 555-55-5555, and you are full-time, nonexempt, and paid at a rate of $34,000 per year. You have elected to contribute 2 percent of your gross pay to your 401(k). Complete the W-4 and the I-9 to start your own employee file. You are single with only one job (claiming two exemptions). You live at 1644 Smitten Road, Woodstock, VT 05001. Your phone number is (555) 555-5555. Your date of birth is 01/01/1991. You are a citizen of the United States and provide a Vermont driver's license #88110009

expiring 01/01/23 in addition to your Social Security card for verification of your identity. Mary Shangraw verified the information for the company. Prevosti Farms and Sugarhouse is located at 820 Westminster Road, Bridgewater, Vermont, 05520.

Form W-4 (2019)

Future developments. For the latest information about any future developments related to Form W-4, such as legislation enacted after it was published, go to *www.irs.gov/FormW4.*

Purpose. Complete Form W-4 so that your employer can withhold the correct federal income tax from your pay. Consider completing a new Form W-4 each year and when your personal or financial situation changes.

Exemption from withholding. You may claim exemption from withholding for 2019 if **both** of the following apply.

- For 2018 you had a right to a refund of **all** federal income tax withheld because you had **no** tax liability, **and**
- For 2019 you expect a refund of **all** federal income tax withheld because you expect to have **no** tax liability.

If you're exempt, complete **only** lines 1, 2, 3, 4, and 7 and sign the form to validate it. Your exemption for 2019 expires February 17, 2020. See Pub. 505, Tax Withholding and Estimated Tax, to learn more about whether you qualify for exemption from withholding.

General Instructions

If you aren't exempt, follow the rest of these instructions to determine the number of withholding allowances you should claim for withholding for 2019 and any additional amount of tax to have withheld. For regular wages, withholding must be based on allowances you claimed and may not be a flat amount or percentage of wages.

You can also use the calculator at ***www.irs.gov/W4App*** to determine your tax withholding more accurately. Consider using this calculator if you have a more complicated tax situation, such as if you have a working spouse, more than one job, or a large amount of nonwage income not subject to withholding outside of your job. After your Form W-4 takes effect, you can also use this calculator to see how the amount of tax you're having withheld compares to your projected total tax for 2019. If you use the calculator, you don't need to complete any of the worksheets for Form W-4.

Note that if you have too much tax withheld, you will receive a refund when you file your tax return. If you have too little tax withheld, you will owe tax when you file your tax return, and you might owe a penalty.

Filers with multiple jobs or working spouses. If you have more than one job at a time, or if you're married filing jointly and your spouse is also working, read all of the instructions including the instructions for the Two-Earners/Multiple Jobs Worksheet before beginning.

Nonwage income. If you have a large amount of nonwage income not subject to withholding, such as interest or dividends, consider making estimated tax payments using Form 1040-ES, Estimated Tax for Individuals. Otherwise, you might owe additional tax. Or, you can use the Deductions, Adjustments, and Additional Income Worksheet on page 3 or the calculator at *www.irs.gov/W4App* to make sure you have enough tax withheld from your paycheck. If you have pension or annuity income, see Pub. 505 or use the calculator at *www.irs.gov/W4App* to find out if you should adjust your withholding on Form W-4 or W-4P.

Nonresident alien. If you're a nonresident alien, see Notice 1392, Supplemental Form W-4 Instructions for Nonresident Aliens, before completing this form.

Specific Instructions

Personal Allowances Worksheet

Complete this worksheet on page 3 first to determine the number of withholding allowances to claim.

Line C. *Head of household please note:* Generally, you may claim head of household filing status on your tax return only if you're unmarried and pay more than 50% of the costs of keeping up a home for yourself and a qualifying individual. See Pub. 501 for more information about filing status.

Line E. Child tax credit. When you file your tax return, you may be eligible to claim a child tax credit for each of your eligible children. To qualify, the child must be under age 17 as of December 31, must be your dependent who lives with you for more than half the year, and must have a valid social security number. To learn more about this credit, see Pub. 972, Child Tax Credit. To reduce the tax withheld from your pay by taking this credit into account, follow the instructions on line E of the worksheet. On the worksheet you will be asked about your total income. For this purpose, total income includes all of your wages and other income, including income earned by a spouse if you are filing a joint return.

Line F. Credit for other dependents. When you file your tax return, you may be eligible to claim a credit for other dependents for whom a child tax credit can't be claimed, such as a qualifying child who doesn't meet the age or social security number requirement for the child tax credit, or a qualifying relative. To learn more about this credit, see Pub. 972. To reduce the tax withheld from your pay by taking this credit into account, follow the instructions on line F of the worksheet. On the worksheet, you will be asked about your total income. For this purpose, total

---

Separate here and give Form W-4 to your employer. Keep the worksheet(s) for your records.

Form **W-4**
Department of the Treasury
Internal Revenue Service

Employee's Withholding Allowance Certificate

▶ Whether you're entitled to claim a certain number of allowances or exemption from withholding is subject to review by the IRS. Your employer may be required to send a copy of this form to the IRS.

OMB No. 1545-0074

2019

1 Your first name and middle initial	Last name	2 Your social security number
Home address (number and street or rural route)	3 ☐ Single ☐ Married ☐ Married, but withhold at higher Single rate. **Note:** If married filing separately, check "Married, but withhold at higher Single rate."	
City or town, state, and ZIP code	4 **If your last name differs from that shown on your social security card, check here. You must call 800-772-1213 for a replacement card.** ▶ ☐	

5 Total number of allowances you're claiming (from the applicable worksheet on the following pages) . . . . | 5 |

6 Additional amount, if any, you want withheld from each paycheck . . . . | 6 | $

7 I claim exemption from withholding for 2019, and I certify that I meet **both** of the following conditions for exemption.
- Last year I had a right to a refund of **all** federal income tax withheld because I had **no** tax liability, **and**
- This year I expect a refund of **all** federal income tax withheld because I expect to have **no** tax liability.

If you meet both conditions, write "Exempt" here . . . . ▶ | 7 |

Under penalties of perjury, I declare that I have examined this certificate and, to the best of my knowledge and belief, it is true, correct, and complete.

Employee's signature
(This form is not valid unless you sign it.) ▶ **Date** ▶

8 Employer's name and address (**Employer:** Complete boxes 8 and 10 if sending to IRS and complete boxes 8, 9, and 10 if sending to State Directory of New Hires.)	9 First date of employment	10 Employer identification number (EIN)

For Privacy Act and Paperwork Reduction Act Notice, see page 4. Cat. No. 10220Q Form **W-4** (2019)

Source: Internal Revenue Service.

Employment Eligibility Verification
Department of Homeland Security
U.S. Citizenship and Immigration Services

USCIS
Form I-9
OMB No. 1615-0047
Expires 08/31/2019

▶ START HERE: Read instructions carefully before completing this form. The instructions must be available, either in paper or electronically, during completion of this form. Employers are liable for errors in the completion of this form.

ANTI-DISCRIMINATION NOTICE: It is illegal to discriminate against work-authorized individuals. Employers **CANNOT** specify which document(s) an employee may present to establish employment authorization and identity. The refusal to hire or continue to employ an individual because the documentation presented has a future expiration date may also constitute illegal discrimination.

Section 1. Employee Information and Attestation *(Employees must complete and sign Section 1 of Form I-9 no later than the* ***first day of employment****, but not before accepting a job offer.)*

Last Name *(Family Name)*	First Name *(Given Name)*	Middle Initial	Other Last Names Used *(if any)*

Address *(Street Number and Name)*	Apt. Number	City or Town	State	ZIP Code

Date of Birth *(mm/dd/yyyy)*	U.S. Social Security Number	Employee's E-mail Address	Employee's Telephone Number
	☐☐☐ - ☐☐ - ☐☐☐☐		

I am aware that federal law provides for imprisonment and/or fines for false statements or use of false documents in connection with the completion of this form.

I attest, under penalty of perjury, that I am (check one of the following boxes):

☐ 1. A citizen of the United States

☐ 2. A noncitizen national of the United States *(See instructions)*

☐ 3. A lawful permanent resident (Alien Registration Number/USCIS Number): ____________

☐ 4. An alien authorized to work until (expiration date, if applicable, mm/dd/yyyy): ____________
Some aliens may write "N/A" in the expiration date field. *(See instructions)*

Aliens authorized to work must provide only one of the following document numbers to complete Form I-9:
An Alien Registration Number/USCIS Number OR Form I-94 Admission Number OR Foreign Passport Number.

1. Alien Registration Number/USCIS Number: ____________

OR

2. Form I-94 Admission Number: ____________

OR

3. Foreign Passport Number: ____________

Country of Issuance: ____________

QR Code - Section 1
Do Not Write In This Space

Signature of Employee	Today's Date *(mm/dd/yyyy)*

Preparer and/or Translator Certification (check one):

☐ I did not use a preparer or translator. ☐ A preparer(s) and/or translator(s) assisted the employee in completing Section 1.

(Fields below must be completed and signed when preparers and/or translators assist an employee in completing Section 1.)

I attest, under penalty of perjury, that I have assisted in the completion of Section 1 of this form and that to the best of my knowledge the information is true and correct.

Signature of Preparer or Translator	Today's Date *(mm/dd/yyyy)*

Last Name *(Family Name)*	First Name *(Given Name)*

Address *(Street Number and Name)*	City or Town	State	ZIP Code

STOP *Employer Completes Next Page* STOP

Employment Eligibility Verification
Department of Homeland Security
U.S. Citizenship and Immigration Services

USCIS
Form I-9
OMB No. 1615-0047
Expires 08/31/2019

Section 2. Employer or Authorized Representative Review and Verification

(Employers or their authorized representative must complete and sign Section 2 within 3 business days of the employee's first day of employment. You must physically examine one document from List A OR a combination of one document from List B and one document from List C as listed on the "Lists of Acceptable Documents.")

Employee Info from Section 1	Last Name *(Family Name)*	First Name *(Given Name)*	M.I.	Citizenship/Immigration Status

List A Identity and Employment Authorization	**OR**	**List B** Identity	**AND**	**List C** Employment Authorization
Document Title		Document Title		Document Title
Issuing Authority		Issuing Authority		Issuing Authority
Document Number		Document Number		Document Number
Expiration Date *(if any)(mm/dd/yyyy)*		Expiration Date *(if any)(mm/dd/yyyy)*		Expiration Date *(if any)(mm/dd/yyyy)*
Document Title		Additional Information		QR Code - Sections 2 & 3 Do Not Write In This Space
Issuing Authority				
Document Number				
Expiration Date *(if any)(mm/dd/yyyy)*				
Document Title				
Issuing Authority				
Document Number				
Expiration Date *(if any)(mm/dd/yyyy)*				

Certification: I attest, under penalty of perjury, that (1) I have examined the document(s) presented by the above-named employee, (2) the above-listed document(s) appear to be genuine and to relate to the employee named, and (3) to the best of my knowledge the employee is authorized to work in the United States.

The employee's first day of employment *(mm/dd/yyyy)*: ____________ ***(See instructions for exemptions)***

Signature of Employer or Authorized Representative	Today's Date *(mm/dd/yyyy)*	Title of Employer or Authorized Representative

Last Name of Employer or Authorized Representative	First Name of Employer or Authorized Representative	Employer's Business or Organization Name

Employer's Business or Organization Address (Street Number and Name)	City or Town	State	ZIP Code

Section 3. Reverification and Rehires *(To be completed and signed by employer or authorized representative.)*

A. New Name *(if applicable)*			**B.** Date of Rehire *(if applicable)*
Last Name *(Family Name)*	First Name *(Given Name)*	Middle Initial	Date *(mm/dd/yyyy)*

C. If the employee's previous grant of employment authorization has expired, provide the information for the document or receipt that establishes continuing employment authorization in the space provided below.

Document Title	Document Number	Expiration Date *(if any) (mm/dd/yyyy)*

I attest, under penalty of perjury, that to the best of my knowledge, this employee is authorized to work in the United States, and if the employee presented document(s), the document(s) I have examined appear to be genuine and to relate to the individual.

Signature of Employer or Authorized Representative	Today's Date *(mm/dd/yyyy)*	Name of Employer or Authorized Representative

Form I-9 07/17/17 N

Page 2 of 3

LISTS OF ACCEPTABLE DOCUMENTS
All documents must be UNEXPIRED

Employees may present one selection from List A
or a combination of one selection from List B and one selection from List C.

LIST A **Documents that Establish Both Identity and Employment Authorization**	OR	**LIST B** **Documents that Establish Identity**	AND	**LIST C** **Documents that Establish Employment Authorization**
1. U.S. Passport or U.S. Passport Card		**1.** Driver's license or ID card issued by a State or outlying possession of the United States provided it contains a photograph or information such as name, date of birth, gender, height, eye color, and address		**1.** A Social Security Account Number card, unless the card includes one of the following restrictions: (1) NOT VALID FOR EMPLOYMENT (2) VALID FOR WORK ONLY WITH INS AUTHORIZATION (3) VALID FOR WORK ONLY WITH DHS AUTHORIZATION
2. Permanent Resident Card or Alien Registration Receipt Card (Form I-551)		**2.** ID card issued by federal, state or local government agencies or entities, provided it contains a photograph or information such as name, date of birth, gender, height, eye color, and address		**2.** Certification of report of birth issued by the Department of State (Forms DS-1350, FS-545, FS-240)
3. Foreign passport that contains a temporary I-551 stamp or temporary I-551 printed notation on a machine-readable immigrant visa		**3.** School ID card with a photograph		**3.** Original or certified copy of birth certificate issued by a State, county, municipal authority, or territory of the United States bearing an official seal
4. Employment Authorization Document that contains a photograph (Form I-766)		**4.** Voter's registration card		**4.** Native American tribal document
5. For a nonimmigrant alien authorized to work for a specific employer because of his or her status: **a.** Foreign passport; and **b.** Form I-94 or Form I-94A that has the following: (1) The same name as the passport; and (2) An endorsement of the alien's nonimmigrant status as long as that period of endorsement has not yet expired and the proposed employment is not in conflict with any restrictions or limitations identified on the form.		**5.** U.S. Military card or draft record		**5.** U.S. Citizen ID Card (Form I-197)
6. Passport from the Federated States of Micronesia (FSM) or the Republic of the Marshall Islands (RMI) with Form I-94 or Form I-94A indicating nonimmigrant admission under the Compact of Free Association Between the United States and the FSM or RMI		**6.** Military dependent's ID card		**6.** Identification Card for Use of Resident Citizen in the United States (Form I-179)
		7. U.S. Coast Guard Merchant Mariner Card		**7.** Employment authorization document issued by the Department of Homeland Security
		8. Native American tribal document		
		9. Driver's license issued by a Canadian government authority		
		For persons under age 18 who are unable to present a document listed above:		
		10. School record or report card		
		11. Clinic, doctor, or hospital record		
		12. Day-care or nursery school record		

Examples of many of these documents appear in Part 13 of the Handbook for Employers (M-274).

Refer to the instructions for more information about acceptable receipts.

Form I-9 07/17/17 N

Page 3 of 3

Source: United States Citizenship and Immigration Services.

2. Complete the employee information form for each employee. Enter the pay rate earnings for each employee.

EMPLOYEE EARNING RECORD

NAME		Hire Date	
ADDRESS		Date of Birth	
CITY/STATE/ZIP		Exempt/Nonexempt	
TELEPHONE		Married/Single	
SOCIAL SECURITY NUMBER		No. of Exemptions	
POSITION		Pay Rate	

Period Ended	Hrs Worked	Reg Pay	OT Pay	Holiday	Comm	Gross Pay	Ins	401(k)	Taxable Pay for Federal	Taxable Pay for FICA

Taxable Wages for Federal	Taxable Wages for FICA	Federal W/H	Social Sec. Tax	Medicare Tax	State Inc. Tax	Total Deduc	Net Pay	YTD Net Pay	YTD Gross Pay

EMPLOYEE EARNING RECORD

NAME		Hire Date	
ADDRESS		Date of Birth	
CITY/STATE/ZIP		Exempt/Nonexempt	
TELEPHONE		Married/Single	
SOCIAL SECURITY NUMBER		No. of Exemptions	
POSITION		Pay Rate	

Period Ended	Hrs Worked	Reg Pay	OT Pay	Holiday	Comm	Gross Pay	Ins	401(k)	Taxable Pay for Federal	Taxable Pay for FICA

Taxable Wages for Federal	Taxable Wages for FICA	Federal W/H	Social Sec. Tax	Medicare Tax	State Inc. Tax	Total Deduc	Net Pay	YTD Net Pay	YTD Gross Pay

EMPLOYEE EARNING RECORD

NAME		Hire Date	
ADDRESS		Date of Birth	
CITY/STATE/ZIP		Exempt/Nonexempt	
TELEPHONE		Married/Single	
SOCIAL SECURITY NUMBER		No. of Exemptions	
POSITION		Pay Rate	

Period Ended	Hrs Worked	Reg Pay	OT Pay	Holiday	Comm	Gross Pay	Ins	401(k)	Taxable Wages for Federal	Taxable Wages for FICA

Taxable Wages for Federal	Taxable Wages for FICA	Federal W/H	Social Sec. Tax	Medicare Tax	State Inc. Tax	Total Deduc	Net Pay	YTD Net Pay	YTD Gross Pay

EMPLOYEE EARNING RECORD

NAME		Hire Date	
ADDRESS		Date of Birth	
CITY/STATE/ZIP		Exempt/Nonexempt	
TELEPHONE		Married/Single	
SOCIAL SECURITY NUMBER		No. of Exemptions	
POSITION		Pay Rate	

Period Ended	Hrs Worked	Reg Pay	OT Pay	Holiday	Comm	Gross Pay	Ins	401(k)	Taxable Pay for Federal	Taxable Pay for FICA

Taxable Wages for Federal	Taxable Wages for FICA	Federal W/H	Social Sec. Tax	Medicare Tax	State Inc. Tax	Total Deduc	Net Pay	YTD Net Pay	YTD Gross Pay

EMPLOYEE EARNING RECORD

NAME		Hire Date	
ADDRESS		Date of Birth	
CITY/STATE/ZIP		Exempt/Nonexempt	
TELEPHONE		Married/Single	
SOCIAL SECURITY NUMBER		No. of Exemptions	
POSITION		Pay Rate	

Period Ended	Hrs Worked	Reg Pay	OT Pay	Holiday	Comm	Gross Pay	Ins	401(k)	Taxable Pay for Federal	Taxable Pay for FICA

Taxable Wages for Federal	Taxable Wages for FICA	Federal W/H	Social Sec. Tax	Medicare Tax	State Inc. Tax	Total Deduc	Net Pay	YTD Net Pay	YTD Gross Pay

EMPLOYEE EARNING RECORD

NAME		Hire Date	
ADDRESS		Date of Birth	
CITY/STATE/ZIP		Exempt/Nonexempt	
TELEPHONE		Married/Single	
SOCIAL SECURITY NUMBER		No. of Exemptions	
POSITION		Pay Rate	

Period Ended	Hrs Worked	Reg Pay	OT Pay	Holiday	Comm	Gross Pay	Ins	401(k)	Taxable Pay for Federal	Taxable Pay for FICA

Taxable Wages for Federal	Taxable Wages for FICA	Federal W/H	Social Sec. Tax	Medicare Tax	State Inc. Tax	Total Deduc	Net Pay	YTD Net Pay	YTD Gross Pay

EMPLOYEE EARNING RECORD

NAME		Hire Date	
ADDRESS		Date of Birth	
CITY/STATE/ZIP		Exempt/Nonexempt	
TELEPHONE		Married/Single	
SOCIAL SECURITY NUMBER		No. of Exemptions	
POSITION		Pay Rate	

Period Ended	Hrs Worked	Reg Pay	OT Pay	Holiday	Comm	Gross Pay	Ins	401(k)	Taxable Pay for Federal	Taxable Pay for FICA

Taxable Wages for Federal	Taxable Wages for FICA	Federal W/H	Social Sec. Tax	Medicare Tax	State Inc. Tax	Total Deduc	Net Pay	YTD Net Pay	YTD Gross Pay

EMPLOYEE EARNING RECORD

NAME		Hire Date	
ADDRESS		Date of Birth	
CITY/STATE/ZIP		Exempt/Nonexempt	
TELEPHONE		Married/Single	
SOCIAL SECURITY NUMBER		No. of Exemptions	
POSITION		Pay Rate	

Period Ended	Hrs Worked	Reg Pay	OT Pay	Holiday	Comm	Gross Pay	Ins	401(k)	Taxable Pay for Federal	Taxable Pay for FICA

Taxable Wages for Federal	Taxable Wages for FICA	Federal W/H	Social Sec. Tax	Medicare	State W/H	Total Deduc	Net Pay	YTD Net Pay	YTD Gross Pay

Answers to Stop & Check Exercises

What's in the File?

1. a, b, d, e
2. b
3. d
4. a
5. c

Who Are You?

1. Student answers will vary. One possible way to prove both identity and employment is a current U.S. passport. Alternatively, a current state-issued driver's license and a Social Security card will work for the purposes of the I-9.
2. Student answers will vary. Many students may underestimate their estimated exemptions.
3. Student answers will vary. Examples of statutory employees include the following: A driver who distributes beverages (other than milk) or meat, vegetable, fruit, or bakery products or who picks up and delivers laundry or dry cleaning, if the driver is a single company's agent or is paid on commission. A full-time life insurance sales agent whose principal business activity is selling life insurance or annuity contracts, or both, primarily for one life insurance company. An individual who works at home on materials or goods that a company supplies and that must be returned to that company or a designated agent in accordance with furnished specifications for the work to be done. A full-time traveling or city salesperson who works on a single company's behalf and turns in orders from wholesalers, retailers, contractors, or operators of hotels, restaurants, or other similar establishments. The goods sold must be merchandise for resale or supplies for use in the buyer's business operation. The work performed for that single company must be the salesperson's principal business activity.

Exempt vs. Nonexempt

1. Exempt workers are exempt from the overtime provisions of FLSA. Exempt workers tend to be employees in a company's managerial or other leadership functions, in which they may need to work more than 40 hours per week to complete their tasks. Exempt workers usually receive a fixed salary per period that is not based on the number of hours worked. Nonexempt workers tend to be compensated on an hourly basis and often do not have managerial or leadership responsibilities. It should be noted that some nonexempt workers do have managerial or leadership responsibilities and may receive a fixed salary; however, these particular employees are covered by the overtime provisions of FLSA.
2. c (40 hours)
3. Nonexempt. When workers are employed on a nonexempt basis, they are paid to perform a specific job regardless of the number of hours worked to accomplish that job. A 2014 Gallup Work and Education poll found that more than half of the nonexempt salaried workers surveyed worked in excess of 40 hours per week.

Worker Facts

1. Hourly workers and nonexempt workers are protected by FLSA
2. Exempt workers receive a fixed amount of money and generally direct the actions of other employees; nonexempt workers are eligible for overtime and generally have their work directed by a manager.
3. Commission workers are typically tied to sales completed by the individual; piece rate pay is determined by the number of pieces the employee completes during a shift or period.

Who Does Which Job?

Student answers will vary. The answer should reflect a clear separation of duties, cross-training, rotation of tasks, and security protocols.

Internal Controls and Audits

1. b
2. c

Destroy and Terminate

1. Paper payroll records should be shredded or burned. Computer records should be purged from the server and all other storage devices.
2. Charlie should receive his final pay on October 11, and no later than October 12. His employer is not required to provide him with a severance package, although he may be eligible for his accrued vacation pay.

3

Chapter Three

Gross Pay Computation

Two important terms in payroll accounting are gross pay and net pay. ***Gross pay*** is the amount of wages earned before deducting amounts for taxes or other deductions. ***Net pay*** is the amount of money the employee actually receives in a paycheck, after all taxes and other deductions have been subtracted. In this chapter, we will focus on computing gross pay.

The calculation of an employee's gross pay is the first step for payroll processing. Employee pay may be calculated in different ways. ***Hourly*** employees are paid for each hour, or fraction thereof, that they work in a given day. Salaried employees are broken into two classifications, based on FLSA classification: ***exempt*** and ***nonexempt***. Salaried exempt employees receive pay based on the job they perform, regardless of the number of hours it takes. Salaried nonexempt employees may receive both ***salary*** and ***overtime***. Another class of employees work on a ***commission*** basis, which means that some or all of their wages are based on sales revenue. A final classification is ***piece-rate*** employees. Typically found in manufacturing environments, employees are paid based upon the number of pieces completed during a work shift.

LEARNING OBJECTIVES

After studying Chapter 3, you should be able to:

LO 3-1 Analyze Minimum Wage Pay for Nonexempt Workers

LO 3-2 Compute Gross Pay for Different Pay Bases

LO 3-3 Calculate Pay Based on Hours and Fractions of Hours

LO 3-4 Calculate Overtime in Various Situations

LO 3-5 Create a Payroll Register

LO 3-6 Apply Combination Pay Methods

LO 3-7 Explain Special Pay Situations

ColorBlind Images/Blend Images LLC

Truck Drivers and Minimum Wage Requirements

The Fair Labor Standards Act (FLSA) established a minimum wage and standard weekly working hours to protect workers. The federal standard for regular weekly working hours is 40 and the act states that employees who work in excess of 40 hours per week must receive overtime wages of at least one and a half times their regular hourly wage. For most nonexempt employees, the 40 hours per week standard is sufficient.

In late 2018, a federal judge in the Western District Court of Arkansas ruled on a case against PAM Transport Inc. that long-distance truck drivers, many of whom are expected to be available to work up to 24 hours per day, should be paid according to FLSA guidelines for every hour worked. In addition, the drivers must receive eight hours of sleep time for each day that they are on the road. This ruling called into question (1) the classification of drivers as employees instead of independent contractors and (2) the question of whether drivers actually receive the FLSA minimum wage for the work they perform. Aside from hourly pay, trucking companies have also paid drivers a per-mile rate, which is akin to piece-rate pay and does not relieve the employer of paying employees the FLSA minimum wage. Trucking companies have argued that the presence of a sleeper berth in long-distance trucks alleviates the need for drivers to be paid for all hours. Drivers have commented that the presence of the sleeping berth leads to them being in and responsible for the employer's property (i.e., the truck and any contents) 24 hours per day during the time they are responsible for transporting said property.

Trucking companies such as CR England have proactively addressed the issue by increasing driver pay and addressing hours worked. Other trucking companies have tried to classify drivers as independent contractors, especially if the driver owns the truck used, therefore avoiding the FLSA mandate. Parts of this issue have been ruled upon by the U.S. Supreme Court, which decided that workers classified as independent contractors may sue employers in court instead of being forced to accept the private arbitration that had been the norm for decades. The case continues to evolve.

(Sources: Business Insider, CNBC, Fleet Owner, Leagle, Trucking Info)

Employee pay is the focus of Chapter 3. We will examine different bases for gross pay computations, discuss how these compensation bases differ, and introduce the use of the payroll register as a tool in pay calculation.

LO 3-1 Analyze Minimum Wage Pay for Nonexempt Workers

flairmicro/123RF

Two primary classifications of employees exist: exempt and nonexempt. These classifications refer to the provisions of the Fair Labor Standards Act (FLSA). The FLSA provisions protect nonexempt employees, including clerical, factory, and other nonmanagerial employees. Nonexempt employees are operative workers whose workdays may vary in duration, whose tasks do not meet the U.S. Department of Labor guidelines for exempt employees, and who do not generally have supervisory or managerial duties. Exempt employees include employees who meet U.S. Department of Labor guidelines for exempt classification, which includes job titles such as Department Supervisor or Warehouse Manager.

For hourly workers, FLSA contains wage provisions that stipulate the ***minimum wage*** an employer may pay an employee. However, the law exempts some employers from the minimum wage requirements. According to the U.S. Department of Labor, the following conditions exempt an employer from paying the federal minimum wage:

- Firms that do not engage in interstate commerce as part of their business production.
- Firms with less than $500,000 of annual business volume.

Note that certain firms are always covered by the FLSA provisions, regardless of their participation in interstate commerce or annual business volume. These businesses include hospitals, schools for mentally or physically disabled or gifted children, preschools, schools of any level, and governmental agencies. Under FLSA section 3(y), law enforcement and fire protection employees may have specified work periods ranging from 7 to 28 days, during which employees would be paid for overtime only after a predefined number of working hours.

FLSA was modified in 1974 to include explicit provisions about domestic workers. Since 1974, minimum wage provisions cover domestic service workers, such as nannies and chauffeurs, who earn more than $2,100 in wages annually (2019 figure). Note that the 1974 modification specifically excluded occasional babysitters and employees who provide domestic companion services for the elderly. In 2015, the U.S. Congress further amended FLSA to include caregivers and other direct care employees who provide in-home companionship services as being subject to the minimum wage. It should be noted that domestic workers who reside on the employer's premises permanently or for an extended time period are exempt from FLSA provisions.

> For live-in domestic service workers who are essentially on duty 24 hours per day, the U.S. Department of Labor has issued a sleep-time requirement of 8 hours per day, of which 5 hours must be consecutive, and adequate sleeping facilities must be provided. According to Fact Sheet 79D, if the employee's sleep time is interrupted for any reason, the employee must be compensated for that time. (Source: DOL)

Minimum Wage

An important consideration with the minimum wage provision of the FLSA is the existence of separate tiers of minimum wage. Wages for ***tipped employees*** are lower than those of nontipped employees. Federal wage and hour laws as of 2019 stipulate a federal minimum wage of $7.25 and a minimum hourly wage of $2.13 for tipped employees. States may enact additional minimum wage laws to address the specific economic needs of their population. This minimizes the legislative need to continually revisit the minimum wage.

> Most American nonexempt employees receive a wage higher than the federal minimum wage, and the majority of minimum wage employees work in the restaurant industry. Certain states such as California and Washington permit municipalities to enact ordinances mandating a higher minimum wage. However, other states such as Iowa and Florida have state constitutions that prohibit cities from instituting higher minimum wages. The challenge for employers, especially for those who operate in multiple areas, is to understand the minimum wage provisions for each location and how they affect the business. (Source: Pew Research Center)

As of 2019, 29 states and the District of Columbia have minimum wage rates that are higher than the federal minimum wage. Note that a few states have a minimum wage that is less than the FLSA minimum wage. These lower minimum wages may be paid by employers who are not subject to FLSA provisions because they do not conduct interstate commerce. A map depicting minimum wages for 2019 is shown in Figure 3-1, and the details of specific minimum wage rates are shown in Table 3-1. Examples involving employee pay with different minimum wages follow.

FIGURE 3-1

Minimum Wage Hourly Rates for 2019

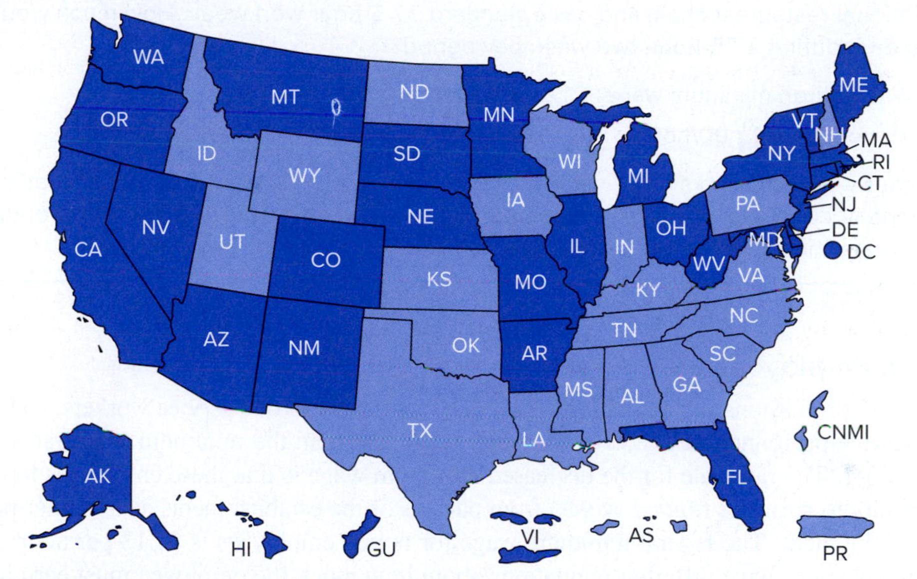

(Source: U.S. Department of Labor, 2019)

Legend: The states highlighted in dark blue have minimum wage amounts that are higher than the federal minimum wage of $7.25 per hour.

TABLE 3-1

Minimum Wage Hourly Rates by State

AK	$9.89	**IA**	$7.25	**MS**	None†	**PA**	$7.25
AL	None†	**ID**	7.25	**MT**	$8.50*	**RI**	10.50
AR	9.25	**IL**	8.25	**NC**	7.25	**SC**	None†
AZ	11.00	**IN**	7.25	**ND**	7.25	**SD**	9.10
CA	11.00*	**KS**	7.25	**NE**	9.00	**TN**	None†
CO	11.10	**KY**	7.25	**NH**	7.25	**TX**	7.25
CT	10.10	**LA**	None†	**NJ**	8.85	**UT**	7.25
D.C.	13.25	**MA**	12.00	**NM**	7.50	**VA**	7.25
DE	8.75	**MD**	10.10	**NV**	8.25*	**VT**	10.78
FL	8.46	**ME**	11.00	**NY**	11.10*	**WA**	12.00*
GA	5.15	**MI**	9.25	**OH**	8.55*	**WI**	7.25
HI	10.10	**MN**	9.86*	**OK**	7.25	**WV**	8.75
		MO	8.60	**OR**	10.75	**WY**	5.15

Source: U.S. Department of Labor, 2019.

*Variances exist depending on metropolitan area, business size, or employee benefits available. Be sure to check with the state revenue department for specific metropolitan areas and businesses.

†In states with no minimum wage, the federal minimum wage prevails.

EXAMPLE 1: STATE MINIMUM WAGE LOWER THAN FEDERAL MINIMUM WAGE

Don Mayer works for a Georgia employer that conducts no interstate commerce and whose annual business volume is less than $300,000. He is a janitor in a manufacturing plant and earns the minimum wage for Georgia. How much would he earn for a 40-hour pay period?

Georgia minimum wage: $5.15 per hour

40 hours × $5.15/hour = $206

Because the employer does not meet the requirements that would force it to pay Don the federal minimum wage, it may pay the state's minimum wage.

EXAMPLE 2: STATE MINIMUM WAGE HIGHER THAN FEDERAL MINIMUM WAGE

Wendy Roberts is a minimum wage worker in the state of Washington. She works for a national restaurant chain and has a standard 37.5-hour workweek. How much would she earn during a 75-hour, two-week pay period?

Washington minimum wage: $12.00 per hour

75 hours × $12.00/hour = $900.00

Because Wendy works for a national chain restaurant, it is safe to assume that the company conducts interstate commerce and earns more than $500,000 in revenues per year. She would be compensated at the state minimum wage in any case.

Tipped Employees

Workers in professions such as waiters, waitresses, bartenders, food service workers, and some hotel service personnel may receive an hourly wage less than the minimum wage rates listed in Table 3-1. The rationale for the decreased minimum wage is that these employees have the opportunity to earn tips (***tipped wages***) from patrons of the establishments as a regular part of their employment. The federal minimum wage for tipped employees is $2.13 per hour; however, many states have different regulations about how much the employee must earn in tips to meet federal wage and hour laws.

In 2018, voters in Washington, DC, approved Initiative 77, which will gradually increase the tipped wage through 2026 until it meets the minimum wage for the area. Initiative 77 was a controversial measure because of the growing restaurant economy and wage gap issues that the measure was intended to remedy. (Source: *Vox*, *Washington Post*)

The difference between the tipped employee minimum wage and the federal minimum wage is known as the *tip credit.* Federal wage and hour laws mandate that the tip credit is $5.12 per hour. Note that the tip credit is the difference between the minimum wage and the tipped employee minimum wage ($7.25 – $2.13 = $5.12). Some states such as Alaska, California, and Montana do not allow tip credit; instead, all workers receive the prevailing federal or local minimum wage. Table 3-2 contains the details about tip credit for each state. Some states have requirements on employers regarding information that needs to be obtained prior to applying a tip credit. For example, North Carolina requires a monthly or per pay period affidavit from employees of the amount of tips received.

TABLE 3-2
Table of 2018 Minimum Hourly Wages for Tipped Employees by State

Jurisdiction	Basic Combined Cash and Tip Minimum Wage Rate	Maximum Tip Credit Against Minimum Wage	Minimum Cash Wage	Definition of Tipped Employee by Minimum Tips Received (monthly unless otherwise specified)
Federal: Fair Labor Standards Act (FLSA)	$7.25	$5.12	$2.13	More than $30
State Law Does Not Allow Tip Credit				
Note: The minimum rate is the same for tipped and non-tipped employees				
Alaska			9.89	
California 25 or fewer employees			11.00	
26 or more employees			12.00	
Minnesota:				
Large employer Annual receipts > $500,000 per year			9.86	
Small employer Annual receipts < $500,000 per year			8.04	
Montana:				
Business with gross annual sales exceeding $110,000			8.50	
Business with gross annual sales of $110,000 or less			4.00	
Nevada			8.25	With no health insurance benefits provided by employer and received by employee
			7.25	With health insurance benefits provided by employer and received by employee
Oregon			10.25	
Washington			12.00	
State Law Allows Tip Credit				
Arizona	11.00	3.00	8.00	Not specified
Arkansas	9.25	6.62	2.63	More than $20
Colorado	11.10	3.02	8.08	More than $30
Connecticut:	10.10			At least $10 weekly for full-time employees or $2.00 daily for part-time in hotels and restaurants. Not specified for other industries.
Hotel, restaurant		36.8% (3.72)	6.38	
Bartenders who customarily receive tips		18.5% (1.87)	8.23	
Delaware	8.25	6.52	2.23	More than $30
District of Columbia (D.C.)[2]	13.25	9.36	3.89	Not specified
Florida	8.46	3.02	5.44	
Hawaii	10.10	0.75	9.35	More than $20
Idaho	7.25	3.90	3.35	More than $30
Illinois	8.25	40% of applicable minimum wage (3.30)	4.95	20
Indiana	7.25	5.12	2.13	Not specified

(continued)

Jurisdiction	Basic Combined Cash and Tip Minimum Wage Rate	Maximum Tip Credit Against Minimum Wage	Minimum Cash Wage	Definition of Tipped Employee by Minimum Tips Received (monthly unless otherwise specified)
Iowa	7.25	2.90	4.35	More than $30
Kansas	7.25	5.12	2.13	More than $20
Kentucky	7.25	5.12	2.13	More than $30
Maine	11.00	5.50	5.50	More than $30
Maryland	10.10	6.47	3.63	More than $30
Massachusetts	11.00	7.25	3.75	More than $20
Michigan	9.45	5.86	3.59	Not specified
Missouri	8.60	50% (4.30)	4.30	Not specified
Nebraska	9.00	6.87	2.13	Not specified
New Hampshire	7.25	55% of applicable minimum wage (3.99)	45% of applicable minimum wage (3.26)	More than 30
New Jersey	8.60	6.47	2.13	Not specified
New Mexico	7.50	5.37	2.13	More than $30
New York	See website[3]			Not specified
North Carolina	7.25	5.12	2.13	More than $20
North Dakota	7.25	33% of applicable minimum wage (2.39)	4.86	More than $30
Ohio: *Applies to employees of businesses with annual gross receipts of greater than $305,000 per year.*	8.55	4.25	4.30	More than $30
Oklahoma	7.25	5.12	2.13	Not specified
Pennsylvania	7.25	4.42	2.83	More than $30
Rhode Island	10.50	6.61	3.89	Not specified
South Carolina			2.13	Not specified
South Dakota	9.10	50% (4.55)	4.55	More than $35
Tennessee			2.13	
Texas	7.25	5.12	2.13	More than $20
Utah	7.25	5.12	2.13	More than $30
Vermont: *Employees in hotels, motels, tourist places, and restaurants who customarily and regularly receive >$120/month in tips for direct and personal customer service*	10.78	5.39	5.39	More than $120
Virginia	7.25	5.12	2.13	Not specified
West Virginia	8.75	70% (6.13)	2.62	Not specified
Wisconsin	7.25	4.92	2.33	Not specified
Wyoming	5.15	3.02	2.13	More than $30

Source: U.S. Department of Labor, 2019.

EXAMPLE: TIPPED EMPLOYEE IN OKLAHOMA, MINIMUM WAGE MET

Abigail Hansford is a tipped employee in Stillwater, Oklahoma. During a 40-hour workweek and pay period, she earned $220 in tips.

Hourly tipped minimum wage: $2.13 per hour

$2.13 per hour × 40 hours = $85.20 in wages

Tips earned: $220

Total wages and tips earned during the pay period:

$220 + $85.20 = $305.20

The federal and state minimum wage are $7.25 per hour. The minimum wage for a 40-hour workweek:

$7.25 per hours × 40 hours = $290

Therefore, Abigail has earned more than the federal and state minimum wage. The employer does not need to contribute to Abigail's pay during the pay period.

In late 2018, the New York City Taxi and Limousine Commission passed an initiative to increase the per-minute and per-mile formula for Uber and Lyft drivers, who are deemed independent contractors and therefore must pay their own employment taxes. The employee minimum wage is $15.00 per hour, and the new minimum hourly earning for app-based taxi services is designed to be $17.22 per hour. This additional amount represents the additional percentage that independent contractors must pay in their employment taxes. (Source: CBS News)

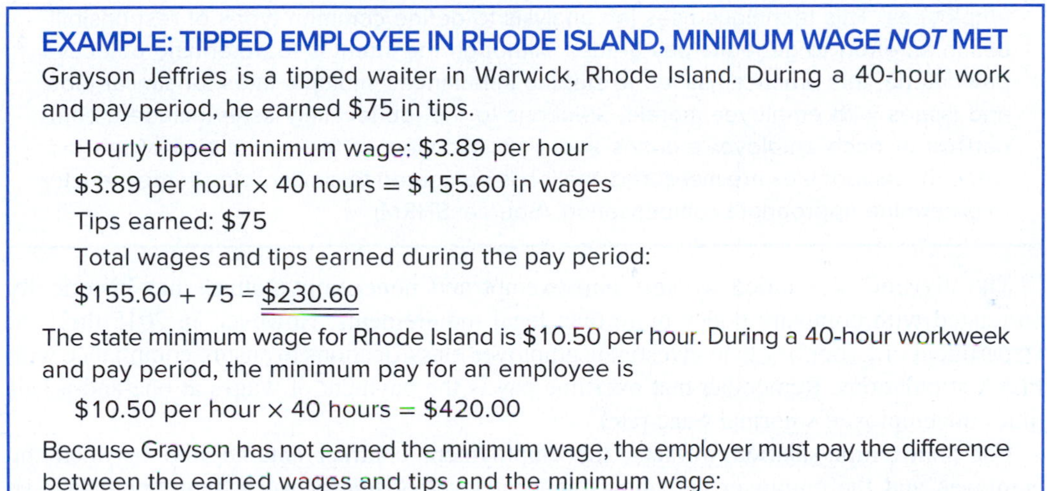

EXAMPLE: TIPPED EMPLOYEE IN RHODE ISLAND, MINIMUM WAGE *NOT* MET

Grayson Jeffries is a tipped waiter in Warwick, Rhode Island. During a 40-hour work and pay period, he earned $75 in tips.

Hourly tipped minimum wage: $3.89 per hour

$3.89 per hour × 40 hours = $155.60 in wages

Tips earned: $75

Total wages and tips earned during the pay period:

$155.60 + 75 = $230.60

The state minimum wage for Rhode Island is $10.50 per hour. During a 40-hour workweek and pay period, the minimum pay for an employee is

$10.50 per hour × 40 hours = $420.00

Because Grayson has not earned the minimum wage, the employer must pay the difference between the earned wages and tips and the minimum wage:

$420.00 – $230.60 = $189.40 to be added to Grayson's pay by the employer to bring his pay to the minimum wage

Pay Your Employees Correctly

Stop & Check

1. Heather Pai works as a clerk receiving minimum wage for a pharmaceutical company in North Carolina that pays its employees on a biweekly basis. She is classified as nonexempt, and her standard workweek is 40 hours. During a two-week period, she worked 88 hours and received $638.00. Was Heather's pay correct? Explain.
2. Tony Dupuis works as a publisher's representative receiving minimum wage in Maryland. He works 39.5 hours during a one-week period. How much should he receive?
3. Mary Lindquist is a temporary worker for a popular radio station, which is a large employer in Minnesota. She receives minimum wage and works 32 hours per week. How much should she receive for two weeks of work?
4. Tony Hardwick is a tipped minimum wage worker for a Minnesota company with $615,000 in annual revenues. He worked 75 hours during a biweekly pay period, in which he earned $1,000 in tips. What is his gross pay (excluding tips)?

Monkey Business Images/
Shutterstock

LO 3-2 Compute Gross Pay for Different Pay Bases

Salaried Workers

Employees in highly technical, qualification-driven positions within a company are generally classified as exempt from FLSA regulations. Accountants, engineers, lawyers, managers, and supervisors are included in this classification. Section 13(a)(1) of the FLSA defines the eligible exempt employees in the following job descriptions: executives, administrative personnel, professionals, and outside sales representatives. Section 13(a)(17) of the FLSA also allows specific computer-related employees to be included in the classification of salaried workers. The FLSA provides a minimum wage for salaried workers of not less than $455 per week, and this amount is currently under review at the federal level with the intent to raise it to recognize the contributions of exempt employees.

> Companies often use a technique called "job leveling" to determine salaries for exempt employees. This technique uses job analysis to define common types of responsibilities in an effort to generate pay grades. Although the intent is to determine objective pay criteria, this practice has led to staffing imbalances, multiple titles for similar jobs, and issues with employee morale. Solutions to the job-leveling issue include a comparison of each employee's duties and a holistic view of the actual size of the job. Once these variables are measured, the job is compared to similar roles in the industry to determine appropriate compensation. (Source: SHRM)

The division of salaried workers into exempt and nonexempt statuses has historically correlated with company policy more than legal requirements. However, in 2015 the U.S. Department of Labor began to investigate employee classifications to ensure compliance with FLSA stipulations. Remember that overtime pay is the payment of wages at one-and-a-half times the employee's normal wage rate.

For nonexempt salaried workers, the employment contract entered into between the employee and the employer determines at what level of hourly work they would receive overtime pay. Many salaried nonexempt worker contracts, when specified, are for 45 hours per week. If the contract stipulates that 45 hours per week is the standard workweek for a salaried, nonexempt employee, then the employee is still subject to FLSA overtime rules for hours worked past 40. For the purpose of this textbook, the standard workweek is five days of a seven-day week.

EXAMPLE: SALARIED, NONEXEMPT EMPLOYEE

Brad Hammond, a salaried, nonexempt employee, earns $1,000 per week and has a standard 45-hour workweek.

Hourly compensation: $1,000/45 hours = $22.22 per hour

Overtime rate = $22.22 × 1.5 = $33.33 per hour

Because this employee is classified as nonexempt according to FLSA guidelines, the employee is subject to overtime compensation, and the hourly rate is needed to compute overtime pay.

For the same salaried, nonexempt employee, if the contract between employee and employer stated that all hours ***exceeding*** 45 were considered for overtime, then the individual would need to work 45.25 hours or more in the week to qualify for overtime.

However, *if* the contract stated that only 40 hours were required before overtime rates applied, then the 5 hours would be paid at overtime rates.

Note: A salaried ***exempt*** worker would be paid $1,000 per week regardless of the number of hours worked.

Employers may not prorate a salaried worker's pay when the number of hours worked is fewer than the contractual hour requirement. An exception to this would be time away from work in accordance with the employer's sick or vacation policy. The company would allow employees to take paid time off under either of these programs to supplement their missed wages. Companies may also offer salaried employees the option of leave without pay for missed days; however, contractual hours covered under leave without pay must be documented and signed by both a manager and the employee.

Salary Translation to Hourly Rates

The calculation of gross pay for salaried employees depends on the firm's choice of pay periods. An employee's gross pay is determined by dividing the annual pay by the number of pay periods in a year. For instance, if a firm paid employees on a monthly basis, then the salary calculation would be $\frac{1}{12}$ of the yearly amount. It is occasionally necessary to determine the hourly rate for salaried employees. To get the hourly rate, you would use the following equation:

$$\text{Hourly rate} = \frac{\text{Annual amount}}{\text{Total hours worked per year}}$$

To arrive at the total number of hours worked per year, multiply the number of weeks in a year (52) by the number of hours worked in a standard workweek without overtime.

$$\text{Hourly rate} = \frac{\text{Annual salary}}{\text{Number of hours in a standard workweek} \times 52 \text{ weeks/year}}$$

Because the calculation of overtime, holiday, or vacation time for salaried workers could be based upon the hourly rate of the individual, knowing how to calculate that amount will enable accurate pay.

EXAMPLE

Jackie Ainsley earns a salary of $60,000 per year for ABD Industries. ABD Industries pays its employees on a monthly basis.

Gross pay = $60,000 per year/12 months = $5,000 per month

If she were a ***nonexempt*** employee, it would become necessary to calculate her hourly rate. When calculating the hourly rate, using the correct number of hours in a regular workweek is critical in determining the overtime pay rate. Note the following examples computing the hourly rate using different regular workweeks.

Number of Hours in the Regular Workweek	Annual salary / Number of hours × 52 weeks	Hourly Rate
40	$\frac{60{,}000}{(40 \times 52)}$	$28.85
37.5	$\frac{60{,}000}{(37.5 \times 52)}$	$30.77
35	$\frac{60{,}000}{(35 \times 52)}$	$32.97

What happens if the salaried employee decides to take unpaid leave during a pay period? That amount must be deducted from the gross pay amount. In the case of unpaid leave, the amount of time taken and the number of regular hours in the pay period are the major factors.

EXAMPLE: UNPAID LEAVE

Michelle Barre wants to take two extra days off around a holiday but has no paid time off remaining for the year. The company pays Michelle on a biweekly basis, and there are 80 hours in a pay period. At 8 hours per day, she will be taking 16 hours of unpaid leave (8 hours × 2 days).

Using the example for Michelle's work with ABD Industries with her regular working hours as 40 hours per week, her normal salary is

80 hours × $28.85/hour = $2,308 per pay period

To calculate her pay, including the unpaid leave, we need the proportion of her paycheck that will be unpaid. We calculate the proportion of the total paycheck she will be taking as unpaid leave.

Unpaid portion: 16 hours

Normal hours per pay period: 80

Unpaid portion = 16/80 = 0.20

That means she will receive 100 – 0.20 = 0.80 (or 80 percent) of her normal gross pay.

Gross pay per period with 16 hours unpaid time:

$2,308 × 0.80 = $1,846.40

Note: Using a rounded hourly rate (as shown in this example) to compute period pay will differ from results using nonrounded hourly rates. We have also not separated out the holiday pay intentionally for this example.

In many instances, nonexempt employees are paid on a salary basis to avoid paperwork such as ***time cards*** or pay sheets if they consistently work a fixed number of hours per week. According to 29 CFR 778.113(a), the employer and employee must agree on the standard number of hours to be worked each week for which the employee shall receive fixed pay. If the employee is classified as a nonexempt worker, however, the FLSA requires that these salaried workers are eligible for overtime. For a nonexempt salaried worker, the hourly rate is necessary to compute pay beyond the agreed-upon weekly hours per 29 CFR 778.113(a).

If the employee works less than the agreed-upon number of hours during the week, some states have provisions by which the employee's salary may be reduced. In this case, the hourly rate is again necessary to make sure the gross pay is correctly calculated.

Salaried Workers and Minimum Wage Comparisons

In the case of a salaried nonexempt worker for whom FLSA provisions apply, the fixed weekly salary must adhere to minimum wage guidelines. The minimum wage applies to salaried nonexempt employees whose wages do not exceed $455 per week. The U.S. Department of Labor has established this salary level as one of the tests for exemption from FLSA provisions.

EXAMPLE: SALARIED NONEXEMPT EMPLOYEE PAY

Sally Albritton is a receptionist for KTC Incorporated, located in California. She is salaried and works 40 hours per week, but she is nonexempt because her job classification is nonmanagerial.

If she were paid $275 per week

Hourly wage = $275/40 hours per week = $6.88/hour

This amount is below the federal minimum wage test for exempt employees. Sally would need to be paid a minimum of $290 per week for her work to meet FLSA minimum wage requirements because of her weekly 40-hour work agreement with her employer. To meet this requirement, the employer must contribute additional money to meet the minimum wage requirement.

Hourly Workers

Hourly workers are paid for any hour or fraction of an hour they work. These employees may be either skilled or unskilled. Hourly employees must receive overtime for hours worked in excess of 40 per week, according to FLSA. Overtime is the same for hourly workers as it is for salaried nonexempt workers. Hourly workers may be paid for each minute worked, and the computation of those minutes depends upon company policy. Companies may offer different work shifts and workday lengths, such as four 10-hour shifts or five 8-hour shifts, to reach the 40 hours needed. State regulations may require the company with the 10-hour shifts to file an election to pay no overtime for the two additional hours per day. The reason stated should not be overtime avoidance, but a deemed economic benefit for the longer schedules. For example, setup time in a manufacturing environment can eliminate anywhere from half an hour to an hour of productive time. By working the longer schedules, manufacturing efficiency can be improved.

In Asheville, North Carolina, the city changed the working hours for employees in the public works department to be 10-hour shifts. The change in working hours has led to increased employee satisfaction. Additionally, the department consumed less electricity and natural gas by closing the office one day per week. Although a four-day workweek is not appropriate for all departments and job functions, it is an option that employers may consider. (Source: WLOS)

Hourly Workers in More Than One Job Classification

An employee working for an hourly wage may work in more than one job classification. When this occurs, the employee's pay per classification may vary. For example, a manufacturing employee may work on the sales counter where the pay differential provides an additional $1.50 per hour. When situations like this occur, the payroll accountant must be informed of hours performed for each of the job classifications to provide accurate pay, classification, and reporting. Methods used to communicate this include notes on the time card, schedules provided to the payroll clerk, or job duty notification forms.

EXAMPLE: HOURLY PAY WITH DIFFERENT RATES

Merrill Cabral is an hourly worker for a fast-food establishment and earns $7.25 per hour. He occasionally is the crew chief, during which he receives a $2.00 per hour differential. During a 40-hour workweek, he worked 16 hours as a crew chief and 24 hours as a regular employee. His pay would be calculated as follows:

Regular pay: 24 hours × $7.25/hour = $174

Crew chief pay: $7.25/hour + $2.00/hour differential = $9.25/hour

16 hours × $9.25/hour = $148

Gross pay = $174 + $148 = $322

Commission Work

Commissions are compensation based on a set percentage of the sales revenue for a product or service that the company provides. Commission-based compensation is appropriate in the following types of situations:

- Retail sales personnel.
- Automotive sales personnel.
- Media databases or monitoring that pertains to media relations.
- Marketing sales agents.

EXAMPLE: COMMISSION WORKER PAY

An ice machine company may have sales representatives earning 5 percent commission on all sales made. If sales representative A sells $100,000 worth of ice machines during July, the commission due is computed as follows:

Sales price × Commission rate = $100,000 × 5% = $5,000

Note: Commissions may be contingent upon the company's commissions return/warranty policy.

If sales representative A had returns of $7,500 during August, the commission for that month could be reduced:

Returns × Commission rate = deduction from commissions $7,500 returns × 5% commission rate = $375 deducted from commissions during August

An important classification of a sales representative's job is the difference between inside and outside sales. An inside sales representative is one who conducts business via telephone, email, or other electronic means and may not travel to customer sites. An outside sales representative meets with customers either at the customer's facility or another agreed-upon location. Some inside sales representatives are covered under the FLSA and must receive at least minimum wage for their labors. Outside sales representatives are excluded from minimum wage requirements under FLSA. In a 2010 circuit court decision, the judge ruled that inside sales representatives are nonexempt from FLSA wage and hour provisions, whereas outside sales and retail sales representatives are exempt.

EXAMPLE: INSIDE SALES REPRESENTATIVE, LESS THAN MINIMUM WAGE

Helen Steinel works as an inside sales representative in the company store and receives 5 percent commission for all sales she makes during her shift. During the week, she made 15 sales via telephone with a total dollar value of $1,500.

Commissions = Dollar value of sales × Commission rate

Commissions = $1,500 × 5% = $75

Based upon a 40-hour workweek, she would have effectively earned **$1.88** per hour; thus, the employer would be responsible for meeting the minimum wage requirements under FLSA. The employer would have to adjust Helen's compensation to meet the minimum wage requirements.

EXAMPLE: OUTSIDE SALES REPRESENTATIVE, LESS THAN MINIMUM WAGE

Samantha Durant works as an outside sales representative for the same company. She made sales this week of $2,000 and has an agreed commission percentage of 10 percent of her total sales revenue. Commission = 2,000 × 10% = $200; $200 per week/40 hours = $5.00 hour. Because she is an outside sales representative, she is exempt from minimum wage regulations under FLSA.

Gross Pay for Commission-Based Employees

In situations where the employee is principally engaged in the sale of a product or service but in no way engaged in the manufacturing of the item, a commission pay basis is appropriate. In some states, the commission-based employee may receive commissions for work even after termination if the sale was completed prior to termination. In many ways, commission-based pay is a contract between the employer and the employee to sell a product. The payment for such a contract may not be reneged upon, even after termination of employment. It should be noted that many states prohibit deductions pertaining to the cost of doing business from an employee's commission. In other words, if a customer received a product that was damaged, lost, or otherwise destroyed, the employee's commission would not be affected.

EXAMPLE

Sonja Hinton works as an outside salesperson with Bayfront Watercraft in California. Her whole function with Bayfront is to sell the company's products to customers at the customer's facility or other agreed-upon locations, for which she receives a commission of 5 percent based on the retail price of all sales she makes. During May, she sold $20,000 of products during one week.

Commission = $20,000 × 0.05 = $1,000

Cultura/Image Source

Commission pay can vary by employer, by client, by sales volume, and by employee based on his or her seniority or experience with the company. For instance, sales made by an employee to Client A may have a different commission rate than sales made to Client B, as well as be different for all other clients. Different products may also have varying commission rates, and changes in sales volume can alter commission rates. A sample of a commission-tracking sheet follows.

EXAMPLE: COMMISSION TRACKING SHEET

Salesperson	Client	Product or Service	Total Sales Price	Rate	Commission
Anthony Bauer	Thompson Milbourne	RR-223	$1,245	2%	$24.90
Anthony Bauer	Kockran Heights	RS-447	$2,016	5%	$100.80
Anthony Bauer	Hoptop Ranges	RT-11	$892	3.5%	$31.22

It is important that commissions earned be tracked closely for a variety of reasons:

- Employee pay accuracy.
- Sales employee performance.
- Sales tracking.
- Job order tracking.
- Returns/reductions of commissions paid accuracy.

Commission pay must still meet FLSA minimum wage standards unless the employee is classified as an exempt worker. Similar to salaried nonexempt employees, commission-based employees are subject to the 40-hour workweek as a basis for FLSA minimum wage computations.

EXAMPLE: EFFECTIVE PAY RATE, EXCEED MINIMUM WAGE

In the example concerning Sonja Hinton at Bayfront, Sonja's pay was $1,000 for 40 hours of work.

Sonja's effective wage = $1,000/40 hours = $25/hour

EXAMPLE: EFFECTIVE PAY RATE, LOWER THAN MINIMUM WAGE

Anita deWard, another inside sales, commission-based employee at Bayfront Watercraft, made only $250 in commission for the week during which she worked 40 hours.

Effective hourly rate = $250/40 hours = $6.25/hour

This amount is below the minimum wage in California. It is the employer's responsibility to compensate the employee at the minimum wage, so Bayfront would have to adjust Anita's compensation to meet FLSA requirements.

Piece-Rate Work

Piece-rate work involves paying employees for each unit they manufacture or each action they perform. This type of pay, based on task completion, is one of the oldest forms of performance-based pay. Dating back to the 16th century, piece-rate pay is thought to have evolved from journeyman artisans whose masters paid them per unit they completed. Prior to computations of hourly wages, piece rate was an accurate measure of how productive an employee was. Frederick Taylor wrote about a piece-rate system in 1896, citing that it placed an emphasis on efficiency and production. A criticism of Taylor's analysis, however, is that the piece-rate system overemphasizes production and may create an adversarial relationship between workers and managers.

California's AB 1513, passed in 2016, amended California Labor Code 226.2 and mandated that piece-rate workers be paid for nonproductive time during the workday. Pay during nonproductive time would be at a different rate than the normal piece-rate work. This nonproductive time includes time that the employee is under the employer's control, but not on a rest or recovery break. The argument for paid nonproductive time for piece-rate workers is that the employee remains under the control of the employer despite the lack of productivity. (Source: California Department of Industrial Relations)

FLSA requirements subjected the piece-rate system to minimum wage requirements. Piece-rate workers must be paid no less than the minimum wage for their location, forcing employers to track their work hours accurately. In many ways, piece-rate pay is more difficult to track and to administer than other types of pay. Not only must the employees be compensated for the work they complete, but they are also subject to FLSA minimum and daily break provisions, including lunch and other breaks. Piece-rate work has also fallen under some suspicion regarding the quality of work being performed, this can add additional review to the completed work.

EXAMPLE: PIECE-RATE PAY, EXCEED MINIMUM WAGE

John Samuelson is a piece-rate worker in Tennessee who receives $15 per completed piece of work. During a week, he completes 30 pieces and works 40 hours.

John's pay = $15/per piece completed × 30 pieces completed = $450

Hourly rate equivalent = $450/40 hours = $11.25/hour

John's pay exceeds the FLSA minimum wage for his location, so the employer does not have to adjust John's compensation.

EXAMPLE: PIECE-RATE WORKER, BELOW MINIMUM WAGE

Sarah McDowell works for the same employer as John and receives the same rate of pay. She completes 15 pieces during the week.

Sarah's pay = $15/piece × 15 = $225

Hourly rate equivalent = $225/40 = $5.63/hour

Sarah's pay does not meet the minimum wage requirement, so the employer would have to examine Sarah's work and pay rates to ensure that she meets the FLSA minimum wage requirements.

Joho/Image Source

A wide variety of occupations benefit from piece-rate pay systems. Some of these occupations include

- Vineyard workers
- Installers
- Machinists/fabricators
- Sheep shearers
- Inspectors
- Customer service agents
- Production workers
- Forest workers

The common thread is that each position has output that is quantifiable and linked to some aspect of a manufacturing or service industry. The important part of piece-rate work is that a quantifiable base must be linked with a specified standard rate per amount of work.

Vineyard workers: Tons of grapes harvested
Inspectors: Number of items inspected
Installers: Number of items installed
Customer service agents: Number of customers assisted
Machinists/fabricators: Number of items produced
Sheep shearers: Pounds of wool gathered
Forest workers: Amount of wood cut

At Bayfront Watercraft, the manufacturing department has different types of fabricators, installers, and other production workers in addition to Pat (the hull maker). Let us assume that Joanna works in the upholstery department where she constructs vinyl covers for seats. Rick is in the assembly department and assembles steering mechanisms for the boats.

EXAMPLE: PIECE-RATE COMPUTATION, DIFFERENT EMPLOYEES

Worker	Number of Items	Rate per Item	Gross Pay
Pat Wu	30 hulls	$100	$3,000
Joanna Yoder	100 seat covers	$ 25	$2,500
Rick Karmaran	25 steering mechanisms	$ 40	$1,000

Each worker is compensated based on the work he or she completes. In some companies, workers may work on multiple items for which different rates exist. In cases where one worker completes multiple pieces at different rates, the rates for each different piece must be computed.

EXAMPLE: TOTAL PAY, ONE PIECE-RATE EMPLOYEE

Worker	Item	Number of Items	Pay per Item	Total Pay
John Brichacek	Motor installation	10 motors	$50 per motor	$500
	Rudder installation	15 rudders	$20 per rudder	$300
			Total pay for John:	$800

A separate record for each employee is important in the case of piece-rate pay, especially when the employee works with multiple production items at different rates. Overtime rates for piece-rate workers are computed differently than for hourly workers. Once the standard number of pieces per hour is determined, the amount per hour per piece can be computed.

EXAMPLE: PIECE RATE WITH OVERTIME PAY

Bayfront determines that 50 ignition assemblies can reasonably be completed in a 40-hour workweek by one worker. Ignition assemblies are paid at a rate of $25 per assembly.

Standard amount paid per 40-hour workweek: $1,250

50 assemblies × $25/assembly = $1,250

Hourly amount = $1,250/40 hours = $31.25/hour

If the employee worked overtime, the rate would be computed as follows:

Overtime rate = Regular hourly rate × 1.5 = $46.875

If an employee worked a 45-hour workweek, the pay would be computed as

Standard amount per week + Overtime pay

= $1,250/40-hour week + ($46.875/hour × 5 hours overtime)

= $1,484.375, which would be $1,484.38 (rounded)

According to FLSA provisions, piece-rate workers must have a standard number of items that can be reasonably completed each day that allows for breaks and rest periods. To increase compensation, it could be very easy for an employee to engage in overwork so that he or she could complete more items. According to 29 CFR 525.12(h)(2)(ii), piece-rate employees must have a standard number of items per period, and most are subject to minimum wage provisions.

Computations for Different Bases

Stop & Check

1. Natasha Uttrecht is a marketing representative who earns a 3 percent commission based on the revenue earned from the marketing campaigns she completes. During the current pay period, she completed a marketing campaign with $224,800 revenue. How much commission will she receive from this campaign?
2. Jeremy Wikander is a specialty artisan for a luxury car maker based in South Carolina. He makes handcrafted dashboards and receives $550.00 per completed assembly. During a semimonthly pay period, he completes two dashboard assemblies and works 90 hours. How much does he receive for the completion of the assemblies? Does this amount comply with minimum wage requirements? Explain.
3. Lanea Kiehn is a salaried worker making $57,000 per year for a company using biweekly payroll. Her standard schedule is 40 hours over five days per week. She has used all of her vacation time prior to this pay period and fell ill for three days. What effect does this have on the current pay period? Will her gross pay be the same as if she had vacation time available? (Note: Only round final calculations.)

Blend Images LLC

LO 3-3 Calculate Pay Based on Hours and Fractions of Hours

Employees, both salaried nonexempt and hourly, are paid based upon the number of hours, or fractions thereof, worked. The payroll accountant must learn how to convert a fraction of a 60-minute clock into a fraction of 100. While accounting software packages are able to convert minutes into payable units, typically the payroll accountant does this math. Fortunately, the math for this calculation is fairly straightforward.

EXAMPLE: CONVERSION OF MINUTES TO DECIMALS AND FRACTIONS

If an employee works 30 minutes, then the computation for pay purposes is

30 minutes ÷ 60 minutes/hour = 0.5 hour or 50/100

If an employee works 33 minutes, the payroll computation is

33 minutes ÷ 60 minutes/hour = 0.55 hour, or 55/100*

Note: This calculation is necessary when the employer pays using the hundredth-hour method instead of the quarter-hour method. If this had been a quarter-hour computation, the number of minutes would have been rounded to the closest 15-minute increment, which is 0.50 hour.

Calculations of employee wages are broken down by the hour or fraction thereof. Regardless of the classification of employee, a determination of pay per pay period causes the payroll accountant to break down all wages. Salaries are determined based upon a yearly salary and therefore need to be broken down per pay period (monthly, bimonthly, weekly, or biweekly). Companies may pay employees by fractions of an hour (hundredth-hour basis) or by the quarter-hour (rounded to the nearest 15-minute interval), depending upon company policy. The next section will walk you through the calculations of both the hundredth and quarterly processes.

Hourly Calculations

Depending on the company's policy, time payments can be paid either by the individual minute or rounded to the nearest designated interval. Hourly calculations are a combination of minutes and hours. Hours are broken into two categories: regular and overtime. When determining the hourly wage for a salaried individual, the number of average hours required under the salary must be known.

EXAMPLE: HOURLY WAGE COMPUTATION, SALARIED EMPLOYEE

If a manager is expected to work 45 hours per week at $75,000 per year, the effective hourly wage would be

$75,000/(45 × 52 weeks) = $75,000/2,340 = $32.05 per hour

EXAMPLE: WEEKLY PAY INCLUDING PAID SICK TIME

Jason Taylor worked four days during the payroll week. He worked 7.5 hours the first day, 8.75 hours the second day, 7 hours the third day, and 9.5 hours the fourth day. He used 8 hours of his paid sick time on one day during the week. He is paid overtime for any hours worked in excess of 40 per week.

Regular hours: 7.5 + 8.75 + 7 + 9.5 = 32.75 hours

He will also receive 8 hours of sick time.

Jason's gross pay = 32.75 regular hours + 8 sick = 40.75 hours

Even though Jason has more than 40 hours on his payroll, 8 are not considered "worked" and would therefore not be included in the calculation for the determination of overtime.

EXAMPLE: WEEKLY PAY INCLUDING PAID HOLIDAY TIME

Karen Golliff worked four days during the week with a holiday on Monday. Her hours worked were 8.25 hours the first day, 9 hours the second day, 7.75 hours the third day, and 8.5 hours the fourth day. The company pays 8 hours for the holiday. She is paid for any hours worked in excess of 40 hours per week.

Regular hours: 8.25 + 9 + 7.75 + 8.5 = 33.5 hours

She will also be paid 8 hours regular pay for the holiday.

Karen's gross pay will contain **41.5** hours of regular pay, which includes **8** hours of holiday pay. Karen has not worked in excess of 40 hours because the holiday is not included in *worked* hours, so she will not receive overtime.

Quarter-Hour System

Some employers compensate employees based upon rounding working hours to the nearest 15 minutes, a system widely known as the ***quarter-hour system***. The payroll accountant becomes responsible for rounding the time either up or down consistently across all individuals

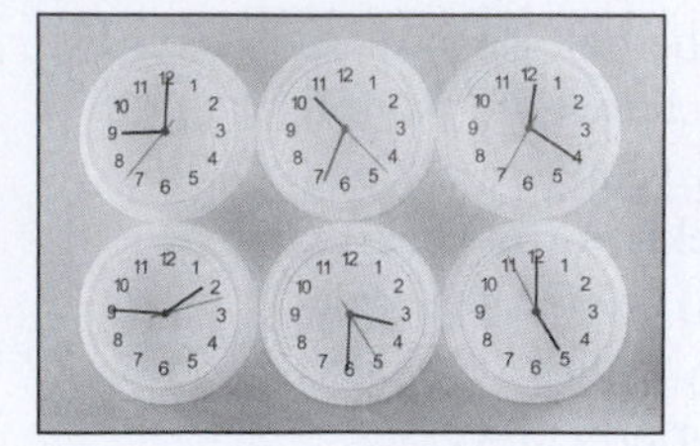
Image Source

and pay periods. If an individual worked 8 hours and 6 minutes, he would be paid for 8 hours. However, if that same individual were to work for 8 hours and 10 minutes, he would be paid for 8 hours plus 15 minutes of overtime, if the company pays for overtime on any hours worked over 8 in a day.

EXAMPLE: ROUNDING MINUTES FOR THE QUARTER HOUR SYSTEM

0–7 minutes past the previous 15-minute interval rounds down to the previous 15-minute interval.

Example: 10:06 a.m. would count as 10:00 a.m. in the quarter-hour system.

8–15 minutes past the previous 15-minute interval rounds up to the next 15-minute interval.

Example: 10:09 a.m. would count as 10:15 a.m. in the quarter-hour system.

EXAMPLE: QUARTER-HOUR SYSTEM COMPUTATION, ROUNDING TO PREVIOUS QUARTER-HOUR

Amanda Leong worked from 8 a.m. until noon. She took one hour for lunch and returned to work at 1 p.m. At the end of the day, Amanda ended up leaving work at 4:20 p.m. Using the quarter-hour system:

From 8 a.m. to noon: 4 hours

From 1 p.m. to 4:20 p.m.: 3.25 hours

because 4:20 p.m. rounds down to 4:15 p.m. under the quarter-hour system.

Total time: 4 + 3.25 = 7.25 hours

EXAMPLE: QUARTER-HOUR SYSTEM COMPUTATION, ROUNDING TO NEXT QUARTER-HOUR

Justin Fretwell worked from 8 a.m. until 12:30 p.m. before taking a half-hour lunch. He returned at 1 p.m. and worked until 4:10 p.m. His employer pays on the quarter-hour system, so Justin would be paid as follows:

From 8 a.m. to 12:30 p.m.: 4 hours, 30 minutes = 4.5 hours

From 1 p.m. to 4:10 p.m.: 3.25 hours

because 4:10 p.m. rounds up to 4:15 p.m. under the quarter-hour system.

Total time for the day: 7.75 hours

Hundredth-Hour System

The ***hundredth-hour system*** is similar to the quarter-hour system in that it calculates partial hours of work performed. Instead of rounding the employee's time to 15-minute intervals, the hundredth-hour system divides the hour into increments. The calculation of partial minutes is simple:

$$\text{Conversion of minutes to hundredth hour} = \frac{\text{Number of minutes in partial hour}}{\text{60 minutes per hour}}$$

EXAMPLE: CONVERSION FROM MINUTES TO HUNDREDTH-HOUR

If an employee worked 4 hours and 16 minutes,

4 hours + 16 minutes/60 minutes per hour = 4.27 hours

EXAMPLE: HUNDREDTH-HOUR TIME COMPUTATION

Leslie Mellor works an 8-hour shift that had 15 minutes of additional overtime. Her normal hourly rate is $10/hour. Her pay would be computed as follows:

8 hours × $10 per hour = $80 regular pay

15 minutes overtime = 15/60 = 0.25 hour

Overtime = 0.25 hours × $10/hour × 1.5 = $3.75

Total pay for the day = $80 + $3.75 = $83.75

Following is an example of how the time may appear on an individual's time card. Note that an employer should choose only one method of computing partial hours—quarter-hours or hundredth-hours—and apply it to all situations and all employees.

EXAMPLE: QUARTER-HOUR COMPUTATION, WEEKLY PAY DETAILS

Amanda Parker: Employee Number 1776M

Clock In	Clock Out	Clock In	Clock Out	Hours Worked
08:00	11:00	12:00	16:54	7 hours 54 minutes = 8.00 hours
08:00	11:30	12:30	17:05	8 hours 5 minutes = 8.00 hours
07:00	12:09	13:15	17:30	9 hours 24 minutes = 9.5 hours
07:30	12:21 rounds down	13:24	17:30	8 hours 57 minutes = 8.75 hours
			Total	34.25 hours

Notice in the next example how the same employee with the same time worked would have different hourly computations based on hundredth-hour computations. The difference in the hourly computations leads to a difference in compensation for the period.

EXAMPLE: HUNDREDTH-HOUR COMPUTATION, WEEKLY PAY DETAILS

Amanda Parker: Employee Number 1776M

Clock In	Clock Out	Clock In	Clock Out	Hours Worked
08:00	11:00	12:00	16:54	7 hours, 54 minutes = 7.9 hours
08:00	11:30	12:30	17:05	8 hours, 5 minutes = 8.08 hours
07:00	12:09	13:15	17:30	9 hours, 24 minutes = 9.4 hours
07:30	12:21	13:24	17:30	8 hours, 57 minutes = 8.95 hours
			Total	34.33 hours

LO 3-4 Calculate Overtime in Various Situations

Nonexempt employee overtime may occur in a variety of situations. When an employee works past the FLSA maximum hours per week, the employee must be compensated at a rate of 1.5 times the regular hourly rate. However, situations exist when employees must be compensated at more than the standard overtime premium, and others exist when exempt employees may receive overtime pay. We will explore examples of overtime compensation in a variety of situations.

Quarter-Hour vs. Hundredth-Hour

Stop & Check

1. Blue Sky Manufacturing has historically paid its employees according to the quarter-hour system. Software changes have caused them to change to the hundredth-hour system. What is the number of hours worked under the quarter-hour system? What is the time worked under the hundredth-hour system?

Employee	Time In	Time Out	Time In	Time Out	Total
Ann Gottlieb	8:06 a.m.	12:25 p.m.	1:20 p.m.	4:57 p.m.	Quarter-hour: Hundredth:
Nevada Lofkin	7:58 a.m.	12:02 p.m.	1:02 p.m.	5:05 p.m.	Quarter-hour: Hundredth:
Pat Blackburn	8:32 a.m.	11:54 a.m.	1:05 p.m.	5:32 p.m.	Quarter-hour: Hundredth:

2. Why do discrepancies exist between the quarter-hour time and the hundredth-hour time totals?
3. Why would it be worthwhile for Blue Sky Manufacturing to switch to the hundredth-hour system?

grinvalds/123RF

Standard Overtime Pay

In general, FLSA-stipulated overtime includes any hours worked in excess of 40 during a 7-day, 168-hour week. No limit on the number of hours that an employee may work per week exists for employees over the age of 16. No legislation stipulates that employees must be paid at overtime rates on Saturdays and Sundays as long as the total number of hours worked is less than 40 during a period of seven consecutive days. An important fact to note is that the regular pay rate may not be below the legal minimum wage, especially in the case when overtime pay has been earned.

According to the Bureau of Labor Statistics, the average number of weekly overtime hours as of 2019 was 3.5 per employee. Although this may seem to be a relatively low number, employee overtime can become a significant amount for a large employer. As an example, corrections officers in King County, Washington, worked in excess of 188,000 overtime hours during 2018. (Sources: BLS, *Seattle Times*)

The first example explains basic overtime pay computation for a nonexempt employee with a 40-hour workweek. The second part of the example reflects the payment of a bonus as a normal part of the employee's pay. Overtime in situations involving commission are computed in the same manner.

EXAMPLE: NONEXEMPT PAY CALCULATION

Monique Martin works as a maintenance worker at a busy office building. She earns $52,000 annually, is paid weekly, and is classified as nonexempt. Her standard workweek is 40 hours. Since Monique is classified as a nonexempt worker, she is eligible to receive overtime for any hours worked in excess of 40 per week per her employment contract.

During the pay period ending April 22, Monique worked 50 hours. As a result, Monique would receive her weekly pay *plus* overtime calculated to include the non-discretionary bonus.

To determine her hourly wage, divide her annual pay by the total hours worked during the year. Her gross earnings for the April 22 pay period would be as follows:

Name	M/S	#W/H	Hourly Rate	No. of Regular Hours	No. of Overtime Hours	Regular Earnings	Overtime Earnings	Gross Earnings	401(k)	Insurance	Taxable Wages for Federal W/H	Taxable Wages for FICA
Monique Martin	S	1	25.00	40	10	1,000.00	375.00	1,375.00				

Note that Monique's regular pay and her overtime pay are calculated separately and then added together to determine the gross pay.

Hourly rate plus bonus

If Monique was eligible for a bonus as part of her employment agreement, her bonus would be added to her regular pay to determine the hourly rate on which the overtime is based. In this example, if Monique received a $120 bonus for her work, the overtime computation would be as follows:

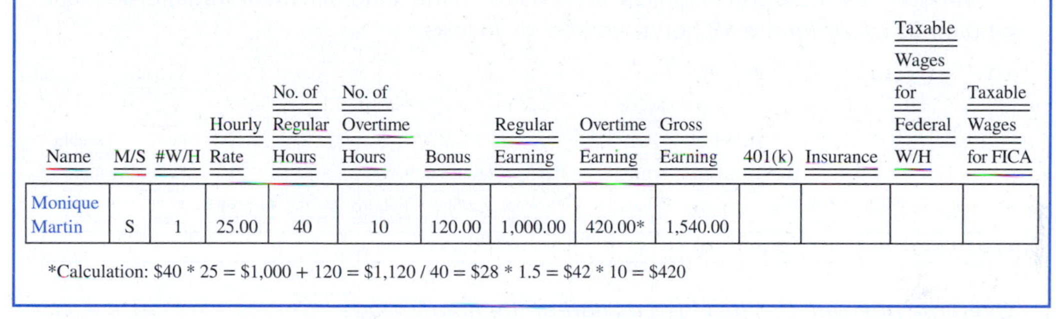

Name	M/S	#W/H	Hourly Rate	No. of Regular Hours	No. of Overtime Hours	Bonus	Regular Earning	Overtime Earning	Gross Earning	401(k)	Insurance	Taxable Wages for Federal W/H	Taxable Wages for FICA
Monique Martin	S	1	25.00	40	10	120.00	1,000.00	420.00*	1,540.00				

*Calculation: $40 * 25 = $1,000 + 120 = $1,120 / 40 = $28 * 1.5 = $42 * 10 = $420

Overtime for Employees of Hospitals and Residential Care Facilities

One instance when the overtime computation differs from the standard rate involves employees who work at hospitals and residential care facilities. FLSA section 7(j) applies a rule to these workers known as the ***Eight and Eighty (8 and 80)*** rule. According to the 8 and 80 rule, the number of consecutive days is 14 instead of 7; similarly, the threshold for overtime is 80 hours during the work period instead of 40. An example reflecting the 8 and 80 rule follows.

EXAMPLE: 8 AND 80 OVERTIME CALCULATION

Victor Garner is a Licensed Professional Nurse (LPN) at Fountainside Hospital. During the period starting June 5 and ending June 18, he worked 95 hours. Victor is classified as nonexempt and earns an hourly wage of $31.50. Victor's pay for the two-week period would be as follows:

Name	M/S	#W/H	Hourly Rate	No. of Regular Hours	No. of Overtime Hours	Regular Earning	Overtime Earning	Gross Earning	401(k)	Insurance	Taxable Wages for Federal W/H	Taxable Wages for FICA
Victor Garner	S	1	31.50	80	15	2,520.00	708.75	3,228.75				

Note that the first 80 hours are paid at the regular hourly rate. The 15 additional hours are paid at the overtime premium rate.

A study conducted by New York University found that new nurses work 12-hours shifts on average and most average 39.4 hours per week. Of these new nurses, about half reported working mandatory overtime. (Source: *Medical Express*)

Tipped Employee Overtime

Another overtime situation involves tipped employees. According to the FLSA, employers may consider tips earned by the employee when computing overtime pay. A best practice when the employer chooses to use the tips earned as part of the overtime computation is to notify the employee in advance that their tips will be included in the overtime pay calculation. An example of both situations, with and without tips included, will show how the wage computations differ.

EXAMPLE: TIPPED EMPLOYEE OVERTIME

Elsie Morales is a nonexempt tipped employee at the Love House Bar and Grill in Arvada, Colorado. The minimum cash wage in Colorado is $8.08 per hour, and the tip credit is $3.02 per hour (i.e., the minimum wage for Colorado is $11.10 per hour). During the pay period beginning January 30, 2019, and ending February 5, 2019, Elsie worked 48 hours and earned $300 in tips.

Without the consideration of tips, and based on the state minimum wage, Elsie must be paid $577.20 for the 48 hours worked, as follows:

Name	M/S	#W/H	Hourly Rate	No. of Regular Hours	No. of Over-time Hours	Tips	Regular Earning	Overtime Earning	Gross Earning	401(k)	Insurance	Taxable Wages for Federal W/H	Taxable Wages for FICA
Elsie Morales	S	1	11.10	40	8		444.00	133.20	577.20				

Overtime pay with tips included as part of the hourly wage

If the employer counted the $300 in tips earned toward the minimum cash overtime wage, Elsie would not be eligible for any further compensation for the overtime because the gross earnings exceed the minimum due.

Name	M/S	#W/H	Hourly Rate	No. of Regular Hours	No. of Over-time Hours	Tips	Regular Earning	Overtime Earning	Gross Earning	401(k)	Insurance	Taxable Wages for Federal W/H	Taxable Wages for FICA
Elsie Morales	S	1	8.08	40	8	300.00	323.20	186.96	810.16				

Earnings calculation

Regular earnings: $300 + 23.20 = $323.20.

Overtime earnings: $623.20/40 = $15.58/hour × 1.5 = $23.37 × 80 = 188.96

Overtime pay excluding tips as part of the hourly wage

If the employer did not count Elsie's tips toward the hourly wage, her pay would be computed as follows:

Name	M/S	#W/H	Hourly Rate	No. of Regular Hours	No. of Over-time Hours	Tips	Regular Earning	Overtime Earning	Gross Earning	401(k)	Insurance	Taxable Wages for Federal W/H	Taxable Wages for FICA
Elsie Morales	S	1	8.08	40	8		323.20	96.96	420.16				

In this case, the employer would need to pay Elsie the difference between the minimum wage and the minimum tipped wage:

$577.20 – $420.16 = $157.04

Piece-Rate Employee Overtime

Piece-rate workers are eligible for overtime on a similar basis to hourly nonexempt employees. However, because they are paid on a piece-rate basis, the overtime computation is based on the number of pieces completed and the total number of productive hours worked during the consecutive seven-day period.

EXAMPLE: PIECE-RATE EMPLOYEE OVERTIME

Edmund Dennis is a piece-rate employee at Snowy Day Sculptures in Terrace Lake, New Mexico. He earns $75 per finished sculpture. During the week of February 27, he worked 48.5 hours and completed 12 sculptures. He is paid minimum wage (i.e., $7.50 per hour) for nonproductive time; during the week of February 27, he had four hours of nonproductive time. His overtime would be calculated based on the productive time of 44.5 hours as follows:

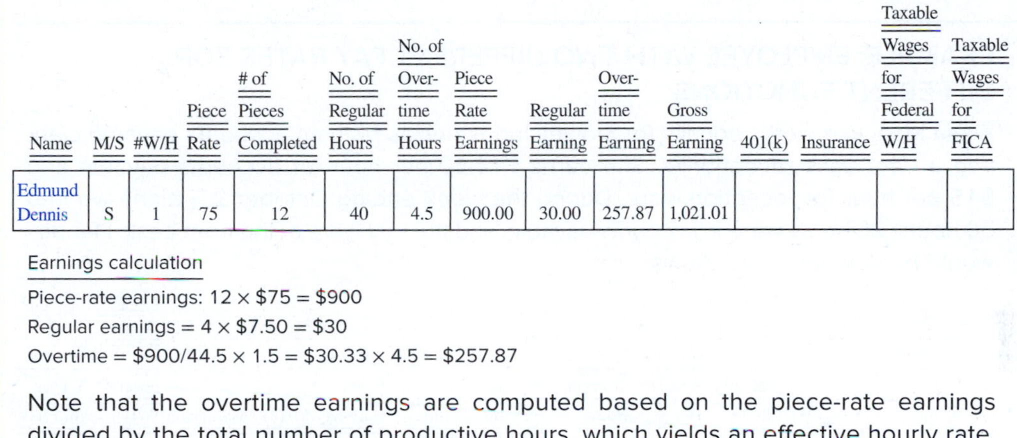

Name	M/S	#W/H	Piece Rate	# of Pieces Completed	No. of Regular Hours	No. of Overtime Hours	Piece Rate Earnings	Regular Earning	Overtime Earning	Gross Earning	401(k)	Insurance	Taxable Wages for Federal W/H	Taxable Wages for FICA
Edmund Dennis	S	1	75	12	40	4.5	900.00	30.00	257.87	1,021.01				

Earnings calculation

Piece-rate earnings: 12 × $75 = $900

Regular earnings = 4 × $7.50 = $30

Overtime = $900/44.5 × 1.5 = $30.33 × 4.5 = $257.87

Note that the overtime earnings are computed based on the piece-rate earnings divided by the total number of productive hours, which yields an effective hourly rate. That hourly rate is multiplied by 1.5 and the number of overtime productive hours to determine the overtime pay.

Salaried Nonexempt Overtime

In cases when the employee is a salaried nonexempt worker, the standard number of working hours per week depends on the hiring agreement. If the number of hours agreed upon is 40 per week, then the standard overtime examples should be followed. However, if the number of agreed-upon hours is 45 per week, then the overtime is calculated using 45 hours to determine the hourly rate and time worked in excess of 45 hours is subject to overtime premiums. The same principle applies to employees who work four 10-hour shifts, shifts that have differential rates, or other similar arrangements.

EXAMPLE: SALARIED NONEXEMPT POSITION WITH A NORMAL 45-HOUR WORK SCHEDULE

Clay Curtis is an administrator for Strickland Farms and earns $52,000 annually, paid biweekly. He is a salaried nonexempt employee with a standard 45-hour workweek. During the two-week pay period ending September 25th, Clay worked 99 hours. His overtime would be computed as follows:

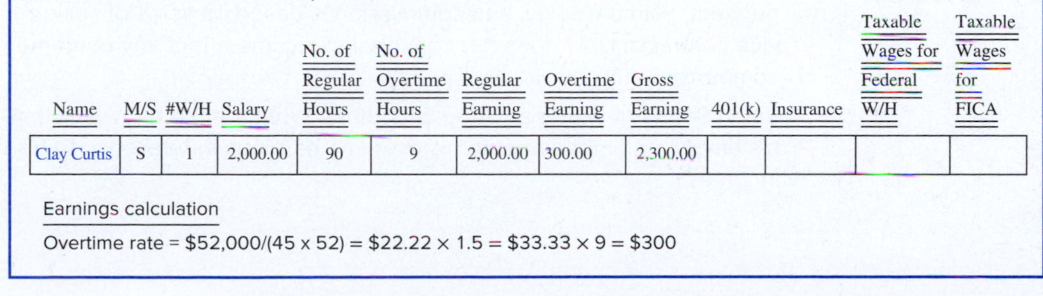

Name	M/S	#W/H	Salary	No. of Regular Hours	No. of Overtime Hours	Regular Earning	Overtime Earning	Gross Earning	401(k)	Insurance	Taxable Wages for Federal W/H	Taxable Wages for FICA
Clay Curtis	S	1	2,000.00	90	9	2,000.00	300.00	2,300.00				

Earnings calculation

Overtime rate = $52,000/(45 x 52) = $22.22 × 1.5 = $33.33 × 9 = $300

Edwin de Luz Trucking and Gravel LLC was ordered to pay nearly $60,000 in back pay and wages due to a failure to record all time worked. The discrepancy resulted from the company's policy of automatically deducting the mandatory 30-minute lunch break from every worker, regardless of the actual time taken. Accurate record keeping is critical for compliance with FLSA regulations. (Source: *KHON*)

Overtime for Employees Who Work in Two or More Separate Functions

Suppose an employee works in two separate functions in the company and earns a different rate for each function. For example, the employee may work in accounts payable and as a front desk receptionist, each with different pay rates. In this case, the overtime rate is calculated using the average of the two pay rates.

EXAMPLE: EMPLOYEE WITH TWO DIFFERENT PAY RATES FOR DIFFERENT FUNCTIONS

Kiana Mancuso works equally for Sidwell Industries as both an accounts payable clerk and a front desk receptionist. She earns $18.50 per hour for accounts payable and $15 per hour for reception work. During the week ending October 27, Kiana worked 50 hours; 26 hours were in accounts payable, and the rest were at the front desk. Her pay would be computed as follows:

Name	M/S	#W/H	Hourly Rate	No. of Regular Hours	No. of Overtime Hours	Regular Earning	Overtime Earning	Gross Earning	401(k)	Insurance	Taxable Wages for Federal W/H	Taxable Wages for FICA
Kiana Mancuso—accounts payable	S	1	18.50	20	6	370.00	166.50	536.50				
Kiana Mancuso—front desk	S	1	15.00	20	4	300.00	90.00	390.00				
Total Earnings								926.50				

Note that company policies on overtime pay may vary from the situations described. When in doubt, the payroll accountant should refer to the FLSA overtime calculator advisor published by the U.S. Department of Labor.

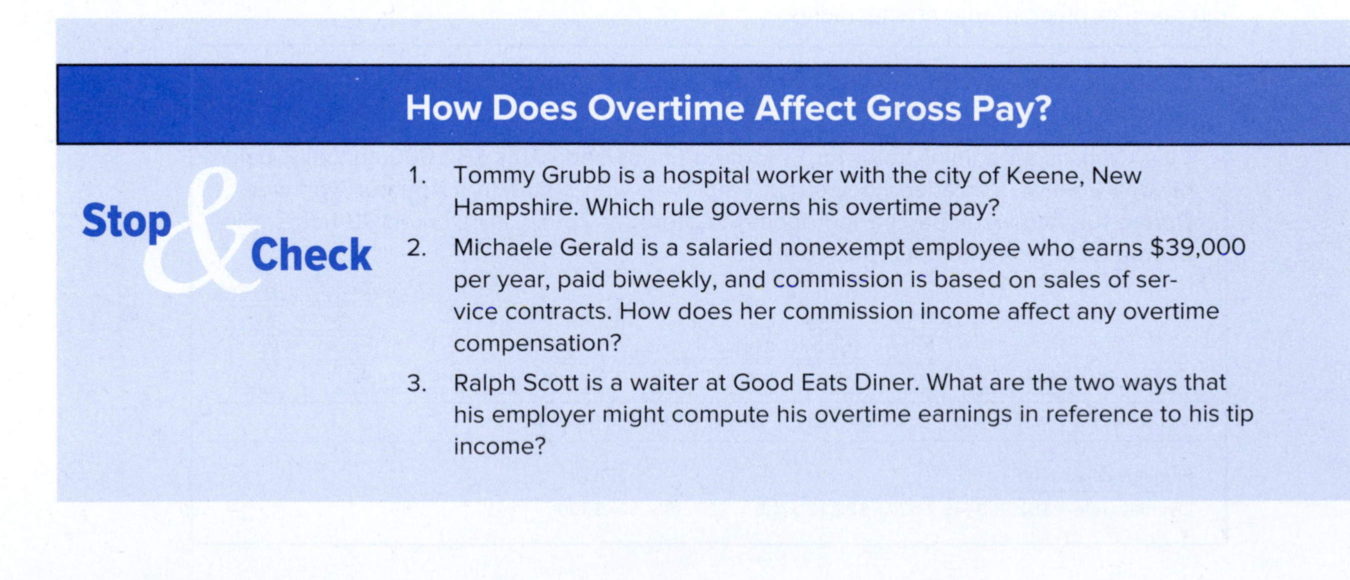

How Does Overtime Affect Gross Pay?

Stop & Check

1. Tommy Grubb is a hospital worker with the city of Keene, New Hampshire. Which rule governs his overtime pay?
2. Michaele Gerald is a salaried nonexempt employee who earns $39,000 per year, paid biweekly, and commission is based on sales of service contracts. How does her commission income affect any overtime compensation?
3. Ralph Scott is a waiter at Good Eats Diner. What are the two ways that his employer might compute his overtime earnings in reference to his tip income?

LO 3-5 Create a Payroll Register

A ***payroll register*** is the payroll accountant's internal tool that helps ensure accuracy of employee compensation. A payroll register can be completed manually, in a spreadsheet program such as Microsoft Excel, in accounting software programs such as QuickBooks, or by payroll outsourcing companies such as ADP or Paychex. Like other worksheets that accountants use, the payroll register is a company confidential document that is subject to the rules about document retention and destruction.

Payroll Register Data

The payroll register is annotated at the top with the beginning and ending dates of the payroll period. Each employee has a separate row in the register. The register contains columns to reflect each employee's specific pay information, such as

1. Employee name.
2. Marital status.
3. Number of withholdings.
4. Salary or hourly rate.
5. Number of regular hours worked.
6. Number of overtime hours worked.
7. Regular pay.
8. Overtime pay.
9. Gross pay.
10. Federal income tax withheld.
11. Social Security tax withheld.
12. Medicare tax withheld.
13. State income tax withheld (where applicable).
14. Other state taxes.
15. Local taxes (if applicable).
16. 401(k) or other retirement plan deductions.
17. Insurance deductions.
18. Garnishments or levies.
19. Union dues.
20. Any other deductions.
21. Net pay.
22. Check or payment ID number.

It may seem tedious to complete a register each payroll period, but the register offers more information than just the employee compensation. The register also contains information about employer liabilities for taxes and the employees' voluntary deductions that the employer must remit to the appropriate places at a future date. A sample payroll register is shown in Figure 3-2.

Note that other columns may be added to meet the company's needs. Other columns that may appear on a payroll register include commission, piece rate, standby hours, and sleep time. The purpose of the payroll register is to both document the employees' time and hours worked and provide totals of the compensation for each category. Employers use these categorizations as part of labor analysis and planning tasks.

A separate payroll register is maintained for each pay period. To ensure accuracy, the accountant totals, proves, and rules the register.

FIGURE 3-2
Sample Payroll Register

P/R End Date
Check Date
Company Name

Name	M/S	# W/H	Hourly Rate or Period Wage	# Regular Hours	# Overtime Hours	# Holiday Hours	Commis-sions	Gross Earnings	401(k)	Sec 125	Taxable Wages for Federal W/H	Taxable Wages for FICA
Totals								-	-	-	-	-

Name	Gross Earnings	Taxable Wages for Federal W/H	Taxable Wages for FICA	Federal W/H	Social Security Tax	State W/H Tax	Medicare W/H	Net Pay	Check No.
Totals	-	-	-	-	-	-	-	-	

WHAT DO *TOTAL, PROVE,* AND *RULE* MEAN?

Total: Each column and row are totaled.

Prove: The column totals are added horizontally *and* row totals are totaled vertically. The aggregate column and row totals must be equal.

Rule: Column totals are double underlined to show that the totals have been totaled.

Track Employee Compensation Using a Payroll Register

The payroll register is a tool used by payroll accountants to ensure accurate tracking of employee compensation. The following examples will demonstrate different scenarios using a payroll register.

EXAMPLE 1: WAGE PAYMENTS, NO OVERTIME

Jon Ames is a nonexempt, hourly employee of CM Bakeries. He receives $12.50/hour and receives overtime for any time worked in excess of 40 hours/week. He is single with one withholding allowance. During the week ending April 25 he worked 37 hours. The payroll register would appear as follows:

Name	M/S	#W/H	Hourly Rate or Period Wage	No. of Regular Hours	No. of Overtime Hours	No. of Holiday Hours	Commissions	Gross Earnings
Jon Ames	S	1	$12.50	37				$462.50

In Example 1, the employee's hourly rate is multiplied by the number of hours worked to obtain the gross pay for the period. The use of the Regular Earnings column is introduced here, although no overtime exists. Example 2 will show how overtime is included in a payroll register.

EXAMPLE 2: WAGE PAYMENT WITH OVERTIME

Mike Brown is a nonexempt, hourly employee of Strong Coffee Company and earns $18.50/hour. He is married with two withholding allowances. He receives overtime for any hours worked in excess of 40 during a weekly period. During the period ended September 20, he worked 45.75 hours. The payroll register would appear as follows:

Name	M/S	#W/H	Hourly Rate or Period Wage	No. of Regular Hours	No. of Overtime Hours	Reg. Earnings	Overtime Earnings	Gross Earnings
Mike Brown	M	2	$18.50	40	5.75	$740.00	$159.56*	$899.56

*Overtime earning = $18.50/hour × 5.75 hours × 1.5 (overtime premium) = $159.56

Notice that the payroll register in Example 2 is expanded to include a breakdown of regular earnings and overtime earnings. The purpose of this practice is to facilitate computations, ensure accuracy, and allow for future analysis of overtime worked during a given period.

Example 3 contains a payroll register for a salaried, exempt employee. Notice the difference in the columns used to record the period salary.

EXAMPLE 3: SALARY PAYMENT

Rae Smith is a manager at Hartshorn Industries. She is a salaried, exempt employee and is married with four withholding allowances. She earns a salary of $2,000 per pay period. For the period ending July 31, the payroll register would appear as follows:

Name	M/S	#W/H	Hourly Rate or Period Wage	No. of Regular Hours	No. of Overtime Hours	No. of Holiday Hours	Commissions	Gross Earnings
Rae Smith	M	4	$2,000.00					$2,000.00

In a company, it is common to have both salaried and hourly employees, and all employees must be represented on a payroll register. Example 4 contains employees with pay variations that commonly exist in business.

EXAMPLE 4: PAYROLL REGISTER FOR MULTIPLE EMPLOYEES

PBL Freight pays its employees on a biweekly basis. The standard workweek for hourly employees is 40 hours, and employees receive overtime pay for any hours worked in excess of 40 during a week. The following payroll register is for the period ending March 22:

Name	M/S	#W/H	Hourly Rate or Period Wage	No. of Regular Hours	No. of Overtime Hours	Reg. Earnings	Overtime Earnings	Gross Earnings
Mary Jahn	S	1	$ 15.25	40		$ 610.00		$ 610.00
John Charles	M	3	$2,750.00			$2.750.00		$ 2.750.00
Ranea Hu	M	5	$ 21.50	40	6	$ 860.00	$193.50	$ 1,053.50
						$4,220.00	$193.50	$ 4,413.50

Notice how the columns are totaled in Example 4. Each earnings column is totaled vertically, and the double underline (i.e., ruling) denotes that the computations are concluded. The total in the bottom-right corner proves that the sum of the rows in the Gross Earnings column equals the total of the Regular Earnings and Overtime Earnings columns. Once the payroll register is totaled, proved, and ruled, then it is ready for the next step in the payroll process.

The Payroll Register

Stop & Check

1. What is the purpose of the payroll register?
2. What are five of the columns that usually appear in a payroll register?
3. Why are computations for regular hours and overtime hours entered in different columns?

LO 3-6 Apply Combination Pay Methods

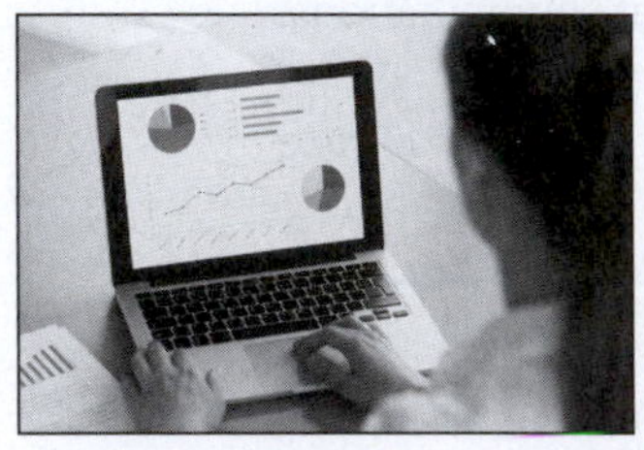

fizkes/Shutterstock

Employers often offer their employees ***combination pay*** methods. Sometimes the employee performs two different jobs for the same employer, and those two tasks have different compensation bases. Other situations involve payroll-based incentives that link to company productivity. Note how the payroll register reflects these combination pay methods.

Base Salary Plus Commission

A common method includes a base salary plus a commission or piece rate, depending on the nature of the work performed. Another method is a combination of salary plus hourly compensation that reflects a standard set of work hours plus additional hours that are paid only when worked. The purpose of the combination pay method is to meet minimum wage requirements and encourage employees to achieve sales or production goals. The base salary offers both the employer and the employee a level of stability in pay amounts because they will know the minimum amount of compensation for each pay period. Whatever the employees earn above the base salary may vary from pay period to pay period, depending on the employee's capabilities, production needs, and customer needs.

EXAMPLE: BASE SALARY PLUS COMMISSION

Henri Jay is a salaried, exempt employee of Night Lights Security. He is single with two withholding allowances. His compensation package includes commission based on sales of security system packages to customers. During the pay period ending January 15, he earned $1,500 in salary and 4 percent commission on $10,000 of sales.

Commission = $10,000 × 0.04 = $400

Name	M/S	#W/H	Hourly Rate or Period Wage	No. of Regular Hours	No. of Overtime Hours	No. of Holiday Hours	Commissions	Gross Earnings
Henri Jay	S	2	$1,500.00				$ 400.00	$1,900.00

Many types of jobs have a combination pay method because it has been found to boost employee productivity and maintain FLSA compliance. Some jobs that use combination pay methods include

Ariel Skelley/Blend Images LLC

- District managers
- Recruiters
- Farm workers
- Account executives
- Retail sales workers
- Real estate salespersons

To compute combination pay methods, knowledge of the employee's base salary plus variable rate is essential.

EXAMPLE: DIFFERENT COMBINATION METHODS, SAME COMPANY

Todd Jones is an account executive for Bayfront Watercraft. He earns a base salary of $36,000 plus a commission of 0.5 percent on each sale he makes. He is married with six withholding allowances. Suppose that Todd sold $100,000 of boats during a two-week pay period ending June 15.

Base salary = $36,000/26 = $1,384.62.

Commission = $100,000 × 0.5% = $500.

Total pay for Todd: $1,884.62

The payroll register for Todd's June 15 pay would appear as

Name	M/S	#W/H	Hourly Rate or Period Wage	No. of Regular Hours	No. of Overtime Hours	Piece Rate Pay	Commissions	Gross Earnings
Todd Jones	M	6	$1,384.62				$500.00	$1,884.62

Maria Dee installs the seating in the boats for Bayfront Watercraft. She is single with one withholding allowance. In her position, she earns a base salary of $26,000 per year plus a piece rate of $100 for each boat completed during the pay period. During the pay period, Maria installed the seating for eight boats.

Salary = $26,000/26 = $1,000

Piece-rate pay = $100 × 8 = $800

Total Pay for Maria: $1,800

The payroll register including both employees for the June 15 pay period would appear as follows:

Name	M/S	#W/H	Hourly Rate or Period Wage	No. of Regular Hours	No. of Overtime Hours	Piece Rate Pay	Commissions	Gross Earnings
Todd Jones	M	6	$1,384.62				$500.00	$1,884.62
Maria Dee	S	1	$1,000.00			$800.00		$1.800.00
Totals						$800.00	$500.00	$3,684.62

Like any other type of pay method, the important element in computing combination pay is accurate maintenance of the base salary, the variable rate, and the number of items or sales for which the variable rate must apply. Use of the payroll register facilitates the computations and ensures the accuracy of the employees' gross pay.

Payroll Draw

A special situation in commission-based pay is a situation called a ***draw***. A draw generally involves an employee whose regular compensation is little more than the minimum wage, such as a retail sales position. Employees have sales goals they must meet and receive compensation on a commission basis once they meet or exceed those sales goals. If the sales goal is not met, the employee may draw salary against future commissions. The expectation with a draw is that the employee will eventually generate enough sales to cover any draws during pay periods when sales revenues were lower than expected.

A draw is generally associated with a commission-only job in which the employer allows new employees to receive money for expected future commissions. With a draw, it is implied that the draw may occur on a regular basis. However, paying employees solely on the basis of commission and draw has been challenged on the basis that it does not recognize employee rest breaks and nonproductive time. In *Bermudez Vaquero v. Stoneledge Furniture LLC,* the court upheld the FLSA rules regarding mandatory rest breaks. (Source: FindLaw)

Salary Plus Commission and Draw

Salaried employees who receive commission may be eligible to draw against that commission at the company's discretion. This pay combination could be for external salespeople who have commission as a relatively large portion of their regular income.

EXAMPLE: SALARY PLUS COMMISSION AND DRAW

Kari Lee is an employee in the sales department of Fastball Sports. She is single with one withholding allowance, and her annual base salary is $12,000, paid monthly. She is expected to earn between $1,000 and $3,000 in sales commissions each month and may draw up to $3,000 per month against future earnings

During October, she earned $1,000 in commissions in addition to her salary. She decided to take an additional $1,000 draw against her future earnings. The payroll register would reflect this compensation as follows:

Name	M/S	#W/H	Hourly Rate or Period Wage	No. of Regular Hours	No. of Overtime Hours	Reg. Earnings	Draw	Commissions	Gross Earnings
Kari Lee	S	1	$1,000.00			$1,000.00	$ 1,000.00	$1,000.00	$3,000.00

In this case, Kari could have withdrawn up to $3,000 against future earnings. If her employment is terminated before she earns enough sales commission to repay the draw, she will have to repay the company for that money. It is important to keep track of employee draws to ensure that the employee repays the draw.

Another example where the company may allow individuals to draw on their payroll exists when the pay period is monthly. In this situation, many employers allow their employees to draw up to 30–40 percent of their wages at mid-month. Some organizations may not withhold taxes from the draw, and the employee will have the full amount of taxes withdrawn upon the next payroll.

EXAMPLE: SALARY PLUS DRAW, EMPLOYEE INELIGIBLE FOR COMMISSION

Scott Fay is a new salesperson with Bayfront Watercraft, hired on September 24. He receives a base salary of $19,500 per year, paid biweekly, plus a 5 percent commission on sales once he achieves his sales quota of $20,000 during a pay period. During the pay period ending September 30, Scott closed $10,000 in sales, making him ineligible for a commission for September. He is eligible to draw up to the minimum commission for the pay period, which is $20,000 × 5%, or $1,000. The payroll register would reflect his pay as follows:

Name	M/S	#W/H	Hourly Rate or Period Wage	No. of Regular Hours	No. of Overtime Hours	Reg. Earnings	Draw	Commissions	Gross Earnings
Scott Fay	S	1	$750.00			$750.00	$1,000.00		$1,750.00

Period salary = $19,500/26 pay periods = $750.00
Commission draw = $20,000 × 0.05 = $1,000.00.

Employers must be careful when allowing employees to draw against future wages. A written and signed authorization must be obtained from the employee that specifies when the draw will be deducted from the employee's future wages to avoid legal issues with deductions, such as wage garnishments, that could be affected by the draw.

tupungato/Getty Images

Incentive Stock Options (ISOs)

Other employee compensation plans, known as ***incentive stock options (ISOs)***, allow an employee to report a small base salary for tax purposes and to be issued company stock that must be held for a certain period before being sold. In some instances, the stock option may be exercised after three months of employment, and in other cases it may be after one year of employment. The purpose of ISO stock option plans is a deferral of taxes and salary liabilities for the employer and employee. This type of compensation is often found in executive pay packages.

In the class action lawsuit *McElrath v. Uber Technologies,* the plaintiff stated that employees were offered an ISO as a significant part of the compensation package. The issue arose because Uber had accelerated the exercisability of its ISOs to make the compensation attractive. However, when employees exercised their options, the company refused to allow employees to receive the promised compensation on a tax-deferred basis that is consistent with an ISO. Instead, Uber changed the ISOs to nonqualified stock options (NSOs), which changed the taxation on the employee compensation. (Source: *Courthouse News*)

EXAMPLE: EXECUTIVE SALARY WITH ISO

Leo Wilde was hired as a regional manager with Amificat International. Amificat International's stock had a market price of $25 per share when Leo was hired. He was offered an annual salary of $78,000 paid biweekly and an ISO of 1,000 shares at $25 per share that could be exercised 1 year after his hire date.

Biweekly salary = $78,000/26 = $3,000

Note that the ISO, valued at $25,000 at the time of hire, may not be exercised for one year. The value of the stock option would depend on the market price on the date that Leo exercised the stock option by selling his shares. In any case, the ISO does not appear on the payroll register but would be included in the total compensation for the employee.

Combination Pay Methods

Stop & Check

1. Shelly Penzo, a service administrator, receives a base salary of $42,000 per year paid semimonthly, plus $100 commission for each service contract she sells to her customers. During a pay period, she sells five contracts. What is her gross pay for the period?
2. Adam Reininger is a new salesperson with S&D Music. He receives a base salary of $36,000 paid monthly. Company policy allows him to draw 35 percent of his salary on the 15th of each month. How much will Adam receive at mid-month if he elects to take a draw? How much will he receive at the end of the month if he takes the 35 percent draw?
3. Joy Mrowicki, an executive for Adarma Chemicals, receives an annual salary of $75,000 plus an additional 3 percent in an ISO. What is the amount of stock she receives annually? What is her total annual compensation?

LO 3-7 Explain Special Pay Situations

Compensation laws have many exceptions. According to the FLSA, every aspect of labor legislation, including minimum wage and overtime provisions, has its less common applications. The introduction of new types of knowledge-based employment during the 21st century, as well as the continuance of more traditional agricultural tasks, necessitates an examination of these special pay situations.

Digital Vision/Getty Images

Compensatory Time

The FLSA allows public employees to receive ***compensatory (comp) time***, often called "comp time," in lieu of overtime. According to section 3(s)(1)(c) of the FLSA, exempt public employees must receive comp time equal to 1.5 times the overtime hours worked. Therefore, if a public employee worked five hours of overtime, the comp time awarded must be 7.5 hours.

Comp time is often misconstrued by the private sector. FLSA provisions for comp time are only for public-sector employees, such as government workers, law enforcement, and seasonally hired laborers. Unless specifically designated by a firm's policies, a private-sector employer is not required to offer comp time. Additionally, many private-sector employers offer comp time on a straight-line basis, meaning that they offer the same number of compensatory hours as the number of overtime hours worked. Firefighters, police, and other emergency workers may receive a maximum of 480 comp hours annually; other public-sector employees are eligible for up to 240 hours of comp time based upon union negotiated contracts. Some union comp time contracts will only cover specific peak periods for the work being performed.

When calculating an employee's gross pay, it is prudent to be aware of any effects that a comp time award may have on overtime pay to ensure that the employee's compensation is accurate.

EXAMPLE: PUBLIC EMPLOYEE COMPENSATORY TIME

David Donahue works as an exempt employee of the federal government. In the course of his work, he accrues 8 hours of overtime during a pay period when he completes additional work for an absent co-worker. According to FLSA regulations, David must receive 12 hours of comp time because he is not eligible for paid overtime as an exempt government employee.

On-Call Time

Some professions require employees to be available for work outside of normal working hours. This availability is known as ***on-call time***, and two classes of on-call time exist: on-call at the employer's premises and on-call away from the employer's premises.

- If the employee is required to remain at the employer's premises, the employee's freedom is restricted, and he or she must be compensated for the on-call time.
- If the employee is not restricted to the employer's premises for the on-call time, compensation is not required.

In California, Proposition 11 in 2018 changed pay for on-call breaks for ambulance providers. Passage of this proposition allowed ambulance providers to be paid at their regular rate of pay during meal breaks and rest breaks. It also required ambulance providers to maintain staffing levels that allow employees to take these paid breaks. (Source: Balletopedia)

In either case, company policy must be specific regarding the conditions of the on-call time. The number of hours specified for on-call compensation must be added to the employee's gross pay. Company policy should also be specific about the pay rate for the on-call time, especially if the pay rate differs from the employee's regular pay rate.

EXAMPLE: ON-CALL TIME

Kevin Gee works as a service representative for Built Strong, an equipment manufacturer. He earns $19.25/hour for a standard 40-hour workweek and is married with two withholding allowances. Built Strong requires that each service representative rotate on-call duties in one-week increments, during which they remain available for service calls outside of working hours but may otherwise engage in personal activities. During this on-call time, company policy stipulates that on-call service representatives receive two hours of regular pay for each on-call day. Kevin was on-call during the biweekly pay period ending February 25 and would receive 14 hours of additional straight-time pay for his on-call time. The payroll register would reflect the on-call pay as follows:

Name	M/S	#W/H	Hourly Rate or Period Wage	No. of Regular Hours	No. of On-Call Hours	Reg. Earnings	On-Call Earnings	Gross Earnings
Kevin Gee	M	2	$19.25	80	14	$1,540.00	$269.50	$1,809.50

Sleep Time, Travel Time, and Wait Time

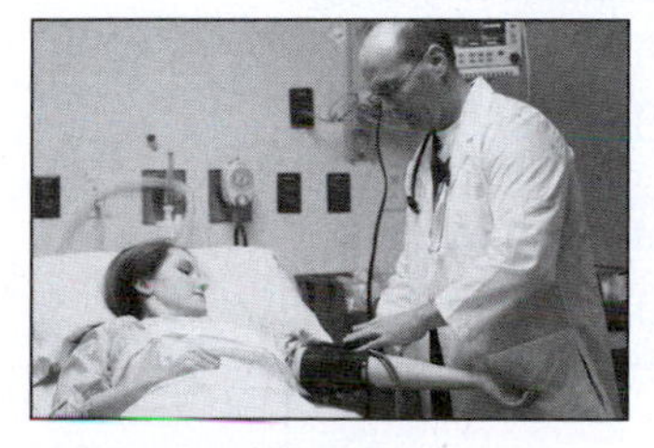

M. Constantini/PhotoAlto

Employees have traditionally commuted to and from work, although a growing trend toward telecommuting exists in the 21st century. Travel to and from an office is not compensable time; however, many employees do not work at a single location. Additionally, many employees travel for their employer's benefit for training or other business requirements. Similarly, employees may be required to wait by their employer, as in the case of a chauffeur or a bus driver. Other employees such as firefighters or medical personnel may be required to work 24-hour shifts and must be given at least five hours of paid ***sleep time*** during that 24-hour period. An agreement between the employer and employee may exist to exclude up to eight hours if the employer provides furnished facilities for uninterrupted sleep.

According to FLSA, the guideline that assists in the determination of compensable activity in these three situations is if the activity is for the employer's benefit. Travel among customer- or business-related sites is compensable as ***travel time*** because it directly benefits the employer. Requiring a driver to wait as part of the job description also benefits the employer and is compensated as ***wait time***. Travel from the employee's home to the office or to the first customer site in the morning and returning home in the evening benefits the employee and is not compensable.

EXAMPLE: SLEEP TIME

Dan Morli is a first-year surgical resident at Mercy Hospital and is classified as an nonexempt employee who earns $124,000 per year, paid semimonthly. The standard workweek is 40 hours. He is single with one withholding allowance. He works two 24-hour shifts per week in the regular course of his employment. His employer provides him a quiet sleeping area, per FLSA requirements. During a single 24-hour shift in the November 15 pay period, he sleeps 7 hours. According to FLSA guidelines, his pay may not be reduced for the first five hours that he sleeps. Dan's gross pay will reflect a two-hour reduction for the additional sleep in excess of the five-hour requirement.

The hourly rate needs to be computed to determine the deduction for the excess sleep time: $124,000/(40 × 52) = $59.62

(continued)

(concluded)

The payroll register would appear as follows:

Name	M/S	#W/H	Hourly Rate or Period Wage	Hourly Rate	Sleep Hours > 5	Reg. Earnings	Less Excess Sleep Time	Gross Earnings
Dan Morli	S	1	$5,166.67	$59.62	2	$5,166.67	$(119.24)	$5,047.43

Note the inclusion of the sleep hours in excess of five and the deduction. The purpose for tracking this information is to highlight specific issues with employee performance and related costs, which leads to stronger managerial control.

moodboard/Getty Images

Jury Duty

Employees may be summoned to serve on a jury for court cases. In the event that an employee is required to serve jury duty, the pay given to employees for the time spent away from work in this capacity is at the discretion of the employer. Some employers pay their employees their full compensation, while others pay a predetermined alternate amount. If an employee receives full compensation while on jury duty, the company may require the employee to return or reject the jury duty pay.

Sub-Minimum Wage Situations

Tipped employees are not the only workers who may legally receive compensation lower than the minimum wage. Other specific classes of employees may receive an hourly wage that is less than the FLSA minimum wage.

A 1996 amendment to the FLSA allows workers younger than the age of 20 to be paid a minimum wage of $4.25 per hour, but only for the first 90 calendar days of employment.

Note that overtime worked by employees who are paid at sub-minimum wage rates may not be less than the federal minimum wage.

EXAMPLE: YOUNG EMPLOYEE

Cady Horn is a new employee of The Big Chicken, a fast-food restaurant in Glendale, Arizona, where new employees are paid minimum wage. Cady is 18 years of age and is single with one withholding allowance. During the weekly pay period ending July 18, she worked 37 hours. The payroll register would appear as follows:

Name	M/S	#W/H	Hourly Rate or Period Wage	No. of Regular Hours	No. of Overtime Hours	Reg. Earnings	Gross Earnings
Cady Horn	S	1	$4.25	37		$157.25	$157.25

Terry Vine/Blend Images

An employer may obtain a certificate to pay a worker with disabilities related to the work performed an amount less than the minimum wage. According to section 14(c) of the FLSA, employers must obtain a certificate to pay less than the minimum wage.

EXAMPLE: DISABLED WORKER

Christi Snow is employed as a call-center representative with OEC Dispatch in Bend, Oregon. She is disabled due to a hearing impairment, and OEC Dispatch has obtained a certificate under section 14(c) of the FLSA in order to pay Christi $10/hour, which is less than the Oregon minimum wage of $10.75/hour. During the weekly pay period ending March 10, Christi worked 44 hours, 4 hours of which were overtime. She is single with three withholding allowances. The payroll register for the period would appear as follows:

Name	M/S	#W/H	Hourly Rate or Period Wage	No. of Regular Hours	No. of Overtime Hours	Reg. Earning	Overtime Earnings	Gross Earnings
Christi Snow	S	3	$10.00	40	4	$400.00	$60.00	$460.00

Full-time students in the employ of retail establishments, agriculture, colleges, and universities may receive a wage that is 85 percent of the federal minimum wage. Like disabled employees, the employer must obtain a certificate authorizing the sub-minimum wage.

EXAMPLE: FULL-TIME STUDENT WAGE

Kay Stone works in the café at Valparaiso University in Valparaiso, Indiana. She is a full-time student of the university and is 20 years old. According to the FLSA, she may receive 85 percent of the minimum wage.

Indiana minimum wage: $7.25/hour

Full-time student wage = $7.25/hour × 0.85 = $6.16/hour

In her employment at the café, Katie may legally be paid $6.16 per hour while she is a full-time student. During the week of May 4, she worked 35 hours. She is single with two withholding allowances. The payroll register would appear as follows:

Name	M/S	#W/H	Hourly Rate or Period Wage	No. of Regular Hours	No. of Overtime Hours	Reg. Earning	Overtime Earnings	Gross Earnings
Kay Stone	S	2	$6.16	35		$215.60		$215.60

According to section 14(a) of the FLSA, student learners in vocational education programs may be paid at a rate of 75 percent of the federal minimum wage. Similar to situations involving disabled employees, the employer must obtain a certificate authorizing the sub-minimum wage.

EXAMPLE: STUDENT WORKER IN VOCATIONAL EDUCATION PROGRAM

Ben Yoo is enrolled at Middlebury High School in Maine and is taking a shop class as part of his program. Ben is 16 and is single with one withholding allowance. He works for Vining's Cabinets as an apprentice woodworker. After obtaining a certificate from the U.S. Department of Labor's Wage and Hour National Certification Team, Vining's Cabinets pays Ben an hourly wage of $8.25 because of his enrollment in the shop class at his high school. During the weekly pay period ending December 18, Ben worked 36 hours. The payroll register would reflect his pay as follows:

Name	M/S	#W/H	Hourly Rate or Period Wage	No. of Regular Hours	No. of Overtime Hours	Reg. Earnings	Overtime Earnings	Gross Earnings
Ben Yoo	S	1	$8.25	36		$297.00		$297.00

Nonqualified Deferred Compensation

Certain employees may be subject to the nonqualified deferred compensation provisions of IRS Code section 409(a). Nonquaified deferred compensation pertains to employees who earn compensation in one period but elect to receive it in a later period. A common example of this practice involves teachers who work during the nine-month academic year but elect to receive compensation for 12 months. Under section 409(a), this type of compensation is taxed like any other employee pay.

Sam Edwards/Glow Images

Pension Payments

Employers occasionally offer pension plans to their employees. The percent of employees who participate in employer-sponsored pensions has decreased due to the availability of alternate retirement plans (i.e., 401(k), 403(b), etc.), and pension funding has experienced shortfalls among both private and governmental employers. When the pension enters the payout period, the retired employee receives their pension less any federal tax due. FICA taxes do not apply to pension plan payments.

Retroactive Pay

If an employee is due pay retroactively ("back pay") because of compensation increases or labor union negotiations, the wages must be issued at the earliest time and all applicable taxes are due. To receive back pay, the FLSA has three methods available:

1. The Department of Labor's Wage and Hour Division may provide supervision for the payment.
2. A lawsuit for back pay *plus* an equal amount of damages may be brought by the Secretary of Labor.
3. The employee may initiate a lawsuit for the back pay *plus* an equal amount of damages *plus* attorney's fees and court costs.

It is important to note that the statute of limitations for back pay lawsuits is two years. However, if willful nonpayment can be proven, the statute of limitations is three years.

In early 2019, the Gilroy (California) Federation of Paraeducators came to an agreement to grant pay raises to educational support staff that was retroactive to July 1, 2017. This pay raise was spread incrementally over two fiscal years to spread the impact on the school district's budget. (Source: *Gilroy Dispatch*)

Wages for Deceased Employees

If an employee dies while a current employee of a firm, it is important to understand the payroll implications associated with gross pay. IRS guidelines stipulate that wages earned prior to the employee's death must be paid as accurately as possible to reflect the amount of work performed. A special note about deceased employee pay is that the employee's pay, if issued specifically in a check form, may need to be reissued to the deceased employee's estate.

What Is the Correct Pay?

Stop & Check

1. Alex Longwith is a nonexempt employee of The Silver Club. He works 10 hours of overtime during a pay period and requests that he receive compensatory time instead of overtime pay. The Silver Club's overtime policy states that that compensatory time may be offered at 1.5 times the number of hours worked in excess of 40. His employer grants his request and offers him 10 hours of compensatory time. How much comp time should Alex receive? Explain.
2. Stacy Albom is a student in a vocational program at a cosmetology school. She accepts employment as a shampooer at Cuts & Styles Hair Salon in Alabama. The agreement between the school and the salon is that students receive the student-learner minimum wage. How much should Stacy be paid per hour?

EMPLOYEE COMPENSATION

Employee compensation tends to be a hot topic because of the way it affects people on a personal level. Some developments since 2015 in employee compensation include the following:

- Increased diligence in overtime tracking and compensation following a lawsuit involving large companies.
- New types of incentive pay to increase employee engagement, including merchandise rewards, additional company benefits, and other nonmonetary awards.
- Discussions of the legality of differential pay levels for travel time by nonexempt employees.
- Discussions about gaps in wages between people with and without a college education.

Some trends to watch in employee compensation include the following:

- Positive exclusion of overtime wages from gross pay to allow employees to realize more of their overtime compensation.
- Work toward establishing consistency in calculations of paid sick leave.
- Further clarification of wage and hour requirements, which were defined by FLSA but have different interpretations among states.
- Guidance about workforce management and alignment with software packages to recognize recent legislation regarding wage and hour laws.
- Flexibility in workforce management software packages to accommodate employee paid time off requests.
- One of the more common payroll errors reported by Department of Labor is the calculation of overtime when bonuses are concerned. There is a proposed clarification to 29 CFR Section 778 and 548 that is currently open for comment. This includes non-discretionary bonuses and commission pay into the determination of regular wage rate for overtime calculations.

Summary of Gross Pay Computation

Gross pay is the employee's compensation before taxes and other withholdings are deducted; net pay is the amount of money an employee receives after taxes and other deductions are subtracted. We discussed the different types of methods for pay computation, including salary, hourly, commission, and piece-rate pay. Gross pay is complex and a variety of combinations exist to meet the needs of the traditional and the gig economies.

We looked at the effect of FLSA provisions and applicability of different compensation methods and offered examples of some job classifications that could be compensated using different methods. We discussed the use of a payroll register in computing gross pay and explored the concepts of total, prove, and rule to ensure accurate computation of gross pay.

We explored a variety of situations involving overtime pay and discussed the computations for different pay bases. We concluded with a discussion of special compensation situations, including on-call time, time spent unoccupied for the employer's benefit, and situations in which an employee may receive less than the FLSA minimum wage. The conclusion had an explanation of retroactive pay and other less-common pay situations.

Key Points

- Gross pay is the total amount earned by an employee prior to the deductions for taxes or other withholdings.
- Employees may be subject to the wage and hour provisions of the FLSA (nonexempt) or they may not (exempt), depending on the type of job and employee duties.
- Nonexempt hourly employees are compensated on a basis that recognizes an economic connection between work performed and wages paid.

- Nonexempt salaried employees work a fixed number of working hours per week and receive overtime compensation.
- Exempt employees receive a fixed salary and may work more hours than their nonexempt colleagues.
- Commission-based pay connects employee compensation with sales revenue.
- Piece-rate pay compensates employees based on the manufacturing or completion of goods or services.
- The payroll register is an integral tool to ensure the accuracy of payroll computations, especially in combination pay situations.
- Employees may have the option to draw against future earnings.
- ISOs are a means of offering compensation on a tax-deferred basis that is connected to the market price of the company's stock.
- Compensatory time is legally required for public-sector exempt employees and may be offered to private-sector employees at the employer's discretion.
- Overtime pay is computed according to the guidelines published by the IRS, as appropriate to the employee's pay base.
- Employees may be compensated for time that they are unoccupied if they are required to be available for the employer's benefit.
- Retroactive "back pay" and pension pay are situations requiring additional care in processing to avoid lawsuits.
- In certain circumstances, employees may receive less than the FLSA minimum wage.

Vocabulary

Combination pay
Commission
Compensatory (comp) time
Draw
Eight and Eighty (8 and 80)
Exempt
Gross pay
Hourly
Hundredth-hour system
Incentive stock options (ISOs)
Minimum wage
Net pay
Nonexempt
On-call time
Overtime
Payroll register
Piece rate
Prove
Quarter-hour system
Rule
Salary
Sleep time
Time card
Tipped employee
Tipped wages
Total
Travel time
Wait time

Review Questions

1. How is overtime pay computed for nonexempt, salaried workers?
2. When do overtime rates apply?
3. How does minimum wage affect commission employees?
4. How does the tipped minimum wage differ from the FLSA minimum wage?
5. What types of occupations are typically salaried?
6. What is an ISO, and how does it affect employee pay?
7. What is the difference between a salary and a draw?
8. How is overtime computed for piece-rate employees?
9. In what situations could a salaried employee receive overtime pay?
10. What is the primary difference between commission work and piece-rate work?
11. In what situations might an employee draw money against his or her future pay?
12. What is the difference between quarter-hour and hundredth-hour pay?
13. Why are companies moving toward the hundredth-hour system?
14. What is comp time?
15. Under what circumstances may an employee receive compensation for on-call time?

16. When are wait time, travel time, and sleep time compensable?
17. Aside from tipped employees, under what circumstances may an employee receive less than the FLSA minimum wage?
18. What is one of the three methods for employees to receive retroactive pay?

Exercises Set A

E3-1A. LO 3-1
Thomas Wilson is a minimum wage worker in Nevada. He is contemplating a move to another state. Which of the following states would be the most favorable in terms of the highest minimum wage? (Select all that apply).
1. Idaho
2. California
3. Utah
4. Arizona

E3-2A. LO 3-1
Certain types of businesses are always covered by FLSA provisions. Which of the following businesses are always covered by FLSA? (Select all that apply.)
1. Fruit stands selling only locally obtained goods that conduct no interstate business.
2. A school for children with learning disabilities.
3. A privately run hospital.
4. A Social Security Administration branch office.

E3-3A. LO 3-1
Marion Barker is a tipped employee in Wisconsin. What is the minimum cash wage for her state?
1. $2.13/hour
2. $2.33/hour
3. $3.32/hour
4. $4.93/hour

E3-4A. LO 3-1
Rick Richards, a waiter at the Misosis Club in Pennsylvania, receives the tipped minimum wage. During a 40-hour workweek, how much must he earn in tips to meet the minimum wage requirement?
1. $85.20
2. $113.20
3. $176.80
4. $204.80

E3-5A. LO 3-2
Marty Burgess works for Hyrolated Sports. His compensation is based on sales of store products to customers. Which type of pay basis represents Marty's pay?
1. Piece rate
2. Hourly
3. Commission
4. Salary

E3-6A. LO 3-3
Lana Reid is an accounting clerk at Tenity Enterprises who is paid $18.15 per hour. During a week's pay period, she worked 39 hours and 41 minutes. Based on a hundredth-hour pay method, what is her gross pay for the period? (Round the final answer to two decimal places.)
1. $726.00
2. $721.46
3. $716.93
4. $720.25

E3-7A. LO 3-4
According to the FLSA, what is the basis used to determine overtime worked for standard nonexempt workers?
1. The 8 and 80 rule.
2. The excess over 40 hours during a pay period.
3. The excess over 40 hours in seven consecutive days.
4. The excess over 8 hours in a 24-hour period.

E3-8A. LO 3-4

Eugene Torres works in a shared role for Multiglass Computers. He works in both the programming and the research departments for the company and splits his time equally in both roles. Eugene is paid $20 per hour in the programming department and $28 per hour in the research department. When he works overtime in the research department, what is his pay rate?

1. $30 per hour
2. $36 per hour
3. $42 per hour
4. $48 per hour

E3-9A. LO 3-5

Of the items in the following list, which one(s) should appear in a payroll register? (Select all that apply.)

1. Name
2. Marital status
3. Shifts worked
4. Hours worked

E3-10A. LO 3-5

Tricia Grey is a salaried, exempt employee with Meganti Inc. She is single with one withholding allowance and earns $45,000 per year. Complete the payroll register for the biweekly pay period ending June 10, 20XX.

Company:							Period Ended:				
Name	M/S	#W/H	Period Wage	Period Salary	Commissions	Draw	No. of Regular Hours	No. of Overtime Hours	Reg. Earnings	Overtime Earnings	Gross Earnings

E3-11A. LO 3-6

Jeremy Ortiz is an employee of Insulor Flooring, where his job responsibilities include selling service contracts to customers. Jeremy is single with two withholding allowances. He receives an annual salary of $36,000 and receives a 3 percent commission on all sales. During the semimonthly pay period ending September 29, 20XX, Jeremy sold $12,500 of service contracts. Complete the payroll register for the September 29 pay period.

Company:							Period Ended:				
Name	M/S	#W/H	Period Wage	Period Salary	Commissions	Draw	No. of Regular Hours	No. of Overtime Hours	Reg. Earnings	Overtime Earnings	Gross Earnings

E3-12A. LO 3-7

Jude Sizemore is a full-time student at Sioux City College in Sioux City, Iowa, where he works in the library. What is the minimum hourly wage that he may receive?

1. $7.25
2. $6.50
2. $6.16
4. $5.44

Problems Set A

P3-1A. LO 3-3

Edie Manson worked the following schedule: Monday, 8 hours; Tuesday, 9 hours; Wednesday, 7 hours 48 minutes; Thursday, 8 hours; Friday, 8 hours. The employer pays overtime for all time worked in excess of 40 hours per week. Complete the following table. Determine Edie's total time worked according to the (a) quarter-hour method and (b) the hundredth-hour method. Which is the more favorable method for Edie, quarter-hour or hundredth-hour?

	Quarter-Hour Time	Hundredth-Hour Time	More Favorable Method
E. Manson			

P3-2A. LO 3-2 Bobby Howard is a salaried exempt employee at Coric Industries. He is married with two withholding allowances. His contract stipulates a 40-hour workweek at $47,500 per year. During the week ending November 27, there was a company paid holiday for one day. Calculate Bobby's weekly pay. Round wages to five decimal points.

Name	M/S	#W/H	Annual Salary	Hourly Rate	No. of Regular Hours	Holiday Hours	Reg. Earnings	Holiday Earnings	Gross Earnings

P3-3A. LO 3-2 Cheryl Bryant completed designing 22 custom cakes on her 18-cake contract as an employee of Frontier Wedding Planners. There is a bonus earned if the individual exceeds 145 percent of her piece contract. How many cakes must Cheryl complete in the remainder of the week to receive the bonus?

P3-4A. LO 3-5 Ernest Miller works for Skyescent Parachutes. He is a shared employee; he works in the manufacturing department and has been trained to work the sales counter in times of need. During other employees' vacations, he was asked to work in the sales department two days for six hours each day. When he works in the manufacturing department, he earns $15.50 per hour. Ernest earns a $2.50 pay differential for working the sales counter. He worked a total of 39 hours and 32 minutes during the week. Ernest is single with one withholding allowance. Compute Ernest's pay for the week ending May 26 using the quarter-hour system. (Use a separate line for each job classification.)

Name	M/S	#W/H	Hourly Rate	No. of Regular Hours	Reg. Earnings	Gross Earnings

P3-5A. LO 3-3 Marcell Teague submitted a pay card reflecting the following hours worked at Kicy Inc. He earns $16.02 per hour. The company pays overtime only on hours worked exceeding 40 per week. The company is considering changing from quarter-hour to hundredth-hour time collection. Under the current quarter-hour system, each time the employee clocks in or out, the time is rounded to the nearest quarter-hour. Calculate Marcell's time for both the quarter-hour and hundredth-hour systems. (Round your intermediate calculations and final answers to two decimal places.)

In	Out	In	Out	Total Hours with Quarter-Hour	Total Hours with Hundredth-Hour
8:00	11:22	12:17	5:22		
7:29	12:30	1:45	4:10		
9:12	11:45	12:28	3:36		
8:00	11:00	12:02	5:00		

What is Marcell's total pay in a quarter-hour system?___________
What is Marcell's total pay in a hundredth-hour system? ___________

P3-6A. LO 3-4 Ranee Tolliver is a nurse at Great Meadows Hospital. She is paid $28 per hour and has a 40-hour standard workweek. During the biweekly pay period from May 15–28, she worked a total of 95 hours. What is her gross pay?

P3-7A.
LO 3-5

Terry McNutt, a single employee with two withholding allowances, is paid $12 per hour and receives commission on net sales. He does not receive a commission until his net sales exceed $150,000. Once the minimum net sales is reached, he receives 4 percent commission on all of his sales at Skidoo Sports. During the week of January 23, he sold $87,000 of ski equipment; however, he had $2,250 of returns from the prior week's sales. Company policy requires that commissions on sales returns are deducted from the employee's pay, regardless of current commission earnings. Compute Terry's gross pay for the 40 hour weekly pay period.

Name	M/S	#W/H	Hourly Rate	No. of Regular Hours	Reg. Earnings	Commissions	Gross Earnings

P3-8A.
LO 3-1, 3-2

Renata McCarter, an outside sales representative for Alinda Publications, receives 15 percent commission on all new magazine subscriptions she sells in her sales territory. During the week of March 27, she sold $4,500 of new subscriptions and worked 40 hours.

What is her gross pay?____________

Is she subject to minimum wage laws?____________

Why or why not?____________

P3-9A.
LO 3-1, 3-2

Telemarketers receive $15 commission on all new customers they sign up for cell phone service through Movill Networks. Each telemarketer works 40 hours. The company ran a competition this week to see who could sign up the most new people and the winner would get a bonus of $75. Because these employees are paid solely on commission, the employer must ensure that they earn the federal minimum wage for 40 hours each week. Compute the gross pay for each of the following outbound sales representatives.

Employee	Number of New Customers Signed	Total Commission	Difference Between Commission and Minimum Pay	Total Gross Pay
S. McCulloch	25			
F. Odell	18			
S. Heller	23			
V. Caro	15			

P3-10A.
LO 3-1, 3-2

For each of the piece-rate workers below, determine gross pay. If the employees have a standard 40-hour workweek, what is their effective hourly wage? Based on the state's minimum wage in South Dakota, calculate each employee's minimum weekly pay. What is the difference the employer must pay between the calculated gross pay and the calculated state's minimum pay? (Reminder: Divide gross pay by 40 hours to determine the hourly wage.)

Worker	Number of Items	Rate per Item	Gross Pay	Gross Pay/ 40 Hours	Minimum Pay	Difference to Be Paid by the Employer
E. McNeal	25 boat hulls	$10				
T. Fair	70 seat covers	$15				
M. Sturgeon	45 steering mechanisms	$ 4				

P3-11A. LO 3-4

Damien Carranza is an nonexempt employee of Verent Enterprises where he is a salesperson, earning a base annual salary of $30,000 with a standard 40-hour workweek. He earns a 3 percent commission on all sales during the pay period. During the weekly pay period ending August 25, Damien closed $25,000 in sales and worked 4 hours overtime. What is his gross pay for the period?

P3-12A. LO 3-1, 3-2, 3-4

Nigel McCloskey is a waiter at Albicious Foods in South Carolina. He is single with one withholding allowance. He receives the standard tipped hourly wage. During the week ending October 22, 20XX, he worked 44 hours and received $170 in tips. Calculate his gross pay, assuming his tips are included in the overtime rate determination.

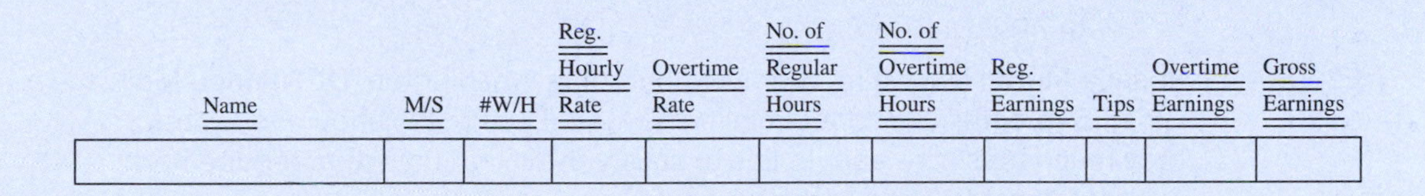

Name	M/S	#W/H	Reg. Hourly Rate	Overtime Rate	No. of Regular Hours	No. of Overtime Hours	Reg. Earnings	Tips	Overtime Earnings	Gross Earnings

Does Albicious Foods need to contribute to Nigel's wages to meet FLSA requirements? _______________

If so, how much should be contributed? _______________

P3-13A. LO 3-5

Stephanie Parker is a salaried, nonexempt administrator for Forise Industries and is paid biweekly. Her annual salary is $63,000, and her standard workweek is 45 hours. During the pay period ending February 3, 20XX, she worked 8 hours overtime. She is single with two withholding allowances. Complete the following payroll register for Stephanie's pay. (Round intermediate calculations to two decimal points.)

Name	M/S	#W/H	Annual Salary	Hourly Rate	Overtime Rate	No. of Overtime Hours	Reg. Earnings	Overtime Earnings	Gross Earnings

P3-14A. LO 3-6

Brigida Masterson is an administrative assistant for Maxilane Fashions. At the end of her shift one day, her employer requires her to deliver a package to a customer before traveling home. Her normal commute is an hour. She spends two hours driving to the customer site, and then another hour driving home for a total of three hours' drive time. How much of Brigida's travel time is compensable?

P3-15A. LO 3-7

Rico Musgrove is an 18-year-old worker in the receiving department of Trynix Inc. in St. Paul, Minnesota. On his first paycheck, he notices that he received $170.00 gross pay for 40 hours of work. Did his employer pay him correctly? Explain.

Exercises Set B

E3-1B. LO 3-1

Barbara Hampton is a minimum wage worker in Ohio. She is contemplating moving to a state with a more favorable minimum wage. Which of the following states should she choose?

1. Indiana
2. New York
3. West Virginia
4. Kentucky

E3-2B. Which of the following workers is covered by FLSA provisions? (Select all that apply.)
LO 3-1

1. Factory manager for an international company.
2. Part-time babysitter earning $1,000 annually.
3. Professional chauffeur earning $25,000 annually.
4. Assistant fire chief for a small town.

E3-3B. Julie Stevens is a tipped employee at the Neovee Resort in Hawaii. What is the minimum cash wage for her area, assuming she receives in excess of $20 in tips per pay period?
LO 3-1

1. $9.35/hour
2. $2.13/hour
3. $3.62/hour
4. $8.25/hour

E3-4B. Rosalie Moran is a waitress at a restaurant in Washington, DC, named Molly's Diner. She earns the tipped minimum wage. During a 40-hour workweek, how much must she earn in tips to satisfy the minimum wage requirement (without consideration of the tip credit)?
LO 3-1

1. $85.20
2. $374.40
3. $190.00
4. $349.20

E3-5B. Austin Sherman is an employee of Divacee Designs. He is an interior designer who is paid based on the number and complexity of the customer designs he generates. What pay basis most accurately describes his compensation?
LO 3-2

1. Hourly
2. Commission
3. Piece rate
4. Salary

E3-6B. Doreen George, a stocker at Dender Factory Outlet, is paid on an hourly basis and earns $12.45/hour. During a one-week period, she worked 39 hours and 19 minutes. How much would her gross pay be under the quarter-hour system? (Round your final answer to two decimal places.)
LO 3-3

1. $485.55
2. $488.66
3. $489.49
4. $491.78

E3-7B. Johnny Clark is a tipped employee at Pyrolia Pizza. What are the two methods his employer may use to determine his overtime compensation?
LO 3-4

1. Compute gross pay based on the minimum cash wage plus tips.
2. Compute gross pay based on an average of the minimum cash wage and the maximum tip credit.
3. Compute gross pay based on the minimum cash wage, excluding tips.
4. Compute gross pay based on the minimum cash wage multiplied by the overtime rate (i.e., 1.5).

E3-8B. Jacques Beasley is a salaried nonexempt accounting clerk for Supplies Enterprises who is contracted to work 45 hours per week. How should his overtime be determined, according to FLSA?
LO 3-4

1. Any hours worked in excess of 40 during a consecutive 7-day period.
2. Any hours worked in excess of 45 during a consecutive 7-day period.
3. Any hours worked in excess of 80 during a consecutive 14-day period.
4. Any hours worked in excess of 45 during a consecutive 14-day period.

E3-9B. LO 3-5

Of the following items listed, which ones should appear in a payroll register? (Select all that apply.)

1. Gross pay
2. Hourly rate
3. Period ending date
4. Office number

E3-10B. LO 3-4, 3-5

Hubert Jennings is an hourly employee working for Symoid Industries. He is married with two withholding allowances and earns $22.15 per hour. During a biweekly pay period ending February 24, 20XX, he worked 88.5 hours. Complete the payroll register with the period's information.

Name	M/S	#W/H	Hourly Rate	Overtime Rate	No. of Regular Hours	No. of Overtime Hours	Regular Earnings	Overtime Earnings	Gross Earnings

E3-11B. LO 3-6

Paula Warren is an employee of Archic Outdoor Gear, where she earns a base salary of $27,200 plus an 8 percent commission on all sales. She is married with four withholding allowances. During the biweekly pay period ended June 16, 20XX, Paula made $15,000 in sales. Complete the payroll register for the pay period.

Name	M/S	#W/H	Period Salary	Sales	Reg. Earnings	Commission Earnings	Gross Earnings

E3-12B. LO 3-7

Sherrill Pullman is 18 years of age and is a new employee of Camicero Bank in Hendersonville, Tennessee. What is the minimum hourly wage that she may receive during the first 90 days of employment?

1. $9.47
2. $2.13
3. $7.25
4. $4.25

Problems Set B

P3-1B. LO 3-3

Ruben Trout worked the following schedule: Monday, 8 hours, 24 minutes; Tuesday, 7 hours, 44 minutes; Wednesday, 9 hours, 8 minutes; Thursday, 8 hours, 2 minutes; Friday, 8 hours, 36 minutes. The employer pays overtime in accordance with FLSA regulations. Determine Ruben's total time worked according to the (a) quarter-hour method and (b) the hundredth-hour method. Which is the more favorable method for Ruben, quarter-hour or hundredth-hour?

	Quarter-Hour Time	Hundredth-Hour Time	More Favorable Method
R. Trout			

P3-2B. LO 3-2

Harvey Ramos is a salaried exempt employee at Duodo Scales with a contract that stipulates 35 hours per week at $52,000 per year. He is married with three withholding allowances. The pay period ending November 26 contained two company-paid holidays. Calculate Harvey's biweekly pay based on a standard five-day workweek. Round wages to five decimal points. (Hint: Determine Harvey's hourly wage to determine holiday pay.)

Name	M/S	#W/H	Period Wage	Hourly Rate	No. of Regular Hours	No. of Holiday Hours	Reg. Earnings	Holiday Earnings	Gross Earnings

P3-3B. Doris Black completed 1,750 pieces on her 2,000-piece contract for Make It Work. There is a bonus earned if the individual exceeds 115 percent of the piece contract. How many more pieces must Doris complete in the remainder of the pay period to receive the bonus?
LO 3-2

P3-4B. Katrina Hughes is a shared employee; she works in the accounting department and has been trained to work at the front desk in times of need. During one weekly pay period, she was asked to work at the front desk on four days for five hours each day. When she works in the accounting department, she earns $17.26 per hour and earns $13.75 per hour for working at the front desk. She worked a total of 45 hours during the week. Complete the payroll register using a separate lines for each job classification, and place the overtime on her accounting department hours.
LO 3-4, 3-5

Name	M/S	#W/H	Hourly Rate	No. of Regular Hours	No. of Overtime Hours	Reg. Earnings	Overtime Earnings	Gross Earnings

P3-5B. Simon Cunningham earns $16.45 per hour at Transist Electronics. Compute his pay under both the hundredth-hour and quarter-hour systems. The company is considering switching from a quarter-hour method to a hundredth-hour method. Simon submitted the following time card:
LO 3-3

In	Out	In	Out	Total Hours with Quarter-Hour	Total Hours with Hundredth-Hour
8:08	11:57	12:59	4:57		
9:04	12:17	1:28	5:18		
7:45	11:45	12:43	4:01		
7:57	12:04	1:03	5:06		

Simon's total pay in the hundredth-hour system: ___________
Simon's total pay in a quarter-hour system: ___________

P3-6B. Shelli Quintanilla is the concierge at Hotel Amize where she is a nonexempt employee earning $18 per hour plus a $250 biweekly bonus based on customer reviews. During the pay period of November 27–December 10, she worked 85 hours and earned the entire bonus. What is her gross pay for the pay period, assuming a 40-hour standard workweek?
LO 3-4

P3-7B. Jesse Daniels is a commission-based employee who is single with one withholding allowance. She is paid $13.50/hour and receives a 5 percent commission on net sales. She does not receive commissions until her net sales exceed $55,500 during a weekly period at Perous Pharmaceuticals. For the week ending May 5, 20XX, she worked 48 hours and sold $67,500 of medicinals but had $900 of returns from last week's sales. Company policy requires that commissions on returned sales be deducted from her pay during the next pay period. Compute her gross pay for the week.
LO 3-4, 3-5

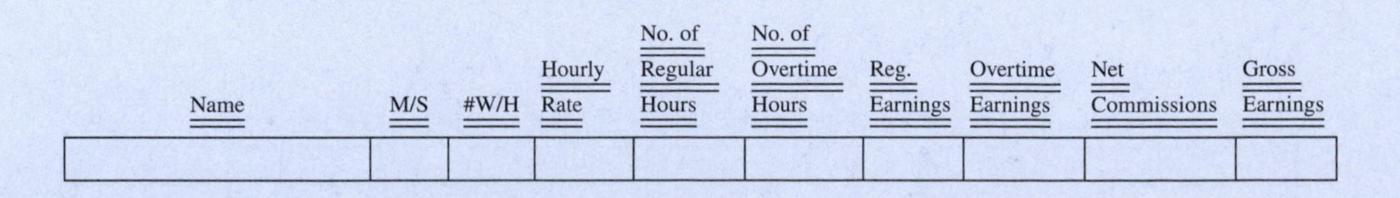

Name	M/S	#W/H	Hourly Rate	No. of Regular Hours	No. of Overtime Hours	Reg. Earnings	Overtime Earnings	Net Commissions	Gross Earnings

P3-8B. LO 3-1, 3-2

Lacie Bingham, an outside sales representative for Redoo Insurance, receives 4 percent commission on all new policies she receives in her sales territory. During the pay period ending April 16, she sold $150,000 of new policies and worked 40 hours.

What is her gross pay? ______

Is she subject to minimum wage laws? ______

Why or why not?______

P3-9B. LO 3-1, 3-2

Outbound sales representatives at Alindu Magazines in Arizona receive a $20 commission on all new customers they sign up for new magazine subscriptions. Each outbound sales representative works 40 hours. During a weekly competition, the outbound sales representative who sold the most subscriptions was awarded a $125 bonus. Because these employees are paid solely on commission, the employer must ensure that they earn the federal minimum wage for 40 hours each week. Compute the gross pay for each of the following outbound sales representatives and the difference when the commission pay is less than the gross pay at minimum wage.

Employee	Number of New Customers Signed	Total Commission	Gross Pay at Minimum Wage	Difference Between Commission and Minimum Pay
H. Meyers	35			
M. Jansen	19			
K. Bartels	42			
T. Macklin	29			

P3-10B. LO 3-1, 3-2

For each of the piece-rate workers at Perigen Snowsports, determine gross pay. If the employees have a standard 37.5-hour workweek, determine their effective hourly rate. Based on the minimum wage for New Hampshire, what is the minimum wage they must receive each week? If they are not receiving the FLSA minimum wage for the pay period, what is the difference that must be paid by the employer? (Remember: Effective hourly rate equals the gross pay divided by 37.5 hours.)

Worker	Number of Items	Rate per Item	Gross Pay	Gross Pay/ 37.5 Hours	Minimum Pay	Difference to Be Paid by the Employer
S. Jackson	25 snowboards	$ 9				
A. Foster	30 helmets	$7.75				
L. Howard	80 bindings	$4.50				

P3-11B. LO 3-4

Latoyia Judge is a piece-rate employee at Anible Computers. She receives $30 for each desktop computer that she assembles and has a standard 40-hour workweek. During the weekly pay period ending December 15, she completed the assembly of 48 computers and worked 44 hours, all of which are productive hours. What is her gross pay for the period?

P3-12B. LO 3-1, 3-2

Clarence Torres is the concierge at the Forise Resort in Oregon. He is single with one withholding allowance. He receives the standard tipped hourly wage for the state. During the week ending December 3, 20XX, he worked 40 hours and received $105 in tips. Compute Clarence's pay for the period.

Name	M/S	#W/H	Hourly Rate	No. of Regular Hours	Reg. Earnings	Tips	Gross Earnings

Does the Forise Resort need to contribute to Clarence's wages to meet FLSA requirements?___________

If so, how much must the employer contribute?___________

P3-13B. LO 3-5
Dennis Murphy is a salaried, nonexempt administrative assistant for Dionti Investments and is paid semimonthly. He is married with two withholding allowances. His annual salary is $65,000, and his standard workweek is 37.5 hours. During the pay period, he worked 10 hours overtime. Compute Dennis's gross pay for the period ending August 18, 20XX.

Name	M/S	#W/H	Annual Salary	Hourly Rate	Overtime Rate	No.of Overtime Hours	Reg. Earnings	Overtime Earnings	Gross Earnings

P3-14B. LO 3-6
Joshua Peterson is a sales assistant at Cogindu Connectors whose normal commute time is 30 minutes in each direction. At the beginning of his shift one day, his employer requires him to pick up a package from a customer before arriving at work. He spends an hour driving to the customer site and then another 30 minutes driving to the office, for a total of 1.5 hours drive time. How much of Joshua's travel time is compensable?

P3-15B. LO 3-7
Annie Adams is a 19-year-old accounting clerk with Quijen Accounting Solutions. During the first month of her employment at Quijen, she noticed that she received $369.75 for her first semimonthly pay covering 87 regular hours. Did the employer pay her correctly? Explain.

Critical Thinking

3-1. West Virginia State University has a policy of hiring students to work in its bookstores and cafeterias. Assuming that 138 students work for the university at minimum wage rates, what is the amount of pay they will receive for a biweekly pay period, assuming they each work 30 hours per week?

3-2. Thomas Campbell owns Veiled Wonders, a firm that makes window treatments. Some merchandise is custom-made to customer specifications, and some is mass-produced in standardized measurements. He has production workers who work primarily on standardized blinds and some employees who additionally work on custom products on an as-needed basis. How should he structure his pay methods for his production workers?

In the Real World: Scenario for Discussion

Many states offer incentives to hire disabled individuals. When doing so, the employer must receive a specific waiver allowing them to pay sub-minimum wage. This can be a great outreach for the employer in assisting the disabled community obtain independence and a sense of self-worth.

Review various state agencies, determine the wages that may be paid to the disabled workers and what benefits a couple of states have. What federal incentives are there for hiring disabled workers?

Internet Activities

3-1. Using a search engine such as Google, Yahoo, or Bing, search "commission-based pay." Sites such as the Society for Human Resource Management (www.shrm.com) have a large volume of articles about commission-based pay and workplace cases. Choose a case and find out as much as you can about the company involved. Why do you think that commission-based pay is such a popular topic among human resource professionals?

3-2. Go to www.accountingtools.com/podcasts and look for payroll-related podcasts. Once you have listened to one or more podcasts, what do you feel was the most interesting information you learned?

3-3. Want to learn more about the concepts in this chapter? Check out:

www.dol.gov/whd/minwage/america.htm

www.flsa.com/coverage.html

http://webapps.dol.gov/elaws/otcalculator.htm

3-4. Would you like to watch a video to learn more about FLSA treatment of minimum wage, hours worked, and overtime? Check out the following links:

Topic 2: Minimum Wage

Topic 4: Hours Worked

Topic 5: Overtime

Continuing Payroll Project: Prevosti Farms and Sugarhouse

The first day of work for Prevosti Farms and Sugarhouse for all employees is February 4, 2019. February 8 is the end of the first pay period and includes work completed during the week of February 4–8. Compute the employee gross pay using 35 hours as the standard workweek for all employees except Mary Shangraw, who works 20 hours per week and receives overtime for any time worked past that point. The other hourly employees receive overtime pay when they work more than 35 hours in one week. Joel Schwartz has made $5,000 in case sales at a 3 percent commission rate during this pay period. Remember that the employees are paid biweekly. Note that the first pay period comprises only one week of work, but the pay frequency for federal income tax purposes is biweekly.

Exempt employee pay information is as follows:

Name	Annual Salary	Notes
Millen	$35,000	
Lewis	$32,000	
Schwartz	$24,000	plus 3% commission on sales
Prevosti	$45,000	

The hours for the nonexempt employees are as follows:

Name	Hourly Rate	Hours Worked 2/4–2/8	Regular Time Pay	Overtime Pay	Commission Pay	Gross Pay
Towle	$12.00	35 hours				
Long	$12.50	40 hours				
Shangraw	$10.50	21 hours				
Success (You)	$16.68	35 hours				

Complete the payroll register for the period's gross pay. Pay will be disbursed on February 13, 2019, starting with check number 6628.

February 22, 2019, is the end of the final pay period for the month. Schwartz has sold $7,500 of product during this pay period at a 3 percent commission. Complete the payroll register for the period's gross pay. Pay will be disbursed on February 27, 2019, and check numbers will continue from prior payroll.

The hours for the nonexempt employees are as follows:

Name	Hourly Rate	Hours Worked 2/11–2/22	Regular Time Pay	Overtime Pay	Commission Pay	Gross Pay
Towle	$12.00	80 hours				
Long	$12.50	70 hours				
Shangraw	$11.00	42 hours				
Success (You)	$16.68	71 hours				

P/R End Date

Check Date

Company Name:

Name	M/S	#W/H	Hourly Rate or Period Wage	No. of Regular Hours	No. of Overtime Hours	No. of Holiday Hours	Commissions	Gross Earning	Sec 125	401(k)	Taxable Wages for Federal W/H
Totals											

Name	Gross Earning	Taxable Wages for Federal W/H	Taxable Wages for FICA	Federal W/H	Social Security Tax	Medicare W/H	State W/H Tax	Garnish-ment	United Way	Net Pay
Totals										

Answers to Stop & Check Exercises

Pay Your Employees Correctly

1. No. Heather should have received time-and-a-half for the additional 8 hours. Her pay should have been $667.00 [(80 × 7.25) + (8 × 1.5 × 7.25)]
2. $398.95 (39.5 × 10.10)
3. $631.40 (32 × 2 × 9.86)
4. $739.50 (75 × 9.86)

Pay Computations for Different Basis

1. $6,744.00 ($224,800 × 3%)
2. $1,100.00. Yes, because $1,100.00/90 hours = $12.22 per hour. South Carolina has no dictated minimum wage so federal minimum wage would apply.
3. With unpaid time, her current pay will be less; if she had vacation time, there would be no difference.

Standard salary per biweekly payroll: $57,000 / 26 = $2,192.310769
($57,000 / (40 × 26 × 2)) = $27.40384 per hour × (8 × 3) for unpaid leave of $657.69216
Current pay $2,192.30769 – 657.69216 = $1,534.62 (rounded)

Quarter-Hour vs. Hundredth-Hour

1. Ann:
   Quarter-hour: 8.25 hours
   Hundredth-hour: 7.93 hours
   Nevada:
   Quarter-hour: 8 hours
   Hundredth-hour: 8.12 hours
   Pat:
   Quarter-hour: 8 hours
   Hundredth-hour: 7.82 hours
2. The difference exists because the time worked during a quarter-hour system is rounded to the nearest quarter hour. In a hundredth-hour system, the worker is paid for the exact number of minutes worked.
3. It would be beneficial to adopt a hundredth-hour system to reduce payroll inaccuracies that may affect both employees and company profits.

How Does Overtime Affect Gross Pay?

1. FLSA Section 7(j) covers the overtime rules for hospital and residential care facilities and would fall under the 8 and 80 rule.
2. Commissions do not have an effect on overtime earnings because overtime only considers worked hours in the calculations.
3. His employer could include Ralph's tips by adding them to his gross pay based on the cash wage. This total with tips becomes the hourly rate used to determine overtime earnings. The other method would be to exclude the tip income, using the cash wage only as the basis for overtime computations.

The Payroll Register

1. To document the employees' time and hours worked as well as to provide totals of the compensation by each category.
2. Name, marital status, number of withholdings, hourly rate, number of regular hours, number of overtime hours, commission, piece rate, regular earnings, overtime earnings, gross earnings.
3. To facilitate calculations of regular and overtime, help ensure accuracy, and allow for analysis of overtime worked.

Combination Pay Methods

1. Base pay = $42,000 ÷ 24 = $1,750
   Commission = $100 × 5 = $500
   Gross pay = $2,250
2. $36,000 ÷ 12 = $3,000 per month
   $3,000 × 0.35 = $1,050 mid-month draw
   $3,000 – $1,050 draw = $1,950 received at the end of the month
3. $75,000 × 0.03 = $2,250 received in stock
   Annual compensation = $75,000 + $2,250 = $77,250

What Is the Correct Pay?

1. 15 hours because compensatory time must be awarded at 1.5 times regular hours.
2. $5.44 per hour ($7.25 × 75%)

Chapter Four

4

Fringe Benefits and Voluntary Deductions

Fringe benefits are noncash forms of compensation that employers use to reward an employee for company service. Examples of fringe benefits include the use of a company car, health and life insurance, dependent care, gym memberships, and many other perks offered as a privilege of working for a particular employer. Employers are not required to offer fringe benefits, and the presence of certain benefits serves as an incentive for potential employees to join the company. By offering fringe benefits, an employer can avoid the need to rely on high salary and wage amounts to attract employees and build morale. However, the cost of offering fringe benefits can impede the company's cash flow. The challenge is to provide a salary and fringe benefit package that attracts the desired employees at a manageable cost to the company.

The IRS classifies fringe benefits as deductible from an employee's pay on either a pre-tax or a post-tax basis, depending on the type of benefit. Pre-tax deductions reduce the current taxable income of the employee and may be taxed at a later time; for example, contributions to a qualifying retirement program would be a pre-tax deduction. Other fringe benefits are deducted from an employee's compensation after computing taxes, which makes the perk a post-tax benefit. The IRS clearly differentiates between taxable and nontaxable fringe benefits in ***Publication 15-b***.

LEARNING OBJECTIVES

After studying Chapter 4, you should be able to:

LO 4-1 Define Fringe Benefits within the Context of Payroll

LO 4-2 Interpret Cafeteria Plan Types

LO 4-3 Describe Fringe Benefit Exclusion Rules

LO 4-4 Explain Fringe Benefit Valuation Rules

dolgachov/123RF

LO 4-5 Differentiate between Pre-Tax and Post-Tax Deductions

LO 4-6 Apply Rules for Withholding, Depositing, and Reporting Benefits

The Hottest Fringe Benefit for Employees

A popular retirement plan enacted by the Revenue Act of 1978 is commonly known as the 401(k) because of its IRS code. The 401(k) is classified as a defined benefit plan characterized by employee contributions and some level of matched contribution by the employer. The purpose of the 401(k) is to help employees set aside money for retirement on a non-taxed basis and is a deferred compensation plan. meaning that employees who elect to contribute to it plan to withdraw money from it at a later date; in this case, that later date is after the employee retires from the workforce.

The 401(k) has grown in popularity among employees over the years but is particularly enticing now because of the IRS private letter ruling in 2018 that allowed employers to connect their employees' student loan repayments with 401(k) contributions. In IRS Letter 201833012, employers may contribute a percentage of employee income to their 401(k) account if the employee paid 2 percent of their eligible compensation toward their student loan repayment during a given pay period. In other words, employers will contribute extra amounts of money toward an employee's retirement if they are making a certain level of payments to reduce their student loan burden.

Companies have already begun to use this opportunity to make their fringe benefits more attractive. Although only 4 percent of employers offer this benefit, companies such as Abbot, Estee Lauder, and Carhartt have already begun to offer the benefit, sometimes contributing an additional 5 percent to employee 401(k) plans. Other companies such as Sotheby's are adding a flat amount to employee 401(k) plans as long as they remain employed in good standing and have qualified student loan obligations.

(Sources: Employer Benefit News, *Forbes*, IRS)

Despite the additional cost involved, fringe benefits are an important part of attracting and retaining high-quality employees. We will explore different types of fringe benefits and their treatment for payroll purposes in Chapter 4.

LO 4-1 Define Fringe Benefits within the Context of Payroll

Mike Kemp/Blend Images LLC

Payroll has been said to be the intersection of human resources and accounting because of the need to include employee information and to record all financial transactions involving work performed for the business. Fringe benefits are an extension of that notion because these benefits are rewards given to employees in return for their service to the company. The correlation between employee satisfaction and retention is often a result of the fringe benefits offered by the employer.

The term *fringe* was applied to these noncash benefits because they were viewed as an insignificant part of employee ***compensation***. Over time, the Bureau of Labor Statistics has proven that fringe benefits actually constitute an additional 25–33 percent of an employee's annual compensation. The importance of fringe benefits, despite the inherent monetary value, is best seen in terms of employee satisfaction and long-term increases in revenue and net income. In this section, we will examine the purpose of fringe benefits and the treatment of this form of noncash compensation as it pertains to pay and taxation.

Purpose of Fringe Benefits

Employees have often been considered a cost of conducting business. The employer's obligation to pay employment taxes and supply additional benefits in order to entice employee engagement was viewed as a necessary, albeit expensive, part of the company's financial structure. Research conducted during the past decade has found that the advantages gained from providing fringe benefits far outweighs the related costs in terms of employee productivity, creativity, and revenue production.

> Over half of U.S. employees report company benefits as a significant factor in their choice of employers. Companies use fringe benefits as an integral part of their staffing strategy. Employers such as Google, Twitter, and Disney are known for offering lavish fringe benefits that include on-site gourmet meals, acupuncture sessions, and entertainment park passes at no additional cost to their employees. This ability to transcend the satisfaction of employees' basic needs by offering luxury as a benefit of employment leads to an increase in worker quality as well as high employee morale and loyalty. (Source: Glassdoor)

Hallmarks of fringe benefits include the following indicators:

- All employees have access to the benefit because of their working relationship with the employer.
- Employees enjoy improved living conditions as a result of the benefit.
- The ability to receive the benefit is not related to employee performance.
- Fringe benefits supplement the employees' cash compensation.
- These benefits may be either deducted pre- or post-tax.
- Fringe benefits promote the welfare of all employees.
- Legislative treatment of fringe benefits involves certain mandatory tax deductions from employee pay.

Fringe benefits may be included in employee pay, although they are not part of the cash compensation package. In the next section, we will explore how fringe benefits appear on an employee's pay advice.

Including Benefits in Pay

In Chapter 3, we discussed the computation of employee gross pay. Some fringe benefits may increase employee pay and would be taxable. Examples of this would include, but are not limited to, employer-provided vehicles, mileage, leasing, and commuting. The items to be included in gross pay are valued at the level as if they were purchased through a third party, often referred to as an *arm's-length transaction.*

> State laws regarding fringe benefits, while based on IRS regulations, may vary regarding paid sick time and paid time off. In New Hampshire, all sick and vacation time is considered to be part of employee wages, and employers must notify employees in writing of these benefits. Furthermore, employees must receive an annual notice that contains details about balances accrued in sick time and paid time off categories. Employers are not required to disburse cash compensation for accrued time at termination and decide if unused time may be rolled over to the next year. (Source: *New Hampshire Business Review*)

Fringe Benefits and Payroll Taxes

Certain fringe benefits change the calculations for tax calculations, such as Federal Withholding, Medicare, or Social Security. Others do not affect the calculation for taxes and are considered post-tax benefits. The IRS requires that all fringe benefits that involve deductions from pay or for which the employee contributes part of regular pay must be listed explicitly on the employee's ***pay advice***. A sample pay advice is contained in Figure 4-1.

FIGURE 4-1

Sample Pay Advice

Hazlitt Industries
2210 Secours Way
Springfield, MA 02312

199203

Stephen Torrisi — Date 11/05/20XX

One-thousand one-hundred twenty-two and 77/100 dollars 1,122.77

Payee: Stephen Torrisi
Address: 3230 Longview Drive
City/State Zip: Agawam, MA 02249

Signed: *Mitchell North*

Payroll End Date 10/31/20XX — Payroll Pay Date 11/05/20XX — Check: 199203

Employee Name Stephen Torrisi — Employee Number 42850 — Rate 21.50

Description	Earnings	YTD Gross	Description	Deductions	YTD Deductions
Regular	1,720.00	32,680.00	Federal W/H	275.47	5,233.93
Holiday			SSI	106.64	2,026.16
Commissions			Medicare	24.94	473.86
			State W/H	88.58	1,683.02
			Pretax Insurance	50.00	950.00
Total Earnings	1,720.00	32,680.00	401(k)	51.60	980.40
			Total Deductions	597.23	11,347.37

The affected taxes include Federal withholding (W/H), SSI, Medicare, and State withholding (W/H), and the fringe benefits include Pretax Insurance and 401(k).

An exception to this requirement involves ***de minimis*** benefits. *De minimis* benefits include items with a value that is so minimal that accounting for it would be unnecessary. These items include an occasional cup of coffee or an isolated postage stamp, both relatively small in value. However, it should be noted that when *de minimis* items become a regular benefit, such as an everyday cup of coffee instead of an occasional one, then the value aggregates to become a sum that could be treated as income.

De minimis benefits, according to IRS Publication 15-b, have such minimal accounting value that the accounting for it is deemed impractical. Examples of de minimis benefits include (but are not limited to):

- Employee use of a company copier, as long as the usage does not exceed 15 percent of the employee's total usage of that equipment for business purposes.
- Noncash, low-value holiday or birthday gifts.
- Similar gifts for family illnesses or birth celebrations.
- Group-term life insurance for the death of a dependent if the life insurance face value does not exceed $2,000.
- Certain meals, occasional picnics, and parties for employees and their guests.
- Occasional tickets to sporting or theater events.
- Personal use of an employer-provided cell phone provided primarily for noncompensatory business purposes.

Notice that *de minimis* benefits are generally classified as occasional use. If the usage becomes more than occasional, such as season tickets to sporting or arts events or club memberships, the benefits is not considered de minimis.

(Source: IRS)

In *Troester v. Starbucks Corp.*, (2018), the question of the *de minimis* doctrine arose when it was applied to work requested of employees who were off the clock but still on the premises. The California Supreme Court ruled that work performed off the clock did not meet the *de minimis* doctrine because of the frequency with which Starbucks requested that its employees perform such tasks. (Sources: APA, Google Scholar)

Voluntary fringe benefits have two basic types of treatments regarding payroll taxes: They may be deducted either before or after ***mandatory deductions*** (i.e., taxes) have been calculated. The IRS specifies which fringe benefits may be deducted on a pre-tax basis and which must be treated as post-tax deductions in Publication 15-b, which is updated annually. Employers are responsible for remitting amounts withheld for fringe benefits in a timely manner and reporting annual totals to employees on Form W-2. Figure 4-2 details the type of fringe benefit and payroll tax treatment follows.

Seb Oliver/Getty Images

EXAMPLE: FRINGE BENEFIT

Amy Zarucki is an employee of Cohen Corporation, a company that offers undergraduate educational assistance as a fringe benefit. According to the IRS, the first $5,250 of Amy's tuition is not subject to payroll taxes. During 2019, Amy received reimbursement from her employer of $7,250 in education assistance. This amount is a fringe benefit that is tax exempt for her employer and subject to taxes over the IRS's cap.

FIGURE 4-2
Fringe Benefits and Payroll Tax Treatment

Fringe Benefits and Payroll Tax Treatment			
Type of Fringe Benefit	Income Tax Exempt	FICA Taxes Exempt	FUTA Tax Exempt
Accident and health benefits*	XX	XX	XX
Achievement awards (up to $1,600 for qualified plan awards, $400 for nonqualified)	XX	XX	XX
Adoption assistance	XX		
Athletic facilities owned or leased by the employer†	XX	XX	XX
De minimis benefits	XX	XX	XX
Dependent care assistance (up to $5,000 annually)	XX	XX	XX
Education (i.e., tuition) assistance (up to $5,250 annually)	XX	XX	XX
Employee discounts (various limits apply)	XX	XX	XX
Employee stock options (depending on the type of option)	XX	XX	XX
Employer-provided cell phone (if not otherwise compensated)	XX	XX	XX
Group term life insurance	XX	XX‡	XX
Health savings accounts (HSAs) for qualified individuals	XX	XX	XX
Lodging on the employer premise (for the employer convenience as condition of employment)	XX	XX	XX
Meals (if *de minimis* or for employer convenience on employer premises)	XX	XX	XX
No-additional-cost services	XX	XX	XX
Retirement planning services	XX	XX	XX
Transportation benefits (commuting and rail passes up to $265, exempt if *de minimis*)	XX	XX	XX
Tuition reduction for undergraduate education (graduate if employee engages in teaching or research)	XX	XX	XX
Working condition benefits	XX	XX	XX

*Does not include long-term care benefits if they are included in flexible spending accounts.
†Exempt if substantially all use during the calendar is by employees, their spouses, and their dependent children and the facility is on the employer's premises or a location owned or leased by the employer.
‡Up to cost of $50,000 of coverage. Excess over $50,000 must appear on the employee's Form W-2.

Fringe Benefits 101

1. What are the two main categories of fringe benefits?
2. Which of the following benefits is not considered a fringe benefit? (Use Figure 4-2 as a reference.)
   a. Educational assistance for undergraduate students.
   b. Group term life insurance over $250,000.
   c. Overtime hours worked during the year.
   d. Cell phones for business purposes.
   e. Retirement planning services.
3. Which of the following fringe benefits would also be exempt for Social Security and Medicare taxes?
   a. Working condition benefits.
   b. Adoption Assistance.
   c. Qualified Health Savings Accounts.
   d. Qualified Achievement Awards.

LO 4-2 Interpret Cafeteria Plan Types

The Internal Revenue Code has a special program to assist workers with necessary health care expenses. Section 125 of the IRS code was initially enacted in 1978 and has been revised several times. It permits employers to offer employees a choice between two or more cash and qualified benefits. The employer must explicitly describe the plan benefit, rules governing the benefit, and ways that the employee may both pay for and obtain the benefits. Employee-elected deductions for qualified cafeteria plan benefits are withheld on a *pre-tax* basis.

Examples of qualified insurance benefits include

- Accident and health benefits.
- Long-term care benefits.
- Group term life insurance (including costs not excluded from wages).
- Health Savings Accounts (HSAs).

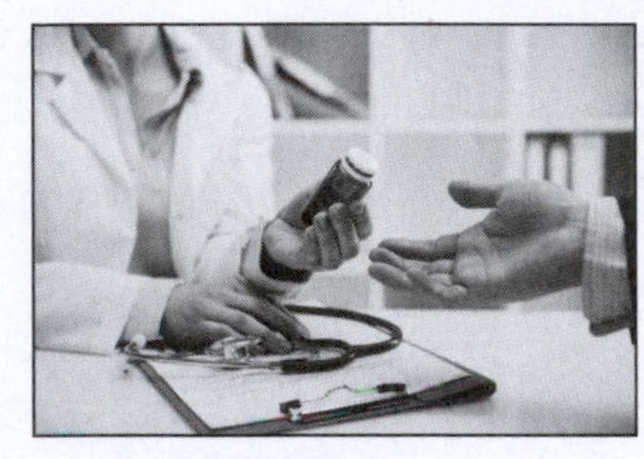
Stasique/Shutterstock

Cafeteria plans, also known as Section 125 plans, are offered by the employer and are usually deducted on a pre-tax basis with the intent of making employer-sponsored benefits more affordable for employees. A cafeteria plan, in essence, allows employees to convert fringe (i.e., non-cash) benefits into tax savings. Although they often pertain to health coverage, cafeteria plans may also include dependent care and other expenses. Participation in cafeteria plans potentially save employees upwards of 7.65 percent (the FICA taxes) and may save more money, depending on the employee's income tax bracket. Note that if an employee chooses to receive benefits under the cafeteria plan this does not convert a fringe benefit to a taxable one.

Premium Only Plan (POP)

A ***premium only plan (POP)*** is a type of cafeteria plan that allows employees to deduct premiums for employer-sponsored group insurance on a pre-tax basis. Deducting the premium on a pre-tax basis allows the employee to have a lower tax liability. A list of POPs that employers may provide and are subject to Section 125 pre-tax provisions is provided in Table 4-1. Note that not all employers offer all types of insurance coverage.

EXAMPLE: PRE-TAX DEDUCTION OF HEALTH INSURANCE PREMIUM

Cathie Hollins, an employee of Wolfe & Associates, has the option to deduct her heath insurance premium on a pre-tax basis. She consulted her payroll accountant about the difference between pre-tax and post-tax premium deduction and received this analysis:

	Pre-Tax vs. Post-Tax	Premium Deduction
	Pre-Tax	Post-Tax
Period gross pay	$2,500	$2,500
Health insurance premium	$ 250	$ 250
Taxable income	$2,250	$2,500

The pre-tax deduction would lead to lower taxable income, which would result in less federal, state, and local income tax being deducted from Cathie's pay.

TABLE 4-1
Types of Insurance that May Be Included in a Premium Only Plan

Health	Dental	Vision
Prescription	Cancer	Medicare Supplement
Accident	Disability	Hospital Indemnity
Employee Group Term Life*		

*Employee Group Term Life insurance premiums are subject to a limit of $50,000 per employee and may be subject to a 10-employee minimum.

Employers benefit by offering POPs because employee premiums deducted on a pre-tax basis reduce the employer's FICA tax liability. Offering pre-tax deductions for group insurance coverage as part of their employee benefits package is also beneficial to employers because participation in health plans has been correlated with reductions in employee sick time and related health care costs. POPs allow employees to offset the cost of rising health care premiums by allowing employees to deduct the premiums on a pre-tax basis.

Flexible Spending Arrangement (FSA)

Another benefit that can be included in the cafeteria plan is a ***flexible spending arrangement (FSA)***. FSAs are available to assist in the payment of medical expenses, including certain co-payments and prescriptions, transportation, and certain child care expenses. According to IRS Publication 502, examples of includible medical expenses are

- Acupuncture.
- Ambulance service.
- Braille books and magazines.
- Chiropractor.
- Hearing aids.
- Lead-based paint removal.
- Wheelchair.

It should be noted that any employee contributions to an FSA in excess of $2,700 annually (2019 amount) are treated as taxable income. The purpose of the FSA is not to defer taxable income or to avoid paying taxes, but to reduce the financial burden of health care costs.

Cafeteria plan–based FSAs generally have a "use it or lose it" provision, meaning that any unused funds at the end of the plan year may not be accessed afterward. However, the IRS permits employers to roll over up to $500 annually per employee at the employer's discretion.

EXAMPLE: FSA EFFECT ON ANNUAL GROSS SALARY

For plans that have a year starting after December 31, 2018, the maximum annual amount that an employee may contribute to an FSA offered under Section 125 is $2,700 per person. As an example, Faith Goldman is an employee of Kuzmeckis Doors. She earns $50,000 annually and elects to contribute $2,700 of her annual pay to an employer-sponsored FSA. Her taxable pay would be reduced as follows:

Annual pay – FSA election = $50,000 – $2,700 = $47,300

At the end of the calendar year, Faith has $500 remaining out of her annual FSA election. Her employer allows her to carry over the balance to next year and requires that it be spent by March 15. She would need to spend the remaining balance on qualified medical expenses and provide documentation as required to support the expenditures. Any amount remaining from the prior year may be forfeited by the employee after March 15.

One benefit of cafeteria plans is that employees may choose two or more benefits that consist of cash and noncash elements. For example, they may elect to have health insurance premiums *and* a flexible spending arrangement deducted on a pre-tax basis.

Health Savings Account (HSA)

Another type of cafeteria plan is a ***health savings account (HSA)*** that can be used to pay for qualified medical expenses. It is important to note that HSAs may only be used in conjunction with a cafeteria plan by employees who have a ***high deductible health plan (HDHP)***. The 2019 definition of a high deductible health plan includes the following deductible limits:

- $1,350 annual deductible (self-coverage).
- $2,700 annual deductible (family).
- $6,750 out-of-pocket expenses maximum (self-coverage).
- $13,500 out-of-pocket expenses maximum (family).

EXAMPLE: PRE-TAX VS. POST-TAX WITH A FLEXIBLE SPENDING ARRANGEMENT (FSA)

Cathie Hollins also has the option to contribute to an FSA for her annual out-of-pocket medical expenses and decides to use that to meet cafeteria plan requirements. She is paid semimonthly and decides to contribute $2,400 to a qualified FSA. Her taxable income would be as follows:

	Pre-Tax vs. Post-Tax	Premium Deduction
	Pre-Tax	Post-Tax
Period gross pay	$2,500	$2,500
Health insurance premium	$ 250	$ 250
FSA	$ 100	-0-
Taxable income	$2,150	$2,500

Note the difference between her taxable income in both situations. The use of pre-tax deductions can significantly reduce Cathie's tax liability.

FSA vs. HSA

FSA	HSA
Must be offered by an employer.	Only permitted for employees with a HDHP (see deductible rules).
Independent Contractors do not qualify.	Independent Contractors do not qualify.
Employees may elect to contribute up to $2,700	Employees may contribute to HSAs as follows: • $3,500 (single) • $7,000 (married) • $1,000 (additional catch-up amount for employees over age 55)
Employees may use any amount of the annual contribution at any time, regardless of how much they have contributed for the year.	Functions like a bank account in that the employee owns the funds contributed, although employers may also contribute funds.
Plan is owned by the employer, and unused annual contributions may be retained by the employer	All funds contributed are the property of the employee
Employer decides if they want to give employees a grace period (up to March 15 in most cases) to use annual elections.	Unused funds rollover each year and continue to grow with the account. Unused funds do not affect the yearly contribution limits.
Employees must provide receipts or provider evidence to support used funds.	Employees may not access more funds than they have contributed to the HSA.
FSA contributions are reported on the W-2	Employees must report all used funds with their personal income tax returns.
Annual contributions must be elected each year.	Employees may change their annual contribution at any time.

numbeos/E+/Getty Images

One aspect of HSAs that differentiates them from FSAs is that the amounts that employees contribute to an HSA may remain in the account for use later in life. These funds may be reserved for medical costs and long-term care and are not taxable when used for medical expenses. Money withdrawn for nonmedical expenses is subject to income taxes. Another difference is that anyone with an HDHP may establish an HSA with a trustee, even if their employer does not offer the benefit. However, not all HSAs can be considered tax exempt. Only HSAs included as part of the company's qualifying Section 125 cafeteria plan are deemed exempt from Social Security, Medicare, and federal income taxes.

A note about HSAs is that the money contributed to the account may roll over from year to year as long as the employee is part of an HDHP. Employees with a single marital status may contribute up to $3,500 tax free, and married employees may

HDHPs are a way for employers to offer affordable insurance premiums for their employees. As of 2019, approximately 79% of employers offer HDHPs. The problem that employers experience is that annual deductibles for these plans can exceed $3,500, which is equivalent to three weeks of an employee's pay. The other issue employers face by offering HDHPs is that pharmaceutical costs cannot always be included in the plan, so employers either offer pharmacy insurance or employees must seek pharmacy-only plans. (Source: PBMI)

contribute up to $7,000. Additionally, employees age 55 and older may contribute an additional $1,000 per year as a catch-up contribution. Certain HSA plans allow participants to invest money into mutual funds or other investments. It should also be noted that HSAs do not have the same restrictions for spending as FSAs.

Employers may make tax-exempt contributions to their employees' HSAs as long as they make comparable contributions to all company employee accounts according to the category or coverage and the employment category (e.g., full-time, part-time). Employer contributions to HSAs are tax exempt as far as federal income tax, FICA, and FUTA because sums contributed are not considered employee wages.

An issue with cafeteria plans is the exclusion of sole proprietors, partners, shareholders in an S-corporation who have greater than a 2 percent share in the company, and members of limited liability companies (LLCs) who elect to be taxed as partnerships. According to Section 125, these individuals may not participate in a cafeteria plan. The problem is that 73 percent of business owners fall into one of these exclusions, which means that many people cannot access the tax privileges that they offer their employees. (Source: *Financial Regulation News*)

What is Served in the Cafeteria Plan?

Stop & Check

1. Which of the following types of insurance may be included in a POP?
   a. Cancer
   b. Vision
   c. Auto
   d. Dental
2. What are two differences between FSAs and HSAs?
3. What constitutes a HDHP?

LO 4-3 Describe Fringe Benefit Exclusion Rules

Remember that fringe benefits are noncash compensation. We have discussed the tax treatment of benefits that may be deducted from employee income on a pre-tax basis using a cafeteria plan. Other fringe benefits may not be included in a cafeteria plan and are also generally not reported as compensation. Employers routinely offer these excluded fringe benefits, and it is important for payroll accountants to understand specific tax rules in order to represent them accurately on employee W-2s when necessary.

Excluded fringe benefits exist that are not part of a cafeteria plan and, despite the cash value, do not generally constitute a taxable portion of employee pay. The value of these fringe benefits are exempt from federal income tax, FICA taxes, FUTA tax, and are not reported on the employee's W-2. The table in Figure 4-2 contains specific details of fringe benefit exclusions and limitations of the exclusions. In this section, we will examine fringe benefits not specifically addressed in Publication 15-b that are commonly offered by companies.

Jetta Productions/Getty Images

Prizes and Awards

Workplace prizes and awards are a way for employers to influence employee morale by offering noncash rewards for winning competitions and achieving milestones such as company tenure. In Publication 15-b, the cash-value limit on achievement awards is $1,600 annually for those given in accordance with a qualified plan; the limit for nonqualified awards is $400. A ***qualified plan*** is one that considers all employees equally, not favoring highly compensated employees. These type of achievement awards, according to IRS Publication 535, is that they are for improvements to safety programs and for longevity of service to the employer. The following example contains context for achievement awards.

Simon Hawkins is a sales employee at Austin Trailers and Motorsports. The company offers achievement awards on a regular basis to reward sales employees for achieving safety goals and longevity of service, All sales staff members are eligible for these awards, including the company officers.

EXCLUDED ACHIEVEMENT AWARD

On June 5, 2019, Simon won an award of $500 for achieving the highest safety record during the month of May. According to Publication 15-b, this achievement award would not be reported on Simon's W-2 as taxable income.

TAXABLE PORTION OF ACHIEVEMENT AWARD: CASH AWARD

As of December 31, 2019, Simon had won the award for compiling a comprehensive safety plan on four separate occasions during the calendar year. The total of his achievement awards is $500 × 4, or $2,000. Because the achievement awards received exceeded $1,600, the additional $400 ($2,000 – $1,600) would be reflected as taxable income on his W-2.

TAXABLE PORTION OF ACHIEVEMENT AWARD: NONCASH AWARD

In addition to winning the cash prizes for safety achievement, Simon received a new smartphone with a value of $1,000 for 10 years of service to the company. As the value of his awards is now $3,000, the excess of value over $1,600 will be reflected as taxable income.

monkeybusinessimages/Getty Images

Gym Memberships

Employee discounts for gym memberships are a common fringe benefit that employers use to promote wellness initiatives. If the employer has on-site athletic facilities (either on the employer's premises or another premises owned or leased by the employer) that are restricted to use by employees, their spouses, and their dependents, then the benefit would be nontaxable. However, if an employer provides gym memberships to off-site clubs at no additional cost to employees on a qualified plan, the cost of the gym membership is taxable. Likewise, if the athletic facility is open to the public as well as to employees and their dependents, the value of the membership would be taxable.

Personal Use of Company Vehicle

Company cars are a common fringe benefit given to employees who drive regularly as part of their job. Business use of these company cars is considered a nontaxable fringe benefit

EXAMPLE: OFF-SITE GYM MEMBERSHIP

Claire Warner is an employee of Althea Productions. Her employer offers memberships at a local gym as an optional benefit for employees. These memberships are at no additional cost to the employee and have a cash value of $75 per month. Because the gym membership has an annual value of $900 and is not an on-site athletic facility, it must be counted as income and reported on Claire's Form W-2.

McGraw-Hill Education/Mark Dierker, photographer

because it is an asset provided to the employee for use that specifically benefits the company, much like a computer or office equipment. The taxable portion occurs when the employee uses the company-provided vehicle for personal business. Employers often request that employees document personal use of the business vehicle at the end of the calendar year to facilitate proper identification of taxable income associated with the company car.

In the case of *Scott v. Scott,* an issue that arose was the value of fringe benefits used to determine the defendant's income for use in divorce proceedings. The plaintiff contended that the use of a company truck was not calculated into the value of the defendant's income that was used as the basis of calculating child support. Upon review of the defendant's total compensation, including all fringe benefits, the Supreme Court of Georgia found that the defendant's actual monthly income was substantially more than previously stated and increased the monthly child support obligation. (Source: *Justia*)

Gift Cards

If an employee received gift cards as a fringe benefit, the cash value of those gift cards must be included as compensation on the employee's Form W-2. For example, if an employee entered a company-sponsored raffle at company functions during the year and won a $100 gift card to a local restaurant, the $100 must be added as compensation to the employee's Form W-2. There is no minimum amount of cash or cash equivalent gift cards that would be excluded under *de minimis* fringe benefits.

Pixtal/AGE Fotostock

Employer-Provided Snacks and Meals

Employers often have coffeemakers and kitchen facilities available for employees. If the employer *occasionally* provides food or beverage as an employee perk, the cash value of the benefit is considered *de minimis* and is not taxable. However, if the employer routinely provides food or beverages for employee consumption at no additional charge to the employees, then the cash value of those items must be reported as compensation on the employee's Form W-2.

EXAMPLE: PIZZA FRIDAYS

Laurie Ortega works for Excellent Embroidery and Screen Printing. On Fridays, the company provides a pizza lunch for all employees. The intent of the pizza is to promote employee morale on Fridays and to celebrate weekly accomplishments. Although the value per employee of Excellent Embroidery for pizza on Fridays is small on a weekly basis, it aggregates to an additional $100 per employee over a year's time. Laurie would see an additional $100 in compensation added to her Form W-2 for this noncash fringe benefit.

Keep in mind that fringe benefits may take many different forms. It is important for the payroll accountant to be aware of the perks offered to employees as well as Publication 15-b guidelines in order to identify potential additions to employee compensation and to provide accurate reports to employees and governmental authorities.

For a fringe benefit to be excluded, the employer must be prepared to prove that providing the benefit, not simply adding it to employee gross pay, substantially improves conditions at the firm. For example, the addition of an on-site gym must provide significant benefit above what it would cost employers to add the amount associated with a gym membership to employee pay. Proving that the benefit is substantial could include tracking the number of employees that use the on-site facility versus those who would request and use an external gym membership. (Source: Mondaq)

Excluded Fringe Benefits

Stop & Check

1. Clayton Clark is an employee at Glazier Foods Inc., where he is in the shipping and receiving department. His employer provides an athletic facility on the premises for employees to use. Would this benefit be taxable on Clayton's W-2? Why or why not?
2. Marcia Zimmerman is an employee of Moeller Gallery, and she has a company-issued vehicle to use in order to conduct business. Does this vehicle represent a fringe benefit? Why or why not?

LO 4-4 Explain Fringe Benefit Valuation Rules

Now that we have an idea about what fringe benefits are and how they fit into a payroll context, it is time to address specific rules about the valuation of fringe benefits. As noted in the case of *Scott v. Scott,* the value of fringe benefits potentially increases the total value of an employee's income without directly affecting the cash they receive. Note that the details for fringe-benefit valuation rules appear in Publication 15-b and are updated annually.

General Valuation Rule

The ***general valuation rule (GVR)*** is the most common way to determine the value of fringe benefits. The GVR uses ***fair market value (FMV)*** as the cornerstone of valuation. Fair market value is defined as the price a person would need to pay to obtain a good or service from a third party in an arm's-length transaction. In other words, if an employee needed to obtain a gym membership, the price paid for that individual membership would constitute the fair market value. In this section, we will explore different applications of the GVR with explanations of the method used to determine value for payroll reporting purposes.

McGraw-Hill Education/Mark Dierker, photographer

Personal Use of Company Vehicle: Lease Value Rule

Access to a company car can present a challenge in terms of evaluation of the specific amount associated with personal use of the asset. To compute the value of the employee's personal use of the asset, the IRS uses a complex method that involves the age of the car, fair market value of the asset, and miles driven. Three primary methods exist for determining value: the ***lease value rule***, the ***commuting rule***, and the ***cents-per-mile rule***. Figure 4-3 contains an example of how a company could derive the valuation using the lease value method. Publication 15-b does provide an annual lease amount for vehicles. After the annual amount of the lease has been determined, the amount is then multiplied by the percentage of personal use of the vehicle. This amount is considered taxable income to the employee. When the employer provides the fuel for the vehicle, this must also be included in the previous calculations. Employer-paid fuel is calculated at FMV or 5.5 cents per mile of personal use. If the employer does not provide fuel, than there is no addition for the fuel.

In the form provided in Figure 4-3, the employee, Irvin Silva, claims that he uses the company car for personal use 20 percent of the time during the calendar year. By obtaining the data requested in the form and computing the value of the fringe benefit, Irvin has received

FIGURE 4-3
Value of the Personal Use of a Company Car: Lease-Value Rule

Champion Process Inc.

Worksheet to Calculate Personal Use of Company Vehicle

(Lease-Value Rule)

Employee Name: Irvin Silva

Vehicle Make: Ford **Vehicle Year:** 2019

Vehicle Model: Taurus

Odometer Mileage on the First Day of Use During the Year: 5,790

Odometer Mileage on the Last Day of Use During the Year: 22,990

Annual Lease Method

Fair Market Value of Vehicle: $40,000

Annual Lease Value: $10,750 ***(Use Table 3-1 in Publication 15b)***

Enter Number of Days Available for Use During the Year: 180

Divide by the Number of Days in the Tax Year: 365

Prorated Annual Lease Percentage: 49.3%

Prorated Annual Lease Value: $5,299.75 ($10,750 x 49.3%)

Percent of Personal Use During the Year (from employee statement): 25%

Personal Annual Lease Value: $1,059.95 **(Annual Lease Value x % Personal Use)**

If fuel is provided by the employer, enter personal miles: 4,300 x $0.055/mile[1] = $236.50

Total Personal Use Taxable Income: $1,059.95 + 236.50 = $1,296.45

[1]Fuel provided by company is valued at $0.055 per mile per personal use purposes.

Note: The number of personal miles is computed by determining the total miles driven during the year (22,990 – 5,790 = 17,200 miles), then multiplying that total by the percentage of personal use (17,200 × 25% = 4300 miles).

$1,263.70 in noncash compensation for this fringe benefit. In addition, the company has provided the fuel for the vehicle (at 5.5 cents per mile), and the number of personal miles is used to compute the personal value of the fuel consumption. The total value of this benefit for Irvin is $1,288.40 and must be added to his Form W-2 as compensation.

Personal Use of a Company Vehicle: Commuting Rule

Like the situation in the lease value rule, the employee has a company vehicle for use. However, the commuting rule applies to employees who are strictly forbidden from using the vehicle outside of work hours and for personal purposes. The vehicle is only available for transport to and from work and during the workday. Under the commuting rule, the employee computes the number of miles driven for commuting to and from work and multiplies that by $1.50 to determine the valuation for this fringe benefit. Figure 4-4 contains an example of how this rule is applied, assuming a 20-mile round-trip commute done each day of the week.

In Figure 4-4, we see that providing a company car and charging an employee based on the amount of miles in the commute can lead to a higher fringe benefit valuation than seen in the lease value rule.

FIGURE 4-4
Value of the Personal Use of a Company Car: Commuting Rule

Champion Process Inc.

Worksheet to Calculate Personal Use of Company Vehicle

(Commuting Rule)

Employee Name: Irvin Silva

Vehicle Make: Ford **Vehicle Year:** 2019

Vehicle Model: Taurus

Odometer Mileage on the First Day of Use During the Year: 871

Odometer Mileage on the Last Day of Use During the Year: 3,115

Commute Rule

Number of miles driven for daily commute to and from work: 20

Number of days worked during the year: 225

Total number of commute miles driven during the year: 4,500

Value of company vehicle for commuting: 4,500 x $1.50/mile = $6,750

Personal Use of a Company Vehicle: Cents-per-Mile Rule

Another way to determine the value of a company car as a fringe benefit is to use the IRS standard mileage rate. This rate is updated each year and for 2019 is sitting at $0.58, and the payroll accountant should refer to Publication 15-b for updated rates. The cents-per-mile rule uses the number of personal miles driven and multiplies it by the standard mileage rate to determine the value of the fringe benefit. The purpose of the cents-per-mile rule is to consider costs of maintenance and insurance for the vehicle, both of which may increase for the company when the vehicle is driven for personal purposes. Figure 4-5 contains an example applying the cents-per-mile rule.

FIGURE 4-5
Value of the Personal Use of a Company Car: Cents-per-Mile Rule

Champion Process Inc.

Worksheet to Calculate Personal Use of Company Vehicle

(Cents-per-Mile Rule)

Employee Name: Irvin Silva

Vehicle Make: Ford **Vehicle Year:** 2019

Vehicle Model: Taurus

Odometer Mileage on the First Day of Use During the Year: 871

Odometer Mileage on the Last Day of Use During the Year: 3,115

Cents-per-Mile Rule

Number of miles driven during the year: 2,244

Number of miles OR percent of miles for personal use: 25%

Value of company vehicle for commuting: 561 x $0.58/mile = $325.38

The choice of company car valuation method rule determines the company's policy and the actual use of the vehicle in terms of total miles driven for business, value of the asset, and primary user of the vehicle. Publication 15-b contains specific details for the payroll accountant to determine which method is the most appropriate. No matter which method is chosen, it is important to be consistent in the application of personal vehicle use valuations.

Stacey Bramhall/Getty Images

Unsafe Conditions

A special rule applies if a company vehicle is provided to an employee only because of unsafe conditions. The foundation of this rule is that the employee would walk, bicycle, or use public transportation under normal conditions. An example of an unsafe condition in which this rule may apply would be in the event of a sudden snowstorm that makes the employee's normal travel mode unsafe. In this case, the IRS rule is that the employee is charged $1.50 for a one-way commute (i.e., to or from home), and this charge should be either added to the employee's wages or reimbursed to the company by the employee.

Other Transportation Benefits

Another transportation benefit that employers can offer is a transit pass. These provide employees access to commuter vehicles (six or more passengers required) through the use of the pass. Employers in larger cities, where parking is a premium, may provide parking subsidies to their employees. When there are toll roads present, an employer may provide prepaid commuter passes to their employees to assist in meeting the cost of toll roads. Employers may exclude up to $265 (2019 value) from the employee's wages for these benefits.

> As of 2020, employers in Seattle will be required to provide employees with commuter passes on a pre-tax basis. Employees will have the option to select the benefit and must provide proof with a request for reimbursement to receive this benefit. (Source: APA)

Fringe Benefit Valuations

Stop & Check

1. Oliver Robertson is a field service representative whose primary job function is to visit customer sites. His primary base for computing mileage is his home. During 2019, he drove a total of 30,250 miles, 15 percent of which was for personal use. Using the IRS standard mileage rate of 58 cents per mile, what is the value of this fringe benefit using the cents-per-mile rule?
2. Katie Turner is a sales representative for a large pharmaceuticals company. She drives a 2019 Lexus ES, which has a fair market value of $47,000 and a lease value of $12,250. Katie has had the use of the vehicle for 180 days during 2019. She drives the vehicle 20 percent for personal use, and fuel is not provided by her employer. Using the lease value rule, what is the value of the fringe benefit? (Round final figure to two decimal places.)

LO 4-5 Differentiate Between Pre-Tax and Post-Tax Deductions

9nong/123RF

Two classes of deductions exist: pre-tax and post-tax. Pre-tax deductions are those deductions that are withheld from an employee's ***gross pay***, which is the amount of compensation prior to computing tax liability or applying deductions. The effect of pre-tax deductions is that they reduce the taxable income of the employee. Pre-tax deductions are ***voluntary deductions*** that have been legislated by the federal government as eligible for pre-tax withholding status, including certain types of insurance, retirement plans, and cafeteria plans.

Post-tax deductions are deducted from employee pay after federal, state, and local income taxes and FICA taxes have been deducted. Amounts deducted on a post-tax basis include both voluntary and court-mandated deductions. The voluntary deductions taken on a post-tax basis involve fringe benefits such as gym memberships, charitable contributions, repayment of company loans, optional insurance (e.g., auto, home), and union dues. Court-mandated deductions deducted on a post-tax basis may include child support garnishments, tax liens, credit card garnishments, and other legally directed items.

Insurance

Employers may provide subsidized health insurance coverage for their employees. The employees pay a portion of these health insurance expenses out of their paycheck, and the company makes up the difference. How much a company pays is determined by the company and could vary greatly, depending on the costs of health insurance and the policy selected by the employee. For health insurance plans to qualify for pre-tax status, they must meet the guidelines stated in the IRS Code:

According to the IRS, the following guidelines are used to determine if a health insurance plan qualifies for pre-tax status:

- Health plans offered through the state's small or large group market.
- An employer's self-insured health plan.
- The Department of Defense's Non-Appropriated Fund Health Benefits Program.

- A governmental plan.
- COBRA health coverage.
- Retiree health coverage.

(Source: IRS)

The IRS specifies these items as pre-tax because it reflects the belief that health insurance is a necessity, allowing employees to reduce their tax liability, and ultimately reducing the financial burden on families and employers by proactively supporting medical care.

EXAMPLE: PRE-TAX MEDICAL PREMIUM

Kelli Dennis works for Gunderson Associates. Her employer offers medical insurance for which the premiums may be taken on a pre-tax basis. Kelli is a salaried employee who earns $48,000 annually and is paid on a semimonthly basis. Her premium for the medical insurance is $125 per pay period. Consider the following difference in taxable income:

	Medical Insurance Deducted on a Pre-Tax Basis	Medical Insurance NOT Deduced on a Pre-Tax Basis
Annual salary	$48,000	$48,000
Period salary	$48,000/24 = $2,000	$48,000/24 = $2,000
Medical insurance deduction	$125	$0
Taxable Income	$1,875	$2,000

In 2010, the Affordable Care Act was passed, providing small businesses a tax credit for providing health insurance coverage when their employees are at low and moderate income levels. The act extended coverage of children until the age of 26 to be included as an option to employees on a pre-tax basis. This is only for employees covered under a qualifying cafeteria plan.

In response to the Affordable Care Act, IRS Code 6056 changed the reporting requirements for health insurance programs provided to employees. Employers with more than 50 employees are required to file an information return with the IRS and must provide a detailed summary of health coverage to employees. The value of the insurance coverage contributed by the employer must be reported on the employee's W-2 year-end tax statement within box 12 using code DD and should reflect the amounts contributed by both the employee and the employer.

According to the Internal Revenue Service, the Affordable Care Act mandates that individuals have "minimum essential coverage." The Tax Cuts and Jobs Act removed the penalty of 2.5 percent after December 31, 2018.

Examples of minimum essential coverage include

- Employer-provided health insurance.
- Health insurance purchased through an approved health insurance exchange.
- Coverage provided under federal auspices such as Medicare and Medicaid.
- Privately purchased health insurance.

Minimum essential coverage does not include the following limited benefit or limited term coverage plans:

- Vision and dental insurance issued on a stand-alone basis (i.e., not grouped with a medical insurance policy).
- Workers' compensation insurance.
- Accidental death and disability plans maintained by the employer.

(Source: Tax Cuts and Job Act, IRS)

It is important to remember that the amounts reported on the W-2 for the employer's contribution to health insurance do not add to the taxable wages of the employee.

Supplemental Health and Disability Insurance

Another option many employers are offering is a flow-through (i.e., the company does not cover any of the costs) of supplemental health and disability insurance. One of the largest providers of this type of insurance is American Family Life Assurance Company of Columbus (AFLAC). There are a variety of policies under AFLAC with separate treatment for taxation purposes (whether pre- or post-tax). The IRS Revision Ruling 2004-55 deals specifically with the tax treatment of short- and long-term disability, and IRS Code Sections 104(a)(3) and 105(a) deal with the exclusion of short- and long-term disability benefits from employees' gross wages. Long-term disability insurance is excluded from taxable income under the ruling. If an employer pays for long-term disability insurance, these amounts may be excluded from or included in gross pay, depending upon the election of the company. When determining the tax treatment for the supplemental health insurance, the IRS guidance provides the following: If the income derived will be estimated to be tax-free, then the cost associated will also be tax-exempt. (Note: Supplemental health and disability plan premiums are not tax-exempt for Social Security and Medicare taxes.)

EXAMPLE: SUPPLEMENTAL HEALTH INSURANCE DEDUCTION

Paul Nichols is a salaried exempt employee of Mark One Restoration Services. He earns $78,000 annually and is paid biweekly. The employer offers him medical insurance and supplemental health insurance with premiums of $150 and $75, respectively. Paul elects to have both premiums withheld on a pre-tax basis.

Salary per period ($78,000/26)	$3,000.00
Less: Medical insurance premium	$ 150.00
Less: Supplemental medical insurance premium	$ 75.00
Taxable income*	$2,775.00

*Note: Taxable income computed here pertains to computations of federal income tax. The taxable income for Social Security and Medicare taxes would be $2,850 because supplemental medical insurance premiums are not exempt for FICA taxes.

Jim Arbogast/Digital Vision/Getty Images

Retirement Plans

Retirement plans were covered under the Employee Retirement Income Security Act (ERISA) of 1974 in conjunction with the Internal Revenue Code. There are two basic types of retirement plans: ***defined benefit*** and ***defined contribution***. In a defined benefit plan, the employer guarantees the employee a specific level of income once retirement has been reached. As an example, under a defined benefit plan, the employer may guarantee 10 percent of average salary earned in the final five years of employment.

In a defined contribution plan, the individual places money from his or her payroll, pre-tax, into a retirement plan and the company may or may not match to a percentage. There are several different types of defined contribution plans, such as ***401(k)***, ***SIMPLE 401(k)***, ***403(b)***, ***457***, ***IRA***, ***SIMPLE***, ***SEP***, ***ESOP***, and profit sharing.

Note: Although some qualified 401(k) plans may be considered as cafeteria plans and may be excluded from FICA tax liability, the IRS states in Publication 15-b that most 401(k) plans are subject to Social Security and Medicare taxes. For the purposes of this text, we will assume that the 401(k) plans are not included in federal or state tax calculations but are included in Social Security and Medicare tax calculations. See Table 4-2 for an explanation of the different retirement plan types.

TABLE 4-2
Retirement Plan Types

Type of Plan	Description
401(k)	A group of investments, typically invested in stock market–based or mutual fund–based plans.
403(b)	Similar to a 401(k), but offered by nonprofit employers such as hospitals and schools.
457	Similar to 401(k) and 403(b), but has no penalty for fund withdrawal before age 59-1/2. Generally offered to governmental and certain nongovernmental employees
Savings Incentive Match Plan for Employees (SIMPLE)	The major limitation is employers may not have more than 100 employees. Funds are specifically set aside for the individual employee in a bank, mutual fund account, or stock market SIMPLE 401(k).
Individual Retirement Account (IRA)	Funds are specifically set aside for the individual employee in a bank or mutual fund account.
Employee Stock Ownership Plan (ESOP)	The company offers employees the ability to earn company stock for the duration of their employment.
Simplified Employee Pension (SEP)	A tax-favorable IRA is set up by or for the employee, and the employer contributes the funds into the account. The SEP is tax-favorable because it reduces the employee's income tax liability.

EXAMPLE: RETIREMENT PLAN EMPLOYEE CONTRIBUTION

Whitney Robinson is a salaried, exempt employee of Hovey Heating and Cooling. She is single with one withholding deduction and receives an annual salary of $60,000, paid semimonthly. She elects to contribute 6 percent of her period pay to the company-sponsored 401(k) plan on a pre-tax basis. Her taxable income would be computed as follows:

Salary per period ($60,000/24)	$2,500.00
Less: 6% contribution to 401(k)*	$ 150.00
Taxable income	$2,350.00

*Note: The 401(k) deduction is *not* exempt from Social Security and Medicare taxes.

Each year, the IRS imposes a cap on pre-tax retirement plan contributions. For 2019, the limit on 401(k) contributions is $19,000. People over 50 years of age may contribute a pre-tax "catch-up" amount up to $6,000. (Source: EBN)

Post-Tax Deductions

After the employer withholds the pre-tax and mandatory amounts from an employee's pay, other withholdings may apply. These other withholdings, known as post-tax deductions, comprise both voluntary and ***mandated deductions***. An example of a voluntary post-tax deduction is a charitable contribution elected by the employee. Mandated post-tax deductions include ***garnishments*** and ***union dues***. Post-tax deductions are amounts that the IRS has declared cannot reduce the employee's tax liability.

Charitable Contributions

Many companies offer to deduct funds for approved charitable organizations directly from the employee's pay. This ***charitable contribution*** is typically withheld *after* taxes have been calculated. The individual will report the charitable contribution on his or her itemized tax return, and there are separate requirements for meeting the deductible percentage that are outside the scope of this text.

EXAMPLE: NET PAY WITH CHARITABLE CONTRIBUTION

Perry Wallace is an employee at Working Environments in Winchester, New Hampshire. He earns $29,000 annually and is paid weekly. He is single with one withholding allowance. He has pre-tax health insurance of $25 and a charitable contribution to the United Way of $10 per pay period. His taxable income would be as follows:

Period pay	$557.69
Less: Health insurance	$ 25.00
Taxable income	$532.69

Note that Perry's taxable income does *not* reflect his United Way contribution. Because that contribution is computed on a post-tax basis, it does not affect taxable income.

Court-Ordered Garnishments

There are several reasons that a court may order an employer to withhold amounts from an employee's pay and redirect those funds to a regulatory agency. The most common garnishments are for child support, alimony, and student loans. Garnishments apply to ***disposable income***, which is the amount of employee pay after legally required deductions such as income taxes have been withheld. If an employee has one garnishment order for 10 percent and receives a second for 15 percent, any further garnishment requests will be deferred until the disposable income is at a level that is available for garnishments.

Consumer credit:

According to Title III of the ***Consumer Credit Protection Act (CCPA)***, garnishments may not be more than: (a) 25 percent of the employee's disposable earnings OR (b) the amount by which an employee's disposable earnings are greater than 30 times the federal minimum wage, or $217.50.

Child support:

Garnishments for child support or alimony may be up to 50 percent of disposable income, with an additional 5 percent for any child support that is more than 12 weeks in arrears.

Nontax debts owed to federal agencies:

Garnishments for nontax amounts to federal agencies may not total more than 15 percent of disposable income.

©McGraw-Hill Education/Ken Cavanagh

Union Dues

When employees are part of a union that requires regular dues, the employer must withhold those dues from the employee as a post-tax payroll deduction. The union uses dues to fund its activities, which include representation in employee–employer negotiations and political activism. Some employers may pay the union dues for their employee as part of their noncash compensation.

Pre-Tax vs. Post-Tax Deductions

Stop & Check

1. Which act offered a small-business tax credit for employees' health insurance premiums?
2. What are examples of different retirement plans that may qualify as pre-tax withdrawals?
3. Otis Singleton has disposable pay of $1,790.00. He receives a court-ordered garnishment for credit card debt of $15,000. Otis Singleton does not have earnings over 30 times the federal minimum wage. What is the maximum amount that may be withheld from Otis's pay?
4. Otis questioned the amount of the garnishment, claiming that he has health insurance of $125 and union dues of $45 that must also be withheld from his pay. How much should be withheld for the garnishment? Explain.

LO 4-6 Apply Rules for Withholding, Depositing, and Reporting Benefits

Providing benefits as a condition of employment is an important part of employee compensation. In many cases, amounts of money associated with benefits are quantifiable such as insurance premiums, employee contributions, or specific mandatory deductions. In other cases, the fringe benefit valuation rules are needed. The next piece of the puzzle is actually withholding, depositing, and reporting the benefits to the necessary people and organizations.

Daimond Shutter/Shutterstock

Rules for Withholding Amounts Related to Benefits

Sums of money related to benefits should be deducted from employee pay in a timely manner. The IRS stipulates that the value of all noncash benefits must be determined no later than January 31 of the following year. This deadline facilitates reporting of the fringe benefits on the employees' W-2s. It additionally allows the employer time to deposit any necessary amounts on time.

As a general rule, money associated with employee benefits should be withheld when the benefit is made available. It is up to the employer's discretion if the money should be withheld during a pay period, monthly, annually, and so forth. Therefore, any employee contributions to cafeteria plans, FSAs, HSAs, or other benefits should be deducted from regular pay. A best practice is to document the amounts involved in voluntary deductions in writing for the employee to acknowledge and sign.

> The IRS reported that the number of employer audits increased because of the reporting of fringe benefits and taxes due. According to the IRS, when an audit is triggered because of red flags in the computer selection program, one of the first areas checked is employer valuation and reporting of fringe benefits. Other items considered include the employer's internal control system and classification of workers as employees or independent contractors. (Source: *Accounting Today*)

An exception to the general rule is the ***special accounting rule*** defined by the IRS for noncash benefits provided only in the last two months of the calendar year. Benefits given during this period may be treated as paid during the following calendar year; however, only the value of the benefits may be treated as such. Although employers may opt to use the special accounting period for specific benefits, all employees who receive that benefit must also have it reported in accordance with the special accounting rule.

EXAMPLE: SPECIAL ACCOUNTING RULE

Marion Morrison is an employee of Connections Inc. and drives a company car. According to the special accounting rule, the company deferred the taxable amount of Marion's personal use of the company car during November and December 2019 until January 2020. This practice would reduce Marion's taxable income for 2019, but she would still be liable for it in her 2020 taxes. Connections Inc. would be required to notify Marion of its use of the special accounting rule for her personal company car use no later than January 31, 2020.

Treatment of Taxable Benefit Withholdings

No matter how the employee receives specific benefits, the employer must treat the benefit as though it was paid annually. The rationale for this treatment is to guarantee that taxable benefits are reflected appropriately on employee W-2s. The employer may change the timing of any amounts withheld for benefits as necessary for the entire company and for individual employees.

One caveat to the rules for withholding involves the transfer of property associated with benefits. For example, if the benefit involved is an investment, any amount withheld from the employee must coincide with the transfer of ownership of the investment.

In regards to the valuation of taxable fringe benefits, employers may choose to add the periodic value of the fringe benefit to period pay and tax it at the employee's regular tax rate. Alternatively, the employer may report the total value and withhold federal income tax at the 25 percent rate. An example of this practice would involve the valuation of personal company car use, if reported annually. In that case, the employer may add the full amount of the benefit valuation to a single pay period and deduct the taxes at that time.

Employees have found that their "free" fringe benefits may be subject to taxes. Wellness programs involving gym memberships, nutritional counseling, and other services provided at no cost to employees may be added to an employee's gross income and subject to income and FICA taxes. (Source: *Forbes*)

Rules for Depositing Amounts Related to Benefits

Employer deposit rules related to benefits are nearly as diverse as the benefits themselves. Like the withholdings, the deposit frequency depends on the timing of deductions from employee pay and recipient requirements (when applicable). A general rule for taxes withheld is that the deposit of these amounts must follow employer deposit rules, which will be covered in Chapter 6. The employer should estimate the amount of the benefit transmitted on a specific date, remit taxes, and transmit any other monies as necessary.

EXAMPLE: DEPOSIT OF EMPLOYEE 401(K) CONTRIBUTIONS

Theresa Bowen, an employee of TMS Physical Therapy, contributes 4 percent of her gross pay to her employer-sponsored employee stock option benefit. Theresa is paid biweekly and earns $52,000 annually. The employer makes quarterly deposits to the stockbroker. In this example, Theresa's contribution is $2,000 × 0.04, or $80, per pay period. The employer would deduct the amounts from Theresa's pay and retain it in a liability account, which they would deposit with the stockbroker at the appropriate time each quarter.

Depositing taxes for noncash fringe benefits will occasionally require an estimate of the taxes due. An example when such an estimate may occur would be employee meals. The employer would estimate the value of the meals and deposit the appropriate amount of tax because it would be a taxable fringe benefit. It is important to note that the estimate needs to be as accurate as possible and that underpayment of taxes associated with noncash fringe benefits will result in IRS penalties.

Rules for Reporting Benefits

Benefit reports occur in two different places: the employee's Form W-2 and the total compensation report. Each report serves a different purpose.

- Form W-2 serves as a report of all wages and associated taxes for a calendar year. All taxable benefits are reported as wages on the employee's Form W-2. This method of reporting ensures that the employer calculates the correct amount of income taxes and that the employee's annual tax return reflects the proper amounts of income.
- The total compensation report is a report given to the employee from the company that details all benefits in monetary terms. This report allows employees to have an accurate statement of the cash and noncash value of their service to the employer.

Rawpixel.com/Shutterstock

Custom benefits software is becoming more popular among employers. Companies specializing in employee benefits provide integrated custom platforms that address employer withholding, depositing, and reporting needs. These platforms sometimes cost more than $100,000, which makes them too expensive for many small- and medium-size employers. Innovations in technology may ultimately make these platforms more affordable. Changes in reporting laws certainly make them necessary. (Source: *Employee Benefit Adviser*)

According to the IRS and the Department of Labor, some of the most common benefits errors are

- Incorrectly defined compensation.
- Delays in the remittance of employees' contributions for benefits.
- Improper definition of employee eligibility and enrollment in benefit plans.
- Incorrect employee vesting in plans.
- Benefit forfeitures.
- Improper use of loans made to participants.
- Incorrect use of hardship distributions.
- Incorrectly recorded plan expenses.

The best way to avoid errors is to involve both the payroll and the human resources departments in benefits determinations to ensure proper implementation and internal classification of related monies. Benefit plans should be reviewed annually to ensure accuracy in legal compliance, remittance procedures, and reconciliation of employee contributions with payroll records.

Employee Benefits Reporting

Stop & Check

1. When should employers withhold amounts of money associated with benefits from employee pay?
2. Brandon McLaughlin is an employee of Creighton Steel and receives several fringe benefits as a result of his employment. He wants to know the value of his employment, both cash and noncash. What report should he request from his employer?
3. Vivian King is an employee of Nabors Drilling. She receives her Form W-2 in January and notices that her gross pay exceeds her annual salary. As the payroll accountant, you are aware of all fringe benefits available to and used by employees. What would you tell Vivian to help her understand the difference?

Trends to Watch

EMPLOYEE BENEFITS

Employers' attitudes toward employee benefits have undergone changes since 2016. Benefits have become important negotiating tools for employees, which has resulted in the following:

- Large companies such as Google, Facebook, and Costco have developed a reputation for offering generous benefits.
- Employees are using sites such as Glassdoor and Salary.com to rate prospective employers' total compensation packages.
- Values associated with fringe benefits have risen in proportion to employee salaries.

Trends to watch in fringe benefits and voluntary deductions include the following:

- Increases to paid family sick leave and flexible or remote work options.
- Increased guidance for student loan repayment connections with employee benefits.
- Increases to onsite wellness benefits such as gyms and healthy eating options coupled with fitness incentives.
- Financial wellness and identity theft education resources.
- Auto-enrollment and automatic diversification plans to help employees save more of their earnings and manage their investments.
- The Department of Labor is clarifying the concepts of discretionary and non-discretionary bonuses. This is in response to a number of incorrect calculations seen within industry. Discretionary bonuses are infrequent and at the discretion of management, so employees are not expecting them year over year. These would not be included in the determination of regular wage rate for overtime. Non-discretionary bonuses are contract driven, commissions, or given frequently enough that employees have come to expect and plan for them. Clarification about inclusion in the calculation of regular wage rate for overtime and retroactive application is under discussion.

Summary of Fringe Benefits and Voluntary Deductions

Fringe benefits are an integral part of employee compensation and often have a significant influence on the cost of an employee. Common forms of fringe benefits are health insurance, and retirement, but can encompass an endless variety of employee perks. Certain noncash fringe benefits are subject to employment taxes, which requires an employer to be aware of the taxes associated with offering certain types of benefits.

A primary category of fringe benefits involves employer-sponsored medical insurance plans. Most medical insurance plans may be deducted from an employee's pay on a pre-tax basis, which reduces the employee's tax liability. Employee medical insurance premiums are deducted on a pre-tax basis; this fringe benefit is often part of a cafeteria plan, and other pre-tax benefits such as flexible spending arrangements (FSA) may be included.

Certain types of noncash fringe benefits are excluded from taxation. A common form of excluded fringe benefits are de minimis benefits that have a value small enough that accounting for the cost would be unrealistic. Other noncash fringe benefits not subject to taxes involve items provided by the employer for their own convenience such as on-site meals and company cars. However, the personal use of company cars is subject to tax, based on the valuation method chosen by the employer.

Many voluntary benefits are deducted from employee pay on a post-tax basis. Other post-tax deductions include court-mandated deductions and garnishments. It is important to note the legal limits involved with garnishing employee pay to ensure that an appropriate amount is deducted. Employers are responsible for withholding, depositing, and reporting all deductions from an employee's pay, especially when those deductions are taxes. The total amount of annual compensation including pay, taxes, and benefits may be reported on the W-2 and the total compensation report.

Key Points

- Fringe benefits are an important part of an employee's compensation package because they help attract and retain high-quality employees.
- Fringe benefits have been correlated with increases in employee productivity and company revenue.
- Fringe benefits may be statutory or voluntary in nature.
- Pre-tax deductions are used for qualified deductions and to reduce the taxable wage base.
- Cafeteria plans allow employees to exclude medical premiums and qualified medical expenses from income tax and FICA taxes.
- Certain pre-tax deductions are subject to FICA taxes.
- Excluded fringe benefits are subject to specific IRS rules that govern amounts and taxation.
- Personal use of company vehicles is evaluated to determine the amount of income the employee is taxed on his or her Form W-2.
- Post-tax deductions include garnishments, union dues, and charitable contributions.
- Garnishments are subject to maximum percentages of disposable income, depending on the type of garnishment.
- Employer withholding of amounts associated with providing employee benefits varies depending on the benefit and if it is subject to taxes.
- Taxes associated with taxable noncash fringe benefits must be deposited when the benefit is transmitted to the employee.
- Employers report the valuation of noncash fringe benefits as part of the employee's Form W-2 and the total compensation report.

Vocabulary

401(k)
403(b)
457
Cafeteria plan
Cents-per-mile rule
Charitable contribution
Commuting rule
Compensation
Consumer Credit Protection Act (CCPA)
De minimis
Defined benefit
Defined contribution
Disposable income
ESOP
Fair market value (FMV)
Flexible spending arrangement (FSA)
Fringe benefit
Garnishments
General valuation rule (GVR)
Gross pay
Health savings account (HSA)
High deductible health plan (HDHP)
IRA
Lease value rule
Mandated deductions
Mandatory deductions
Pay advice
Post-tax deductions
Premium only plan (POP)
Publication 15-b
Qualified plan
SEP
SIMPLE
SIMPLE 401(k)
Special accounting rule
Union dues
Voluntary deductions

Review Questions

1. Why do companies offer fringe benefits to their employees?
2. Approximately what percentage of employee compensation includes fringe benefits?
3. What are three examples of voluntary fringe benefits?
4. What are the two reports associated with fringe benefits?
5. What are two examples of voluntary deductions?
6. What are two examples of pre-tax deductions?
7. What are two types of insurance that may be deducted pre-tax under a cafeteria plan?

8. What are the four categories of cafeteria plans?
9. How does an FSA affect an employee's taxable wages?
10. What are three examples of excluded fringe benefits?
11. What are the ways that the value of a company vehicle as a fringe benefit is determined?
12. What are garnishments and how must they be handled?
13. How do post-tax deductions differ from pre-tax deductions?
14. How does the special accounting rule affect withholding of benefits?
15. How often must employers deposit taxes associated with taxable fringe benefits?

Exercises Set A

E4-1A. LO 4-1, 4-4

Caroline Watts is an employee of Lavender Creek Farm. She has come to you, the payroll accountant, for advice about her health insurance premiums, specifically if she should have them deducted pre-tax or post-tax. What reason(s) would you give her for having the medical premiums deducted on a pre-tax basis?

a. The premium amounts are reduced by deducting them on a pre-tax basis
b. The employee's income that is subject to income tax(es) is reduced
c. The income subject to Social Security and Medicare taxes is reduced
d. All health insurance premiums must be deducted on a pre-tax basis

E4-2A. LO 4-1

Nora Wade is an employee of WGLO-TV, where she is an on-air news presenter. Which of the following would likely be fringe benefits that her employer would provide because they would be needed as part of her job? (Select all that apply.)

a. Wardrobe consulting services
b. On-site cafeteria
c. Hair and makeup services
d. Personal accounting services

E4-3A. LO 4-2

Examples of qualified insurance benefits include which of the following? (Select all that apply.)

a. Long-term care benefits
b. Health savings accounts
c. Pet insurance premiums
d. Group term life insurance (up to $50,000)

E4-4A. LO 4-2

What is a significant difference between flexible spending arrangements (FSAs) and health savings accounts (HSAs)?

a. Only FSAs may be included as part of a cafeteria plan
b. HSAs may accompany any type of employer-sponsored health insurance
c. Amounts contributed to HSAs may remain in the account for use later in life
d. No annual pre-tax contribution limit exists for FSAs

E4-5A. LO 4-3

Dallas Wong is an employee who receives educational assistance in the amount of $10,250 per year. How is this amount treated for tax purposes?

a. None of it is taxable
b. All of it is taxable
c. $5,000 is taxable
d. $5,250 is taxable

E4-6A. LO 4-4

Ana Cole is an employee of Wilson In-Home Healthcare Services. She is issued a company vehicle so that she may drive to customer sites. Which of the general valuation rules would be appropriate to compute the value of the asset for any personal use? (Select all that apply.)

a. Cents-per-mile rule
b. Commuting rule
c. Unsafe conditions rule
d. Lease value rule

E4-7A. LO 4-5
Which of the following describes the primary difference between a 401(k) and a 403(b) retirement plan?
a. The 401(k) is a defined benefit only plan
b. The 403(b) is a defined contribution only plan
c. The 401(k) is restricted to investments in stocks only
d. The 403(b) is restricted to use by nonprofit companies

E4-8A LO 4-5
Which of the following is true about fringe benefits?
a. They represent additional cash paid directly to employees
b. They are only available for employees
c. They represent additional compensation given for services performed
d. The amount of the fringe benefit is never subject to income tax

E4-9A. LO 4-5
How is disposable income computed?
a. Gross pay less pre-tax deductions
b. Gross pay less pre-tax deductions and income taxes
c. Gross pay less mandatory deductions
d. Gross pay less Social Security and Medicare taxes

E4-10A. LO 4-6
By what date must a company declare the value of noncash benefits used in 2019?
a. January 1, 2020
b. December 31, 2020
c. February 1, 2020
d. January 31, 2020

Problems Set A

P4-1A. LO 4-1, 4-2
Karen Wilson and Katie Smith are looking at the company's health care options and trying to determine how much their net pay will decrease if they sign up for the qualified cafeteria plan offered by the company. Explain the calculations of taxable income when qualified health care deductions are involved. Karen, a married woman with four exemptions, earns $2,000 per biweekly payroll. Katie, a single woman with one exemption, also earns $2,000 per biweekly payroll. The biweekly employee contribution to health care that would be subject to the cafeteria plan is $100.

Karen's taxable income if she declines to participate in the cafeteria plan: ___________

Karen's taxable income if she participates in the cafeteria plan: ___________

Katie's taxable income if she declines to participate in the cafeteria plan: ___________

Katie's taxable income if she participates in the cafeteria plan: ___________

P4-2A. LO 4-1
Joe Ramsey is a computer programmer at Biosphere Communications. He approaches you, the payroll accountant, about his garnishment for child support, claiming that he wishes to remit it personally because he needs to increase his net pay. What advice should you offer him?

P4-3A. LO 4-1, 4-2
Yvette Bradbury is an account representative at Commerce Savings Bank, earning $42,000 annually, paid semimonthly. She contributes 3 percent of her gross pay to her qualified 401(k) plan on a pre-tax basis and has a pre-tax medical premium of $120. What is her taxable income per pay period?

P4-4A. LO 4-3
Keren Wiseman is an employee of Dimensionworks Designs in New Mexico. She received the following achievement awards from her employer during 2019:

- Best safety plan, Santa Fe County: $1,200
- Top emergency plan layout, New Mexico: $1,600
- Ten-year employee award: $750

How much of her achievement award income is taxable?

P4-5A. LO 4-1, 4-3

Trinidad Schwab is an employee at the Kyletown Fire Department. He received the following benefits from his employer during 2019 for company purposes:

- On-site housing: $250 per month
- Employer-provided cell phone: $50 per month
- Meals: $100 per month

What amount of these benefits are taxable for 2019?

P4-6A. LO 4-4

Judi Pendergrass is an account representative at Ever Pharmaceuticals. She has a company car for customer visits, which she uses to commute from work to home on Friday nights and from home to work on Monday mornings, 50 weeks per year. Her commute is 25 miles each direction. Using the commuting rule, what is the valuation of the fringe benefit?

P4-7A. LO 4-4

Brent Bishop is the Vice President of Operations for Southern Sweets Bakery. He drives a 2019 Toyota Prius Prime as his company car, and it has a fair market value of $37,500. The prorated annual lease value per Publication 15-b for the vehicle is $9,750. He reported driving 34,750 miles during 2019, of which 20 percent were for personal reasons. The company pays his fuel and charges him five cents per mile for fuel charges. Using the lease value rule, what is the valuation of Brent's company car benefit?

P4-8A. LO 4-5

Geraldine Wolfe is a supervisor at Fantastigifts. She has an annual salary of $45,000, paid biweekly, and a garnishment for consumer credit of $375. Assuming that her disposable income is 80 percent of her gross pay per period, does the garnishment follow the CCPA? If not, what is the maximum garnishment allowed for Geraldine's consumer credit garnishment?

P4-9A. LO 4-1, 4-2, 4-5

Christine Boone is an employee at Americamp Vehicles. She earns a salary of $34,750 annually, paid biweekly. She contributes to the following fringe benefits and other deductions:

- Medical insurance: $80 per pay period
- Dental insurance: $15 per pay period
- 401(k): 5 percent of gross pay
- Union dues: $100 per month
- Additional withholding: $75 per month

What is the total annual amount of Christine's fringe benefits and other deductions?

P4-10A. LO 4-6

Gavin Range is the payroll accountant for Comptech Industries. His employer decided to use the special accounting rule for 2019. Which months may be included in the special accounting rule?

P4-11A. LO 4-1, 4-2, 4-3, 4-5

Elijah Hamilton is the payroll accountant at White Box Builders. He is preparing an information package about voluntary and fringe benefits. Using the following list of fringe benefits, classify each benefit as pre-tax or post-tax *and* if it is taxable or tax exempt for federal income taxes.

Employee Benefits

Benefit	Pre-tax	Post-tax	Taxable	Tax-exempt
401(k)				
Medical insurance				
Off-site gym membership				
United Way contributions				
AFLAC				
Tuition assistance up to $5,250 annually				
Commuter passes				

Exercises Set B

E4-1B. LO 4-1
Which of the following fringe benefits is exempt from federal income tax but subject to FICA tax?
a. Moving expense reimbursements
b. Tuition reduction for undergraduate education
c. Adoption assistance
d. Working condition benefits

E4-2B. LO 4-1
Robin Mendez is an employee of Pharmiceutics LLC. She is a traveling salesperson who routinely meets with customers at their places of business. Which of the following fringe benefits would be appropriate for her employer to provide for Robin to conduct business? (Select all that apply.)
a. Laptop computer
b. Company car
c. Personal stylist
d. Clothing allowance

E4-3B. LO 4-2
Which of the following is a co-requisite of a health savings account (HSA)?
a. No employer-provided insurance
b. A high deductible health plan
c. Multiple health insurance plans held by the same employee
d. A flexible spending arrangement

E4-4B. LO 4-2
What is the annual maximum amount that an employee may contribute to a flexible savings arrangement, before it becomes taxable income?
a. $2,200
b. $2,400
c. $2,700
d. $2,800

E4-5B. LO 4-3
Alejandro McCarthy is an employee of Shiloh Bakery. His regular commute includes paying a toll for a portion of his route. Shiloh Bakery offers commuter passes as a fringe benefit. What is the maximum amount that may be excluded from taxes as a fringe benefit?
a. $155
b. $205
c. $265
d. $305

E4-6B. LO 4-4
Juan Potter is an employee of Convergent Technologies whose job is strictly based in the company's office. His employer has authorized his use of a company vehicle for commuting purposes, as necessary. Which of the general valuation rules would be appropriate to evaluate the value of this fringe benefit?
a. Lease value rule
b. Unsafe conditions rule
c. Commuting rule
d. Cents-per-mile rule

E4-7B. LO 4-2
Cameron Levitt is the payroll accountant for Glowing Yoga. He is preparing a presentation about the Section 125 cafeteria plans. Which of the following items may qualify for inclusion in a cafeteria plan?
a. Health benefits
b. Adoption assistance
c. Child care expenses
d. Education assistance

E4-8B. LO 4-5

Gabrielle Jackson is the payroll accountant of Choice Bakeries. She is researching retirement plan options for her employer. Choice Bakeries has 77 employees and is a for-profit company. Which of the following plans should she consider? (Select all that apply.)

a. 403(b)
b. 401(k)
c. SIMPLE 401(k)
d. IRA

E4-9B. LO 4-1

Which of the following is/are examples of fringe benefits? (Select all that apply.)

a. Education assistance (up to $5,250 annually)
b. Dependent care assistance (up to $5,000 annually)
c. Vacation packages
d. Retirement planning services

E4-10B. LO 4-5

Which of the following are always post-tax deductions? (Select all that apply.)

a. Garnishments
b. Qualified health insurance
c. Charitable contributions
d. Retirement plan contributions

E4-11B. LO 4-6

To which two months does the special accounting rule pertain?

a. January and February
b. November and December
c. The last two months of the company's fiscal year
d. December and January of the following year

Problems Set B

P4-1B. LO 4-1, 4-2

Will Barrett and Eric Martin are looking at the company's health care options and trying to determine what their taxable income will be if they sign up for the qualified cafeteria plan offered by the company, which will allow them to deduct the health care contributions pre-tax. Will, a single man with one exemption, earns $1,600 per semimonthly payroll. Eric, a married man with six exemptions, earns $1,875 per semimonthly pay period. The semimonthly employee contribution to health care that would be subject to the cafeteria plan is $75 for Will, $250 for Eric. Calculate the taxable income when qualified health care deductions are involved.

Will's taxable income if he declines to participate in the cafeteria plan: __________

Will's taxable income if he participates in the cafeteria plan: __________

Eric's taxable income if he declines to participate in the cafeteria plan: __________

Eric's taxable income if he participates in the cafeteria plan: __________

P4-2B. LO 4-1

Orlando Collier is employed as a concierge at Strawberry Lodge, an upscale resort in the Adirondack Mountains. He wants to know which deductions from his pay are considered voluntary fringe benefits. As the payroll accountant, where would you tell him to look on his pay stub?

P4-3B. LO 4-1, 4-2

Todd Redden is a supervisor at Pinebank Construction. He contributes $2,400 annually to a FSA and has medical insurance that has a $250 monthly premium. He earns a salary of $64,000 and is paid semimonthly. What is his taxable income per period?

P4-4B. LO 4-3

Kareem Espinal is employed as a copywriter at Jacksaw Publications. He is receiving education assistance of $10,000 per year from his employer to complete his bachelor's degree from an accredited college. How much of that assistance is taxable?

P4-5B.
LO 4-1, 4-3

Jewel Lyman is an employee in the office of Salvaggio & Wheelers, Attorneys at Law. She received the following benefits during 2019:

- Medical insurance: $250 per month
- Commuter pass: $500 per month
- Employer-paid membership to Anytime Gym: $75 per year
- Dependent care assistance: $3,600 per year

What is the total taxable amount for Jewel's 2019 benefits?

P4-6B.
LO 4-4

Rodney Atwater is a sales representative for American Silk Mills. Because he visits customer sites, he has a company car. He drove 25,500 miles during 2019, of which he reported 15 percent was personal miles. Using the cents-per-mile rule, what is the valuation of this benefit for 2019?

P4-7B.
LO 4-4

Janice Lucas is the president of Miller Custom Coffee Roasters. She drives a 2018 Mercedes E300 with a fair market value of $57,500. The lease value is $14,750. The odometer started at 655 and was reported at 32,855 at the end of the year. The car was available all of 2019. Janice reported that she drove 32,200 miles during 2019, of which 9,800 were for personal reasons. The company pays all her fuel and charges her five cents per personal mile for fuel costs. What is her 2019 valuation using the lease value rule?

P4-8B.
LO 4-5

Doug Barton is an employee at Artlee Collections. He earns a salary of $36,000 per year, paid semimonthly, and has a child support garnishment. Assuming that Doug's disposable income is 80 percent of his gross pay, what is the maximum amount per period that may be deducted for the garnishment?

P4-9B.
LO 4-2, 4-5

Gwen Evans is an employee at Findley Street Financial, where she earns an annual salary of $125,500, paid semimonthly. She has the following fringe and voluntary benefits:

- Medical insurance: $150 per month
- 401(k): 6 percent of gross pay
- Flexible spending arrangement: $2,000 annually
- United Way contribution: $25 per pay period

What is the total amount she contributes to fringe benefits and voluntary deductions annually?

P4-10B.
LO 4-6

Arla Dodson is the payroll accountant for Penn & Associates Investments. The company owner decided on December 15, 2019, that he would invoke the special accounting rule. By what date does Arla need to notify affected employees that the rule is being used?

P4-11B.
LO 4-1, 4-2, 4-3, 4-5

Kerry Palmer is reviewing benefits with you, the payroll accountant for Silly Lemon Films. Based on the following benefits in which she is interested, classify them as pre-tax or post-tax deductions *and* if they are taxable or tax exempt for federal income tax.

K. Palmer Benefits				
Benefit	**Pre-Tax**	**Post-Tax**	**Taxable**	**Tax Exempt**
Medical insurance				
FSA				
AFLAC				
Graduate School Tuition at $11,000 annually				
On-site meals				

Critical Thinking

4-1. Malcolm Figueroa is a sales employee of Carefree Pools and Spas Inc. During 2019, he was issued a company car with a fair market value of $35,000. He drove a total of 22,000 miles; used the car for 2,000 miles for personal use; and his employer paid for fuel, charging Malcolm 5.5 cents per mile. Under the lease-value rule, what is the amount that must be added to Malcolm's gross pay for 2019? (Use the following table for lease values.)

4-2. Malcolm's employer offers him the option to use the cents-per-mile rule instead of the lease-value rule for 2019. Which method will yield the lower gross income for Malcolm? (Use 58 cents per mile in your calculations.)

(1) Automobile FMV	(2) Annual Lease
$ 0 to 999	$ 600
1,000 to 1,999	850
2,000 to 2,999	1,100
3,000 to 3,999	1,350
4,000 to 4,999	1,600
5,000 to 5,999	1,850
6,000 to 6,999	2,100
7,000 to 7,999	2,350
8,000 to 8,999	2,600
9,000 to 9,999	2,850
10,000 to 10,999	3,100
11,000 to 11,999	3,350
12,000 to 12,999	3,600
13,000 to 13,999	3,850
14,000 to 14,999	4,100
15,000 to 15,999	4,350
16,000 to 16,999	4,600
17,000 to 17,999	4,850
18,000 to 18,999	5,100
19,000 to 19,999	5,350
20,000 to 20,999	5,600
21,000 to 21,999	5,850
22,000 to 22,999	6,100
23,000 to 23,999	6,350
24,000 to 24,999	6,600
25,000 to 25,999	6,850
26,000 to 27,999	7,250
28,000 to 29,999	7,750
30,000 to 31,999	8,250
32,000 to 33,999	8,750
34,000 to 35,999	9,250
36,000 to 37,999	9,750
38,000 to 39,999	10,250
40,000 to 41,999	10,750
42,000 to 43,999	11,250
44,000 to 45,999	11,750

(1) Automobile FMV	(2) Annual Lease
46,000 to 47,999	12,250
48,000 to 49,999	12,750
50,000 to 51,999	13,250
52,000 to 53,999	13,750
54,000 to 55,999	14,250
56,000 to 57,999	14,750
58,000 to 59,999	15,250

In the Real World: Scenario for Discussion

Project labor agreements (PLAs) are used in certain states to promote pay and benefit equity for construction workers. Specifically, PLAs ensure that construction workers who choose not to join a union have access to the same pay and benefits as their union-affiliated colleagues. PLAs ensure that the presence or absence of a labor union is not a factor in the contract bidding process, therefore encouraging more contractors to bid on construction projects. Proponents of PLAs contend that they expand employment opportunities. Opponents claim that the PLA cannot exist in at-will employment states.

Which side is more correct? How can the at-will employment laws exist where PLAs are allowed?

Internet Activities

4-1. Health insurance is a rapidly changing and evolving field. Employers have many options and concerns to consider. Check out www.npr.org/sections/health-care/ to listen to podcasts about health insurance and employer issues. What issues do employers currently face?

4-2. Using a site such as Google, Yahoo, or Safari, search for the term "fringe benefits." Sites such as HR360 at www.hr360.com contain insights into fringe benefits and guidance about the tax treatment for benefits. Why do you think that fringe benefits are important enough to influence an employee's choice of employer?

4-3. Go to www.benefitspro.com and search for benefits-related podcasts. Once you have listened to one or more podcast, what insights did you gain from the information presented?

4-4. Want to know more about the topics discussed in this chapter? Go to the following links:

www.healthcare.gov/law/index.html
www.aflac.com
www.investopedia.com
www.irs.gov/pub/irs-pdf/p15b.pdf
www.dol.gov/general/topic/wages/garnishments

4-5. Can employers charge employees for their uniforms? Check out the U.S. Department of Labor video at https://www.youtube.com/watch?v=PoZCux0rTN8&feature=youtu.be

Continuing Payroll Project: Prevosti Farms and Sugarhouse

Although the company has already established medical and retirement plan benefits, Toni Prevosti wants to consider other benefits to attract employees. As the company's accountant, you have been tasked with annotating employee earnings records with benefit elections for each employee. The following sheet contains details of employee choices. These costs are employer paid and will take effect on the first pay period of March.

To calculate the Life Insurance benefit, multiply the employee's annual salary by 1 percent. For example, if an employee earned $50,000 per year, the life insurance would be $50,000 × 0.01 = $500.

Employee	Flex-Time	Child Care Assistance (under $5,000 annually)	FSA (annual)	Educational Assistance ($4,000 annually)	Life Insurance (at 1% of annual salary value)	Long-Term Care Insurance ($15 per period)	Gym Membership ($15 per month)
Millen	Yes	Yes	$500.00	No	Yes	No	Yes
Towle	No	No	1,200.00	Yes	No	No	Yes
Long	Yes	Yes	700.00	Yes	Yes	No	Yes
Shangraw	Yes	No	200.00	No	Yes	No	No
Lewis	No	No	1,600.00	No	Yes	Yes	No
Schwartz	No	No	450.00	Yes	Yes	No	Yes
Prevosti	Yes	No	900.00	No	Yes	No	Yes
Student	No	No	300.00	Yes	No	No	Yes

Annotate the Employee Earning Records with payroll-related benefit elections. The amount per period should be included in the record. As an example, if an employee elected to contribute $1,300 to his or her FSA, the period payroll deduction would be $1,300/26, or $50.

EMPLOYEE EARNING RECORD (Partial)

NAME	Thomas Millen	Hire Date	2/1/2019
ADDRESS	1022 Forest School Rd	Date of Birth	12/16/1982
CITY/STATE/ZIP	Woodstock/VT/05001	Exempt/Nonexempt	Exempt
TELEPHONE	802-478-5055	Married/Single	M
SOCIAL SECURITY NUMBER	031-11-3456	No. of Exemptions	4
POSITION	Production Manager	Pay Rate	$35,000/year

Flex-Time	Child Care	FSA Amount	Educational Assistance	Life Ins.	Long-Term Care	Gym Membership	Total Benefit

EMPLOYEE EARNING RECORD (Partial)

NAME	Avery Towle	Hire Date	2/1/2019
ADDRESS	4011 Route 100	Date of Birth	7/14/1991
CITY/STATE/ZIP	Plymouth/VT/05102	Exempt/Nonexempt	Nonexempt
TELEPHONE	802-967-5873	Married/Single	S
SOCIAL SECURITY NUMBER	089-74-0974	No. of Exemptions	1
POSITION	Production Worker	Pay Rate	$12.00/hour

Flex-Time	Child Care	FSA Amount	Educational Assistance	Life Ins.	Long-Term Care	Gym Membership	Total Benefit

EMPLOYEE EARNING RECORD (Partial)

NAME	Charlie Long	Hire Date	2/1/2019
ADDRESS	242 Benedict Rd	Date of Birth	3/6/1987
CITY/STATE/ZIP	S. Woodstock/VT/05002	Exempt/Nonexempt	Nonexempt
TELEPHONE	802-429-3846	Married/Single	M
SOCIAL SECURITY NUMBER	056-23-4593	No. of Exemptions	2
POSITION	Production Worker	Pay Rate	$12.50/hour

Flex-Time	Child Care	FSA Amount	Educational Assistance	Life Ins.	Long-Term Care	Gym Membership	Total Benefit

EMPLOYEE EARNING RECORD (Partial)

NAME	Mary Shangraw	Hire Date	2/1/2019
ADDRESS	1901 Main St #2	Date of Birth	8/20/1994
CITY/STATE/ZIP	Bridgewater/VT/05520	Exempt/Nonexempt	Nonexempt
TELEPHONE	802-575-5423	Married/Single	S
SOCIAL SECURITY NUMBER	075-28-8945	No. of Exemptions	1
POSITION	Administrative Assistant	Pay Rate	$10.50/hour

Flex-Time	Child Care	FSA Amount	Educational Assistance	Life Ins.	Long-Term Care	Gym Membership	Total Benefit

EMPLOYEE EARNING RECORD (Partial)

NAME	Kristen Lewis	Hire Date	2/1/2019
ADDRESS	840 Daily Hollow Rd	Date of Birth	4/6/1960
CITY/STATE/ZIP	Bridgewater/VT/05523	Exempt/Nonexempt	Exempt
TELEPHONE	802-390-5572	Married/Single	M
SOCIAL SECURITY NUMBER	076-39-5673	No. of Exemptions	3
POSITION	Office Manager	Pay Rate	$32,000/year

Flex-Time	Child Care	FSA Amount	Educational Assistance	Life Ins.	Long-Term Care	Gym Membership	Total Benefit

EMPLOYEE EARNING RECORD (Partial)

NAME	Joel Schwartz	Hire Date	2/1/2019
ADDRESS	55 Maple Farm Wy	Date of Birth	5/23/1985
CITY/STATE/ZIP	Woodstock/VT/05534	Exempt/Nonexempt	Exempt
TELEPHONE	802-463-9985	Married/Single	M
SOCIAL SECURITY NUMBER	021-34-9876	No. of Exemptions	2
POSITION	Sales	Pay Rate	$24,000/year + commission

Flex-Time	Child Care	FSA Amount	Educational Assistance	Life Ins.	Long-Term Care	Gym Membership	Total Benefit

EMPLOYEE EARNING RECORD (Partial)

NAME	Toni Prevosti	Hire Date	2/1/2019
ADDRESS	10520 Cox Hill Rd	Date of Birth	9/18/1967
CITY/STATE/ZIP	Bridgewater/VT/05521	Exempt/Nonexempt	Exempt
TELEPHONE	802-673-2636	Married/Single	M
SOCIAL SECURITY NUMBER	055-22-0443	No. of Exemptions	5
POSITION	Owner/President	Pay Rate	$45,000/year

Flex-Time	Child Care	FSA Amount	Educational Assistance	Life Ins.	Long-Term Care	Gym Membership	Total Benefit

EMPLOYEE EARNING RECORD (Partial)

NAME	Student Success	Hire Date	2/1/2019
ADDRESS	1644 Smittin Rd	Date of Birth	1/1/1991
CITY/STATE/ZIP	Woodstock/VT/05001	Exempt/Nonexempt	Nonexempt
TELEPHONE	(555) 555-5555	Married/Single	S
SOCIAL SECURITY NUMBER	555-55-5555	No. of Exemptions	2
POSITION		Pay Rate	$34,000/year

Flex-Time	Child Care	FSA Amount	Educational Assistance	Life Ins.	Long-Term Care	Gym Membership	Total Benefit

Answers to Stop & Check Exercises

Fringe Benefits 101

1. Fringe benefits will fall under the pre-tax or post-tax category.
2. b and c
3. a, c, and d

What Is Served in the Cafeteria Plan?

1. a, b, d
2. A flexible spending account (FSA) can be taxable when contributions are over $2,700 annually by the employee. The purpose is to defer, not avoid paying taxes, and there is typically a use it or lose it policy where the funds expire at a point in time when not used. Health savings accounts (HSAs) may only be used in conjunction with a cafeteria plan where there is a high deductible, and the funds may be available longer for related medical care.
3. A HDHP has the following limits: $1,350 annual deductible (single), $2,700 annual deductible (family), $6,750 out-of-pocket expenses maximum (single), $13,500 out-of-pocket expenses maximum (family).

Excluded Fringe Benefits

1. No, because it is provided on the employer's premises and is operated by the company and restricted to use by its employees, their spouses, and dependents.
2. A portion of the cost of the car will be included in Marcia's gross income that would represent the personal use portion of mileage. However, any amount that is directly related to the job would be excluded under the Working Conditions Benefits.

Fringe Benefit Valuations

1. $2,631.75 (rounded) (30,250 miles × 15% × 0.58).
2. The value of the fringe benefit is $813.70, computed as follows (round final figure to two decimals):

Fair market value of vehicle:	$ 47,000
Annual lease value:	12,250
Prorated annual lease value:	49.315%
Percent of personal use during the year:	20%
Personal annual lease value:	$1,208.22

Pre-Tax vs. Post-Tax Deductions

1. Affordable Care Act.
2. 401(k); 403(b); Savings Incentive Match Plan for Employees (SIMPLE); Individual Retirement Account (IRA); Employee Stock Ownership Plan (ESOP); Simplified Employee Pension (SEP).
3. $447.50 calculated as: $1,790 disposable income × 25%.
4. Union dues and health insurance are not legally required and thus would not affect the amount of the disposable income available for garnishments.

Employee Benefits Reporting

1. Monies should be withheld from the employee when the benefit is made available; normal practice is to deduct these as the employees receive their pay (daily, weekly, biweekly, semimonthly, monthly, annually).
2. The total compensation report can be given to Brandon to explain the total cost of benefits and compensation received.
3. There are several fringe benefits that must be included in taxable income to the employees. These include personal use of a company provided vehicle, commuting paid by the employer, or lease of a vehicle.

Chapter Five

Employee Net Pay and Pay Methods

Death and taxes are the two certainties in life. Taxes are withheld from employees' earnings and remitted to the governing body. Companies operate as the collector and depositor of income taxes, garnishments, and other deductions on behalf of the employee. The tax code permits certain qualifying deductions to be taken out of an employee's pay prior to the income taxes being calculated. These deductions are called pre-tax deductions. Other deductions come out of the employee's pay after income taxes have been calculated; these are called post-tax deductions. Circular E, also known as Publication 15 (and all supplemental materials), from the Internal Revenue Service provides a comprehensive list of employee taxes, employer responsibilities, and guidance for special situations.

Taxes, voluntary, and mandated deductions all reduce the gross pay that we computed in Chapter 3. In this chapter, we will explore the effects of these deductions and any other fringe benefits on employee take-home pay, also called ***net pay***.

LEARNING OBJECTIVES

After studying Chapter 5, you should be able to:

LO 5-1 Compute Employee Net Pay

LO 5-2 Determine Federal Income Tax Withholding Amounts

LO 5-3 Compute Social Security and Medicare Tax Withholding

LO 5-4 Calculate State and Local Income Taxes

LO 5-5 Apply Post-Tax Deductions

LO 5-6 Discuss Employee Pay Methods

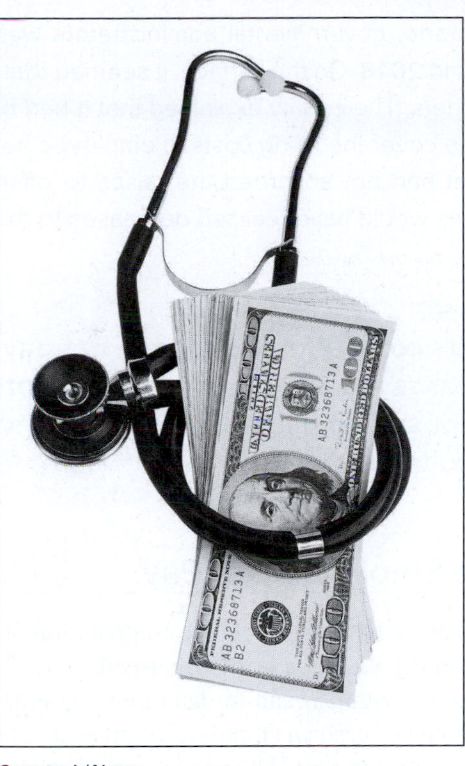

Comstock/Alamy

Pay Raises Do Not Keep Pace with Rising Health Insurance Costs

Rising health insurance costs are an issue for most American employees. For many people, it seems that take-home (net) pay is less each year. The simple truth of the matter is that the average pay raise of 3 percent is lower than the 4 to 5 percent increase in employee health insurance premiums. The graph in Figure 5-1 depicts the change in employee health care premiums from 2000 to 2017.

FIGURE 5-1

Health Premium Cost vs. Median Family Income, 2000–2017

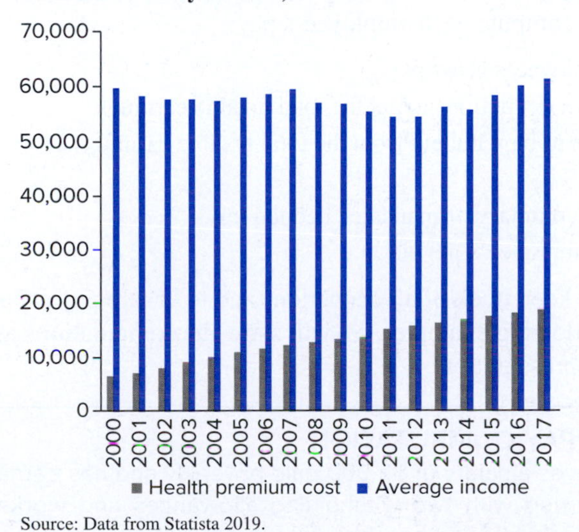

Source: Data from Statista 2019.

In Mesa County, Colorado, governmental administrators were criticized for receiving relatively large pay raises in 2018. On the surface, it seemed that the raises were larger for some officials than for others. The county explained that it had been absorbing employee raises in previous years to cover the rising costs of employee health insurance premiums. If the county government had not absorbed the raises to offset increases in insurance premium costs, employees would have realized decreases to their net pay since 2012.

(Sources: Kaiser Family Foundation, *The Daily Sentinel*)

Changes to benefits costs affect employee net pay in the form of increases or decreases in take-home pay. In Chapter 5, we will explore computations of employee net pay and the methods used to transmit that pay to the employees.

LO 5-1 Compute Employee Net Pay

Andriy Popov/123RF

Now that we have discussed the computation of gross income, it is time to focus on the various taxes and miscellaneous voluntary or court-ordered deductions withheld and to determine the employee's ***net pay***, which is the amount of cash an employee receives in a physical check, cash, direct deposit, or a paycard. The process of computing gross pay involves several steps, each of which must be completed accurately. We will explore the details of pre-tax deductions, tax computations, and post-tax deductions in the following sections of this chapter.

Once the employer has computed the employee's gross pay, the next step is to deduct mandatory, voluntary, and mandated amounts. These deductions include federal income tax, Medicare, and Social Security taxes, which are the primary mandatory deductions. Other mandatory deductions that the employee may be subject to include ***state income taxes***, city or county income taxes, and regional taxes. For example, Denver has a "head tax" for those employees working within the city and county; Mountain View, California, instituted a similar tax because of Google's presence in the city. Federal Unemployment Tax is the sole employer-only tax. Some states require employees to contribute for the State Unemployment Tax, whereas other states consider it an employer-only tax.

Pay Computation Steps

This is the process to compute each employee's pay:

1. Start with the employee's gross pay.
2. Subtract the pre-tax deductions to get the total taxable earnings.
3. Compute the taxes to be withheld from the total taxable earnings.
4. Deduct the taxes.
5. Deduct any other voluntary or mandated deductions.
6. The result is the employee's net pay.

The easiest way to keep track of all deductions and to ensure pay accuracy is to use a payroll register. In the following examples, we will show the computations as well as a sample of the payroll register representation.

EXAMPLE: NET PAY COMPUTATION

Marco Myles receives a salary of $2,000 paid biweekly and has earned $46,000 year-to-date. He is married with two withholding allowances and works for KOR Inc. in Charleston, West Virginia, where his state income tax is 6 percent. His pre-tax deductions include medical insurance of $50, a cafeteria plan of $75, and a 401(k) of 3 percent of his gross salary per pay period. He has charitable contributions of $10, union dues of $62, and a court-ordered garnishment for $120. Taxable income computation is the same for both federal and state income tax purposes. Let us compute Marco's net pay step-by-step:

Gross pay	$2,000.00
Less: pre-tax medical insurance deduction	−50.00
Less: cafeteria plan	−75.00
Less: 401(k) contribution	−60.00
Total taxable earnings	$1,815.00
Less: federal income tax (using wage-bracket method)	−110.00
Less: Social Security tax*	−116.25
Less: Medicare tax†	−27.19
Less: West Virginia state income tax***	−108.90
Less: charitable contribution	−10.00
Less: union dues	−62.00
Less: garnishment	−120.00
Net pay	$1,260.66

*2,000 − 50 − 75 = 1,875 × .062 = 116.25
†2,000 − 50 − 75 = 1,875 × .0145 = 27.19
***1,815 × 0.06 = 108.90

The payroll register for Marco Myles's pay would appear as follows:

Name	M/S	# W/H	Hourly Rate or Period Wage	No. of Regular Hours	No. of Overtime Hours	No. of Holiday Hours	Gross Earnings	401(k)	Insurance	Cafeteria Plan	Taxable Wages for Federal W/H	Taxable Wages for FICA
Marco Myles	M	2	2,000.00				2,000.00	60.00	50.00	75.00	1,815.00	1,875.00

Name	Gross Earning	Taxable Wages for Federal W/H	Taxable Wages for FICA	Federal W/H	Social Security Tax	Medicare W/H	State W/H Tax	Charitable Contribution	Union Dues	Garnishment	Net Pay
Marco Myles	2,000.00	1,815.00	1,875.00	110.00	116.25	27.19	108.90	10.00	62.00	120.00	1,260.66

Mayuree Moonhirun/Shutterstock

Grossed-Up Pay

An employer will occasionally want to pay an employee a specific net amount, perhaps as a bonus. However, all federal, state, and local taxes must be applied. The amount of the employee's pay must be "grossed up" to satisfy tax liabilities and achieve the net pay desired.

EXAMPLE: "GROSSING UP" AN EMPLOYEE'S PAY

Caitlyn Lanneker is an employee of Pacifica Enterprises, located in the state of Washington. The firm's president wants to award Caitlyn a $150 bonus at the end of the year to reward her. Use the following steps to compute the gross-up amount:

1. Compute the tax rate for federal income tax and FICA. The tax rate on bonuses is 22 percent (IRS Notice 1036). The Social Security (6.2%) and Medicare taxes (1.45%)

(continued)

(concluded)

must be added to this rate. For bonuses, the total tax rate equals 22% + 6.2% + 1.45%, or 29.65%. (For nonbonus gross-up, compute the tax rate using amounts from Appendix C). Add any state or local income tax rates to this computation as necessary.

2. To calculate the net tax rate, subtract the tax rate percentage from 100 percent (i.e., 100% − tax rate) to get the net tax rate. For this bonus, it is 100% – 29.65%, or 70.35%, because no state or local income tax rates apply.
3. Gross-up amount equals the net pay divided by the net tax rate.

For example, for Caitlyn to receive a $150 bonus, the equation to calculate the gross pay is $150/70.35% = $213.22.

Note: Typically, voluntary pre-tax or post-tax deductions are not withheld from bonus checks.

Differentiating Between Gross and Net Pay

Stop & Check

1. What is the difference between gross pay and net pay?
2. What are three items that may be deducted from gross pay?
3. What does it mean to "gross up" an amount paid to an employee?

LO 5-2 Determine Federal Income Tax Withholding Amounts

one photo/Shutterstock

Now let us shift our focus to ***mandatory deductions*** that must be withheld from employee pay. The first class of mandatory deductions is the federal income tax. This is an employee-only tax, meaning that the employer does not contribute a matching amount for the federal income tax withheld from an employee's pay.

Federal Income Taxes

The first tax we will cover is the ***federal income tax***. The federal income tax represents amounts to be withheld from employed persons, calculated using the information reported by the employee on Form W-4. The withheld tax is the employee's deposit against income taxes. The employee's federal income tax is determined by four factors:

1. Gross pay.
2. Pay frequency (weekly, biweekly, semimonthly, etc.).
3. Marital status.
4. Number of withholding allowances claimed on Form W-4.

Jirapong Manustrong/Shutterstock

The highest taxed federal income tax bracket is single with zero dependents. Employees who work more than one job or have additional income for which no income tax is withheld may request additional amounts as either percentages or dollars to be withheld and submitted to the IRS on their behalf. The employee makes these requests on Form W-4.

The employer acts as a collector and depositor for these funds. When an individual files the income tax return, the amount withheld from his or her pay during the year reduces the amount he or she may have to pay with the return. Federal taxable income is reduced by pre-tax deductions discussed previously.

Federal Income Tax Computation Examples

EXAMPLE: GROSS PAY LESS 401(K) AND INSURANCE

Amanda Brady's gross wages are $950, she has subscribed to the company's cafeteria plan, and she has agreed to a 10 percent investment of her gross wages in a qualified 401(k) plan. Her portion of the health insurance is $56.90 per pay period. To calculate her taxable pay, we must first determine the 401(k) deduction: $950 × 10% = $95. Therefore, her taxable pay is

$950.00	gross pay
–95.00	401(k) deduction
–56.90	health insurance
$798.10	taxable income

EXAMPLE: EFFECT OF FIXED AMOUNT VS. PERCENTAGE DEDUCTION FOR 401(K) CONTRIBUTION ON TAXABLE WAGES

Daniel Cain has gross wages of $1,125, participates in the company's 401(k) program at $100 per pay period, and has health insurance and AFLAC (all pre-tax) totaling $113.80. The calculation of Daniel's taxable income is

$1,125.00	gross pay
–100.00	401(k) deduction
–113.80	health insurance and AFLAC
$ 911.20	taxable income

Had Daniel participated in the company's 401(k) as a percentage instead of a fixed dollar, the percent would be calculated prior to other deductions. For instance, if he elected to invest 3 percent of his gross pay, his taxable income would be

$1,125.00	
× 0.03	
33.75	401(k) contribution

$1,125.00	gross pay
–33.75	401(k) contribution
–113.80	health insurance and AFLAC
$ 977.45	taxable income

Note: Gross Pay – qualified medical = taxable wages for FICA. $1125 – 113.80 = $1,011.20 would be the taxable amount for Social Security and Medicare because retirement contributions are not exempt from FICA taxes.

Regardless of the method used for calculating federal income taxes, the reduction for pre-tax items will remain the same. In manual systems, there are two commonly used methods to calculate the employee's federal income tax: wage bracket and percentage.

Wage-Bracket Method

Using the ***wage-bracket method***, the payroll clerk identifies the individual's marital status, number of exemptions, and taxable income level and then follows the chart located in Publication 15 for the amount to be withheld. If manually calculating the wage-bracket method, it is important to apply the appropriate number of withholding allowances prior to calculating the tax amounts. The wage-bracket method is useful for manual payroll preparation

FIGURE 5-2

Biweekly Payroll Period—Married Persons, Wage-Bracket Method

Valerie Ball is married and has three withholding allowance. The employee is paid biweekly and earned $1,839. What is the Federal Income Tax for Valerie?

Wage Bracket Method Tables for Income Tax Withholding

MARRIED Persons—**BIWEEKLY** Payroll Period

(For Wages Paid through December 31, 2018)

And the wages are–		And the number of withholding allowances claimed is—									
At least	But less than	0	1	2	3	4	5	6	7	8	9
		The amount of income tax to be withheld is—									
$1,765	$1,785	$145	$126	$107	$88	$69	$53	$37	$21	$5	
1,785	1,805	147	128	109	90	71	55	39	23	7	
1,805	1,825	150	131	112	92	73	57	41	25	9	
1,825	1,845	152	133	114	95	76	59	43	27	11	
1,845	1,865	155	135	116	97	78	61	45	29	13	
1,865	1,885	157	138	119	100	80	63	47	31	15	
1,885	1,905	159	140	121	102	83	65	49	33	17	
1,905	1,925	162	143	124	104	85	67	51	35	19	
1,925	1,945	164	145	126	107	88	69	53	37	21	
1,945	1,965	167	147	128	109	90	71	55	39	23	
1,965	1,985	169	150	131	112	92	73	57	41	25	
1,985	2,005	171	152	133	114	95	76	59	43	27	
2,005	2,025	174	155	136	116	97	78	61	45	29	

Important facts:

- The employee is married
- Has 3 withholding allowances
- Pay frequency is biweekly
- Earned $1,839

The page of the table is for married employees with biweekly pay

Go to the row that contains the bracket containing the employee's pay. In this example, the pay is $1,839, which is in the $1,825-$1,845 row.

Go to the column that contains the number of withholding allowances. In this case, the employee has 3 withholding allowances.

*The intersection of the table **row and column** is the **withholding tax**, which is **$95**

because the process of federal tax withholding is an estimate for the year-end amount of taxes due. To determine taxes to withhold using the wage-bracket method in Appendix C, see Figure 5-2, which is for married persons who are paid on a biweekly basis, using Publication 15. The wage-bracket method may be programmed into an automated payroll system. If the payroll clerk is using an automated system, periodic checking and ensuring year-end updates do not run prior to the last payroll are important to ensuring validity in the system.

A married person with three withholding allowances and with $1,839 in biweekly earnings will have $95 of federal income tax withheld. Note that the amount of tax withheld decreases as the number of withholding allowances increases.

EXAMPLE: WAGE-BRACKET COMPUTATION OF FEDERAL INCOME TAX, MARRIED, SEMIMONTHLY

Jessa Cunningham is an employee of Rowan Trees. She earns $48,000 per year and is paid semimonthly. She is married with three withholding allowances. Using the wage-bracket tables in Appendix C, we will determine Jessa's federal income tax in different situations.

1. NO VOLUNTARY PRE-TAX DEDUCTIONS

Period pay ($48,000/24)	$2,000.00
Taxable income	2,000.00
Federal income tax	101.00

2. PRE-TAX HEALTH INSURANCE DEDUCTION, $150

Period pay ($48,000/24)	$2,000.00
Less: health insurance	150.00
Taxable income	$1,850.00
Federal income tax	$ 84.00

3. PRE-TAX HEALTH INSURANCE DEDUCTION, $150, AND 401(K) CONTRIBUTION, 4%

Period pay ($48,000/24)	$2,000.00
Less: health insurance	150.00
Less: 401(k) contribution	80.00
Taxable income*	$1,770.00
Federal income tax	$ 76.00

***Note:** The taxable income for Social Security and Medicare tax is $2,000 – 150 = $1,850

The process of using wage-bracket tables for employees claiming single marital status is similar. Figure 5-3 is a sample of the wage-bracket table for a single person with semimonthly wages.

Using the table in Figure 5-3, a single person earning a semimonthly wage of $1,088 with one withholding allowance will have a federal income tax of $84.

EXAMPLE: WAGE-BRACKET COMPUTATION OF FEDERAL INCOME TAX, SINGLE, BIWEEKLY

Alex Castro is an employee at Milliken Metals. He is single with three withholding allowances and earns $45,500 annually, paid biweekly. Using the wage-bracket tables in Appendix C, we will determine Alex's federal income tax in different situations.

1. NO PRE-TAX DEDUCTIONS

Period pay ($45,500/26)	$1,750.00
Taxable income	1,750.00
Federal income tax	128.00

2. PRE-TAX HEALTH INSURANCE, $75, PRE-TAX SUPPLEMENTAL HEALTH INSURANCE, $55

Period pay ($45,500/26)	$1,750.00
Less: health insurance	75.00
Less: supplemental health insurance	55.00
Taxable income	$1,620.00
Federal income tax	$ 111.00

(continued)

(concluded)

3. PRE-TAX HEALTH INSURANCE, $75, PRE-TAX SUPPLEMENTAL HEALTH INSURANCE, $55, 401(K) CONTRIBUTION, $100

Period pay ($45,500/26)	$1,750.00
Less: health insurance	75.00
Less: supplemental health insurance	55.00
Less: 401(k) contribution	100.00
Taxable income	$1,520.00
Federal income tax*	$ 99.00

***Note:** The taxable income for Social Security and Medicare tax is $1,750-75-55 = $1,620

FIGURE 5-3

Semimonthly Payroll Period—Single Persons

Emanuel Simon is single and has one withholding allowance. The employee is paid semimonthly and earned $1,338. What is the Federal Income Tax for Emanuel?

Wage Bracket Method Tables for Income Tax Withholding

SINGLE Persons—SEMIMONTHLY Payroll Period

(For Wages Paid through December 2019)

And the wages are–		And the number of withholding allowances claimed is—									
At least	But less than	0	1	2	3	4	5	6	7	8	9
		The amount of income tax to be withheld is—									
1,250	1,270	124	103	82	61	40	23	5	0	0	0
1,270	1,290	127	106	85	64	43	25	7	0	0	0
1,290	1,310	129	108	87	66	45	27	9	0	0	0
1,310	1,330	131	110	89	68	47	29	11	0	0	0
1,330	1,350	134	113	92	71	50	31	13	0	0	0
1,350	1,370	136	115	94	73	52	33	15	0	0	0
1,370	1,390	139	118	97	76	55	35	17	0	0	0
1,390	1,410	141	120	99	78	57	37	19	2	0	0
1,410	1,430	143	122	101	80	59	39	21	4	0	0
1,430	1,450	146	125	104	83	62	41	23	6	0	0

Important facts:

- The employee is single
- Has 1 withholding allowance
- Pay frequency is semimonthly
- Earned $1,338

The page of the table is for single employees with semimonthly pay

Go to the row that contains the bracket containing the employee's pay. In this example, the pay is $1,338, which is in the $1,330-$1,350 row.

Go to the column that contains the number of withholding allowances. In this case, the employee has 1 withholding allowance.

*The intersection of the table **row and column** is the **withholding tax**, which is **$113**

When using the wage-bracket tables, it should be noted that many wage amounts are the same number as the beginning and the end of a range. In these events, if the number is the exact number of the range, the next bracket should be used For example, refer to the below image. What is important to notice is the language at the top of the column: "And the wages are—At least . . . But less than." If the wages were $1,269.99, then the top row would be used. If the wages were precisely $1,270, then the second row would be used.

Wage Bracket Method Tables for Income Tax Withholding

SINGLE Persons—**SEMIMONTHLY** Payroll Period

(For Wages Paid through December 2019)

And the wages are–		And the number of withholding allowances claimed is—										
At least	But less than	0	1	2	3	4	5	6	7	8	9	10
		The amount of income tax to be withheld is—										
1,250	1,270	124	103	82	61	40	23	5	0	0	0	0
1,270	1,290	127	106	85	64	43	25	7	0	0	0	0

Percentage Method

There are many tables in Publication 15 from the IRS to assist employers with the correct amount of withholding given the variety of pay period, marital status, and exemption options that can be available. The ***percentage method*** for calculating employee withholding is tiered, with each layer building upon the previous layer. The table that reflects the amount for one withholding allowance using the percentage method is contained in Figure 5-4. It is important to select the withholding allowance amount that corresponds to the correct pay frequency. Note that if the employee has more than one withholding allowance, the amount in the table should be multiplied by the number of withholding allowances claimed on the employee's Form W-4.

When using the percentage method, the deduction for each withholding allowance is subtracted prior to computing the taxes. Note that the wage-bracket and percentage methods will yield similar results as to income tax withholding; the percentage method shown in Figure 5-5 allows more flexibility for calculations involving high-wage earners or uncommon pay periods.

FIGURE 5-4

Percentage Method for One Withholding Allowance—2019

Payroll Period	One Withholding Allowance
Weekly	$ 80.80
Biweekly	161.50
Semimonthly	175.00
Monthly	350.00
Quarterly	1,050.00
Semiannually	2,100.00
Annually	4,200.00
Daily or miscellaneous (each day of the payroll period)	16.20

FIGURE 5-5

Percentage Method Tables for Income Tax

Percentage Method Tables for Income Tax Withholding

(For Wages Paid in 2018)

TABLE 1—WEEKLY Payroll Period

(a) SINGLE person (including head of household)—

If the amount of wages (after subtracting withholding allowances) is: Not over $71 — The amount of income tax to withhold is: $0

Over—	But not over—		of excess over—
$71	—$254	$0.00 plus 10%	—$71
$254	—$815	$18.30 plus 12%	—$254
$815	—$1,658	$85.62 plus 22%	—$815
$1,658	—$3,100	$271.08 plus 24%	—$1,658
$3,100	—$3,917	$617.16 plus 32%	—$3,100
$3,917	—$9,687	$878.60 plus 35%	—$3,917
$9,687		$2,898.10 plus 37%	—$9,687

(b) MARRIED person—

If the amount of wages (after subtracting withholding allowances) is: Not over $222 — The amount of income tax to withhold is: $0

Over—	But not over—		of excess over—
$222	—$588	$0.00 plus 10%	—$222
$588	—$1,711	$36.60 plus 12%	—$588
$1,711	—$3,395	$171.36 plus 22%	—$1,711
$3,395	—$6,280	$541.84 plus 24%	—$3,395
$6,280	—$7,914	$1,234.24 plus 32%	—$6,280
$7,914	—$11,761	$1,757.12 plus 35%	—$7,914
$11,761		$3,103.57 plus 37%	—$11,761

TABLE 2—BIWEEKLY Payroll Period

(a) SINGLE person (including head of household)—

If the amount of wages (after subtracting withholding allowances) is: Not over $142 — The amount of income tax to withhold is: $0

Over—	But not over—		of excess over—
$142	—$509	$0.00 plus 10%	—$142
$509	—$1,631	$36.70 plus 12%	—$509
$1,631	—$3,315	$171.34 plus 22%	—$1,631
$3,315	—$6,200	$541.82 plus 24%	—$3,315
$6,200	—$7,835	$1,234.22 plus 32%	—$6,200
$7,835	—$19,373	$1,757.42 plus 35%	—$7,835
$19,373		$5,795.72 plus 37%	—$19,373

(b) MARRIED person—

If the amount of wages (after subtracting withholding allowances) is: Not over $444 — The amount of income tax to withhold is: $0

Over—	But not over—		of excess over—
$444	—$1,177	$0.00 plus 10%	—$444
$1,177	—$3,421	$73.30 plus 12%	—$1,177
$3,421	—$6,790	$342.58 plus 22%	—$3,421
$6,790	—$12,560	$1,083.76 plus 24%	—$6,790
$12,560	—$15,829	$2,468.56 plus 32%	—$12,560
$15,829	—$23,521	$3,514.64 plus 35%	—$15,829
$23,521		$6,206.84 plus 37%	—$23,521

TABLE 3—SEMIMONTHLY Payroll Period

(a) SINGLE person (including head of household)—

If the amount of wages (after subtracting withholding allowances) is: Not over $154 — The amount of income tax to withhold is: $0

Over—	But not over—		of excess over—
$154	—$551	$0.00 plus 10%	—$154
$551	—$1,767	$39.70 plus 12%	—$551
$1,767	—$3,592	$185.62 plus 22%	—$1,767
$3,592	—$6,717	$587.12 plus 24%	—$3,592
$6,717	—$8,488	$1,337.12 plus 32%	—$6,717
$8,488	—$20,988	$1,903.84 plus 35%	—$8,488
$20,988		$6,278.84 plus 37%	—$20,988

(b) MARRIED person—

If the amount of wages (after subtracting withholding allowances) is: Not over $481 — The amount of income tax to withhold is: $0

Over—	But not over—		of excess over—
$481	—$1,275	$0.00 plus 10%	—$481
$1,275	—$3,706	$79.40 plus 12%	—$1,275
$3,706	—$7,356	$371.12 plus 22%	—$3,706
$7,356	—$13,606	$1,174.12 plus 24%	—$7,356
$13,606	—$17,148	$2,674.12 plus 32%	—$13,606
$17,148	—$25,481	$3,807.56 plus 35%	—$17,148
$25,481		$6,724.11 plus 37%	—$25,481

TABLE 4—MONTHLY Payroll Period

(a) SINGLE person (including head of household)—

If the amount of wages (after subtracting withholding allowances) is: Not over $308 — The amount of income tax to withhold is: $0

Over—	But not over—		of excess over—
$308	—$1,102	$0.00 plus 10%	—$308
$1,102	—$3,533	$79.40 plus 12%	—$1,102
$3,533	—$7,183	$371.12 plus 22%	—$3,533
$7,183	—$13,433	$1,174.12 plus 24%	—$7,183
$13,433	—$16,975	$2,674.12 plus 32%	—$13,433
$16,975	—$41,975	$3,807.56 plus 35%	—$16,975
$41,975		$12,557.56 plus 37%	—$41,975

(b) MARRIED person—

If the amount of wages (after subtracting withholding allowances) is: Not over $963 — The amount of income tax to withhold is: $0

Over—	But not over—		of excess over—
$963	—$2,550	$0.00 plus 10%	—$963
$2,550	—$7,413	$158.70 plus 12%	—$2,550
$7,413	—$14,713	$742.26 plus 22%	—$7,413
$14,713	—$27,213	$2,348.26 plus 24%	—$14,713
$27,213	—$34,296	$5,348.26 plus 32%	—$27,213
$34,296	—$50,963	$7,614.82 plus 35%	—$34,296
$50,963		$13,448.27 plus 37%	—$50,963

Percentage Method Tables for Income Tax Withholding (continued)

(For Wages Paid in 2018)

TABLE 5—QUARTERLY Payroll Period

(a) SINGLE person (including head of household)—

If the amount of wages (after subtracting withholding allowances) is: Not over $925 — The amount of income tax to withhold is: $0

Over—	But not over—		of excess over—
$925	—$3,306	$0.00 plus 10%	—$925
$3,306	—$10,600	$238.10 plus 12%	—$3,306
$10,600	—$21,550	$1,113.38 plus 22%	—$10,600
$21,550	—$40,300	$3,522.38 plus 24%	—$21,550
$40,300	—$50,925	$8,022.38 plus 32%	—$40,300
$50,925	—$125,925	$11,422.38 plus 35%	—$50,925
$125,925		$37,672.38 plus 37%	—$125,925

(b) MARRIED person—

If the amount of wages (after subtracting withholding allowances) is: Not over $2,888 — The amount of income tax to withhold is: $0

Over—	But not over—		of excess over—
$2,888	—$7,650	$0.00 plus 10%	—$2,888
$7,650	—$22,238	$476.20 plus 12%	—$7,650
$22,238	—$44,138	$2,226.76 plus 22%	—$22,238
$44,138	—$81,638	$7,044.76 plus 24%	—$44,138
$81,638	—$102,888	$16,044.76 plus 32%	—$81,638
$102,888	—$152,888	$22,844.76 plus 35%	—$102,888
$152,888		$40,344.76 plus 37%	—$152,888

TABLE 6—SEMIANNUAL Payroll Period

(a) SINGLE person (including head of household)—

If the amount of wages (after subtracting withholding allowances) is: Not over $1,850 — The amount of income tax to withhold is: $0

Over—	But not over—		of excess over—
$1,850	—$6,613	$0.00 plus 10%	—$1,850
$6,613	—$21,200	$476.30 plus 12%	—$6,613
$21,200	—$43,100	$2,226.74 plus 22%	—$21,200
$43,100	—$80,600	$7,044.74 plus 24%	—$43,100
$80,600	—$101,850	$16,044.74 plus 32%	—$80,600
$101,850	—$251,850	$22,844.74 plus 35%	—$101,850
$251,850		$75,344.74 plus 37%	—$251,850

(b) MARRIED person—

If the amount of wages (after subtracting withholding allowances) is: Not over $5,775 — The amount of income tax to withhold is: $0

Over—	But not over—		of excess over—
$5,775	—$15,300	$0.00 plus 10%	—$5,775
$15,300	—$44,475	$952.50 plus 12%	—$15,300
$44,475	—$88,275	$4,453.50 plus 22%	—$44,475
$88,275	—$163,275	$14,089.50 plus 24%	—$88,275
$163,275	—$205,775	$32,089.50 plus 32%	—$163,275
$205,775	—$305,775	$45,689.50 plus 35%	—$205,775
$305,775		$80,689.50 plus 37%	—$305,775

TABLE 7—ANNUAL Payroll Period

(a) SINGLE person (including head of household)—

If the amount of wages (after subtracting withholding allowances) is: Not over $3,700 — The amount of income tax to withhold is: $0

Over—	But not over—		of excess over—
$3,700	—$13,225	$0.00 plus 10%	—$3,700
$13,225	—$42,400	$952.50 plus 12%	—$13,225
$42,400	—$86,200	$4,453.50 plus 22%	—$42,400
$86,200	—$161,200	$14,089.50 plus 24%	—$86,200
$161,200	—$203,700	$32,089.50 plus 32%	—$161,200
$203,700	—$503,700	$45,689.50 plus 35%	—$203,700
$503,700		$150,689.50 plus 37%	—$503,700

(b) MARRIED person—

If the amount of wages (after subtracting withholding allowances) is: Not over $11,550 — The amount of income tax to withhold is: $0

Over—	But not over—		of excess over—
$11,550	—$30,600	$0.00 plus 10%	—$11,550
$30,600	—$88,950	$1,905.00 plus 12%	—$30,600
$88,950	—$176,550	$8,907.00 plus 22%	—$88,950
$176,550	—$326,550	$28,179.00 plus 24%	—$176,550
$326,550	—$411,550	$64,179.00 plus 32%	—$326,550
$411,550	—$611,550	$91,379.00 plus 35%	—$411,550
$611,550		$161,379.00 plus 37%	—$611,550

TABLE 8—DAILY or MISCELLANEOUS Payroll Period

(a) SINGLE person (including head of household)—

If the amount of wages (after subtracting withholding allowances) divided by the number of days in the payroll period is: Not over $14.20 — The amount of income tax to withhold per day is: $0

Over—	But not over—		of excess over—
$14.20	—$50.90	$0.00 plus 10%	—$14.20
$50.90	—$163.10	$3.67 plus 12%	—$50.90
$163.10	—$331.50	$17.13 plus 22%	—$163.10
$331.50	—$620.00	$54.18 plus 24%	—$331.50
$620.00	—$783.50	$123.42 plus 32%	—$620.00
$783.50	—$1,937.30	$175.74 plus 35%	—$783.50
$1,937.30		$579.57 plus 37%	—$1,937.30

(b) MARRIED person—

If the amount of wages (after subtracting withholding allowances) divided by the number of days in the payroll period is: Not over $44.40 — The amount of income tax to withhold per day is: $0

Over—	But not over—		of excess over—
$44.40	—$117.70	$0.00 plus 10%	—$44.40
$117.70	—$342.10	$7.33 plus 12%	—$117.70
$342.10	—$679.00	$34.26 plus 22%	—$342.10
$679.00	—$1,256.00	$108.38 plus 24%	—$679.00
$1,256.00	—$1,582.90	$246.86 plus 32%	—$1,256.00
$1,582.90	—$2,352.10	$351.47 plus 35%	—$1,582.90
$2,352.10		$620.69 plus 37%	—$2,352.10

Source: Internal Revenue Service

Using the percentage method tables can be confusing, so let's look at a step-by-step example.

How to calculate federal income tax using the percentage method: Caroline is single and claims two withholding allowances on her Form W-4. She is paid semimonthly and earns $48,000 per year.

Step 1:	**Total wage payment**	**$48,000 ÷ 24**	**=**	**$ 2,000**
Step 2:	**One withholding allowance for semimonthly pay (Figure 5-3)**			$ 175.00
Step 3:	**Allowances claimed on W-4**			2
Step 4:	**Multiply Step 2 by Step 3**			$ 350.00
Step 5:	**Amount subject to withholding**	$2,000 – $350	=	$1,650.00
Step 6:	**See Table 3a in Figure 5-5 (Semimonthly wages for single person). Look at the column labeled "of excess over" and choose line 2 "$563.00"**		–	$ 563.00
Step 7:	**Subtract Step 6 from Step 5**		=	$1,087.00
Step 8:	**Multiply Step 7 by 12% (from line 2 in Table 3a)**	$1,087.00 × 0.12	=	$ 130.44
Step 9:	**Add Step 8 plus $40.50 (from line 2 in Table 3a) to compute the federal income tax to withhold**	$130.44 + $40.50	=	$ 170.94

The amount of federal income tax withholding may differ slightly between the wage-bracket and percentage methods. Let's revisit the tax computation for the married employee, this time using the percentage method.

EXAMPLE: MARRIED EMPLOYEE, PERCENTAGE METHOD VS. WAGE-BRACKET TABLE

Valerie Ball earns $1,839 biweekly and is married with three withholding allowances. We will use Table 2b of the percentage method for this computation.

Gross pay	$1,839.00
Less withholding allowances (3 × $161.50)	484.50
Taxable base	1,354.50
Less: "of excess over $1,200" (line 2)	1,200.00
Adjusted taxable base	$ 154.50
Multiplied by tax rate (12% or 0.12)	18.54
Plus marginal tax	74.60
Total tax	$ 93.14

Note that the wage-bracket method ended with a result of $93. The reason for the difference in the cents is the rounding used in wage-bracket table computations.

Let's now revisit the single employee and compare the percentage method computations to the wage-bracket table.

EXAMPLE: SINGLE EMPLOYEE, PERCENTAGE METHOD VS. WAGE-BRACKET TABLE

Emanuel Simon earns $1,088 semimonthly and is single with one withholding allowance. We will use Table 3a of the percentage method tables for this computation.

Gross pay	$1,088.00
Less: withholding allowance (1 × $175.00)	175.00
Taxable base	$ 913.00
Less: "of excess over $551" (line 2)	551.00
Adjusted taxable base	$ 362.00
Multiplied by tax rate (12% or 0.12)	43.44
Plus marginal tax	39.70
Total tax	$ 83.14

Note that the wage-bracket method resulted in $83.14. Again, the reason for the difference is the rounding used in wage-bracket table computations.

How Much Tax to Withhold?

Stop & Check

1. Jennifer Parsons earns $52,000 annually. She is married with two allowances and is paid semimonthly. Calculate the amount to be withheld using (a) the wage-bracket method and (b) the percentage method.
2. If Jennifer elected to deduct $100 per pay period for her 401(k), how much would that change the tax withheld from her paycheck? (Use the wage-bracket method.)
3. How much would Jennifer's federal income tax be if her $75 health insurance and $55 AFLAC premiums were deducted each pay period pre-tax? (Use the wage-bracket method, independent of question 2.)

LO 5-3 Compute Social Security and Medicare Tax Withholding

zimmytws/iStockphoto/Getty Images

The Social Security Act of 1935 mandated the withholding of certain taxes in addition to federal income tax. Two different taxes were part of the Social Security Act legislation: Social Security tax and Medicare tax. Employers collect only federal income taxes on employees without making a corresponding contribution. Social Security and Medicare, collectively known as ***FICA (Federal Insurance Contributions Act) taxes***, contain both the employer's and the employee's portion. When the employer deposits the federal withholding tax, it deposits the Social Security and Medicare amounts at the same time. The deposits are usually done online but may be made by standard mail in certain circumstances. The report provided to the IRS does not provide a breakdown of tax amounts for individual employees. Specific questions about Social Security or Medicare tax situations should be directed to the Social Security Administration at www.ssa.gov or via telephone at 800-772-1213.

kreinick/123RF

Social Security Tax

Social Security tax, formerly known as OASDI, was designed to cover people for illness, retirement, disability, and old age. As a method of social insurance by which communities will help provide for people who are unable to work, Social Security has evolved into a tax that is levied upon all employees until their annual income reaches a specified level. The maximum income, known as the ***wage base***, for the Social Security tax changes annually. In 2019, the wage base is $132,900. This means only the first $132,900 of wages earned are subject to the 6.2% tax. Every dollar earned above $132,900 will not be subject to social security tax. The tax rate on employee pay is 6.2 percent of eligible wages. Remember that eligible wages can be different from gross pay because of pre-tax deductions and the wage base maximum.

Examples of Social Security Tax Computations

Employee	Period Wages	YTD Salary at End of Previous Pay Period	Social Security Tax Computation	Social Security Tax Amount to Be Withheld
1	$ 1,700	$ 55,600	$1,700 × 6.2%	$105.40
2	2,850	90,000	2,850 × 6.2%	176.70
3	7,200	125,800	7,100 × 6.2%*	440.20
4	6,200	131,200	1.700 × 6.2%†	105.40
5	10,500	195,000	0††	0

* The employee's wage base reaches the maximum during this pay period; thus, only the amount under the $132,900 cap is taxed for Social Security: $132,900 – $125,800 = $7,100, so only the $7,100 is taxed.

† The employee's wage base reaches the maximum during this pay period; thus, only the amount under the $132,900 cap is taxed for Social Security: $132,900 – $131,200 = $1.700, so only the $1,700 is taxed.

†† The employee's wage base maximum was met prior to the current pay period, so no Social Security taxes are withheld.

The employee earnings record is especially important in computing and tracking the Social Security taxes due for each employee. Current records allow payroll accountants to keep track of annual salaries for each employee to avoid exceeding the maximum wage base, preventing excess deductions from employees' pay.

The employer and employee pay the same amount for the Social Security tax. Remember that the Social Security tax has a maximum annual wage amount, the ***wage base***, for which taxes may be withheld. After reaching that maximum annual wage, neither the employee nor the employer pay any more Social Security tax for the remainder of the year.

Medicare Tax

Medicare taxes differ from Social Security taxes in a couple of significant ways. ***Medicare taxes*** were levied on employers and employees to help provide basic health coverage for all individuals qualified to enroll in Medicare benefits. The Medicare tax amount for employee wages is 1.45 percent on all wages earned; there is **no maximum wage base** for Medicare taxes. The Affordable Care Act of 2010 levied an ***additional Medicare tax*** of 0.9 percent on certain workers Who earn more than $200,000 annually. This made the simple computations and tracking for Medicare taxes a little more challenging for payroll accountants and increased the need for accuracy on the employee earnings report. Note that the additional Medicare tax is levied only on the employees, so there is no employer match.

Highly compensated employees are subject to an additional 0.9 percent of Medicare tax as a result of the Affordable Care Act. This additional tax is only paid by the employee, and no employer match is required. The wage base for this additional Medicare tax depends on the marital and tax filing statuses reported on the employee's Form W-4 as follows:

- $200,000 for employees who report that they are single.
- $250,000 for employees who report that they are married and file taxes jointly.
- $125,000 for employees who report that they are married and file taxes separately.

Examples of Medicare Tax Computations

Employee	Period Wages	YTD Salary at End of Previous Pay Period	Medicare Tax Computation	Total Medicare Tax Liability (Employee and Employer)
1	$1,700	$ 55,600	$ 1,700 × 1.45%	$ 24.65 × 2 = $49.30
2	2,850	90,000	2,850 × 1.45%	41.33 × 2 = 82.66
3	7,200	112,600	7,200 × 1.45%	104.40 × 2 = 208.80
4	6,200	118,000	6,200 × 1.45%	89.90 × 2 = 179.80
5	10,500	195,000	Employee: (10,500 × 0.0145***) + (5,500** × 0.009) = $201.75	Employee: $201.75 + Employer: $152.25* Total = $354.00

*The employer does not pay the additional Medicare tax.
**195,000 + 10,500 = 205,500. 205,500–200,000 = 5,500.
***10,500*.0145 = 152.25

Remember that the applicable wages may have pre-tax deductions. Social Security and Medicare taxes apply to the employee's gross pay if an employee elects to have a 401(k) deduction. However, qualified Section 125 (cafeteria) plans are exempt from FICA taxes. When computing employee taxes, understanding the tax effect of the pre-tax deductions is important in computing accurate FICA deductions.

EXAMPLE: COMPUTATION OF SOCIAL SECURITY AND MEDICARE TAXES WITH PRE-TAX DEDUCTIONS

Chris McBride is an employee who earns an annual salary of $58,000, paid biweekly. He is single with one withholding allowance. Chris has pre-tax deductions including $155 for health insurance and a contribution of 5 percent of his gross pay to a 401(k) plan. Let's compute Chris's net pay using the wage-bracket tables in Appendix C to determine federal income tax.

Gross pay per period (58,000/26)	$2,230.77
Less: health insurance	155.00
Less: 401(k) (2,230.77 × 0.05)	111.54
Taxable income*	$1,964.23
Federal income tax	204.00
Social Security tax†	128.70
Medicare tax†	30.10
Net pay	$1,601.43

*This taxable income is for federal income tax only.
†Social Security and Medicare taxes are computed on taxable income of $2,230.77 – $155.00 = $2,075.77, then $2,075.77 × 0.062 (Social Security) and $2,075.77 × 0.0145 (Medicare)

EXAMPLE: COMPUTATION OF NET PAY, HIGHLY COMPENSATED EMPLOYEE

Morris Malone is the CEO and president of Martens Flooring. His annual salary is $320,000, and he is paid semimonthly. He is married with five withholding allowances, files taxes jointly, and has pre-tax deductions for health insurance of $250 and 401(k) of $1,000.

Note that because he is a highly compensated employee, we will need to use the percentage method to compute his federal income tax. He will exceed the Social Security wage base in May 20XX and will incur the additional Medicare tax in September. Let's look at his net pay computations on January 15, May 31, and October 31.

(continued)

(concluded)

FEDERAL INCOME TAX COMPUTATION

Federal income tax is computed as follows, using Table 3b from Appendix C:

Gross pay per period	$ 13,333.33
Less: health Insurance	250.00
Less: 401(k)	1,000.00
Taxable income	$ 12,083.33
Less: withholding allowance (5 × $175.00)	875.00
Taxable base	$ 11,208.33
Less: "of excess over $7,508" (line 4)	7,508.00
Adjusted taxable base	$ 3,700.33
Multiplied by tax rate (24% or 0.24)	888.08
Plus marginal tax	1,198.46
Total federal income tax	$ 2,086.54

JANUARY 15 PAY PERIOD

Gross pay per period	$ 13,333.33
Less: health Insurance	250.00
Less: 401(k)	1,000.00
Taxable income*	$ 12,083.33
Federal income tax	2,086.54
Social Security tax†	811.17
Medicare tax†	189.71
Net pay	$ 8,995.91

* This taxable income is for federal income tax only.
† Social Security and Medicare taxes are computed using a base of $13,333 – 250 = $13,083.33.

MAY 31 PAY PERIOD

As of May 15, Morris has earned year-to-date gross pay of $119,999.97 ($13,333.33 × 9 pay periods). This means that he will exceed the Social Security wage base during the next pay period, which ends May 31. Morris's salary is only taxable for Social Security wages up to the wage base of $132,900 (2019 amount), so the amount that may be taxed is $132,900 – $119,999.97 = $12,900.03. After the May 31 pay period, Morris will have no more Social Security tax deducted from his pay. His net pay for May 31 will be as follows:

Gross pay per period	$ 13,333.33
Less: health Insurance	250.00
Less: 401(k)	1,000.00
Taxable income*	$ 12,083.33
Federal income tax	2,086.54
Social Security tax†	799.80
Medicare tax††	189.71
Net pay	$ 9,007.28

* This taxable income is for federal income tax only.
† Social Security tax is computed as $12,900.03 × 0.062 = $799.80.
††Medicare tax is computed using a base of $13,083.33 as $13,083.33 * .0145 = $189.71.

OCTOBER 31 PAY PERIOD

As of October 15, Morris has earned year-to-date pay of $253,333.27 (13,333.33*19 pay periods). His pay is now subject to the Additional Medicare tax of 0.9 percent, levied only on employees (i.e., no employer match). His net pay for October 31 will be computed as follows:

Gross pay per period	$ 13,333.33
Less: health insurance	250.00
Less: 401(k)	1,000.00
Taxable income*	$ 12,083.33
Federal income tax	2,086.54
Social Security tax	-0-
Medicare tax†	307.46
Net pay	$ 9,689.34

* This taxable income is for federal income tax only.
†Medicare taxes are computed as: $13,333.33-250.00 = $13,083.33 * (.0145 + .009) = $307.46

Maintaining accurate records of taxes withheld through payroll registers and employee earnings records is a critical part of calculating proper FICA tax deductions. Whether a company uses a manual system, an automated system, or outsources the payroll duties, it remains responsible for the accuracy of the deductions and maintenance of associated records.

zimmytws/123RF

As of 2018, the average annual amount per employee that was paid into FICA taxes was $8,770. This includes both employee and employer contributions for Social Security and Medicare. The average annual payout from Social security to recipients in 2019 is $17,532. (Source: Investopedia, The Motley Fool)

FICA Taxes

Stop & Check

1. Trent Powell is an employee whose annual salary prior to the current pay period is $63,500. His gross pay for the current pay period is $5,280. What amount must be withheld for Social Security tax? For Medicare tax?
2. For Trent's FICA taxes, what is the total tax liability including employee and employer share?
3. Sarah Erickson is the CEO of a company, and she earns $250,000 per year. Her year-to-date salary for the 19th pay period of the year was $197,916.67. She is single and contributes 5 percent of her pay to her 401(k) and has a qualified Section 125 deduction of $75 per semi-monthly pay period.
    a. For the 20th pay period, what is her Social Security tax liability? Medicare tax liability?
    b. For the 21st pay period, what is her Medicare tax liability?

LO 5-4 Calculate State and Local Income Taxes

Many states and localities apply taxes in addition to the federal income tax, Social Security, and Medicare. According to the IRS, all but nine states withhold income taxes. As budgets become tighter and the unfunded pension liabilities come due, these states may look to income tax as a means for covering budget or pension shortfalls. The nine states are

Alaska	New Hampshire*	Tennessee*
Florida	South Dakota	Washington
Nevada	Texas	Wyoming

* New Hampshire and Tennessee do not charge a payroll tax, but obtain revenue from individual taxpayers through taxes on dividends and investments.

State-Specific Taxes

All other states (except the nine above) withhold income tax from their employees, and many apply other taxes as well. For instance, employees in the state of California have State Disability Insurance (SDI) of 1.0 percent of gross pay (up to a maximum wage of $118,371 in 2019), in addition to the personal income tax (PIT) that the state levies. Like federal income tax, California's PIT amounts vary by income level, pay frequency, and marital status. California, like many other states, offers both the wage-bracket and the percentage method of determining the PIT amount due. In contrast, Illinois charges a flat rate of 4.95 percent on all employees for its state withholding tax. (See Appendix D for state income tax information.)

If a firm operates only in one state, deciphering state income tax requirements is reasonably simple but becomes increasingly complex as the firm does business in more locations. State income tax information is readily available through each state's department of revenue as well as through most computerized payroll software programs. (See Appendix E for a state revenue department list.)

EastVillage Images/Shutterstock

New York ranks as the highest state in *per capita* state and local income tax. The marginal tax rate in 2018 was 6.57% and many localities charge income taxes. Workers who reside or earn income in New York City pay a tax that ranges from approximately 2.9 to 3.9 percent in addition to any federal and state income taxes. (Source: The Balance)

Some states require the collection and remittance of income taxes based upon all wages earned within their state. This could result in the company having several state employer identification numbers, even if the company does not have a physical presence in the state. For example, if a Floridian paper mill worker is stationed at the St. Marys, Georgia, location, the employer could be required to remit the employee's income taxes in Georgia. Other types of payroll taxes can include items like Oregon's public transportation payroll tax, starting in 2018 for any services performed within the state, regardless of residency status.

EXAMPLE: NET PAY WITH STATE INCOME TAX

Jeremy Underwood receives a salary of $850 per week at his job in Joliet, Illinois. He is married with three withholding allowances and is paid weekly. We will use the wage-bracket tables in Appendix C to obtain Jeremy's federal income tax. He has pre-tax deductions of $50 for insurance and $50 for 401(k). Using the Illinois state tax rate of 4.95 percent,

Taxable income ($850 – 50 – 50)	$750.00
State income tax ($750 × .0495)	$ 37.13

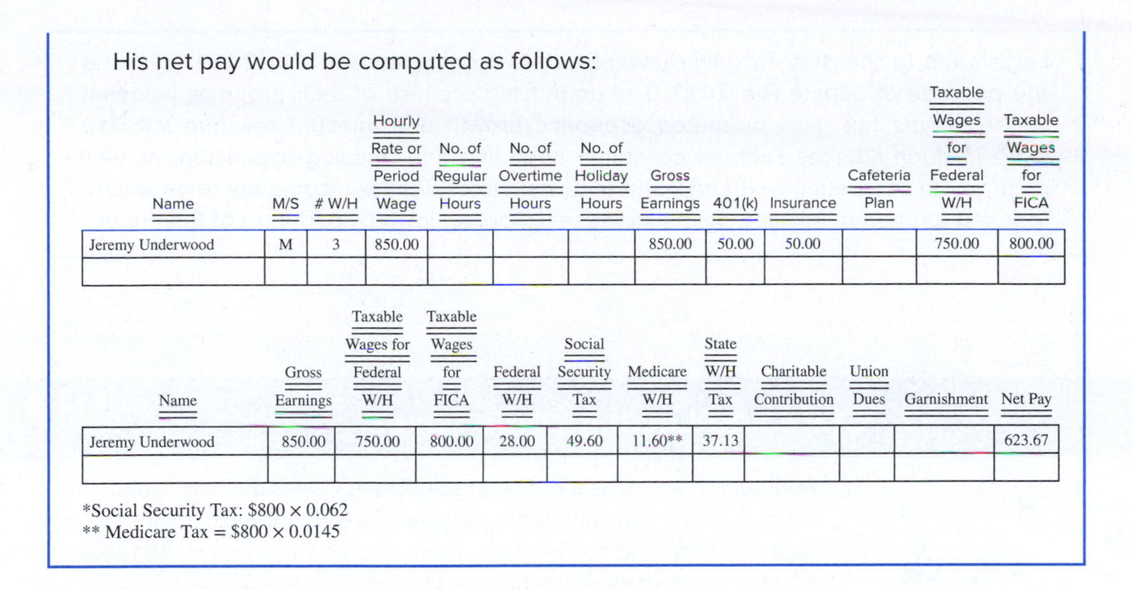

His net pay would be computed as follows:

Name	M/S	# W/H	Hourly Rate or Period Wage	No. of Regular Hours	No. of Overtime Hours	No. of Holiday Hours	Gross Earnings	401(k)	Insurance	Cafeteria Plan	Taxable Wages for Federal W/H	Taxable Wages for FICA
Jeremy Underwood	M	3	850.00				850.00	50.00	50.00		750.00	800.00

Name	Gross Earnings	Taxable Wages for Federal W/H	Taxable Wages for FICA	Federal W/H	Social Security Tax	Medicare W/H	State W/H Tax	Charitable Contribution	Union Dues	Garnishment	Net Pay
Jeremy Underwood	850.00	750.00	800.00	28.00	49.60	11.60**	37.13				623.67

*Social Security Tax: $\$800 \times 0.062$
** Medicare Tax = $\$800 \times 0.0145$

Local Income Taxes

Another mandatory tax is ***local income tax*** levied by certain municipalities and counties. Payroll accountants need to be aware of any local taxes that apply to their business. Information about applicable local taxes may be found through city and county governments, often through their Internet sites.

Denver, Colorado, has a local tax called the Occupational Privilege Tax (OPT), also known as the "head tax." The OPT is $5.75 per month for employees and $4.00 for employers of any business that has any activity in Denver, even if the employee or business does not exist or reside in Denver itself, on wages exceeding $500. The local income tax is applied after any pre-tax deductions. (Source: Denver Treasury Division)

EXAMPLE: NET PAY WITH LOCAL INCOME TAX

Shalie Rice is an employee at Keiser and Sons in Denver, Colorado. She earns $39,000 annually and is paid biweekly. She is married with two withholding allowances. She has pre-tax deductions including $100 for health insurance and a contribution of 6 percent of her gross pay to a 401(k) plan. We will use the wage-bracket tables in Appendix C to compute Shalie's federal income tax. Colorado's state income tax is 4.63 percent. Her net pay would be as follows:

Name	M/S	# W/H	Hourly Rate or Period Wage	No. of Regular Hours	No. of Overtime Hours	No. of Holiday Hours	Gross Earnings	401(k)	Insurance	Cafeteria Plan	Taxable Wages for Federal W/H	Taxable Wages for FICA
Shalie Rice	M	2	1,500.00				1,500.00	90.00	100.00		1,310.00	1,400.00

Name	Gross Earnings	Taxable Wages for Federal W/H	Taxable Wages for FICA	Federal W/H Tax	Social Security Tax	Medicare W/H Tax	State W/H Tax	Denver OPT	Union Dues	Garnishment	Net Pay
Shalie Rice	1,500.00	1,310.00	1,400.00	54.00	86.80*	20.30**	60.65***	5.75			1,082.50

*$\$1{,}400 \times 0.062 = 86.80$
**$\$1{,}400 \times 0.0145 = 20.30$
***$\$1{,}310 \times 0.0463 = 60.65$

Legislators in the state of Iowa lowered state income tax rates in 2019 following the passage of Senate File 2417. The underlying premise of their proposal was that lower income tax rates promoted economic growth and injected revenue into the state through sources such as consumer spending and housing expansion, as well as promote competition with adjacent Midwest states. Future income tax rates will be indexed to prevent inflation-based increases. (Source: Iowa Department of Revenue)

State and Local Income Taxes

Stop & Check

1. April Griffith works as a research scientist in Coeur d'Alene, Idaho. She is married with two withholding allowances and earns $62,500 annually, paid biweekly. She has a pre-tax deduction of $150 for her 401(k) and $80 for qualified health insurance. Using the state tax listed in Appendix D, what is her state income tax?
2. Rick Barker works as an accountant in Denver, Colorado. Colorado has a state income tax of a flat 4.63 percent. Colorado's OPT is $5.75 per month per employee. If Rick is paid monthly and earns $2,850 after pre-tax deductions, what are his state and local taxes?

LO 5-5 Apply Post-Tax Deductions

Once the payroll clerk determines each employee's gross pay, pre-tax deductions, and taxes withheld, the post-tax deductions are applied to the remaining amount. All deductions, both voluntary and mandatory, should be listed on an attachment to the paycheck, in both pay-period and year-to-date amounts.

Post-tax deductions may include court-mandated or governmental debts as well as employee repayments of advances or overpayments. In this section, we will explore examples of post-tax deductions and how they are included in net pay computations.

Charitable Conributions

Employees may choose to contribute part of their pay to charitable organizations as an automatic deduction. This deduction is taken on a post-tax basis because the employee may deduct it from gross income on the annual tax return.

EXAMPLE: CHARITABLE CONTRIBUTION

Perry Wallace is an employee at Working Environments in Winchester, New Hampshire. He earns $29,000 annually and is paid weekly. He is single with one withholding allowance. He has a pre-tax health insurance premium of $25 and a charitable contribution to the United Way of $10 per pay period. His net pay would be as follows:

Name	M/S	# W/H	Hourly Rate or Period Wage	No. of Regular Hours	No. of Overtime Hours	No. of Holiday Hours	Gross Earnings	401(k)	Insurance	Cafeteria Plan	Taxable Wages for Federal W/H	Taxable Wages for FICA
Perry Wallace	S	1	557.69				557.69		25.00		532.69	532.69

Name	Gross Earnings	Taxable Wages for Federal W/H	Taxable Wages for FICA	Federal W/H	Social Security Tax	Medicare W/H	State W/H Tax	Charitable Contribution	Union Dues	Garnishment	Net Pay
Perry Wallace	557.69	532.69	532.69	41.00	33.03	7.72		10.00			440.94

Garnishments

Remember that garnishments are for court-mandated deductions such as child support obligations, liens, and consumer credit repayment. These deductions are taken on a post-tax basis because they are viewed as an obligation of the employee that must be paid out of post-tax income. Garnishments are subject to a maximum of 25 percent of disposable income for many situations. However, child support garnishment may be up to 60 percent, depending on how many people the person supports financially.

EXAMPLE: CHILD SUPPORT

Andrew Malowitz is an employee of Kennesaw Mills. He earns $49,500 annually, paid semimonthly. He is single with three withholding allowances. He has a pre-tax health insurance deduction of $100 and contributes 3 percent of his gross pay to his 401(k) per pay period. The state income tax rate is 6 percent. He has a court-ordered garnishment of $300 per pay period for child support. His net pay would appear as follows (amounts rounded to nearest dollar). Specific computations used in the payroll register follow immediately below the register.

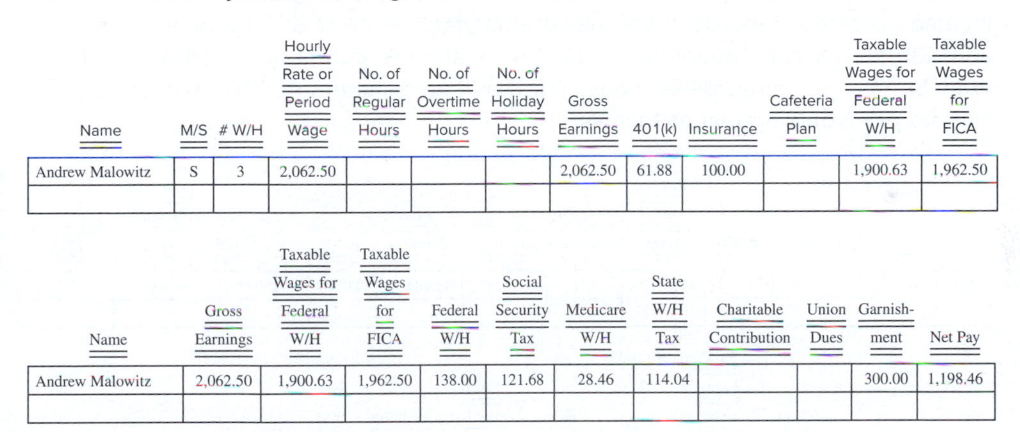

Name	M/S	# W/H	Hourly Rate or Period Wage	No. of Regular Hours	No. of Overtime Hours	No. of Holiday Hours	Gross Earnings	401(k)	Insurance	Cafeteria Plan	Taxable Wages for Federal W/H	Taxable Wages for FICA
Andrew Malowitz	S	3	2,062.50				2,062.50	61.88	100.00		1,900.63	1,962.50

Name	Gross Earnings	Taxable Wages for Federal W/H	Taxable Wages for FICA	Federal W/H	Social Security Tax	Medicare W/H	State W/H Tax	Charitable Contribution	Union Dues	Garnishment	Net Pay
Andrew Malowitz	2,062.50	1,900.63	1,962.50	138.00	121.68	28.46	114.04			300.00	1,198.46

Payroll Register Computations

Payroll Register Column	Computation
Period Wage	$49,500/24 = $2,062.50
401(k)	$2,062.50 × 0.03 = $61.88
Taxable Wages for Federal and State	$2,062.50 – 61.88 – 100 = $1,900.63
Taxable Wages for FICA	$2,062.50 – 100 = $1,962.50
Social Security tax	$1,962.50 × 0.062 = $121.68
Medicare tax	$1,962.50 × 0.0145 = $24.68
State tax	$1,900.63 × 0.06 = $114.04
Net Pay	$2,062.50 – 61.88 – 100 – 138 – 121.68 – 28.46 – 114.04 – 300 = $1,198.46

(continued)

(concluded)

DISPOSABLE INCOME: CHILD SUPPORT

It is important to consider Andrew's disposable income to ensure that the garnishment does not exceed legal maximums. His disposable income is computed as follows:

Gross pay	$2,062.50
Less: federal income tax	138.00
Less: state income tax	114.04
Less: Social Security tax	121.68
Less: Medicare tax	28.46
Total disposable income	$1,660.32
Percent of garnishment to disposable income	18.1%*

* $300/1,660.32 = 0.181 = 18.1% (rounded)

MIKA Images/Alamy

Consumer Credit

Like other post-tax deductions such as student loans, consumer credit is considered to be an obligation to be paid out of a person's after-tax earnings. The next example shows the effect of a consumer credit garnishment on an employee's wages. In this case, the 25 percent maximum garnishment rule applies.

EXAMPLE: CONSUMER CREDIT

Mona Todd is an employee of Level Two Gallery in Ogden, Utah. She earns $38,500 annually, paid biweekly. She is single with two withholding allowances. The state income tax rate is 5 percent. She has pre-tax deductions of $50 for health insurance and $30 for her contribution to a 401(k) plan, and she contributes $15 to the United Way. She has a court-ordered consumer credit garnishment of $100 per pay period. Her net pay would appear as follows:

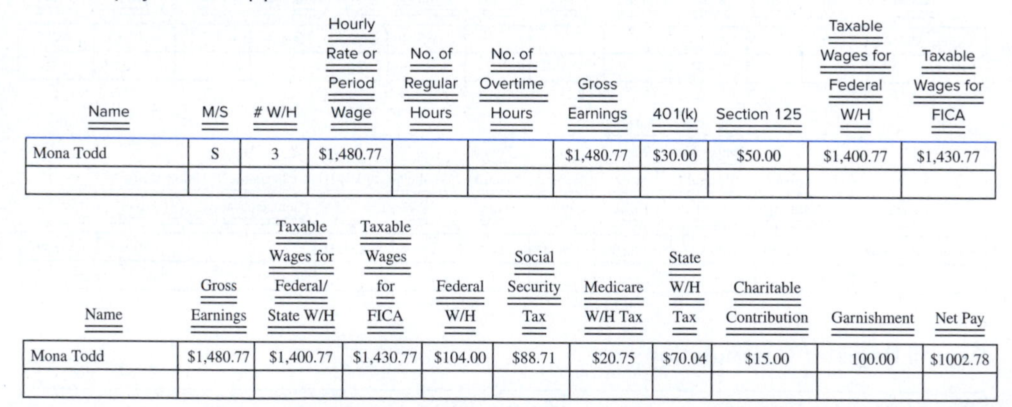

Name	M/S	# W/H	Hourly Rate or Period Wage	No. of Regular Hours	No. of Overtime Hours	Gross Earnings	401(k)	Section 125	Taxable Wages for Federal W/H	Taxable Wages for FICA
Mona Todd	S	3	$1,480.77			$1,480.77	$30.00	$50.00	$1,400.77	$1,430.77

Name	Gross Earnings	Taxable Wages for Federal/ State W/H	Taxable Wages for FICA	Federal W/H	Social Security Tax	Medicare W/H Tax	State W/H Tax	Charitable Contribution	Garnishment	Net Pay
Mona Todd	$1,480.77	$1,400.77	$1,430.77	$104.00	$88.71	$20.75	$70.04	$15.00	100.00	$1002.78

DISPOSABLE INCOME: CONSUMER CREDIT

Let's ensure that Mona's consumer credit garnishment is within legal guidelines:

Gross pay	$1,480.77
Less: federal income tax	104.00
Less: state income tax	70.04
Less: Social Security tax	88.71
Less: Medicare tax	20.75
Total disposable income	$1,197.27
Percent of garnishment to disposable income	8.4%*

* $100/$1,197.27 = .0835 = 8.4% (rounded)

A topic of discussion between the American Payroll Association and the Wage and Hour Division of the Department of Labor has been the treatment of lump-sum distributions when a garnishment is imposed on an employee. The general guideline for considering a distribution as subject to garnishment is the concept of "personal service." If the distribution was for services rendered by the employee, then the amount may be garnished. Specific examples of lump-sum distributions that are subject to garnishment include the following:

- Sign-on bonuses
- Any performance or productivity bonus
- Commissions
- Holiday pay
- Retroactive pay
- Termination pay
- Any other bonuses or incentive payments

(Source: American Payroll Association)

Union Dues

Employees who belong to a collective bargaining unit usually pay dues to the unit for their representation. The CCPA disposable income limits do not pertain to union dues because those dues are not court mandated. The following example shows how union dues affect employee pay. It should be noted that the employee's deduction for union dues is voluntary.

EXAMPLE: UNION DUES

Forester Greer is an employee of Pacific High School in Washington state, where he is a member of a collective bargaining unit (i.e., union) that negotiates his salary, benefits, and working conditions and has dues of $50 per pay period. He earns $67,500 annually and is paid biweekly. He is married with four withholding allowances. He has pre-tax deductions of $150 for a 401(k) plan and $100 for a qualified Section 125 cafeteria plan. His net pay would appear as follows:

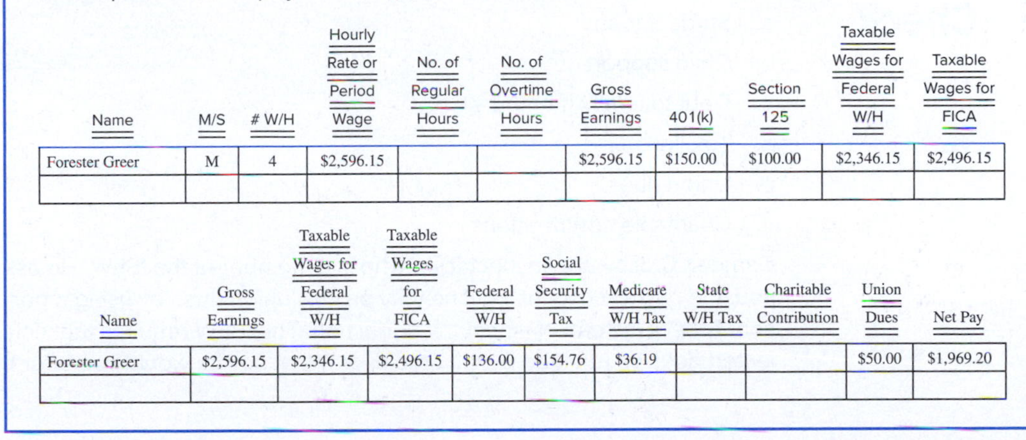

Name	M/S	# W/H	Hourly Rate or Period Wage	No. of Regular Hours	No. of Overtime Hours	Gross Earnings	401(k)	Section 125	Taxable Wages for Federal W/H	Taxable Wages for FICA
Forester Greer	M	4	$2,596.15			$2,596.15	$150.00	$100.00	$2,346.15	$2,496.15

Name	Gross Earnings	Taxable Wages for Federal W/H	Taxable Wages for FICA	Federal W/H	Social Security Tax	Medicare W/H Tax	State W/H Tax	Charitable Contribution	Union Dues	Net Pay
Forester Greer	$2,596.15	$2,346.15	$2,496.15	$136.00	$154.76	$36.19			$50.00	$1,969.20

According to ADP, approximately 7.2 percent of employees had amounts garnished from their pay as of 2013. In 2016, the estimated amount of employee wages subject to garnishments totaled over $665 million. E-Garnishments are becoming more popular through the use of electronic income withholding orders (e-IWOs), which states transmit to employers for enforcement. (Source: ADP, Debt.org)

Employee Advances and Overpayments

Employees may have an opportunity for an advance of money in anticipation of their pay. Timing of the repayment of advances depends on the agreement between the employee and employer. When the advance becomes due for repayment, it is treated as a post-tax deduction. The same concept applies to situations in which the employee is overpaid due to an error in computation or reporting.

dotshock/Shutterstock

At Maricopa County Community College, a payroll system upgrade caused employees to be under- or overpaid, sometimes by thousands of dollars. Rollout of the new payroll system caused issues with understanding the differences between the new and old systems. Accountants worked with managers and employees to ensure that all discrepancies were addressed in a timely manner. (Source: AZCentral)

Stop & Check

Post-Tax Deductions

1. Which of the following is a debt that may be collected via wage garnishment?
   a. Student loans
   b. Child support
   c. Debt to family members
   d. Tax liens
   e. Union dues
   f. Charitable contributions
2. Camden Crosby is a an electrician who is a member of the IBEW. He asks you, the payroll accountant, if he may pay his union dues by using a personal check instead of a post-tax deduction. The IBEW requires that collected dues be remitted by the employer. What advice would you offer him?

LO 5-6 Discuss Employee Pay Methods

Once the net pay is computed, the next step is to give the employees access to their money. Four common types of payment methods are available: cash, check, direct deposit, and paycard. Each method has its benefits and drawbacks. We will explore each method separately.

Tetra Images/Tetra Images/Corbis

Cash

Cash is one of the oldest forms of paying employees but is not widely used as a contemporary payroll practice. The most common use of cash as a payment method involves paying for day laborers, temporary helpers, and odd jobs. Cash is one of the most difficult forms of payroll to manage because it is difficult to track and control. Payments for wages in cash should involve a written receipt signed by the employee. Companies paying by cash must physically have the cash on hand for payroll, which increases the risk of theft from both internal and external sources. Payroll taxes must be withheld, which requires prior preparation so that the appropriate amount of cash is available to pay precisely what is due for each employee. For employees, cash is a very convenient pay method because of its inherent liquidity.

Cash wage payment challenges in security of the funds for both the employer and the employee. For the employer, ensuring that the employee receives and acknowledges the appropriate pay amount is the key. When using cash as a payment method for employees, a receipt that contains information about the gross pay, deductions, and net pay (called the ***pay advice***) is important. The critical piece is to have the employee sign and date a copy of the pay advice, acknowledging receipt of the correct amount of cash on the specific date. Obtaining the employee's signature and date received can prevent future problems with perceived problems involving timely payments of employee compensation.

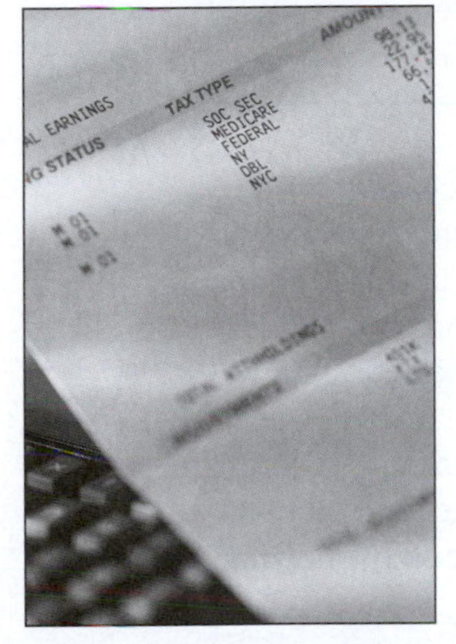

Comstock Images/Getty Images

Check

Paper checks are a common method of remitting employee compensation. For the employer, a paper check offers traceability and simplicity of accounting records. The use of checks instead of cash means that the employer does not have to maintain large amounts of cash, reducing the vulnerability of keeping currency on hand. Programs such as QuickBooks and Sage100 Standard allow employers to print paychecks directly from the program on specifically designed, preprinted forms. Checks offer a level of security that cash does not because they are issued to a specific employee, the only person who can legally convert the check into cash.

The disadvantage to using paper checks for payroll purposes involves bank account reconciliation. Once issued, the employee may choose not to deposit it into his or her bank account, which can complicate the firm's reconciliation process. Paper checks could be lost or destroyed, requiring voiding of the old check and issuance of a new one. Additionally, employees may not have a bank account, which makes cashing paychecks challenging and potentially costly. Paper checks may soon be phased out of current practice as other methods of employee pay grow in popularity because of the convenience for both the employer and the employee.

According to the Pew Internet and American Life Project in 2014, more than 53 million consumers in the United States use online banking. As of 2017, that number grew to more than two-thirds of Americans. The practice of payroll disbursement using paper checks is declining as people shift from traditional banking methods to a culture of electronic money management. (Sources: Pew Research Center, *American Banking Journal*)

For employers who use paper checks as a compensation method, two significant best practices exist: (1) The use of a payroll-only checking account and (2) a procedure for the handling of the payroll checks themselves. A separate payroll-dedicated checking account

Ingram Publishing

prevents problems that could occur if the company has difficulties (such as insufficient funds) in the business's main account. For the checks themselves, the payroll accountant needs to maintain a record that notes the use of each and every check, especially for checks that are voided, lost, or never cashed. If a company issues checks, it needs to maintain an unclaimed property account for payroll checks that are never cashed by the employee. The process of leaving a check uncashed, especially if it is a payroll check, results in the ***escheatment*** of the payroll check because the payee of the the check has never claimed the property (i.e., the payroll money) and is subject to state laws about the handling and distribution of such unclaimed money. Compliance with state escheatment laws is mandatory but not largely enforced—but that does not relieve the employer of the obligation to pay its employee. Use of a record in which the payroll accountant annotates each check's use (i.e., cashed, voided, lost) is imperative.

> According to the office of the State Comptroller of New York, the policy for escheatment is that uncashed payroll checks are escheated as of predetermined dated. For example, any payroll check issued during 2016 that remained uncashed as of February 21, 2018, was moved to an escheated status and marked as unclaimed property. (Source: New York Office of the State Comptroller).

When a company pays employees by check, the numerical amount of the check must also be represented in specific words for the bank to accept the check for payment to the payee. It is important to note that banks pay the check based on the amount written in words on the check. The highlighted area in the image in Figure 5-6 shows how the information should appear on the face of the check, specifically the written-out amount of the check. Figure 5-6 contains a sample of a paycheck.

A relevant concept in using checks for payroll is the potential for fraud by manipulating the information on checks. The check issuer (i.e., the employer) may be liable for the funds until the fraudulent activity is proven. Some red flags that may indicate check fraud include the following:

- Changes in font type between the company's address and the employee's name.
- Low check numbers (e.g., 1001–1500) because payroll fraud often involves new accounts.

FIGURE 5-6
Sample Paycheck

Wings of the North
121 Nicholas Street
North Pole, AK 99705

Check No.
23445

Petra Smith

Date 1/3/20XX

One Thousand One Hundred Twenty-four and 13/100 dollars 1,124.13

Payee: Petra Smith
Address: 426 Candy Cane Lane
City/State Zip: North Pole, AK 99705

Signed: *Rudolph Donner*

- Evidence of typewriter use on the check (most payroll checks are generated via computerized programs).
- Stains or discolorations on the check.
- Notations in the memo line that contain the word "payroll" or "load."
- Handwritten additions to the check, such as the recipient's phone number.
- Absence of the bank's or the recipient's address.
- Check number is either absent or is the same on all checks.

(Source: National Check Fraud Center)

Paper checks are more vulnerable to fraud than electronic transfers because of the ease of obtaining preprinted checks. Many employers are transitioning to either direct deposits or paycards to protect company assets.

Direct Deposit

Direct deposit of employee compensation into the individual's bank account offers employers some of the same advantages as checks. Like checks, employee compensation is traceable through both the employer's bank and the optional paper pay advice issued to the employee. Employees often prefer direct deposit because their pay is immediately available in their bank account, eliminating the need to travel to the bank to deposit the paper check. However, for employees to receive their pay through direct deposit, they must have a bank account.

An advantage of direct deposit is that it prevents paper waste, promoting "green" business practices. The savings per employee per pay period is approximately $1.35, according to the National Federation of Independent Business. Although this may seem like a small amount, when multiplied by the number of employees and pay periods annually it creates a potentially large saving for employers. These savings came from lower waste collection, paper usage, and recycling costs. Not only does direct deposit save a company money, it reduces the time needed for payroll processing, which frees payroll accountants to complete other tasks.

Comstock/PunchStock

When using direct deposit as an employee compensation method, a suggested best practice is to grant the employees access to a website or online portal by which they can securely view their pay advice and pay history, as this may substitute for paper payroll advices. Because direct deposit involves the use of electronic data transmittal, the posting of the pay advice on a secure site could be linked with the human resources data, allowing the employee an element of self-maintenance in payroll records. The potential pitfall in the use of a website for these highly sensitive records is the vulnerability of the information to computer hacking. If an employer chooses to use a website in this manner, he or she must take steps to prevent hacking through data encryption, identity verification, and site security.

> The Federal Communications Commission (FCC) has published guidelines for employer data security procedures, especially as pertains to employee information on websites and the use of paycards. The FCC guidelines include advice about the selection of data to be included on employee-accessible websites, password strength guidelines, update intervals, and data archiving. (Source: FCC)

Paycards

Paycards have been growing in popularity since the beginning of the 21st century. These cards are debit cards onto which an employer electronically transmits the employee's pay. The use of payroll cards started in the 1990s as a convenient way to compensate over-the-road

TARIK KIZILKAYA/Getty Images

truck drivers who could not be in a predictable place on each payday. Comerica started issuing the paycards that could be used anywhere a conventional MasterCard was accepted, which is nearly everywhere. Unlike the use of paper checks or direct deposit, the paycard does not require an employee to maintain a bank account to access his or her pay. The convenience and ease of use for employees makes the paycard an option that millions of workers in the United States have opted to use.

Paycards have grown in popularity because of their inherent flexibility for sending and receiving money. The paycard may be used as a debit card by people without bank accounts, which also grants them the ability to participate in online purchases even if they cannot qualify for a credit card. For the 9 million unbanked households in the United States, paycards grant the financial freedom and accessibility that they may otherwise not have and allow unbanked employees to avoid check cashing fees. (Sources: Symmetry Software, Innovations for Poverty Action)

What is the disadvantage to paycard use? Unlike the limits to access that a bank has for its account holders, a paycard can be lost or stolen. Some employees may encounter challenges such as withdrawal limits or cash back at point-of-sale (POS) purchases. Like paper checks, paycards may be subject to state escheatment laws that govern unclaimed funds.

An issue that haunted the early use of paycards was ***Regulation E*** of the Federal Deposit Insurance Corporation (FDIC), which protects consumers from loss of the availability of their funds on deposit in the event of bank losses. Until 2006, Regulation E applied to funds on deposit in an FDIC-insured institution. Regulation E was extended to cover payroll funds transferred to paycards, according to 12 CFR Part 205. As a pay method that is growing in popularity among employers and employees, paycards offer more compensation options for employers.

Paycards require different types of security than the other types of employee compensation, but most elements remain the same. In addition to tracking hours and accurately compensating employees based on their marital status and withholdings, the employer must keep the employee's paycard number in a secure file. Software such as QuickBooks offers password encryption abilities for the files of employees who have paycards. Like any other debit card, the funds are electronically coded to the account number. The card issuer (not the employer) must remain compliant with Regulation E as far as card loss or theft is concerned, but the employer is responsible to ensure this extra step of payroll security.

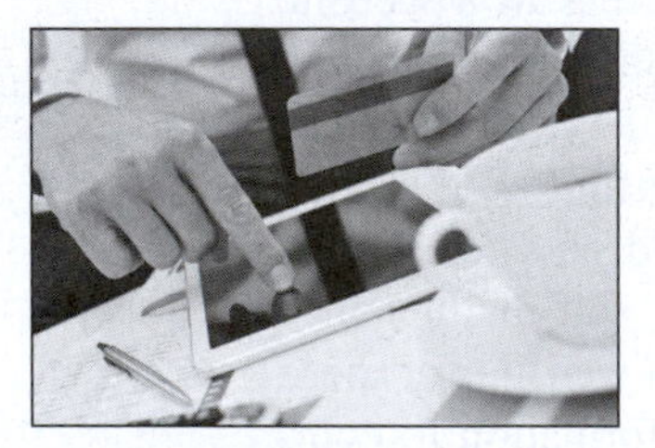
nito/Shutterstock

In late 2013, Visa Inc. introduced an improvement to its Visa Advanced Authorization technology, making compensation via paycards more secure and reliable. This new technology improved real-time fraud detection and was projected to prevent nearly $200 million in fraud within a five-year period. Since its inception, the technology has evolved to include predictive analytics that detect unusual card usage. (Source: Visa)

Zapp2Photo/Shutterstock

Cryptocurrency

An emerging wage payment method involves ***cryptocurrency***, such as Bitcoin, and ***blockchain*** technology. Cryptocurrency uses Internet technology to transmit money securely from one "wallet," or account, to a recipient. The Bitcoin itself is not a physical currency, as it exists only in electronic form. Transmission of wages is thought to be secure because the blockchain technology makes it very difficult for wages to be diverted from the intended recipient because the blockchain involves the transmission of packets of data through a very large number of computers, making a single transaction difficult to isolate.

The advantage of using Bitcoin is that it is not subject to international exchange rates and it is transferred nearly instantaneously. The problem with using cryptocurrency is that no central authority oversees the value of the currency, making it extremely volatile in value, which could lead to the underpayment of employees if the currency loses value. As cryptocurrency becomes more accepted as a payroll payment form, additional governmental guidance will likely emerge.

The state of Ohio started accepting employer remittance of payroll taxes via blockchain technology in late 2018. The state's revenue department allots a 15-minute time period for the employer to complete entering the data associated with the remittance and a third-party company insures the state against the risk of loss in value during the transmission time. (Source: American Payroll Association)

Pay Methods

Stop & Check

1. What are the different employee pay methods?
2. What regulation governs paycard loss or theft?
3. For which pay method(s) must an employee have a bank account?

Trends to Watch

TAXES AND PAYMENT METHODS

Employee net pay changes each year because of legal developments regarding deductions and pay methods. Developments in employee withholdings since 2015 include the following:

- Changes to employee net pay because of the Affordable Care Act health insurance requirements for employers.
- Changes to sick-leave compensation at the state and local levels.
- Changes in the amounts that employees may contribute on a tax-deferred basis to pension plans.
- Increased public awareness of the effect of pay raises, especially for cost of living, on net pay.
- State-level legislation about the percent of disposable earnings that may be subject to garnishments.

Some trends to watch in employee net pay include the following:

- Expanded regulatory guidance regarding data privacy and security, similar to the General Data Protection Regulation (GDPR) mandated in the European Union, to protect electronic employee payroll transmission.
- Evolving use of mobile payments and electronic wallets to facilitate the transmission of employee pay.
- The increase in legislative guidance regarding the use of artificial intelligence (AI) and cryptocurrency for payroll transmission.
- Increased standardization of payroll methods using cloud-based technologies.
- An increase in borderless payroll accounts that make the transmission of employee pay and employer tax obligations more seamless.

Summary of Employee Net Pay and Pay Methods

Employee pay is subject to a variety of deductions that can be mandatory, mandated by a court or other authority, or voluntary. Deductions such as federal income tax and Medicare tax are virtually inescapable. Other taxes such as Social Security, state taxes, and local taxes are not applicable in every employee's situation and depend on a variety of factors such as year-to-date pay and state of residence. Of the other deductions, some can be withheld from an employee's pay before taxes are deducted, which benefits an employee by reducing their payroll tax liability. Other deductions must be taken after taxes are withheld. Understanding the difference between gross pay and net pay is vital for payroll accountants because the net pay, not the gross, is the pay that the employee actually receives.

The question of employee pay methods is complex. Which pay method is the best? It is not an easy answer. An employer should consider the needs of the employees, as well as the business, to decide if one method will suit everyone. Sometimes a combination of payment methods is the best solution, although it adds complexity for the payroll accountant. The most appropriate method for the organization will depend on many different factors. Attention to these factors, which include payroll frequency, employee types, and the nature of the business itself, helps inform employer decisions about employee pay methods.

Key Points

- Net pay is gross pay less all deductions.
- Federal income tax applies to all workers, and the amount varies based on wages, pay frequency, marital status, and number of withholdings.
- Social Security tax has a maximum wage base that can change each year.
- Medicare tax has no maximum wage base, and an additional Medicare tax is levied on highly compensated employees.
- Employees who are subject to mandated deductions such as garnishments for child support and consumer credit liens have certain protections as to the percent of disposable income that may be withheld.
- Employees' pay may be disbursed in cash, by check, by paycard, or via direct deposit.
- Uncashed employee paychecks are turned over to state authorities as escheatments and become unclaimed property.
- Electronic means of transmitting pay such as paycards are growing in popularity because of the ease of access and transmittal.

Vocabulary

Additional Medicare tax
Blockchain
Cryptocurrency
Direct deposit
Escheatment
Federal income tax
FICA tax
Local income tax
Mandatory deductions
Medicare tax
Net pay
Pay advice
Paycard
Percentage method
Regulation E
Social Security tax
State income taxes
Wage base
Wage-bracket method

Review Questions

1. What are the four factors that affect how much federal income tax is withheld from an employee's pay?
2. How is Social Security tax computed? What is the maximum wage base?
3. How is Medicare tax computed? What is the maximum wage base?
4. Name four states that do not have an income tax for employees.
5. How is an employee's net income computed?

6. Why is the difference between gross pay and taxable income important?
7. What are five different pay methods?
8. What are an advantage and disadvantage of paycards?
9. What are an advantage and disadvantage of direct deposit?
10. How does the percentage method work?
11. When should the percentage method be used instead of the wage-bracket method?
12. What are two examples of garnishments?
13. Why are garnishments deducted on a post-tax basis?
14. Why are union dues not considered a garnishment?
15. How does cryptocurrency function as a payroll payment method?
16. Why has cryptocurrency not yet been fully adopted as an employee payment method?

Exercises Set A

E5-1A.
LO 5-1

Lyle Ingram, the payroll accountant, needs to compute net pay for the employees for Hay Industries. Place the following steps in the proper order.

a. Compute income taxes
b. Subtract pre-tax deductions from gross pay
c. Compute Social Security and Medicare taxes
d. Subtract taxes and all other deductions from gross pay
e. Determine gross pay. Order: ______

E5-2A.
LO 5-1

Daryl Simpson is the owner of Padua Products. During the holiday season, he wants to reward his employees for their work during the year, and he has asked you to gross up their bonuses so that they receive the full amount as net pay. What amount(s) should you consider when computing the grossed-up pay? (Select all that apply.)

a. Desired bonus amount
b. Garnishments
c. Mandated deductions
d. Income tax(es)

E5-3A.
LO 5-2

Teddy Harrington is a new payroll clerk with B&H Farms. As he prepares to use the wage-bracket tables to determine federal income tax withholdings, what information does he need for each employee? (Select all that apply.)

a. Age
b. Taxable income
c. Pay date
d. Pay frequency

E5-4A.
LO 5-3

Under which circumstances could the percentage method be used to determine federal income tax withholding amounts? (Select all that apply.)

a. When the employee's taxable income exceeds the maximum amount on the appropriate wage-bracket table
b. When using a computerized accounting system to compute payroll deductions
c. When using a manual accounting system for a small number of low-pay employees
d. When computational accuracy is critical

E5-5A.
LO 5-3

Which of the following is true about Social Security and Medicare taxes as they pertain to earnings limits? (Select all that apply.)

a. Social Security tax applies to all earnings, regardless of year-to-date amounts
b. Highly compensated employees are subject to additional Medicare tax withholding
c. Once an employee's year-to-date earnings exceed the wage base, no additional Social Security tax is withheld
d. Employers contribute equally on all Social Security and Medicare taxes

E5-6A. LO 5-3
Which of the following are the rates for Social Security and Medicare taxes, respectively?
a. 4.4 percent, 6.2 percent
b. 4.2 percent, 1.5 percent
c. 6.2 percent, 1.45 percent
d. 1.45 percent, 6.2 percent

E5-7A. LO 5-4
Which of the following statements are true about state and local income taxes? (Select all that apply.)
a. All states tax employee earnings
b. State tax rates on employee earnings vary among states
c. Certain states have no personal income tax deduction
d. Some localities levy income tax on employees

E5-8A. LO 5-6
Petra Stevens is the accountant for FAB Products, a newly formed company. She is exploring employee pay methods. Which of the following describes a method in which employee earnings are transferred automatically from the employer's bank account to the employee's bank account?
a. Check
b. Paycard
c. Cash
d. Direct deposit

E5-9A. LO 5-2
What are the two methods payroll accountants use to determine federal income tax withholding amounts? (Select all that apply.)
a. Percentage method
b. Salary-bracket method
c. Wage-salary method
d. Wage-bracket method

E5-10A. LO 5-3
At what income level do many employees contribute an additional percentage to their Medicare tax deduction?
a. $128,400
b. $150,000
c. $175,000
d. $200,000

Problems Set A

P5-1A. LO 5-1,5-2, 5-3
Compute the net pay for Karen Wilson and Katie Smith. Assume that they are paid biweekly, subject to federal income tax (use the wage-bracket method) and FICA taxes, and have no other deductions from their pay. They have a state tax rate of 3 percent. If they choose to participate in the cafeteria plan, the deduction for the pay period is $100; otherwise, there is no deduction for the cafeteria plan. The cafeteria plan qualifies under Section 125. You do not need to complete the number of hours.

Name	M/S	#W/H	Hourly Rate or Period Wage	No. of Regular Hours	No. of Overtime Hours	No. of Holiday Hours	Commissions	Gross Earnings	Cafeteria Plan	Taxable Wages for Federal W/H	Taxable Wages for FICA
Karen Wilson—no cafeteria plan	M	4	2,000.00								
Karen Wilson—cafeteria plan	M	4	2,000.00								
Katie Smith—no cafeteria plan	S	1	2,000.00								
Katie Smith—cafeteria plan	S	1	2,000.00								

Name	Gross Earnings	Taxable Wages for Federal W/H	Taxable Wages for FICA	Federal W/H	Social Security Tax	Medicare W/H Tax	State W/H Tax	Net Pay
Karen Wilson—no cafeteria plan								
Karen Wilson—cafeteria plan								
Katie Smith—no cafeteria plan								
Katie Smith—cafeteria plan								

P5-2A.
LO 5-1, 5-2, 5-3, 5-5

Tooka's Trees in Auburn, Tennessee, has six employees who are paid biweekly. Calculate the net pay from the information provided below for the November 15 pay date. Assume that all wages are subject to Social Security and Medicare taxes. Use the wage-bracket method of determining federal income tax. All 401(k) and Section 125 amounts are pre-tax deductions. The wages are not subject to state taxes. You do not need to complete the number of hours.

a. T. Taylor
   Single, four withholdings
   Gross pay: $1,500 per period
   401(k) deduction: $125 per pay period
b. B. Walburn
   Married, six withholdings
   Gross pay: $2,225 per period
   401(k) deduction: $250 per period
c. H. Carpenter
   Single, no withholdings
   Gross pay: $2,100 per period
   Section 125 deduction: $75 per period
   401(k) deduction: $50 per period
d. J. Knight
   Married, three withholdings
   Gross pay: $1,875 per period
   United Way deduction: $50 per period
   Garnishment: $50 per period
e. C. Lunn
   Single, one withholding
   Gross pay: $1,200 per period
   Section 125 withholding: $50 per period
   401(k) deduction: 6 percent of gross pay
f. E. Smooter
   Married, eight withholdings
   Gross pay: $2,425 per period
   401(k) deduction: $75 per period

Name	M/S	#W/H	Hourly Rate or Period Wage	No. of Regular Hours	No. of Overtime Hours	No. of Holiday Hours	Commiss-ions	Gross Earnings	401(k)	Section 125	Taxable Wages for Federal W/H	Taxable Wages for FICA

Name	Gross Earnings	Taxable Wages for Federal W/H	Taxable Wages for FICA	Federal W/H	Social Security Tax	Medicare W/H Tax	State W/H Tax	Garnish-ments	United Way	Net Pay

P5-3A. LO 5-1, 5-2, 5-3, 5-4, 5-5

The following employees of CIBA Ironworks in Bristol, Illinois, are paid in different frequencies. Some employees have union dues or garnishments deducted from their pay. Calculate their net pay using the wage-bracket method to determine federal income tax, and including Illinois income tax of 4.95 percent of taxable pay. No employee has exceeded the maximum FICA limits. You do not need to complete the number of hours.

Employee	Frequency	Marital Status/ Withholdings	Pay	Union Dues per Period	Garnishment per Period	Net Pay
C. Whaley	Weekly	M, 2	$ 850		$ 50	
F. Paguaga	Semimonthly	M, 6	2,800	$120		
K. Harvey	Monthly	S, 3	8,000	240	75	
L. Bolling	Biweekly	M, 0	2,500		100	

Name	Frequency	M/S	#W/H	Hourly Rate or Period Wage	No. of Regular Hours	No. of Overtime Hours	No. of Holiday Hours	Commiss-ions	Gross Earnings	401(k)	Section 125	Taxable Wages for Federal W/H	Taxable Wages for FICA

Name	Gross Earnings	Taxable Wages for Federal/ State W/H	Taxable Wages for FICA	Federal W/H	Social Security Tax	Medicare W/H Tax	State W/H Tax	Union Dues	Garnish-ment	Net Pay

P5-4A. LO 5-1, 5-2, 5-3, 5-4, 5-5

Frances Newberry is the payroll accountant for Pack-It Services of Jackson, Arizona. The employees of Pack-It Services are paid semimonthly. An employee, Glen Riley, comes to her on November 6 and requests a pay advance of $750, which he will pay back in equal parts on the November 15 and December 15 paychecks. Glen is married with eight withholding allowances and is paid $50,000 per year. He contributes 3 percent of his pay to a 401(k) and has $25 per paycheck deducted for a Section 125 plan. Compute his net pay on his November 15 paycheck. The applicable state income tax rate is 2.88 percent.

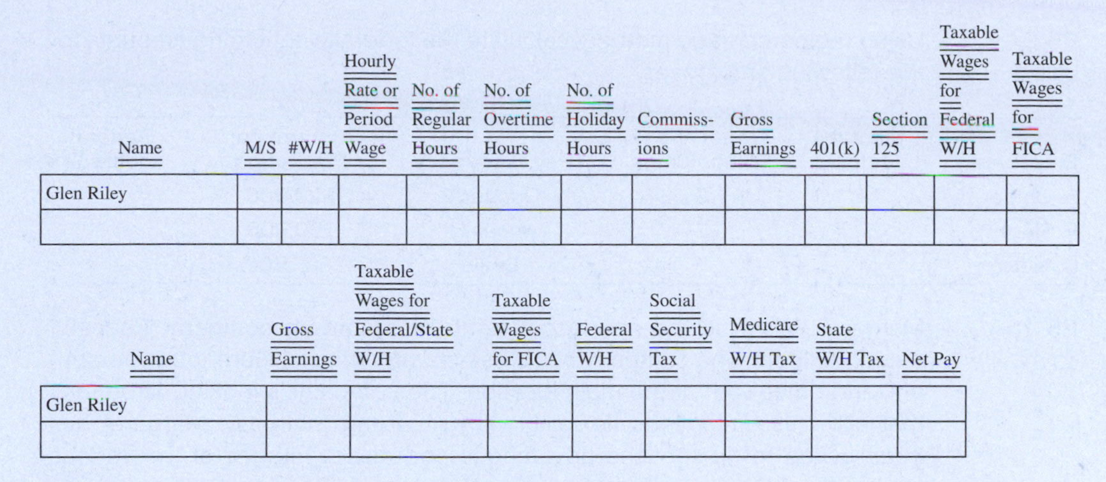

Name	M/S	#W/H	Hourly Rate or Period Wage	No. of Regular Hours	No. of Overtime Hours	No. of Holiday Hours	Commiss-ions	Gross Earnings	401(k)	Section 125	Taxable Wages for Federal W/H	Taxable Wages for FICA
Glen Riley												

Name	Gross Earnings	Taxable Wages for Federal/State W/H	Taxable Wages for FICA	Federal W/H	Social Security Tax	Medicare W/H Tax	State W/H Tax	Net Pay
Glen Riley								

P5-5A. LO 5-1, 5-2

Milligan's Millworks pays its employees on a weekly basis. Using the wage-bracket tables from Appendix C, compute the federal income tax withholdings for the following employees of Milligan's Millworks:

Employee	Marital Status	No. of Exemptions	Weekly Pay	Federal Tax
D. Balestreri	S	4	$ 845	
Y. Milligan	S	2	$1,233	
H. Curran	M	7	$ 682	
D. Liberti	M	0	$ 755	

P5-6A. LO 5-2

Wynne and Associates has employees with pay schedules that vary based on job classification. Compute the federal income tax withholding for each employee using the percentage method.

Employee	Marital Status	No. of Exemptions	Pay Frequency	Pay Amount	Federal Income Tax
S. Turner	S	1	Weekly	$ 3,000	
D. McGorray	S	4	Monthly	15,000	
A. Kennedy	M	3	Daily	500	
R. Thomas	M	5	Annually	$120,000	

P5-7A. LO 5-3

The employees of Agonnacultis Inc. are paid on a semimonthly basis. Compute the FICA taxes for the employees for the November 15 payroll. All employees have been employed for the entire calendar year.

Employee	Semimonthly Pay	YTD Pay for Oct 31 Pay Date	Social Security Tax for Nov. 15 Pay Date	Medicare Tax for Nov. 15 Pay Date
T. Newberry	$7,500			
S. Smith	$3,500			
D. Plott	$4,225			
I. Ost	$6,895			
D. Bogard	$10,250			
M. Mallamace	$4,100			

P5-8A. LO 5-4

Fannon's Chocolate Factory operates in North Carolina. Using the state income tax rate of 5.5 percent, calculate the income tax for each employee.

Employee	Amount per Pay Period	North Carolina Income Tax
K. Jamieson	$ 550	
D. Macranie	$4,895	
G. Lockhart	$3,225	
K. McIntyre	$1,795	

P5-9A. LO 5-2 Using the percentage method, calculate the federal withholding amounts for the following employees.

Employee	Marital Status	Withholdings	Pay Frequency	Amount per Pay Period	Federal Income Tax
S. Calder	M	6	Quarterly	$20,000	
P. Singh	S	2	Annually	90,000	
B. Nelson	M	0	Daily	500	

P5-10A. LO 5-6 Margaret Wilson is the new accountant for a start-up company, Peaceful Skunk Builders. The company has cross-country drivers, warehouse personnel, and office staff at the main location. The company is looking at options that allow its employees flexibility with receiving their pay. Margaret has been asked to present the advantages and disadvantages of the various pay methods to senior management. Which would be the best option for each class of workers?

Exercises Set B

E5-1B. LO 5-1 Chastity Santos is in the process of computing net pay for the employees of Happy Crab Marketing. Place the following steps in order after Chastity has determined the amount of gross pay.

a. Compute Social Security and Medicare tax withholding
b. Compute income tax withholding(s)
c. Compute pre-tax deductions
d. Compute post-tax deductions

E5-2B. LO 5-1 Joey Martel is an employee of Overclock Watches. His employer would like to give him a bonus and has asked you to gross it up to ensure that Joey receives the full amount of the desired award. Which of the following should be considered in the denominator to compute the grossed-up amount? (Select all that apply.)

a. Social Security and Medicare taxes
b. 401(k) contribution
c. Health insurance premium
d. Income tax(es)

E5-3B. LO 5-2 Liam Figueroa is the payroll accountant for Chop Brothers Coffee. As he prepares to use wage-bracket tables to determine federal income tax withholdings for each employee, which information should he have available? (Select all that apply.)

a. Marital status
b. Job title
c. Year-to-date earnings
d. Number of withholding allowances

E5-4B. LO 5-2 Which of the following are steps in computing federal income tax withholding using the percentage method? (Select all that apply.)

a. Compute and deduct withholding allowance
b. Apply the tax rate to the taxable portion of the earnings
c. Determine if the employee is exempt or nonexempt
d. Add the marginal tax

E5-5B. LO 5-3 Which of the following are true about Social Security and Medicare tax deductions? (Select all that apply.)

a. They are applied to the gross pay
b. Contributions to a 401(k) plan are exempt from these taxes
c. Medicare taxes apply to all earnings equally
d. Certain pre-tax deductions are exempt from Social Security and Medicare tax computations

E5-6B. LO 5-3

Scout Freeman is the vice president for marketing at Sun Field Industries. She earns $140,000 annually and is paid on a semimonthly basis. As of October 31, Scout has year-to-date earnings of $126,666.67. The Social Security wage base is $132,900. What is the maximum amount of her taxable earnings that may be subject to Social Security tax for the November 15 pay period?

a. $5,833.33
b. $1,833.33
c. $4,000.33
d. $0

E5-7B. LO 5-4

Which of the following is true about state and local income tax? (Select all that apply.)

a. Pre-tax deduction rules for federal income tax are generally the same for state and local income taxes
b. Nine states do not have a personal income tax on earnings
c. All localities levy income taxes on employees
d. State income tax computations vary among states

E5-8B. LO 5-6

Which of the following is true about employee pay methods? (Select all that apply.)

a. Employees must be able to access the full amount of their net pay upon demand
b. Employers must keep a record of all pay disbursements
c. Employees do not need to own a bank account to receive their pay via direct deposit
d. Paycards may be reloaded with an employee's net pay on the pay date

E5-9B. LO 5-4

Which of the following states does not withhold employee income tax? (Select all that apply.)

a. Washington
b. North Dakota
c. Tennessee
d. Alabama

E5-10B. LO 5-6

Margarita Sutton is preparing a training session for her colleagues about payroll check fraud. Which of the following may be indicators of check fraud? (Select all that apply.)

a. Changes in font type between company address and employee name
b. Company logo on the face of the check
c. Check number is missing from the check
d. Only one signature is required from the company

Problems Set B

P5-1B. LO 5-1, 5-2, 5-3

Compute the net pay for Will Barrett and Eric Martin. Assume that they are paid biweekly, subject to federal income tax (use wage bracket method) and FICA taxes, and have no other deductions from their pay. Will's deduction if he chooses to participate in the cafeteria plan is $75; Eric's is $250. There is no deduction if they do not participate in the cafeteria plan. The cafeteria plan qualifies for Section 125. There are no state income taxes and you do not need to complete the number of hours.

Name	M/S	#W/H	Hourly Rate or Period Wage	No. of Regular Hours	No. of Overtime Hours	No. of Holiday Hours	Commissions	Gross Earnings	Cafeteria Plan	Taxable Wages for Federal W/H	Taxable Wages for FICA
Will Barrett—no cafeteria plan	S	1	1,600.00								
Will Barrett—cafeteria plan	S	1	1,600.00								
Eric Martin—no cafeteria plan	M	6	1,875.00								
Eric Martin—cafeteria plan	M	6	1,875.00								

Name	Gross Earnings	Taxable Wages for Federal W/H	Taxable Wages for FICA	Federal W/H	Social Security Tax	Medicare W/H	State W/H Tax	Net Pay
Will Barrett—no cafeteria plan								
Will Barrett—cafeteria plan								
Eric Martin—no cafeteria plan								
Eric Martin—cafeteria plan								

P5-2B. LO 5-1, 5-2, 5-3, 5-5, 5-6

Hark Enterprises in Taft, Wyoming, has six employees who are paid on a semimonthly basis. Calculate the net pay from the information provided for the August 15 pay date. Assume that all wages are subject to Social Security and Medicare taxes. Use the wage-bracket tables in Appendix C to determine the federal income tax withholding. You do not need to complete the number of hours.

a. L. Fletcher:
   Married, five withholdings
   Gross pay: $1,320 per period
   401(k) deduction: 2 percent of gross pay per pay period
b. S. Lince
   Single, no withholdings
   Gross pay: $1,745 per period
   401(k) deduction: $220 per pay period
c. A. Brown
   Single, five withholdings
   Gross pay: $2,120 per period
   Section 125 deduction: $25 per pay period
   401(k) deduction: $150 per pay period
d. R. Kimble
   Married, six withholdings
   Gross pay: $1,570 per period
   United Way deduction: $25 per pay period
   Garnishment: $75 per period
e. F. Monteiro
   Married, no withholdings
   Gross pay: $2,200 per period
   Section 125 deduction: $100 per period
   401(k) deduction: 4 percent of gross pay
f. K. Giannini
   Single, two withholdings
   Gross pay: $1,485 per period
   401(k) deduction: $120 per period

Name	M/S	#W/H	Hourly Rate or Period Wage	No. of Regular Hours	No. of Overtime Hours	No. of Holiday Hours	Commissions	Gross Earnings	401(k)	Section 125	Taxable Wages for Federal W/H	Taxable Wages for FICA

Name	Gross Earnings	Taxable Wages for Federal/State W/H	Taxable Wages for FICA	Federal W/H	Social Security Tax	Medicare Tax	State Tax	United Way	Garnishment	Net Pay

P5-3B.
LO 5-1, 5-2, 5-3, 5-4, 5-5

The following employees of Memory Bytes of Titusville, Washington, are paid in different frequencies. Some employees have union dues or garnishments deducted from their pay. Calculate their net pay. Use the wage-bracket tables in Appendix C to determine federal income tax unless the amount is over the table. No employee has exceeded the maximum FICA limits. You do not need to complete the number of hours.

Employee	Frequency	Marital Status/ Withholdings	Pay	Union Dues per Period	Garnishment per Period	Net Pay
N. Lawrence	Biweekly	M, 5	$1,680	$102		
D. Gaitan	Weekly	S, 0	1,300		$70	
N. Ruggieri	Semimonthly	M, 2	2,525	110	90	
P. Oceguera	Monthly	S, 2	6,600		45	

Name	M/S	#W/H	Hourly Rate or Period Wage	No. of Regular Hours	No. of Overtime Hours	No. of Holiday Hours	Commissions	Gross Earnings	401(k)	Section 125	Taxable Wages for Federal W/H	Taxable Wages for FICA

Name	Gross Earnings	Taxable Wages for Federal/State W/H	Taxable Wages for FICA	Federal W/H Tax	Social Security Tax	Medicare W/H Tax	State W/H	Union Dues	Garnishment	Net Pay

P5-4B.
LO 5-1, 5-2, 5-3, 5-4, 5-5

Jane Heinlein is the payroll accountant for Sia Lights of Carter, Nebraska. The employees of Sia Lights are paid biweekly. An employee, Melinda Gunnarson, comes to her on September 13 and requests a pay advance of $825, which she will pay back in equal parts on the September 27 and October 11 paychecks. Melinda is single with one withholding allowance and is paid $32,500 per year. She contributes 1 percent of her pay to a 401(k) plan and has $25 per paycheck deducted for a court-ordered garnishment. Compute her net pay for her September 27th paycheck. Her state income tax rate is 6.84 percent. Use the wage-bracket tables in Appendix C to determine the federal income tax withholding amount. You do not need to complete the number of hours.

Name	M/S	#W/H	Hourly Rate or Period Wage	No. of Regular Hours	No. of Overtime Hours	No. of Holiday Hours	Commissions	Gross Earnings	401(k)	Section 125	Taxable Wages for Federal W/H	Taxable Wages for FICA
Melinda Gunnarson												

Name	Gross Earnings	Taxable Wages for Federal W/H	Taxable Wages for FICA	Federal W/H	Social Security Tax	Medicare Tax	State Tax	Garnishment	Advance	Net Pay
Melinda Gunnarson										

P5-5B. LO 5-2 Wolfe Industries pays its employees on a semimonthly basis. Using the wage-bracket tables from Appendix C, compute the federal income tax deductions for the following employees of Wolfe Industries:

Employee	Marital Status	No. of Exemptions	Semimonthly Pay	Federal Income Tax
T. Canter	M	1	$1,050	
M. McCollum	M	5	1,390	
C. Hammond	S	2	1,295	
T. Elliott	S	4	1,165	

P5-6B. LO 5-2 GL Kennels has employees with pay schedules that vary based on job classification. Compute the federal income tax liability for each employee using the percentage method.

Employee	Marital Status	No. of Exemptions	Pay Frequency	Pay Amount	Percentage Method
C. Wells	M	2	Biweekly	$1,825	
L. Decker	M	0	Weekly	750	
J. Swaby	S	5	Weekly	875	
M. Ohlson	M	3	Semimonthly	2,025	

P5-7B. LO 5-3 The employees of Black Cat Designs are paid on a semimonthly basis. Compute the FICA taxes for the employees for the November 30, 2019, payroll. All employees have been employed for the entire calendar year.

Employee	Semimonthly Pay	YTD Pay for 11-15-2019	Social Security Tax for 11-30-2019 Pay	Medicare Tax for 11-30-2019 Pay
P. Gareis	$4,250			
E. Siliwon	6,275			
G. De La Torre	5,875			
L. Rosenthal	2,850			
C. Bertozzi	5,105			
T. Gennaro	2,940			

P5-8B. LO 5-4 Christensen Ranch operates in Pennsylvania. Using the state income tax rate of 3.07 percent, calculate the state income tax for each employee.

Employee	Amount per Pay Period	Pennsylvania Income Tax
G. Zonis	$1,325	
V. Sizemore	1,710	
R. Dawson	925	
C. Couture	2,550	

P5-9B. LO 5-2 Using the percentage method, calculate the federal withholding amounts for the following employees.

Employee	Marital Status	Withholdings	Pay Frequency	Amount per Pay Period	Federal Income Tax
L. Abbey	S	3	Annually	$63,500	
G. Narleski	M	0	Quarterly	14,000	
T. Leider	S	1	Monthly	1,200	

P5-10B LO 5-6 David Adams has been retained as a consultant for Marionet Industries. The company has had difficulty with its cross-country drivers receiving their pay in a timely fashion because they are often away from their home banks. The company is looking at options that allow its employees flexibility with receiving their pay. Prepare a presentation for senior management depicting the advantages and disadvantages of the various pay methods.

Critical Thinking

For the Critical Thinking problems, use the following steps to compute the gross-up amount:

1. Compute tax rate: The tax rate on bonuses is 22 percent. The Social Security (6.2%) and Medicare taxes (1.45%) must be added to this rate. For bonuses, the total tax rate equals 22% + 6.2% + 1.45%, or 29.65%.
2. Subtract 100 percent – tax rate percentage to get the net tax rate. For bonuses, it is 100% – 29.65%, or 70.35%.
3. Gross-up amount = net pay / net tax rate. For example, if you want the employee to receive a $150 bonus, the equation is $150 / 70.35% = $213.22.
   (Note: Typically voluntary pre-tax and post-tax deductions are not withheld from bonus checks.)

5-1 Vicky Le, an employee of Sweet Shoppe Industries, receives a bonus of $5,000 for her stellar work. Her boss wants Vicky to receive $5,000 on the check. She contributes 3 percent of her pay in a pre-tax deduction to her 401(k). Calculate the gross pay amount that would result in $5,000 paid to Vicky.

5-2 Your boss approaches you in mid-December and requests that you pay certain employees their gross pay amount as if there were no deductions as their year-end bonuses. None of the employees have reached the Social Security wage base for the year. What is the gross-up amount for each of the following employees? (Use the tax rate for bonuses and no state taxes.)

Employee	Regular Gross Pay per Period	Grossed-Up Amount
Yves St. John	$2,500	
Kim Johnson	3,380	
Michael Hale	3,178	

In the Real World: Scenario for Discussion

The state of Kansas passed legislation in 2007 that allowed employers to select their employee pay method. The legislation was known as the "paperless payroll law," and many employers opted to give their employees paycards instead of cash, check, or direct deposit. This practice spread to many other states, including New York. In 2017, the law was revoked because it made employers into *de facto* financial institutions.

What are the issues with this practice? What are the benefits?

Internet Activities

5-1. Did you know that you can use an online calculator to see how your voluntary deductions will affect your paycheck? Many different payroll calculators exist. Go to one or more of the following sites and use the payroll calculator:

www.paycheckcity.com/

www.surepayroll.com/resources/calculator

www.adp.com/tools-and-resources/calculators-and-tools/payroll-calculators.aspx

5-2. Want to know more about the concepts in this chapter? Check out these sites:

www.irs.gov/pub/irs-pdf/p15.pdf

www.americanpayroll.org/Visa-Paycard-Portal/

5-3. Would you like to preview employee apps used to enter time and to calculate payroll disbursements? Check out these links:

DOL Timesheet: https://itunes.apple.com/us/app/dol-timesheet/id433638193?mt=8

Intuit payroll: https://payroll.intuit.com/additional-services/mobile-payroll-apps/

Sure payroll: https://www.surepayroll.com/payroll/mobile

Continuing Payroll Project: Prevosti Farms and Sugarhouse

For the February 8, 2019, pay period, use the gross pay totals from the end of Chapter 4 and compute the net pay for each employee. Once you have computed the net pay (using the wage-bracket tables in Appendix C), state withholding tax for Vermont is computed at 3.35 percent of taxable wages (i.e., gross pay less pre-tax deductions). Note that the first pay period comprises only one week of work during the February 8 pay period and that the federal income tax should be determined using the biweekly tables in Appendix C.

Initial pre-tax deductions for each employee are as follows:

Name	Deduction
Millen	Insurance: $155/paycheck/401(k): 3% of gross pay
Towle	Insurance: $100/paycheck/401(k): 5% of gross pay
Long	Insurance: $155/paycheck/401(k): 2% of gross pay
Shangraw	Insurance: $100/paycheck/401(k): 3% of gross pay
Lewis	Insurance: $155/paycheck/401(k): 4% of gross pay
Schwartz	Insurance: $100/paycheck/401(k): 5% of gross pay
Prevosti	Insurance: $155/paycheck/401(k): 6% of gross pay
You	Insurance: $100/paycheck/401(k): 2% of gross pay

Compute the net pay for the February 8 pay period using the payroll register. All insurance and 401(k) deductions are pre-tax. Update the Employee Earnings Records as of February 8, 2019.

Name	M/S	# W/H	Hourly Rate or Period Wage	No. of Regular Hours	No. of Overtime Hours	No. of Holiday Hours	Commissions	Gross Earnings	401(k)	Sec 125	Taxable Wages for Federal W/H	Taxable Wages for FICA

Name	Gross Earnings	Taxable Wages for Federal/State W/H	Taxable Wages for FICA	Federal W/H Tax	Social Security Tax	Medicare W/H Tax	State W/H Tax	Total Deduc	Net Pay	Check No.

Compute the net pay for the February 22 pay period using the payroll register. All insurance and 401(k) deductions are pre-tax. Update the Employee Earnings Records as of February 22, 2019.

Name	M/S	# W/H	Hourly Rate or Period Wage	No. of Regular Hours	No. of Overtime Hours	No. of Holiday Hours	Commissions	Gross Earnings	401(k)	Sec 125	Taxable Wages for Federal W/H	Taxable Wages for FICA
Thomas Millen	M	4		70								
Avery Towle	S	1		70	10							
Charlie Long	M	2		70								
Mary Shangraw	S	1		40	2							
Kristen Lewis	M	3		70								
Joe Schwartz	M	2		70			225.00					
Toni Prevosti	M	5		70								
Student Success	S	2		70	1							

Name	Gross Earnings	Taxable Wages for Federal/State W/H	Taxable Wages for FICA	Federal W/H Tax	Social Security Tax	Medicare W/H Tax	State W/H Tax	Total Deduc	Net Pay	Check No.
Thomas Millen										
Avery Towle										
Charlie Long										
Mary Shangraw										
Kristen Lewis										
Joe Schwartz										
Toni Prevosti										
Student Success										

EMPLOYEE EARNING RECORD

NAME	Thomas Millen	Hire Date	2/1/2019
ADDRESS	1022 Forest School Rd	Date of Birth	12/16/1982
CITY/STATE/ZIP	Woodstock/VT/05001	Exempt/Nonexempt	Exempt
TELEPHONE	802-478-5055	Married/Single	M
SOCIAL SECURITY NUMBER	031-11-3456	No. of Exemptions	4
POSITION	Production Manager	Pay Rate	$35,000/Year

Flex-Time	Child Care	FSA Amount	Educ. Assist.	Life Ins.	Long-Term Care	Gym

Period Ended	Hrs Worked	Reg Pay	OT Pay	Holiday	Comm	Gross Pay	401(k)	Sec 125	Taxable Wages for Federal W/H	Taxable Wages for FICA

Taxable Wages for Federal	Taxable Wages for FICA	Federal W/H	Social Security Tax	Medicare Tax	State W/H	Total Deduc	Net Pay	YTD Net Pay	YTD Gross Pay	Benefits Election

EMPLOYEE EARNING RECORD

NAME	Avery Towle	Hire Date	2/1/2019
ADDRESS	4011 Route 100	Date of Birth	7/14/1991
CITY/STATE/ZIP	Plymouth/VT/05102	Exempt/Nonexempt	Nonexempt
TELEPHONE	802-967-5873	Married/Single	S
SOCIAL SECURITY NUMBER	089-74-0974	No. of Exemptions	1
POSITION	Production Worker	Pay Rate	$12.00/hour

Flex-Time	Child Care	FSA Amount	Educ. Assist.	Life Ins.	Long-Term Care	Gym

Period Ended	Hrs Worked	Reg Pay	OT Pay	Holiday	Comm	Gross Pay	401(k)	Sec 125	Taxable Wages for Federal W/H	Taxable Wages for FICA

Taxable Wages for Federal	Taxable Wages for FICA	Federal W/H	Social Security Tax	Medicare Tax	State W/H	Total Deduc	Net Pay	YTD Net Pay	YTD Gross Pay	Benefits Election

EMPLOYEE EARNING RECORD

NAME	Charlie Long	Hire Date	2/1/2019
ADDRESS	242 Benedict Rd	Date of Birth	3/16/1987
CITY/STATE/ZIP	S. Woodstock/ VT/05002	Exempt/Nonexempt	Nonexempt
TELEPHONE	802-429-3846	Married/Single	M
SOCIAL SECURITY NUMBER	056-23-4593	No. of Exemptions	2
POSITION	Production Worker	Pay Rate	$12.50/hour

Flex-Time	Child Care	FSA Amount	Educ. Assist.	Life Ins.	Long-Term Care	Gym

Period Ended	Hrs Worked	Reg Pay	OT Pay	Holiday	Comm	Gross Pay	401(k)	Sec 125	Taxable Wages for Federal W/H	Taxable Wages for FICA

Taxable Wages for Federal	Taxable Wages for FICA	Federal W/H	Social Security Tax	Medicare Tax	State W/H	Total Deduc	Net Pay	YTD Net Pay	YTD Gross Pay	Benefits Election

EMPLOYEE EARNING RECORD

NAME	Mary Shangraw	Hire Date	2/1/2019
ADDRESS	1901 Main St #2	Date of Birth	8/20/1994
CITY/STATE/ZIP	Bridgewater/VT/05520	Exempt/Nonexempt	Exempt
TELEPHONE	802-575-5423	Married/Single	S
SOCIAL SECURITY NUMBER	075-28-8945	No. of Exemptions	1
POSITION	Administrative Assistant	Pay Rate	$10.50/hour

Flex-Time	Child Care	FSA Amount	Educ. Assist.	Life Ins.	Long-Term Care	Gym

Period Ended	Hrs Worked	Reg Pay	OT Pay	Holiday	Comm	Gross Pay	401(k)	Sec 125	Taxable Wages for Federal W/H	Taxable Wages for FICA

Taxable Wages for Federal	Taxable Wages for FICA	Federal W/H	Social Security Tax	Medicare Tax	State W/H	Total Deduc	Net Pay	YTD Net Pay	YTD Gross Pay	Benefits Election

EMPLOYEE EARNING RECORD

NAME	Kristen Lewis	Hire Date	2/1/2019
ADDRESS	840 Daily Hollow Rd	Date of Birth	4/6/1950
CITY/STATE/ZIP	Bridgewater/VT/05523	Exempt/Nonexempt	Exempt
TELEPHONE	802-390-5572	Married/Single	M
SOCIAL SECURITY NUMBER	076-39-5673	No. of Exemptions	3
POSITION	Office Manager	Pay Rate	$32,000/year

Flex-Time	Child Care	FSA Amount	Educ. Assist.	Life Ins.	Long-Term Care	Gym

Period Ended	Hrs Worked	Reg Pay	OT Pay	Holiday	Comm	Gross Pay	401(k)	Sec 125	Taxable Wages for Federal W/H	Taxable Wages for FICA

Taxable Wages for Federal	Taxable Wages for FICA	Federal W/H	Social Security Tax	Medicare Tax	State W/H	Total Deduc	Net Pay	YTD Net Pay	YTD Gross Pay	Benefits Election

EMPLOYEE EARNING RECORD

NAME	Joel Schwartz	Hire Date	2/1/2019
ADDRESS	55 Maple Farm Wy	Date of Birth	5/23/1985
CITY/STATE/ZIP	Woodstock/VT/05534	Exempt/Nonexempt	Exempt
TELEPHONE	802-463-9985	Married/Single	M
SOCIAL SECURITY NUMBER	021-34-9876	No. of Exemptions	2
POSITION	Sales	Pay Rate	$24,000/year + commission

Flex-Time	Child Care	FSA Amount	Educ. Assist.	Life Ins.	Long-Term Care	Gym

Period Ended	Hrs Worked	Reg Pay	OT Pay	Holiday	Comm	Gross Pay	401(k)	Sec 125	Taxable Wages for Federal W/H	Taxable Wages for FICA

Taxable Wages for Federal	Taxable Wages for FICA	Federal W/H	Social Security Tax	Medicare Tax	State W/H	Total Deduc	Net Pay	YTD Net Pay	YTD Gross Pay	Benefits Election

EMPLOYEE EARNING RECORD

NAME	Toni Prevosti	Hire Date	2/1/2019
ADDRESS	10520 Cox Hill Rd	Date of Birth	9/18/1967
CITY/STATE/ZIP	Bridgewater/VT/05521	Exempt/Nonexempt	Exempt
TELEPHONE	802-673-2636	Married/Single	M
SOCIAL SECURITY NUMBER	055-22-0443	No. of Exemptions	5
POSITION	Owner/President	Pay Rate	$45,000/year

Flex-Time	Child Care	FSA Amount	Educ. Assist.	Life Ins.	Long-Term Care	Gym

Period Ended	Hrs Worked	Reg Pay	OT Pay	Holiday	Comm	Gross Pay	401(k)	Sec 125	Taxable Wages for Federal W/H	Taxable Wages for FICA

Taxable Wages for Federal	Taxable Wages for FICA	Federal W/H	Social Security Tax	Medicare Tax	State W/H	Total Deduc	Net Pay	YTD Net Pay	YTD Gross Pay	Benefits Election

EMPLOYEE EARNING RECORD

NAME	Student Success	Hire Date	2/1/2019
ADDRESS	1644 Smittin Rd	Date of Birth	1/1/1991
CITY/STATE/ZIP	Woodstock/VT/05001	Exempt/Nonexempt	Nonexempt
TELEPHONE	(555) 555-5555	Married/Single	S
SOCIAL SECURITY NUMBER	555-55-5555	No. of Exemptions	2
POSITION		Pay Rate	$34,000/year

Flex-Time	Child Care	FSA Amount	Educ. Assist.	Life Ins.	Long-Term Care	Gym

Period Ended	Hrs Worked	Reg Pay	OT Pay	Holiday	Comm	Gross Pay	401(k)	Sec 125	Taxable Wages for Federal W/H	Taxable Wages for FICA

Taxable Wages for Federal	Taxable Wages for FICA	Federal W/H	Social Security Tax	Medicare Tax	State W/H	Total Deduc	Net Pay	YTD Net Pay	YTD Gross Pay	Benefits Election

Answers to Stop & Check Exercises

Differentiating between Gross and Net Pay

1. Gross pay consists of wages or commissions earned by the employee before deductions. Net pay consists of an employee's salary or wages less all mandatory and voluntary deductions.
2. Student answers may vary but could include: Qualifying medical or dental plans, Internal Revenue Code Section 125 plans, 401(k) retirement plans, federal income tax, Medicare tax, Social Security tax, state income tax, garnishments, charitable contributions, union dues.
3. To "gross up" a payroll amount is to calculate the amount of gross pay necessary to receive a net pay result. This is most often done for bonuses.

How Much Tax to Withhold?

1. (a) $143; (b) (($2,166.67 − (2 × $175) − $1,200) × 0.12) + $80.80 = $144.90.
2. $2,166.67 gross pay − $100 for 401(k) deduction per pay period = $2,066.67 taxable pay. This is the amount used in conjunction with the wage-bracket table to calculate the federal income tax withheld of $131. The difference in taxes with the 401(k) deduction is $12 = $143 − $131.
3. $127 = $2,166.67 gross pay − $75 health insurance − $55 AFLAC = $2,036.67 taxable pay.

FICA Taxes

1. Social Security = $327.36 = $5,280 × .062; Medicare = $76.56 = $5,280 × 0.0145.
2. Total Liability = $807.84 = ($327.36 + $76.56) × 2.
3. a. $0 Social Security tax; Medicare taxable would be reduced by the qualified insurance deduction. Year-to-date salary $197,916.73 less the qualified deduction $1,425 ($75 × 19) gives $196,491.73. Medicare base for this payroll, $3,508.27 to reach the $200,000 cap and $6,833.40 ($10,416.67 − $3,508.27 − $75.00) that will be charged the surcharge. ($3,508.27 × 1.45%) + ($6,833.40 × 2.35%) = $50.87 + $160.58 = $211.45 Medicare tax.
   b. ($10,416.67 − $75.00) × 2.35% = $243.03 Medicare tax.

State and Local Income Taxes

1. $24.35 ($62,500 annual salary/26 biweekly = $2,403.85 gross pay − $150 for 401(k) pre-tax deduction − $80 health insurance pre-tax deduction = $2,173.85 taxable pay × 1.12%. From Appendix D, Married.
2. $131.96 ($2,850 × 4.63%) state, $5.75 local.

Post-Tax Deductions

1. a, b, d
2. Because the IBEW requires that employees' union dues be remitted by the employer, the amount due must be deducted on a post-tax basis from his period pay.

Pay Methods

1. Cash, check, direct deposit, paycard, and cryptocurrencies.
2. Regulation E.
3. Direct deposit.

6

Chapter Six

Employer Payroll Taxes and Labor Planning

All facets of payroll accounting are important because they affect the success of the company and its employees. A particularly important piece of the payroll puzzle is the employer's payroll tax responsibility. The reporting and remittance of payroll taxes is a significant aspect that requires scrupulous attention to detail. Many different tax forms exist that must be filed at regular intervals and with varying governmental bodies. Tax filing requires organizational skills, time management, and continued accuracy. Tax reporting is a huge responsibility of the business and its payroll accountant because of governmental oversight. Additionally, employment tax revenue remittances represent 70 percent of all federal revenue. Therefore, employment tax remittances are a vital part of the U.S. economy.

Employers must also consider payroll responsibilities as part of labor planning. Besides taxes, other aspects of an employer's payroll responsibilities include maintaining workers' compensation insurance, forwarding amounts withheld through employees' voluntary and mandated deductions, and determining both labor expenses and employee benefits. The Internal Revenue Service and state employment departments have websites that contain important information about filing requirements, due dates, guidelines, and penalties (see Appendix E for state employment department contact information). Insurance responsibilities are a vital consideration when determining labor expenses and employee benefits because they are a significant element in the cost of doing business.

LEARNING OBJECTIVES

After studying Chapter 6, you should be able to:

LO 6-1 List Employer-Paid and Employee-Paid Obligations

LO 6-2 Discuss Reporting Periods and Requirements for Employer Tax Deposits

Cineberg/Shutterstock

LO 6-3 Prepare Mid-Year and Year-End Employer Tax Reporting and Deposits

LO 6-4 Describe Payroll Within the Context of Business Expenses

LO 6-5 Relate Labor Expenses to Company Profitability

LO 6-6 Complete Benefit Analysis as a Function of Payroll

Climate Change and Construction Labor Costs

The notion of climate change as an economic challenge is a reality that is gaining in popularity. Many people think of climate change primarily in terms of temperature and meteorological conditions. The economic implications of changes in weather could significantly impact industries that are limited by outdoor conditions. The construction industry represents one large group of workers—as well as being a large sector of the U.S. economy—who will feel the effect of a changing climate.

One issue facing the construction industry is weather extremes, both on the hot and the cold side. Construction employers will need to be sure that employees have appropriate, specialized equipment that can handle weather extremes. Depending on the temperature, more employees may need to be available to rotate during projects in order to guarantee worker safety. As the amount of weather-related destruction increases, employers need to meet rising labor costs associated with needed rebuilding efforts. Finally, employers' insurance costs are increasing because of the potential for harm or delay in completing construction projects. All in all, rising labor costs in the construction industry are a significant concern, especially since much of it is connected with the uncontrollable force of nature; furthermore, it affects the employer's payroll costs and labor planning functions.

(Sources: For Construction Pros, Planeitzen)

Labor costs potentially constitute a significant portion of a company's expense. Employee benefits such as company contributions to retirement plans, temporary disability insurance, and educational reimbursements represent additional business expenses. In this chapter, we will examine employer payroll tax responsibilities and how payroll is a tool in labor planning.

LO 6-1 List Employer-Paid and Employee-Paid Obligations

Employers must pay some of the same taxes that the employees do. However, a firm has additional liabilities that employees do not, such as certain unemployment taxes and workers' compensation insurance. A comparison of employee-paid and employer-paid taxes is given in Table 6-1.

The taxes that an employer must pay are often known as ***statutory deductions***, meaning that governmental statutes have made the tax a mandatory, legally obligated deduction. An important element of employer tax responsibility is that it continues after disbursing the employees' pay, often extending well after an employee leaves the firm. Employers must file mandatory reconciliation reports detailing the amounts they have withheld from employee pay, tracking the employees throughout the company's accounting system, and maintaining the personnel files for both current and terminated employees in accordance with the firm's payroll practices and governmental regulations.

Social Security and Medicare Taxes

The ***FICA*** taxes, which include both the Social Security and Medicare taxes, are among the statutory withholdings that employees and employers pay. Employees and employers must each contribute 6.2 percent (for a total of 12.4%) of the employee's pay up to the maximum withholding amount for Social Security. Additionally, employers must match the employees' payroll deductions for the Medicare tax in the amount of 1.45 percent (for a total of 2.9%) of the employees' gross pay less applicable deductions. In addition, the Affordable Care Act has mandated an additional 0.9 percent of Medicare tax for employees whose wages exceed $200,000 annually. The employer does not match this additional Medicare tax.

Let us look at an example of how the employer's share of the FICA tax works.

EXAMPLE: EMPLOYEE AND EMPLOYER SHARE, SOCIAL SECURITY TAX

Courtney Russo works as an hourly worker who earns an annual salary of $36,000 and is paid biweekly. Her gross pay is $1,384.62 per pay period ($36,000 per year/26 pay periods).

Courtney's share of the Social Security tax:	$1,384.62 × 6.2% = $ 85.85
Her employer's share of the Social Security tax:	$1,384.62 × 6.2% = $ 85.85
Total Social Security tax liability for Courtney's pay this period:	$ 171.70

As shown in the example, the employer and employee contribute the same amounts for the Social Security tax. Remember that the Social Security tax has a maximum withholding per year based on the employee's salary, which is $132,900 for 2019. After reaching that maximum, neither the employee nor the employer contributes any more Social Security tax.

TABLE 6-1
Employee-Paid and Employer-Paid Taxes

Tax	Employee Pays	Employer Pays
Social Security	XX	XX
Medicare	XX	XX
Federal Income Tax	XX	
Federal Unemployment Tax (FUTA)		XX
State Income Tax (where applicable)	XX	
State Unemployment Tax (SUTA)	Sometimes both are responsible at different percentages; see your local taxation authority for specific details.	XX
Local Income Taxes	XX	
Local Occupational Taxes (where applicable)	XX	XX
Workers' Compensation Premiums		XX
401(k)/Pension (if matching policy exists)	XX	XX
Other Voluntary Deductions	XX	

EXAMPLE: EMPLOYEE AND EMPLOYER SHARE SOCIAL SECURITY TAXES, HIGHLY COMPENSATED EMPLOYEE

William Perry is the vice president of Sunny Glassworks. His annual salary is $225,000, which is paid semimonthly. His gross pay per period is $9,375.00 ($225,000/24 pay periods). For the 13th pay period of the year, the Social Security tax withholding is as follows:

William's share of the Social Security tax:	$9,375 × 6.2% = $ 581.25
Sunny Glasswork's share of William's Social Security tax:	$9,375 × 6.2% = $ 581.25
Total Social Security tax liability for William's pay this period:	$1,162.50

After the 14th pay period, William's year-to-date pay is $9,375 × 14 = $131,250. After the 15th pay period, William's year-to-date pay will be $9,375 × 15 = $140,625, which exceeds the Social Security wage base. The amount subject to Social Security tax for the 15th pay period equals the wage base minus the 14th pay period YTD pay:

$132,900 – $131,250 = $1,650 of William's pay during the 14th pay period is excluded from Social Security tax, which means that he is only taxed on $7,725.

William's share of the Social Security tax:	$7,725 × 6.2% = $ 478.95
Sunny Glasswork's share of William's Social Security tax:	$7,725 × 6.2% = $ 478.95
Total Social Security tax liability for William's pay this period that must be remitted by Sunny Glassworks:	$ 957.90

Medicare tax, the other piece of the FICA taxes, has no maximum but does have an additional tax for high-wage employees. Let us look at Courtney Russo's pay again to see how the Medicare tax works.

EXAMPLE: EMPLOYEE AND EMPLOYER SHARE, MEDICARE TAXES

Courtney's share of the Medicare tax:	$ 1,384.62 × 1.45% = $ 20.08
Her employer's share of the Medicare tax:	$ 1,384.62 × 1.45% = $ 20.08
Total Medicare tax liability for Courtney's pay this period that must be remitted by Sunny Glassworks:	$ 40.16
Total FICA responsibility from Courtney's pay this period ($171.70 + $40.16):	$ 211.86

Now let's look at the employee and employer share of Medicare taxes for William, who is a highly compensated employee.

EXAMPLE: EMPLOYEE AND EMPLOYER SHARE MEDICARE TAXES, HIGHLY COMPENSATED EMPLOYEE

As of the 22nd pay period of the year, William's YTD pay is $206,250. Amount subject to the additional Medicare tax: $6,250.

Medicare tax amounts:	
William's standard Medicare tax liability:	$9,375 × 1.45% = $135.94
Sunny Glasswork's Medicare tax liability:	$9,375 × 1.45% = $135.94
William's additional Medicare tax liability:	$6,250 × 0.9% = $ 56.25
Total Medicare tax liability:	$328.13
Total FICA responsibility for William's pay this period:	$328.13

Remember, no Social Security tax applies because William has already exceeded the wage base.

Social Security and Medicare amounts may be listed separately when the company makes its tax deposit. The employer's tax deposit will also include the amount deducted from the employee for federal income tax.

Maintaining accurate records of taxes withheld through payroll registers and employee earnings records is a critical part of calculating proper FICA tax deductions. Whether a company uses a manual system, has an automated system, or outsources the payroll duties, it remains responsible for the accuracy of the deductions and maintenance of associated records.

Federal and State Unemployment Taxes

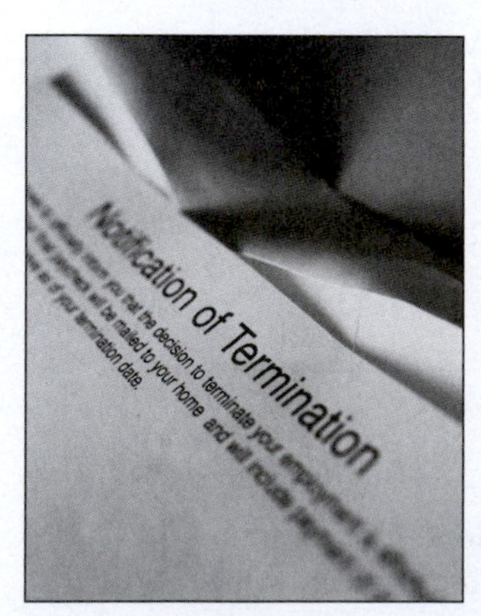

Janis Christie/Getty Images

Another set of employer-paid payroll taxes includes those mandated by the ***Federal Unemployment Tax Act (FUTA)*** and ***State Unemployment Tax Act (SUTA)***. FUTA and SUTA are unemployment compensation funds established to provide for workers who have lost their jobs. Generally, the rate for FUTA tax is lower than that for SUTA tax because the states govern the disbursement of unemployment funds and because unemployment rates vary by region. FUTA taxes pay for the administrative expenses of the unemployment insurance fund. SUTA tax rates provide a localized and individual focus for employer taxes. The unemployment insurance fund pays for half of extended unemployment benefits and provides a fund of additional benefits against which states may borrow as necessary to cover unemployment claims. An interesting note is that FUTA and SUTA are employer-only taxes in all *but* three states: Alaska, New Jersey, and Pennsylvania.

FUTA pertains only to U.S. citizens and workers employed by American companies. According to the IRS, to be classified as an American company, an employer must meet the following criteria:

- An individual who is a resident of the United States,
- A partnership, if two-thirds or more of the partners are residents of the United States,
- A trust, if all of the trustees are residents of the United States, or
- A corporation organized under the laws of the United States, of any state, or the District of Columbia.

American citizens who work for companies outside of the United States who are not classified as American employers are not subject to FUTA provisions. Certain resident aliens and professions are exempt from FUTA provisions, as stipulated by Income Tax Regulation §31.3301-1. The professions from which employee compensation is exempt from FUTA provisions are

- Compensation paid to agricultural workers.
- Compensation paid to household employees unless the compensation exceeds $1,000 during any calendar quarter of the current year or prior year.
- Compensation paid to employees of religious, charitable, educational, or certain other tax-exempt organizations.
- Compensation paid to employees of the U.S. government or any of its agencies.
- Compensation paid to employees of the government of any state of the United States, or any of its political subdivisions.
- Compensation paid to employees of the government of the District of Columbia, or any of its political subdivisions.

The full 2019 rate for FUTA tax is 6.0 percent of the first $7,000 of an employee's wages paid during a calendar year. FUTA is paid by the employer. Employees who move to a different company will have the new employer paying additional FUTA taxes. Therefore, if an employer has a high turnover rate among its employees (i.e., a large number of employees remain employed for only a short period before terminating employment), the firm will pay FUTA tax for all employees for the first $7,000 of earnings, including the ones who remained in their employ for only a short time. FUTA is subject to a 5.4 percent reduction, for which employers may qualify on two conditions:

- Employers make SUTA deposits on time and in full.
- As long as the state is not a credit reduction state.

With the credit, the employer's FUTA rate will be 0.6 percent on the first $7,000 of every employee's wage. The minimum FUTA tax rate is 0.6 percent, which means that a minimum of $42 ($7,000 × 0.006) may be paid per employee. Note that FUTA tax liability is always reported for the prior year, which means that the the FUTA tax liability in 2020 will increase with the first payroll and thus reflect both 2019 and 2020 liability if the 940 has not been filed

EXAMPLE: FUTA TAX COMPUTATION, ALL EMPLOYEES EARNING IN EXCESS OF $7,000

Snowborn Inc. is a company based in Great Falls, Montana. During 2019, the company had 178 employees, all of whom earned in excess of $7,000 in wages and salaries. At the end of the year, only 145 employees remained with the company. The 2019 FUTA tax liability for Snowborn Inc. would be computed as follows:

Number of employees during 2019	Multiplied by the first $7,000 of wages	Multiplied by 0.6% tax rate	FUTA tax liability for 2019
178	$7,000	0.006	$7,476

Note that Snowborn Inc. is liable for the FUTA tax on all employees who worked for the company, even if they left employment with the company. The FUTA tax filing is due on January 31, 2020.

yet. If the employer makes quarterly deposits, then the full 2019 liability would not be part of the FUTA Tax Payable account in 2020.

What happens when the employees earn less than $7,000 during the calendar year? The employer is still responsible for the FUTA tax on the employees' earnings, but only the amount earned during the calendar year.

EXAMPLE: FUTA TAX, EMPLOYEES WITH EARNINGS LESS THAN $7,000 DURING THE YEAR

Baja Brothers Wines, based in Tucson, Arizona, has 62 employees and the following employee data for FUTA taxes:

Number of employees during 2019	Multiplied by the first $7,000 of wages	Multiplied by 0.6% tax rate	FUTA tax liability for 2019
59	$7,000	0.006	$2,478.00
Employees who earned less than $7,000 during 2019:	**Multiplied by the amount of wages earned in 2019**	**Multiplied by 0.6% tax rate**	
Employee A	$ 5,894.00	0.006	$ 35.36
Employee B	3,198.00	0.006	19.19
Employee C	975.00	0.006	5.85
		Total FUTA tax	**$2,538.40**

belterz/iStockphoto

Establishment of the SUTA in each state provided states with local authority to offer unemployment or jobless benefits. Designed as an unemployment insurance program after the Great Depression of the 1930s, the remittance of SUTA payments follows many of the same procedures as other payroll taxes. As a state-run fund, each state can establish its own qualification requirements for both individual claims and business payments, the wage base for employers in the state, and the tax rate. The SUTA wage base and rate fluctuates among states and can be an incentive for businesses to change operations from one state to another. Note that all states' wage bases exceed the minimum required by the law, but the tax rate is variable.

FUTA Credit Reduction

As we noted, the nominal FUTA tax is 6.0 percent, of which the employer remits 0.6 percent to the federal government. A caveat to this 0.6 percent employer rate involves Title XII advances issued from the federal government to assist with payments of unemployment liabilities. This can occur when a high period of unemployment happens due to layoffs or economic downturns.

In the event that a state defaults on its repayment of these federal loans, the credit taken against the 6.0 percent FUTA rate may be reduced. Each year, states have until November 10 to repay the prior year's loan. If the loan remains unpaid for more than one year, the FUTA credit will continue to be reduced in the third and fifth year after the loan is due. An example of the FUTA credit reduction follows.

EXAMPLE: FUTA CREDIT REDUCTION

State Z had a loan taken during 2018 to supplement amounts paid for unemployment insurance liabilities. The balance of that loan would be due on November 10, 2019. If the balance is not paid by that date, the credit against the FUTA rate for the next calendar year would be as follows:

FUTA rate	Standard FUTA rate after credit	FUTA rate after credit reduction
6.0%	0.6%	2.4%

The credit would be reduced further in future years if the loan remains unpaid. The credit reduction is reported by employers on Form 940. For 2019, the FUTA credit reductions only applies to the U.S. Virgin Islands (2.4%). (Source: EY)

State Unemployment Taxes

SUTA is limited to wages collected and the 5.4 percent rate is a guideline. State rates vary based on employee retention and other factors. States examine employee turnover during an established period and determine if employers qualify for a credit against the nominal SUTA rate. Depending upon the state the company is operating in, this limit may be equal to, higher, or lower than the SUTA rate. For example, Alaska's SUTA wage base was $39,900 in 2019. A chart containing the SUTA wage base and rates is shown in Table 6-2.

TABLE 6-2
SUTA Wage Base and Rates 2019

State	Wage Base	Min/Max Rate
Alabama	$ 8,000	0.65%–6.8%
Alaska	$39,900	1.0%–5.4%
Arizona	$ 7,000	0.04%–11.80%
Arkansas	$10,000	0.4%–14.3%
California	$ 7,000	1.5%–6.2%
Colorado	$13,100	0.62%–8.15%
Connecticut	$15,000	1.9%–6.8%
Delaware	$16,500	0.3%–8.2%
District of Columbia	$ 9,000	1.6%–7.0%
Florida	$ 7,000	0.1%–5.4%
Georgia	$ 9,500	0.04%–8.1%
Hawaii	$46,800	0.0%–5.6%
Idaho	$40,000	0.251%–5.4%
Illinois	$12,960	0.475%–6.875%
Indiana	$ 9,500	0.5%–7.4%
Iowa	$30,600	0.0%–7.5%
Kansas	$14,000	0.0%–7.1%
Kentucky	$10,500	0.225%–8.925%
Louisiana	$ 7,700	0.1%–6.2%
Maine	$12,000	0.6%–5.46%
Maryland	$ 8,500	0.3%–7.5%
Massachusetts	$15,000	0.94%–14.37%
Michigan	$ 9,500	0.06%–10.3%
Minnesota	$34,000	0.2%–9.1%
Mississippi	$14,000	0.2%–5.6%
Missouri	$12,000	0.0%–9.45%
Montana	$33,000	0.13%–6.25%
Nebraska	$ 9,000	0.0%–5.4%
Nevada	$31,200	0.3%–5.4%

(continued)

TABLE 6-2

SUTA Wage Base and Rates 2019 *(concluded)*

State	Wage Base	Min/Max Rate
New Hampshire	$14,000	0.1%–7.0%
New Jersey	$34,400	0.4%–5.4%
New Mexico	$24,800	0.33%–5.4%
New York	$11,400	0.6%–7.9%
North Carolina	$24,300	0.06%–5.76%
North Dakota	$36,400	0.15%–9.75%
Ohio	$ 9,500	0.3%–9.2%
Oklahoma	$18,100	0.1%–5.5%
Oregon	$40,600	0.9%–5.4%
Pennsylvania	$10,000	2.3905%–11.0333%
Rhode Island	$23,600	1.1%–9.7%
South Carolina	$14,000	0.06%–5.46%
South Dakota	$15,000	0.0%–9.35%
Tennessee	$ 7,000	0.01%–10.0%
Texas	$ 9,000	0.36%–6.36%
Utah	$35,300	0.1%–7.1%
Vermont	$15,600	0.8%–6.5%
Virginia	$ 8,000	0.11%–6.21%
Washington	$49,800	0.13%–7.73%
West Virginia	$12,000	1.5%–8.5%
Wisconsin	$14,000	0.0%–12.0%
Wyoming	$25,400	0.18%–8.72%

Sources: American Payroll Association, ADP

An employer's SUTA rate is determined by a mix of state unemployment rates and company experience ratings. The SUTA rate for company A may be different from the rate for company B. For example, a construction company may experience higher unemployment claims because of the seasonal nature and higher risk associated with the industry; therefore, the company's rate may be 4.54 percent, whereas a similar-sized company in a professional services industry may have an unemployment rate of 3.28 percent. States issue letters on an annual basis to companies with the individually determined SUTA rate for the following year.

The first example is a company that has a SUTA rate of 5.4 percent and all employees have earned in excess of $7,000 for the year.

EXAMPLE: FUTA AND SUTA LIABILITY, SUTA = 5.4 PERCENT

JayMac Communications, a California company, has 15 employees, all of whom have met the $7,000 threshold for the FUTA tax. The state portion for which JayMac is liable is 5.4 percent. The unemployment tax obligations are

FUTA:	15 employees × $7,000 × 0.006 =	$ 630
SUTA:	15 employees × $7,000 × 0.054 =	5,670
Total unemployment tax liability:		$6,300

The next example is a company in Georgia that has a SUTA rate of 2.3 percent and some employees who have earned less than $7,000 during the year.

EXAMPLE: FUTA AND SUTA LIABILITY, SUTA = 2.3 PERCENT

Charmer Industries of Georgia has 20 employees: 18 employees have met the FUTA and SUTA thresholds, and 2 employees have not, earning $5,400 and $2,500, respectively. The state obligation for Charmer is 2.3 percent owing to a favorable employer rating. Charmer's unemployment taxes would be computed as follows:

FUTA:	18 × $7,000 × 0.006 =	$ 756.00
	($5,400 + $2,500) × 0.006 =	$ 47.40
	Total FUTA liability:	$ 803.40
SUTA:	18 × $9,500 × 0.023 =	$3,933.00
	($5,400 + $2,500) × 0.023 =	$ 181.70
	Total SUTA liability:	$4,114.70
Total unemployment tax liability:		$4,918.10

Other State and Local Employer-Only Payroll Taxes

Some states have employer-only taxes unique to the area. Delaware, Colorado, Hawaii, and several other states have additional taxes that are remitted under different names. Some examples of these types of taxes include

- Georgia employers pay an administrative assessment of 0.06 percent on employee gross wages with a wage base of $9,500 (2019 figure).
- Maine has an employer-paid Competitive Skills Scholarship Program tax of 0.06 percent.
- In California, employers pay an Employment Training Tax (ETT) of 0.1 percent on all wages up to the first $7,000 of wages.

As a payroll accountant, it is very important to be familiar with the tax withholding and employer responsibilities for each state in which the company has employees residing, even if there is not a business office located there. It is also important to be aware of any forms that are required within the state the company has employees.

Individual counties and cities can also impose occupational taxes on the businesses within their jurisdiction. The reporting periods for the local and city taxes are separate from the filing requirements for federal or state taxes. The payroll accountant must review all tiers of taxes to ensure compliance in collection, submission, and reporting.

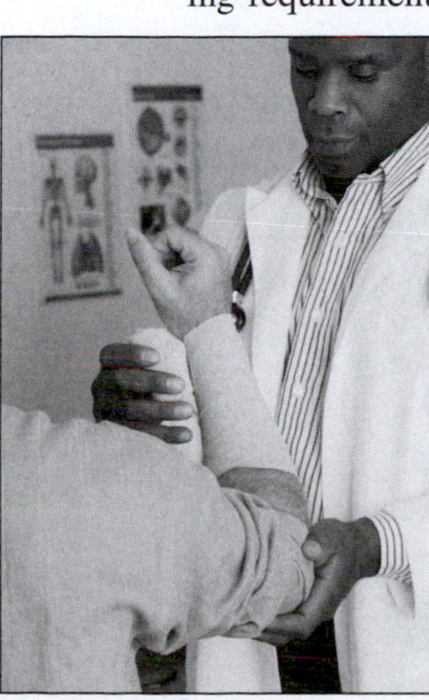

Radius Images/Alamy

Workers' Compensation Insurance

Workers' compensation insurance is another type of employer payroll responsibility. Although it is not considered a tax, states enforce workers' compensation statutes; federal employees are protected by the Federal Employment Compensation Act. Workers' compensation statutes are designed to protect workers who are injured (temporarily or permanently) or killed during the performance of their job-related duties.

Because workers' compensation is an insurance policy maintained by employers, premiums vary based on employees' job classifications and the risk of injury they typically encounter in the normal course of work. Premium amounts are expressed as amounts per $100 of payroll for each job classification. Premium amounts are estimated based on expected payroll amounts for the coming year and then adjusted at the end of the year once the actual payroll amounts are finalized.

EXAMPLE: WORKERS' COMPENSATION PREMIUM COMPUTATION

Jesse Hildreth is the owner of Eastern Freight Lines. She has three categories of employees: drivers, loaders, and administrative staff. The workers' compensation premium rates are as follows:

- Drivers: $1.45/$100 of payroll
- Loaders: $2.50/$100 of payroll
- Administrative staff: $0.40/$100 of payroll

For 20XX, Eastern Freight Lines payroll is expected to be the following:

Job Classification	Premium per $100 of Payroll	Estimated Payroll	Premium Due Jan. 1
Driver	$1.45	$387,500	$ 5,618.75*
Loader	2.50	435,200	10,880†
Administrative Staff	0.40	320,000	1,280††
Total Premium Due, Jan. 1			$ 17,778.75

*($387,500/$100) × $1.45 = $5,618.75
†($435,200/$100) × $2.50 = $10,880
††($320,000/$100) × $0.40 = $1,280

The 20XX premium is adjusted based on actual payroll. The difference between the paid estimated premium and the premium based on actual payroll results must either be remitted to the insurance company or refunded to the employer. An analysis of the actual payroll as of December 31, 20XX, revealed the following results:

Job Classification	Premium per $100 of Payroll	Actual Payroll	Premium Due Dec. 31
Driver	$1.45	$410,563	$ 5,953.16*
Loader	2.50	478,290	11,957.25†
Administrative staff	0.40	338,945	1,355.78††
Total actual premium due December 31			$19,266.19
Less: Premium paid on Jan. 1			17,778.75
Difference to be remitted to the insurance company			$ 1,487.44

*($410,563/$100) × $1.45 = $5,953.16
†($478,290/$100) × $2.50 = $11,957.25
††($338,945/$100) × $0.40 = $1,355.78

Eastern Freight Lines must remit $1,487.44 to the insurance company due to the difference between the estimated and the actual payroll for 20XX.

Workers' compensation premium rates may also vary based on the employer's safety record. For example, a company with multiple job-related injuries would have a higher premium than another company with few or no injuries. Employer compliance with OSHA guidelines is important to control the cost of workers' compensation insurance.

The majority of workers' compensation insurance claims occur in five main categories of injuries:

1. Sprains and strains.
2. Punctures or cuts.
3. Bruises or other contusions.
4. Inflammation.
5. Fractured bones.

Most work-related injuries can be avoided through employee safety training, attention to the walking and working conditions of the facility, and employer diligence. (Source: Insurance Journal)

FUTA, SUTA, and Workers' Compensation

1. AMS Enterprises in New Mexico has 30 employees. Of these, 25 have exceeded the FUTA and SUTA wage bases. This is the first quarter of the year, and AMS Enterprises has not yet paid FUTA or SUTA taxes for the year. The other five employees' YTD wages are as follows: Employee A, $15,800; Employee B, $7,800; Employee C, $11,115; Employee D, $22,800; Employee E, $2,575. AMS Enterprises receives the full FUTA tax credit and pays a SUTA rate of 4.2 percent (See Table 6-2 for SUTA taxable wage maximum). How much are AMS Enterprises' FUTA and SUTA liabilities?
2. Noodle Noggins of Maine has 12 employees and is eligible for the full FUTA tax credit; the SUTA rate is 3.26 percent. Ten of the 12 employees have exceeded the FUTA wage base. Eight employees have exceeded the SUTA wage base (See Table 6-2 for the SUTA taxable wage maximum). The remaining employees have the following YTD wages: $5,500, $6,800, $11,100, and $9,850. The Competitive Skills Scholarship tax applies to all employees. Noodle's YTD total wages are $279,580. What are the FUTA, SUTA, and Competitive Skills Scholarship tax liabilities for Noodle Noggins?
3. High Flyers Jump School has two classifications of employees: clerical employees and jump instructors. The workers' compensation premium rates are $0.45/$100 for clerical employees and $3.75/$100 for jump instructors. During 20XX, the estimated payroll amounts were $104,550 for clerical employees and $215,690 for jump instructors. How much would the estimated workers' compensation insurance policy cost High Flyers Jump School during 20XX?

Comstock/Getty Images

LO 6-2 Discuss Reporting Periods and Requirements for Employer Tax Deposits

The frequency of depositing federal income tax and FICA taxes depends on the size of the company's payroll. The depositing schedules have nothing to do with a company's pay frequency, although some of the names are similar. The IRS stipulates five different schedules for an employer's deposit of payroll taxes:

- Annually
- Quarterly
- Monthly
- Semiweekly
- Next business day

Of these, the most common deposit schedules are monthly and semiweekly. Electronic tax deposits are usually processed through the ***Electronic Federal Tax Payment System (EFTPS)*** website, although the IRS allows employers to transmit payments through certain financial institutions via ***Automated Clearing House (ACH)*** or wire transfer. When using the EFTPS, the employer must register with the IRS to access the site. The EFTPS is used for both Form 941 (federal income tax, Social Security tax, and Medicare tax) and the quarterly/annual Form 940 FUTA tax deposit. The website for EFTPS is www.eftps.gov.

Lookback Period

The frequency of each company's deposits is determined through a ***lookback period***, which is the amount of payroll taxes an employer has reported in the 12-month period prior to June 30

TABLE 6-3
Lookback Period

Lookback Period for 2019 Taxes			
July 1, 2017, through	October 1, 2017, through	January 1, 2018, through	April 1, 2018, through
September 30, 2017	December 31, 2017	March 31, 2018	June 30, 2018

Source: Internal Revenue Service

of the previous year. For example, the lookback period that the IRS would use for 2019 tax deposit frequency would be the July 1, 2017, through June 30, 2018, period. Employers receive notification about their deposit requirements in writing from the IRS in October of each year. Table 6-3 shows the lookback period.

Deposit Frequencies

The IRS informs businesses in writing if they need to deposit their payroll taxes annually, monthly, or semiweekly based on the deposits during the lookback period. All new companies are monthly schedule depositors unless they have a total payroll liability in excess of $100,000 during any pay period. It is important to note that the tax deposit due date is based on the payroll disbursement date, not the pay period ending date. For example, if a company's pay period ended on June 28, but the payroll was not disbursed until July 1, the payroll tax deposit date would be based on the July 1 disbursement. Table 6-4 outlines the criteria for differences among deposit frequencies.

EXAMPLE: MONTHLY SCHEDULE DEPOSITOR

Generational Coffee is a company based in Wenatchee, Washington. During the lookback period ending June 30, 2018, the company had **$36,549** in total payroll tax liability. Generational Coffee would be a *monthly* schedule depositor. Payroll tax deposits would be due on the *15th* of the following month (e.g., June 15 for May payroll taxes).

TABLE 6-4
Criteria for Deposit Frequencies

Frequency	Criteria	Due Date
Annually	$2,500 or less in employment taxes to be remitted annually with Form 944.	January 31 of the following year.
Quarterly	For any amounts not deposited during the quarter that may be due to rounding errors or other undeposited amounts.	15th of the month following the end of the quarter.
Monthly	$50,000 or less in payroll tax liability during the lookback period. The amount of total tax liability is also found on Form 941, line 10. All new businesses are monthly schedule depositors unless they accrue in excess of $100,000 in payroll taxes for any pay period. (See the Next Business Day rule frequency.)	15th of the month following the month during which the company accrued payroll tax deposits. For example, taxes on March payroll would be due on **April 15**, or the next business day if April 15 falls on a weekend or a holiday.
Semiweekly	More than $50,000 in payroll tax liability during the lookback period. The amount of total tax liability is also found on Form 941, line 10. The exception to the semiweekly deposit schedule is the Next Business Day rule.	For payroll paid on a Wednesday, Thursday, or Friday, the payroll tax deposit is due by the following **Wednesday**. For payroll paid on a Saturday, Sunday, Monday, or Tuesday, the payroll tax is due by the following **Friday**.
Next business day	$100,000 or more in payroll tax liability for any payroll period.	The payroll tax deposit is due on the **next business day**.

Notice the amount of total payroll tax for Generational Coffee. Because the total amount was less than $50,000, it is classified as a monthly schedule payroll tax depositor, and due dates are the 15th of the following month.

EXAMPLE: SEMIWEEKLY SCHEDULE DEPOSITOR

Pollak Woolens is a company based in Sault Ste. Marie, Michigan. During the lookback period ending June 30, 2018, it had **$75,984** in total payroll tax liability. Pollak Woolens would be a ***semiweekly*** schedule depositor. Depending on the payroll date, tax deposits are due on either the ***Wednesday*** or the ***Friday*** following the payroll date.

Notice the total tax liability during the lookback period. For Pollak Woolens, the amount exceeded $50,000 but is less than $100,000; this makes it a semiweekly schedule depositor. Because payroll tax deposits for semiweekly depositors are driven by the day of the week upon which payroll was paid, deposits may be due either on Wednesday or on Friday. For companies with a biweekly payroll frequency, the tax deposit date may remain the same with few exceptions due to holidays. For companies with semimonthly payroll frequencies, the day of the tax deposit will likely vary.

EXAMPLE: NEXT BUSINESS DAY DEPOSITOR

Cornell Companies, based in Ohio, is a semiweekly schedule payroll tax depositor because of the total payroll tax liability of $693,259 during the lookback period ending June 30, 2018. The company had a total payroll tax liability of **$110,290** during the August 23, 2019, payroll period. August 23 is a Friday, so the payroll deposit would be due on ***Monday, August 26*** because it exceeds $100,000.

In this example, Cornell Companies is already a semiweekly schedule depositor because of its payroll tax liability during the lookback period. Because the company's tax liability exceeds $100,000 for the payroll period, Cornell Companies must deposit those payroll taxes by the next business day.

EXAMPLE: ANNUAL SCHEDULE DEPOSITOR

Wallflower Guitars is based in Ocean Springs, Mississippi. During the lookback period ending June 30, 2018, the company had a total payroll tax liability of $2,154. The payroll tax deposit schedule for Wallflower Guitars would be annual because of the small amount of total tax liability. As long as the total payroll tax liability remains less than $2,500 during 2019, the company may deposit its payroll taxes with its annual payroll tax return.

In this example, Wallflower Guitars has a very small payroll tax liability. It should be noted that ***annual schedule depositors*** are assumed to have very small tax liability. If the company's payroll tax liability grows during the calendar year, the schedule depositors should be mindful of the monthly schedule deposit rules. However, the company will not become a monthly schedule depositor until notified in writing by the IRS.

Reporting Periods

Stop & Check

1. Perry Plastics had $46,986 in payroll taxes during the lookback period. How often must the company deposit its payroll taxes?
2. For Perry Plastics, when is the deposit for June payroll taxes due?
3. Charlie's Kitchens has a payroll tax liability of $126,463 on its Friday payroll. When is the payroll tax deposit due?

LO 6-3 Prepare Mid-Year and Year-End Employer Tax Reporting and Deposits

anekoho/Shutterstock

Companies and payroll accountants are responsible for timely filing of the various tax documents required by governmental authorities. Note that the dates for depositing and reporting taxes are not always the same. For example, an employer may be required to file payroll tax deposits through the EFTPS on a daily, semiweekly, or monthly basis, depending upon their payroll tax liability during the lookback period. However, that same employer would not be required to file tax forms until after the end of the quarter. Like personal tax reporting, business reporting of statutory tax obligations has specific forms that employers must use. The most common forms used to deposit federal income tax and FICA taxes are Forms 941 (quarterly) and 944 (annual). An additional form used by agricultural businesses is Form 943, which serves the same purpose as Form 941.

Form 941

Monthly payroll tax depositors file ***Form 941*** (see Figure 6-1), which is the employer's quarterly report of taxes deposited and taxes due. The form is used to reconcile the firm's deposits with the tax liability derived through mathematical computations on the form. It is common to encounter minor adjustments during the process of completing the form owing to rounding differences incurred during monthly tax deposits. Form 941 has specific instructions for its completion, as shown in Table 6-5.

Schedule B

Semiweekly depositors must file Schedule B (Figure 6-2) in addition to Form 941. This form allows firms to enter the details of payroll tax liabilities that occur multiple times during a month. On ***Schedule B***, the payroll tax liability is entered on the days of the month on which the payroll occurred. The total tax liability for each month is entered in the right column. The total tax liability for the quarter must equal line 10 of Form 941.

EXAMPLE: PAYROLL TAX LIABILITY

Nicholas Lindeman is the owner of a company that pays its employees on the 15th and the last day of the month. All employees are salaried, exempt workers. Pay dates that fall on the weekend are paid on the preceding Friday. According to the lookback period, the company is required to deposit payroll taxes on a semiweekly basis. Because Lindeman is a semiweekly schedule depositor, he must file Schedule B in addition to Form 941. For the first quarter of 2019, Lindeman's company had the following pay dates and payroll tax liabilities:

Pay Date	Payroll Tax Liability
January 15	$ 41,486.47
January 31	41,486.47
February 15	41,486.47
February 28	41,486.47
March 15	41,486.47
March 30	41,486.47
Total Tax Liability for the Quarter	$248,918.82

Note that the payroll tax liability is (a) listed on the payroll date and (b) includes the FICA taxes (employee and employer share) and the federal income tax withheld.

TABLE 6-5
Instructions for Completing Form 941

Part 1: Data for Chalmette Company

Susan Wagner is the President of Chalmette Company, EIN 67-3983240, located at 572 Rue Bon Temps, New Orleans, Louisiana, 70116. The company phone number is 504-555-2039. The following Form 941 is for the second quarter of the year.

Name	Gross Earning	Taxable Wages for Federal W/H	Taxable Wages for FICA	Taxable Wages for FUTA	Total Federal W/H	Total Social Security Tax	Total Medicare W/H	FUTA Tax	SUTA Tax	Net Pay
YTD Totals	$128,356.74	$128,356.74	$94,569.00	$84,000.00	$18,432.50	$11,726.56	$2,742.50	$504.00	$5,106.73	
Line on Form 941		2	5a & 5c		3	5a	5c			

Line 1: The number of employees during the quarter reported, as indicated in the box in the upper right-hand corner.
Line 2: Total wages subject to federal income tax (less pre-tax deductions) for the quarter.
Line 3: Federal income tax withheld from wages paid during the quarter.
Line 4: Check box only if no wages paid during the quarter were subject to taxes. (This is uncommon.)
Lines 5a–5d: Column 1 is for the wages and tips subject to Social Security and Medicare taxes; column 2 is the amount of wages multiplied by the tax percent specified on the form.
Line 5e: Total of column 2, lines 5a–5d.
Line 5f: Tax on unreported tips.
Line 6: Total taxes due before adjustments.
Lines 7–9: Quarterly tax adjustments.
Line 10: Total tax less adjustments: line 6 minus lines 7, 8, and 9.
Line 11: Qualified business tax credit for research activities
Line 12: Total taxes due, after adjustments and credits
Line 13: Total taxes deposited during the quarter.
Line 14: Balance due.
Line 15: Overpayment.

Part 2:
Check the first box if the tax liability for the quarter is less than $2,500.
OR
Check the second box if the tax liability is greater than $2,500 and enter the taxes deposited each month during the quarter.
The total deposits must equal the total liability in Part 1.
If the business is a semiweekly depositor, then Schedule B must be completed.

FIGURE 6-1
Form 941

Form **941 for 2019: Employer's QUARTERLY Federal Tax Return** 950117
(Rev. January 2019) Department of the Treasury — Internal Revenue Service OMB No. 1545-0029

Employer identification number (EIN) 6 7 – 3 9 8 3 2 4 0

Name *(not your trade name)* Susan Wagner

Trade name *(if any)* Chalmette Company

Address 572 Rue Bon Temps
Number Street Suite or room number

New Orleans | LA | 70116
City State ZIP code

Foreign country name | Foreign province/county | Foreign postal code

Report for this Quarter of 2019
(Check one.)

- ☐ **1:** January, February, March
- ☒ **2:** April, May, June
- ☐ **3:** July, August, September
- ☐ **4:** October, November, December

Go to *www.irs.gov/Form941* for instructions and the latest information.

Read the separate instructions before you complete Form 941. Type or print within the boxes.

Part 1: Answer these questions for this quarter.

Line	Description		Column 1		Column 2	Line	Amount
1	**Number of employees who received wages, tips, or other compensation for the pay period including:** *Mar. 12* (Quarter 1), *June 12* (Quarter 2), *Sept. 12* (Quarter 3), or *Dec. 12* (Quarter 4)					1	12
2	**Wages, tips, and other compensation**					2	128356. 74
3	**Federal income tax withheld from wages, tips, and other compensation**					3	18432. 50
4	**If no wages, tips, and other compensation are subject to social security or Medicare tax**						☐ **Check and go to line 6.**
5a	**Taxable social security wages**		94569. 00	× 0.124 =	11726. 56		
5b	**Taxable social security tips**		.	× 0.124 =	.		
5c	**Taxable Medicare wages & tips**		94569. 00	× 0.029 =	2742. 50		
5d	**Taxable wages & tips subject to Additional Medicare Tax withholding**		.	× 0.009 =	.		
5e	**Add Column 2 from lines 5a, 5b, 5c, and 5d**					5e	14469. 06
5f	**Section 3121(q) Notice and Demand—Tax due on unreported tips** (see instructions)					5f	.
6	**Total taxes before adjustments.** Add lines 3, 5e, and 5f					6	32901. 56
7	**Current quarter's adjustment for fractions of cents**					7	. 01
8	**Current quarter's adjustment for sick pay**					8	.
9	**Current quarter's adjustments for tips and group-term life insurance**					9	.
10	**Total taxes after adjustments.** Combine lines 6 through 9					10	32901. 57
11	**Qualified small business payroll tax credit for increasing research activities.** Attach Form 8974					11	.
12	**Total taxes after adjustments and credits.** Subtract line 11 from line 10					12	32901. 57
13	**Total deposits for this quarter, including overpayment applied from a prior quarter and overpayments applied from Form 941-X, 941-X (PR), 944-X, or 944-X (SP) filed in the current quarter**					13	32901. 57
14	**Balance due.** If line 12 is more than line 13, enter the difference and see instructions					14	.

15 **Overpayment.** If line 13 is more than line 12, enter the difference [.] Check one: ☐ Apply to next return. ☐ Send a refund.

▶ **You MUST complete both pages of Form 941 and SIGN it.** Next ▶

For Privacy Act and Paperwork Reduction Act Notice, see the back of the Payment Voucher. Cat. No. 17001Z Form **941** (Rev. 1-2019)

950217

Name *(not your trade name)*	**Employer identification number (EIN)**
Susan Wagner	67-3983240

Part 2: Tell us about your deposit schedule and tax liability for this quarter.

If you are unsure about whether you are a monthly schedule depositor or a semiweekly schedule depositor, see section 11 of Pub. 15.

16 Check one: ☐ **Line 12 on this return is less than $2,500 or line 12 on the return for the prior quarter was less than $2,500, and you didn't incur a $100,000 next-day deposit obligation during the current quarter.** If line 12 for the prior quarter was less than $2,500 but line 12 on this return is $100,000 or more, you must provide a record of your federal tax liability. If you are a monthly schedule depositor, complete the deposit schedule below; if you are a semiweekly schedule depositor, attach Schedule B (Form 941). Go to Part 3.

☒ **You were a monthly schedule depositor for the entire quarter.** Enter your tax liability for each month and total liability for the quarter, then go to Part 3.

Tax liability:	**Month 1**	10967. 19
	Month 2	10967. 19
	Month 3	10967. 19
Total liability for quarter		32901. 57 **Total must equal line 12.**

☐ **You were a semiweekly schedule depositor for any part of this quarter.** Complete Schedule B (Form 941), Report of Tax Liability for Semiweekly Schedule Depositors, and attach it to Form 941.

Part 3: Tell us about your business. If a question does NOT apply to your business, leave it blank.

17 If your business has closed or you stopped paying wages . . . . ☐ Check here, and

enter the final date you paid wages / / .

18 If you are a seasonal employer and you don't have to file a return for every quarter of the year . . ☐ Check here.

Part 4: May we speak with your third-party designee?

Do you want to allow an employee, a paid tax preparer, or another person to discuss this return with the IRS? See the instructions for details.

☐ Yes. Designee's name and phone number

Select a 5-digit Personal Identification Number (PIN) to use when talking to the IRS.

☒ No.

Part 5: Sign here. You MUST complete both pages of Form 941 and SIGN it.

Under penalties of perjury, I declare that I have examined this return, including accompanying schedules and statements, and to the best of my knowledge and belief, it is true, correct, and complete. Declaration of preparer (other than taxpayer) is based on all information of which preparer has any knowledge.

Sign your name here Susan Wagner

Print your name here: Susan Wagner

Print your title here: President

Date 7/12/2019

Best daytime phone 504-555-2039

Paid Preparer Use Only

Check if you are self-employed . . . ☐

Preparer's name		PTIN	
Preparer's signature		Date	/ /
Firm's name (or yours if self-employed)		EIN	
Address		Phone	
City	State	ZIP code	

Source: Internal Revenue Service

FIGURE 6-2

Schedule B for Form 941

Schedule B (Form 941):

960311

Report of Tax Liability for Semiweekly Schedule Depositors

OMB No. 1545-0029

(Rev. January 2017) Department of the Treasury — Internal Revenue Service

Employer identification number (EIN) 1 3 – 2 5 6 9 9 0 4

Name *(not your trade name)* Nicholas Lindeman

Calendar year 2 0 1 9 (Also check quarter)

Report for this Quarter... (Check one.)

- [X] **1:** January, February, March
- [ ] **2:** April, May, June
- [ ] **3:** July, August, September
- [ ] **4:** October, November, December

Use this schedule to show your TAX LIABILITY for the quarter; don't use it to show your deposits. When you file this form with Form 941 or Form 941-SS, don't change your tax liability by adjustments reported on any Forms 941-X or 944-X. You must fill out this form and attach it to Form 941 or Form 941-SS if you're a semiweekly schedule depositor or became one because your accumulated tax liability on any day was $100,000 or more. Write your daily tax liability on the numbered space that corresponds to the date wages were paid. See Section 11 in Pub. 15 for details.

Month 1

Day	Amount	Day	Amount	Day	Amount	Day	Amount
1	.	9	.	17	.	25	.
2	.	10	.	18	.	26	.
3	.	11	.	19	.	27	.
4	.	12	.	20	.	28	.
5	.	13	.	21	.	29	.
6	.	14	.	22	.	30	.
7	.	15	41486.47	23	.	31	41486.47
8	.	16	.	24	.		

Tax liability for Month 1 82972.94

Month 2

Day	Amount	Day	Amount	Day	Amount	Day	Amount
1	.	9	.	17	.	25	.
2	.	10	.	18	.	26	.
3	.	11	.	19	.	27	.
4	.	12	.	20	.	28	41486.47
5	.	13	.	21	.	29	.
6	.	14	.	22	.	30	.
7	.	15	41486.47	23	.	31	.
8	.	16	.	24	.		

Tax liability for Month 2 82972.94

Month 3

Day	Amount	Day	Amount	Day	Amount	Day	Amount
1	.	9	.	17	.	25	.
2	.	10	.	18	.	26	.
3	.	11	.	19	.	27	.
4	.	12	.	20	.	28	.
5	.	13	.	21	.	29	41486.47
6	.	14	.	22	.	30	.
7	.	15	41486.47	23	.	31	.
8	.	16	.	24	.		

Tax liability for Month 3 82972.94

Fill in your total liability for the quarter (Month 1 + Month 2 + Month 3) ▶

Total must equal line 12 on Form 941 or Form 941-SS.

Total liability for the quarter 248918.82

For Paperwork Reduction Act Notice, see separate instructions. IRS.gov/form941 Cat. No. 11967Q **Schedule B (Form 941) (Rev. 1-2017)**

Source: Internal Revenue Service

State Tax Remittance

Each state that charges income tax has its own form that it uses for employee income ***tax remittance*** purposes. State tax forms are similar to federal forms as far as the information included is concerned and generally have similar due dates. An important note is that each state has its own unique taxes. For example, California has an employee-only State Disability Insurance (SDI) tax of 1.0 percent on earnings up to $118,371 per employee (2019 figure), as well as an employer-only Employment Training Tax (ETT) of 0.1 percent on the first $7,000 of each employee's earnings. These additional taxes are included on the state's payroll tax return. Figure 6-3 Contains an example of a completed California quarterly tax return.

Additionally, employers are responsible for reporting any other local or regional taxes. Employers must abide by the filing requirements for each of the taxes or face fines or penalties depending upon state/local tax code. The purpose of these taxes can include the provision of social services and the funding of infrastructure costs. The Denver Head Tax was designed to fulfill both of these purposes in response to the increase of infrastructure and the availability of municipal programs for residents. An example of the Denver Occupational Privilege Tax Return quarterly form is located in Figure 6-4.

Form 944

Firms with a total annual tax liability of less than $2,500 use ***Form 944*** (see Figure 6-5). Like Form 941, the firm enters the details of wages paid and computes the taxes due. The firm reports the monthly deposits and liabilities in Part 2. However, instead of entering a quarterly liability, the firm enters the annual liability, which is the sum of all the monthly liabilities. The IRS must notify a company in writing of the requirement to file Form 944 prior to its use.

EXAMPLE: FORM 944

Sophie Jennings owns Forest Dog Walkers. Forest Dog Walkers is a sole proprietorship with one part-time employee who works only five months of the year. The IRS has notified Ms. Jennings that Forest Dog Walkers is required to report federal payroll tax liabilities using Form 944. The total wages paid to the employee during 2018 were $8,952.20. The federal income tax liability was $800, and total payroll tax liability for the year was $2,169.98. Because the total annual payroll tax liability is less than $2,500, Forest Dog Walkers must file an annual return. The due date for Form 944 is January 31 of the following year.

Unemployment Tax Reporting

Form 940 is the employer's annual report of federal unemployment taxes due, based on employee wages paid during the year. This report is for a calendar year and is due by January 31 of the following year.

According to 26 IRC Section 3306, certain fringe benefits are not subject to federal unemployment taxes because they represent non-cash compensation that is not intended to be used as disposable income. Specific examples of these fringe benefits are employer contributions to employee retirement plans, such as the 401(k) and 403(b), and payments for benefits excluded under qualified Section 125 cafeteria plans.

EXAMPLE: EMPLOYER CONTRIBUTIONS TO RETIREMENT PLANS

Winterguard Products offers its employees a matching 401(k) contribution of 0.5 percent for each 1 percent of salary that the employee contributes. During 2019, Susanna Stark, an employee of Winterguard Products, contributed 4 percent of her $36,500 annual salary to her 401(k) plan.

Susanna's contribution	$36,500 × 0.04 =	$1,460.00
Winterguard's contribution match	Half of employee's contribution =	730.00
Amount exempt from FUTA tax		$ 730.00

The $730 would be listed on line 4 of Form 940 as an amount exempt from FUTA taxes.

FIGURE 6-3

Example of Completed California Quarterly Contribution Return and Report of Wages

EDD Employment Development Department State of California

QUARTERLY CONTRIBUTION RETURN AND REPORT OF WAGES

REMINDER: File your DE 9 and DE 9C together.

PLEASE TYPE THIS FORM—DO NOT ALTER PREPRINTED INFORMATION

00090112

QUARTER ENDED 09/30/2019 DUE 10/15/2019 DELINQUENT IF NOT POSTMARKED OR RECEIVED BY 10/15/2019

YR 19 QTR 3

EMPLOYER ACCOUNT NO. 392-1002-3

Four Mountains Inn
19283 Aracita Blvd
Jackson, CA 94453

DEPT. USE ONLY — DO NOT ALTER THIS AREA

P1 P2 C P U S A T

EFFECTIVE DATE Mo. Day Yr.

FEIN 58-3020493

ADDITIONAL FEINS

A. NO WAGES PAID THIS QUARTER ☐ B. OUT OF BUSINESS/NO EMPLOYEES ☐

B1. OUT OF BUSINESS DATE M M D D Y Y Y Y

C. TOTAL SUBJECT WAGES PAID THIS QUARTER 48,394.78

D. UNEMPLOYMENT INSURANCE (UI) (Total Employee Wages up to $ per employee per calendar year)

(D1) UI Rate % 3.8 TIMES (D2) UI TAXABLE WAGES FOR THE QUARTER 19,840.62 = (D3) UI CONTRIBUTIONS 753.94

E. EMPLOYMENT TRAINING TAX (ETT)

(E1) ETT Rate % 0.1 TIMES UI Taxable Wages for the Quarter (D2) ...... = (E2) ETT CONTRIBUTIONS 19.84

F. STATE DISABILITY INSURANCE (SDI) (Total Employee Wages up to $ per employee per calendar year)

(F1) SDI Rate % 1 TIMES (F2) SDI TAXABLE WAGES FOR THE QUARTER 19,840.62 = (F3) SDI EMPLOYEE CONTRIBUTIONS WITHHELD 198.41

G. CALIFORNIA PERSONAL INCOME TAX (PIT) WITHHELD 3,275.29

H. **SUBTOTAL** (Add Items D3, E2, F3, and G) 4,247.48

I. LESS: CONTRIBUTIONS AND WITHHOLDINGS PAID FOR THE QUARTER 0.00
(**DO NOT** INCLUDE PENALTY AND INTEREST PAYMENTS)

J. TOTAL TAXES DUE OR OVERPAID (Item H minus Item I) 4,247.48

If amount due, prepare a *Payroll Tax Deposit* (DE 88), include the correct payment quarter, and mail to: Employment Development Department, P.O. Box 826276, Sacramento, CA 94230-6276. **NOTE:** Do not mail payments along with the DE 9 and *Quarterly Contribution Return and Report of Wages (Continuation)* (DE 9C), as this may delay processing and result in erroneous penalty and interest charges. **Mandatory Electronic Funds Transfer (EFT)** filers must remit all SDI/PIT deposits by EFT to avoid a noncompliance penalty.

K. I declare that the above, to the best of my knowledge and belief, is true and correct. If a refund was claimed, a reasonable effort was made to refund any erroneous deductions to the affected employee(s).

Signature *Benjamin Blanco* Title Owner (Owner, Accountant, Preparer, etc.) Phone (530) 2931004 Date 10/11/2019

SIGN AND MAIL TO: State of California / Employment Development Department / P.O. Box 989071 / West Sacramento CA 95798-9071

DE 9 Rev. 1 (1-12) **(INTERNET)** Page 1 of 2

e-Services Fast, Easy, and Convenient! Visit EDD's Web site at **www.edd.ca.gov**

Sources: American Payroll Association, ADP

FIGURE 6-4

Example of a Denver Occupational Privilege Tax Return

Denver Occupational Privilege Tax Return
Quarterly

City and County of Denver
Department of Finance, Treasury Division
P.O. Box 660859
Dallas, TX 75266-0859
www.DenverGov.org/eBizTax

Business Name	Account Number	Phone Number
Mile High Gifts	203-1495010	303-555-8883

Primary Business Location	Period End Date
6637 16th Avenue, Denver, CO	3/31/2019

► YOU MUST FILE A RETURN EVEN IF YOU HAVE DETERMINED NO TAX IS DUE

► IMPORTANT INFORMATION IS ON THE BACK

If the number of employees for which the business is liable (Line 2) is different from the number of employees from whom the tax was withheld (Line 3) or if no tax is due, you must attach an explanation.

I. BUSINESS OCCUPATIONAL PRIVILEGE TAX

Line 1. Enter the number of self-employed individuals, owners, partners or managers. Multiply this number by $4.00 and enter the total.

NOTE: This line is for self-employed proprietors, partners, or managers of the business. There is no minimum level of monthly earnings required for self-employed proprietors, partners, or managers to be liable.

NOTE: All businesses located in Denver or performing work in Denver, regardless of the length or duration, are required to pay the minimum $4.00 Business Occupational Privilege Tax (OPT) for each month even when there are no taxable employees.

Line 2. Enter the number of employees for which the business is liable. Multiply this number by $4.00 and enter the total.

Liable employees are those who worked all or part of their time in Denver and received gross compensation of at least $500 for the month for services performed in Denver. Include all qualifying employees, even if some have another employer that is withholding this tax. The business is still liable for the business portion if the compensation was $500 or more. In the case of corporations for purposes of this tax, everyone, including all corporate officers, are considered employees.

II. EMPLOYEE OCCUPATIONAL PRIVILEGE TAX

Line 3. Enter the number of employees liable for this tax. Multiply this number by $5.75 and enter the total.

This line is for all employees who received gross compensation of at least $500 for the month for services performed in Denver. Corporations under the Business OPT ordinance are considered to only have employees, not owners. Therefore all corporate officers meeting the earnings requirement in Denver, should be included here. If any employee has another employer who is withholding this tax, Form TD-269 must be furnished to the secondary employer verifying the primary employer is withholding the tax.

Line 4a. If the return is filed or paid after the due date, enter 15% of Line 4, or $25.00, whichever is greater.

Line 4b. If the return is filed or paid after the due date enter 1% of Line 4 for each month or part of a month past due.

Line 5. Add Line 3, Line 4a, Line 4b. Enter the total. This is the total amount owed. Include a check or money order made payable to **Manager of Finance.**

RETURN LOWER PORTION - DETACH HERE

☐ CHECK HERE IF THIS IS AN AMENDED RETURN

DENVER OCCUPATIONAL PRIVILEGE TAX RETURN

ACCOUNT NUMBER	TaxType	Period End	Due Date	Media #
2031495010	Occupational Privilege Tax	3/31	4/15	000000000005

000000000005

NAME

PRIMARY BUSINESS LOCATION 6637 16th Avenue, Denver, CO 80244

I hereby certify, under penalty of perjury, that the statements made herein are to the best of my knowledge true and correct.

Signature (Required) Kira Gardner **Title** President **Date** 4/5/2019

BUSINESS OCCUPATIONAL PRIVILEGE TAX

1	Enter the number of liable self-employed individuals, owners, partners or managers for each month, add across and enter the total.						
	Month 1	Month 2	Month 3	Total			
	1	1	1	1	Multiply Total by $4.00	4	00
2	Enter the number of employees the business is liable for each month, add across and enter total.						
	Month 1	Month 2	Month 3	Total			
	5	5	5	5	Multiply Total by $4.00	20	00
	EMPLOYEE OCCUPATIONAL PRIVILEGE TAX						
3	Enter the number of liable employees for each month, add across and enter total.						
	Month 1	Month 2	Month 3	Total			
	-5	-5	-5	-5	Multiply Total by $5.75	28	75
4	**Total Tax: Add Lines 1, 2 and 3**					52	75
5	Late Filing - if return is filed after the due date - Add:	**a** Penalty: the greater of 15% of Line 4 or $25.00					
		b Interest: 1% of Line 4 for each month that the return is late					
6	TOTAL DUE AND PAYABLE: Add Line 4, 5a, 5b. This is the total due. Include a check or money order payable to **MANAGER OF FINANCE**					52	75

0000000000050000000000005

Sources: American Payroll Association, ADP

FIGURE 6-5
Form 944

Form **944 for 2018: Employer's ANNUAL Federal Tax Return**

Department of the Treasury — Internal Revenue Service

OMB No. 1545-2007

Employer identification number (EIN) 3 2 – 9 8 7 0 9 8 0

Name *(not your trade name)* Sophie Jennings

Trade name *(if any)* Forest Dog Walkers

Address 403 Lake Road
Number Street Suite or room number

Rouse Point | NY | 12809
City State ZIP code

Foreign country name Foreign province/county Foreign postal code

Who Must File Form 944

You must file annual Form 944 instead of filing quarterly Forms 941 **only if the IRS notified you in writing.**

Go to *www.irs.gov/Form944* for instructions and the latest information.

Read the separate instructions before you complete Form 944. Type or print within the boxes.

Part 1: Answer these questions for this year. Employers in American Samoa, Guam, the Commonwealth of the Northern Mariana Islands, the U.S. Virgin Islands, and Puerto Rico can skip lines 1 and 2, unless you have employees who are subject to U.S. income tax withholding.

1	**Wages, tips, and other compensation**	1	2380.78
2	**Federal income tax withheld from wages, tips, and other compensation**	2	274.00
3	**If no wages, tips, and other compensation are subject to social security or Medicare tax**	3	☐ **Check and go to line 5.**

4 **Taxable social security and Medicare wages and tips:**

	Column 1		Column 2
4a **Taxable social security wages**	2380.78	× 0.124 =	295.22
4b **Taxable social security tips**	.	× 0.124 =	.
4c **Taxable Medicare wages & tips**	2380.78	× 0.029 =	69.04
4d **Taxable wages & tips subject to Additional Medicare Tax withholding**	.	× 0.009 =	.

4e	**Add Column 2 from lines 4a, 4b, 4c, and 4d**	4e	364.26
5	**Total taxes before adjustments.** Add lines 2 and 4e	5	638.26
6	**Current year's adjustments** (see instructions)	6	.
7	**Total taxes after adjustments.** Combine lines 5 and 6	7	638.26
8	**Qualified small business payroll tax credit for increasing research activities.** Attach Form 8974	8	.
9	**Total taxes after adjustments and credits.** Subtract line 8 from line 7	9	638.26
10	**Total deposits for this year, including overpayment applied from a prior year and overpayments applied from Form 944-X, 944-X (SP), 941-X, or 941-X (PR)**	10	.
11	**Balance due.** If line 9 is more than line 10, enter the difference and see instructions	11	.

12 **Overpayment.** If line 10 is more than line 9, enter the difference ______ . Check one: ☐ Apply to next return. ☐ Send a refund.

▶ **You MUST complete both pages of Form 944 and SIGN it.**

Next ▶

For Privacy Act and Paperwork Reduction Act Notice, see the back of the Payment Voucher. Cat. No. 39316N Form **944** (2018)

Note that a company that files Form 944 has the opportunity to remit payroll taxes using Form 944-V, payment voucher.

Name *(not your trade name)*	Employer identification number (EIN)
Sophie Jennings	32-9870980

Part 2: Tell us about your deposit schedule and tax liability for this year.

13 **Check one:** [X] **Line 9 is less than $2,500. Go to Part 3.**

[ ] **Line 9 is $2,500 or more. Enter your tax liability for each month. If you're a semiweekly depositor or you became one because you accumulated $100,000 or more of liability on any day during a deposit period, you must complete Form 945-A instead of the boxes below.**

	Jan.		Apr.		July		Oct.
13a	.	13d	.	13g	.	13j	.
	Feb.		May		Aug.		Nov.
13b	.	13e	.	13h	.	13k	.
	Mar.		June		Sept.		Dec.
13c	.	13f	.	13i	.	13l	.

Total liability for year. Add lines 13a through 13l. Total must equal line 9. **13m** .

Part 3: Tell us about your business. If question 14 does NOT apply to your business, leave it blank.

14 **If your business has closed or you stopped paying wages...**

[ ] Check here and enter the final date you paid wages.

Part 4: May we speak with your third-party designee?

Do you want to allow an employee, a paid tax preparer, or another person to discuss this return with the IRS? See the instructions for details.

[ ] Yes. Designee's name and phone number

Select a 5-digit Personal Identification Number (PIN) to use when talking to the IRS.

[X] No.

Part 5: Sign here. You MUST complete both pages of Form 944 and SIGN it.

Under penalties of perjury, I declare that I have examined this return, including accompanying schedules and statements, and to the best of my knowledge and belief, it is true, correct, and complete. Declaration of preparer (other than taxpayer) is based on all information of which preparer has any knowledge.

Sign your name here *Sophie Jennings*

Date *1/28/2019*

Print your name here **Sophie Jennings**

Print your title here **Owner**

Best daytime phone **518-555-4395**

Paid Preparer Use Only

Check if you're self-employed [ ]

Preparer's name		PTIN	
Preparer's signature		Date	
Firm's name (or yours if self-employed)		EIN	
Address		Phone	
City	State	ZIP code	

Page **2** Form **944** (2018)

Detach Here and Mail With Your Payment and Form 944.

Form **944-V** — **Payment Voucher** — OMB No. 1545-2007 — **2018**

Department of the Treasury Internal Revenue Service

▶ **Don't staple this voucher or your payment to Form 944.**

1 Enter your employer identification number (EIN). **32-9870980**

2 **Enter the amount of your payment.** ▶ Make your check or money order payable to **"United States Treasury"**

Dollars	Cents
638	26

3 Enter your business name (individual name if sole proprietor).
Forest Dog Walkers

Enter your address.
403 Lake Road

Enter your city, state, and ZIP code; or your city, foreign country name, foreign province/county, and foreign postal code.
Rouse Point, NY 12809

Source: Internal Revenue Service

Fringe benefits that may be exempt from FUTA taxes are those excluded from cafeteria plans, such as the ones in the following example:

EXAMPLE: EXCLUDED FRINGE BENEFITS NOT SUBJECT TO FUTA TAXES

Hutcheson Medical Products offers its employees the following fringe benefits:

Benefit	Annual Value	Amount Paid During the Calendar Year
Adoption assistance	$5,000 per employee	$15,000.00
Achievement awards	$250 per employee	10,000.00
Meals	$300 per employee	15,000.00
Total annual value of excluded fringe benefits		$40,000.00

Hutcheson Medical Products would list $40,000 on Form 940 line 4, "Payments exempt from FUTA tax."

Other fringe benefits specifically exempt from FUTA tax and reported on line 4 include

- Dependent care (up to $2,500 per employee or $5,000 per married couple).
- Employer contributions to group term life insurance.
- Certain other noncash payments, as outlined in the Instructions for Form 940.

For tax reporting purposes, amounts contributed by employees to these exempt items must be treated in one of two ways on Form 940:

- Deducted from Line 3 "Total payments to all employees."
- Reported on Line 4 "Payments exempt from FUTA taxes."

EXAMPLE: ANNUAL FUTA TAX LIABILITY LESS THAN $500

Kimbro Painting has an annual FUTA liability of $392 during 2018. During the first three quarters of 2018, they would leave Part 5 blank because the tax liability is less than $500 and the liability would rollover to the next quarter. They would complete Part 5 to report the year-end FUTA deposit.

According to the IRS Tax Topic 759, they should deposit since it is year end. "If your total FUTA tax liability for the year is $500 or less, you can either deposit the amount or pay the tax with your Form 940 by January 31." Because they have a total liability of $392 for the year, they should have an amount in Section 5 and make the payment with the year-end filing.

An example of Form 940 for L&L Hay and Grain is found in Figure 6-6.

EXAMPLE: FORM 940

Paige Laparchay owns L&L Hay and Grain, EIN 39-7482936. She filed the Annual FUTA Tax Return (Form 940) to report unemployment tax contributions during 2018. L&L Hay and Grain has 12 employees, all of whom earned over the FUTA wage base. Lines 9 through 11 are adjustments to the FUTA deposited, which are rare and do not apply in this scenario. (See pages 8–10 of Publication 15 for more details.)

Name	Gross Earnings (Including fringe benefits and retirement)	Fringe Benefits	Retirement/ Pension	Payments Exempt from FUTA	Payments in Excess of $7,000 per Employee	Taxable Wages for FUTA	FUTA Tax
YTD Totals	$364,039.32	$24,868.00	$38,496.00	$63,364.00	$216,675.32	$84,000.00	$504.00
Line on Form 940	3			4	5	7	8

Line 1a: If the company pays unemployment tax in only one state, then the state abbreviation is entered here; otherwise, the company must check the box on line 1b and complete schedule A. L&L Hay and Grain has only one location, in Oklahoma.

Line 3: All wages paid during the calendar year are entered here ($364,039.32).

Line 4: Payments exempt from FUTA Tax. L&L has fringe benefits ($24,868.00) and retirement plan contributions ($38,496.00) that are exempt from FUTA.

Line 5: Wages for the year that are in excess of $7,000 per employee are entered here. The FUTA wage base is $7,000 per employee. In this example, all employees worked for the entire calendar year, so L&L is responsible for FUTA tax on $7,000 per employee. To compute Line 5:

Total wages	$364,039.32
Less: payments exempt from FUTA	(63,364.00)
Less: FUTA wage base ($7,000 × 12 employees)	(84,000.00)
Wages in excess of $7,000	$216,675.32

Line 6: This is the sum of lines 4 and 5.

Line 7: FUTA Taxable wages, which are $84,000 for L&L Hay and Grain.

Line 8: FUTA Tax ($84,000 × .006) or $504.

Line 12: Total FUTA Tax of $504.

Line 13: Total FUTA Tax deposited during the year. This total must match Line 17 (side 2). Because all of L&L Hay and Grain's employees exceeded their wage base by the end of the second quarter of 2018, all FUTA tax for the year has been deposited prior to completion of the tax return.

Lines 16a and 16b: Tax liability during each quarter. These boxes report the employer's FUTA tax liability based on wages paid or accrued during the quarter. In this case, L&L Hay and Grain had a FUTA liability of $350 for the first quarter of 2018 and $104 for the second quarter of 2018. The sum of these liabilities (and any other quarterly liability, which does not exist in this example) is recorded on Line 17. The total on Line 17 must match the total on Line 13 (side 1).

Matching Final Annual Pay to Form W-2

One of the more common questions payroll accountants receive following the release of W-2s from the employees at the end of the year is, "why doesn't this match my final paycheck?" In short, it should—if you know how to calculate the income that belongs in each block of the W-2. The W-2 reflects all gross wages received by the employee, less any pre-tax deductions: health insurance, qualified retirement contributions, and other deductions adding any taxable

FIGURE 6-6
Form 940

Form **940 for 2018: Employer's Annual Federal Unemployment (FUTA) Tax Return** 850113
Department of the Treasury — Internal Revenue Service OMB No. 1545-0028

Employer identification number (EIN) 3 9 – 7 4 8 2 9 3 6

Name *(not your trade name)* Paige Laparchay

Trade name *(if any)* L&L Hay and Grain

Address 1534 Route 19 West
Number Street Suite or room number

Burlington OK 73722
City State ZIP code

Foreign country name Foreign province/county Foreign postal code

Type of Return
(Check all that apply.)

- ☐ **a.** Amended
- ☐ **b.** Successor employer
- ☐ **c.** No payments to employees in 2018
- ☐ **d.** Final: Business closed or stopped paying wages

Go to *www.irs.gov/Form940* for instructions and the latest information.

Read the separate instructions before you complete this form. Please type or print within the boxes.

Part 1: Tell us about your return. If any line does NOT apply, leave it blank. See instructions before completing Part 1.

1a	**If you had to pay state unemployment tax in one state only, enter the state abbreviation** .	1a	O K
1b	**If you had to pay state unemployment tax in more than one state, you are a multi-state employer** . . .	1b	☐ Check here. Complete Schedule A (Form 940).
2	**If you paid wages in a state that is subject to CREDIT REDUCTION** . . .	2	☐ Check here. Complete Schedule A (Form 940).

Part 2: Determine your FUTA tax before adjustments. If any line does NOT apply, leave it blank.

3	**Total payments to all employees** . . .			3	364069. 32
4	**Payments exempt from FUTA tax** . . .	4	63364. 00		
	Check all that apply: 4a ☒ Fringe benefits; 4b ☐ Group-term life insurance; 4c ☒ Retirement/Pension; 4d ☐ Dependent care; 4e ☐ Other				
5	**Total of payments made to each employee in excess of $7,000** . . .	5	216675. 32		
6	**Subtotal** (line 4 + line 5 = line 6) . . .			6	280039. 32
7	**Total taxable FUTA wages** (line 3 – line 6 = line 7). See instructions. . . .			7	84000. 00
8	**FUTA tax before adjustments** (line 7 x 0.006 = line 8) . . .			8	504. 00

Part 3: Determine your adjustments. If any line does NOT apply, leave it blank.

9	**If ALL of the taxable FUTA wages you paid were excluded from state unemployment tax, multiply line 7 by 0.054** (line 7 × 0.054 = line 9). Go to line 12 . . .	9	.
10	**If SOME of the taxable FUTA wages you paid were excluded from state unemployment tax, OR you paid ANY state unemployment tax late** (after the due date for filing Form 940), complete the worksheet in the instructions. Enter the amount from line 7 of the worksheet . .	10	.
11	**If credit reduction applies,** enter the total from Schedule A (Form 940) . . .	11	.

Part 4: Determine your FUTA tax and balance due or overpayment. If any line does NOT apply, leave it blank.

12	**Total FUTA tax after adjustments** (lines 8 + 9 + 10 + 11 = line 12) . . .	12	504. 00
13	**FUTA tax deposited for the year, including any overpayment applied from a prior year** .	13	504. 00
14	**Balance due.** If line 14 is more than line 13, enter the excess on line 14. • If line 14 is more than $500, you must deposit your tax. • If line 14 is $500 or less, you may pay with this return. See instructions . . .	14	.
15	**Overpayment.** If line 13 is more than line 12, enter the excess on line 15 and check a box below	15	.

► You **MUST** complete both pages of this form and **SIGN** it. Check one: ☐ Apply to next return. ☐ Send a refund.

Next ►

For Privacy Act and Paperwork Reduction Act Notice, see the back of the Payment Voucher. Cat. No. 11234O Form **940** (2018)

850212

Name *(not your trade name)*	**Employer identification number (EIN)**
Paige Laparchay	39-7482936

Part 5: Report your FUTA tax liability by quarter only if line 12 is more than $500. If not, go to Part 6.

16 Report the amount of your FUTA tax liability for each quarter; do NOT enter the amount you deposited. If you had no liability for a quarter, leave the line blank.

16a 1st quarter (January 1 – March 31)	**16a**	350 . 00
16b 2nd quarter (April 1 – June 30)	**16b**	154 . 00
16c 3rd quarter (July 1 – September 30)	**16c**	.
16d 4th quarter (October 1 – December 31)	**16d**	.
17 Total tax liability for the year (lines 16a + 16b + 16c + 16d = line 17)	**17**	504 . 00 **Total must equal line 12.**

Part 6: May we speak with your third-party designee?

Do you want to allow an employee, a paid tax preparer, or another person to discuss this return with the IRS? See the instructions for details.

☐ **Yes.** Designee's name and phone number

Select a 5-digit Personal Identification Number (PIN) to use when talking to IRS

☒ **No.**

Part 7: Sign here. You MUST complete both pages of this form and SIGN it.

Under penalties of perjury, I declare that I have examined this return, including accompanying schedules and statements, and to the best of my knowledge and belief, it is true, correct, and complete, and that no part of any payment made to a state unemployment fund claimed as a credit was, or is to be, deducted from the payments made to employees. Declaration of preparer (other than taxpayer) is based on all information of which preparer has any knowledge.

✗ Sign your name here *Paige Laparchay*

Print your name here: Paige Laparchay

Print your title here: President

Date: 1/28/2019

Best daytime phone: 580-555-4932

Paid Preparer Use Only

Check if you are self-employed ☐

Preparer's name		PTIN	
Preparer's signature		Date	/ /
Firm's name (or yours if self-employed)		EIN	
Address		Phone	
City	State	ZIP code	

Source: Internal Revenue Service

fringe benefits. The total federal income taxes that the employer withheld from the employee and remitted as part of the 941 tax deposits also appears on the W-2 and acts as supporting documentation for the total wages reported on Forms 941 and 940.

As a result of the Affordable Care Act, the employer must report their contributions to employee health coverage on Form W-2. Amounts contributed by the employer should appear in Box 12 using code DD to designate that it is the employer's share of the health care premium.

REPORTING OF EMPLOYER-SPONSORED HEALTH CARE COVERAGE

	Form W-2, Box 12, Code DD		
Type of Coverage	**Must Report**	**Optional**	**Do Not Report**
Major medical insurance	X		
Dental insurance, either as part of major medical or a separate, voluntary election		X	
Health FSA funded only by salary reduction (reported in Box 14)			X
Health FSA value in excess of employee salary deduction for qualified benefits	X		
Health saving arrangement contribution (employer or employee funded)			X
Hospital indemnity or specified illness funded by employee pre-tax deduction or by employer	X		
Multi-employer plans		X	
Domestic partner coverage included in gross income	X		
Governmental plan provided for members of the military and their families			X
Federally recognized Indian tribal government plans			X
Accident or disability income			X
Long-term care			X
Workers' compensation			X
Excess reimbursement to highly compensated individual			X
Payment or reimbursement of premium to 2% shareholder-employee, included in gross income			X
Employers required to file fewer than 250 W-2 forms in preceding calendar year		X	
Form W-2 furnished to terminated employee prior to end of calendar year		X	
Form W-2 provided by third-party sick-pay provider to employees of other employers		X	

Source: Internal Revenue Service

Similarly, Form W-2 contains the employee's Social Security and Medicare wages. These wages are not reduced by contributions by the employee to qualified pension accounts (401(k), 403(b), etc.), and therefore may be higher than box 1. The only difference between boxes 3 and 5 will come when employees earn more than the maximum Social Security wage in the given year, or $132,900 for 2019. When this occurs, the Medicare wages reported in box 5 will be greater than the Social Security wages displayed in box 3. Boxes 4 and 6 contain the Social Security and Medicare taxes withheld from the employee and remitted through 941 deposits.

Tipped employees will have amounts represented in boxes 7 and 8 for their reported tips. Box 10 is used to report Dependent Care Benefits. Contributions to nonqualifying retirement plans will be represented in box 11. Employee contributions to qualifying plans are represented in box 12. An alphabetical code is assigned to the specific type of qualified retirement plan the contributions are made to (A through EE). Box 13 denotes specific contributions to deferred compensation plans. Box 14 is used to report other information to employees, such as union dues, health insurance premiums (not pre-tax), educational assistance payments, and other similar items. State and local taxes and wages are represented in boxes 15 through 20.

The following is an explanation of each box and its contents for Form W-2.

Instructions for Completing Form W-2

Box	Explanation
a	Employee's Social Security number based on their Social Security card and/or Form W-4.
b	Employer Identification Number (EIN)
c	Employer address: This should match the address reported on other tax reports such as the Form 941 and Form 940.
d	Optional. This could be used for the company's employee number.
e–f	Employee's name and address as shown on the Social Security card and Form W-4.
1	Wages paid during the calendar year, including any additional amounts from • Bonuses • Cash value of prizes • Awards • Noncash value of fringe benefits • Educational assistance programs (over $5,250) • Group-term life insurance • Roth contributions made to certain retirement plans • Payments to statutory employees • HSA contributions • Nonqualified moving expenses and expense reimbursements • Any other compensation
2	Federal income tax withheld during the year.
3	Social Security wages: Wages paid subject to employees Social Security tax but not including Social Security and allocated tips. • Educational assistance programs (over $5,250)
4	Social Security tax withheld (employee share only)
5	Medicare wages and tips: This should be the same as the Social Security wages in box 3, unless employees reach the Social Security wage cap. • Educational assistance programs (over $5,250)
6	Medicare tax withheld (employee share only)
7	Social Security tips: Any tips reported to you by the employee go in this box.
8	Allocated tips: Use this box if the company allocates tips among employees.
9	Verification code: Used if the employer participates in the W-2 Verification Code pilot.
10	Dependent care benefits: Report all dependent care benefits paid during the calendar year under a dependent care benefit program.
11	Nonqualified plans: Used by the Social Security Administration.
12	Codes (see Figure 6-7)
13	Check boxes for the following circumstances • Statutory employee: Earnings are subject to Social Security and Medicare taxes but not federal income tax. • Retirement plan: If the employee was an active participant in a defined benefit or defined contribution plan. • Third-party sick pay: Used when reporting sick pay benefits.
14	Other: Used to report annual leave value of an employee's company car is the employer paid 100%.
15–20	Used for reporting state and local tax information. Deductions and inclusions would follow state laws.

Source: Internal Revenue Service

When completing a ***Form W-2***, you will have several copies of the same form. A sample Form W-2 is found in Figure 6-8. According to the order in which they print, the copies of Form W-2 are as follows:

Which Copy?	What Is It For?
Copy A	Social Security Administration
Copy 1	State, City, or Local Tax Department
Copy B	Filing with the Employee's Federal Tax Return
Copy C	Employee's Records
Copy 2	State, City, or Local Tax Department
Copy D	Employer

FIGURE 6-7
Box 12 Codes for Form W-2

Form W-2 Reference Guide for Box 12 Codes

A	Uncollected social security or RRTA tax on tips	L	Substantiated employee business expense reimbursements	Y	Deferrals under a section 409A nonqualified deferred compensation plan
B	Uncollected Medicare tax on tips (but not Additional Medicare Tax)	M	Uncollected social security or RRTA tax on taxable cost of group-term life insurance over $50,000 (former employees only)	Z	Income under a nonqualified deferred compensation plan that fails to satisfy section 409A
C	Taxable cost of group-term life insurance over $50,000	N	Uncollected Medicare tax on taxable cost of group-term life insurance over $50,000 (but not Additional Medicare Tax) (former employees only)	AA	Designated Roth contributions under a section 401(k) plan
D	Elective deferrals under a section 401(k) cash or deferred arrangement plan (including a SIMPLE 401(k) arrangement)	P	Excludable moving expense reimbursements paid directly to members of the Armed Forces	BB	Designated Roth contributions under a section 403(b) plan
E	Elective deferrals under a section 403(b) salary reduction agreement	Q	Nontaxable combat pay	DD	Cost of employer-sponsored health coverage
F	Elective deferrals under a section 408(k)(6) salary reduction SEP	R	Employer contributions to an Archer MSA	EE	Designated Roth contributions under a governmental section 457(b) plan
G	Elective deferrals and employer contributions (including nonelective deferrals) to a section 457(b) deferred compensation plan	S	Employee salary reduction contributions under a section 408(p) SIMPLE plan	FF	Permitted benefits under a qualified small employer health reimbursement arrangement
H	Elective deferrals to a section 501(c)(18)(D) tax-exempt organization plan	T	Adoption benefits	GG	Income from qualified equity grants under section 83(i)
J	Nontaxable sick pay	V	Income from exercise of nonstatutory stock option(s)	HH	Aggregate deferrals under section 83(i) elections as of the close of the calendar year
K	20% excise tax on excess golden parachute payments	W	Employer contributions (including employee contributions through a cafeteria plan) to an employee's health savings account (HSA)		

Source: Internal Revenue Service

Figure 6-8 is an example of a Form W-2 for Joseph A. Balestreri.

FIGURE 6-8
Form W-2

22222	a Employee's social security number	OMB No. 1545-0008	
b Employer identification number (EIN) 45-3392039		1 Wages, tips, other compensation 36,523.34	2 Federal income tax withheld 3,671.04
c Employer's name, address, and ZIP code Crystal GM & Buick 882 First Street Pawtucket, RI 02862		3 Social security wages 38,523.34	4 Social security tax withheld 2,388.45
		5 Medicare wages and tips 38,523.34	6 Medicare tax withheld 558.89
		7 Social security tips	8 Allocated tips
d Control number		9	10 Dependent care benefits
e Employee's first name and initial Last name Suff. Joseph A. Balestreri 3949 Winchester Street Pawtucket, RI 02862		11 Nonqualified plans	12a Code D 2,000.00
		13 Statutory employee ☐ Retirement plan ☒ Third-party sick pay ☐	12b Code
		14 Other	12c Code
f Employee's address and ZIP code			12d Code

15 State	Employer's state ID number	16 State wages, tips, etc.	17 State income tax	18 Local wages, tips, etc.	19 Local income tax	20 Locality name
RI	382948374	36,523.34	1,369.63			

Form **W-2** **Wage and Tax Statement** 2019 Department of the Treasury—Internal Revenue Service

Copy 1—For State, City, or Local Tax Department

Source: Internal Revenue Service

EXAMPLE: FORM W-2

Joseph A. Balestren worked for Crystal GM & Buick during 2019. The following is on his W-2 for 2019:

Box 1 contains the wages, tips, and other compensation. Joseph earned $36,523.34 during 2019.

Box 2 contains the federal income tax withheld: Joseph had $3,671.04 withheld based on his W-4 information.

Boxes 3 and 5 contain the Social Security and Medicare wages. Note that these two boxes contain a higher amount than box 1. Joseph has a retirement plan into which he contributed $2,000 during 2019.

Boxes 4 and 6 contain the Social Security tax withheld ($2,388.45) and the Medicare tax withheld ($558.59).

Box 12 contains amounts for nontaxable items. Codes for box 12 are contained in Figure 6-7.

Boxes 15–17 contain the state tax information. Joseph had $1,369.63 withheld for state taxes based on the state withholding certificate that he filed in January 2019.

Form W-3 is the transmittal form that accompanies the submission of Copy A to the Social Security Administration. It contains the aggregate data for all W-2s issued by an employer. Form W-3 and all accompanying W-2s must be mailed or electronically transmitted by January 31 of the following year (i.e., W-2s and W-3s for 2019 are due on January 31, 2020). The total annual wages reported on the W-3 must match the annual wages reported on Forms 941 and 940. The following is an explanation of the boxes on Form W-3.

Instructions for Completing Form W-3

Box	Explanation
a	Control number (optional)
b	Kind of payer: The employer indicates if one or more of the following applies: • Form 941 *and* no other category applies • Military • Form 943 (agricultural employers) • Form 944 *and* no other category applies • CT-1 (railroad employers) • Hshld. Emp. (Household employers) • Medicare govt. emp. (if the Forms W-2 are for employees subject only to Medicare tax) Kind of employer: The employer checks the box that applies to them: • None, if none of the situations apply • 501c non-govt (for tax-exempt non-governmental employers, such as private foundations, charities, social and recreational clubs, and veterans organizations) • State/local non-501c (for state/local governments or other entities with governmental authority) • State/local 501c (for state/local governments that have a tax-exempt designation) • Federal govt. (for federal government entities) Third-party sick pay: Employers who have indicated on the Form W-2 that they issue third-party sick pay must check this box
c	Total number of Forms W-2 submitted with the W-3
d	Establishment number: Used to identify separate establishments within the same business.
e	Employer Identification Number (EIN)
f–g	Employer name and address

(continued)

Instructions for Completing Form W-3

Box	Explanation
h	Any other EIN used during the year
	Employer contact information
1–8	Same as boxes 1–8 on Form W-2. The numbers in these boxes should reflect the total of each box for all forms submitted with Form W-3.
9	Leave blank
10	Dependent care benefits: Report all dependent care benefits paid during the calendar year under a dependent care benefit program as a total of all Forms W-2.
11	The total reported in box 11 of Forms W-2
12a	Deferred Compensation: Enter the total of all amounts reported with codes D-H, S, Y, AA, BB, and EE in Box 12 of Forms W-2. No code should be entered in Box 12a.
13	For third-party sick pay use only. Leave the box blank.
15	State/Employer's state ID number: Place the two-letter state abbreviation and the ID number. If the Forms W-2 are from more than one state, enter X in this box and omit the ID number.
16–19	Enter the state/local total wages and income tax withheld in the corresponding boxes.

The following example from Ferrigno Day Spa depicts the completion of Form W-3 for a company. (See Figure 6-9.)

EXAMPLE

Marlene Ferrigno is the owner of Ferrigno Day Spa, 2849 Water Street, Falls Church, Virginia, 22043, EIN 84-9943043, phone number 703-555-0904, fax number 703-555-0906. Her email address is mferrigno@ferrignodayspa.com.

Box b: Ferrigno Day Spa will file Form 941 to report quarterly tax liability, so box 941 is checked.

Box c: Ferrigno Day Spa had 25 employees who received W-2s.

Box 1: Wages and tips for 2019 were $654,087.35.

Box 2: The amount of federal income tax withheld for the 2019 wages was $117,735.

Box 3: Social Security wages were $546,333.35.

Box 4: Social Security tax withheld was $33,872.67.

Box 5: Medicare wages and tips were $570,838.25.

Box 6: Medicare tax withheld was $8,277.16.

Box 7: Social Security tips were $24,505.

Box 12a: Deferred compensation was $83,249.

Box 15: VA; Employer's State ID number: 66-2245538849A-238

Box 16: State wages, tips, etc. were $654,087.35

Box 17: State income tax withheld was $41,403.73

Note: Taxable tips reported in Box 7 should be reported on IRS form 4070.

(Source: Internal Revenue Service)

Employers may occasionally need to correct filed tax forms. In this case, the employer should use the X version of the form (i.e., Form 941-X, Form 940-X, etc.). Note that any additional tax amounts owed that are discovered during the correction process should be remitted as soon as the employer completes the correction form. During the correction process, if an employer has withheld too much federal income tax or FICA from one or more employees, the employee has the option to recover these overages using IRS Form 843.

FIGURE 6-9

Form W-3

33333	a Control number	For Official Use Only ▶ OMB No. 1545-0008	
b Kind of Payer (Check one): 941 [X], Military [ ], 943 [ ], 944 [ ], CT-1 [ ], Hshld. emp. [ ], Medicare govt. emp. [ ]		Kind of Employer (Check one): None apply [ ], 501c non-govt. [ ], State/local non-501c [ ], State/local 501c [ ], Federal govt. [ ]	Third-party sick pay (Check if applicable) [ ]
c Total number of Forms W-2 25	d Establishment number	1 Wages, tips, other compensation 654,087.35	2 Federal income tax withheld 117,735.00
e Employer identification number (EIN) 84-9943043		3 Social security wages 546,333.35	4 Social security tax withheld 33,872.67
f Employer's name Ferrigno Day Spa		5 Medicare wages and tips 570,838.25	6 Medicare tax withheld 8,277.16
2849 Water Street Falls Church, VA 22043		7 Social security tips 24,505.00	8 Allocated tips
		9	10 Dependent care benefits
g Employer's address and ZIP code		11 Nonqualified plans	12a Deferred compensation 83,249.00
h Other EIN used this year		13 For third-party sick pay use only	12b
15 State VA	Employer's state ID number 66-2245538849A-238	14 Income tax withheld by payer of third-party sick pay	
16 State wages, tips, etc. 654,087.35	17 State income tax 41,403.73	18 Local wages, tips, etc.	19 Local income tax
Employer's contact person Marlene Ferrigno		Employer's telephone number 703-555-0904	For Official Use Only
Employer's fax number 703-555-0906		Employer's email address mferrigno@ferrignodayspa.com	

Under penalties of perjury, I declare that I have examined this return and accompanying documents, and, to the best of my knowledge and belief, they are true, correct, and complete.

Signature ▶ Title ▶ Date ▶

Form **W-3 Transmittal of Wage and Tax Statements** 2019 Department of the Treasury Internal Revenue Service

Source: Internal Revenue Service

Tax Forms

Stop & Check

1. Jacobucci Enterprises is a monthly schedule depositor. According to the information it reported on Form 941, its quarterly tax liability is $8,462.96. During the quarter, it made deposits of $2,980.24 and $3,068.24. How much must it remit with its tax return?
2. Corrado's Corrals paid annual wages totaling $278,452.76 to 15 employees. Assuming that all employees were employed for the entire year, what is the amount of FUTA wages?
3. For Corrado's Corrals in the previous question, what is the FUTA tax liability?
4. Skyrockets Inc. had the following wage information reported in box 1 of its W-2s:

   Employee A: $25,650

   Employee B: $30,025

   Employee C: $28,550

   Employee D: $31,970

   What amount must it report as total wages on its Form W-3?

LO 6-4 Describe Payroll within the Context of Business Expenses

vetkit/Shutterstock

Understanding employer payroll expenses is important because of the wide range of mandatory activities and lesser-known expenses associated with maintaining employees. Compensation expenses and employer payroll-related liabilities must be accurately maintained in an accounting system. The scope of payroll-related employer responsibilities contributes to the need for knowledgeable payroll accountants.

According to the Bureau of Labor Statistics, employers' average hourly cost for employees was $36.63, of which wages were $25.03 and benefits totaled $11.60. For private-sector employers, the average hourly cost was $34.53; for governmental employers, the average hourly cost was $50.03. (Source: BLS)

The amounts withheld from employee pay and the employer liabilities must be deposited in a timely manner with the appropriate authorities. The omission of any of the required filings, activities, or any inaccuracy in the accounting system can lead to problems that could include governmental sanctions and penalties. No statute of limitations exists for unpaid taxes. If a company outsources its payroll processing, it is still liable for any late or unremitted payroll taxes.

The IRS will waive penalties under two conditions:

1. The amount of the shortfall does not exceed the greater of $100 or 2 percent of the required tax deposit.
2. The amount of the shortfall is deposited either (a) by the due date of the period return (monthly and semiweekly depositors) or (b) the first Wednesday or Friday that falls after the 15th of the month (semiweekly depositors only).

Penalties fall into two classifications: (1) failure to deposit and (2) failure to file. The following penalties apply when a ***failure to deposit*** occurs:

2%	Deposits made 1 to 5 days late.
5%	Deposits made 6 to 15 days late.
10%	Deposits made 16 or more days late. Also applies to amounts paid within 10 days of the date of the first notice the IRS sent asking for the tax due.
10%	Amounts (that should have been deposited) paid directly to the IRS, or paid with your tax return. See payment with return, earlier in this section, for an exception.
15%	Amounts still unpaid more than 10 days after the date of the first notice the IRS sent asking for the tax due or the day on which you received notice and demand for immediate payment, whichever is earlier.

Source: Internal Revenue Service

EXAMPLE: FAILURE TO DEPOSIT PENALTY

Mane Street Hairstylists is a monthly schedule payroll tax depositor. The company owed $4,552 in payroll tax liabilities during the month of July. The owner, Billy James, failed to deposit the July payroll taxes until August 27.

The failure to deposit penalty would be calculated as follows:

Tax Due	Number of Days Late	% Penalty	Total Penalty
$ 4,552.00	12	5%	$ 227.60

The ***failure to file*** penalty applies to amounts on Form 941 and is 5 percent of the unpaid tax due with the return. This penalty accrues for each month or partial month that the tax remains unpaid.

EXAMPLE: FAILURE TO FILE AND FAILURE TO DEPOSIT PENALTIES

Mary Warren, president of Great Meadows Farms, outsourced the payroll for the company in October 2019. She received a notice on February 15, 2020, that Form 941 for the fourth quarter of 2019 was not filed. After contacting the payroll service, she determined that $32,860 in payroll taxes due with Form 941 were never deposited. The penalties for this oversight would be as follows:

Failure to File Penalty

Tax Due	Number of Months Late	% Penalty per Month	Penalty
$32,860.00	2*	5%	$3,286.00

Failure to Deposit Penalty

Tax Due	Number of Days Late	% Penalty	Penalty
$32,860.00	30	10%	$ 3,286.00
		Total penalties due	$6,572.00

* The number of months is two because the failure to file penalty is based on both months and partial months. Because the notice was issued in February, the penalty would be for 2 months.

Notice how quickly the penalties can accrue for unfiled and undeposited taxes. The maximum penalty rate for the failure to file is 25% and the maximum for failure to deposit is 15%. Also keep in mind that the penalties may be subject to interest charges.

A quick summary of general employer payroll expenses and responsibilities follows:

Employee Compensation	Tax Withholding	Tax Matching
Tax remittance	Voluntary deductions from employee pay	Remittance of voluntary deductions
Tax reporting	Tax deposits	Accountability

Singkham/Shutterstock

Employees and Company Framework

Beyond the expenses and responsibilities of the payroll accounting system is the understanding of how the employees fit within the larger framework of the company. Payroll is one part of the cost of employing people. Before the employee ever becomes productive for a company, employers will incur recruiting, hiring, and training costs that vary based on the company's location and minimum job requirements. Other costs include any tools, uniforms, and specific equipment that employees need to perform their jobs. Expenses associated with hiring and retaining well-qualified employees may comprise a significant amount of a company's overhead.

According to a study conducted by Hundred5, the cost to hire and train new employees averages 15 to 25 percent of the employee's salary. For a manager earning $36,000 per year, the cost to hire and train could total approximately $9,000. (Source: Hundred5)

It is important to understand the responsibility that employers have for remitting the federal income tax and FICA tax amounts withheld from employees. According to IRS §6672, any responsible person within the company who *willfully* does not remit the withheld employee taxes—meaning that they did not remit the taxes due to something as innocuous as a lack of funds—is subject to a 100% penalty for those non-remitted funds. It is important to note that this penalty only applies to employee federal income tax and FICA taxes, not the employer's share of the FICA taxes or FUTA tax. The following diagram explains who is considered a responsible party for payroll tax deposits.

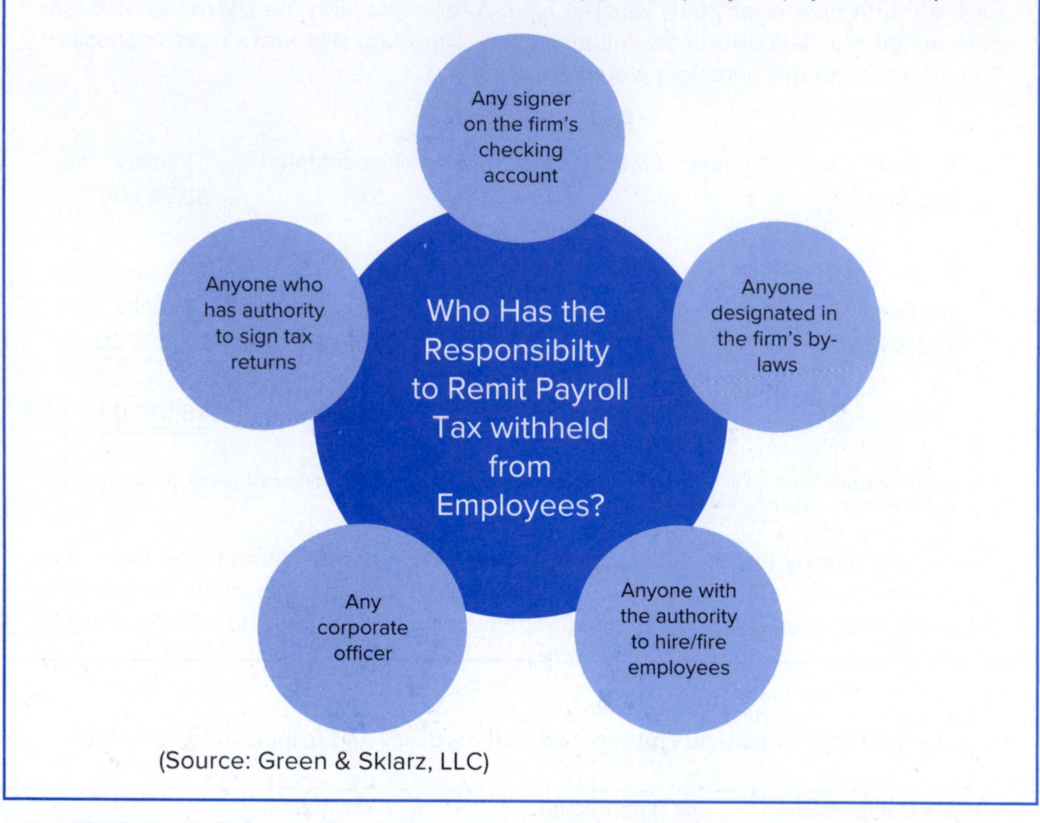

(Source: Green & Sklarz, LLC)

Tracking employee payroll expenses is an important duty of payroll accountants. The use of payroll reports fosters cost analysis that informs accounting and human resource professionals of specific details needed for budget purposes. Companies need the information generated by payroll records to ensure profitability and competitiveness.

Payroll-Related Business Expenses

Stop & Check

1. What are the two types of penalties associated with payroll taxes?
2. How do payroll expenses relate to other business functions?

LO 6-5 Relate Labor Expenses to Company Profitability

Compensating employees is far more complex than simply paying the hourly wage. The employer's expenses related to taxes, insurance, and benefits are an addition to the employee's annual salary. (See Figure 6-10.) Having employees affects the profitability of a company but is a vital part of doing business. Managers need to associate the proper amount of payroll costs with their department so they can make informed decisions about employee productivity and future budgets.

kitzcorner/Shutterstock

The Labor Distribution Report

The number of employees in a department is known as the ***labor distribution***. Payroll accounting is a powerful tool in understanding the labor distribution of a company. Accounting records facilitate departmental identification of the number and type of employees, time worked, overtime used, and benefits paid. Integrating the department information into the employee earnings records facilitates labor distribution analysis.

For example, ABD Industries has three departments: administration, sales, and manufacturing. The employees are distributed as follows:

Administration: 15	Sales: 10	Manufacturing: 60

Without ***departmental classification***, the payroll costs associated with the 85 employees at ABD would be allocated evenly among the departments. This allocation would result in the administration and sales departments absorbing an amount of the payroll costs that is disproportionate to the number of employees. The departmental classification yields an accurate picture of how the labor is distributed across a company.

EXAMPLE: LABOR DISTRIBUTION, NO DEPARTMENTAL CLASSIFICATION

Total payroll amount for ABD Industries = $500,000
Number of departments = 3
Payroll cost assigned to each department:
$500,000/3 = $166,666.67

Assigning payroll costs without departmental classification works when each department is composed of an equal number of employees with reasonably similar skills and job titles.

EXAMPLE: LABOR DISTRIBUTION WITH DEPARTMENTAL CLASSIFICATION

Total payroll for ABD: $500,000 or
Payroll cost per employee: $500,000/85 employees = $5,882.35 per employee (if allocated evenly per employee).

Departmental allocation:

Administration payroll costs = $5,882.35 × 15 = $88,235
Sales payroll costs = $5,882.35 × 10 = $58,824
Manufacturing payroll costs = $5,882.35 × 60 = $352,941

FIGURE 6-10
Percent of Employee Compensation Component to Total Payroll Expense

Compensation Component	Civilian Workers	Private Industry	State and Local Government
Wages and salaries	68.3%	69.7%	62.4%
Benefits	31.7%	30.3%	37.6%
Paid leave	7.1%	7.0%	7.5%
Supplemental pay	3.3%	3.8%	1.0%
Insurance	8.7%	7.9%	11.9%
Health benefits	8.2%	7.5%	11.6%
Retirement and savings	5.3%	3.9%	11.6%
Defined benefit	3.3%	1.6%	10.8%
Defined contribution	2.0%	2.3%	0.8%
Legally required	7.3%	7.7%	5.5%

Source: Bureau of Labor Statistics, 2018

Allocating costs according to the number of employees in each department yields a more accurate amount than equal distribution of the labor costs across the three departments at ABD. However, allocating by number of departmental employees assumes that each employee has equal compensation, which is improbable. A payroll accounting system allows accurate allocation based on the precise amounts paid to each employee per payroll period. Labor distribution reports are among the tools that managers use to determine the productivity and costs specifically associated with their department.

Labor distribution reports may be used to reveal whatever information is important to a business. Funding sources, payroll accuracy, and budget projections are three common uses of labor distribution reports. Vanderbilt University uses a labor distribution report to ensure that payroll costs are linked to appropriate departments and to specific grant funding. (Source: *Small Business Chronicle*)

Labor Distribution Report

Stop & Check

1. Pine Banks Tree Farms has 10 employees on staff: three office staff, five agricultural workers, and two drivers. The annual payroll expense is $300,000.
   a. What would be the labor distribution if Pine Banks Tree Farms uses departmental classification?
   b. What would be the labor distribution if Pine Banks Tree Farms does not use departmental classification?
2. Which method—departmental classification or nondepartmental classification—is most appropriate? Why?

LO 6-6 Complete Benefit Analysis as a Function of Payroll

Triangle Images/Getty Images

Companies offer employee benefits both to retain employees after the initial hire and to remain competitive within their industry. The problem with offering benefits is that the cost of the benefits directly affects a company's profitability. The challenge is to find ways to promote employee engagement, reduce employee turnover, and maintain company profitability. Payroll data plays an important role in completing an analysis of benefits offered and their strategic advantage.

Wages and salaries are often a company's largest employee expense. The second largest expense to employers is employee benefits. According to Paychex, employee benefits potentially add an additional 25–33 percent to an employee's base pay. Benefits can include paid time off, holiday pay, bonuses, and insurance. Many companies pay a percentage of the employee's insurance benefits, ranging from 70 percent to 100 percent in some cases. With the rising costs and mandatory nature of health insurance for certain employers, employee costs have become a major budget concern for many managers.

Payroll-related employee costs need to be compared to the advantages of maintaining the employee, namely, the profitability of the department and the company. To achieve the analysis required, a ***benefit analysis*** report needs to be compiled. Compiling a benefit analysis report is an important tool in maintaining a balance between employee retention and profitability. The payroll records of the company facilitate the compilation of the benefit analysis report.

The analysis of employee benefits considers all of the variables that comprise their compensation. Many managers are unaware of the full cost of having an employee added to or removed from their department, so the benefit analysis report serves the following purposes:

Dragon Images/Shutterstock

- Benefit analysis helps employers benchmark their employees' compensation to other companies with similar profiles or in certain geographic locations.
- The report helps employers with labor distribution and budgeting tasks by providing data for decision making.
- The benefit analysis facilitates managerial understanding of departmental impacts prior to hiring or dismissing employees.

Accurate reporting of the benefits costs to employers provides the management with guidance for budget analysis and employee compensation. A sample benefit analysis report is contained in Figure 6-11.

FIGURE 6-11
Sample Benefit Analysis Report

Statement for: Elizabeth M. Charette

Annual Gross Salary: **$44,137.60**

Total Hours Worked Annually: **2,080 Hours**

Health & Welfare Benefits:	Annual Employee Cost	Annual Employer Cost
Medical/Dental:	$600	$6,000
Life Insurance:	$0	$1,200
AD&D Coverage:	$0	$980
Dependent Life Insurance:	$300	$600
Disability Insurance:	$600	$3,000
Total Health & Welfare:	$1,500	$11,780
Retirement Plan Benefits:	**Employee Cost**	**Employer Cost**
401(k) Employee Contribution:	$1,324.13	$662.07
Profit Sharing:	$0	$3,000
Total Retirement Plan:	$1,324.13	$3,662.07
PTO & Holiday Pay	**Employee Cost**	**Employer Cost**
Paid Time Off:	$0	$1,697.60
Holiday Pay:	$0	$1,867.36
Total PTO and Holiday Pay:	$0	$3,564.96
Additional Compensation:	**Employee Cost**	**Employer Cost**
Annual Bonus:	$0	$2,500
Bereavement Pay:	$0	$509.28
Production Bonus:	$0	$500
Tuition Reimbursement:	$0	$5,250
Total Additional Comp:	$0	$8,759.28
Government Mandated:	**Employee Cost**	**Employer Cost**
Social Security:	$2,736.53	$2,736.53
Medicare:	$640.00	$640.00
Federal Unemployment:	$0	$253.28
State Unemployment:	$0	$2,279.53
Workers' Compensation:	$0	$353.10
Total Government Mandated:	$3,376.53	$6,262.44
Total Cost of Benefit Provided by WLA Industries	$6,200.66	$34,028.75
Total Cost of Employing E. M. Charette*		$78,166.35

*44137.60+34028.75 = $78,166.35

Sources: American Payroll Association, ADP

Note the differences between total employee benefit costs and total employer benefit costs. Mandatory and voluntary employee payroll deduction represent a significant monetary investment. When added to the employee's wages and the costs involved with recruitment and hiring, the amount of money dedicated to labor costs becomes a significant portion of a company's expenses.

Taking the information prepared above, the payroll accountant can determine the cost of each employee to the company. This information can also be used to determine the total cost of offering a particular benefit to the employees. The latter is used when the company is looking at annual renewals of health insurance benefits for comparison.

Annual Total Compensation Report

Some companies provide their employees with an ***annual total compensation report***. The annual total compensation report is similar to the benefit analysis report because it contains detailed analysis of employee costs. The difference between the two reports is the intended audience. The benefit analysis report is an internal report for the company's management, and the annual total compensation report is meant to be distributed to the employee. The work going into the total compensation report can come from either the human resources department or the accounting department, depending on the structure of the company. Either way, the payroll accountant contributes vital information to the report.

> The Credit Union National Association (CUNA) publishes annual total compensation reports that contain the details of CEOs and senior executives at credit unions in the United States. Information from these reports informs each credit union's decisions about base salary, benefits, and retirement packages by providing an industry-wide benchmark. (Source: CUNA)

Andrey_Popov/Shutterstock

To prepare the information for the benefit analysis and total compensation reports, the payroll accountant will gather information from many sources: payroll registers, accounts payable invoices, ***payroll tax reports***, and contributions to retirement programs (when employer matching is involved). The payroll accountant will start by printing the annual earnings report for the employee in question. A computerized earnings register can be configured to include taxes and other deductions from the employee's pay. When the total compensation report covers periods greater than one year, it may be necessary for the payroll accountant to obtain Social Security and Medicare tax rates for the years in question. Employer portions of unemployment insurance, workers' compensation, and taxes are added to the benefits provided to the employees in the determination of the total cost.

The payroll accountant will request copies of invoices for health insurance, life insurance, and any other benefits the employer provides, such as on-site meals and gym facilities/memberships, from the accounts payable accountant. Other items that may be added to the cost per employee for benefit analysis could be company-provided awards, meals, clothing, or special facilities (break room, locker room, etc.). Once complete, the annual compensation report is distributed to employees to help them understand the total value of their annual compensation. A sample total compensation report is in Figure 6-12.

FIGURE 6-12

Total Compensation Report

CASH COMPENSATION AND BENEFITS SUMMARY

The amount of your total compensation from ABC Company is much more than what is indicated in your yearly earnings statement. In addition to direct pay, it includes the value of your health care insurance, disability and life insurance, retirement benefits, and government mandated benefits. Below, we break out your total compensation.

CASH COMPENSATION	Amount
Base Salary	$52,000.00
Total:	**$52,000.00**

BENEFITS	Plan	Coverage	Your Contribution	Company Contribution
Medical Insurance	ABC One		$600.00	$5,400.00
Vision Insurance	ABC Vision		$0.00	$600.00
Dental Insurance	NL Dental		$120.00	$1,080.00
Total:			**$720.00**	**$7,080.00**

Your Contribution 9.23%

Company Contribution 90.77%

TOTAL COMPENSATION VALUE

The true value of your ABC Company total compensation includes your direct pay, the company's contribution to your benefits, and the consequent tax savings to you.

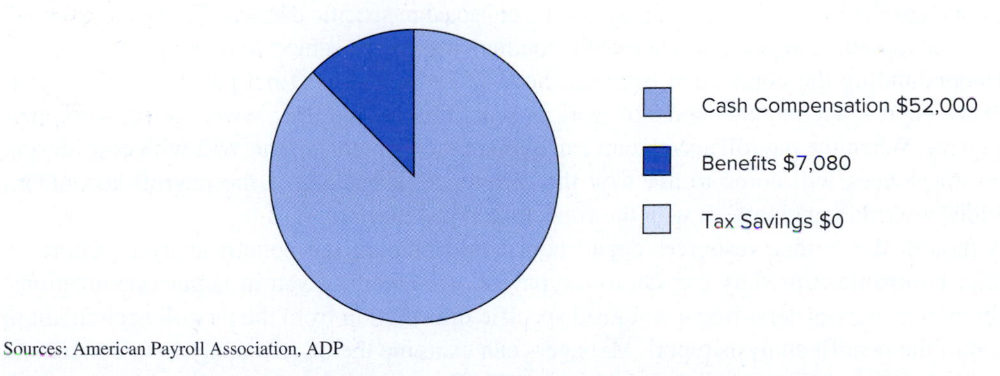

Sources: American Payroll Association, ADP

Benefit Analysis Report

Stop & Check

1. What are the purposes of compiling a benefit analysis report?
2. What is the difference between a benefit analysis report and an annual total compensation report?

EMPLOYER TAXES AND BENEFIT ANALYSIS

Tax rates and remittance methods for employers tend to change annually based on directives issued by federal, state, and local governments. Some developments in employer taxes that have changed since 2015 include the following:

- The use of the EFTPS as a mandatory tax remittance method for new employers and the preferred method for existing employers.
- Additional guidance from the Financial Accounting Standards Board about the reporting of defined benefit and defined contribution plan accounting.
- Increased automation of employer taxes to improve and streamline remittance procedures.
- Continuing focus on employee wellness that includes health incentives as part of employees' total compensation package.

Some trends to watch in employer taxes and benefit analysis include the following:

- The addition of financial wellness platforms to help employees understand their income, benefits, and investments
- Transparency in pay and benefits in an effort to prove equality of pay and benefits in response to equal pay legislation.
- Changes to corporate law that affects the employer's cost of worker's compensation insurance.
- Increasing governmental guidance about tax deductions for employee benefits.

Summary of Employer Payroll Taxes and Labor Planning

Taxes are a part of conducting business. Whether taxes are income or employee related, a business must abide by the regulations for the timely submission and reporting of taxes. Employers have responsibilities for collecting federal income tax, Social Security, and Medicare taxes from their employees. In addition, the company is responsible for setting aside federal unemployment taxes per employee based upon taxable wages. Apart from the federal taxes, employers may be liable for the collecting, reporting, and submission of state and local income and unemployment taxes. Privilege taxes, such as the Denver Head Tax, may also be collected in specific districts. Employers who fail to meet the reporting, deposit, or submission requirements may be subject to fines and penalties.

Understanding the connection between the W-2 Form and the final paycheck of the year can save payroll accountants hours of work in searching to find the answers to each employee's query. When the payroll accountant can explain the elements of the W-2 with confidence, fewer employees will come to ask why the difference, especially if the payroll accountant provides a written explanation with the final annual paycheck or W-2.

Although the human resources department could prepare the benefit analysis report, in smaller companies this duty can fall to the payroll accountant. Even in larger organizations, the human resources department will need specific information from the payroll accountant to feed into the benefit analysis report. Managers can examine the benefit analysis to understand how much their employees cost their department. Once receiving a total annual compensation report, the employee has a more complete understanding of their compensation package, thereby feeding wage discussions and building a data-driven understanding of cost changes.

Key Points

- Employers share some of the same tax obligations as their employees. Some examples are the Social Security, Medicare, and (in some states) SUTA taxes.
- FUTA taxes are paid only on the first $7,000 of each employee's annual taxable wage; SUTA tax wage base limits vary by state.
- Workers' compensation is state-mandated insurance that employers carry to protect employees who are injured or killed while performing normal work duties.

- Workers' compensation insurance premium costs vary according to labor classifications.
- Payroll tax deposit frequency is determined by the amount of payroll taxes paid during a "lookback" period.
- All new employers are monthly schedule depositors until the next lookback period.
- Most employers file quarterly payroll tax returns on Form 941.
- Employers who deposit payroll taxes on a semiweekly basis must also file a Schedule B with their Form 941.
- Employers with less than $2,500 of annual tax liability file a Form 944 at the end of the calendar year.
- Employers report FUTA tax liability on an annual basis by using Form 940.
- Employers file an annual Form W-2 for each employee with the Social Security Administration.
- Form W-3 is the transmittal form used to report a company's aggregate annual wages and withholdings.
- Labor distribution has an effect on company profitability, and benefit costs are a significant factor in managerial decisions.
- A total annual compensation report is used to communicate to employees the complete compensation package that they receive.

Vocabulary

Annual schedule depositors
Annual total compensation report
Automated Clearing House (ACH)
Benefit analysis
Departmental classification
Electronic Federal Tax Payment System (EFTPS)
FICA
Form 940
Form 941
Form 944
Form W-2
Form W-3
FUTA
Labor distribution
Lookback period
Monthly depositors
Next business day depositors
Payroll tax reports
Quarterly depositors
Schedule B
Semiweekly depositors
Statutory deductions
SUTA
Tax remittance

Review Questions

1. What taxes are paid only by the employer in most states?
2. What taxes are the shared responsibility of the employer and employee?
3. What taxes are paid by the employee only?
4. What determines the deposit requirements for employer taxes?
5. How often must a company report Form 941 earnings/withholdings?
6. How often must a company report Form 940 earnings/withholdings?
7. Which of the mandatory taxes have a maximum wage base?
8. How did the Affordable Care Act change Medicare tax withholding percentages?
9. What is the purpose of Form 941?
10. Which employers must use Schedule B?
11. How do employers know that they must use Form 944?
12. What is the purpose of Form 940?
13. What is the difference between Form W-2 and Form W-3?
14. What are the employer's payroll responsibilities as far as taxes and other withholdings are concerned?
15. How does payroll relate to a company's costs of doing business?
16. What is meant by the term *labor distribution*?
17. How do payroll records inform managers about labor distribution?
18. What is a benefit analysis report?
19. How can a manager use the benefit analysis report in the decision-making process?
20. How do the payroll reports inform managers about department and company profitability?

Exercises Set A

E6-1A. LO 6-1

Which of the following are employer-only payroll obligations? (Select all that apply.)

a. Social Security tax
b. SUTA
c. Medicare tax
d. FUTA

E6-2A. LO 6-1

As of 2019, which of the following accurately represents the full FUTA rate and wage base?

a. 0.6 percent, $132,900
b. Varies by state
c. 6.0 percent, $7,000
d. 0.6 percent, $7,000

E6-3A. LO 6-1

Davis Reyes is the accounting for Heads Up Hat Corporation. As he prepares the payroll for the semimonthly pay period ending December 15, he notices that some of the year-to-date executives' salaries have exceeded $200,000. What payroll tax responsibilities does Heads Up Hat Corporation have, especially regarding FICA taxes? (Select all that apply.)

a. Social Security tax must be deducted from the executives' pay for those under the cap and matched by the corporation
b. An additional 0.9 percent Medicare tax must be deducted from the employees' pay for those over the base and matched by the corporation
c. An additional 0.9 percent Medicare tax must be deducted from the executives' pay for those over the base, but no corporate match is required
d. Medicare taxes should be deducted from all employees' pay and matched by the corporation

E6-4A. LO 6-2

Rosa Pierce is a payroll clerk at Hot Tree Hand Tools. She receives a written notice from the IRS that the company is a semiweekly schedule depositor. How is the deposit schedule determined?

a. The number of employees in the company
b. The payroll frequency used by the company
c. The amount of FUTA taxes paid
d. The payroll tax liability during the lookback period

E6-5A. LO 6-2

Match the amount of payroll tax liabilities from the lookback period with the appropriate tax deposit schedule.

a. $42,300 annual payroll taxes	1. Annual
b. $145,033 annual payroll taxes	2. Monthly
c. $128,450 payroll tax for one pay period	3. Semiweekly
d. $1,580 annual payroll taxes	4. Next business day

E6-6A. LO 6-3

Which form(s) should be prepared and filed by companies with employees and payroll tax liabilities exceeding $50,000 as of December 31, 20XX? (Select all that apply.)

a. Form 940
b. Form W-4
c. Form 941
d. Form W-2

E6-7A. LO 6-4

Wade Pools Company made its required tax deposits. However, it filed its second-quarter Form 941 on August 21, after receiving notice from the IRS of the missing form. What is the failure to file penalty?

a. 2 percent
d. 5 percent
c. 10 percent
d. 15 percent

E6-8A. LO 6-4, 6-5
Which of the following is true about the cost of employees within a business context? (Select all that apply.)
a. Employees comprise a significant cost of conducting business
b. Hiring employees involves a significant overhead cost
c. Costs associated with employees include only salary and limited hiring expenses
d. The cost of providing employee benefits is minimal and of little importance

E6-9A. LO 6-6
Which of the following represent the purpose(s) of the benefit analysis report? (Select all that apply.)
a. Benchmarking with other companies
b. Understanding of employer and employee benefits costs
c. Billing employees for benefits costs
d. Identification of opportunities for increasing profitability

E6-10A. LO 6-6
Why is it important to prepare the benefit analysis report or the total compensation report? (Select all that apply.)
a. The reports promote employee education about the total value of their salary and benefits
b. The reports inform labor planning and employer cost strategies
c. The reports may be used as employee contracts
d. The reports may be used to accompany benefits billing

E6-11A. LO 6-1, 6-4
Which of the following is a characteristic of workers' compensation? (Select all that apply.)
a. Workers' compensation is an insurance policy
b. Private employers are federally mandated to provide workers' compensation
c. The cost of workers' compensation represents a labor expense to the business
d. Workers' compensation is provided to cover employees who are injured or killed while performing work duties

Problems Set A

P6-1A. LO 6-1
Bob Higgins works for Red Apple Engines, which pays employees on a semimonthly basis. Bob's annual salary is $150,000. Calculate the following:

Pay Date	Prior YTD Earnings	Social Security Taxable Wages	Medicare Taxable Wages	Employer Share Social Security Tax	Employer Share Medicare Tax
November 15					
December 31					

P6-2A. LO 6-1 6-3
White Lemon Cameras has the following employees:

Employee Name	Annual Taxable Wages
Mia Haskell	$26,000
Viktor Papadopoulos	35,000
Puja Anderson	32,000
Cady Billingmeier	29,000
Carl Johnson	46,000

White Lemon Cameras' SUTA tax rate is 5.4 percent and applies to the first $8,000 of employee wages. What is the annual amount due for each employee?

Employee Name	FUTA Due	SUTA Due
Mia Haskell		
Viktor Papadopoulos		
Puja Anderson		
Cady Billingmeier		
Carl Johnson		

P6-3A. LO 6-1, 6-2, 6-3

Freedom Inc. has 16 employees within Denver City and County. All of the employees worked a predominant number of hours within the city. The employees earned $7.25 per hour and worked 160 hours each during the month. The employer must remit $4.00 per month per employee who earns more than $500 per month. Additionally, employees who earn more than $500 per month must have $5.75 withheld from their pay. What is the employee and company Occupational Privilege Tax for these employees?

Employee: ______________

Employer: ______________

P6-4A. LO 6-1, 6-3

Joseph Farmer earned $128,000 in 2019 for a company in Kentucky. He is single with one withholding allowance and is paid annually. Compute the following employee share of the taxes using the percentage method in Appendix C and the state information in Appendix D.

Federal income tax withholding: ______________

Social Security tax: ______________

Medicare tax: ______________

State income tax withholding: ______________

P6-5A. LO 6-3

Using the information from P6-4A, compute the employer's share of the taxes. The FUTA rate in Kentucky for 2019 is 0.6 percent on the first $7,000 of employee wages, and the SUTA rate is 5.4 percent with a wage base of $10,200.

Federal income tax withholding: ______________

Social Security tax: ______________

Medicare tax: ______________

FUTA tax: ______________

SUTA tax: ______________

State income tax withholding: ______________

P6-6A. LO 6-2

Veryclear Glassware is a new business owned by Samantha Peoples, the company president. Her first year of operation commenced on April 1, 2019. What schedule depositor would she be for the first year of operations?

P6-7A. LO 6-3

Using the information from P6-6A, complete the following Form 941 for second quarter 2019.

EIN: 78-7654398

Address: 23051 Old Redwood Highway, Sebastopol, California 95482, phone 707-555-5555

Number of employees: 7

Wages, tips, and other compensation paid during second quarter 2019: $244,798

Income tax withheld from employees: $48,000

Social Security tax withheld from employees: $15,177.48

Medicare tax withheld from employees: $3,549.57

Monthly tax liability:

April	$28,484.79
May	28,484.79
June	28,484.80

P6-8A. LO 6-3

Using the information from P6-6A and P6-7A for VeryClear Glassware (California Employer Account Number 999-9999-9), complete the following State of California Form DE-9, Quarterly Contribution and Report of Wages Report. Use 5.4 percent as the UI rate with a cap of $7,000 per employee, 0.1 percent as the ETT rate also with a cap of $7,000 per employee, and 0.9 percent as the SDI rate with a cap of $110,902 per employee. All employees have worked the full quarter with the company, and all wages are subject to UI, ETT, and SDI. The California PIT taxes withheld for the quarter are $4,068. The company has deposited $6,656.18 for the quarter. Samantha Peoples submitted the form on 7/6/2019.

950117

Form **941 for 2019: Employer's QUARTERLY Federal Tax Return**
(Rev. January 2019) Department of the Treasury — Internal Revenue Service

OMB No. 1545-0029

Employer identification number (EIN) [ ][ ] – [ ][ ][ ][ ][ ][ ][ ]

Name *(not your trade name)*

Trade name *(if any)*

Address

Number Street Suite or room number

City State ZIP code

Foreign country name Foreign province/county Foreign postal code

Report for this Quarter of 2019
(Check one.)

☐ **1:** January, February, March

☐ **2:** April, May, June

☐ **3:** July, August, September

☐ **4:** October, November, December

Go to *www.irs.gov/Form941* for instructions and the latest information.

Read the separate instructions before you complete Form 941. Type or print within the boxes.

Part 1: Answer these questions for this quarter.

1	**Number of employees who received wages, tips, or other compensation for the pay period including:** ***Mar. 12*** **(Quarter 1),** ***June 12*** **(Quarter 2),** ***Sept. 12*** **(Quarter 3), or** ***Dec. 12*** **(Quarter 4)**		1	
2	**Wages, tips, and other compensation**		2	.
3	**Federal income tax withheld from wages, tips, and other compensation**		3	.
4	**If no wages, tips, and other compensation are subject to social security or Medicare tax**		☐	**Check and go to line 6.**

		Column 1		Column 2
5a	**Taxable social security wages**	.	× 0.124 =	.
5b	**Taxable social security tips**	.	× 0.124 =	.
5c	**Taxable Medicare wages & tips**	.	× 0.029 =	.
5d	**Taxable wages & tips subject to Additional Medicare Tax withholding**	.	× 0.009 =	.

5e	**Add Column 2 from lines 5a, 5b, 5c, and 5d**	5e	.
5f	**Section 3121(q) Notice and Demand—Tax due on unreported tips** (see instructions)	5f	.
6	**Total taxes before adjustments.** Add lines 3, 5e, and 5f	6	.
7	**Current quarter's adjustment for fractions of cents**	7	.
8	**Current quarter's adjustment for sick pay**	8	.
9	**Current quarter's adjustments for tips and group-term life insurance**	9	.
10	**Total taxes after adjustments.** Combine lines 6 through 9	10	.
11	**Qualified small business payroll tax credit for increasing research activities.** Attach Form 8974	11	.
12	**Total taxes after adjustments and credits.** Subtract line 11 from line 10	12	.
13	**Total deposits for this quarter, including overpayment applied from a prior quarter and overpayments applied from Form 941-X, 941-X (PR), 944-X, or 944-X (SP) filed in the current quarter**	13	.
14	**Balance due.** If line 12 is more than line 13, enter the difference and see instructions	14	.

15 **Overpayment.** If line 13 is more than line 12, enter the difference [.] Check one: ☐ Apply to next return. ☐ Send a refund.

► **You MUST complete both pages of Form 941 and SIGN it.**

Next ►

For Privacy Act and Paperwork Reduction Act Notice, see the back of the Payment Voucher. Cat. No. 17001Z Form **941** (Rev. 1-2019)

950217

Name *(not your trade name)* | **Employer identification number (EIN)**

Part 2: Tell us about your deposit schedule and tax liability for this quarter.

If you are unsure about whether you are a monthly schedule depositor or a semiweekly schedule depositor, see section 11 of Pub. 15.

16 Check one: ☐ **Line 12 on this return is less than $2,500 or line 12 on the return for the prior quarter was less than $2,500, and you didn't incur a $100,000 next-day deposit obligation during the current quarter.** If line 12 for the prior quarter was less than $2,500 but line 12 on this return is $100,000 or more, you must provide a record of your federal tax liability. If you are a monthly schedule depositor, complete the deposit schedule below; if you are a semiweekly schedule depositor, attach Schedule B (Form 941). Go to Part 3.

☐ **You were a monthly schedule depositor for the entire quarter.** Enter your tax liability for each month and total liability for the quarter, then go to Part 3.

Tax liability: Month 1 ____ .

Month 2 ____ .

Month 3 ____ .

Total liability for quarter ____ . **Total must equal line 12.**

☐ **You were a semiweekly schedule depositor for any part of this quarter.** Complete Schedule B (Form 941), Report of Tax Liability for Semiweekly Schedule Depositors, and attach it to Form 941.

Part 3: Tell us about your business. If a question does NOT apply to your business, leave it blank.

17 If your business has closed or you stopped paying wages . . . . ☐ Check here, and

enter the final date you paid wages ___ / ___ / ___ .

18 If you are a seasonal employer and you don't have to file a return for every quarter of the year . . ☐ Check here.

Part 4: May we speak with your third-party designee?

Do you want to allow an employee, a paid tax preparer, or another person to discuss this return with the IRS? See the instructions for details.

☐ Yes. Designee's name and phone number ____ ____

Select a 5-digit Personal Identification Number (PIN) to use when talking to the IRS. ☐☐☐☐☐

☐ No.

Part 5: Sign here. You MUST complete both pages of Form 941 and SIGN it.

Under penalties of perjury, I declare that I have examined this return, including accompanying schedules and statements, and to the best of my knowledge and belief, it is true, correct, and complete. Declaration of preparer (other than taxpayer) is based on all information of which preparer has any knowledge.

✗ **Sign your name here** ____

Print your name here ____

Print your title here ____

Date ___ / ___ / ___

Best daytime phone ____

Paid Preparer Use Only

Check if you are self-employed . . . ☐

Preparer's name		PTIN	
Preparer's signature		Date	/ /
Firm's name (or yours if self-employed)		EIN	
Address		Phone	
City	State	ZIP code	

Page **2** Form **941** (Rev. 1-2019)

Source: Internal Revenue Service

P6-9A. LO 6-3

The Content Rabbit Graphics Company paid its 25 employees a total of $863,428.49 during 2018. Of these wages, $5,400 is exempt fringe benefits (Section 125 cafeteria plans) and $9,850 is exempt retirement benefits (employer contributions to 401(k) plans). All employees have worked there for the full calendar year and reached the FUTA wage base during the first quarter; taxes were deposited then. The Content Rabbit Graphics Company is located at 3874 Palm Avenue, Sebring, Florida, 20394. The owner is Eula Parks, EIN is 99-2039485, phone number is 461-555-9485. Complete Form 940, submitting it on January 13, 2019.

P6-10A. LO 6-3

Leda Inc. is located at 433 Augusta Road, Caribou, Maine, 04736, phone number 207-555-1212. The Federal EIN is 54-3910394, and it has a Maine Revenue Services number of 3884019. Owner Amanda Leda has asked you to prepare Form W-2 for each of the following employees of Leda Inc. as of December 31, 2019.

Sarah C. Niehaus 122 Main Street, #3 Caribou, ME 04736 SSN: 477-30-2234 Dependent Care Benefit: $1,800.00	Total 2019 wages: $34,768.53 401(k) contribution: $1,043.06 Section 125 contribution: $1,500.00 Federal income tax withheld: $4,833.82 Social Security tax withheld: $2,062.65 Medicare tax withheld: $482.39 State income tax withheld $1,869.08
Maxwell S. Law 1503 22nd Street New Sweden, ME 04762 SSN: 493-55-2049	Total 2019 wages: $36,729.37 401(k) contribution: $1,469.18 Section 125 contribution: $1,675.00 Federal income tax withheld: $4,407.52 Social Security tax withheld: $2,173.37 Medicare tax withheld: $508.29 State income tax withheld $1,947.94
Siobhan E. Manning 1394 West Highway 59 Woodland, ME 04694 SSN: 390-39-1002 Tuition in excess of $5,250: $1,575.00 (Include in boxes 1, 3, 5, 16)	Total 2019 wages: $30,034.87 401(k) contribution: $712.75 Section 125 contribution: $1,000.00 Federal income tax withheld: $4,833.82 Social Security tax withheld: $1,897.81 Medicare tax withheld: $443.84 State income tax withheld $1,734.03
Donald A. Hendrix 1387 Rimbaud Avenue Caribou, ME 04736 SSN: 288-30-5940	Total 2019 wages: $22,578.89 401(k) contribution: $1,354.73 Section 125 contribution: $2,250.00 Federal income tax withheld: $2,709.47 Social Security tax withheld: $1,260.39 Medicare tax withheld: $294.77 State income tax withheld $1,231.00
Alison K. Sutter 3664 Fairfield Street Washburn, ME 04786 SSN: 490-55-0293	Total 2019 wages: $45,908.34 401(k) contribution: $2,754.50 Section 125 contribution: $1,750.00 Federal income tax withheld: $5,509.00 Social Security tax withheld: $2,737.82 Medicare tax withheld: $640.30 State income tax withheld $2,401.42

P6-11A. LO 6-3

Using the information from P6-10A for Leda Inc., complete Form W-3 that must accompany the company's W-2 Forms. Leda Inc. is a 941-ss payer and is a private, for-profit company. Amanda Leda is the owner; phone number is 207-555-1212; no e-mail address to disclose; fax number is 207-555-9898. No third-party sick pay applied for 2019. The form was signed on January 20, 2020.

EDD Employment Development Department State of California

QUARTERLY CONTRIBUTION RETURN AND REPORT OF WAGES

REMINDER: File your DE 9 and DE 9C together.

PLEASE TYPE THIS FORM—DO NOT ALTER PREPRINTED INFORMATION

00090112

QUARTER ENDED DUE DELINQUENT IF NOT POSTMARKED OR RECEIVED BY YR QTR

EMPLOYER ACCOUNT NO.

DEPT. USE ONLY — DO NOT ALTER THIS AREA

P1 P2 C P U S A T

EFFECTIVE DATE Mo. Day Yr.

FEIN

A. NO WAGES PAID THIS QUARTER ☐ B. OUT OF BUSINESS/NO EMPLOYEES ☐

ADDITIONAL FEINS

B1. OUT OF BUSINESS DATE M M D D Y Y Y Y

C. TOTAL SUBJECT WAGES PAID THIS QUARTER ....

D. UNEMPLOYMENT INSURANCE (UI) (Total Employee Wages up to $ per employee per calendar year)

(D1) UI Rate % TIMES (D2) UI TAXABLE WAGES FOR THE QUARTER = (D3) UI CONTRIBUTIONS 0.00

E. EMPLOYMENT TRAINING TAX (ETT)

(E1) ETT Rate % TIMES UI Taxable Wages for the Quarter (D2)...... = (E2) ETT CONTRIBUTIONS 0.00

F. STATE DISABILITY INSURANCE (SDI) (Total Employee Wages up to $ per employee per calendar year)

(F1) SDI Rate % TIMES (F2) SDI TAXABLE WAGES FOR THE QUARTER = (F3) SDI EMPLOYEE CONTRIBUTIONS WITHHELD 0.00

G. CALIFORNIA PERSONAL INCOME TAX (PIT) WITHHELD ....

H. **SUBTOTAL** (Add Items D3, E2, F3, and G)...................................... 0.00

I. LESS: CONTRIBUTIONS AND WITHHOLDINGS PAID FOR THE QUARTER ....
(**DO NOT** INCLUDE PENALTY AND INTEREST PAYMENTS)

J. TOTAL TAXES DUE OR OVERPAID (Item H minus Item I) 0.00

If amount due, prepare a *Payroll Tax Deposit* (DE 88), include the correct payment quarter, and mail to: Employment Development Department, P.O. Box 826276, Sacramento, CA 94230-6276. **NOTE:** Do not mail payments along with the DE 9 and *Quarterly Contribution Return and Report of Wages (Continuation)* (DE 9C), as this may delay processing and result in erroneous penalty and interest charges. **Mandatory Electronic Funds Transfer (EFT)** filers must remit all SDI/PIT deposits by EFT to avoid a noncompliance penalty.

K. I declare that the above, to the best of my knowledge and belief, is true and correct. If a refund was claimed, a reasonable effort was made to refund any erroneous deductions to the affected employee(s).

Signature Required Title (Owner, Accountant, Preparer, etc.) Phone ( ) Date

SIGN AND MAIL TO: State of California / Employment Development Department / P.O. Box 989071 / West Sacramento CA 95798-9071

DE 9 Rev. 1 (1-12) **(INTERNET)** Page 1 of 2

e-Services — Fast, Easy, and Convenient! Visit EDD's Web site at **www.edd.ca.gov**

Source: Internal Revenue Service

Form **940 for 2018: Employer's Annual Federal Unemployment (FUTA) Tax Return** 850113

Department of the Treasury — Internal Revenue Service OMB No. 1545-0028

Employer identification number (EIN) ☐☐ – ☐☐☐☐☐☐☐

Name *(not your trade name)*

Trade name *(if any)*

Address

Number Street Suite or room number

City State ZIP code

Foreign country name Foreign province/county Foreign postal code

Type of Return
(Check all that apply.)

☐ **a.** Amended

☐ **b.** Successor employer

☐ **c.** No payments to employees in 2018

☐ **d.** Final: Business closed or stopped paying wages

Go to *www.irs.gov/Form940* for instructions and the latest information.

Read the separate instructions before you complete this form. Please type or print within the boxes.

Part 1: Tell us about your return. If any line does NOT apply, leave it blank. See instructions before completing Part 1.

1a **If you had to pay state unemployment tax in one state only, enter the state abbreviation** . **1a** ☐☐

1b **If you had to pay state unemployment tax in more than one state, you are a multi-state employer** . . . . . **1b** ☐ Check here. Complete Schedule A (Form 940).

2 **If you paid wages in a state that is subject to CREDIT REDUCTION** . . . . . **2** ☐ Check here. Complete Schedule A (Form 940).

Part 2: Determine your FUTA tax before adjustments. If any line does NOT apply, leave it blank.

3 **Total payments to all employees** . . . . . **3** _____ .

4 **Payments exempt from FUTA tax** . . . . . **4** _____ .

Check all that apply: **4a** ☐ Fringe benefits **4c** ☐ Retirement/Pension **4e** ☐ Other

4b ☐ Group-term life insurance **4d** ☐ Dependent care

5 **Total of payments made to each employee in excess of $7,000** . . . . . **5** _____ .

6 **Subtotal** (line 4 + line 5 = line 6) . . . . . **6** _____ .

7 **Total taxable FUTA wages** (line 3 – line 6 = line 7). See instructions . . . . . **7** _____ .

8 **FUTA tax before adjustments** (line 7 x 0.006 = line 8) . . . . . **8** _____ .

Part 3: Determine your adjustments. If any line does NOT apply, leave it blank.

9 **If ALL of the taxable FUTA wages you paid were excluded from state unemployment tax, multiply line 7 by 0.054** (line 7 × 0.054 = line 9). Go to line 12 . . . . . **9** _____ .

10 **If SOME of the taxable FUTA wages you paid were excluded from state unemployment tax, OR you paid ANY state unemployment tax late** (after the due date for filing Form 940), complete the worksheet in the instructions. Enter the amount from line 7 of the worksheet . . **10** _____ .

11 **If credit reduction applies,** enter the total from Schedule A (Form 940) . . . . . **11** _____ .

Part 4: Determine your FUTA tax and balance due or overpayment. If any line does NOT apply, leave it blank.

12 **Total FUTA tax after adjustments** (lines 8 + 9 + 10 + 11 = line 12) . . . . . **12** _____ .

13 **FUTA tax deposited for the year, including any overpayment applied from a prior year** . **13** _____ .

14 **Balance due.** If line 12 is more than line 13, enter the excess on line 14.

- If line 14 is more than $500, you must deposit your tax.
- If line 14 is $500 or less, you may pay with this return. See instructions . . . . . **14** _____ .

15 **Overpayment.** If line 13 is more than line 12, enter the excess on line 15 and check a box below **15** _____ .

▶ You **MUST** complete both pages of this form and **SIGN** it. Check one: ☐ Apply to next return. ☐ Send a refund.

Next ▶

For Privacy Act and Paperwork Reduction Act Notice, see the back of the Payment Voucher. Cat. No. 11234O Form **940** (2018)

850212

Name *(not your trade name)* | **Employer identification number (EIN)**

Part 5: Report your FUTA tax liability by quarter only if line 12 is more than $500. If not, go to Part 6.

16 Report the amount of your FUTA tax liability for each quarter; do NOT enter the amount you deposited. If you had no liability for a quarter, leave the line blank.

16a 1st quarter (January 1 – March 31) . . . . **16a** [.]

16b 2nd quarter (April 1 – June 30) . . . . **16b** [.]

16c 3rd quarter (July 1 – September 30) . . . . **16c** [.]

16d 4th quarter (October 1 – December 31) . . . . **16d** [.]

17 Total tax liability for the year (lines 16a + 16b + 16c + 16d = line 17) **17** [.] **Total must equal line 12.**

Part 6: May we speak with your third-party designee?

Do you want to allow an employee, a paid tax preparer, or another person to discuss this return with the IRS? See the instructions for details.

☐ **Yes.** Designee's name and phone number

Select a 5-digit Personal Identification Number (PIN) to use when talking to IRS

☐ **No.**

Part 7: Sign here. You MUST complete both pages of this form and SIGN it.

Under penalties of perjury, I declare that I have examined this return, including accompanying schedules and statements, and to the best of my knowledge and belief, it is true, correct, and complete, and that no part of any payment made to a state unemployment fund claimed as a credit was, or is to be, deducted from the payments made to employees. Declaration of preparer (other than taxpayer) is based on all information of which preparer has any knowledge.

✗ **Sign your name here**

Print your name here

Print your title here

Date / /

Best daytime phone

Paid Preparer Use Only

Check if you are self-employed ☐

Preparer's name | PTIN

Preparer's signature | Date / /

Firm's name (or yours if self-employed) | EIN

Address | Phone

City | State | ZIP code

Source: Internal Revenue Service

22222	a Employee's social security number	OMB No. 1545-0008	
b Employer identification number (EIN)		1 Wages, tips, other compensation	2 Federal income tax withheld
c Employer's name, address, and ZIP code		3 Social security wages	4 Social security tax withheld
		5 Medicare wages and tips	6 Medicare tax withheld
		7 Social security tips	8 Allocated tips
d Control number		9	10 Dependent care benefits
e Employee's first name and initial Last name Suff.		11 Nonqualified plans	12a Code
		13 Statutory employee / Retirement plan / Third-party sick pay	12b Code
		14 Other	12c Code
f Employee's address and ZIP code			12d Code

15 State Employer's state ID number	16 State wages, tips, etc.	17 State income tax	18 Local wages, tips, etc.	19 Local income tax	20 Locality name

Form **W-2 Wage and Tax Statement** 2019 Department of the Treasury—Internal Revenue Service

Copy 1—For State, City, or Local Tax Department

Source: Internal Revenue Service

DO NOT STAPLE

33333	a Control number	**For Official Use Only ▶** **OMB No. 1545-0008**	
b **Kind of Payer** (Check one): 941, Military, 943, 944, CT-1, Hshld. emp., Medicare govt. emp.		**Kind of Employer** (Check one): None apply, 501c non-govt., State/local non-501c, State/local 501c, Federal govt.	Third-party sick pay (Check if applicable)
c Total number of Forms W-2	d Establishment number	1 Wages, tips, other compensation	2 Federal income tax withheld
e Employer identification number (EIN)		3 Social security wages	4 Social security tax withheld
f Employer's name		5 Medicare wages and tips	6 Medicare tax withheld
		7 Social security tips	8 Allocated tips
		9	10 Dependent care benefits
g Employer's address and ZIP code		11 Nonqualified plans	12a Deferred compensation
h Other EIN used this year		13 For third-party sick pay use only	12b
15 State Employer's state ID number		14 Income tax withheld by payer of third-party sick pay	
16 State wages, tips, etc.	17 State income tax	18 Local wages, tips, etc.	19 Local income tax
Employer's contact person		Employer's telephone number	For Official Use Only
Employer's fax number		Employer's email address	

Under penalties of perjury, I declare that I have examined this return and accompanying documents, and, to the best of my knowledge and belief, they are true, correct, and complete.

Signature ▶ Title ▶ Date ▶

Form **W-3 Transmittal of Wage and Tax Statements** 2019 Department of the Treasury Internal Revenue Service

Source: Internal Revenue Service

P6-12A.
LO 6-4, 6-6

Clark Patrick owns Camel Customs, a company that restores vintage Ford Mustangs. He has seven employees. Clark wants to perform a benefits analysis report for one of his employees, Gayle Rowe, for the year. Gayle's benefits package is as follows:

Annual salary: $40,000

401(k) contribution: 3 percent of annual salary, company match is 50 percent of employee contribution

Medical insurance deduction: $150 per month

Dental insurance: $25 per month

Complete the following Benefits Analysis Report for Gayle Rowe for the year. Do not include FUTA and SUTA taxes.

Yearly Benefit Costs	Company Cost	Gayle's Cost
Medical insurance	$7,200	$
Dental insurance	$1,000	$
Life insurance	200	-0-
AD&D	50	-0-
Short-term disability	500	-0-
Long-term disability	250	-0-
401(k)	$	$
Social Security	$	$
Medicare	$	$
Tuition reimbursement	2,000	-0-
Total yearly benefit costs	$	$
Gayle's annual salary	$	
Total yearly benefit costs	$	
Total value of Gayle's compensation	$	

P6-13A.
LO 6-4, 6-5

Black Sheep Printing has 35 employees distributed among the following departments:

Sales: 10	Factory: 15	Administration: 10

The total annual payroll for Black Sheep Printing is $700,000.
Compute the labor distribution based on equal distribution among the departments.

Sales: ______________

Factory: ______________

Administration: ______________

P6-14A.
LO 6-4, 6-5

For Black Sheep Printing in P6-13A, compute the labor distribution based on the number of employees per department:

Sales: ______________

Factory: ______________

Administration: ______________

P6-15A.
LO 6-1, 6-4

Small Orange Fine Foods is a specialty grocery store. The employees are classified according to job titles for workers' compensation insurance premium computation purposes.

a. Based on the payroll estimates as of January 1, what is the total estimated workers' compensation premium for 20XX?

Employee Classification	Rate per $100 of Payroll	Estimated Payroll for 20XX	Workers' Compensation Premium
Grocery Clerk	$0.75	$192,500	
Shelf Stocker	1.90	212,160	
Stock Handler	2.40	237,120	
		Total Premium =	

b. The actual payroll for 20XX is listed below. What is the workers' compensation premium based on the actual payroll?

Employee Classification	Rate per $100 of Payroll	Actual Payroll for 20XX	Workers' Compensation Premium
Grocery Clerk	$0.75	$196,588	
Shelf Stocker	1.90	215,220	
Stock Handler	2.40	242,574	
		Total Premium =	

c. What is the difference between the actual and the estimated premiums?
____

Exercises Set B

E6-1B. LO 6-1
Of the following taxes, which one(s) is/are examples of statutory deductions that pertain to employers? (Select all that apply.)
a. Social Security tax
b. Employee federal income tax
c. FUTA
d. 401(k) contributions

E6-2B. LO 6-1
Which of the following is/are true about FUTA obligations? (Select all that apply.)
a. FUTA is an employer-only tax.
b. FUTA is subject to a 5.4 percent reduction based on employer and state factors.
c. FUTA is subject to a $7,000 wage base per employee.
d. FUTA applies to all companies.

E6-3B. LO 6-1
Of the IRS-stipulated lookback periods, which one(s) is/are the most commonly used? (Select all that apply.)
a. Monthly
b. Semiweekly
c. Quarterly
d. Annual

E6-4B. LO 6-2
The Foggy Snail Theater has annual payroll taxes of $49,250 during the most recent lookback period. Which payroll deposit frequency will the company have, based on that lookback period?
a. Quarterly
b. Monthly
c. Semiweekly
d. Annual

E6-5B. LO 6-3
Joyce Hunter is the new payroll accountant with Rainy Snake Products in Sparks, Nevada. The company had a payroll tax liability of $250,350 during the most recent lookback period. For the quarter ending September 30, 20XX, which federal form(s) should she file? (Select all that apply.)
a. Form 940
b. Form W-2
c. Form SS-8
d. Form 941

E6-6B. LO 6-3
Which of the following is a form that must accompany all Forms W-2 submitted to the Social Security Administration?
a. Form 941
b. Form 940
c. Form W-3
d. Form W-4

E6-7B. LO 6-4
What are the penalties associated with the lack of reporting and remitting payroll taxes? (Select all that apply.)
a. Failure to report
b. Failure to file
c. Failure to deposit
d. Failure to remit

E6-8B. LO 6-4
Winston Briggs is the accounting supervisor for Cheeky Cat Furnishings, which has chosen to maintain its payroll on an in-house basis for this purpose and has hired new accounting clerks. Which of the following are payroll responsibilities of Cheeky Cat Furnishings? (Select all that apply.)
a. Timely remittance of payroll taxes
b. Remittance of voluntary deductions
c. Accountability to employees and governmental agencies
d. Publication of salary data in company-wide publications

E6-9B. LO 6-5
Which of the following represents the difference between the benefit analysis report and the annual total compensation report? (Select all that apply.)
a. The benefit analysis report is designed for review by employees
b. The annual total compensation report's intended audience is company managers
c. The benefit analysis report reflects actual benefit costs, and the annual total compensation report includes salary data
d. The reports are maintained as public records

E6-10B. LO 6-5
Which of the following represent(s) the purpose(s) of the labor distribution report? (Select all that apply.)
a. Accurate payroll cost allocation among departments
b. Explanation of individual employee costs
c. Evaluation of labor planning efforts
d. Determination of departmental performance

E6-11B. LO 6-1, 6-4
Sunny Day Flooring has employees in its manufacturing, sales, and administrative departments. Which department will have the highest rate for its workers' compensation insurance?
a. Manufacturing
b. Sales
c. Administrative
d. All departments will have the same rate

Problems Set B

P6-1B. LO 6-1
Doyle Watson works for Clear Pencil Accounting, which pays employees on a semimonthly basis. Doyle's annual salary is $210,000. Calculate the following:

Pay Date	Prior YTD Earnings	Social Security Taxable Wages	Medicare Taxable Wages	Employer Share Social Security Tax	Employer Share Medicare Tax
November 30					
December 31					

P6-2B.
LO 6-1, 6-3

Black Robot Grill of Andrews, Texas, has the following employees as of December 31:

Employee Name	Annual Taxable Wages
Mark English	$45,750
Shelly Morris	21,250
TL Radford	29,850
James Morrow	36,280
Trella Lyons	34,900

The company's SUTA tax rate is 6.25 percent and wage base is $9,000. What is the annual amount of FUTA and SUTA taxes due for each employee?

Employee Name	FUTA Due	SUTA Due
Mark English		
Shelly Morris		
TL Radford		
James Morrow		
Trella Lyons		

P6-3B.
LO 6-1, 6-2, 6-3

Deep Mouse Designs has 22 employees within Denver City and County. The employees earned $11.50 per hour and worked 160 hours each during the month. The employer must remit $4.00 per month per employee who earns more than $500 per month. Additionally, employees who earn more than $500 per month must have $5.75 withheld from their pay. What is the employee and company Occupational Privilege Tax for these employees?

Employee: ______________

Employer: ______________

P6-4B.
LO 6-1, 6-2, 6-3

Rosalie Watts earned $155,000 in 2019 for Sad Orange Web Design in King of Prussia, Pennsylvania. Sad Orange's SUTA rate is 4.8 percent and has a wage base for 2019 of $9,750. Compute Sad Orange Web Designs' share of Rosalie's salary.

Social Security tax:______________

Medicare tax:______________

FUTA tax:______________

SUTA tax:______________

P6-5B.
LO 6-2, 6-3

Howard Murphy is the owner of Stormy Banana Films in West Hollywood, California. Stormy Banana Films had 15 employees with total annual wages of $214,750 (no one exceeded the Medicare tax surcharge or Social Security cap). The FUTA rate for California in 2019 is 2.2 percent because it is a credit reduction state. Stormy Banana Films has a SUTA rate of 3.2 percent for 2019 with a wage base of $7,000. Compute the following employer taxes:

Social Security tax:______________

Medicare tax:______________

FUTA tax:______________

SUTA tax:______________

P6-6B.
LO 6-1

Peaceful Cat Pet Foods is a new business owned by Sylvester Hammond. His first year of operations commenced on June 1, 2019. What schedule depositor would his company be for the first year of operations?

P6-7B.
LO 6-3

Using the information from P6-6B, complete the following Form 941 for third quarter 2019. The form was signed by the owner on October 10, 2019.

EIN: 98-0050036

Address: 1021 Old Plainfield Road, Salina, California 95670

Phone: 707-555-0303

Number of employees: 8

Wages, tips, and other compensation paid during third quarter 2019: $302,374

Income tax withheld: $51,000

Monthly tax liability:

July	$32,421.08
August	32,421.08
September	32,421.07

P6-8B.
LO 6-3

Using the information from P6-6B and P6-7B for Peaceful Cat Pet Foods, complete the following State of California Form DE-9, Quarterly Contribution Return and Report of Wages. The California employer account number is 989-8877-1. Use 5.4 percent as the UI rate, 0.1 percent as the ETT rate, and 0.9 percent as the SDI rate. California UI and ETT wage cap is $7,000 while SDI cap is $118,371. No employee has reached the SDI limit. All employees have worked since July 1 with the company. The California PIT taxes withheld for the quarter are $40,000. The company has deposited no taxes for the quarter. Form DE-9 was completed and signed on October 10, 2019, with a due date of October 15, 2019.

P6-9B.
LO 6-3

Jealous Frog Toys paid its nine employees a total of $432,586.40 during 2018. Included in these wages is the $12470 fringe benefit. All employees have worked there for the full calendar year and reached the FUTA wage base during the first quarter. Taxes were deposited on time. The employer contributed $12,470 to Section 125 plans during the year (payments exempt from FUTA). Jealous Frog Toys is located at 783 Morehead Street, Fargo, ND 68383, phone number 701-555-3432. The owner is Noah Jackson, and the EIN is 73-4029848. Complete Form 940. The form was signed and submitted on January 10, 2019.

Form **941 for 2019: Employer's QUARTERLY Federal Tax Return**
(Rev. January 2019) Department of the Treasury — Internal Revenue Service

950117
OMB No. 1545-0029

Employer identification number (EIN) ☐☐ – ☐☐☐☐☐☐☐

Name *(not your trade name)*

Trade name *(if any)*

Address
Number Street Suite or room number
City State ZIP code
Foreign country name Foreign province/county Foreign postal code

Report for this Quarter of 2019
(Check one.)

☐ **1:** January, February, March
☐ **2:** April, May, June
☐ **3:** July, August, September
☐ **4:** October, November, December

Go to *www.irs.gov/Form941* for instructions and the latest information.

Read the separate instructions before you complete Form 941. Type or print within the boxes.

Part 1: Answer these questions for this quarter.

1	**Number of employees who received wages, tips, or other compensation for the pay period including:** ***Mar. 12*** **(Quarter 1),** ***June 12*** **(Quarter 2),** ***Sept. 12*** **(Quarter 3), or** ***Dec. 12*** **(Quarter 4)**	1	
2	**Wages, tips, and other compensation**	2	.
3	**Federal income tax withheld from wages, tips, and other compensation**	3	.
4	**If no wages, tips, and other compensation are subject to social security or Medicare tax**	☐ **Check and go to line 6.**	

		Column 1		Column 2
5a	**Taxable social security wages**	.	× 0.124 =	.
5b	**Taxable social security tips**	.	× 0.124 =	.
5c	**Taxable Medicare wages & tips**	.	× 0.029 =	.
5d	**Taxable wages & tips subject to Additional Medicare Tax withholding**	.	× 0.009 =	.

5e	**Add Column 2 from lines 5a, 5b, 5c, and 5d**	5e	.
5f	**Section 3121(q) Notice and Demand—Tax due on unreported tips** (see instructions)	5f	.
6	**Total taxes before adjustments.** Add lines 3, 5e, and 5f	6	.
7	**Current quarter's adjustment for fractions of cents**	7	.
8	**Current quarter's adjustment for sick pay**	8	.
9	**Current quarter's adjustments for tips and group-term life insurance**	9	.
10	**Total taxes after adjustments.** Combine lines 6 through 9	10	.
11	**Qualified small business payroll tax credit for increasing research activities.** Attach Form 8974	11	.
12	**Total taxes after adjustments and credits.** Subtract line 11 from line 10	12	.
13	**Total deposits for this quarter, including overpayment applied from a prior quarter and overpayments applied from Form 941-X, 941-X (PR), 944-X, or 944-X (SP) filed in the current quarter**	13	.
14	**Balance due.** If line 12 is more than line 13, enter the difference and see instructions	14	.

15 **Overpayment.** If line 13 is more than line 12, enter the difference . Check one: ☐ Apply to next return. ☐ Send a refund.

▶ **You MUST complete both pages of Form 941 and SIGN it.** Next ▶

For Privacy Act and Paperwork Reduction Act Notice, see the back of the Payment Voucher. Cat. No. 17001Z Form **941** (Rev. 1-2019)

950217

Name *(not your trade name)*	**Employer identification number (EIN)**

Part 2: Tell us about your deposit schedule and tax liability for this quarter.

If you are unsure about whether you are a monthly schedule depositor or a semiweekly schedule depositor, see section 11 of Pub. 15.

16 Check one: ☐ **Line 12 on this return is less than $2,500 or line 12 on the return for the prior quarter was less than $2,500, and you didn't incur a $100,000 next-day deposit obligation during the current quarter.** If line 12 for the prior quarter was less than $2,500 but line 12 on this return is $100,000 or more, you must provide a record of your federal tax liability. If you are a monthly schedule depositor, complete the deposit schedule below; if you are a semiweekly schedule depositor, attach Schedule B (Form 941). Go to Part 3.

☐ **You were a monthly schedule depositor for the entire quarter.** Enter your tax liability for each month and total liability for the quarter, then go to Part 3.

Tax liability: Month 1 ________ .

Month 2 ________ .

Month 3 ________ .

Total liability for quarter ________ . **Total must equal line 12.**

☐ **You were a semiweekly schedule depositor for any part of this quarter.** Complete Schedule B (Form 941), Report of Tax Liability for Semiweekly Schedule Depositors, and attach it to Form 941.

Part 3: Tell us about your business. If a question does NOT apply to your business, leave it blank.

17 If your business has closed or you stopped paying wages . . . . ☐ Check here, and

enter the final date you paid wages ____ / / ____ .

18 If you are a seasonal employer and you don't have to file a return for every quarter of the year . . ☐ Check here.

Part 4: May we speak with your third-party designee?

Do you want to allow an employee, a paid tax preparer, or another person to discuss this return with the IRS? See the instructions for details.

☐ Yes. Designee's name and phone number ________ ________

Select a 5-digit Personal Identification Number (PIN) to use when talking to the IRS. ☐☐☐☐☐

☐ No.

Part 5: Sign here. You MUST complete both pages of Form 941 and SIGN it.

Under penalties of perjury, I declare that I have examined this return, including accompanying schedules and statements, and to the best of my knowledge and belief, it is true, correct, and complete. Declaration of preparer (other than taxpayer) is based on all information of which preparer has any knowledge.

X Sign your name here ________

Print your name here ________

Print your title here ________

Date ____ / / ____

Best daytime phone ________

Paid Preparer Use Only

Check if you are self-employed . . . ☐

Preparer's name		PTIN	
Preparer's signature		Date	/ /
Firm's name (or yours if self-employed)		EIN	
Address		Phone	
City	State	ZIP code	

Source: Internal Revenue Service

EDD Employment Development Department State of California

QUARTERLY CONTRIBUTION RETURN AND REPORT OF WAGES

REMINDER: File your DE 9 and DE 9C together.

PLEASE TYPE THIS FORM—DO NOT ALTER PREPRINTED INFORMATION

00090112

YR QTR

QUARTER ENDED

DUE

DELINQUENT IF NOT POSTMARKED OR RECEIVED BY

EMPLOYER ACCOUNT NO.

DEPT. USE ONLY

DO NOT ALTER THIS AREA

P1 P2 C P U S A

T

EFFECTIVE DATE Mo. Day Yr.

FEIN

ADDITIONAL FEINS

A. NO WAGES PAID THIS QUARTER ☐

B. OUT OF BUSINESS/NO EMPLOYEES ☐

B1. OUT OF BUSINESS DATE M M D D Y Y Y Y

C. TOTAL SUBJECT WAGES PAID THIS QUARTER ....

D. UNEMPLOYMENT INSURANCE (UI) (Total Employee Wages up to $ per employee per calendar year)

(D1) UI Rate % TIMES (D2) UI TAXABLE WAGES FOR THE QUARTER = (D3) UI CONTRIBUTIONS

E. EMPLOYMENT TRAINING TAX (ETT)

(E1) ETT Rate % TIMES UI Taxable Wages for the Quarter (D2) ...... = (E2) ETT CONTRIBUTIONS

F. STATE DISABILITY INSURANCE (SDI) (Total Employee Wages up to $ per employee per calendar year)

(F1) SDI Rate % TIMES (F2) SDI TAXABLE WAGES FOR THE QUARTER = (F3) SDI EMPLOYEE CONTRIBUTIONS WITHHELD

G. CALIFORNIA PERSONAL INCOME TAX (PIT) WITHHELD ....

H. **SUBTOTAL** (Add Items D3, E2, F3, and G) ....

I. LESS: CONTRIBUTIONS AND WITHHOLDINGS PAID FOR THE QUARTER ....
(**DO NOT** INCLUDE PENALTY AND INTEREST PAYMENTS)

J. TOTAL TAXES DUE OR OVERPAID (Item H minus Item I) ....

If amount due, prepare a *Payroll Tax Deposit* (DE 88), include the correct payment quarter, and mail to: Employment Development Department, P.O. Box 826276, Sacramento, CA 94230-6276. **NOTE:** Do not mail payments along with the DE 9 and *Quarterly Contribution Return and Report of Wages (Continuation)* (DE 9C), as this may delay processing and result in erroneous penalty and interest charges. **Mandatory Electronic Funds Transfer (EFT)** filers must remit all SDI/PIT deposits by EFT to avoid a noncompliance penalty.

K. I declare that the above, to the best of my knowledge and belief, is true and correct. If a refund was claimed, a reasonable effort was made to refund any erroneous deductions to the affected employee(s).

Signature *Required* ______ Title ______ (Owner, Accountant, Preparer, etc.) Phone (____) ______ Date ______

SIGN AND MAIL TO: State of California / Employment Development Department / P.O. Box 989071 / West Sacramento CA 95798-9071

DE 9 Rev. 1 (1-12) **(INTERNET)**

Page 1 of 2

e-Services Fast, Easy, and Convenient! Visit EDD's Web site at **www.edd.ca.gov**

Source: Internal Revenue Service

Form **940 for 2018: Employer's Annual Federal Unemployment (FUTA) Tax Return** 850113

Department of the Treasury — Internal Revenue Service

OMB No. 1545-0028

Employer identification number (EIN) ☐☐ – ☐☐☐☐☐☐☐

Name *(not your trade name)*

Trade name *(if any)*

Address

Number Street Suite or room number

City State ZIP code

Foreign country name Foreign province/county Foreign postal code

Type of Return
(Check all that apply.)

☐ **a.** Amended

☐ **b.** Successor employer

☐ **c.** No payments to employees in 2018

☐ **d.** Final: Business closed or stopped paying wages

Go to *www.irs.gov/Form940* for instructions and the latest information.

Read the separate instructions before you complete this form. Please type or print within the boxes.

Part 1: Tell us about your return. If any line does NOT apply, leave it blank. See instructions before completing Part 1.

1a If you had to pay state unemployment tax in one state only, enter the state abbreviation . 1a ☐☐

1b If you had to pay state unemployment tax in more than one state, you are a multi-state employer . . . . 1b ☐ Check here. Complete Schedule A (Form 940).

2 If you paid wages in a state that is subject to CREDIT REDUCTION . . . . 2 ☐ Check here. Complete Schedule A (Form 940).

Part 2: Determine your FUTA tax before adjustments. If any line does NOT apply, leave it blank.

3 Total payments to all employees . . . . 3 ______ .

4 Payments exempt from FUTA tax . . . . 4 ______ .

Check all that apply: **4a** ☐ Fringe benefits **4c** ☐ Retirement/Pension **4e** ☐ Other

4b ☐ Group-term life insurance **4d** ☐ Dependent care

5 Total of payments made to each employee in excess of $7,000 . . . . 5 ______ .

6 Subtotal (line 4 + line 5 = line 6) . . . . 6 ______ .

7 Total taxable FUTA wages (line 3 – line 6 = line 7). See instructions . . . . 7 ______ .

8 FUTA tax before adjustments (line 7 x 0.006 = line 8) . . . . 8 ______ .

Part 3: Determine your adjustments. If any line does NOT apply, leave it blank.

9 If ALL of the taxable FUTA wages you paid were excluded from state unemployment tax, multiply line 7 by 0.054 (line 7 × 0.054 = line 9). Go to line 12 . . . . 9 ______ .

10 If SOME of the taxable FUTA wages you paid were excluded from state unemployment tax, OR you paid ANY state unemployment tax late (after the due date for filing Form 940), complete the worksheet in the instructions. Enter the amount from line 7 of the worksheet . . 10 ______ .

11 If credit reduction applies, enter the total from Schedule A (Form 940) . . . . 11 ______ .

Part 4: Determine your FUTA tax and balance due or overpayment. If any line does NOT apply, leave it blank.

12 Total FUTA tax after adjustments (lines 8 + 9 + 10 + 11 = line 12) . . . . 12 ______ .

13 FUTA tax deposited for the year, including any overpayment applied from a prior year . 13 ______ .

14 Balance due. If line 12 is more than line 13, enter the excess on line 14.

- If line 14 is more than $500, you must deposit your tax.
- If line 14 is $500 or less, you may pay with this return. See instructions . . . . 14 ______ .

15 Overpayment. If line 13 is more than line 12, enter the excess on line 15 and check a box below 15 ______ .

► You **MUST** complete both pages of this form and **SIGN** it. Check one: ☐ Apply to next return. ☐ Send a refund.

Next ►

850212

Name *(not your trade name)* | **Employer identification number (EIN)**

Part 5: **Report your FUTA tax liability by quarter only if line 12 is more than $500. If not, go to Part 6.**

16 **Report the amount of your FUTA tax liability for each quarter; do NOT enter the amount you deposited. If you had no liability for a quarter, leave the line blank.**

16a **1st quarter** (January 1 – March 31) . . . . **16a** .

16b **2nd quarter** (April 1 – June 30) . . . . **16b** .

16c **3rd quarter** (July 1 – September 30) . . . . **16c** .

16d **4th quarter** (October 1 – December 31) . . . . **16d** .

17 **Total tax liability for the year** (lines 16a + 16b + 16c + 16d = line 17) **17** . **Total must equal line 12.**

Part 6: **May we speak with your third-party designee?**

Do you want to allow an employee, a paid tax preparer, or another person to discuss this return with the IRS? See the instructions for details.

☐ **Yes.** Designee's name and phone number

Select a 5-digit Personal Identification Number (PIN) to use when talking to IRS

☐ **No.**

Part 7: **Sign here. You MUST complete both pages of this form and SIGN it.**

Under penalties of perjury, I declare that I have examined this return, including accompanying schedules and statements, and to the best of my knowledge and belief, it is true, correct, and complete, and that no part of any payment made to a state unemployment fund claimed as a credit was, or is to be, deducted from the payments made to employees. Declaration of preparer (other than taxpayer) is based on all information of which preparer has any knowledge.

✗ **Sign your name here**

Print your name here

Print your title here

Date / /

Best daytime phone

Paid Preparer Use Only

Check if you are self-employed ☐

Preparer's name

PTIN

Preparer's signature

Date / /

Firm's name (or yours if self-employed)

EIN

Address

Phone

City

State

ZIP code

Source: Internal Revenue Service

P6-10B. LO 6-3

Philip Castor, owner of Castor Corporation, is located at 1310 Garrick Way, Sun Valley, Arizona, 86029, phone number 928-555-8842. The federal EIN is 20-1948348, and the state employer identification number is 9040-2038-1. Prepare Form W-2 (below) for each of the following employees of Castor Corporation as of December 31, 2019. The same deductions are allowed for state income tax as for federal.

Employee	Payroll information
Paul M. Parsons 5834 Moon Drive Sun Valley, AZ 86029 SSN: 578-33-3049	Total 2019 wages: $47,203.78 401(k) contribution: $2,832.23 Section 125 contribution: $1,400.00 Federal income tax withheld: $5,664.45 Social Security tax withheld: $2,839.83 Medicare tax withheld: $664.15 State income tax withheld: $1,443.84
Rachel Y. Maddox 32 Second Street Holbrook, AZ 86025 SSN: 734-00-1938 Tuition in excess of $5,250: $750 (Include in boxes 1, 3, 5, 16)	Total 2019 wages: $37,499.02 401(k) contribution: $1,124.97 Section 125 contribution: $500.00 Federal income tax withheld: $4,409.88 Social Security tax withheld: $2,340.44 Medicare tax withheld: $547.36 State income tax withheld: $1,180.92
Ari J. Featherstone 7784 Painted Desert Road Sun Valley, AZ 86029 SSN: 290-03-4992	Total 2019 wages: $41,904.29 401(k) contribution: $1,885.69 Federal income tax withheld: $5,028.52 Social Security tax withheld: $2,598.07 Medicare tax withheld: $607.61 State income tax withheld: $1,344.63
Connor L. Clearwater 7384 Ridge Road Woodruff, AZ 85942 SSN: 994-20-4837	Total 2019 wages: $29,874.37 401(k) contribution: $597.49 Section 125 contribution: $250.00 Federal income tax withheld: $3,584.92 Social Security tax withheld: $1,836.71 Medicare tax withheld: $429.55 State income tax withheld: $975.30
Tieya L. Millen 229 Second Street #4A Holbrook, AZ 86025 SSN: 477-30-2234	Total 2019 wages: $15,889.04 Federal income tax withheld: $1,906.69 Social Security tax withheld: $985.12 Medicare tax withheld: $230.39 State income tax withheld: $533.87

22222	a Employee's social security number	OMB No. 1545-0008	
b Employer identification number (EIN)		1 Wages, tips, other compensation	2 Federal income tax withheld
c Employer's name, address, and ZIP code		3 Social security wages	4 Social security tax withheld
		5 Medicare wages and tips	6 Medicare tax withheld
		7 Social security tips	8 Allocated tips
d Control number		9	10 Dependent care benefits
e Employee's first name and initial Last name Suff.		11 Nonqualified plans	12a Code
		13 Statutory employee ☐ Retirement plan ☐ Third-party sick pay ☐	12b Code
		14 Other	12c Code
f Employee's address and ZIP code			12d Code

15 State Employer's state ID number	16 State wages, tips, etc.	17 State income tax	18 Local wages, tips, etc.	19 Local income tax	20 Locality name

Form **W-2** **Wage and Tax Statement** 2019 Department of the Treasury—Internal Revenue Service

Copy 1—For State, City, or Local Tax Department

(Source: Internal Revenue Service)

DO NOT STAPLE

33333	a Control number	For Official Use Only ▶ OMB No. 1545-0008	
b Kind of Payer (Check one) ▶ 941 ☐ Military ☐ 943 ☐ 944 ☐ CT-1 ☐ Hshld. emp. ☐ Medicare govt. emp. ☐		Kind of Employer (Check one) ▶ None apply ☐ 501c non-govt. ☐ State/local non-501c ☐ State/local 501c ☐ Federal govt. ☐	Third-party sick pay (Check if applicable) ☐
c Total number of Forms W-2	d Establishment number	1 Wages, tips, other compensation	2 Federal income tax withheld
e Employer identification number (EIN)		3 Social security wages	4 Social security tax withheld
f Employer's name		5 Medicare wages and tips	6 Medicare tax withheld
		7 Social security tips	8 Allocated tips
		9	10 Dependent care benefits
g Employer's address and ZIP code		11 Nonqualified plans	12a Deferred compensation
h Other EIN used this year		13 For third-party sick pay use only	12b
15 State Employer's state ID number		14 Income tax withheld by payer of third-party sick pay	
16 State wages, tips, etc.	17 State income tax	18 Local wages, tips, etc.	19 Local income tax
Employer's contact person		Employer's telephone number	For Official Use Only
Employer's fax number		Employer's email address	

Under penalties of perjury, I declare that I have examined this return and accompanying documents, and, to the best of my knowledge and belief, they are true, correct, and complete.

Signature ▶ Title ▶ Date ▶

Form **W-3 Transmittal of Wage and Tax Statements** 2019 Department of the Treasury Internal Revenue Service

Source: Internal Revenue Service

P6-11B. LO 6-3 Using the information from P6-10B for Castor Corporation, complete Form W3 (above) that must accompany the company's Form W2s. Castor Corporation is a 941-SS payer and is a private, for-profit company. No third-party sick pay was applied for 2019. The W-3 was signed and submitted January 12, 2020.

P6-12B. LO 6-5, 6-6 Cloudy Night Signs is a company that makes custom signs and has 12 employees. The owner wants to perform a benefits analysis report for the year for one of its employees, Howard Nelson. Howard's benefits package is as follows:

Annual Salary: $38,950

401(k) contribution: 5 percent of annual salary, company match is half of employee's contribution up to 6 percent

Medical insurance deduction: $140 per month

Dental insurance: $36 per month

Complete the following Benefits Analysis Report for Howard Nelson for the year.

Yearly Benefit Costs	Company Cost	Howard's Cost
Medical insurance	$9,600	$
Dental insurance	800	$
Life insurance	1,200	-0-
AD&D	125	-0-
Short-term disability	500	-0-
Long-term disability	250	-0-
401(k)	$	$
Social Security	$	$
Medicare	$	$
Tuition reimbursement	5,000	-0-
Total yearly benefit costs	$	
Howard's annual salary	$	
Total yearly benefit costs	$	
Total value of Howard's compensation	$	

P6-13B. LO 6-4, 6-5

Happy Panda Fashions has 52 employees distributed among the following departments:

Sales: 14	Factory: 26	Administration: 12

The total annual payroll for Happy Panda Fashions is $1,280,550. Compute the labor distribution based on equal distribution among the departments.

Sales: ______________

Factory: ______________

Administration: ______________

P6-14B. LO 6-4, 6-5

For Happy Panda Fashions in P6-13B, compute the labor distribution based on the number of employees per department:

Sales:

Factory:

Administration:

P6-15B. LO 6-1, 6-4

At Fox Furniture, employees are classified according to job title for workers' compensation insurance premium computation purposes.

a. Based on the following payroll estimates as of January 1, what is the estimated workers' compensation insurance premium for the year 20XX?

Employee Classification	Rate per $100 of Payroll	Estimated Payroll for 20XX	Workers' Compensation Premium
Sales Associate	$0.55	$213,680	
Loader	2.15	155,240	
Furniture Builder	2.95	102,590	
		Total Premium =	

b. The actual payroll for 20XX is listed below. What is the workers' compensation premium based on the actual payroll?

Employee Classification	Rate per $100 of Payroll	Actual Payroll for 20XX	Workers' Compensation Premium
Sales Associate	$0.55	$228,944	
Loader	2.15	163,743	
Furniture Builder	2.95	105,389	
		Total Premium =	

c. What is the difference between the actual and the estimated premiums?

____

Critical Thinking

6-1. Burton Book Memorabilia is a semiweekly depositor. Following the success of a special project, Kelly Burton, the owner, pays each of the 250 employees a $20,000 bonus on August 16, 2019. Assuming a 25 percent income tax rate, when will Kelly need to deposit the payroll taxes?

6-2. Claude Lopez is the president of Zebra Antiques. His employee, Dwight Francis, is due a raise. Dwight's current benefit analysis is as follows:

Yearly Benefit Costs	Company Cost (Current)	Employee Cost (Current)
Medical insurance	$ 8,000	$ 1,200
Dental insurance	120	120
Life insurance	300	-0-
AD&D	50	-0-
Short-term disability	60	-0-
Long-term disability	30	-0-
401(k)	750	1,500
Social Security	3,018.16	3,018.16
Medicare	705.86	705.86
Tuition reimbursement	2,000	-0-
Total yearly benefit costs (employer)	15,134.02	
Employee's annual salary	50,000	
Total value of employee's compensation	65,134.02	

Compute the benefit analysis assuming:

- 7 percent increase in pay.
- 3 percent contribution to 401(k) will remain the same with a company match of 50 percent.
- 10 percent increase in medical and dental insurance premiums.

Yearly Benefit Costs	Company Cost (New)	Employee Cost (New)
Medical insurance	$	$
Dental insurance	$	$
Life insurance	$	-0-
AD&D	$	-0-
Short-term disability	$	-0-
Long-term disability	$	-0-
401(k)	$	$
Social Security	$	$
Medicare	$	$
Tuition reimbursement	$	-0-
Total yearly benefit costs (employer)	$	
Dwight's annual salary	$	
Total value of employee's compensation	$	

In the Real World: Scenario for Discussion

In Shavertown, Pennsylvania, the owner of Wilkes-Barre Bookkeeping LLC was indicted for embezzling over $375,000 of his clients' payroll tax remittances between 2010 and 2016 and for lying to clients about his actions. Additionally, he embezzled nearly $70,000 from a nonprofit for which he was the treasurer. He was sentenced to 38 months in prison and ordered to pay restitution totaling nearly $500,000. Do you think this was a fair sentence? Why or why not?

Internet Activities

6-1. Would you like to know more about the Employment Cost Index? Check out the videos from the Bureau of Labor Statistics: www.bls.gov/eci/videos.htm

6-2. Go to www.bizfilings.com/toolkit/sbg/tax-info/payroll-taxes/unemployment.aspx and check out the unemployment tax laws for your state.

6-3. Want to know more about the concepts in this chapter? Go to one or more of the following sites. What are two or three things you notice about the information on the site?

 www.smallbusiness.chron.com/example-employee-compensation-plan-10068.html

 http://yourbusiness.azcentral.com/labor-cost-distribution-report-26061.html

 www.irs.gov/publications/p80/ar02.html

6-4. Check out the employer payroll tax estimation tool at https://gusto.com/tools/employer-tax-calculator

6-5. Would you like to explore specific topics about being an employer in more depth? Check out https://www.employer.gov/

Continuing Payroll Project: Prevosti Farms and Sugarhouse

The first quarter tax return needs to be filed for Prevosti Farms and Sugarhouse by April 15, 2019. For the purpose of the taxes, assume the second February payroll amounts were duplicated for the March 9 and March 23 payroll periods and the new benefit elections went into effect as planned (see Chapter 4). The form was completed and signed on April 10, 2019.

Benefit Information	Exclude: Federal	FICA
Health Insurance	Yes	Yes
Life Insurance	Yes	Yes
Long-term care	Yes	Yes
FSA	Yes	Yes
401(k)	Yes	No
Gym	No	No

Number of employees	8
Gross quarterly wages	$32,085.15
Federal income tax withheld	628.00
401(k) contributions	1,259.90
Insurance withheld	4,080.00
Gym membership	90.00
Month 1	-0-
Month 2	2,008.18
Month 3	2,904.72

Complete Form 941 for Prevosti Farms and Sugarhouse. Prevosti Farms and Sugarhouse was assigned EIN 22-6654454.

950117

Form **941 for 2019: Employer's QUARTERLY Federal Tax Return**
(Rev. January 2019) Department of the Treasury — Internal Revenue Service
OMB No. 1545-0029

Employer identification number (EIN) [ ][ ] – [ ][ ][ ][ ][ ][ ][ ]

Name *(not your trade name)*

Trade name *(if any)*

Address
Number Street Suite or room number
City State ZIP code
Foreign country name Foreign province/county Foreign postal code

Report for this Quarter of 2019
(Check one.)

☐ **1:** January, February, March
☐ **2:** April, May, June
☐ **3:** July, August, September
☐ **4:** October, November, December

Go to *www.irs.gov/Form941* for instructions and the latest information.

Read the separate instructions before you complete Form 941. Type or print within the boxes.

Part 1: Answer these questions for this quarter.

1	**Number of employees who received wages, tips, or other compensation for the pay period including:** ***Mar. 12*** **(Quarter 1),** ***June 12*** **(Quarter 2),** ***Sept. 12*** **(Quarter 3), or** ***Dec. 12*** **(Quarter 4)**	1	
2	**Wages, tips, and other compensation**	2	.
3	**Federal income tax withheld from wages, tips, and other compensation**	3	.
4	**If no wages, tips, and other compensation are subject to social security or Medicare tax**	☐	**Check and go to line 6.**

		Column 1		Column 2
5a	**Taxable social security wages**	.	× 0.124 =	.
5b	**Taxable social security tips**	.	× 0.124 =	.
5c	**Taxable Medicare wages & tips**	.	× 0.029 =	.
5d	**Taxable wages & tips subject to Additional Medicare Tax withholding**	.	× 0.009 =	.

5e	**Add Column 2 from lines 5a, 5b, 5c, and 5d**	5e	.
5f	**Section 3121(q) Notice and Demand—Tax due on unreported tips** (see instructions)	5f	.
6	**Total taxes before adjustments.** Add lines 3, 5e, and 5f	6	.
7	**Current quarter's adjustment for fractions of cents**	7	.
8	**Current quarter's adjustment for sick pay**	8	.
9	**Current quarter's adjustments for tips and group-term life insurance**	9	.
10	**Total taxes after adjustments.** Combine lines 6 through 9	10	.
11	**Qualified small business payroll tax credit for increasing research activities.** Attach Form 8974	11	.
12	**Total taxes after adjustments and credits.** Subtract line 11 from line 10	12	.
13	**Total deposits for this quarter, including overpayment applied from a prior quarter and overpayments applied from Form 941-X, 941-X (PR), 944-X, or 944-X (SP) filed in the current quarter**	13	.
14	**Balance due.** If line 12 is more than line 13, enter the difference and see instructions	14	.

15 **Overpayment.** If line 13 is more than line 12, enter the difference [.] Check one: ☐ Apply to next return. ☐ Send a refund.

▶ **You MUST complete both pages of Form 941 and SIGN it.** Next ▶

For Privacy Act and Paperwork Reduction Act Notice, see the back of the Payment Voucher. Cat. No. 17001Z Form **941** (Rev. 1-2019)

950217

Name *(not your trade name)* | **Employer identification number (EIN)**

Part 2: Tell us about your deposit schedule and tax liability for this quarter.

If you are unsure about whether you are a monthly schedule depositor or a semiweekly schedule depositor, see section 11 of Pub. 15.

16 Check one: ☐ **Line 12 on this return is less than $2,500 or line 12 on the return for the prior quarter was less than $2,500, and you didn't incur a $100,000 next-day deposit obligation during the current quarter.** If line 12 for the prior quarter was less than $2,500 but line 12 on this return is $100,000 or more, you must provide a record of your federal tax liability. If you are a monthly schedule depositor, complete the deposit schedule below; if you are a semiweekly schedule depositor, attach Schedule B (Form 941). Go to Part 3.

☐ **You were a monthly schedule depositor for the entire quarter.** Enter your tax liability for each month and total liability for the quarter, then go to Part 3.

Tax liability: Month 1 ______ .

Month 2 ______ .

Month 3 ______ .

Total liability for quarter ______ . **Total must equal line 12.**

☐ **You were a semiweekly schedule depositor for any part of this quarter.** Complete Schedule B (Form 941), Report of Tax Liability for Semiweekly Schedule Depositors, and attach it to Form 941.

Part 3: Tell us about your business. If a question does NOT apply to your business, leave it blank.

17 If your business has closed or you stopped paying wages . . . . ☐ Check here, and

enter the final date you paid wages ___ / ___ / ___ .

18 If you are a seasonal employer and you don't have to file a return for every quarter of the year . . ☐ Check here.

Part 4: May we speak with your third-party designee?

Do you want to allow an employee, a paid tax preparer, or another person to discuss this return with the IRS? See the instructions for details.

☐ Yes. Designee's name and phone number ______ ______

Select a 5-digit Personal Identification Number (PIN) to use when talking to the IRS. ☐☐☐☐☐

☐ No.

Part 5: Sign here. You MUST complete both pages of Form 941 and SIGN it.

Under penalties of perjury, I declare that I have examined this return, including accompanying schedules and statements, and to the best of my knowledge and belief, it is true, correct, and complete. Declaration of preparer (other than taxpayer) is based on all information of which preparer has any knowledge.

X **Sign your name here** ______

Print your name here ______

Print your title here ______

Date ___ / ___ / ___

Best daytime phone ______

Paid Preparer Use Only

Check if you are self-employed . . . ☐

Preparer's name		PTIN	
Preparer's signature		Date	/ /
Firm's name (or yours if self-employed)		EIN	
Address		Phone	
City	State	ZIP code	

Source: Internal Revenue Service

Answers to Stop & Check Exercises

FUTA, SUTA, and Workers' Compensation

1.

FUTA: $7,000 × 29 × 0.006 =	$ 1,218.00
$2,575 × 0.006 =	15.45
FUTA liability	$ 1,233.45
SUTA: $24,800 × 25 × 0.042 =	$26,040.00
$60,090 × 0.042 =	2,523.78
(under the cap: 15,800 + 7,800 + 11,115 + 22,800 + 2,575)	
SUTA liability	$28,563.78
Total combined FUTA/SUTA liability	$29,787.23

2.

FUTA: $7,000 × 10 × 0.006 =	$ 420.00
($5,500 + 6,800) × 0.006 =	73.80
Total FUTA liability	$ 493.80
SUTA: $12,000 × 8 × 0.0326 =	$ 3,129.60
$33,250 × 0.0326 =	$ 1,083.95
(under the cap: 5,500 + 6,800 + 11,100 + 9,850)	
Total SUTA liability	$ 4,213.55
Competitive Skills Scholarship tax liability: $279,580 × 0.0006 =	$ 167.75

3.

Job Classification	Premium per $100 of Payroll	Estimated Payroll	Premium Due
Clerical Workers	$0.45	$104,550	$ 470.48
Jump Instructors	3.75	215,690	8,088.38
			$8,558.86

Reporting Periods

1. Monthly.
2. July 15.
3. Monday, the next business day.

Tax Forms

1. $2,414.48.
2. $105,000 (15 employees × $7,000).
3. $630.00 ($105,000 (from problem 2) × 0.006 FUTA rate).
4. $116,195.

Payroll-Related Business Expenses

1. Failure to file and failure to deposit penalties.
2. Payroll expenses relate to the company's profitability, worker productivity analyses, employee retention, and business competitiveness.

Labor Distribution Report

1. a. $300,000/10 employees = $30,000 per employee; Office, $90,000; agricultural, $150,000; drivers, $60,000.
   b. Each department would be allocated $100,000 of the payroll.
2. Department classification is the most appropriate because it matches the costs more closely to each department.

Benefit Analysis Report

1. One of the purposes of compiling a benefit analysis report is to represent graphically all of the variables that make up an employee's compensation package. The benefit analysis report provides managers and supervisors a budgetary tool to understand the full cost of hiring or dismissing employees. Additionally, the benefit analysis allows companies to compare benefits and employee costs to geographic or industry standards.
2. The benefit analysis report is an internal report for the company's management, and the annual total compensation report is meant to be distributed to the employee.

7

Chapter Seven

The Payroll Register, Employees' Earnings Records, and Accounting System Entries

In this chapter, we will integrate the payroll register with the employees' earnings records and financial statements. In previous chapters, we have examined the effects of payroll on employees, employers, and governmental agencies. This chapter links ***Generally Accepted Accounting Principles (GAAP)*** with payroll elements we have explored in Chapters 1–6. We will discuss the debits and credits associated with payroll accrual and payment. For this chapter, we will use the accrual basis of accounting, which means that transactions are recognized at the time that they are incurred.

Accounting entries are the transactions that place the payroll amounts into the correct ledger accounts. In automated systems, the software is designed to code each payroll item automatically to the correct General Ledger account. However, for the payroll accountant to record accurate expenses and period-end accruals in the correct month, manual entries are necessary. This is the final step of the payroll cycle for each pay period and is the most important piece of the process from an accounting perspective. The final piece of this chapter will include the examination of the ways that payroll costs affect a company's financial reports.

LEARNING OBJECTIVES

After studying Chapter 7, you should be able to:

LO 7-1 Connect the Payroll Register to the Employees' Earnings Records

LO 7-2 Describe Financial Accounting Concepts

Michael Shake/Shutterstock

LO 7-3 Complete Payroll-Related General Journal Entries

LO 7-4 Generate Payroll-Related General Ledger Entries

LO 7-5 Describe Payroll Effects on the Accounting System

LO 7-6 Explain Payroll Entries in Accounting Reports

Large Financial Accounting Fraud in a Small Town

In the small town of Dixon, Illinois, Rita Crundwell was the town's comptroller from 1983 until 2012. During her tenure in town administration, the town had experienced financial shortfalls, and review of the financial statements never revealed anything wrong. However, one day Ms. Crundwell was away from the office and one of her assistants needed the current bank statements to complete a required report. Ms. Crundwell usually handled the bank statements, but the task fell to her assistant in this instance. After contacting the bank, the statements arrived and the assistant noticed an extra bank account that had never been reported previously.

During her time in Dixon, Ms. Crundwell had built a large horse-breeding business that was well known for its high-quality show horses and for the lavish lifestyle that Ms. Crundwell enjoyed. The problem was that Ms. Crundwell's annual town salary of approximately $80,000 could not have supported her lifestyle. Once the bank statements were analyzed, the FBI started examining Ms. Crundwell's finances more closely and noticed that she had been siphoning money, approximately $53 million in total, out of the town's coffers. After being found guilty of wire fraud, Ms. Crundwell was sentenced to 19.5 years in prison in 2013. Inspection of the town's financial accounting records was the key to recouping the money that had been stolen.

(Source: Fraud Magazine, *All the Queen's Horses*)

Payroll-related accounting entries are often investigated during company audits. Accurate reporting of payroll costs in the financial statement is a key part of GAAP compliance and decision making. In Chapter 7, we will examine the accounting system entries for payroll costs, then the effect on the company's financial reports, and finally how those reports influence managerial decisions.

LO 7-1 Connect the Payroll Register to the Employees' Earnings Records

Ingram Publishing/SuperStock

In previous chapters, we have completed the payroll register, which is the primary tool used to compute payroll amounts. The payroll register has a related set of documents called the employee earnings records. The employees' earnings records form the link between the accounting and the human resource departments. The information contained within each row of the payroll register is transferred to the employees' earnings records. Additionally, information from the payroll register is used to complete payroll entries in the General Journal.

Employee earnings records form the link between the accounting and the human resource departments and connect closely with the payroll register. The information contained within each row of the payroll register is transferred to the employee's earnings record, an example of which is shown in Figure 7-1.

FIGURE 7-1
Employee Earnings Record

EMPLOYEE EARNING RECORD

NAME		Hire Date	
ADDRESS		Date of Birth	
CITY/STATE/ZIP		Exempt/Nonexempt	
TELEPHONE		Married/Single	
SOCIAL SECURITY NUMBER		No. of Exemptions	
POSITION		Pay Rate	

Period Ended	Hrs Worked	Reg Pay	OT Pay	Holiday	Comm	Gross Pay	Ins	401(k)	Taxable Pay for Federal W/H	Taxable Pay for FICA

Taxable Wages for Federal W/H	Taxable Wages for FICA	Fed W/H	Social Sec. Tax	Medicare Tax	State W/H	Total Deduc	Net Pay	YTD Net Pay	YTD Sec. Tax

The employee earnings record is the master document accountants use to track employees' marital status, deductions (mandatory, voluntary, and mandated), and year-to-date earnings. Remember that Social Security, FUTA, and SUTA taxes have annual earnings limits for each employee. Accountants update the employees' earnings records during each pay period to track all pay and tax deductions. Any employee changes, including pay rate, marital status, and number of withholding allowances, should be annotated in the earnings records as soon as possible to ensure the accuracy of the payroll.

EXAMPLE: EMPLOYEE EARNINGS RECORD, INDIVIDUAL EMPLOYEE

Using the example of Stanley Nobles at Cornerstone Graniteworks, we will enter his data into his employee earnings record.

EMPLOYEE EARNING RECORD

NAME	Stanley Nobles	Hire Date	4/22/2019
ADDRESS	2845 Arapahoe Boulevard	Date of Birth	7/15/1988
CITY/STATE/ZIP	Boulder, CO 80305	Exempt/Nonexempt	Nonexempt
TELEPHONE	303-555-1034	Married/Single	Single
SOCIAL SECURITY NUMBER	204-33-5439	No. of Exemptions	1
POSITION	Granite Tech III	Pay Rate	$22.00/hour

Period Ended	Hours Worked	Reg Pay	OT Pay	Holiday	Comm	Gross Pay	Ins	Cafeteria	Taxable Wages for Federal W/H	Taxable Wages for FICA
9/30/xx	88	1,760.00	264.00			2,024.00	100.00	25.00	1,899.00	1,924.00

Taxable Wages for Federal W/H	Taxable Wages for FICA	Fed W/H	Social Sec. Tax	Medicare Tax	State W/H	Union Dues	Total Deduc	Net pay	YTD Net Pay	YTD Gross Pay
1,899.00	1,924.00	180.00	119.29	27.90	87.92	75.00	615.11	1,408.89	24,118.03	36,432.00

Note how the following employee information is reflected in the employee earnings record:

- Address.
- Telephone number.
- Social Security number.
- Full-time status.
- Marital status.
- Pay basis (i.e., hourly).
- Hire date.
- Birth date.
- Position.
- Pay rate.
- Pay period date.

(continued)

(concluded)

- Year-to-date net pay.
- Year-to-date gross pay.

These items are common to most employee earnings records because of the connection between payroll and human resources. The information contained in the employee earnings record is used as the basis for the employee's Form W-2 as well as other company tax and benefits reporting.

The Employees' Earnings Records and Periodic Tax Reports

Period totals are also included on the earnings record. These totals facilitate the preparation of the quarterly and annual reports. Like any payroll record, the earnings records should be retained and destroyed at the same interval as other accounting records. Earnings records are typically included as supporting documents for internal copies of quarterly filings of Form 941 as well as state and local tax returns (where applicable). During a payroll audit, the documentation attached to the tax returns provides verification of the information contained in the reports. A secondary use is that, in the event of computer data failure, documents attached to payroll records can be used to re-create files.

An audit of the accounting records for the city of Oakdale, Louisiana, and the Allen Parish Office found that the payroll withholdings were not remitted to governmental authorities and that accounting reports were not filed for 2016. The Ward Marshal's office claimed that it did not have enough money to pay the delinquent taxes and lacked the personnel to complete the required reports. The recommendation from the auditor was to employ a person who understood Generally Accepted Accounting Principles. (Source: *American Press*)

Employees' Earnings Register

Stop & Check

1. How do the employees' earnings records relate to the payroll register?
2. Which of the following fields exist on both the payroll register and the employees' earnings records?
   a. Name
   b. Pay rate
   c. Job title
   d. Net pay
   e. Address
3. What reports and forms use information from the employees' earnings records?

LO 7-2 Describe Financial Accounting Concepts

Now that we have explored the principles of computing and reporting payroll data, it is time to connect the information to financial accounting concepts. In financial accounting, the fundamental accounting equation is **Assets = Liabilities + Owners' Equity.**

EXAMPLE: FINANCIAL ACCOUNTING CATEGORIES

Assets: Cash or other items that are used in the operation of the business and amounts owed to the business by customers.

Liabilities: Amounts owed by the business to other people or companies.

Owners' equity: The net investment that the owner has in the business, including earnings kept in the business.

Warakorn Harnprasop/123RF

Financial business transactions, such as the movement of cash used in paying employees and remitting amounts to third parties, are tracked using the accounting system. A fundamental concept in accounting involves the accounting equation, which must remain in balance at all times. As such, transactions will either increase an account (or multiple accounts), decrease an account (or multiple accounts), or a combination thereof. To understand the concept of equation balance, T-accounts are the first step in understanding the classification process that is part of transaction analysis.

EXAMPLE: TRANSACTION ANALYSIS USING T-ACCOUNTS

Barry Larson, the owner of Riptide Sails, paid an independent contractor $4,000 for work done during the course of business on August 1, 2019. Accountants classify the transaction into two accounts: assets and owners' equity. The cash account would decrease because the money was paid from the business. Barry's expenses would increase because he paid a contractor, which appears as an expense of the company and decreases the amount of equity Barry has in the business. Using the T-account approach, the transaction would look like this:

Contractor Expense	
Dr.	Cr.
4,000	

Cash	
Dr.	Cr.
	4,000

Debits and Credits

If accountants were to maintain T-accounts for all of a business's transactions, their work would be tedious and vulnerable to a large number of errors. To simplify the addition and subtraction involved, accountants use the terms *debit* (abbreviated Dr.) and *credit* (abbreviated Cr.) to explain the transaction. In accounting parlance, ***debit*** simply means "the left side of the T-account," and ***credit*** simply means "the right side of the T-account." No connotation exists about good or bad with the use of these terms in accounting.

EXAMPLE: DEBIT AND CREDIT RULES

Debits Increase:	Credits Increase:
Expenses	Liabilities
Assets	Equity (Capital)
Dividends	Revenue

The General Journal

To simplify the use of T-accounts, accountants use a journal (called the ***General Journal***) to record the daily financial transactions. The General Journal is maintained in chronological order. The General Journal is essentially one big T-account, has columns to record the debits and credits involved in each transaction, and contains a chronologically ordered list of transactions. Complementing the General Journal is the ***General Ledger***, in which all journal transactions are recorded chronologically in their specific accounts.

In the transaction above, the transaction would appear in the General Journal as follows:

EXAMPLE: TRANSACTION IN THE GENERAL JOURNAL

Trans.	Date	Account Name & Description	Post Ref	Debit	Credit
1	8/1/2019	Contractor Expense	501	4,000.00	
		Cash	101		4,000.00
		Paid Contractor			

Note certain accounting conventions present in the journal entry:

- The date of the transaction is noted.
- The debit part of the transaction is on the first line and is flush left in the column.
- The credit part of the transaction is on the second line and is indented slightly.
- A brief description of the transaction is on line three.
- Account numbers are annotated in the Post Reference (Post Ref) column.
- The post reference in the General Journal is the General Ledger account number.

The General Ledger

Once the transaction has been recorded in the General Journal, the accountant posts the entry to corresponding General Ledger accounts. In the following table, note that (1) the transaction itself is listed, and (2) the balance of each account is adjusted accordingly.

EXAMPLE: GENERAL LEDGER POSTING

			Account: 101 – Cash		
Date	Description	Post Ref.	Debit	Credit	Balance
8/1/2019	Paid Contractor	J1		4,000.00	4,000.00
			Account: 501 – Contractor Expense		
Date	Description	Post Ref.	Debit	Credit	Balance
8/1/2019	Paid Contractor	J1	4,000.00		4,000.00

The General Ledger account balances are used to generate the payroll reports that we have been discussing so far. The elements of the General Ledger and specific posting practices will appear later in this chapter.

Despite the increase in the use of accounting software, the need for payroll accountants is growing in importance. Accountants are needed to monitor accuracy in recorded transactions and to adapt to industry changes, especially the integration of technology and the growing use of artificial intelligence. Payroll accountants are particularly in demand because of the specific skills involved in and increasing complexity of payroll accounting. (Source: *Bloomberg BNA, In the Black*)

Stop & Check

Financial Accounting Concepts

1. What is the fundamental accounting equation?
2. What increases the Wages and Salaries Payable account: a debit or a credit?
3. What increases the Wages and Salaries Expense account: a debit or a credit?

Jetta Productions/Blend Images LLC

LO 7-3 Complete Payroll-Related General Journal Entries

Recording the specific General Journal entries that correspond to payroll activities is the next step in the process. General Journal entries are the original entry point for events to be recorded within the accounting system. A sample period payroll for NC Bikes follows.

EXAMPLE: NC BIKES PAYROLL DATA

NC Bikes pays its employees biweekly and operates on a calendar fiscal year (i.e., the year-end is December 31). The payroll accountant for NC Bikes has completed the payroll register for the January 25, 2019, payroll. Paychecks will be issued on January 31. Payroll totals are as follows:

Gross pay: $18,050.00
Federal income tax withheld: $1,500.00
Social Security tax withheld: $1,084.38
Medicare tax withheld: $253.61
State income tax withheld: $577.60
401(k) contributions withheld: $750.00
Health insurance premiums withheld: $560.00
United Way contributions withheld: $180.00
Net pay: $13,144.41

The totals row of the payroll register would appear as follows:

Name	Gross Earnings	401(k) Contributions	Insurance	Federal W/H	Social Security Tax	Medicare Tax	State W/H	United Way	Net Pay	Check No.
Totals	$18,050.00	$750.00	$560.00	$1,500.00	$1,084.38	$253.61	$577.60	$180.00	$13,144.41	

The payroll register is the tool used by payroll accountants to create the pay-related journal entries. Here's how it works:

EXAMPLE: PAYROLL REGISTER TO GENERAL JOURNAL ENTRIES

Payroll Register Column	General Journal Account	NC Bikes Amount
Gross Earnings	Salaries and Wages Expense	$18,050.00
401(k) Contributions	401(k) Contributions Payable	750.00
Insurance	Health Insurance Premiums Payable	560.00
Federal W/H	FIT Payable	1,500.00
Social Security Tax	Social Security Tax Payable	1,084.38
Medicare Tax	Medicare Tax Payable	253.61
State W/H	State Income Tax Payable	577.60
United Way	United Way Contributions Payable	180.00
Net Pay	Salaries and Wages Payable	13,144.41

As the payroll data is transferred from the payroll register to the General Journal, notice the following accounting categories:

- Account names ending with the word "expense" are classified as Expense accounts (remember Debit increases).
- Account names ending with the word "payable" are classified as Liability accounts (remember Credit increases).

Employee Pay-Related Journal Entries

The General Journal entry to record the employee's portion of the payroll and the issuance of the checks to employees is in two parts:

EXAMPLE: NC BIKES GENERAL JOURNAL PAYROLL ENTRIES—EMPLOYEE PAYROLL TRANSACTION

Date	Description	Account	Debit	Credit
Jan. 25	Salaries and Wages Expense	511	$18,050.00	
	FIT Payable	221		$1,500.00
	Social Security Tax Payable	222		1,084.38
	Medicare Tax Payable	223		253.61
	State Income Tax Payable	224		577.60
	401(k) Contributions Payable	225		750.00
	Health Insurance Premiums Payable	226		560.00
	United Way Contributions Payable	227		180.00
	Salaries and Wages Payable	231		13,144.41
Jan. 31	Salaries and Wages Payable	231	13,144.41	
	Cash	101		13,144.41

Employer Payroll-Related Journal Entries

The employer's share of the payroll is similarly recorded. NC Bikes's share of the payroll expenses follows:

EXAMPLE: NC BIKES EMPLOYER PAYROLL TAX OBLIGATIONS DATA

Social Security tax: $1,084.38
Medicare tax: $253.61
FUTA tax: $104.94
SUTA tax: $974.70

The General Journal entry for the employer's share of the payroll taxes follows:

EXAMPLE: NC BIKES GENERAL JOURNAL PAYROLL ENTRIES—EMPLOYER PAYROLL TAX TRANSACTION

Date	Description	Account	Debit	Credit
Jan. 25	Payroll Taxes Expense	512	$2,417.63	
	Social Security Tax Payable	222		$1,084.38
	Medicare Tax Payable	223		253.61
	FUTA Tax Payable	228		104.94
	SUTA Tax Payable	229		974.70

Other Payroll-Related Journal Entries

What about the other deductions that NC Bikes withheld from its employees' pay? These other deductions, including federal and state income tax, 401(k) contributions, health insurance premiums, and United Way contributions, are liabilities of the company. These amounts will remain in the liability accounts until NC Bikes ***remits*** them, which means that the company sends the collected money to the appropriate entity. Upon remittance, the General Journal entries will appear as a debit (decrease) to the Liability account and a credit (decrease) to Cash. An example for the January 25 payroll's voluntary deductions, paid to the appropriate companies on January 31, follows:

EXAMPLE: NC BIKES GENERAL JOURNAL PAYROLL ENTRIES—VOLUNTARY DEDUCTIONS REMITTANCE

Date	Description	Account	Debit	Credit
Jan. 31	401(k) Contributions Payable	225	$750.00	
	Health Insurance Payable	226	560.00	
	United Way Contribution Payable	227	180.00	
	Cash	101		$1,490.00

Remember that the remittance for the governmental taxes has a specific schedule. The General Journal entry for the tax remittances would follow the same pattern as the voluntary deductions: debit the Liability account(s) and credit Cash.

Payroll Accruals and Reversals

A common occurrence is that a payroll may be split between two months, as will be the case for NC Bikes. For example, the majority of the pay for the end of February will be paid on the March 1, 2019, payday. For accounting purposes, the accountant needs to record the ***accrual*** of the payroll for February to represent accurately the ***expenses*** and liabilities incurred during the period. Some companies choose to record the period's expenses through ***adjusting entries*** and then reverse the entries after the start of the next period to prevent confusion in the payroll accounting process.

In the case of NC Bikes, the adjusting entry would appear as follows for the end of February:

EXAMPLE: NC BIKES ADJUSTING ENTRY—EMPLOYEE PAYROLL DATA

Gross pay: $16,245.00
Federal income tax withheld: $1,350.00
Social Security tax withheld: $1,007.19
Medicare tax withheld: $235.55
State income tax withheld: $519.84
Net pay: $13,132.42

The adjusting entry for February 28, 2019, would look like this:

EXAMPLE: NC BIKES GENERAL JOURNAL—EMPLOYEE DATA ADJUSTING ENTRIES

Date	Description	Account	Debit	Credit
Feb. 28	Salaries and Wages Expense	511	$16,245.00	
	FIT Payable	221		$1,350.00
	Social Security Tax Payable	222		1,007.19
	Medicare Tax Payable	223		235.55
	State Income Tax Payable	224		519.84
	Salaries and Wages Payable	231		13,132.42

The amount for the employer's share would be as follows:

EXAMPLE: NC BIKES GENERAL JOURNAL—EMPLOYER PAYROLL TAX DATA ADJUSTING ENTRIES

Date	Description	Account	Debit	Credit
Feb. 28	Payroll Taxes Expense	512	$2,217.17	
	Social Security Tax Payable	222		$1,007.19
	Medicare Tax Payable	223		235.55
	FUTA Tax Payable (16,245 × 0.006)	228		97.47
	SUTA Tax Payable (16,245 × .0.53983)	229		876.96

On March 1, 2019, the accountant could record a reversing entry as follows:

EXAMPLE: NC BIKES GENERAL JOURNAL—EMPLOYEE DATA REVERSING ENTRIES

Date	Description	Account	Debit	Credit
Mar. 1	FIT Payable	221	$1,350.00	
	Social Security Tax Payable	222	1,007.19	
	Medicare Tax Payable	223	235.55	
	State Income Tax Payable	224	519.84	
	Salaries and Wages Payable	231	13,132.42	
	Salaries and Wages Expense	511		$16,245.00

The ***reversal*** of the General Journal entries, used in accrual-based accounting to represent accrued employer payroll expenditures and liabilities at the end of the prior month, would look like this:

EXAMPLE: NC BIKES GENERAL JOURNAL—EMPLOYER PAYROLL TAX DATA REVERSING ENTRIES

Date	Description	Account	Debit	Credit
Mar. 1	Social Security Tax Payable	222	$1,007.19	
	Medicare Tax Payable	223	235.55	
	FUTA Tax Payable	224	97.47	
	SUTA Tax Payable	229	876.96	
	Payroll Taxes Expense	512		$2,217.17

Note that not all companies and accountants use reversing entries. An advantage of using the reversing entry is that it simplifies the payroll process by avoiding calculating partial payroll periods that occur due to the period end. A disadvantage is that the reversing entry becomes additional entries that the accountant has to journalize and post. The use of reversing entries is at the company's discretion.

Payroll and the General Journal

Stop & Check

1. In the following General Journal entry, which account represents the employees' gross pay?

Description	Debit	Credit
Wages and Salaries Expense	$124,785.00	
Federal Income Tax Payable		$15,280.00
Social Security Tax Payable		7,736.67
Medicare Tax Payable		1,809.38
State Income Tax Payable		4,741.83
Wages and Salaries Payable		95,217.12

(continued)

(concluded)

2. Based on the preceding General Journal entry, what would be the entry for the employer's share of the payroll taxes? Omit FUTA/SUTA taxes.
3. Davidson Custom Windows has accrued gross pay of $42,795 that will be paid out in the following period. The accrual amounts are as follows:

Wages and Salaries Expense	$42,795.00	
Federal Income Tax Payable		$15,280.00
Social Security Tax Payable		2,653.29
Medicare Tax Payable		620.53
State Income Tax Payable		1,626.21
Wages and Salaries Payable		22,614.97

What would be the reversing entry?

LO 7-4 Generate Payroll-Related General Ledger Entries

As mentioned before, the process of updating the General Ledger accounts with the transactions that the accountant records in the General Journal is called ***posting***. Each account used in the General Journal has a corresponding General Ledger account used to track individual balances of a firm.

For the January 25 payroll and January 31 remittances for NC Bikes that we discussed in the previous section, the postings to the General Ledger would appear as depicted in Figure 7-2. Note that the entries shown reflect only the payroll entries for the end of January and for the end of February.

General Ledger Posting Practices

Note that the columns in the General Ledger are similar to those in the General Journal. Some specific practices in the General Ledger are worth noting:

- Each line has a date. (In the General Journal, only the first line of each transaction is dated.)
- The description is usually left blank, except for adjusting, closing, and reversing entries.

The post reference number is a combination of letters and numbers. The letters denote which journal the entry correlates. In this case, "J" means that the original entry may be found in the General Journal. The number in the Post Ref column reflects the page of the journal on which the entry is recorded.

Conejota/Shutterstock

The first pair of Debit and Credit columns is used to record the General Journal entry. If the account had a debit in the General Journal transaction, then the amount would appear in the Debit column in the first pair of columns in the General Ledger. The same practice is used for credits.

The second pair of Debit and Credit columns is used to maintain a running balance of the total in the account. These account balances are the foundation for the financial reports generated by the accountant and reviewed by managers, officers, customers, vendors, and governmental agencies.

FIGURE 7-2

NC Bikes General Ledger

Account: 101 – Cash							
						Balance	
Date		Description	Post Ref	Debit	Credit	Debit	Credit
Jan	31	Beginning Balance				122,367.43	
Jan	31		J1		13,144.91	109,222.52*	
Jan	31		J4		750.00	108,472.52	
Jan	31		J4		560.00	107,912.52	
Jan	31		J4		180.00	107,732.52	

* Cash has a normal debit balance. It will decrease when the account is credited. 122,367.43 − 13,144.91 = 109.222.52.

Account: 221 – FIT Payable							
						Balance	
Date		Description	Post Ref	Debit	Credit	Debit	Credit
Jan	25		J1		1,500.00		1,500.00
Feb	28	Accrue Payroll	J5		1,350.00		2,850.00*
Mar	1	Reverse Payroll	J7	1,350.00			1,500.00

* FIT Payable is a liability account. It will increase with a credit. 1,500 + 1,350 = 2,850.

Account: 222 – Social Security Tax Payable							
						Balance	
Date		Description	Post Ref	Debit	Credit	Debit	Credit
Jan	25		J1		1,084.38		1,084.38
Jan	25		J1		1,084.38		2,168.76
Feb	28	Accrue Payroll	J5		974.70		3,143.46
Feb	28	Accrue Payroll – Employer	J6		974.70		4,118.16
Mar	1	Reverse Payroll	J7	974.70			3,143.46
Mar	1	Reverse Payroll – Employer	J7	974.70			2,168.76

Account: 223 – Medicare Tax Payable							
						Balance	
Date		Description	Post Ref	Debit	Credit	Debit	Credit
Jan	25		J1		253.61		253.61
Jan	25		J1		253.61		507.22
Feb	28	Accrue Payroll	J5		235.55		742.77
Feb	28	Accrue Payroll – Employer	J6		235.55		978.32
Mar	1	Reverse Payroll	J7	235.55			742.77
Mar	1	Reverse Payroll – Employer	J8	235.55			507.22

Account: 224 – State Income Tax Payable							
						Balance	
Date		Description	Post Ref	Debit	Credit	Debit	Credit
Jan	25		J1		577.60		577.60
Feb	28	Accrue Payroll	J5		519.84		1,097.44
Mar	1	Reverse Payroll	J7	519.84			577.60

Account: 225 – 401(k) Contributions Payable							
						Balance	
Date		Description	Post Ref	Debit	Credit	Debit	Credit
Jan	25		J1		750.00		750.00
Jan	30		J4	750.00			—

(*continued*)

FIGURE 7-2

NC Bikes General Ledger *(concluded)*

Account: 226 – Health Insurance Payable							
Date		Description	Post Ref	Debit	Credit	Balance Debit	Balance Credit
Jan	25		J1		560.00		560.00
Jan	30		J4	560.00			—

Account: 227 – United Way Contributions Payable							
Date		Description	Post Ref	Debit	Credit	Balance Debit	Balance Credit
Jan	25		J1		180.00		180.00
Jan	30		J4	180.00			—

Account: 228 – FUTA Tax Payable							
Date		Description	Post Ref	Debit	Credit	Balance Debit	Balance Credit
Jan	25		J1		144.40		144.40
Feb	28	Accrue Payroll – Employer	J6		129.96		274.36
Mar	1	Reverse Payroll – Employer	J8	129.96			144.40

Account: 229 – SUTA Tax Payable							
Date		Description	Post Ref	Debit	Credit	Balance Debit	Balance Credit
Jan	25		J1		974.40		974.40
Feb	28	Accrue Payroll – Employer	J6		876.96		1,851.36
Mar	1	Reverse Payroll – Employer	J8	876.96			974.40

Account: 231 – Salaries and Wages Payable							
Date		Description	Post Ref	Debit	Credit	Balance Debit	Balance Credit
Jan	25		J1		13,144.41		13,144.41
Jan	31		J1	13,144.41			—
Feb	28	Accrue Payroll	J5		13,164.91		13,164.91
Mar	1	Reverse Payroll	J7	13,164.91			—

Account: 512 – Payroll Taxes Expense							
Date		Description	Post Ref	Debit	Credit	Balance Debit	Balance Credit
Jan	25		J1	2,457.09		2,457.09	
Feb	28	Accrue Payroll	J6	2,217.17		4,674.26	
Mar	1	Reverse Payroll	J7		2,217.17	2,457.09	

Account: 511 – Salaries and Wages Expense							
Date		Description	Post Ref	Debit	Credit	Balance Debit	Balance Credit
Jan	25		J1	18,050.00		18,050.00	
Feb	28	Accrue Payroll	J6	16,245.00		34,295.00	
Mar	1	Reverse Payroll	J7		16,245.00	18,050.00	

Artificial Intelligence is becoming a growing part of the accounting industry. The use of AI allows accountants to focus less on the data input and management by completing the low-level information processing tasks such as paying invoices, generating reports, and updating accounts. This leaves the accountant available to engage in analytical tasks and collaboration with other aspects of company management. (Source: *Accounting Today*)

General Ledger Entries

Stop & Check

1. The Medicare Tax Payable account for Wild Bear Films had a credit balance on June 22 of $2,540. As of the June 30 payroll, credits totaling $220 were posted to the Medicare Tax Payable account. What is the balance in the account as of June 30?
2. The post reference for the June 30 journal entry is J34. What does this post reference mean?

LO 7-5 Describe Payroll Effects on the Accounting System

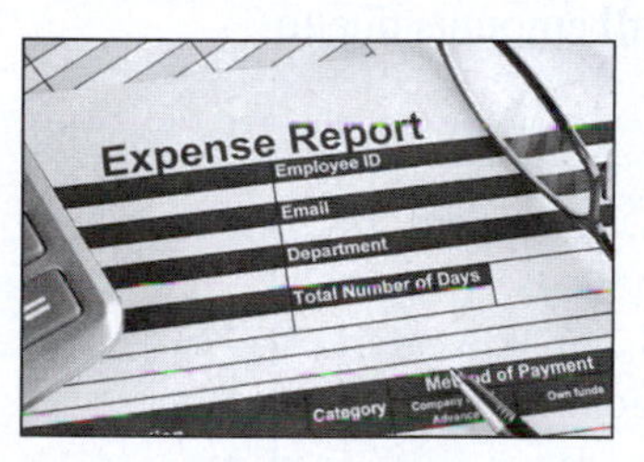

Murat Sarica/Getty Images

Entries in the payroll system are posted into the General Ledger. When a company has an automated payroll system, the journal entries discussed previously are automatically updated to the General Ledger. A payroll accountant needs to understand how the accounts should look after a payroll is completed to ensure the automated system has performed correctly. Glitches within computer programs may cause the payroll entry to be one sided, in which only the debit or credit entry will flow through to the General Ledger. When this occurs, the payroll accountant must discover what has not posted to ensure the entire transaction posts correctly.

Payroll-Related Business Expenses

Payroll represents an expense to the business. As such, it reduces the company's profitability proportional to the wages earned and taxes paid. When the payroll accountant accrues the expenses related to the payroll, the company's expenses will also increase. Companies that operate using a cash basis (i.e., recording activities only when cash is received or spent) will witness the payroll expenses reducing the income when wages and salaries are paid to the employees and when taxes are remitted to governmental agencies.

Payroll issues have affected at least 82 million Americans, according to a study by Kronos Inc. During 2019, the partial federal government shutdown impacted many more people than during "normal" times. These issues involve being shortchanged on a paycheck, missing a paycheck, or having a payroll check bounce when presented at a bank. These issues reduce employee engagement and lead to problems with the remittance of taxes and other payroll deductions. (Source: *Employee Benefits News*)

Besides administering specific payroll tasks, a responsibility of the payroll accountant is to allocate the employee expenses to specific accounts, departments, or business activities. Regardless of the employee's job description, some amount of time can be allocable to jobs or customers. For example, a fabric manufacturing company will have sewing, accounting, and managerial staff. The bulk of the sewing staff's time will be allocable to specific jobs; however, some time will be considered overhead—cleaning or meetings, for example. The bulk of the accounting department's time will be considered overhead. However, if the accountant is working on the analysis of a specific client's project, that time may be billed to the client. Managerial positions may also have specific times allocated to jobs depending upon the needs of the client and the position.

bacho12345/123RF

Payroll-Related Liabilities

Unpaid payroll obligations represent a liability to the company. These liabilities include not only amounts due to employees, but also money to be remitted for voluntary, mandatory, and mandated deductions. Until the money is remitted, the company holds it in its accounts. Specific examples of payroll liabilities include, but are certainly not limited to, the following:

- Federal income tax
- FICA taxes
- Health insurance premiums
- Retirement plan contributions
- Child support garnishments
- Union dues

Employers have a ***fiduciary*** responsibility to remit all amounts withheld from employee pay. Remember that the Current Tax Payment Act requires employers to remit taxes in a timely manner, according to governmental guidelines. For the other deductions, according to 29 CFR 2510, employers are subject to the provisions of ERISA to protect all amounts due to employees and other recipients.

> The Employee Benefits Security Administration, a division of the Department of Labor, oversees employee contributions and estimated that approximate 67 million participants in employer-sponsored 401(k) plans had invested over $4.7 trillion as of December 2016. The number of participants has historically increased at a rate of about 3 percent per year since 1975. (Source: DOL)

The Business Effects of Payroll

Stop & Check

1. Does the payment of employee wages increase or decrease the profitability of a business?
2. Why is it important to allocate payroll-related expenses properly?

LO 7-6 Explain Payroll Entries in Accounting Reports

wrangler/Shutterstock

When examining the ***income statement***, ***balance sheet***, and post-closing ***trial balance*** (Figures 7-3, 7-4, and 7-5), the payroll accountant must know what effect his or her work has on each statement. The financial statements are the key to integrating payroll accounting data and human resources information.

Let's start with the income statement, which reports all revenue and expenses for a specific time period. These periods are usually monthly,

FIGURE 7-3
Income Statement Presentation (Partial)

NC Bikes Income Statement For the Quarter Ended March 31, 20XX		
Revenue:		
Sales Revenue		$78,303.40
Expenses:		
Salaries and Wages Expense	$34,295.00	
Payroll Taxes Expense	4,674.26	
Utilities Expense	1,725.00	
Telephone Expense	884.00	
Rent Expense	5,175.00	
Total Expenses		46,753.26
Net Income for Quarter		$31,550.14

FIGURE 7-4
Balance Sheet Presentation (Partial)

NC Bikes Balance Sheet March 31, 20XX		
Assets:		
Cash		$ 78,507.89
Accounts Receivable		39,723.67
Equipment		15,289.00
Inventory		225,960.00
Total Assets		$359,480.56
Liabilities:		
Accounts Payable		4,085.27
FIT Payable		2,850.00
Social Security Tax Payable		4,118.16
Medicare Tax Payable		978.32
State Income Tax Payable		1,097.44
Health Insurance Payable		560.00
FUTA Tax Payable		274.36
SUTA Tax Payable		1,851.36
Salaries and Wages Payable		13,164.91
Total Liabilities		28,979.82
Owner's Equity		
J. Nelson, Capital		330,500.74
Total Owner's Equity		330,500.74
Total Liabilities and Owner's Equity		$359,480.56

quarterly, and annually. The function of the income statement is to correlate all money received during the course of business operations with the money spent to earn that income. Within the expense section of the income statement, you will see several accounts that relate to payroll. The Salaries and wages expense represents the gross pay from the period. Each of the taxes we have discussed is listed. Note that the expenses related to the taxes are paid by

FIGURE 7-5
Post-Closing Trial Balance Presentation

NC Bikes Post-Closing Trial Balance March 31, 20XX		
Account	**Debit**	**Credit**
Cash	$ 78,507.89	
Accounts Receivable	39,723.67	
Inventory	225,960.00	
Equipment	15,289.00	
Accounts Payable		$ 4,085.27
FIT Payable		2,850.00
Social Security Tax Payable		4,118.16
Medicare Tax Payable		978.32
State Income Tax Payable		1,097.44
Health Insurance Payable		560.00
FUTA Tax Payable		274.36
SUTA Tax Payable		1,851.36
Salaries and Wages Payable		13,164.91
J. Nelson, Capital		162,755.23
A. Nelson, Capital		136,195.37
Retained Earnings		31,550.14
	$359,480.56	$359,480.56

the employer and forwarded to the taxing authority; thus, there is no accrued federal income tax expense. Expenses related to the employer portion of retirement fund matching, health benefits, or other benefits are also located within the income statement.

Moving on to the balance sheet, any unpaid liabilities to be paid during the next 12 months will be reported in the current liability section. In accrual accounting, there may also be end-of-period entries to accrue for payroll earned by the employees. Additional liability accounts for accrued salaries, accrued hourly wages, accrued holiday pay, and accrued paid time off could also appear, depending on the timing of the end of the period and the types of employees and benefits with which the company operates. If there are employees who have taken payroll advances, which are amounts to be repaid by the employee, these are reported in the current assets section as receivables.

The trial balance contains all accounts the company uses, spanning all of the financial statements. The accounts listed on the trial balance appear in the order of the chart of accounts. In the United States, these are typically listed assets first: short-term and then long-term. Following are liabilities: short-term and then long-term. Equity accounts are listed next, followed by revenues and expenses. The important thing to remember when examining the trial balance is that it should balance: Debits must equal credits. Should one side not balance with the other, the accountant must determine why and correct the error. A post-closing trial balance will have already closed the revenue and expense accounts into the retained earnings account.

The purpose of all financial statements is to provide information to the stakeholders of a company. Stakeholders of a company include (but are certainly not limited to) company managers, governmental agencies, creditors, and employees who use the information to make decisions about the business. Financial statements are prepared in accordance with GAAP guidelines to facilitate the presentation of the statements among the wide variety of businesses that exist. Managers of a company, in particular, use the financial reports to make decisions about labor and benefits planning.

The Internet of Things (IoT) is a term that encompasses all connected devices such as computers, smartphones, and artificial intelligence technology. Accountants are beginning to leverage the IoT to prevent audits by using blockchain technology, reduce the labor involved in generating financial reports, and communicating transparent and accurate financial information with stakeholders. (Source: Sage)

Labor Reports

©Nonwarit Pruetisirirot/123RF

The payroll accountant may provide specific ***labor reports*** to management or department heads. These reports may have a variety of names and content depending on the needs of the business.

- The ***labor usage*** report designates where the labor is used within the company. When a company has several employees who work in different departments, the labor usage report can be useful in determining overhead ***allocations*** by department and the need for increased or decreased staff within a specific department.
- The ***billable vs. nonbillable*** report tracks the time employees have spent specifically on projects for which customers are paying. This report allows managers to determine if the time allocated to the job in the job costing process is accurate, the company is operating efficiently, or if the employee is taking too long on a specific job.
- ***Overtime*** reports allow managers to determine how much overtime has been paid to employees during a specified time period. This report allows managers to monitor labor distribution and scheduling to ensure adherence with budget guidelines.
- Employers can also make use of ***trend*** reports for payroll staffing needs. Trend reports of income over the period of the year or two can reveal seasonal increases or decreases in business. An informed business manager will know if the company needs to have seasonal or temporary workers for short-term increases. If the trend reflects a steady increase in business, the manager may determine that hiring a new employee would be beneficial. Analyzing the staffing needs of the company compared to income projections may also lead managers to know if they need to lay off personnel, reduce hours of existing employees, or restructure company operations.

The level of employment in the United States has grown since 2010 and is projected to continue doing so, according to the Bureau of Labor Statistics. As the number of employees grows, the need for payroll professionals will also increase because of the complexity in compensating workers. Understanding payroll accounting is a vital skill needed by all industries, government employers, and private-sector and private-sector companies. It is safe to state that payroll accounting is a profession that will continue to be needed for the foreseeable future. (Source: BLS)

Labor Reports

Stop & Check

1. Which of the following reports are affected by the payroll of an organization?
   a. Trial balance
   b. Statement of owners' equity
   c. Interest statement
   d. Income statement
   e. Balance sheet
2. What is a specific type of report that the payroll accountant provides to managerial staff?
3. What are trend reports?

Trends to Watch

ECONOMIC EFFECTS OF PAYROLL

Although payroll accounting principles remain relatively stable, the role that payroll plays in the broader context of a business is subject to change. Some developments in payroll accounting in the business context that have changed since 2015 include the following:

- Accountants seeking roles as consultants (as opposed to technicians) because of increases in automation and technology that foster completion of lower-level work.
- Increases in labor costs for employers resulting from changes to the minimum wage.
- Technology use such as cloud-based payroll services has fostered employee mobility and created challenges to work–life balance.
- Employer-sponsored wellness programs have become a part of strategic human resource management because of the correlation with employee sick time and retention.

Some trends to watch in payroll's economic effects include the following:

- Increases to the "gig" economy, in which employees have a contract or freelance position either in addition to or replacing full-time employment.
- Expanded access to data analytics in accounting to improve a company's competitive position among their competitors.
- Increased use of cloud-based accounting software that may be accessed through multiple portals to analyze real-time data.
- Advancements in accounting software that will further integrate payroll accounting with enterprise resource planning (ERP) efforts that promote an informed approach to business decision making.

Summary of the Payroll Register, Employees' Earnings Records, and Accounting System Entries

The payroll register and employees' earnings records are two tools that payroll accountants need to maintain their work accurately. Both records track employee compensation and contain information about company liabilities to governmental agencies and other organizations. These records also provide information for company decision makers by yielding data about labor distribution and cost allocation. Payroll records provide information about benefits given to employees and how those benefits affect a business's profitability. Information contained in these sources and tools used by payroll accountants provides integral insights for managerial functions.

The final piece of the payroll cycle is the creation of accounting system entries. Similar to other business transactions, recording, paying the payroll, remitting money to governmental agencies and other firms requires General Journal and General Ledger entries. Business owners and departmental managers use this accounting information to measure the effectiveness of business plans and to plan both short- and long-term strategies. As an integral part of business operations, payroll-related expenses and liabilities represent an employer's financial duty, affect the financial reports, and influence the company's viability.

With this chapter's explanation of accounting system entries, we have now completed our journey through the payroll process. We have investigated the history of payroll, its many aspects and functions, and the importance of employee compensation within a business context.

We hope that on finishing this book you will have gained the understanding that payroll accounting is complex, involves many different decisions along the way, and deserves your close attention. Figure 7-6 is a depiction of the basic elements of the payroll process that we have discussed.

FIGURE 7-6
Payroll Process Flowchart

Key Points

- The payroll register connects directly to the employees' earnings records.
- The employees' earnings records are the link between accounting and human resources and contain information from the payroll register.
- Accounting principles assist in the classification of payroll costs and organizational performance.

- Payroll transactions are recorded in the General Journal and posted to General Ledger accounts.
- The balances in the General Ledger accounts form the foundation of financial reports.
- Payroll costs represent an expense of the business.
- Employees are assigned to departments to foster accurate measurements of business segment profitability.
- Accounting reports provide managers with insights into company profitability and stability.
- Payroll-related transactions contain both expenses and liabilities of a company.
- Employers have a fiduciary duty to ensure that all amounts deducted from employee pay are remitted to the appropriate entity.
- Trend reports offer business leaders insight about changes in labor costs over a period.
- Financial reports contain the data that connects the payroll and human resources functions within a company.

Vocabulary

Accrual
Adjusting entries
Allocation
Assets
Balance sheet
Credit
Debit
Expense
Fiduciary
Generally Accepted Accounting Principles (GAAP)
General Journal
General Ledger
Income statement
Labor reports
Liabilities
Owners' equity
Posting
Remit
Reversal
Trial balance

Review Questions

1. What types of accounts does a debit increase?
2. What types of accounts does a credit increase?
3. Where are daily accounting entries recorded?
4. Once recorded, to what are the entries posted?
5. What is the purpose of the payroll register?
6. What information is contained in employees' earnings records?
7. How are the payroll register and the employees' earnings records related?
8. What type of account is debited for the gross pay?
9. What are three of the accounts that may be credited for the employee payroll?
10. What two accounts are affected upon issuance of paychecks?
11. What accounts are debited and credited for the employer share of the payroll expenses?
12. How do payroll expenses affect the income statement and balance sheet?
13. How can companies use payroll information that is reported in the financial statements to determine labor distribution?
14. How can a company's payroll information contained in financial reports assist in corporate planning?
15. How do the payroll register and employees' earnings records help employers meet their responsibilities to different groups, such as the employees and governmental agencies?
16. What is the term for the responsibility that employers have for payroll deductions under ERISA?

Exercises Set A

E7-1A. Which column exists in the employees' earnings records but not in the payroll register?
LO 7-1
a. Gross pay
b. Net pay
c. YTD net pay
d. 401(k) contributions

E7-2A. What is the connection between the employees' earnings records and payroll tax reporting? (Select all that apply.)
LO 7-1
a. Employees' earnings records do not connect with payroll tax reporting
b. Employees' earnings records may be used to ensure the accuracy of payroll tax reporting
c. Employees' earnings records contain details of payroll tax reporting and may be considered as source documents
d. Employees' earnings records contain year-to-date gross pay, which reflects when employees reach tax bases

E7-3A. A debit increases which of the following types of accounts? (Select all that apply.)
LO 7-2
a. Liabilities
b. Expenses
c. Revenue
d. Assets

E7-4A. The total of the Gross Earnings column of the payroll register for a given pay period will appear in which account for the payroll-related General Journal entry?
LO 7-3
a. Salaries and Wages Payable
b. Cash
c. Salaries and Wages Expense
d. Expenses

E7-5A. What is always true about the General Ledger? (Select all that apply.)
LO 7-4
a. The process of transferring amounts from the General Journal to the General Ledger is called posting
b. The General Ledger is a way to represent monthly groupings of entire General Journal entries
c. The General Ledger contains information about the individual accounts used in General Journal transactions
d. A debit to an account in a General Journal transaction is a debit to that account in the General Ledger

E7-6A. How does a payroll accountant use the information in the General Ledger? (Select all that apply.)
LO 7-4, 7-5, 7-6
a. The account balances form the basis for accounting reports
b. The payroll accountant uses General Ledger balances to determine the effectiveness of individual employees
c. General Ledger account balances aggregate data to determine payroll costs
d. Payroll expenses contained in the General Ledger are not used to make personnel decisions

E7-7A. Which of the following accounts would appear on the income statement? (Select all that apply.)
LO 7-6
a. Payroll taxes expense
b. 401(k) contributions payable
c. 401(k) employer contributions expense
d. Social Security tax payable

E7-8A. What is always true about trial balance reports? (Select all that apply.)
LO 7-6
a. Only accounts with activity during the period are included on the report
b. All accounts with balances are included in the report
c. The total of the debit column must equal the total of the credit column
d. The report is prepared for a range of dates

E7-9A. The purpose of a labor report is to do what? (Select all that apply.)
LO 7-6
a. Report an individual employee's regular time and overtime
b. Reflect all expenses of a firm
c. Promote analysis of payroll expenses
d. Update managers about payroll on a daily basis

E7-10A. Which law governs the fiduciary responsibility that employers have with regards to employees' payroll deductions?
LO 7-5, 7-6
a. FICA
b. FLSA
c. ERISA
d. ACA

Problems Set A

P7-1A. Charles Merrill owns a housekeeping service, Charles' Cleaners, in Florida. For the weekly payroll ending July 12, 2019, checks dated July 17, 2019, complete the payroll register. Use the wage bracket method in the federal tax table in Appendix C. No employee has exceeded the Social Security tax wage base. Total, prove, and rule the entries.
LO 7-1

P/R End Date 7/12/2019 Company Name Charles' Cleaners
Check Date 7/17/2019

Name	M/S	# W/H	Hourly Rate or Period Wage	No. of Regular Hours	No. of Overtime Hours	No. of Holiday Hours	Commissions	Gross Earnings	401(k)	Cafeteria Plan	Taxable Wages for Federal W/H	Taxable Wages for FICA
Clark, M.	M	3	$ 8.50	40	3				$50.00			
Toonen, B.	S	1	$ 9.20	35					$75.00			
Dahl, P.	S	0	$ 10.10	37.5								
Steverman, S.	S	1	$ 8.74	40								
Bromley, L	M	4	$ 8.90	38					$60.00	$20.00		
Matte, R.	S	2	$ 10.50	40	5				$75.00			
Maddox, F.	S	1	$ 9.95	40						$15.00		
Totals												

Name	Gross Earnings	Taxable Wages for Federal W/H	Taxable Wages for FICA	Federal W/H	Social Security Tax	Medicare Tax	State W/H	Garnishment	United Way	Net Pay	Check No.
Clark, M.											
Toonen, B.									$10.00		
Dahl, P.								$100.00			
Steverman, S.									$25.00		
Bromley, L											
Matte, R.									$10.00		
Maddox, F.											
Totals											

P7-2A. What follows is the employee earnings record for Sean Steverman of Charles' Cleaners. Record his earnings from the July 12 weekly pay in P7-1A.

LO 7-1

EMPLOYEE EARNING RECORD

NAME	Sean Steverman	Hire Date	May 22, 2011
ADDRESS	2326 Vinings Drive	Date of Birth	November 15, 1991
CITY/STATE/ZIP	Lodi, FL 32039	Exempt/Nonexempt	Nonexempt
TELEPHONE	305-555-5698	Married/Single	Single
SOCIAL SECURITY NUMBER	188-56-7316	No. of Exemptions	1
POSITION	House Cleaner	Pay Rate	8.74/hour

Period Ended	Hours Worked	Regular Pay	OT Pay	Holiday	Comm	Gross Pay	401(k)	Section 125	Taxable Wages for Federal W/H	Taxable Wages for FICA
7/5/2019	40	$321.60				$321.60	—	—	$321.60	$321.60

Taxable Wages for Federal	Taxable Wages for FICA W/H	Fed W/H	Social Sec. Tax	Medicare Tax	State W/H	United Way	Net Pay	YTD Net Pay	YTD Sec. Tax
$321.60	$321.60	$17.00	$19.94	$4.66	—	$25.00	$252.00	$3,500.00	$4,502.40

P7-3A. Using the payroll register from P7-1A for Charles' Cleaners, complete the General Journal entry for the employees' pay for the July 12 pay date. Paychecks will be issued on July 17.

LO 7-2, 7-3

	Date	Description	Post Ref.	Debit	Credit	
1						1
2						2
3						3
4						4
5						5
6						6
7						7
8						8
9						9
10						10
11						11
12						12

P7-4A. LO 7-2, 7-3

Using the payroll register from P7-1A for Charles' Cleaners, complete the General Journal entry for the employer's share of the payroll taxes for the July 12 pay date. Assume 5.4 percent SUTA and 0.6 percent FUTA tax rates and that $1,352.40 is subject to FUTA/SUTA taxes.

	Date	Description	Post Ref.	Debit	Credit	
1						1
2						2
3						3
4						4
5						5
6						6
7						7
8						8
9						9

P7-5A. LO 7-2, 7-3

Using the employee payroll entry from P7-3A, post the July 12 employee pay for Charles' Cleaners to the selected General Ledger accounts shown next.

Account: Salaries and Wages Payable

	Date	Description	Post Ref.	Debit	Credit	Balance		
						Debit	Credit	
1								1
2								2
3								3
4								4
5								5
6								6

Account: Employee Federal Income Tax Payable

	Date	Description	Post Ref.	Debit	Credit	Balance		
						Debit	Credit	
1								1
2								2
3								3
4								4
5								5
6								6

Account: Social Security Tax Payable

	Date	Description	Post Ref.	Debit	Credit	Balance		
						Debit	Credit	
1								1
2								2
3								3
4								4
5								5
6								6

Account: Medicare Tax Payable

	Date	Description	Post Ref.	Debit	Credit	Balance		
						Debit	Credit	
1								1
2								2
3								3
4								4
5								5
6								6

Account: Salaries and Wages Expense

	Date	Description	Post Ref.	Debit	Credit	Balance		
						Debit	Credit	
1								1
2								2
3								3
4								4
5								5
6								6
7								7

P7-6A. LO 7-2, 7-3 Using the employee payroll entry from P7-3A, complete the General Journal entry for the issuance of the pay for the July 12 pay date. The date of the checks is July 17, 2019.

	Date	Description	Post Ref.	Debit	Credit	
1						1
2						2
3						3
4						4
5						5

P7-7A. LO 7-2, 7-3, 7-4 Using the employer payroll entry from P7-4A, post the employer's share of payroll taxes for the July 12 pay at Charles' Cleaners to the appropriate General Ledger accounts. Assume that $1,352.40 is subject to FUTA/SUTA taxes.

Account: Social Security Tax Payable

	Date	Description	Post Ref.	Debit	Credit	Balance		
						Debit	Credit	
1								1
2								2
3								3
4								4
5								5
6								6
7								7

Account: Medicare Tax Payable

	Date	Description	Post Ref.	Debit	Credit	Balance		
						Debit	Credit	
1								1
2								2
3								3
4								4
5								5
6								6
7								7

Account: Federal Unemployment Tax Payable

	Date	Description	Post Ref.	Debit	Credit	Balance		
						Debit	Credit	
1								1
2								2
3								3
4								4
5								5
6								6
7								7

Account: State Unemployment Tax Payable

	Date	Description	Post Ref.	Debit	Credit	Balance		
						Debit	Credit	
1								1
2								2
3								3
4								4
5								5
6								6
7								7

Account: Payroll Taxes Expense

	Date	Description	Post Ref.	Debit	Credit	Balance		
						Debit	Credit	
1								1
2								2
3								3
4								4
5								5
6								6
7								7

P7-8A.
LO 7-2, 7-3

KMH Industries is a monthly schedule depositor of payroll taxes. For the month of August 2019, the payroll taxes (employee and employer share combined) were as follows:

Social Security tax: $3,252.28

Medicare tax: $760.61

Employee federal income tax: $2,520

Create the General Journal entry for the remittance of the taxes. The entry should be dated September 13. Use check 2052 in the description.

	Date		Description	Post Ref.	Debit	Credit	
1							1
2							2
3							3
4							4
5							5
6							6
7							7
8							8

P7-9A.
LO 7-2, 7-3

Sophie Sue Breeders has the following voluntary withholdings to remit:

AFLAC payable: $560.00

401(k) payable: $1,280.00

Garnishments payable: $375.00

United Way contributions payable: $200.00

Create the General Journal entry on June 14, 2019, for the remittance of these withheld amounts.

	Date		Description	Post Ref.	Debit	Credit	
1							1
2							2
3							3
4							4
5							5
6							6
7							7

P7-10A.
LO 7-5, 7-6

Sheronda Rowe is the payroll accountant for Great Lake Lamps. The company's management has requested an analysis of the payroll effects on the expenses of the company. Explain which accounting report(s) you would use to construct your analysis. How would you explain the purpose of labor expenses as they affect company productivity?

P7-11A.
LO 7-6

The new vice president of marketing for your company has asked to meet with you regarding the purpose and location of payroll entries in accounting reports. What will you tell the vice president?

Exercises Set B

E7-1B. LO 7-1
Which of the following information exists in both the employees' earnings records and the payroll register? (Select all that apply.)
a. Marital status
b. Social Security number
c. Hourly rate or period wage
d. Employee home address

E7-2B. LO 7-1
How do the payroll register and employees' earnings records connect with payroll tax determination and remittance? (Select all that apply.)
a. Payroll register column totals contain information about pay period tax withholdings
b. Employees' earnings records have pertinent information to determine individual taxable wage base attainment
c. Payroll registers records reflect which employees have reached the Medicare additional tax
d. Payroll registers contain specific information about each employee's raise history

E7-3B. LO 7-2
Which of the following are categories contained in the fundamental accounting equation? (Select all that apply.)
a. Assets
b. Liabilities
c. Expenses
d. Owners' Equity

E7-4B. LO 7-2
Which of the following principles are always true about financial accounting? (Select all that apply.)
a. Assets = Owners' Equity
b. Debits = Credits
c. Assets = Liabilities + Owners' Equity
d. Debits + Credits = Owners' Equity

E7-5B. LO 7-3
What is true about expenses and liabilities? (Select all that apply.)
a. Expenses usually have the word *expense* in the account title
b. Expenses represent additional sums earned by the company
c. Liabilities represent sums of money owed by third parties to the company
d. Liabilities usually have the word *payable* in the account title

E7-6B. LO 7-3, 7-4, 7-5
How do payroll-related expenses affect financial statements? (Select all that apply.)
a. Payroll expenses may be allocable to work performed for a firm's vendors
b. Payroll expense accounts are reported on the Income Statement
c. The period's gross earnings are reported on the Balance Sheet
d. Payroll expenses reduce the net income of a company

E7-7B. LO 7-6
Which of the following payroll-related accounts appear on the Balance Sheet? (Select all that apply.)
a. Wages and salaries expense
b. Medicare tax payable
c. Employee federal income tax payable
d. Health insurance premiums payable

E7-8B. LO 7-2, 7-5
What is the purpose of payroll-related accrual and reversal entries on financial statements? (Select all that apply.)
a. Accrual entries represent payroll amounts earned but not yet paid
b. Reversing entries represent disbursement of accrued payroll prior to the end of the payroll period
c. Accrual entries are used to improve the accuracy of the net income for a period
d. Reversing entries are omitted from financial statements

E7-9B. LO 7-6

Managers use labor reports to do which of the following? (Select all that apply.)

a. Analyze labor trends
b. Determine staffing needs
c. Ensure FLSA wage and hour compliance
d. Formulate strategic plans for the company

E7-10B. LO 7-5, 7-6

To which parties does an employer have fiduciary duty when it incurs payroll liabilities? (Select all that apply.)

a. Customers
b. Employees
c. Government
d. Vendors

Problems Set B

P7-1B. LO 7-1

Tony Stanford owns Cosmic Comics in Greensboro, North Carolina. For the weekly payroll dated September 13, 2019, complete the payroll register. Checks will be issued on September 18, 2019. Use the wage bracket method in the federal tax table in Appendix C. Assume 5.25 percent state income tax. No employee has exceeded the Social Security wage base. Total, prove, and rule the entries.

P/R End Date	9/13/2019	Company Name	Cosmic Comics
Check Date	9/18/2019	Check Date	

Name	M/S	# W/H	Hourly Rate or Period Wage	No. of Regular Hours	No. of Overtime Hours	No. of Holiday Hours	Commissions	Gross Earnings	401(k)	Sec 125	Taxable Wages for Federal W/H	Taxable Wages for FICA
Camacho, N.	M	2	$ 12.20	40	2				$50.00			
Rea, A.	S	4	$ 9.45	39						$20.00		
Dahl, P.	M	5	$ 11.30	40	5				$35.00	$10.00		
Hayes, K.	S	1	$ 8.95	37					$20.00			
Fortanier, Y.	S	0	$ 10.05	38.5								
Cronan, S.	M	2	$ 13.45	40	6							
Murner, A.	S	2	$ 10.65	37					$45.00	$10.00		
Zinsli, E.	M	0	$ 9.50	40	1				$25.00			
Totals												

Name	Gross Earnings	Taxable Wages for Federal W/H	Taxable Wages for FICA	Federal W/H	Social Security Tax	Medicare W/H	State W/H Tax	Garnishment	United Way	Net Pay	Check No.
Camacho, N.									$ 10.00		
Rea, A.											
Dahl, P.											
Hayes, K.								$ 60.00			
Fortanier, Y.								$ 50.00			
Cronan, S.											
Murner, A.											
Zinsli, E.											
Totals											

P7-2B. What follows is the employee earnings record for Ally Murner of Cosmic Comics. Record her earnings on the September 13, 2019, pay from P7-1B.
LO 7-1

EMPLOYEE EARNING RECORD

NAME	Ally Murner	Hire Date	4/2/2019
ADDRESS	522 Shady Lane	Date of Birth	7/1/1989
CITY/STATE/ZIP	Winslow, NC 22203	Exempt/Nonexempt	Nonexempt
TELEPHONE	704-553-5967	Married/Single	Single
SOCIAL SECURITY NUMBER	680-30-2983	No. of Exemptions	2
POSITION	Night Cashier	Pay Rate	$10.65/hour

Period Ended	Hrs Worked	Reg Pay	OT Pay	Holiday	Comm	Gross Pay	401(K)	Sec 125	Taxable Pay for Federal W/H	Taxable Pay for FICA
9/6/2019	40	$426.00				$426.00	$ 45.00	$ 10.00	$371.00	$416.00

Taxable Pay for Federal W/H	Taxable Pay for FICA	Fed Inc. Tax	Social Sec. Tax	Medicare	State Inc. Tax	Garnishment	United Way	Net Pay	YTD Net Pay	YTD Gross Pay
$371.00	$461.00	$14.00	$25.79	$6.03	$19.48			305.70	5,808.30	$8,256.90

P7-3B. Using the payroll register from P7-1B for Cosmic Comics, complete the General Journal entry for the employees' pay for the September 13, 2019, pay date. Employees' paychecks will be issued on September 18.
LO 7-1, 7-2, 7-3

	Date	Description	Post Ref.	Debit	Credit
1					
2					
3					
4					
5					
6					
7					
8					
9					

P7-4B. Using the payroll register from P7-1B for Cosmic Comics, complete the General Journal entry for the employer's share of the payroll taxes for the September 13, 2019, pay date. Assume a 5.4 percent SUTA rate and 0.6 percent FUTA rate, and assume that $954.05 of the gross pay is subject to SUTA/FUTA taxes.
LO 7-1, 7-2, 7-3

	Date	Description	Post Ref.	Debit	Credit
1					
2					
3					
4					
5					
6					
7					
8					
9					

P7-5B. LO 7-3, 7-4 Using the employee payroll entry from P7-3B, post the September 13 employee pay for Cosmic Comics to the selected General Ledger accounts.

Account: Salaries and Wages Payable

	Date	Description	Post Ref.	Debit	Credit	Balance	
						Debit	Credit
1							
2							
3							
4							
5							
6							

Account: Employee Federal Income Tax Payable

	Date	Description	Post Ref.	Debit	Credit	Balance	
						Debit	Credit
1							
2							
3							
4							
5							
6							

Account: Social Security Tax Payable

	Date	Description	Post Ref.	Debit	Credit	Balance	
						Debit	Credit
1							
2							
3							
4							
5							
6							

Account: Medicare Tax Payable

	Date	Description	Post Ref.	Debit	Credit	Balance	
						Debit	Credit
1							
2							
3							
4							
5							
6							

Account: Employee State Income Tax Payable

	Date	Description	Post Ref.	Debit	Credit	Balance Debit	Balance Credit
1							
2							
3							
4							
5							
6							

Account: Salaries and Wages Expense

	Date	Description	Post Ref.	Debit	Credit	Balance Debit	Balance Credit
1							
2							
3							
4							
5							
6							
7							

P7-6B. LO 7-3, 7-4 Using the employee payroll entry from P7-3B, complete the General Journal entry for the issuance of Cosmic Comics pay on September 18, 2019.

	Date	Description	Post Ref.	Debit	Credit	
1						1
2						2
3						3
4						4
5						5

P7-7B. LO 7-3, 7-4 Using the employer payroll entry from P7-4B, post the employer's share of payroll taxes for the September 13 pay period at Cosmic Comics to the appropriate General Ledger accounts.

Account: Payroll Taxes Expense

	Date	Description	Post Ref.	Debit	Credit	Balance Debit	Balance Credit	
1								1
2								2
3								3
4								4
5								5
6								6
7								7

Account: Social Security Tax Payable

	Date	Description	Post Ref.	Debit	Credit	Balance		
						Debit	Credit	
1								1
2								2
3								3
4								4
5								5
6								6
7								7

Account: Medicare Tax Payable

	Date	Description	Post Ref.	Debit	Credit	Balance		
						Debit	Credit	
1								1
2								2
3								3
4								4
5								5
6								6
7								7

Account: Federal Unemployment Tax Payable

	Date	Description	Post Ref.	Debit	Credit	Balance		
						Debit	Credit	
1								1
2								2
3								3
4								4
5								5
6								6
7								7

Account: State Unemployment Tax Payable

	Date	Description	Post Ref.	Debit	Credit	Balance		
						Debit	Credit	
1								1
2								2
3								3
4								4
5								5
6								6
7								7

P7-8B.
LO 7-2, 7-3

Legends Leadworks is a monthly schedule depositor of payroll taxes. For the month of April 2019, the payroll taxes (employee and employer share) were as follows:

Social Security tax: $5,386.56

Medicare tax: $1,259.76

Employee federal income tax: $4,978

Create the General Journal entry for the remittance of the taxes on May 15, 2019. Use check 1320 in the description.

	Date	Description	Post Ref.	Debit	Credit	
1						1
2						2
3						3
4						4
5						5
6						6
7						7
8						8

P7-9B.
LO 7-2, 7-3

Candy Farms Inc. has the following voluntary withholdings to remit as of September 30, 2019:

AFLAC payable: $687.00

Workers' compensation insurance payable: $1,042.00

401(k) payable: $2,104.00

Garnishments payable: $450.00

U.S. savings bonds payable: $200.00

Create the General Journal entry for the remittance of these withheld amounts on October 11, 2019.

	Date	Description	Post Ref.	Debit	Credit	
1						1
2						2
3						3
4						4
5						5
6						6
7						7
8						8

P7-10B.
LO 7-5, 7-6

Pujah Srinivasan is the controller for HHT Industries. She has been asked to explain the payroll accounts on the financial statements for the preceding month. What information will she find about payroll on the financial statements?

P7-11B.
LO 7-5, 7-6

You are interviewing for a position with Limelight Photography. The president of the company, Emma Jankiewicz, asks you to explain how payroll is both an expense and a liability of the company. How will you answer her?

Critical Thinking

7-1. Your boss asks you for a five-year labor cost trend chart. The labor costs per year are as follows:

2015	$178,967
2016	185,923
2017	172,245
2018	179,905
2019	182,478

Construct a line chart to depict the data. What conclusions can you derive from the data about labor costs and trends over the past five years? Why?

7-2. Giblin's Goodies pays employees weekly on Fridays. However, the company notices that October 31 is a Thursday and the pay period will end on November 1. The payroll data for October 28–October 31 is as follows:

Gross pay: $4,500

Federal income tax: $520

Social Security tax: $279

Medicare tax: $65.25

State income tax: $90

Give the adjusting entry in the General Journal to recognize the employee and employer share of the payroll for October 28-31. Date the entry October 31. Then give the journal entry to reverse the adjustment on November 1, 2019.

	Date		Description	Post Ref.	Debit	Credit	
1							1
2							2
3							3
4							4
5							5
6							6
7							7
8							8
9							9
10							10
11							11
12							12
13							13
14							14
15							15

In the Real World: Scenario for Discussion

An ongoing discussion among business managers is the return on employee investment (ROEI). Employers want to maximize business profitability, and employees are a significant part of organizational success. Investments into employee training and professional development comprise a significant part of many companies' budgets. Measures including providing tablet computers for employees to pursue flexible learning opportunities and self-paced classes give employers the opportunity to reduce training and development costs. What are the pros and cons of this practice?

Internet Activities

7-1. Would you like to know about personal experiences as a payroll accountant? How about videos that detail the completion of payroll-related forms? Go to www.youtube.com and search the term *payroll accounting* to read personal perspectives about payroll practice, outsourcing, and tax form completion. What were three insights you found that were new to you?

7-2. Would you like to build your own favorites list of payroll accounting tools? Go to one or more of the following sites. What are three important items you noticed?

www.accountingtools.com

www.accountantsworld.com

www.americanpayroll.org

7-3. Join a conversation about payroll accounting with industry professionals. Go to www.linkedin.com and establish a profile (if you do not have one). Search groups for payroll accounting and follow the conversations. Which topics did you choose? Why?

7-4. Want to know more about the concepts in this chapter? Check out

www.moneyinstructor.com/lesson/accountingconcepts.asp

https://www.accountingcoach.com/accounting-basics/outline

Continuing Payroll Project: Prevosti Farms and Sugarhouse

Complete the Payroll Register for the February and March biweekly pay periods, assuming benefits went into effect as anticipated. Use the Wage Bracket Method Tables for Income Tax Withholding in Appendix C. Complete the General Journal entries as follows:

February 8	Journalize the employee pay.
February 8	Journalize the employer payroll tax for the February 8 pay period. Use 5.4 percent SUTA and 0.6 percent FUTA. No employees will exceed the FUTA or SUTA wage base.
February 13	Issue the employee pay.
February 22	Journalize the employee pay.
February 22	Journalize the employer payroll tax for the February 22 pay period. Use 5.4 percent SUTA and 0.6 percent FUTA. No employee will exceed the FUTA or SUTA wage base.
February 27	Issue the employee pay.
March 9	Journalize employee pay.
March 9	Journalize employer payroll tax for the March 9 pay period. Use 5.4 percent SUTA and 0.6 percent FUTA. No employees will exceed the FUTA or SUTA wage base.
March 14	Issue employee pay.
March 23	Journalize employee pay.
March 23	Journalize employer payroll tax for the March 23 pay period. Use 5.4 percent SUTA and 0.6 percent FUTA. No employees will exceed FUTA or SUTA wage base.
March 28	Issue employee pay.

	Date	Description	Post Ref.	Debit	Credit	
1						1
2						2
3						3
4						4
5						5
6						6
7						7
8						8
9						9
10						10
11						11
12						12
13						13
14						14
15						15
16						16
17						17
18						18
19						19
20						20
21						21
22						22
23						23
24						24
25						25
26						26
27						27
28						28
29						29
30						30
31						31
32						32
33						33
34						34
35						35

Post all journal entries to the appropriate General Ledger accounts.

Account: Cash **101**

						Balance		
	Date	Description	Post Ref.	Debit	Credit	Debit	Credit	
1		Beg. Bal.				47 0 0 0 00		1
2								2
3								3
4								4
5								5
6								6

Account: Employee Federal Income Tax Payable **203**

	Date	Description	Post Ref.	Debit	Credit	Balance		
						Debit	Credit	
1								1
2								2
3								3
4								4
5								5
6								6

Account: Social Security Tax Payable **204**

	Date	Description	Post Ref.	Debit	Credit	Balance		
						Debit	Credit	
1								1
2								2
3								3
4								4
5								5
6								6

Account: Medicare Tax Payable **205**

	Date	Description	Post Ref.	Debit	Credit	Balance		
						Debit	Credit	
1								1
2								2
3								3
4								4
5								5
6								6

Account: Employee State Income Tax Payable **206**

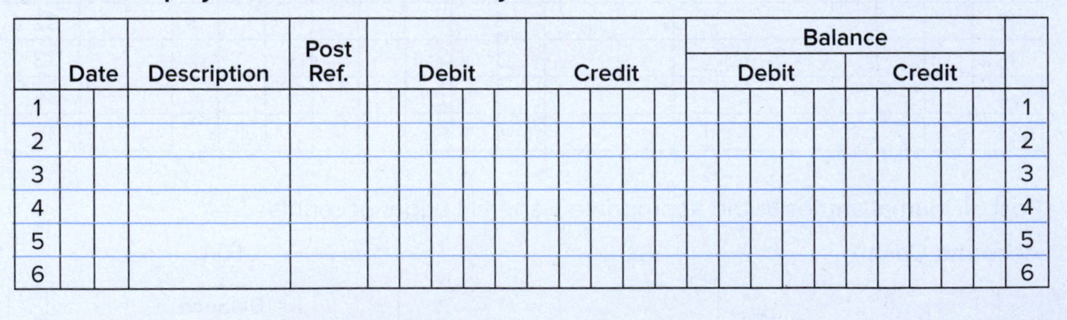

	Date	Description	Post Ref.	Debit	Credit	Balance		
						Debit	Credit	
1								1
2								2
3								3
4								4
5								5
6								6

Account: 401(k) Contributions Payable **208**

	Date	Description	Post Ref.	Debit	Credit	Balance		
						Debit	Credit	
1								1
2								2
3								3
4								4
5								5
6								6

Account: Health Insurance Payable **209**

	Date	Description	Post Ref.	Debit	Credit	Balance		
						Debit	Credit	
1								1
2								2
3								3
4								4
5								5
6								6

Account: Salaries and Wages Payable **210**

	Date	Description	Post Ref.	Debit	Credit	Balance		
						Debit	Credit	
1								1
2								2
3								3
4								4
5								5
6								6

Account: FUTA Tax Payable **211**

	Date	Description	Post Ref.	Debit	Credit	Balance		
						Debit	Credit	
1								1
2								2
3								3
4								4
5								5
6								6

Account: SUTA Tax Payable **212**

	Date	Description	Post Ref.	Debit	Credit	Balance		
						Debit	Credit	
1								1
2								2
3								3
4								4
5								5
6								6

Account: Payroll Taxes Expense **514**

	Date	Description	Post Ref.	Debit	Credit	Balance		
						Debit	Credit	
1								1
2								2
3								3
4								4
5								5
6								6

Account: Salaries and Wages Expense **515**

	Date	Description	Post Ref.	Debit	Credit	Balance Debit	Balance Credit	
1								1
2								2
3								3
4								4
5								5
6								6

Answers to Stop & Check Exercises

Employees' Earnings Records

1. The payroll register contains the period payroll information for all employees. The employees' earnings record lists all payroll data for a single employee.
2. a. Name
   b. Pay rate
   c. Net pay
3. Quarterly and annual tax reports use the totals from the employees' earnings records.

Financial Accounting Concepts

1. Assets = Liabilities + Owners' Equity
2. Credit
3. Debit

Payroll and the General Journal

1. Wages and Salaries Expense
2.

Account	Debit	Credit
Payroll Taxes Expense	$9,546.05	
Social Security Tax Payable		$7,736.67
Medicare Tax Payable		$1,809.38

3.

Account	Debit	Credit
Federal Income Tax Payable	$15,280.00	
Social Security Tax Payable	2,653.29	
Medicare Tax Payable	620.53	
State Income Tax Payable	1,626.21	
Wages and Salaries Payable	22,614.97	
Wages and Salaries Expense		$42,795.00

General Ledger Entries

1. $2,760 Cr.
2. The transaction may be found in the General Journal earlier in this section.

The Business Effects of Payroll

1. The payment of employee wages decreases profitability because it increases the expenses of a business.
2. Allocation of payroll expenses to specific jobs, clients, and so on allows the company to understand the costs associated with the activity.

Labor Reports

1. a. Trial balance
   b. Statement of owners' equity
   c. Income summary
   d. Balance sheet
2. Labor reports
3. Trend reports are used by managers to identify business patterns, needs, and opportunities.

Appendix A

Comprehensive Payroll Project: Wayland Custom Woodworking

Wayland Custom Woodworking is a firm that manufactures custom cabinets and woodwork for business and residential customers. Students will have the opportunity to establish payroll records and to complete a month of payroll information for Wayland.

Wayland Custom Woodworking is located at 1716 Nichol Street, Logan, Utah, 84321, phone number 435-555-9877. The owner is Mark Wayland. Wayland's EIN is 91-7444533, and the Utah Employer Account Number is 99992901685WTH. Wayland has determined it will pay its employees on a semimonthly basis. Federal income tax should be computed using the ***percentage*** method.

Students will complete the payroll for the final quarter of 2019 and will file fourth quarter and annual tax reports on the appropriate dates. At the instructor's discretion, students may complete a short version, which contains the payroll transactions beginning December 4. Directions for completion of the short version follow the November 30 transactions.

The SUTA (UI) rate for Wayland Custom Woodworking is 2.6 percent on the first $35,300, and the state withholding rate is a calculation of 4.95 percent for all income levels, deductions, and marital statuses (use Table A-1 for the calculation of state tax due for employees).

Rounding can create a challenge. For these exercises, the rate for the individuals is not rounded. So take their salary and divide by 2,080 (52 weeks at 40 hours per week) for full-time, nonexempt employees.

EXAMPLE: ANNUAL SALARY TO HOURLY RATE, NONEXEMPT EMPLOYEE

Employee Varden's annual salary is $42,000, and he is a nonexempt employee.

Hourly rate = $42,000/ (52 × 40) = $42,000/2,080

Hourly rate = $20.19231 per hour

After the gross pay has been calculated, round the result to only two decimal points prior to calculating taxes or other withholdings.

EXAMPLE: PERIOD GROSS PAY, SALARIED EMPLOYEE

Employee Chinson earns an annual salary of $24,000 and is paid semimonthly.

Period gross pay = $24,000/24 = $1,000 gross pay

For pay periods with holiday hours: determine the amount paid per day, multiply by the number of days applicable to each pay.

Annual salary: $24,000/(52*5) = $24,000/260 = $92.30769 (rounded to 5 decimal points) per day.

Employees are paid for the following holidays occurring during the final quarter:

- Thanksgiving day and the day after, Thursday and Friday, November 28–29.
- Christmas, which is a Wednesday. Employees receive holiday pay for Tuesday, December 24, and Wednesday, December 25.

For the completion of this project, the following information can be located in Appendix C. Students will use the percentage method for federal income tax and the tax tables have been provided for Utah. Both 401(k) and insurance are pre-tax for federal income tax and Utah income tax. Round calculations to get to final tax amounts and 401(k) contributions after calculating gross pay.

Federal Withholding Allowance (less 401(k), Section 125)	$175.00 per allowance claimed
Federal Unemployment Rate (employer only) (less Section 125)	0.6% on the first $7,000 of wages
Semimonthly Federal Percentage Method Tax Table	Appendix C Table 3
State Unemployment Rate (employer only) (less Section 125)	2.6% on the first $35,300 of wages
State Withholding Rate (less 401(k), Section 125)	See Utah Schedule 3, Table A-1

Utah Schedule 3 SEMIMONTHLY Payroll Period *(24 pay periods per year)*

Example: Married

1. Utah taxable wages	5,075	
2. Multiply line 1 by .0495 (4.95%)	251	
3. Base allowance	30	
4. Line 1 minus $297 (not less than 0)		4,778
5. Multiply line 4 by .013 (1.3%)		62
6. Line 3 minus line 5 (not less than 0)		-
7. Withholding tax line 2 minus line 6 (not less than 0)	251	

Federal taxable wages (also for state) $5,075.

TABLE A-1

Utah Schedule 3 SEMIMONTHLY Payroll Period *(24 pay periods per year)*

Single

1. Utah taxable wages		
2. Multiply line 1 by .0495 (4.95%)		
3. Base allowance	15	
4. Line 1 minus $297 (not less than 0)		
5. Multiply line 4 by .013 (1.3%)		
6. Line 3 minus line 5 (not less than 0)		
7. Withholding tax line 2 minus line 6 (not less than 0)		

Married

1. Utah taxable wages		
2. Multiply line 1 by .0495 (4.95%)		
3. Base allowance	30	
4. Line 1 minus $594 (not less than 0)		
5. Multiply line 4 by .013 (1.3%)		
6. Line 3 minus line 5 (not less than 0)		
7. Withholding tax line 2 minus line 6 (not less than 0)		

October 1

Wayland Custom Woodworking (WCW) pays its employees according to their job classification. The following employees comprise Wayland's staff:

Employee Number	Name and Address	Payroll information
00-Chins	Anthony Chinson	Married, 1 withholding allowance
	530 Sylvann Avenue	Exempt
	Logan, UT 84321	$24,000/year + commission
	435-555-1212	Start Date: 10/1/2019
	Job title: Account Executive	SSN: 511-22-3333
00-Wayla	Mark Wayland	Married, 5 withholding allowances
	1570 Lovett Street	Exempt
	Logan, UT 84321	$75,000/year
	435-555-1110	Start Date: 10/1/2019
	Job title: President/Owner	SSN: 505-33-1775
01-Peppi	Sylvia Peppinico	Married, 7 withholding allowances
	291 Antioch Road	Exempt
	Logan, UT 84321	$43,500/year
	435-555-2244	Start Date: 10/1/2019
	Job title: Craftsman	SSN: 047-55-9951
01-Varde	Stevon Varden	Married, 2 withholding allowances
	333 Justin Drive	Nonexempt
	Logan, UT 84321	$42,000/year
	435-555-9981	Start Date: 10/1/2019
	Job title: Craftsman	SSN: 022-66-1131
02-Hisso	Leonard Hissop	Single, 4 withholding allowances
	531 5th Street	Nonexempt
	Logan, UT 84321	$49,500/year
	435-555-5858	Start Date: 10/1/2019
	Job title: Purchasing/Shipping	SSN: 311-22-6698

Complete the headers of the Employees' Earnings Register for all company employees. Enter the YTD earnings for each employee. The departments are as follows:

Department 00: Sales and Administration

Department 01: Factory Workers

Department 02: Delivery and Customer Service

1. You have been hired as of October 1 as the new accounting clerk. Your employee number is 00-SUCCE. Your name is STUDENT SUCCESS. Your address is 1650 South Street, Logan, UT 84321. Your phone number is 435-556-1211, you were born July 16, 1985, your Utah driver's license number is 887743 expiring in 7/2024, and your Social Security number is 555-55-5555. You are nonexempt and paid at a rate of $36,000 per year. Complete the W-4 and, using the given information, complete the I-9 form to start your employee file. Complete it as if you are single with one withholding, you contribute 3 percent to a 401(k), and health insurance is $50 per pay period.

The balance sheet for WCW as of September 30, 2019, is as follows:

Wayland Custom Woodworking
Balance Sheet
September 30, 2019

Assets		***Liabilities & Equity***	
Cash	$1,125,000.00	Accounts Payable	$ 112,490.00
Supplies	27,240.00	Salaries and Wages Payable	
Office Equipment	87,250.00	Federal Unemployment Tax Payable	
Inventory	123,000.00	Social Security Tax Payable	
Vehicle	25,000.00	Medicare Tax Payable	
Accumulated Depreciation, Vehicle		State Unemployment Tax Payable	
Building	164,000.00	Employee Federal Income Tax Payable	
Accumulated Depreciation, Building		Employee State Income Tax Payable	
Land	35,750.00	401(k) Contributions Payable	
Total Assets	1,587,240.00	Employee Medical Premiums Payable	
		Notes Payable	224,750.00
		Utilities Payable	
		Total Liabilities	337,240.00
		Owners' Equity	1,250,000.00
		Retained Earnings	—
		Total Equity	1,250,000.00
		Total Liabilities and Equity	1,587,240.00

October 15

October 15 is the end of the first pay period for the month of October. Employee pay will be disbursed on October 18, 2019. Any time worked in excess of 88 hours during this pay period is considered overtime for nonexempt employees. Remember that the employees are paid on a semimonthly basis. The hours for the employees are as follows:

Name	Hourly Rate (round to 5 decimals)	Pay Period Hours 10/1–10/15	Regular (round to 2 decimals)	Overtime (round to 2 decimals)	Commission
Chinson		88 hours (exempt)			$1,500.00
Wayland		88 hours (exempt)			
Peppinico		88 hours (exempt)			
Varden		88 hours			
Hissop		93.25 hours			
Student		90 hours			

October

Sunday	Monday	Tuesday	Wednesday	Thursday	Friday	Saturday
		1	2	3	4	5
6	7	8	9	10	11	12
13	14	15	16	17	18	19
20	21	22	23	24	25	26
27	28	29	30	31		

Complete the Payroll Register for October 15. Round wages to five decimal points and all other final answers to two decimal points. Update the Employees' Earnings Records for the period's pay and update the YTD amount. Insurance qualifies for Section 125 treatment.

Voluntary deductions for each employee are as follows:

Name	Deduction
Chinson	Insurance: $50/paycheck 401(k): 3% of gross pay
Wayland	Insurance: $75/paycheck 401(k): 6% of gross pay
Peppinico	Insurance: $75/paycheck 401(k): $50 per paycheck
Varden	Insurance: $50/paycheck 401(k): 4% of gross pay
Hissop	Insurance: $75/paycheck 401(k): 3% of gross pay
Student	Insurance: $50/paycheck 401(k): 3% of gross pay

Complete the Payroll Register for October 15.

P/R End Date | | Company Name Wayland Custom Woodworking

Check Date | |

Name	M/S	# W/H	Hourly Rate or Period Wage	No. of Regular Hours	No. of Overtime Hours	No. of Holiday Hours	Commissions	Gross Earnings	Insurance	401(k)	Taxable Wages for Federal W/H	Taxable Wages for FICA
Anthony Chinson												
Mark Wayland												
Sylvia Peppinico												
Stevon Varden												
Leonard Hissop												
Student												
Total												

Name	Gross Earnings	Taxable Wages for Federal W/H	Taxable Wages for FICA	Federal W/H	Social Security Tax	Medicare W/H	State W/H Tax	Union Dues	Net Pay	Check No.
Anthony Chinson										
Mark Wayland										
Sylvia Peppinico										
Stevon Varden										
Leonard Hissop										
Student										
Total										

EMPLOYEE EARNING RECORD

NAME		Hire Date	
ADDRESS		Date of Birth	
CITY/STATE/ZIP		Exempt/Nonexempt	
TELEPHONE		Married/Single	
SOCIAL SECURITY NUMBER		No. of Exemptions	
POSITION		Pay Rate	

Period Ended	Hrs. Worked	Reg Pay	OT Pay	Holiday	Comm	Gross Pay	Ins	401(k)	Taxable Pay for Federal W/H	Taxable Pay for FICA

Taxable Pay for Federal W/H	Taxable Pay for FICA	Fed Inc. Tax	Social Sec. Tax	Medicare	State Inc. Tax	Total Deduc	Net Pay	YTD Net Pay	YTD Sec. Tax	YTD FUTA

EMPLOYEE EARNING RECORD

NAME		Hire Date	
ADDRESS		Date of Birth	
CITY/STATE/ZIP		Exempt/Nonexempt	
TELEPHONE		Married/Single	
SOCIAL SECURITY NUMBER		No. of Exemptions	
POSITION		Pay Rate	

Period Ended	Hrs. Worked	Reg Pay	OT Pay	Holiday	Comm	Gross Pay	Ins	401(k)	Taxable Pay for Federal W/H	Taxable Pay for FICA

Taxable Pay for Federal W/H	Taxable Pay for FICA	Fed Inc. Tax	Social Sec. Tax	Medicare	State Inc. Tax	Total Deduc	Net Pay	YTD Net Pay	YTD Sec. Tax	YTD FUTA

EMPLOYEE EARNING RECORD

NAME		Hire Date	
ADDRESS		Date of Birth	
CITY/STATE/ZIP		Exempt/Nonexempt	
TELEPHONE		Married/Single	
SOCIAL SECURITY NUMBER		No. of Exemptions	
POSITION		Pay Rate	

Period Ended	Hrs. Worked	Reg Pay	OT Pay	Holiday	Comm	Gross Pay	Ins	401(k)	Taxable Pay for Federal W/H	Taxable Pay for FICA

Taxable Pay for Federal W/H	Taxable Pay for FICA	Fed Inc. Tax	Social Sec. Tax	Medicare	State Inc. Tax	Total Deduc	Net Pay	YTD Net Pay	YTD Sec. Tax	YTD FUTA

EMPLOYEE EARNING RECORD

NAME		Hire Date	
ADDRESS		Date of Birth	
CITY/STATE/ZIP		Exempt/Nonexempt	
TELEPHONE		Married/Single	
SOCIAL SECURITY NUMBER		No. of Exemptions	
POSITION		Pay Rate	

Period Ended	Hrs. Worked	Reg Pay	OT Pay	Holiday	Comm	Gross Pay	Ins	401(k)	Taxable Pay for Federal W/H	Taxable Pay for FICA

Taxable Pay for Federal W/H	Taxable Pay for FICA	Fed Inc. Tax	Social Sec. Tax	Medicare	State Inc. Tax	Total Deduc	Net Pay	YTD Net Pay	YTD Sec. Tax	YTD FUTA

EMPLOYEE EARNING RECORD

NAME		Hire Date	
ADDRESS		Date of Birth	
CITY/STATE/ZIP		Exempt/Nonexempt	
TELEPHONE		Married/Single	
SOCIAL SECURITY NUMBER		No. of Exemptions	
POSITION		Pay Rate	

Period Ended	Hrs. Worked	Reg Pay	OT Pay	Holiday	Comm	Gross Pay	Ins	401(k)	Taxable Pay for Federal W/H	Taxable Pay for FICA

Taxable Pay for Federal W/H	Taxable Pay for FICA	Fed Inc. Tax	Social Sec. Tax	Medicare	State Inc. Tax	Total Deduc	Net Pay	YTD Net Pay	YTD Sec. Tax	YTD FUTA

EMPLOYEE EARNING RECORD

NAME		Hire Date	
ADDRESS		Date of Birth	
CITY/STATE/ZIP		Exempt/Nonexempt	
TELEPHONE		Married/Single	
SOCIAL SECURITY NUMBER		No. of Exemptions	
POSITION		Pay Rate	

Period Ended	Hrs. Worked	Reg Pay	OT Pay	Holiday	Comm	Gross Pay	Ins	401(k)	Taxable Pay for Federal W/H	Taxable Pay for FICA

Taxable Pay for Federal W/H	Taxable Pay for FICA	Fed Inc. Tax	Social Sec. Tax	Medicare	State Inc. Tax	Total Deduc	Net Pay	YTD Net Pay	YTD Sec. Tax	YTD FUTA

General Journal Entries

Complete the General Journal entries as follows:

15-Oct	Journalize employee pay including the issuance of paychecks (use one entry for all checks).
15-Oct	Journalize employer payroll tax for the October 15 pay date.
18-Oct	Journalize the payment of payroll.

Post all journal entries to the appropriate General Ledger accounts.

Date		Description	Post Ref.	Debit	Credit

October 31

October 31 is the end of the final pay period for the month. Employee pay will be disbursed on November 4, 2019. Any hours exceeding 96 during this pay period are considered overtime for nonexempt employees. Compute the employee pay. Update the Employees' Earnings Records for the period's pay and update the YTD amount.

Complete the Payroll Register for October 31. Round wages to five decimal points and all other final answers to two decimal points.

The hours for the employees are as follows:

Name	Hourly rate (round to 5 decimals)	Hours Worked 10/16–10/31	Regular (round to 2 decimals)	Overtime (round to 2 decimals)	Commission
Chinson		96 hours (exempt)			$ 1,750.00
Wayland		96 hours (exempt)			
Peppinico		96 hours (exempt)			
Varden		100 hours			
Hissop		103 hours			
Student		98 hours			

October

Sunday	Monday	Tuesday	Wednesday	Thursday	Friday	Saturday
		1	2	3	4	5
6	7	8	9	10	11	12
13	14	15	16	17	18	19
20	21	22	23	24	25	26
27	28	29	30	31		

Complete the Payroll Register for October 31.

Run End Date		Company Name	Wayland Custom Woodworking
P/R Date			

Name	M/S	# W/H	Hourly Rate or Period Wage	No. of Regular Hours	No. of Overtime Hours	No. of Holiday Hours	Commissions	Gross Earnings	Insurance	401(k)	Taxable Wages for Federal W/H	Taxable Wages for FICA
Anthony Chinson												
Mark Wayland												
Sylvia Peppinico												
Stevon Varden												
Leonard Hissop												
Student												
Total												

Name	Gross Earnings	Taxable Wages for Federal W/H	Taxable Wages for FICA	Federal W/H	Social Security Tax	Medicare W/H	State W/H Tax	Union Dues	Net Pay	Check No.
Anthony Chinson										
Mark Wayland										
Sylvia Peppinico										
Stevon Varden										
Leonard Hissop										
Student										
Total										

General Journal Entries

Complete the General Journal entries as follows:

31-Oct	Journalize employee pay for the period.
31-Oct	Journalize employer payroll tax for the October 31 pay date.
04-Nov	Journalize the payment of payroll to employees. (Use one entry for all disbursements.)
04-Nov	Journalize remittance of 401(k) and Section 125 health insurance premiums deducted.
04-Nov	Journalize remittance of monthly payroll taxes.

Post all journal entries to the appropriate General Ledger accounts

Date		Description	Post Ref.	Debit	Credit

November 15

Compute the pay for each employee. Update the Employees' Earnings Record for the period's pay and the new YTD amount. Employee pay will be disbursed on November 19, 2019. Any hours exceeding 88 during this pay period are considered overtime for nonexempt employees. Remember that the employees are paid semimonthly.

Complete the Payroll Register for November 15. Round wages to five decimal points and all other final answers to two decimal points.

The hours for the employees are as follows:

Name	Hourly rate (round to 5 decimals)	Pay Period Hours 11/01–11/15	Regular (round to 2 decimals)	Overtime (round to 2 decimals)	Commission
Chinson		88 hours (exempt)			$1,050.00
Wayland		88 hours (exempt)			
Peppinico		88 hours (exempt)			
Varden		96 hours			
Hissop		91 hours			
Student		93 hours			

November						
Sunday	Monday	Tuesday	Wednesday	Thursday	Friday	Saturday
					1	2
3	4	5	6	7	8	9
10	11	12	13	14	15	16
17	18	19	20	21	22	23
24	25	26	27	28	29	30

Complete the Payroll Register for November 15.

Run Date ______ Company Name Wayland Custom Woodworking

P/R Date ______

Name	M/S	# W/H	Hourly Rate or Period Wage	No. of Regular Hours	No. of Overtime Hours	No. of Holiday Hours	Commissions	Gross Earnings	Insurance	401(k)	Taxable Wages for Federal W/H	Taxable Wages for FICA
Anthony Chinson												
Mark Wayland												
Sylvia Peppinico												
Stevon Varden												
Leonard Hissop												
Student												
Total												

Name	Gross Earnings	Taxable Wages for Federal W/H	Taxable Wages for FICA	Federal W/H	Social Security Tax	Medicare W/H	State W/H Tax	Union Dues	Net Pay	Check No.
Anthony Chinson										
Mark Wayland										
Sylvia Peppinico										
Stevon Varden										
Leonard Hissop										
Student										
Total										

General Journal Entries

Complete the General Journal entries as follows:

15-Nov	Journalize employee pay including the issuance of paychecks (use one entry for all checks).
15-Nov	Journalize employer payroll tax for the November 15 pay date.
19-Nov	Journalize payment of payroll to employees.

Post all journal entries to the appropriate General Ledger accounts.

Date		Description	Post Ref.	Debit	Credit

Post all journal entries to the appropriate General Ledger accounts.

November 30

Compute the Net Pay for each employee. Employee pay will be disbursed on December 4, 2019. Update the Employees' Earnings Records with the November 30 pay and the new YTD amount.

The company is closed and pays for the Friday following Thanksgiving. The employees will receive holiday pay for Thanksgiving and the Friday following. All the hours over 88 are eligible for overtime for nonexempt employees as they were worked during the non-holiday week.

The hours for the employees are as follows:

Name	Hourly rate (round to 5 decimals)	Pay Period Hours 11/16—11/30	Regular (round to 2 decimals)	Overtime (round to 2 decimals)	Holiday (round to 2 decimals)	Commission
Chinson		80 hours (exempt — 16 hours Holiday)				$2,325.00
Wayland		80 hours (exempt — 16 hours Holiday)				
Peppinico		80 hours (exempt — 16 hours Holiday)				
Varden		82 hours (exempt — 16 hours Holiday)				
Hissop		83 hours (exempt — 16 hours Holiday)				
Student		81 hours (exempt — 16 hours Holiday)				

November						
Sunday	Monday	Tuesday	Wednesday	Thursday	Friday	Saturday
					1	2
3	4	5	6	7	8	9
10	11	12	13	14	15	16
17	18	19	20	21	22	23
24	25	26	27	28	29	30

Complete the Payroll Register for November 30. Round wages to five decimal points and all other final answers to two decimal points.

Complete the Payroll Register for November 30.

Run Date ______ Company Name Wayland Custom Woodworking

P/R Date ______

Name	M/S	# W/H	Hourly Rate or Period Wage	No. of Regular Hours	No. of Overtime Hours	No. of Holiday Hours	Commissions	Gross Earnings	Insurance	401(k)	Taxable Wages for Federal W/H	Taxable Wages for FICA
Anthony Chinson												
Mark Wayland												
Sylvia Peppinico												
Stevon Varden												
Leonard Hissop												
Student												
Total												

Name	Gross Earnings	Taxable Wages for Federal W/H	Taxable Wages for FICA	Federal W/H	Social Security Tax	Medicare W/H	State W/H Tax	Union Dues	Net Pay	Check No.
Anthony Chinson										
Mark Wayland										
Sylvia Peppinico										
Stevon Varden										
Leonard Hissop										
Student										
Total										

General Journal Entries

Complete the General Journal entries as follows:

30-Nov	Journalize employee pay including the issuance of paychecks (use one entry for all checks).
30-Nov	Journalize employer payroll tax for the November 30 pay date.
04-Dec	Journalize payment of payroll to employees.
04-Dec	Journalize remittance of 401(k) and health insurance premiums deducted.
04-Dec	Journalize remittance of monthly payroll taxes.

Post all journal entries to the appropriate General Ledger accounts.

Date		Description	Post Ref.	Debit	Credit

December 15

Compute the net pay and update the Employees' Earnings Records with the December 15 pay and the new YTD information. Employee pay will be disbursed on December 19, 2019. Any hours worked in excess of 80 hours during this pay period are considered overtime for nonexempt employees.

The hours for the employees are as follows:

Name	Hourly rate (round to 5 decimals)	Pay Period Hours 12/16–12/31	Regular (round to 2 decimals)	Overtime (round to 2 decimals)	Holiday (round to 2 decimals)	Commission
Chinson		80 hours (exempt)				$1,680.00
Wayland		80 hours (exempt)				
Peppinico		80 hours (exempt)				
Varden		84 hours				
Hissop		80 hours				
Student		83 hours				

December						
Sunday	Monday	Tuesday	Wednesday	Thursday	Friday	Saturday
1	2	3	4	5	6	7
8	9	10	11	12	13	14
15	16	17	18	19	20	21
22	23	24	25	26	27	28
29	30	31				

Complete the Payroll Register for December 15. Round wages to five decimal points and all other final answers to two decimal points.

Run Date		Company Name	Wayland Custom Woodworking
P/R Date			

Name	M/S	# W/H	Hourly Rate or Period Wage	No. of Regular Hours	No. of Overtime Hours	No. of Holiday Hours	Commissions	Gross Earnings	Insurance	401(k)	Taxable Wages for Federal W/H	Taxable Wages for FICA
Anthony Chinson												
Mark Wayland												
Sylvia Peppinico												
Stevon Varden												
Leonard Hissop												
Student												
Total												

Name	Gross Earnings	Taxable Wages for Federal W/H	Taxable Wages for FICA	Federal W/H	Social Security Tax	Medicare W/H	State W/H Tax	Union Dues	Net Pay	Check No.
Anthony Chinson										
Mark Wayland										
Sylvia Peppinico										
Stevon Varden										
Leonard Hissop										
Student										
Total										

General Journal Entries

Complete the General Journal entries as follows:

15-Dec	Journalize employee pay including the issuance of paychecks (use one entry for all checks).
15-Dec	Journalize employer payroll tax for the December 15 pay date.
19-Dec	Journalize payment of payroll to employees.

Post all journal entries to the appropriate General Ledger accounts.

Date		Description	Post Ref.	Debit	Credit

December 31

The final pay period of the year will not be paid to employees until January 3, 2020. The company will accrue the wages for the final pay period only. Because the pay period is complete, there will not be a reversing entry for the accrual.

The company pays for Christmas Eve and the day of Christmas for 2019. Employees will be paid for both Tuesday and Wednesday as holiday pay.

Employee pay will be disbursed and reflected on the Employees' Earnings Register when paid. The remainder of the employer liability will be paid with the final filing for the year. Complete all state and federal tax forms for year-end. Generate W-2 and W-3 for employees, and recall that these forms only reflect wages actually paid during the year. Accrued wages should not be included on Forms W-2 and W-3. Employer amounts for health coverage should be reported as 1.5 times the employee's premium in Box 12, using Code DD.

The hours for the employees are as follows:

Name	Hourly rate (round to 5 decimals)	Pay Period Hours 12/16–12/31	Regular (round to 2 decimals)	Overtime (round to 2 decimals)	Holiday (round to 2 decimals)	Commission
Chinson		96 hours (exempt — 16 hours Holiday)				$1,015.00
Wayland		96 hours (exempt — 16 hours Holiday)				
Peppinico		96 hours (exempt — 16 hours Holiday)				
Varden		98 hours (16 Holiday)*				
Hissop		97 hours (16 Holiday)*				
Student		99 hours (16 Holiday)*				

*Employees worked extra hours on Saturday during the week of 12/23–12/27. Reminder, holidays and vacations are not included as hours *worked* for calculation of overtime.

December						
Sunday	Monday	Tuesday	Wednesday	Thursday	Friday	Saturday
1	2	3	4	5	6	7
8	9	10	11	12	13	14
15	16	17	18	19	20	21
22	23	24	25	26	27	28
29	30	31				

Complete the Payroll Register for December 31.

Run Date ______ Company Name Wayland Custom Woodworking

P/R Date ______

Name	M/S	# W/H	Hourly Rate or Period Wage	No. of Regular Hours	No. of Overtime Hours	No. of Holiday Hours	Commissions	Gross Earnings	Insurance	401(k)	Taxable Wages for Federal W/H	Taxable Wages for FICA
Anthony Chinson												
Mark Wayland												
Sylvia Peppinico												
Stevon Varden												
Leonard Hissop												
Student												
Total												

Name	Gross Earnings	Taxable Wages for Federal W/H	Taxable Wages for FICA	Federal W/H	Social Security Tax	Medicare W/H	State W/H Tax	Union Dues	Net Pay	Check No.
Anthony Chinson										
Mark Wayland										
Sylvia Peppinico										
Stevon Varden										
Leonard Hissop										
Student										
Total										

General Journal Entries

Complete the General Journal entries as follows:

31-Dec Accrue employee pay including the issuance of paychecks (use one entry for all checks).

31-Dec Accrue employer payroll tax for the December 31 pay date.

Post all journal entries to the appropriate General Ledger accounts.

Date		Description	Post Ref.	Debit	Credit

Employment Eligibility Verification

Department of Homeland Security

U.S. Citizenship and Immigration Services

USCIS
Form I-9
OMB No. 1615-0047
Expires 08/31/2019

▶START HERE: Read instructions carefully before completing this form. The instructions must be available, either in paper or electronically, during completion of this form. Employers are liable for errors in the completion of this form.

ANTI-DISCRIMINATION NOTICE: It is illegal to discriminate against work-authorized individuals. Employers **CANNOT** specify which document(s) an employee may present to establish employment authorization and identity. The refusal to hire or continue to employ an individual because the documentation presented has a future expiration date may also constitute illegal discrimination.

Section 1. Employee Information and Attestation

*(Employees must complete and sign Section 1 of Form I-9 no later than the **first day of employment**, but not before accepting a job offer.)*

Last Name *(Family Name)*	First Name *(Given Name)*	Middle Initial	Other Last Names Used *(if any)*

Address *(Street Number and Name)*	Apt. Number	City or Town	State	ZIP Code

Date of Birth *(mm/dd/yyyy)*	U.S. Social Security Number	Employee's E-mail Address	Employee's Telephone Number
	☐☐☐ - ☐☐ - ☐☐☐☐		

I am aware that federal law provides for imprisonment and/or fines for false statements or use of false documents in connection with the completion of this form.

I attest, under penalty of perjury, that I am (check one of the following boxes):

☐ 1. A citizen of the United States

☐ 2. A noncitizen national of the United States *(See instructions)*

☐ 3. A lawful permanent resident (Alien Registration Number/USCIS Number): ____________

☐ 4. An alien authorized to work until (expiration date, if applicable, mm/dd/yyyy): ____________
Some aliens may write "N/A" in the expiration date field. *(See instructions)*

Aliens authorized to work must provide only one of the following document numbers to complete Form I-9: An Alien Registration Number/USCIS Number OR Form I-94 Admission Number OR Foreign Passport Number.

1. Alien Registration Number/USCIS Number: ____________

OR

2. Form I-94 Admission Number: ____________

OR

3. Foreign Passport Number: ____________

Country of Issuance: ____________

QR Code - Section 1
Do Not Write In This Space

Signature of Employee	Today's Date *(mm/dd/yyyy)*

Preparer and/or Translator Certification (check one):

☐ I did not use a preparer or translator. ☐ A preparer(s) and/or translator(s) assisted the employee in completing Section 1.

(Fields below must be completed and signed when preparers and/or translators assist an employee in completing Section 1.)

I attest, under penalty of perjury, that I have assisted in the completion of Section 1 of this form and that to the best of my knowledge the information is true and correct.

Signature of Preparer or Translator	Today's Date *(mm/dd/yyyy)*

Last Name *(Family Name)*	First Name *(Given Name)*

Address *(Street Number and Name)*	City or Town	State	ZIP Code

STOP *Employer Completes Next Page* STOP

Employment Eligibility Verification
Department of Homeland Security
U.S. Citizenship and Immigration Services

USCIS
Form I-9
OMB No. 1615-0047
Expires 08/31/2019

Section 2. Employer or Authorized Representative Review and Verification

(Employers or their authorized representative must complete and sign Section 2 within 3 business days of the employee's first day of employment. You must physically examine one document from List A OR a combination of one document from List B and one document from List C as listed on the "Lists of Acceptable Documents.")

Employee Info from Section 1	Last Name *(Family Name)*	First Name *(Given Name)*	M.I.	Citizenship/Immigration Status

List A Identity and Employment Authorization	**OR**	**List B** Identity	**AND**	**List C** Employment Authorization
Document Title		Document Title		Document Title
Issuing Authority		Issuing Authority		Issuing Authority
Document Number		Document Number		Document Number
Expiration Date *(if any)(mm/dd/yyyy)*		Expiration Date *(if any)(mm/dd/yyyy)*		Expiration Date *(if any)(mm/dd/yyyy)*
Document Title		Additional Information		QR Code - Sections 2 & 3 Do Not Write In This Space
Issuing Authority				
Document Number				
Expiration Date *(if any)(mm/dd/yyyy)*				
Document Title				
Issuing Authority				
Document Number				
Expiration Date *(if any)(mm/dd/yyyy)*				

Certification: I attest, under penalty of perjury, that (1) I have examined the document(s) presented by the above-named employee, (2) the above-listed document(s) appear to be genuine and to relate to the employee named, and (3) to the best of my knowledge the employee is authorized to work in the United States.

The employee's first day of employment *(mm/dd/yyyy)*: ______________ ***(See instructions for exemptions)***

Signature of Employer or Authorized Representative	Today's Date *(mm/dd/yyyy)*	Title of Employer or Authorized Representative

Last Name of Employer or Authorized Representative	First Name of Employer or Authorized Representative	Employer's Business or Organization Name

Employer's Business or Organization Address (Street Number and Name)	City or Town	State	ZIP Code

Section 3. Reverification and Rehires *(To be completed and signed by employer or authorized representative.)*

A. New Name *(if applicable)*			**B.** Date of Rehire *(if applicable)*
Last Name *(Family Name)*	First Name *(Given Name)*	Middle Initial	Date *(mm/dd/yyyy)*

C. If the employee's previous grant of employment authorization has expired, provide the information for the document or receipt that establishes continuing employment authorization in the space provided below.

Document Title	Document Number	Expiration Date *(if any) (mm/dd/yyyy)*

I attest, under penalty of perjury, that to the best of my knowledge, this employee is authorized to work in the United States, and if the employee presented document(s), the document(s) I have examined appear to be genuine and to relate to the individual.

Signature of Employer or Authorized Representative	Today's Date *(mm/dd/yyyy)*	Name of Employer or Authorized Representative

Internal Revenue Service

LISTS OF ACCEPTABLE DOCUMENTS
All documents must be UNEXPIRED

Employees may present one selection from List A
or a combination of one selection from List B and one selection from List C.

LIST A **Documents that Establish Both Identity and Employment Authorization**	**OR**	**LIST B** **Documents that Establish Identity**	**AND**	**LIST C** **Documents that Establish Employment Authorization**
1. U.S. Passport or U.S. Passport Card		1. Driver's license or ID card issued by a State or outlying possession of the United States provided it contains a photograph or information such as name, date of birth, gender, height, eye color, and address		1. A Social Security Account Number card, unless the card includes one of the following restrictions: (1) NOT VALID FOR EMPLOYMENT (2) VALID FOR WORK ONLY WITH INS AUTHORIZATION (3) VALID FOR WORK ONLY WITH DHS AUTHORIZATION
2. Permanent Resident Card or Alien Registration Receipt Card (Form I-551)		2. ID card issued by federal, state or local government agencies or entities, provided it contains a photograph or information such as name, date of birth, gender, height, eye color, and address		2. Certification of report of birth issued by the Department of State (Forms DS-1350, FS-545, FS-240)
3. Foreign passport that contains a temporary I-551 stamp or temporary I-551 printed notation on a machine-readable immigrant visa		3. School ID card with a photograph		3. Original or certified copy of birth certificate issued by a State, county, municipal authority, or territory of the United States bearing an official seal
4. Employment Authorization Document that contains a photograph (Form I-766)		4. Voter's registration card		4. Native American tribal document
5. For a nonimmigrant alien authorized to work for a specific employer because of his or her status: a. Foreign passport; and b. Form I-94 or Form I-94A that has the following: (1) The same name as the passport; and (2) An endorsement of the alien's nonimmigrant status as long as that period of endorsement has not yet expired and the proposed employment is not in conflict with any restrictions or limitations identified on the form.		5. U.S. Military card or draft record 6. Military dependent's ID card 7. U.S. Coast Guard Merchant Mariner Card 8. Native American tribal document 9. Driver's license issued by a Canadian government authority **For persons under age 18 who are unable to present a document listed above:**		5. U.S. Citizen ID Card (Form I-197) 6. Identification Card for Use of Resident Citizen in the United States (Form I-179) 7. Employment authorization document issued by the Department of Homeland Security
6. Passport from the Federated States of Micronesia (FSM) or the Republic of the Marshall Islands (RMI) with Form I-94 or Form I-94A indicating nonimmigrant admission under the Compact of Free Association Between the United States and the FSM or RMI		10. School record or report card 11. Clinic, doctor, or hospital record 12. Day-care or nursery school record		

Examples of many of these documents appear in Part 13 of the Handbook for Employers (M-274).

Refer to the instructions for more information about acceptable receipts.

Form W-4 (2019)

Future developments. For the latest information about any future developments related to Form W-4, such as legislation enacted after it was published, go to *www.irs.gov/FormW4*.

Purpose. Complete Form W-4 so that your employer can withhold the correct federal income tax from your pay. Consider completing a new Form W-4 each year and when your personal or financial situation changes.

Exemption from withholding. You may claim exemption from withholding for 2019 if **both** of the following apply.

- For 2018 you had a right to a refund of **all** federal income tax withheld because you had **no** tax liability, **and**
- For 2019 you expect a refund of **all** federal income tax withheld because you expect to have **no** tax liability.

If you're exempt, complete **only** lines 1, 2, 3, 4, and 7 and sign the form to validate it. Your exemption for 2019 expires February 17, 2020. See Pub. 505, Tax Withholding and Estimated Tax, to learn more about whether you qualify for exemption from withholding.

General Instructions

If you aren't exempt, follow the rest of these instructions to determine the number of withholding allowances you should claim for withholding for 2019 and any additional amount of tax to have withheld. For regular wages, withholding must be based on allowances you claimed and may not be a flat amount or percentage of wages.

You can also use the calculator at ***www.irs.gov/W4App*** to determine your tax withholding more accurately. Consider using this calculator if you have a more complicated tax situation, such as if you have a working spouse, more than one job, or a large amount of nonwage income not subject to withholding outside of your job. After your Form W-4 takes effect, you can also use this calculator to see how the amount of tax you're having withheld compares to your projected total tax for 2019. If you use the calculator, you don't need to complete any of the worksheets for Form W-4.

Note that if you have too much tax withheld, you will receive a refund when you file your tax return. If you have too little tax withheld, you will owe tax when you file your tax return, and you might owe a penalty.

Filers with multiple jobs or working spouses. If you have more than one job at a time, or if you're married filing jointly and your spouse is also working, read all of the instructions including the instructions for the Two-Earners/Multiple Jobs Worksheet before beginning.

Nonwage income. If you have a large amount of nonwage income not subject to withholding, such as interest or dividends, consider making estimated tax payments using Form 1040-ES, Estimated Tax for Individuals. Otherwise, you might owe additional tax. Or, you can use the Deductions, Adjustments, and Additional Income Worksheet on page 3 or the calculator at *www.irs.gov/W4App* to make sure you have enough tax withheld from your paycheck. If you have pension or annuity income, see Pub. 505 or use the calculator at *www.irs.gov/W4App* to find out if you should adjust your withholding on Form W-4 or W-4P.

Nonresident alien. If you're a nonresident alien, see Notice 1392, Supplemental Form W-4 Instructions for Nonresident Aliens, before completing this form.

Specific Instructions

Personal Allowances Worksheet

Complete this worksheet on page 3 first to determine the number of withholding allowances to claim.

Line C. *Head of household please note:* Generally, you may claim head of household filing status on your tax return only if you're unmarried and pay more than 50% of the costs of keeping up a home for yourself and a qualifying individual. See Pub. 501 for more information about filing status.

Line E. Child tax credit. When you file your tax return, you may be eligible to claim a child tax credit for each of your eligible children. To qualify, the child must be under age 17 as of December 31, must be your dependent who lives with you for more than half the year, and must have a valid social security number. To learn more about this credit, see Pub. 972, Child Tax Credit. To reduce the tax withheld from your pay by taking this credit into account, follow the instructions on line E of the worksheet. On the worksheet you will be asked about your total income. For this purpose, total income includes all of your wages and other income, including income earned by a spouse if you are filing a joint return.

Line F. Credit for other dependents. When you file your tax return, you may be eligible to claim a credit for other dependents for whom a child tax credit can't be claimed, such as a qualifying child who doesn't meet the age or social security number requirement for the child tax credit, or a qualifying relative. To learn more about this credit, see Pub. 972. To reduce the tax withheld from your pay by taking this credit into account, follow the instructions on line F of the worksheet. On the worksheet, you will be asked about your total income. For this purpose, total

Separate here and give Form W-4 to your employer. Keep the worksheet(s) for your records.

Form **W-4**
Department of the Treasury
Internal Revenue Service

Employee's Withholding Allowance Certificate

▶ Whether you're entitled to claim a certain number of allowances or exemption from withholding is subject to review by the IRS. Your employer may be required to send a copy of this form to the IRS.

OMB No. 1545-0074

2019

1 Your first name and middle initial	Last name	**2 Your social security number**
Home address (number and street or rural route)	**3** ☐ Single ☐ Married ☐ Married, but withhold at higher Single rate. **Note:** If married filing separately, check "Married, but withhold at higher Single rate."	
City or town, state, and ZIP code	**4 If your last name differs from that shown on your social security card, check here. You must call 800-772-1213 for a replacement card.** ▶ ☐	

5 Total number of allowances you're claiming (from the applicable worksheet on the following pages) **5**

6 Additional amount, if any, you want withheld from each paycheck . . . . **6** $

7 I claim exemption from withholding for 2019, and I certify that I meet **both** of the following conditions for exemption.

- Last year I had a right to a refund of **all** federal income tax withheld because I had **no** tax liability, **and**
- This year I expect a refund of **all** federal income tax withheld because I expect to have **no** tax liability.

If you meet both conditions, write "Exempt" here . . . . ▶ **7**

Under penalties of perjury, I declare that I have examined this certificate and, to the best of my knowledge and belief, it is true, correct, and complete.

Employee's signature
(This form is not valid unless you sign it.) ▶ **Date ▶**

8 Employer's name and address (**Employer:** Complete boxes 8 and 10 if sending to IRS and complete boxes 8, 9, and 10 if sending to State Directory of New Hires.)	**9** First date of employment	**10** Employer identification number (EIN)

For Privacy Act and Paperwork Reduction Act Notice, see page 4. Cat. No. 10220Q Form **W-4** (2019)

Internal Revenue Service

Account: Cash **101**

	Date		Description	Post Ref.	Debit	Credit	Balance		
							Debit	Credit	
Beg Bal									
1									1
2									2
3									3
4									4
5									5
6									6
7									7
8									8
9									9
10									10
11									11
12									12
13									13
14									14
15									15

Account: Employee Federal Income Tax Payable **203**

	Date		Description	Post Ref.	Debit	Credit	Balance		
							Debit	Credit	
1									1
2									2
3									3
4									4
5									5
6									6
7									7
8									8
9									9

Account: Social Security Tax Payable **204**

	Date		Description	Post Ref.	Debit	Credit	Balance		
							Debit	Credit	
1									1
2									2
3									3
4									4
5									5
6									6
7									7
8									8
9									9
10									10
11									11
12									12
13									13
14									14
15									15

Account: Medicare Tax Payable **205**

	Date		Description	Post Ref.	Debit	Credit	Balance		
							Debit	Credit	
1									1
2									2
3									3
4									4
5									5
6									6
7									7
8									8
9									9
10									10
11									11
12									12
13									13
14									14
15									15

Account: Employee State Income Tax Payable **206**

	Date		Description	Post Ref.	Debit	Credit	Balance		
							Debit	Credit	
1									1
2									2
3									3
4									4
5									5
6									6
7									7
8									8
9									9
10									10

Account: 401(k) Contributions Payable **208**

	Date		Description	Post Ref.	Debit	Credit	Balance		
							Debit	Credit	
1									1
2									2
3									3
4									4
5									5
6									6
7									7
8									8
9									9
10									10

Account: Employee Medical Premiums Payable **209**

	Date		Description	Post Ref.	Debit	Credit	Balance		
							Debit	Credit	
1									1
2									2
3									3
4									4
5									5
6									6
7									7
8									8
9									9
10									10

Account: Salaries and Wages Payable **210**

	Date		Description	Post Ref.	Debit	Credit	Balance		
							Debit	Credit	
1									1
2									2
3									3
4									4
5									5
6									6
7									7
8									8
9									9
10									10
11									11
12									12

Account: Federal Unemployment Tax Payable **211**

	Date		Description	Post Ref.	Debit	Credit	Balance		
							Debit	Credit	
1									1
2									2
3									3
4									4
5									5
6									6
7									7
8									8
9									9
10									10

Account: State Unemployment Tax Payable **212**

	Date		Description	Post Ref.	Debit	Credit	Balance		
							Debit	Credit	
1									1
2									2
3									3
4									4
5									5
6									6
7									7
8									8
9									9
10									10

Account: Payroll Taxes Expense **514**

	Date		Description	Post Ref.	Debit	Credit	Balance		
							Debit	Credit	
1									1
2									2
3									3
4									4
5									5
6									6
7									7
8									8
9									9
10									10

Account: Salaries and Wages Expense **515**

	Date		Description	Post Ref.	Debit	Credit	Balance		
							Debit	Credit	
1									1
2									2
3									3
4									4
5									5
6									6
7									7
8									8
9									9
10									10

950117

Form **941 for 2019: Employer's QUARTERLY Federal Tax Return**
(Rev. January 2019) Department of the Treasury — Internal Revenue Service

OMB No. 1545-0029

Employer identification number (EIN) ☐☐ – ☐☐☐☐☐☐☐

Name *(not your trade name)*

Trade name *(if any)*

Address
Number Street Suite or room number
City State ZIP code
Foreign country name Foreign province/county Foreign postal code

Report for this Quarter of 2019
(Check one.)

☐ **1:** January, February, March
☐ **2:** April, May, June
☐ **3:** July, August, September
☐ **4:** October, November, December

Go to *www.irs.gov/Form941* for instructions and the latest information.

Read the separate instructions before you complete Form 941. Type or print within the boxes.

Part 1: Answer these questions for this quarter.

1	**Number of employees who received wages, tips, or other compensation for the pay period including:** *Mar. 12* **(Quarter 1),** *June 12* **(Quarter 2),** *Sept. 12* **(Quarter 3), or** *Dec. 12* **(Quarter 4)**		1	
2	**Wages, tips, and other compensation**		2	.
3	**Federal income tax withheld from wages, tips, and other compensation**		3	.
4	**If no wages, tips, and other compensation are subject to social security or Medicare tax**		☐	**Check and go to line 6.**

		Column 1		Column 2
5a	**Taxable social security wages**	.	× 0.124 =	.
5b	**Taxable social security tips**	.	× 0.124 =	.
5c	**Taxable Medicare wages & tips**	.	× 0.029 =	.
5d	**Taxable wages & tips subject to Additional Medicare Tax withholding**	.	× 0.009 =	.

5e	**Add Column 2 from lines 5a, 5b, 5c, and 5d**	5e	.
5f	**Section 3121(q) Notice and Demand—Tax due on unreported tips** (see instructions)	5f	.
6	**Total taxes before adjustments.** Add lines 3, 5e, and 5f	6	.
7	**Current quarter's adjustment for fractions of cents**	7	.
8	**Current quarter's adjustment for sick pay**	8	.
9	**Current quarter's adjustments for tips and group-term life insurance**	9	.
10	**Total taxes after adjustments.** Combine lines 6 through 9	10	.
11	**Qualified small business payroll tax credit for increasing research activities.** Attach Form 8974	11	.
12	**Total taxes after adjustments and credits.** Subtract line 11 from line 10	12	.
13	**Total deposits for this quarter, including overpayment applied from a prior quarter and overpayments applied from Form 941-X, 941-X (PR), 944-X, or 944-X (SP) filed in the current quarter**	13	.
14	**Balance due.** If line 12 is more than line 13, enter the difference and see instructions	14	.

15 **Overpayment.** If line 13 is more than line 12, enter the difference ______ . Check one: ☐ Apply to next return. ☐ Send a refund.

▶ **You MUST complete both pages of Form 941 and SIGN it.**

Next ▶

For Privacy Act and Paperwork Reduction Act Notice, see the back of the Payment Voucher. Cat. No. 17001Z Form **941** (Rev. 1-2019)

Internal Revenue Service

950217

Name *(not your trade name)* | **Employer identification number (EIN)**

Part 2: Tell us about your deposit schedule and tax liability for this quarter.

If you are unsure about whether you are a monthly schedule depositor or a semiweekly schedule depositor, see section 11 of Pub. 15.

16 Check one: ☐ **Line 12 on this return is less than $2,500 or line 12 on the return for the prior quarter was less than $2,500, and you didn't incur a $100,000 next-day deposit obligation during the current quarter.** If line 12 for the prior quarter was less than $2,500 but line 12 on this return is $100,000 or more, you must provide a record of your federal tax liability. If you are a monthly schedule depositor, complete the deposit schedule below; if you are a semiweekly schedule depositor, attach Schedule B (Form 941). Go to Part 3.

☐ **You were a monthly schedule depositor for the entire quarter.** Enter your tax liability for each month and total liability for the quarter, then go to Part 3.

Tax liability: Month 1 ________ .

Month 2 ________ .

Month 3 ________ .

Total liability for quarter ________ . **Total must equal line 12.**

☐ **You were a semiweekly schedule depositor for any part of this quarter.** Complete Schedule B (Form 941), Report of Tax Liability for Semiweekly Schedule Depositors, and attach it to Form 941.

Part 3: Tell us about your business. If a question does NOT apply to your business, leave it blank.

17 If your business has closed or you stopped paying wages . . . . ☐ Check here, and

enter the final date you paid wages ___ / ___ / ___ .

18 If you are a seasonal employer and you don't have to file a return for every quarter of the year . . ☐ Check here.

Part 4: May we speak with your third-party designee?

Do you want to allow an employee, a paid tax preparer, or another person to discuss this return with the IRS? See the instructions for details.

☐ Yes. Designee's name and phone number ________ ________

Select a 5-digit Personal Identification Number (PIN) to use when talking to the IRS. ☐☐☐☐☐

☐ No.

Part 5: Sign here. You MUST complete both pages of Form 941 and SIGN it.

Under penalties of perjury, I declare that I have examined this return, including accompanying schedules and statements, and to the best of my knowledge and belief, it is true, correct, and complete. Declaration of preparer (other than taxpayer) is based on all information of which preparer has any knowledge.

Sign your name here ________

Print your name here ________

Print your title here ________

Date ___ / ___ / ___

Best daytime phone ________

Paid Preparer Use Only

Check if you are self-employed . . . ☐

Preparer's name		PTIN	
Preparer's signature		Date	/ /
Firm's name (or yours if self-employed)		EIN	
Address		Phone	
City	State	ZIP code	

Internal Revenue Service

Form **940 for 2019: Employer's Annual Federal Unemployment (FUTA) Tax Return** 850113

Department of the Treasury — Internal Revenue Service

OMB No. 1545-0028

Employer identification number (EIN) ☐☐ – ☐☐☐☐☐☐☐

Name *(not your trade name)*

Trade name *(if any)*

Address

Number Street Suite or room number

City State ZIP code

Foreign country name Foreign province/county Foreign postal code

Type of Return
(Check all that apply.)

- ☐ **a.** Amended
- ☐ **b.** Successor employer
- ☐ **c.** No payments to employees in 2018
- ☐ **d.** Final: Business closed or stopped paying wages

Go to *www.irs.gov/Form940* for instructions and the latest information.

Read the separate instructions before you complete this form. Please type or print within the boxes.

Part 1: Tell us about your return. If any line does NOT apply, leave it blank. See instructions before completing Part 1.

1a	**If you had to pay state unemployment tax in one state only, enter the state abbreviation**	1a	
1b	**If you had to pay state unemployment tax in more than one state, you are a multi-state employer**	1b	☐ Check here. Complete Schedule A (Form 940).
2	**If you paid wages in a state that is subject to CREDIT REDUCTION**	2	☐ Check here. Complete Schedule A (Form 940).

Part 2: Determine your FUTA tax before adjustments. If any line does NOT apply, leave it blank.

3	**Total payments to all employees**			3	.
4	**Payments exempt from FUTA tax**	4	.		
	Check all that apply: 4a ☐ Fringe benefits; 4b ☐ Group-term life insurance; 4c ☐ Retirement/Pension; 4d ☐ Dependent care; 4e ☐ Other				
5	**Total of payments made to each employee in excess of $7,000**	5	.		
6	**Subtotal** (line 4 + line 5 = line 6)			6	.
7	**Total taxable FUTA wages** (line 3 – line 6 = line 7). See instructions			7	.
8	**FUTA tax before adjustments** (line 7 x 0.006 = line 8)			8	.

Part 3: Determine your adjustments. If any line does NOT apply, leave it blank.

9	**If ALL of the taxable FUTA wages you paid were excluded from state unemployment tax, multiply line 7 by 0.054** (line 7 × 0.054 = line 9). Go to line 12	9	.
10	**If SOME of the taxable FUTA wages you paid were excluded from state unemployment tax, OR you paid ANY state unemployment tax late** (after the due date for filing Form 940), complete the worksheet in the instructions. Enter the amount from line 7 of the worksheet	10	.
11	**If credit reduction applies,** enter the total from Schedule A (Form 940)	11	.

Part 4: Determine your FUTA tax and balance due or overpayment. If any line does NOT apply, leave it blank.

12	**Total FUTA tax after adjustments** (lines 8 + 9 + 10 + 11 = line 12)	12	.
13	**FUTA tax deposited for the year, including any overpayment applied from a prior year**	13	.
14	**Balance due.** If line 12 is more than line 13, enter the excess on line 14. • If line 14 is more than $500, you must deposit your tax. • If line 14 is $500 or less, you may pay with this return. See instructions	14	.
15	**Overpayment.** If line 13 is more than line 12, enter the excess on line 15 and check a box below	15	.

▶ You **MUST** complete both pages of this form and **SIGN** it. Check one: ☐ Apply to next return. ☐ Send a refund.

Next ▶

For Privacy Act and Paperwork Reduction Act Notice, see the back of the Payment Voucher. Cat. No. 11234O Form **940** (2018)

Internal Revenue Service

850212

Name *(not your trade name)*	**Employer identification number (EIN)**

Part 5: Report your FUTA tax liability by quarter only if line 12 is more than $500. If not, go to Part 6.

16 Report the amount of your FUTA tax liability for each quarter; do NOT enter the amount you deposited. If you had no liability for a quarter, leave the line blank.

16a 1st quarter (January 1 – March 31)	**16a**	.
16b 2nd quarter (April 1 – June 30)	**16b**	.
16c 3rd quarter (July 1 – September 30)	**16c**	.
16d 4th quarter (October 1 – December 31)	**16d**	.

17 Total tax liability for the year (lines 16a + 16b + 16c + 16d = line 17) **17** . **Total must equal line 12.**

Part 6: May we speak with your third-party designee?

Do you want to allow an employee, a paid tax preparer, or another person to discuss this return with the IRS? See the instructions for details.

☐ **Yes.** Designee's name and phone number

Select a 5-digit Personal Identification Number (PIN) to use when talking to IRS

☐ **No.**

Part 7: Sign here. You MUST complete both pages of this form and SIGN it.

Under penalties of perjury, I declare that I have examined this return, including accompanying schedules and statements, and to the best of my knowledge and belief, it is true, correct, and complete, and that no part of any payment made to a state unemployment fund claimed as a credit was, or is to be, deducted from the payments made to employees. Declaration of preparer (other than taxpayer) is based on all information of which preparer has any knowledge.

✗ Sign your name here

Print your name here

Print your title here

Date / /

Best daytime phone

Paid Preparer Use Only

Check if you are self-employed ☐

Preparer's name		PTIN	
Preparer's signature		Date	/ /
Firm's name (or yours if self-employed)		EIN	
Address		Phone	
City	State	ZIP code	

Internal Revenue Service

Utah State Tax Commission

TC-941

Last Revised 2/13/2018

All Periods							December Periods Only (Reconciliation)		
Filing Period End Date	Federal EIN	Utah Withholding Account Number	Amended Return	Utah Wages	Federal Tax Withheld	Utah Tax Withheld	Annual Total of Utah Tax Withheld	Total Number of W2s with Utah Wages or Withholding	Total Number of 1099s with Utah Withholding

State of Utah

DWS-UIC
Form 33H
REV 1213

Utah Employer Quarterly Wage List and Contribution Report

Utah Department of Workforce Services, Unemployment Insurance
140 E. 300 S., PO Box 45233, Salt Lake City UT 84145-0233
1-801-526-9235 option 5; 1-800-222-2857 option 5

The preferred method of filing this report is on-line at our website:
http://jobs.utah.gov

Instructions on Back

Registration #: ____________
FEIN: ____________
FEIN change: ____________

EMPLOYER NAME & ADDRESS:

A report must be filed even if no wages are paid for the quarter. See Instructions

Yr/Quarter: ____________
Qtr End Date: ____________
Due Date: ____________

Number of Employees this quarter:

1st Month	2nd Month	3rd Month

Type or machine print preferred.

Employee Social Security Number	Employee Name First	Middle Initial	Last	Total Wages Paid to Employee for this Qtr

The Taxable Wage Base for each employee is $ ____________

Close account, last payroll date: ____________
Please Select Reason
☐ Out of Business
☐ New Owner

Change name, address, or phone:
Please Select Reason
☐ New Owner
☐ Current Owner

Please enter phone number if missing or incorrect.

Current Phone

Name: ____________
Address: ____________
Phone: ____________

Grand Total Wages (All Pages)		
Wages in Excess (See Instruction 9)		
Subject Wages		
Contribution Rate	X	
Contribution Due		
Interest (1% per month)		
Late Penalty ($25.00 min)		
Total Payment Due		

(Make check payable to Utah Unemployment Compensation Fund)

( ) -

Name	Title	Date	Contact Phone Number

I certify the information on this report is true and correct to the best of my knowledge.

Signature

Utah Department of Workforce Services

22222
a Employee's social security number
OMB No. 1545-0008
b Employer identification number (EIN)
1 Wages, tips, other compensation
2 Federal income tax withheld
c Employer's name, address, and ZIP code
3 Social security wages
4 Social security tax withheld
5 Medicare wages and tips
6 Medicare tax withheld
7 Social security tips
8 Allocated tips
d Control number
9
10 Dependent care benefits
e Employee's first name and initial Last name Suff.
11 Nonqualified plans
12a Code
13 Statutory employee Retirement plan Third-party sick pay
12b Code
14 Other
12c Code
12d Code
f Employee's address and ZIP code
15 State Employer's state ID number
16 State wages, tips, etc.
17 State income tax
18 Local wages, tips, etc.
19 Local income tax
20 Locality name

Form **W-2** **Wage and Tax Statement** 2019
Department of the Treasury—Internal Revenue Service
Copy 1—For State, City, or Local Tax Department
Internal Revenue Service

22222
a Employee's social security number
OMB No. 1545-0008
b Employer identification number (EIN)
1 Wages, tips, other compensation
2 Federal income tax withheld
c Employer's name, address, and ZIP code
3 Social security wages
4 Social security tax withheld
5 Medicare wages and tips
6 Medicare tax withheld
7 Social security tips
8 Allocated tips
d Control number
9
10 Dependent care benefits
e Employee's first name and initial Last name Suff.
11 Nonqualified plans
12a Code
13 Statutory employee Retirement plan Third-party sick pay
12b Code
14 Other
12c Code
12d Code
f Employee's address and ZIP code
15 State Employer's state ID number
16 State wages, tips, etc.
17 State income tax
18 Local wages, tips, etc.
19 Local income tax
20 Locality name

Form **W-2** **Wage and Tax Statement** 2019
Department of the Treasury—Internal Revenue Service
Copy 1—For State, City, or Local Tax Department
Internal Revenue Service

22222
a Employee's social security number
OMB No. 1545-0008
b Employer identification number (EIN)
1 Wages, tips, other compensation
2 Federal income tax withheld
c Employer's name, address, and ZIP code
3 Social security wages
4 Social security tax withheld
5 Medicare wages and tips
6 Medicare tax withheld
7 Social security tips
8 Allocated tips
d Control number
9
10 Dependent care benefits
e Employee's first name and initial Last name Suff.
11 Nonqualified plans
12a Code
13 Statutory employee ☐ Retirement plan ☐ Third-party sick pay ☐
12b Code
14 Other
12c Code
12d Code
f Employee's address and ZIP code

15 State	Employer's state ID number	16 State wages, tips, etc.	17 State income tax	18 Local wages, tips, etc.	19 Local income tax	20 Locality name

Form **W-2** **Wage and Tax Statement** **2019**
Department of the Treasury—Internal Revenue Service
Copy 1—For State, City, or Local Tax Department
Internal Revenue Service

22222
a Employee's social security number
OMB No. 1545-0008
b Employer identification number (EIN)
1 Wages, tips, other compensation
2 Federal income tax withheld
c Employer's name, address, and ZIP code
3 Social security wages
4 Social security tax withheld
5 Medicare wages and tips
6 Medicare tax withheld
7 Social security tips
8 Allocated tips
d Control number
9
10 Dependent care benefits
e Employee's first name and initial Last name Suff.
11 Nonqualified plans
12a Code
13 Statutory employee ☐ Retirement plan ☐ Third-party sick pay ☐
12b Code
14 Other
12c Code
12d Code
f Employee's address and ZIP code

15 State	Employer's state ID number	16 State wages, tips, etc.	17 State income tax	18 Local wages, tips, etc.	19 Local income tax	20 Locality name

Form **W-2** **Wage and Tax Statement** **2019**
Department of the Treasury—Internal Revenue Service
Copy 1—For State, City, or Local Tax Department
Internal Revenue Service

22222

a Employee's social security number

OMB No. 1545-0008

b Employer identification number (EIN)

1 Wages, tips, other compensation

2 Federal income tax withheld

c Employer's name, address, and ZIP code

3 Social security wages

4 Social security tax withheld

5 Medicare wages and tips

6 Medicare tax withheld

7 Social security tips

8 Allocated tips

d Control number

9

10 Dependent care benefits

e Employee's first name and initial Last name Suff.

11 Nonqualified plans

12a Code

13 Statutory employee Retirement plan Third-party sick pay

12b Code

14 Other

12c Code

12d Code

f Employee's address and ZIP code

15 State Employer's state ID number	16 State wages, tips, etc.	17 State income tax	18 Local wages, tips, etc.	19 Local income tax	20 Locality name

Form **W-2 Wage and Tax Statement** 2019

Department of the Treasury—Internal Revenue Service

Copy 1—For State, City, or Local Tax Department

Internal Revenue Service

DO NOT STAPLE

33333

a Control number

For Official Use Only ▶

OMB No. 1545-0008

b **Kind of Payer** (Check one): 941, Military, 943, 944, CT-1, Hshld. emp., Medicare govt. emp.

Kind of Employer (Check one): None apply, 501c non-govt., State/local non-501c, State/local 501c, Federal govt.

Third-party sick pay (Check if applicable)

c Total number of Forms W-2

d Establishment number

1 Wages, tips, other compensation

2 Federal income tax withheld

e Employer identification number (EIN)

3 Social security wages

4 Social security tax withheld

f Employer's name

5 Medicare wages and tips

6 Medicare tax withheld

7 Social security tips

8 Allocated tips

9

10 Dependent care benefits

11 Nonqualified plans

12a Deferred compensation

g Employer's address and ZIP code

h Other EIN used this year

13 For third-party sick pay use only

12b

15 State Employer's state ID number

14 Income tax withheld by payer of third-party sick pay

16 State wages, tips, etc.

17 State income tax

18 Local wages, tips, etc.

19 Local income tax

Employer's contact person

Employer's telephone number

For Official Use Only

Employer's fax number

Employer's email address

Under penalties of perjury, I declare that I have examined this return and accompanying documents, and, to the best of my knowledge and belief, they are true, correct, and complete.

Signature ▶ Title ▶ Date ▶

Form **W-3 Transmittal of Wage and Tax Statements** 2019

Department of the Treasury Internal Revenue Service

Internal Revenue Service

Appendix B

Special Classes of Federal Tax Withholding

Special Classes of Employment and Special Types of Payments	Treatment Under Employment Taxes		
	Income Tax Withholding	Social Security and Medicare (Including Additional Medicare Tax when Wages are Paid in Excess of $200,000)	FUTA
Aliens, Nonresident:	See Publication 515, "Withholding of Tax on Nonresident Aliens and Foreign Entitie Publication 519, "U.S. Tax Guide for Aliens."		
Aliens, Resident:			
1. Service performed in the United States.	Same as U.S. citizen.	Same as U.S. citizen. (Exempt if any part of service as crew member of foreign vessel or aircraft is performed outside United States.)	Same as U.S. citizen.
2. Service performed outside United States.	Withhold	Taxable if (1) working for an American employer or (2) an American employer by agreement covers U.S. citizens and residents employed by its foreign affiliates.	Exempt unless on or in connection with an Ame vessel or aircraft and pe under contract made in U States, or alien is employ such vessel or aircraft w touches U.S. port.
Cafeteria Plan Benefits Under Section 125:	If employee chooses cash, subject to all employment taxes. If employee chooses a benefit, the treatment is the same as if the benefit was provided outside the plan. Publication 15-B for more information.		
Deceased Worker:			
1. Wages paid to beneficiary or estate in same calendar year as worker's death. See the "Instructions for Forms W-2 and W-3" for details.	Exempt	Taxable	Taxable
2. Wages paid to beneficiary or estate after calendar year of worker's death.	Exempt	Exempt	Exempt
Dependent Care Assistance Programs:	Exempt to the extent it is reasonable to believe amounts are excludable from gros income under Section 129.		

Special Classes of Employment and Special Types of Payments	Treatment Under Employment Taxes		
	Income Tax Withholding	**Social Security and Medicare (Including Additional Medicare Tax when Wages are Paid in Excess of $200,000)**	**FUTA**
Disabled Worker's Wages paid after year in which worker became entitled to disability insurance benefits under the Social Security Act.	Withhold	Exempt, if worker did not perform service for employer during period for which payment is made.	Taxable
Employee Business Expense Reimbursement:			
1. Accountable plan.			
a. Amounts not exceeding specified government rate for per diem or standard mileage.	Exempt	Exempt	Exempt
b. Amounts in excess of specified government rate for per diem or standard mileage.	Withhold	Taxable	Taxable
2. Nonaccountable plan. See Section 5 of IRS Publication 15 for details.	Withhold	Taxable	Taxable
Family Employees:			
1. Child employed by parent (or partnership in which each partner is a parent of the child).	Withhold	Exempt until age 18; age 21 for domestic service.	Exempt until age 21.
2. Parent employed by child.	Withhold	Taxable if in course of the son's or daughter's business. For domestic services, see Section 3 of IRS Publication 15.	Exempt
3. Spouse employed by spouse. See Section 3 of IRS Publication 15 for more information.	Withhold	Taxable if in course of spouse's business.	Exempt
Fishing and Related Activities:	See Publication 334, "Tax Guide for Small Business."		
Foreign Governments and International Organizations:	Exempt	Exempt	Exempt
Foreign Service by U.S. Citizens:			
1. As U.S. government employees.	Withhold	Same as within United States.	Exempt
2. For foreign affiliates of American employers and other private employers.	Exempt if at time of payment (1) it is reasonable to believe employee is entitled to exclusion from income under Section 911 or (2) the employer is required by law of the foreign country to withhold income tax on such payment.	Exempt unless (1) an American employer by agreement covers U.S. citizens employed by its foreign affiliates or (2) U.S. citizen works for American employer.	Exempt unless (1) on American vessel or aircraft and work is performed under contract made in United States or worker is employed on vessel when it touches U.S. port or (2) U.S. citizen works for American employer (except in a contiguous country with which the United States has an agreement for unemployment compensation) or in the U.S. Virgin Islands.
Fringe Benefits:	Taxable on excess of fair market value of the benefit over the sum of an amount paid for it by the employee and any amount excludable by law. However, special valuation rules may apply. Benefits provided under cafeteria plans may qualify for exclusion from wages for Social Security, Medicare, and FUTA taxes. See Publication 15-B for details.		

Special Classes of Employment and Special Types of Payments	Treatment Under Employment Taxes		
	Income Tax Withholding	Social Security and Medicare (Including Additional Medicare Tax when Wages are Paid in Excess of $200,000)	FUTA
Government Employment: State/local governments and political subdivisions, employees of:			
1. Salaries and wages (includes payments to most elected and appointed officials).	Withhold	Generally taxable for (1) services performed by employees who are either (a) covered under a Section 218 agreement or (b) not covered under a Section 218 agreement and not a member of a public retirement system (mandatory Social Security and Medicare coverage), and (2) (Medicare tax only) services performed by employees hired or rehired after 3/31/86 who are not covered under a Section 218 agreement or the mandatory Social Security provisions, unless specifically excluded by law. See Publication 963.	Exempt
2. Election workers. Election workers are individuals who are employed to perform services for state or local governments at election booths in connection with national, state, or local elections. **Note.** File Form W-2 for payments of $600 or more even if no Social Security or Medicare taxes were withheld.	Exempt	Taxable if paid $1,800 or more in 2019 (lesser amount if specified by a Section 218 Social Security agreement). See Revenue Ruling 2000-6.	Exempt
3. Emergency workers. Emergency workers who were hired on a temporary basis in response to a specific unforeseen emergency and are not intended to become permanent employees.	Withhold	Exempt if serving on a temporary basis in case of fire, storm, snow, earthquake, flood, or similar emergency.	Exempt
U.S. federal government employees.	Withhold	Taxable for Medicare. Taxable for Social Security unless hired before 1984. See Section 3121(b)(5).	Exempt
Homeworkers (Industrial, Cottage Industry):			
1. Common law employees.	Withhold	Taxable	Taxable
2. Statutory employees. See Section 2 of IRS Publication 15 for details.	Exempt	Taxable if paid $100 or more in cash in a year.	Exempt
Hospital Employees:			
1. Interns.	Withhold	Taxable	Exempt
2. Patients.	Withhold	Taxable (exempt for state or local government hospitals).	Exempt

Special Classes of Employment and Special Types of Payments	Treatment Under Employment Taxes		
	Income Tax Withholding	**Social Security and Medicare (Including Additional Medicare Tax when Wages are Paid in Excess of $200,000)**	**FUTA**
Household Employees:			
1. Domestic service in private homes. Farmers, see Publication 51 (Circular A).	Exempt (withhold if both employer and employee agree).	Taxable if paid $2,000 or more in cash in 2019. Exempt if performed by an individual younger than age 18 during any portion of the calendar year and is not the principal occupation of the employee.	Taxable if employer paid total cash wages of $1,000 or more in any quarter in the current or preceding calendar year.
2. Domestic service in college clubs, fraternities, and sororities.	Exempt (withhold if both employer and employee agree).	Exempt if paid to regular student; also exempt if employee is paid less than $100 in a year by an income-tax-exempt employer.	Taxable if employer paid total cash wages of $1,000 or more in any quarter in the current or preceding calendar year.
Insurance for Employees:			
1. Accident and health insurance premiums under a plan or system for employees and their dependents generally or for a class or classes of employees and their dependents.	Exempt (except 2% shareholder-employees of S corporations).	Exempt	Exempt
2. Group-term life insurance costs. See Publication 15-B for details.	Exempt	Exempt, except for the cost of group-term life insurance includible in the employee's gross income. Special rules apply for former employees.	Exempt
Insurance Agents or Solicitors:			
1. Full-time life insurance salesperson.	Withhold only if employee under common law. See Section 2 of IRS Publication 15.	Taxable	Taxable if (1) employee under common law and (2) not paid solely by commissions.
2. Other salesperson of life, casualty, and so on, insurance.	Withhold only if employee under common law.	Taxable only if employee under common law.	Taxable if (1) employee under common law and (2) not paid solely by commissions.
Interest on Loans with Below-Market Interest Rates (foregone interest and deemed original issue discount):	See Publication 15-A.		
Leave-Sharing Plans: Amounts paid to an employee under a leave-sharing plan.	Withhold	Taxable	Taxable
Newspaper Carriers and Vendors: Newspaper carriers younger than age 18; newspaper and magazine vendors buying at fixed prices and retaining receipts from sales to customers. See Publication 15-A for information on statutory nonemployee status.	Exempt (withhold if both employer and employee voluntarily agree).	Exempt	Exempt

Special Classes of Employment and Special Types of Payments	Treatment Under Employment Taxes		
	Income Tax Withholding	Social Security and Medicare (Including Additional Medicare Tax when Wages are Paid in Excess of $200,000)	FUTA
Noncash Payments:			
1. For household work, agricultural labor, and service not in the course of the employer's trade or business.	Exempt (withhold if both employer and employee voluntarily agree).	Exempt	Exempt
2. To certain retail commission salespersons ordinarily paid solely on a cash commission basis.	Optional with employer, except to the extent employee's supplemental wages during the year exceed $1 million.	Taxable	Taxable
Nonprofit Organizations:	See Publication 15-A.		
Officers or Shareholders of an S Corporation: Distributions and other payments by an S corporation to a corporate officer or shareholder must be treated as wages to the extent the amounts are reasonable compensation for services to the corporation by an employee. See the instructions for Form 1120S.	Withhold	Taxable	Taxable
Partners: Payments to general or limited partners of a partnership. See Publication 541, "Partnerships," for partner reporting rules.	Exempt	Exempt	Exempt
Railroads: Payments subject to the Railroad Retirement Act. See Publication 915, Social Security and Equivalent Railroad Retirement Benefits, for more details.	Withhold	Exempt	Exempt
Religious Exemptions:	See Publication 15-A and Publication 517, "Social Security and Other Information for Members of the Clergy and Religious Workers."		
Retirement and Pension Plans:			
1. Employer contributions to a qualified plan.	Exempt	Exempt	Exempt
2. Elective employee contributions and deferrals to a plan containing a qualified cash or deferred compensation arrangement (for example, 401(k)).	Generally exempt, but see Section 402(g) for limitation.	Taxable	Taxable
3. Employer contributions to individual retirement accounts under simplified employee pension plan (SEP).	Generally exempt, but see Section 402(g) for salary reduction SEP limitation.	Exempt, except for amounts contributed under a salary reduction SEP agreement.	
4. Employer contributions to Section 403(b) annuities.	Generally exempt, but see Section 402(g) for limitation.	Taxable if paid through a salary reduction agreement (written or otherwise).	
5. Employee salary reduction contributions to a SIMPLE retirement account.	Exempt	Taxable	Taxable

(*Continued*)

Special Classes of Employment and Special Types of Payments	Treatment Under Employment Taxes		
	Income Tax Withholding	Social Security and Medicare (Including Additional Medicare Tax when Wages are Paid in Excess of $200,000)	FUTA
6. Distributions from qualified retirement and pension plans and Section 403(b) annuities. See Publication 15-A for information on pensions, annuities, and employer contributions to nonqualified deferred compensation arrangements.	Withhold, but recipient may elect exemption on Form W-4P in certain cases; mandatory 20% withholding applies to an eligible rollover distribution that is not a direct rollover; exempt for direct rollover. See Publication 15-A.	Exempt	Exempt
7. Employer contributions to a Section 457(b) plan.	Generally exempt, but see Section 402(g) limitation.	Taxable	Taxable
8. Employee salary reduction contributions to a Section 457(b) plan.	Generally exempt, but see Section 402(g) salary reduction limitation.	Taxable	Taxable
Salespersons:			
1. Common law employees.	Withhold	Taxable	Taxable
2. Statutory employees.	Exempt	Taxable	Taxable, except for full-time life insurance sales agents.
3. Statutory nonemployees (qualified real estate agents, direct sellers, and certain companion sitters). See Publication 15-A for details.	Exempt	Exempt	Exempt
Scholarships and Fellowship Grants (Includible in Income Under Section 117(c)):	Withhold	Taxability depends on the nature of the employment and the status of the organization. See Students, scholars, trainees, teachers, etc., below	
Severance or Dismissal Pay:	Withhold	Taxable	Taxable
Service Not in the Course of the Employer's Trade or Business (Other Than on a Farm Operated for Profit or for Household Employment in Private Homes):	Withhold only if employee earns $50 or more in cash in a quarter and works on 24 or more different days in that quarter or in the preceding quarter.	Taxable if employee receives $100 or more in cash in a calendar year.	Taxable only if employee earns $50 or more in cash in a quarter and works on 24 or more different days in that quarter or in the preceding quarter.
Sick Pay: See Publication 15-A for more information.	Withhold	Exempt after the end of 6 calendar months after the calendar month employee last worked for employer.	
Students, Scholars, Trainees, Teachers, etc.: 1. Student enrolled and regularly attending classes, performing services for:			
a. Private school, college, or university	Withhold	Exempt	Exempt
b. Auxiliary nonprofit organization operated for and controlled by school, college, or university	Withhold	Exempt unless services are covered by a Section 218 (Social Security Act) agreement.	Exempt
c. Public school, college, or university	Withhold	Exempt unless services are covered by a Section 218 (Social Security Act) agreement.	Exempt

Special Classes of Employment and Special Types of Payments	Treatment Under Employment Taxes		
	Income Tax Withholding	Social Security and Medicare (Including Additional Medicare Tax when Wages are Paid in Excess of $200,000)	FUTA
2. Full-time student performing service for academic credit, combining instruction with work experience as an integral part of the program.	Withhold	Taxable	Exempt unless program was established for or on behalf of an employer or group of employers.
3. Student nurse performing part-time services for nominal earnings at hospital as incidental part of training.	Withhold	Exempt	Exempt
4. Student employed by organized camps.	Withhold	Taxable	Exempt
5. Student, scholar, trainee, teacher, and so on, as nonimmigrant alien under Section 101(a)(15)(F), (J), (M), or (Q) of Immigration and Nationality Act (that is, aliens holding F-1, J-1, M-1, or Q-1 visas).	Withhold unless excepted by regulations.	Exempt if service is performed for purpose specified in Section 101(a)(15)(F), (J), (M), or (Q) of Immigration and Nationality Act. However, these taxes may apply if the employee becomes a resident alien. See the special residency tests for exempt individuals in Chapter 1 of Pub. 519, Tax Guide for Aliens.	
Supplemental Unemployment Compensation Plan Benefits:	Withhold	Exempt under certain conditions. See Publication 15-A.	
Tips:			
1. If $20 or more in a month.	Withhold	Taxable	Taxable for all tips reported in writing to employer.
2. If less than $20 in a month. See Section 6 of IRS Publication 15 for more information.	Exempt	Exempt	Exempt
Workers' Compensation:	Exempt	Exempt	Exempt

Source: Internal Revenue Service

Appendix C

Federal Income Tax Tables*

The following is information about federal income tax withholding for 2019. Specific questions about federal income taxes and business situations may be directed to the Internal Revenue Service via the IRS website at https://www.irs.gov/businesses.

Payroll Period	One Withholding Allowance
Weekly	$ 80.80
Biweekly	161.50
Semimonthly	175.00
Monthly	350.00
Quarterly	1,050.00
Semiannually	2,100.00
Annually	4,200.00
Daily or miscellaneous (each day of the payroll period)	16.20

**Note:* Appendix C is derived from IRS Publication 15. A comment to refer to pages 44 and 47 exists at the section end for wage-bracket tables when the taxable wages exceed the table. These page references are for Publication 15 itself and not to pages within this text.

Source: Internal Revenue Service

Percentage Method Tables for Income Tax Withholding

(For Wages Paid in 2019)

TABLE 1—WEEKLY Payroll Period

(a) SINGLE person (including head of household)—

If the amount of wages (after subtracting withholding allowances) is: Not over $73 .... The amount of income tax to withhold is: $0

Over—	But not over—		of excess over—
$73	—$260	$0.00 plus 10%	—$73
$260	—$832	$18.70 plus 12%	—$260
$832	—$1,692	$87.34 plus 22%	—$832
$1,692	—$3,164	$276.54 plus 24%	—$1,692
$3,164	—$3,998	$629.82 plus 32%	—$3,164
$3,998	—$9,887	$896.70 plus 35%	—$3,998
$9,887	....	$2,957.85 plus 37%	—$9,887

(b) MARRIED person—

If the amount of wages (after subtracting withholding allowances) is: Not over $227 .... The amount of income tax to withhold is: $0

Over—	But not over—		of excess over—
$227	—$600	$0.00 plus 10%	—$227
$600	—$1,745	$37.30 plus 12%	—$600
$1,745	—$3,465	$174.70 plus 22%	—$1,745
$3,465	—$6,409	$553.10 plus 24%	—$3,465
$6,409	—$8,077	$1,259.66 plus 32%	—$6,409
$8,077	—$12,003	$1,793.42 plus 35%	—$8,077
$12,003	....	$3,167.52 plus 37%	—$12,003

TABLE 2—BIWEEKLY Payroll Period

(a) SINGLE person (including head of household)—

If the amount of wages (after subtracting withholding allowances) is: Not over $146 .... The amount of income tax to withhold is: $0

Over—	But not over—		of excess over—
$146	—$519	$0.00 plus 10%	—$146
$519	—$1,664	$37.30 plus 12%	—$519
$1,664	—$3,385	$174.70 plus 22%	—$1,664
$3,385	—$6,328	$553.32 plus 24%	—$3,385
$6,328	—$7,996	$1,259.64 plus 32%	—$6,328
$7,996	—$19,773	$1,793.40 plus 35%	—$7,996
$19,773	....	$5,915.35 plus 37%	—$19,773

(b) MARRIED person—

If the amount of wages (after subtracting withholding allowances) is: Not over $454 .... The amount of income tax to withhold is: $0

Over—	But not over—		of excess over—
$454	—$1,200	$0.00 plus 10%	—$454
$1,200	—$3,490	$74.60 plus 12%	—$1,200
$3,490	—$6,931	$349.40 plus 22%	—$3,490
$6,931	—$12,817	$1,106.42 plus 24%	—$6,931
$12,817	—$16,154	$2,519.06 plus 32%	—$12,817
$16,154	—$24,006	$3,586.90 plus 35%	—$16,154
$24,006	....	$6,335.10 plus 37%	—$24,006

TABLE 3—SEMIMONTHLY Payroll Period

(a) SINGLE person (including head of household)—

If the amount of wages (after subtracting withholding allowances) is: Not over $158 .... The amount of income tax to withhold is: $0

Over—	But not over—		of excess over—
$158	—$563	$0.00 plus 10%	—$158
$563	—$1,803	$40.50 plus 12%	—$563
$1,803	—$3,667	$189.30 plus 22%	—$1,803
$3,667	—$6,855	$599.38 plus 24%	—$3,667
$6,855	—$8,663	$1,364.50 plus 32%	—$6,855
$8,663	—$21,421	$1,943.06 plus 35%	—$8,663
$21,421	....	$6,408.36 plus 37%	—$21,421

(b) MARRIED person—

If the amount of wages (after subtracting withholding allowances) is: Not over $492 .... The amount of income tax to withhold is: $0

Over—	But not over—		of excess over—
$492	—$1,300	$0.00 plus 10%	—$492
$1,300	—$3,781	$80.80 plus 12%	—$1,300
$3,781	—$7,508	$378.52 plus 22%	—$3,781
$7,508	—$13,885	$1,198.46 plus 24%	—$7,508
$13,885	—$17,500	$2,728.94 plus 32%	—$13,885
$17,500	—$26,006	$3,885.74 plus 35%	—$17,500
$26,006	....	$6,862.84 plus 37%	—$26,006

TABLE 4—MONTHLY Payroll Period

(a) SINGLE person (including head of household)—

If the amount of wages (after subtracting withholding allowances) is: Not over $317 .... The amount of income tax to withhold is: $0

Over—	But not over—		of excess over—
$317	—$1,125	$0.00 plus 10%	—$317
$1,125	—$3,606	$80.80 plus 12%	—$1,125
$3,606	—$7,333	$378.52 plus 22%	—$3,606
$7,333	—$13,710	$1,198.46 plus 24%	—$7,333
$13,710	—$17,325	$2,728.94 plus 32%	—$13,710
$17,325	—$42,842	$3,885.74 plus 35%	—$17,325
$42,842	....	$12,816.69 plus 37%	—$42,842

(b) MARRIED person—

If the amount of wages (after subtracting withholding allowances) is: Not over $983 .... The amount of income tax to withhold is: $0

Over—	But not over—		of excess over—
$983	—$2,600	$0.00 plus 10%	—$983
$2,600	—$7,563	$161.70 plus 12%	—$2,600
$7,563	—$15,017	$757.26 plus 22%	—$7,563
$15,017	—$27,771	$2,397.14 plus 24%	—$15,017
$27,771	—$35,000	$5,458.10 plus 32%	—$27,771
$35,000	—$52,013	$7,771.38 plus 35%	—$35,000
$52,013	....	$13,725.93 plus 37%	—$52,013

Internal Revenue Service

Percentage Method Tables for Income Tax Withholding (continued)

(For Wages Paid in 2019)

TABLE 5—QUARTERLY Payroll Period

(a) SINGLE person (including head of household)—

If the amount of wages (after subtracting withholding allowances) is: Not over $950 — The amount of income tax to withhold is: $0

Over—	But not over—		of excess over—
$950	—$3,375	$0.00 plus 10%	—$950
$3,375	—$10,819	$242.50 plus 12%	—$3,375
$10,819	—$22,000	$1,135.78 plus 22%	—$10,819
$22,000	—$41,131	$3,595.60 plus 24%	—$22,000
$41,131	—$51,975	$8,187.04 plus 32%	—$41,131
$51,975	—$128,525	$11,657.12 plus 35%	—$51,975
$128,525		$38,449.62 plus 37%	—$128,525

(b) MARRIED person—

If the amount of wages (after subtracting withholding allowances) is: Not over $2,950 — The amount of income tax to withhold is: $0

Over—	But not over—		of excess over—
$2,950	—$7,800	$0.00 plus 10%	—$2,950
$7,800	—$22,688	$485.00 plus 12%	—$7,800
$22,688	—$45,050	$2,271.56 plus 22%	—$22,688
$45,050	—$83,313	$7,191.20 plus 24%	—$45,050
$83,313	—$105,000	$16,374.32 plus 32%	—$83,313
$105,000	—$156,038	$23,314.16 plus 35%	—$105,000
$156,038		$41,177.46 plus 37%	—$156,038

TABLE 6—SEMIANNUAL Payroll Period

(a) SINGLE person (including head of household)—

If the amount of wages (after subtracting withholding allowances) is: Not over $1,900 — The amount of income tax to withhold is: $0

Over—	But not over—		of excess over—
$1,900	—$6,750	$0.00 plus 10%	—$1,900
$6,750	—$21,638	$485.00 plus 12%	—$6,750
$21,638	—$44,000	$2,271.56 plus 22%	—$21,638
$44,000	—$82,263	$7,191.20 plus 24%	—$44,000
$82,263	—$103,950	$16,374.32 plus 32%	—$82,263
$103,950	—$257,050	$23,314.16 plus 35%	—$103,950
$257,050		$76,899.16 plus 37%	—$257,050

(b) MARRIED person—

If the amount of wages (after subtracting withholding allowances) is: Not over $5,900 — The amount of income tax to withhold is: $0

Over—	But not over—		of excess over—
$5,900	—$15,600	$0.00 plus 10%	—$5,900
$15,600	—$45,375	$970.00 plus 12%	—$15,600
$45,375	—$90,100	$4,543.00 plus 22%	—$45,375
$90,100	—$166,625	$14,382.50 plus 24%	—$90,100
$166,625	—$210,000	$32,748.50 plus 32%	—$166,625
$210,000	—$312,075	$46,628.50 plus 35%	—$210,000
$312,075		$82,354.75 plus 37%	—$312,075

TABLE 7—ANNUAL Payroll Period

(a) SINGLE person (including head of household)—

If the amount of wages (after subtracting withholding allowances) is: Not over $3,800 — The amount of income tax to withhold is: $0

Over—	But not over—		of excess over—
$3,800	—$13,500	$0.00 plus 10%	—$3,800
$13,500	—$43,275	$970.00 plus 12%	—$13,500
$43,275	—$88,000	$4,543.00 plus 22%	—$43,275
$88,000	—$164,525	$14,382.50 plus 24%	—$88,000
$164,525	—$207,900	$32,748.50 plus 32%	—$164,525
$207,900	—$514,100	$46,628.50 plus 35%	—$207,900
$514,100		$153,798.50 plus 37%	—$514,100

(b) MARRIED person—

If the amount of wages (after subtracting withholding allowances) is: Not over $11,800 — The amount of income tax to withhold is: $0

Over—	But not over—		of excess over—
$11,800	—$31,200	$0.00 plus 10%	—$11,800
$31,200	—$90,750	$1,940.00 plus 12%	—$31,200
$90,750	—$180,200	$9,086.00 plus 22%	—$90,750
$180,200	—$333,250	$28,765.00 plus 24%	—$180,200
$333,250	—$420,000	$65,497.00 plus 32%	—$333,250
$420,000	—$624,150	$93,257.00 plus 35%	—$420,000
$624,150		$164,709.50 plus 37%	—$624,150

TABLE 8—DAILY or MISCELLANEOUS Payroll Period

(a) SINGLE person (including head of household)—

If the amount of wages (after subtracting withholding allowances) divided by the number of days in the payroll period is: Not over $14.60 — The amount of income tax to withhold per day is: $0

Over—	But not over—		of excess over—
$14.60	—$51.90	$0.00 plus 10%	—$14.60
$51.90	—$166.40	$3.73 plus 12%	—$51.90
$166.40	—$338.50	$17.47 plus 22%	—$166.40
$338.50	—$632.80	$55.33 plus 24%	—$338.50
$632.80	—$799.60	$125.96 plus 32%	—$632.80
$799.60	—$1,977.30	$179.34 plus 35%	—$799.60
$1,977.30		$591.54 plus 37%	—$1,977.30

(b) MARRIED person—

If the amount of wages (after subtracting withholding allowances) divided by the number of days in the payroll period is: Not over $45.40 — The amount of income tax to withhold per day is: $0

Over—	But not over—		of excess over—
$45.40	—$120.00	$0.00 plus 10%	—$45.40
$120.00	—$349.00	$7.46 plus 12%	—$120.00
$349.00	—$693.10	$34.94 plus 22%	—$349.00
$693.10	—$1,281.70	$110.64 plus 24%	—$693.10
$1,281.70	—$1,615.40	$251.90 plus 32%	—$1,281.70
$1,615.40	—$2,400.60	$358.68 plus 35%	—$1,615.40
$2,400.60		$633.50 plus 37%	—$2,400.60

Internal Revenue Service

Wage Bracket Method Tables for Income Tax Withholding

SINGLE Persons—WEEKLY Payroll Period

(For Wages Paid through December 2019)

And the wages are–		And the number of withholding allowances claimed is—										
At least	But less than	0	1	2	3	4	5	6	7	8	9	10
		The amount of income tax to be withheld is—										
$ 0	$73	$0	$0	$0	$0	$0	$0	$0	$0	$0	$0	$0
73	84	1	0	0	0	0	0	0	0	0	0	0
84	95	2	0	0	0	0	0	0	0	0	0	0
95	106	3	0	0	0	0	0	0	0	0	0	0
106	117	4	0	0	0	0	0	0	0	0	0	0
117	128	5	0	0	0	0	0	0	0	0	0	0
128	139	6	0	0	0	0	0	0	0	0	0	0
139	150	7	0	0	0	0	0	0	0	0	0	0
150	161	8	0	0	0	0	0	0	0	0	0	0
161	172	9	0	0	0	0	0	0	0	0	0	0
172	183	10	2	0	0	0	0	0	0	0	0	0
183	194	12	3	0	0	0	0	0	0	0	0	0
194	205	13	5	0	0	0	0	0	0	0	0	0
205	216	14	6	0	0	0	0	0	0	0	0	0
216	227	15	7	0	0	0	0	0	0	0	0	0
227	238	16	8	0	0	0	0	0	0	0	0	0
238	249	17	9	1	0	0	0	0	0	0	0	0
249	260	18	10	2	0	0	0	0	0	0	0	0
260	271	19	11	3	0	0	0	0	0	0	0	0
271	282	21	12	4	0	0	0	0	0	0	0	0
282	293	22	13	5	0	0	0	0	0	0	0	0
293	304	23	14	6	0	0	0	0	0	0	0	0
304	315	25	16	7	0	0	0	0	0	0	0	0
315	326	26	17	9	1	0	0	0	0	0	0	0
326	337	27	18	10	2	0	0	0	0	0	0	0
337	348	29	19	11	3	0	0	0	0	0	0	0
348	359	30	20	12	4	0	0	0	0	0	0	0
359	370	31	22	13	5	0	0	0	0	0	0	0
370	381	33	23	14	6	0	0	0	0	0	0	0
381	392	34	24	15	7	0	0	0	0	0	0	0
392	403	35	26	16	8	0	0	0	0	0	0	0
403	414	37	27	17	9	1	0	0	0	0	0	0
414	425	38	28	18	10	2	0	0	0	0	0	0
425	436	39	29	20	12	3	0	0	0	0	0	0
436	447	40	31	21	13	5	0	0	0	0	0	0
447	458	42	32	22	14	6	0	0	0	0	0	0
458	469	43	33	24	15	7	0	0	0	0	0	0
469	480	44	35	25	16	8	0	0	0	0	0	0
480	491	46	36	26	17	9	1	0	0	0	0	0
491	502	47	37	28	18	10	2	0	0	0	0	0
502	513	48	39	29	19	11	3	0	0	0	0	0
513	524	50	40	30	21	12	4	0	0	0	0	0
524	535	51	41	32	22	13	5	0	0	0	0	0
535	546	52	43	33	23	14	6	0	0	0	0	0
546	557	54	44	34	25	16	7	0	0	0	0	0
557	568	55	45	36	26	17	9	0	0	0	0	0
568	579	56	47	37	27	18	10	2	0	0	0	0
579	590	58	48	38	29	19	11	3	0	0	0	0
590	601	59	49	40	30	20	12	4	0	0	0	0
601	612	60	51	41	31	22	13	5	0	0	0	0
612	623	62	52	42	33	23	14	6	0	0	0	0
623	634	63	53	44	34	24	15	7	0	0	0	0
634	645	64	55	45	35	25	16	8	0	0	0	0
645	656	66	56	46	36	27	17	9	1	0	0	0
656	667	67	57	47	38	28	18	10	2	0	0	0
667	678	68	59	49	39	29	20	11	3	0	0	0
678	689	70	60	50	40	31	21	13	5	0	0	0
689	700	71	61	51	42	32	22	14	6	0	0	0
700	711	72	62	53	43	33	24	15	7	0	0	0
711	722	73	64	54	44	35	25	16	8	0	0	0
722	733	75	65	55	46	36	26	17	9	1	0	0
733	744	76	66	57	47	37	28	18	10	2	0	0
744	755	77	68	58	48	39	29	19	11	3	0	0
755	766	79	69	59	50	40	30	21	12	4	0	0
766	777	80	70	61	51	41	32	22	13	5	0	0
777	788	81	72	62	52	43	33	23	14	6	0	0
788	799	83	73	63	54	44	34	25	16	7	0	0
799	810	84	74	65	55	45	36	26	17	9	0	0
810	821	85	76	66	56	47	37	27	18	10	2	0
821	832	87	77	67	58	48	38	29	19	11	3	0

Internal Revenue Service

Wage Bracket Method Tables for Income Tax Withholding

SINGLE Persons—**WEEKLY** Payroll Period

(For Wages Paid through December 2019)

And the wages are–		And the number of withholding allowances claimed is—										
At least	But less than	0	1	2	3	4	5	6	7	8	9	10
		The amount of income tax to be withheld is—										
832	**843**	89	78	69	59	49	40	30	20	12	4	0
843	**854**	91	80	70	60	51	41	31	21	13	5	0
854	**865**	93	81	71	62	52	42	32	23	14	6	0
865	**876**	96	82	73	63	53	43	34	24	15	7	0
876	**887**	98	84	74	64	55	45	35	25	16	8	0
887	**898**	101	85	75	66	56	46	36	27	17	9	1
898	**909**	103	86	77	67	57	47	38	28	18	10	2
909	**920**	105	88	78	68	58	49	39	29	20	11	3
920	**931**	108	90	79	69	60	50	40	31	21	13	4
931	**942**	110	93	80	71	61	51	42	32	22	14	6
942	**953**	113	95	82	72	62	53	43	33	24	15	7
953	**964**	115	97	83	73	64	54	44	35	25	16	8
964	**975**	118	100	84	75	65	55	46	36	26	17	9
975	**986**	120	102	86	76	66	57	47	37	28	18	10
986	**997**	122	105	87	77	68	58	48	39	29	19	11
997	**1,008**	125	107	89	79	69	59	50	40	30	21	12
1,008	**1,019**	127	109	92	80	70	61	51	41	32	22	13
1,019	**1,030**	130	112	94	81	72	62	52	43	33	23	14
1,030	**1,041**	132	114	97	83	73	63	54	44	34	25	15
1,041	**1,052**	135	117	99	84	74	65	55	45	36	26	17
1,052	**1,063**	137	119	101	85	76	66	56	47	37	27	18
1,063	**1,074**	139	122	104	87	77	67	58	48	38	28	19
1,074	**1,085**	142	124	106	88	78	69	59	49	40	30	20
1,085	**1,096**	144	126	109	91	80	70	60	51	41	31	21
1,096	**1,107**	147	129	111	93	81	71	62	52	42	32	23
1,107	**1,118**	149	131	113	96	82	73	63	53	43	34	24
1,118	**1,129**	151	134	116	98	84	74	64	54	45	35	25
1,129	**1,140**	154	136	118	101	85	75	65	56	46	36	27
1,140	**1,151**	156	139	121	103	86	76	67	57	47	38	28
1,151	**1,162**	159	141	123	105	88	78	68	58	49	39	29
1,162	**1,173**	161	143	126	108	90	79	69	60	50	40	31
1,173	**1,184**	164	146	128	110	92	80	71	61	51	42	32
1,184	**1,195**	166	148	130	113	95	82	72	62	53	43	33
1,195	**1,206**	168	151	133	115	97	83	73	64	54	44	35
1,206	**1,217**	171	153	135	118	100	84	75	65	55	46	36
1,217	**1,228**	173	155	138	120	102	86	76	66	57	47	37
1,228	**1,239**	176	158	140	122	105	87	77	68	58	48	39
1,239	**1,250**	178	160	143	125	107	89	79	69	59	50	40
1,250	**1,261**	180	163	145	127	109	92	80	70	61	51	41
1,261	**1,272**	183	165	147	130	112	94	81	72	62	52	43
1,272	**1,283**	185	168	150	132	114	96	83	73	63	54	44
1,283	**1,294**	188	170	152	134	117	99	84	74	65	55	45
1,294	**1,305**	190	172	155	137	119	101	85	76	66	56	47
1,305	**1,316**	193	175	157	139	122	104	87	77	67	58	48
1,316	**1,327**	195	177	159	142	124	106	88	78	69	59	49
1,327	**1,338**	197	180	162	144	126	109	91	80	70	60	50
1,338	**1,349**	200	182	164	147	129	111	93	81	71	61	52
1,349	**1,360**	202	184	167	149	131	113	96	82	73	63	53
1,360	**1,371**	205	187	169	151	134	116	98	84	74	64	54
1,371	**1,382**	207	189	172	154	136	118	100	85	75	65	56
1,382	**1,393**	210	192	174	156	138	121	103	86	76	67	57
1,393	**1,404**	212	194	176	159	141	123	105	88	78	68	58
1,404	**1,415**	214	197	179	161	143	126	108	90	79	69	60
1,415	**1,426**	217	199	181	163	146	128	110	92	80	71	61
1,426	**1,437**	219	201	184	166	148	130	113	95	82	72	62
1,437	**1,448**	222	204	186	168	151	133	115	97	83	73	64
1,448	**1,459**	224	206	189	171	153	135	117	100	84	75	65
1,459	**1,470**	226	209	191	173	155	138	120	102	86	76	66
1,470	**1,481**	229	211	193	176	158	140	122	105	87	77	68
1,481	**1,492**	231	214	196	178	160	142	125	107	89	79	69
1,492	**1,503**	234	216	198	180	163	145	127	109	92	80	70
1,503	**1,514**	236	218	201	183	165	147	130	112	94	81	72
1,514	**1,525**	239	221	203	185	167	150	132	114	96	83	73
1,525	**1,536**	241	223	205	188	170	152	134	117	99	84	74
1,536	**1,547**	243	226	208	190	172	155	137	119	101	85	76
1,547 and over		Use Table 1(a) for a SINGLE person on page 46. Also see the instructions on page 44.										

Wage Bracket Method Tables for Income Tax Withholding

MARRIED Persons—**WEEKLY** Payroll Period

(For Wages Paid through December 2019)

And the wages are–		And the number of withholding allowances claimed is—										
At least	But less than	0	1	2	3	4	5	6	7	8	9	10
		The amount of income tax to be withheld is—										
$ 0	$227	$0	$0	$0	$0	$0	$0	$0	$0	$0	$0	$0
227	238	1	0	0	0	0	0	0	0	0	0	0
238	249	2	0	0	0	0	0	0	0	0	0	0
249	260	3	0	0	0	0	0	0	0	0	0	0
260	271	4	0	0	0	0	0	0	0	0	0	0
271	282	5	0	0	0	0	0	0	0	0	0	0
282	293	6	0	0	0	0	0	0	0	0	0	0
293	304	7	0	0	0	0	0	0	0	0	0	0
304	315	8	0	0	0	0	0	0	0	0	0	0
315	326	9	1	0	0	0	0	0	0	0	0	0
326	337	10	2	0	0	0	0	0	0	0	0	0
337	348	12	3	0	0	0	0	0	0	0	0	0
348	359	13	5	0	0	0	0	0	0	0	0	0
359	370	14	6	0	0	0	0	0	0	0	0	0
370	381	15	7	0	0	0	0	0	0	0	0	0
381	392	16	8	0	0	0	0	0	0	0	0	0
392	403	17	9	1	0	0	0	0	0	0	0	0
403	414	18	10	2	0	0	0	0	0	0	0	0
414	425	19	11	3	0	0	0	0	0	0	0	0
425	436	20	12	4	0	0	0	0	0	0	0	0
436	447	21	13	5	0	0	0	0	0	0	0	0
447	458	23	14	6	0	0	0	0	0	0	0	0
458	469	24	16	8	0	0	0	0	0	0	0	0
469	480	25	17	9	1	0	0	0	0	0	0	0
480	491	26	18	10	2	0	0	0	0	0	0	0
491	502	27	19	11	3	0	0	0	0	0	0	0
502	513	28	20	12	4	0	0	0	0	0	0	0
513	524	29	21	13	5	0	0	0	0	0	0	0
524	535	30	22	14	6	0	0	0	0	0	0	0
535	546	31	23	15	7	0	0	0	0	0	0	0
546	557	32	24	16	8	0	0	0	0	0	0	0
557	568	34	25	17	9	1	0	0	0	0	0	0
568	579	35	27	19	10	2	0	0	0	0	0	0
579	590	36	28	20	12	3	0	0	0	0	0	0
590	601	37	29	21	13	5	0	0	0	0	0	0
601	612	38	30	22	14	6	0	0	0	0	0	0
612	623	39	31	23	15	7	0	0	0	0	0	0
623	634	41	32	24	16	8	0	0	0	0	0	0
634	645	42	33	25	17	9	1	0	0	0	0	0
645	656	43	34	26	18	10	2	0	0	0	0	0
656	667	45	35	27	19	11	3	0	0	0	0	0
667	678	46	36	28	20	12	4	0	0	0	0	0
678	689	47	38	30	21	13	5	0	0	0	0	0
689	700	49	39	31	23	14	6	0	0	0	0	0
700	711	50	40	32	24	16	7	0	0	0	0	0
711	722	51	42	33	25	17	9	0	0	0	0	0
722	733	53	43	34	26	18	10	2	0	0	0	0
733	744	54	44	35	27	19	11	3	0	0	0	0
744	755	55	46	36	28	20	12	4	0	0	0	0
755	766	57	47	37	29	21	13	5	0	0	0	0
766	777	58	48	39	30	22	14	6	0	0	0	0
777	788	59	50	40	31	23	15	7	0	0	0	0
788	799	61	51	41	32	24	16	8	0	0	0	0
799	810	62	52	42	34	25	17	9	1	0	0	0
810	821	63	53	44	35	27	18	10	2	0	0	0
821	832	64	55	45	36	28	20	11	3	0	0	0
832	843	66	56	46	37	29	21	13	5	0	0	0
843	854	67	57	48	38	30	22	14	6	0	0	0
854	865	68	59	49	39	31	23	15	7	0	0	0
865	876	70	60	50	41	32	24	16	8	0	0	0
876	887	71	61	52	42	33	25	17	9	1	0	0
887	898	72	63	53	43	34	26	18	10	2	0	0
898	909	74	64	54	45	35	27	19	11	3	0	0
909	920	75	65	56	46	36	28	20	12	4	0	0
920	931	76	67	57	47	38	29	21	13	5	0	0
931	942	78	68	58	49	39	31	22	14	6	0	0
942	953	79	69	60	50	40	32	24	16	7	0	0
953	964	80	71	61	51	42	33	25	17	9	0	0
964	975	82	72	62	53	43	34	26	18	10	2	0
975	986	83	73	64	54	44	35	27	19	11	3	0

Internal Revenue Service

Wage Bracket Method Tables for Income Tax Withholding

MARRIED Persons—**WEEKLY** Payroll Period

(For Wages Paid through December 2019)

And the wages are–		And the number of withholding allowances claimed is—										
At least	But less than	0	1	2	3	4	5	6	7	8	9	10
		The amount of income tax to be withheld is—										
986	**997**	84	75	65	55	46	36	28	20	12	4	0
997	**1,008**	86	76	66	57	47	37	29	21	13	5	0
1,008	**1,019**	87	77	68	58	48	38	30	22	14	6	0
1,019	**1,030**	88	79	69	59	49	40	31	23	15	7	0
1,030	**1,041**	90	80	70	60	51	41	32	24	16	8	0
1,041	**1,052**	91	81	72	62	52	42	33	25	17	9	1
1,052	**1,063**	92	83	73	63	53	44	35	27	18	10	2
1,063	**1,074**	94	84	74	64	55	45	36	28	20	11	3
1,074	**1,085**	95	85	75	66	56	46	37	29	21	13	4
1,085	**1,096**	96	86	77	67	57	48	38	30	22	14	6
1,096	**1,107**	97	88	78	68	59	49	39	31	23	15	7
1,107	**1,118**	99	89	79	70	60	50	41	32	24	16	8
1,118	**1,129**	100	90	81	71	61	52	42	33	25	17	9
1,129	**1,140**	101	92	82	72	63	53	43	34	26	18	10
1,140	**1,151**	103	93	83	74	64	54	45	35	27	19	11
1,151	**1,162**	104	94	85	75	65	56	46	36	28	20	12
1,162	**1,173**	105	96	86	76	67	57	47	38	29	21	13
1,173	**1,184**	107	97	87	78	68	58	49	39	31	22	14
1,184	**1,195**	108	98	89	79	69	60	50	40	32	24	15
1,195	**1,206**	109	100	90	80	71	61	51	42	33	25	17
1,206	**1,217**	111	101	91	82	72	62	53	43	34	26	18
1,217	**1,228**	112	102	93	83	73	64	54	44	35	27	19
1,228	**1,239**	113	104	94	84	75	65	55	45	36	28	20
1,239	**1,250**	115	105	95	86	76	66	56	47	37	29	21
1,250	**1,261**	116	106	97	87	77	68	58	48	38	30	22
1,261	**1,272**	117	108	98	88	79	69	59	49	40	31	23
1,272	**1,283**	119	109	99	90	80	70	60	51	41	32	24
1,283	**1,294**	120	110	101	91	81	71	62	52	42	33	25
1,294	**1,305**	121	112	102	92	82	73	63	53	44	35	26
1,305	**1,316**	123	113	103	93	84	74	64	55	45	36	28
1,316	**1,327**	124	114	105	95	85	75	66	56	46	37	29
1,327	**1,338**	125	116	106	96	86	77	67	57	48	38	30
1,338	**1,349**	127	117	107	97	88	78	68	59	49	39	31
1,349	**1,360**	128	118	108	99	89	79	70	60	50	41	32
1,360	**1,371**	129	119	110	100	90	81	71	61	52	42	33
1,371	**1,382**	130	121	111	101	92	82	72	63	53	43	34
1,382	**1,393**	132	122	112	103	93	83	74	64	54	45	35
1,393	**1,404**	133	123	114	104	94	85	75	65	56	46	36
1,404	**1,415**	134	125	115	105	96	86	76	67	57	47	38
1,415	**1,426**	136	126	116	107	97	87	78	68	58	49	39
1,426	**1,437**	137	127	118	108	98	89	79	69	60	50	40
1,437	**1,448**	138	129	119	109	100	90	80	71	61	51	41
1,448	**1,459**	140	130	120	111	101	91	82	72	62	52	43
1,459	**1,470**	141	131	122	112	102	93	83	73	64	54	44
1,470	**1,481**	142	133	123	113	104	94	84	75	65	55	45
1,481	**1,492**	144	134	124	115	105	95	86	76	66	56	47
1,492	**1,503**	145	135	126	116	106	97	87	77	67	58	48
1,503	**1,514**	146	137	127	117	108	98	88	78	69	59	49
1,514	**1,525**	148	138	128	119	109	99	89	80	70	60	51
1,525	**1,536**	149	139	130	120	110	101	91	81	71	62	52
1,536	**1,547**	150	141	131	121	112	102	92	82	73	63	53
1,547	**1,558**	152	142	132	123	113	103	93	84	74	64	55
1,558	**1,569**	153	143	134	124	114	104	95	85	75	66	56
1,569	**1,580**	154	145	135	125	115	106	96	86	77	67	57
1,580	**1,591**	156	146	136	126	117	107	97	88	78	68	59
1,591	**1,602**	157	147	138	128	118	108	99	89	79	70	60
1,602	**1,613**	158	149	139	129	119	110	100	90	81	71	61
1,613	**1,624**	160	150	140	130	121	111	101	92	82	72	63
1,624	**1,635**	161	151	141	132	122	112	103	93	83	74	64
1,635	**1,646**	162	152	143	133	123	114	104	94	85	75	65
1,646	**1,657**	163	154	144	134	125	115	105	96	86	76	67
1,657	**1,668**	165	155	145	136	126	116	107	97	87	78	68
1,668	**1,679**	166	156	147	137	127	118	108	98	89	79	69
1,679	**1,690**	167	158	148	138	129	119	109	100	90	80	71
1,690	**1,701**	169	159	149	140	130	120	111	101	91	82	72
1,701	**1,711**	170	160	151	141	131	122	112	102	92	83	73
1,711 and over		Use Table 1(b) for a MARRIED person on page 46. Also see the instructions on page 44.										

Wage Bracket Method Tables for Income Tax Withholding

SINGLE Persons—BIWEEKLY Payroll Period

(For Wages Paid through December 2019)

And the wages are–		And the number of withholding allowances claimed is—										
At least	But less than	0	1	2	3	4	5	6	7	8	9	10
		The amount of income tax to be withheld is—										
$ 0	$146	$0	$0	$0	$0	$0	$0	$0	$0	$0	$0	$0
146	157	1	0	0	0	0	0	0	0	0	0	0
157	168	2	0	0	0	0	0	0	0	0	0	0
168	179	3	0	0	0	0	0	0	0	0	0	0
179	190	4	0	0	0	0	0	0	0	0	0	0
190	201	5	0	0	0	0	0	0	0	0	0	0
201	212	6	0	0	0	0	0	0	0	0	0	0
212	223	7	0	0	0	0	0	0	0	0	0	0
223	234	8	0	0	0	0	0	0	0	0	0	0
234	245	9	0	0	0	0	0	0	0	0	0	0
245	256	10	0	0	0	0	0	0	0	0	0	0
256	267	12	0	0	0	0	0	0	0	0	0	0
267	278	13	0	0	0	0	0	0	0	0	0	0
278	289	14	0	0	0	0	0	0	0	0	0	0
289	300	15	0	0	0	0	0	0	0	0	0	0
300	311	16	0	0	0	0	0	0	0	0	0	0
311	322	17	1	0	0	0	0	0	0	0	0	0
322	333	18	2	0	0	0	0	0	0	0	0	0
333	344	19	3	0	0	0	0	0	0	0	0	0
344	355	20	4	0	0	0	0	0	0	0	0	0
355	366	21	5	0	0	0	0	0	0	0	0	0
366	377	23	6	0	0	0	0	0	0	0	0	0
377	388	24	7	0	0	0	0	0	0	0	0	0
388	399	25	9	0	0	0	0	0	0	0	0	0
399	410	26	10	0	0	0	0	0	0	0	0	0
410	421	27	11	0	0	0	0	0	0	0	0	0
421	432	28	12	0	0	0	0	0	0	0	0	0
432	443	29	13	0	0	0	0	0	0	0	0	0
443	454	30	14	0	0	0	0	0	0	0	0	0
454	465	31	15	0	0	0	0	0	0	0	0	0
465	476	32	16	0	0	0	0	0	0	0	0	0
476	487	34	17	1	0	0	0	0	0	0	0	0
487	498	35	18	2	0	0	0	0	0	0	0	0
498	509	36	20	3	0	0	0	0	0	0	0	0
509	529	37	21	5	0	0	0	0	0	0	0	0
529	549	40	23	7	0	0	0	0	0	0	0	0
549	569	42	25	9	0	0	0	0	0	0	0	0
569	589	44	27	11	0	0	0	0	0	0	0	0
589	609	47	29	13	0	0	0	0	0	0	0	0
609	629	49	31	15	0	0	0	0	0	0	0	0
629	649	52	33	17	1	0	0	0	0	0	0	0
649	669	54	35	19	3	0	0	0	0	0	0	0
669	689	56	37	21	5	0	0	0	0	0	0	0
689	709	59	39	23	7	0	0	0	0	0	0	0
709	729	61	42	25	9	0	0	0	0	0	0	0
729	749	64	44	27	11	0	0	0	0	0	0	0
749	769	66	47	29	13	0	0	0	0	0	0	0
769	789	68	49	31	15	0	0	0	0	0	0	0
789	809	71	51	33	17	1	0	0	0	0	0	0
809	829	73	54	35	19	3	0	0	0	0	0	0
829	849	76	56	37	21	5	0	0	0	0	0	0
849	869	78	59	39	23	7	0	0	0	0	0	0
869	889	80	61	42	25	9	0	0	0	0	0	0
889	909	83	63	44	27	11	0	0	0	0	0	0
909	929	85	66	47	29	13	0	0	0	0	0	0
929	949	88	68	49	31	15	0	0	0	0	0	0
949	969	90	71	51	33	17	1	0	0	0	0	0
969	989	92	73	54	35	19	3	0	0	0	0	0
989	1,009	95	75	56	37	21	5	0	0	0	0	0
1,009	1,029	97	78	59	39	23	7	0	0	0	0	0
1,029	1,049	100	80	61	42	25	9	0	0	0	0	0
1,049	1,069	102	83	63	44	27	11	0	0	0	0	0
1,069	1,089	104	85	66	46	29	13	0	0	0	0	0
1,089	1,109	107	87	68	49	31	15	0	0	0	0	0
1,109	1,129	109	90	71	51	33	17	0	0	0	0	0
1,129	1,149	112	92	73	54	35	19	2	0	0	0	0
1,149	1,169	114	95	75	56	37	21	4	0	0	0	0
1,169	1,189	116	97	78	58	39	23	6	0	0	0	0
1,189	1,209	119	99	80	61	41	25	8	0	0	0	0
1,209	1,229	121	102	83	63	44	27	10	0	0	0	0

Internal Revenue Service

Wage Bracket Method Tables for Income Tax Withholding

SINGLE Persons—**BIWEEKLY** Payroll Period

(For Wages Paid through December 2019)

And the wages are–		And the number of withholding allowances claimed is—										
At least	But less than	0	1	2	3	4	5	6	7	8	9	10
		The amount of income tax to be withheld is—										
1,229	**1,249**	124	104	85	66	46	29	12	0	0	0	0
1,249	**1,269**	126	107	87	68	49	31	14	0	0	0	0
1,269	**1,289**	128	109	90	70	51	33	16	0	0	0	0
1,289	**1,309**	131	111	92	73	53	35	18	2	0	0	0
1,309	**1,329**	133	114	95	75	56	37	20	4	0	0	0
1,329	**1,349**	136	116	97	78	58	39	22	6	0	0	0
1,349	**1,369**	138	119	99	80	61	41	24	8	0	0	0
1,369	**1,389**	140	121	102	82	63	44	26	10	0	0	0
1,389	**1,409**	143	123	104	85	65	46	28	12	0	0	0
1,409	**1,429**	145	126	107	87	68	48	30	14	0	0	0
1,429	**1,449**	148	128	109	90	70	51	32	16	0	0	0
1,449	**1,469**	150	131	111	92	73	53	34	18	2	0	0
1,469	**1,489**	152	133	114	94	75	56	36	20	4	0	0
1,489	**1,509**	155	135	116	97	77	58	39	22	6	0	0
1,509	**1,529**	157	138	119	99	80	60	41	24	8	0	0
1,529	**1,549**	160	140	121	102	82	63	43	26	10	0	0
1,549	**1,569**	162	143	123	104	85	65	46	28	12	0	0
1,569	**1,589**	164	145	126	106	87	68	48	30	14	0	0
1,589	**1,609**	167	147	128	109	89	70	51	32	16	0	0
1,609	**1,629**	169	150	131	111	92	72	53	34	18	2	0
1,629	**1,649**	172	152	133	114	94	75	55	36	20	4	0
1,649	**1,669**	174	155	135	116	97	77	58	38	22	6	0
1,669	**1,689**	178	157	138	118	99	80	60	41	24	8	0
1,689	**1,709**	182	159	140	121	101	82	63	43	26	10	0
1,709	**1,729**	187	162	143	123	104	84	65	46	28	12	0
1,729	**1,749**	191	164	145	126	106	87	67	48	30	14	0
1,749	**1,769**	196	167	147	128	109	89	70	50	32	16	0
1,769	**1,789**	200	169	150	130	111	92	72	53	34	18	2
1,789	**1,809**	204	171	152	133	113	94	75	55	36	20	4
1,809	**1,829**	209	174	155	135	116	96	77	58	38	22	6
1,829	**1,849**	213	178	157	138	118	99	79	60	41	24	8
1,849	**1,869**	218	182	159	140	121	101	82	62	43	26	10
1,869	**1,889**	222	186	162	142	123	104	84	65	45	28	12
1,889	**1,909**	226	191	164	145	125	106	87	67	48	30	14
1,909	**1,929**	231	195	167	147	128	108	89	70	50	32	16
1,929	**1,949**	235	200	169	150	130	111	91	72	53	34	18
1,949	**1,969**	240	204	171	152	133	113	94	74	55	36	20
1,969	**1,989**	244	208	174	154	135	116	96	77	57	38	22
1,989	**2,009**	248	213	177	157	137	118	99	79	60	40	24
2,009	**2,029**	253	217	182	159	140	120	101	82	62	43	26
2,029	**2,049**	257	222	186	162	142	123	103	84	65	45	28
2,049	**2,069**	262	226	190	164	145	125	106	86	67	48	30
2,069	**2,089**	266	230	195	166	147	128	108	89	69	50	32
2,089	**2,109**	270	235	199	169	149	130	111	91	72	52	34
2,109	**2,129**	275	239	204	171	152	132	113	94	74	55	36
2,129	**2,149**	279	244	208	174	154	135	115	96	77	57	38
2,149	**2,169**	284	248	212	177	157	137	118	98	79	60	40
2,169	**2,189**	288	252	217	181	159	140	120	101	81	62	43
2,189	**2,209**	292	257	221	186	161	142	123	103	84	64	45
2,209	**2,229**	297	261	226	190	164	144	125	106	86	67	47
2,229	**2,249**	301	266	230	195	166	147	127	108	89	69	50
2,249	**2,269**	306	270	234	199	169	149	130	110	91	72	52
2,269	**2,289**	310	274	239	203	171	152	132	113	93	74	55
2,289	**2,309**	314	279	243	208	173	154	135	115	96	76	57
2,309	**2,329**	319	283	248	212	177	156	137	118	98	79	59
2,329	**2,349**	323	288	252	217	181	159	139	120	101	81	62
2,349	**2,369**	328	292	256	221	185	161	142	122	103	84	64
2,369	**2,389**	332	296	261	225	190	164	144	125	105	86	67
2,389	**2,409**	336	301	265	230	194	166	147	127	108	88	69
2,409	**2,429**	341	305	270	234	199	168	149	130	110	91	71
2,429	**2,449**	345	310	274	239	203	171	151	132	113	93	74
2,449	**2,469**	350	314	278	243	207	173	154	134	115	96	76
2,469	**2,489**	354	318	283	247	212	176	156	137	117	98	79
2,489	**2,509**	358	323	287	252	216	181	159	139	120	100	81
2,509	**2,529**	363	327	292	256	221	185	161	142	122	103	83
2,529 and over		Use Table 2(a) for a SINGLE person on page 46. Also see the instructions on page 44.										

Internal Revenue Service

Wage Bracket Method Tables for Income Tax Withholding

MARRIED Persons—**BIWEEKLY** Payroll Period

(For Wages Paid through December 2019)

And the wages are–		And the number of withholding allowances claimed is—										
At least	But less than	0	1	2	3	4	5	6	7	8	9	10
		The amount of income tax to be withheld is—										
$ 0	**$454**	$0	$0	$0	$0	$0	$0	$0	$0	$0	$0	$0
454	**464**	1	0	0	0	0	0	0	0	0	0	0
464	**474**	2	0	0	0	0	0	0	0	0	0	0
474	**484**	3	0	0	0	0	0	0	0	0	0	0
484	**494**	4	0	0	0	0	0	0	0	0	0	0
494	**504**	5	0	0	0	0	0	0	0	0	0	0
504	**524**	6	0	0	0	0	0	0	0	0	0	0
524	**544**	8	0	0	0	0	0	0	0	0	0	0
544	**564**	10	0	0	0	0	0	0	0	0	0	0
564	**584**	12	0	0	0	0	0	0	0	0	0	0
584	**604**	14	0	0	0	0	0	0	0	0	0	0
604	**624**	16	0	0	0	0	0	0	0	0	0	0
624	**644**	18	2	0	0	0	0	0	0	0	0	0
644	**664**	20	4	0	0	0	0	0	0	0	0	0
664	**684**	22	6	0	0	0	0	0	0	0	0	0
684	**704**	24	8	0	0	0	0	0	0	0	0	0
704	**724**	26	10	0	0	0	0	0	0	0	0	0
724	**744**	28	12	0	0	0	0	0	0	0	0	0
744	**764**	30	14	0	0	0	0	0	0	0	0	0
764	**784**	32	16	0	0	0	0	0	0	0	0	0
784	**804**	34	18	2	0	0	0	0	0	0	0	0
804	**824**	36	20	4	0	0	0	0	0	0	0	0
824	**844**	38	22	6	0	0	0	0	0	0	0	0
844	**864**	40	24	8	0	0	0	0	0	0	0	0
864	**884**	42	26	10	0	0	0	0	0	0	0	0
884	**904**	44	28	12	0	0	0	0	0	0	0	0
904	**924**	46	30	14	0	0	0	0	0	0	0	0
924	**944**	48	32	16	0	0	0	0	0	0	0	0
944	**964**	50	34	18	2	0	0	0	0	0	0	0
964	**984**	52	36	20	4	0	0	0	0	0	0	0
984	**1,004**	54	38	22	6	0	0	0	0	0	0	0
1,004	**1,024**	56	40	24	8	0	0	0	0	0	0	0
1,024	**1,044**	58	42	26	10	0	0	0	0	0	0	0
1,044	**1,064**	60	44	28	12	0	0	0	0	0	0	0
1,064	**1,084**	62	46	30	14	0	0	0	0	0	0	0
1,084	**1,104**	64	48	32	16	0	0	0	0	0	0	0
1,104	**1,124**	66	50	34	18	1	0	0	0	0	0	0
1,124	**1,144**	68	52	36	20	3	0	0	0	0	0	0
1,144	**1,164**	70	54	38	22	5	0	0	0	0	0	0
1,164	**1,184**	72	56	40	24	7	0	0	0	0	0	0
1,184	**1,204**	74	58	42	26	9	0	0	0	0	0	0
1,204	**1,224**	76	60	44	28	11	0	0	0	0	0	0
1,224	**1,244**	79	62	46	30	13	0	0	0	0	0	0
1,244	**1,264**	81	64	48	32	15	0	0	0	0	0	0
1,264	**1,284**	83	66	50	34	17	1	0	0	0	0	0
1,284	**1,304**	86	68	52	36	19	3	0	0	0	0	0
1,304	**1,324**	88	70	54	38	21	5	0	0	0	0	0
1,324	**1,344**	91	72	56	40	23	7	0	0	0	0	0
1,344	**1,364**	93	74	58	42	25	9	0	0	0	0	0
1,364	**1,384**	95	76	60	44	27	11	0	0	0	0	0
1,384	**1,404**	98	79	62	46	29	13	0	0	0	0	0
1,404	**1,424**	100	81	64	48	31	15	0	0	0	0	0
1,424	**1,444**	103	83	66	50	33	17	1	0	0	0	0
1,444	**1,464**	105	86	68	52	35	19	3	0	0	0	0
1,464	**1,484**	107	88	70	54	37	21	5	0	0	0	0
1,484	**1,504**	110	91	72	56	39	23	7	0	0	0	0
1,504	**1,524**	112	93	74	58	41	25	9	0	0	0	0
1,524	**1,544**	115	95	76	60	43	27	11	0	0	0	0
1,544	**1,564**	117	98	78	62	45	29	13	0	0	0	0
1,564	**1,584**	119	100	81	64	47	31	15	0	0	0	0
1,584	**1,604**	122	103	83	66	49	33	17	1	0	0	0
1,604	**1,624**	124	105	86	68	51	35	19	3	0	0	0
1,624	**1,644**	127	107	88	70	53	37	21	5	0	0	0
1,644	**1,664**	129	110	90	72	55	39	23	7	0	0	0
1,664	**1,684**	131	112	93	74	57	41	25	9	0	0	0
1,684	**1,704**	134	115	95	76	59	43	27	11	0	0	0
1,704	**1,724**	136	117	98	78	61	45	29	13	0	0	0
1,724	**1,744**	139	119	100	81	63	47	31	15	0	0	0
1,744	**1,764**	141	122	102	83	65	49	33	17	1	0	0
1,764	**1,784**	143	124	105	85	67	51	35	19	3	0	0

Internal Revenue Service

Wage Bracket Method Tables for Income Tax Withholding

MARRIED Persons—**BIWEEKLY** Payroll Period

(For Wages Paid through December 2019)

And the wages are–		And the number of withholding allowances claimed is—										
At least	But less than	0	1	2	3	4	5	6	7	8	9	10
		The amount of income tax to be withheld is—										
1,784	**1,804**	146	127	107	88	69	53	37	21	5	0	0
1,804	**1,824**	148	129	110	90	71	55	39	23	7	0	0
1,824	**1,844**	151	131	112	93	73	57	41	25	9	0	0
1,844	**1,864**	153	134	114	95	76	59	43	27	11	0	0
1,864	**1,884**	155	136	117	97	78	61	45	29	13	0	0
1,884	**1,904**	158	139	119	100	80	63	47	31	15	0	0
1,904	**1,924**	160	141	122	102	83	65	49	33	17	1	0
1,924	**1,944**	163	143	124	105	85	67	51	35	19	3	0
1,944	**1,964**	165	146	126	107	88	69	53	37	21	5	0
1,964	**1,984**	167	148	129	109	90	71	55	39	23	7	0
1,984	**2,004**	170	151	131	112	92	73	57	41	25	9	0
2,004	**2,024**	172	153	134	114	95	75	59	43	27	11	0
2,024	**2,044**	175	155	136	117	97	78	61	45	29	13	0
2,044	**2,064**	177	158	138	119	100	80	63	47	31	15	0
2,064	**2,084**	179	160	141	121	102	83	65	49	33	17	0
2,084	**2,104**	182	163	143	124	104	85	67	51	35	19	2
2,104	**2,124**	184	165	146	126	107	87	69	53	37	21	4
2,124	**2,144**	187	167	148	129	109	90	71	55	39	23	6
2,144	**2,164**	189	170	150	131	112	92	73	57	41	25	8
2,164	**2,184**	191	172	153	133	114	95	75	59	43	27	10
2,184	**2,204**	194	175	155	136	116	97	78	61	45	29	12
2,204	**2,224**	196	177	158	138	119	99	80	63	47	31	14
2,224	**2,244**	199	179	160	141	121	102	82	65	49	33	16
2,244	**2,264**	201	182	162	143	124	104	85	67	51	35	18
2,264	**2,284**	203	184	165	145	126	107	87	69	53	37	20
2,284	**2,304**	206	187	167	148	128	109	90	71	55	39	22
2,304	**2,324**	208	189	170	150	131	111	92	73	57	41	24
2,324	**2,344**	211	191	172	153	133	114	94	75	59	43	26
2,344	**2,364**	213	194	174	155	136	116	97	77	61	45	28
2,364	**2,384**	215	196	177	157	138	119	99	80	63	47	30
2,384	**2,404**	218	199	179	160	140	121	102	82	65	49	32
2,404	**2,424**	220	201	182	162	143	123	104	85	67	51	34
2,424	**2,444**	223	203	184	165	145	126	106	87	69	53	36
2,444	**2,464**	225	206	186	167	148	128	109	89	71	55	38
2,464	**2,484**	227	208	189	169	150	131	111	92	73	57	40
2,484	**2,504**	230	211	191	172	152	133	114	94	75	59	42
2,504	**2,524**	232	213	194	174	155	135	116	97	77	61	44
2,524	**2,544**	235	215	196	177	157	138	118	99	80	63	46
2,544	**2,564**	237	218	198	179	160	140	121	101	82	65	48
2,564	**2,584**	239	220	201	181	162	143	123	104	84	67	50
2,584	**2,604**	242	223	203	184	164	145	126	106	87	69	52
2,604	**2,624**	244	225	206	186	167	147	128	109	89	71	54
2,624	**2,644**	247	227	208	189	169	150	130	111	92	73	56
2,644	**2,664**	249	230	210	191	172	152	133	113	94	75	58
2,664	**2,684**	251	232	213	193	174	155	135	116	96	77	60
2,684	**2,704**	254	235	215	196	176	157	138	118	99	79	62
2,704	**2,724**	256	237	218	198	179	159	140	121	101	82	64
2,724	**2,744**	259	239	220	201	181	162	142	123	104	84	66
2,744	**2,764**	261	242	222	203	184	164	145	125	106	87	68
2,764	**2,784**	263	244	225	205	186	167	147	128	108	89	70
2,784	**2,804**	266	247	227	208	188	169	150	130	111	91	72
2,804	**2,824**	268	249	230	210	191	171	152	133	113	94	74
2,824	**2,844**	271	251	232	213	193	174	154	135	116	96	77
2,844	**2,864**	273	254	234	215	196	176	157	137	118	99	79
2,864	**2,884**	275	256	237	217	198	179	159	140	120	101	82
2,884	**2,904**	278	259	239	220	200	181	162	142	123	103	84
2,904	**2,924**	280	261	242	222	203	183	164	145	125	106	86
2,924	**2,944**	283	263	244	225	205	186	166	147	128	108	89
2,944	**2,964**	285	266	246	227	208	188	169	149	130	111	91
2,964	**2,984**	287	268	249	229	210	191	171	152	132	113	94
2,984	**3,004**	290	271	251	232	212	193	174	154	135	115	96
3,004	**3,024**	292	273	254	234	215	195	176	157	137	118	98
3,024	**3,044**	295	275	256	237	217	198	178	159	140	120	101
3,044	**3,064**	297	278	258	239	220	200	181	161	142	123	103
3,064	**3,084**	299	280	261	241	222	203	183	164	144	125	106
3,084	**3,104**	302	283	263	244	224	205	186	166	147	127	108
3,104 and over		Use Table 2(b) for a MARRIED person on page 46. Also see the instructions on page 44.										

Internal Revenue Service

Wage Bracket Method Tables for Income Tax Withholding

SINGLE Persons—SEMIMONTHLY Payroll Period

(For Wages Paid through December 2019)

And the wages are–		And the number of withholding allowances claimed is—										
At least	But less than	0	1	2	3	4	5	6	7	8	9	10
		The amount of income tax to be withheld is—										
$ 0	$158	$0	$0	$0	$0	$0	$0	$0	$0	$0	$0	$0
158	169	1	0	0	0	0	0	0	0	0	0	0
169	180	2	0	0	0	0	0	0	0	0	0	0
180	191	3	0	0	0	0	0	0	0	0	0	0
191	202	4	0	0	0	0	0	0	0	0	0	0
202	213	5	0	0	0	0	0	0	0	0	0	0
213	224	6	0	0	0	0	0	0	0	0	0	0
224	235	7	0	0	0	0	0	0	0	0	0	0
235	246	8	0	0	0	0	0	0	0	0	0	0
246	257	9	0	0	0	0	0	0	0	0	0	0
257	268	10	0	0	0	0	0	0	0	0	0	0
268	279	12	0	0	0	0	0	0	0	0	0	0
279	290	13	0	0	0	0	0	0	0	0	0	0
290	301	14	0	0	0	0	0	0	0	0	0	0
301	312	15	0	0	0	0	0	0	0	0	0	0
312	323	16	0	0	0	0	0	0	0	0	0	0
323	334	17	0	0	0	0	0	0	0	0	0	0
334	345	18	1	0	0	0	0	0	0	0	0	0
345	356	19	2	0	0	0	0	0	0	0	0	0
356	367	20	3	0	0	0	0	0	0	0	0	0
367	378	21	4	0	0	0	0	0	0	0	0	0
378	389	23	5	0	0	0	0	0	0	0	0	0
389	400	24	6	0	0	0	0	0	0	0	0	0
400	411	25	7	0	0	0	0	0	0	0	0	0
411	422	26	8	0	0	0	0	0	0	0	0	0
422	433	27	9	0	0	0	0	0	0	0	0	0
433	444	28	11	0	0	0	0	0	0	0	0	0
444	455	29	12	0	0	0	0	0	0	0	0	0
455	466	30	13	0	0	0	0	0	0	0	0	0
466	477	31	14	0	0	0	0	0	0	0	0	0
477	488	32	15	0	0	0	0	0	0	0	0	0
488	499	34	16	0	0	0	0	0	0	0	0	0
499	510	35	17	0	0	0	0	0	0	0	0	0
510	530	36	19	1	0	0	0	0	0	0	0	0
530	550	38	21	3	0	0	0	0	0	0	0	0
550	570	40	23	5	0	0	0	0	0	0	0	0
570	590	43	25	7	0	0	0	0	0	0	0	0
590	610	45	27	9	0	0	0	0	0	0	0	0
610	630	47	29	11	0	0	0	0	0	0	0	0
630	650	50	31	13	0	0	0	0	0	0	0	0
650	670	52	33	15	0	0	0	0	0	0	0	0
670	690	55	35	17	0	0	0	0	0	0	0	0
690	710	57	37	19	2	0	0	0	0	0	0	0
710	730	59	39	21	4	0	0	0	0	0	0	0
730	750	62	41	23	6	0	0	0	0	0	0	0
750	770	64	43	25	8	0	0	0	0	0	0	0
770	790	67	46	27	10	0	0	0	0	0	0	0
790	810	69	48	29	12	0	0	0	0	0	0	0
810	830	71	50	31	14	0	0	0	0	0	0	0
830	850	74	53	33	16	0	0	0	0	0	0	0
850	870	76	55	35	18	0	0	0	0	0	0	0
870	890	79	58	37	20	2	0	0	0	0	0	0
890	910	81	60	39	22	4	0	0	0	0	0	0
910	930	83	62	41	24	6	0	0	0	0	0	0
930	950	86	65	44	26	8	0	0	0	0	0	0
950	970	88	67	46	28	10	0	0	0	0	0	0
970	990	91	70	49	30	12	0	0	0	0	0	0
990	1,010	93	72	51	32	14	0	0	0	0	0	0
1,010	1,030	95	74	53	34	16	0	0	0	0	0	0
1,030	1,050	98	77	56	36	18	1	0	0	0	0	0
1,050	1,070	100	79	58	38	20	3	0	0	0	0	0
1,070	1,090	103	82	61	40	22	5	0	0	0	0	0
1,090	1,110	105	84	63	42	24	7	0	0	0	0	0
1,110	1,130	107	86	65	44	26	9	0	0	0	0	0
1,130	1,150	110	89	68	47	28	11	0	0	0	0	0
1,150	1,170	112	91	70	49	30	13	0	0	0	0	0
1,170	1,190	115	94	73	52	32	15	0	0	0	0	0
1,190	1,210	117	96	75	54	34	17	0	0	0	0	0
1,210	1,230	119	98	77	56	36	19	1	0	0	0	0
1,230	1,250	122	101	80	59	38	21	3	0	0	0	0

Internal Revenue Service

Wage Bracket Method Tables for Income Tax Withholding

SINGLE Persons—**SEMIMONTHLY** Payroll Period

(For Wages Paid through December 2019)

And the wages are–		And the number of withholding allowances claimed is—										
At least	But less than	0	1	2	3	4	5	6	7	8	9	10
		The amount of income tax to be withheld is—										
1,250	**1,270**	124	103	82	61	40	23	5	0	0	0	0
1,270	**1,290**	127	106	85	64	43	25	7	0	0	0	0
1,290	**1,310**	129	108	87	66	45	27	9	0	0	0	0
1,310	**1,330**	131	110	89	68	47	29	11	0	0	0	0
1,330	**1,350**	134	113	92	71	50	31	13	0	0	0	0
1,350	**1,370**	136	115	94	73	52	33	15	0	0	0	0
1,370	**1,390**	139	118	97	76	55	35	17	0	0	0	0
1,390	**1,410**	141	120	99	78	57	37	19	2	0	0	0
1,410	**1,430**	143	122	101	80	59	39	21	4	0	0	0
1,430	**1,450**	146	125	104	83	62	41	23	6	0	0	0
1,450	**1,470**	148	127	106	85	64	43	25	8	0	0	0
1,470	**1,490**	151	130	109	88	67	46	27	10	0	0	0
1,490	**1,510**	153	132	111	90	69	48	29	12	0	0	0
1,510	**1,530**	155	134	113	92	71	50	31	14	0	0	0
1,530	**1,550**	158	137	116	95	74	53	33	16	0	0	0
1,550	**1,570**	160	139	118	97	76	55	35	18	0	0	0
1,570	**1,590**	163	142	121	100	79	58	37	20	2	0	0
1,590	**1,610**	165	144	123	102	81	60	39	22	4	0	0
1,610	**1,630**	167	146	125	104	83	62	41	24	6	0	0
1,630	**1,650**	170	149	128	107	86	65	44	26	8	0	0
1,650	**1,670**	172	151	130	109	88	67	46	28	10	0	0
1,670	**1,690**	175	154	133	112	91	70	49	30	12	0	0
1,690	**1,710**	177	156	135	114	93	72	51	32	14	0	0
1,710	**1,730**	179	158	137	116	95	74	53	34	16	0	0
1,730	**1,750**	182	161	140	119	98	77	56	36	18	1	0
1,750	**1,770**	184	163	142	121	100	79	58	38	20	3	0
1,770	**1,790**	187	166	145	124	103	82	61	40	22	5	0
1,790	**1,810**	189	168	147	126	105	84	63	42	24	7	0
1,810	**1,830**	193	170	149	128	107	86	65	44	26	9	0
1,830	**1,850**	197	173	152	131	110	89	68	47	28	11	0
1,850	**1,870**	202	175	154	133	112	91	70	49	30	13	0
1,870	**1,890**	206	178	157	136	115	94	73	52	32	15	0
1,890	**1,910**	211	180	159	138	117	96	75	54	34	17	0
1,910	**1,930**	215	182	161	140	119	98	77	56	36	19	1
1,930	**1,950**	219	185	164	143	122	101	80	59	38	21	3
1,950	**1,970**	224	187	166	145	124	103	82	61	40	23	5
1,970	**1,990**	228	190	169	148	127	106	85	64	43	25	7
1,990	**2,010**	233	194	171	150	129	108	87	66	45	27	9
2,010	**2,030**	237	199	173	152	131	110	89	68	47	29	11
2,030	**2,050**	241	203	176	155	134	113	92	71	50	31	13
2,050	**2,070**	246	207	178	157	136	115	94	73	52	33	15
2,070	**2,090**	250	212	181	160	139	118	97	76	55	35	17
2,090	**2,110**	255	216	183	162	141	120	99	78	57	37	19
2,110	**2,130**	259	221	185	164	143	122	101	80	59	39	21
2,130	**2,150**	263	225	188	167	146	125	104	83	62	41	23
2,150	**2,170**	268	229	191	169	148	127	106	85	64	43	25
2,170	**2,190**	272	234	195	172	151	130	109	88	67	46	27
2,190	**2,210**	277	238	200	174	153	132	111	90	69	48	29
2,210	**2,230**	281	243	204	176	155	134	113	92	71	50	31
2,230	**2,250**	285	247	208	179	158	137	116	95	74	53	33
2,250	**2,270**	290	251	213	181	160	139	118	97	76	55	35
2,270	**2,290**	294	256	217	184	163	142	121	100	79	58	37
2,290	**2,310**	299	260	222	186	165	144	123	102	81	60	39
2,310	**2,330**	303	265	226	188	167	146	125	104	83	62	41
2,330	**2,350**	307	269	230	192	170	149	128	107	86	65	44
2,350	**2,370**	312	273	235	196	172	151	130	109	88	67	46
2,370	**2,390**	316	278	239	201	175	154	133	112	91	70	49
2,390	**2,410**	321	282	244	205	177	156	135	114	93	72	51
2,410	**2,430**	325	287	248	210	179	158	137	116	95	74	53
2,430	**2,450**	329	291	252	214	182	161	140	119	98	77	56
2,450	**2,470**	334	295	257	218	184	163	142	121	100	79	58
2,470	**2,490**	338	300	261	223	187	166	145	124	103	82	61
2,490	**2,510**	343	304	266	227	189	168	147	126	105	84	63
2,510	**2,530**	347	309	270	232	193	170	149	128	107	86	65
2,530	**2,550**	351	313	274	236	197	173	152	131	110	89	68

2,550 and over Use Table 3(a) for a SINGLE person on page 46. Also see the instructions on page 44.

Wage Bracket Method Tables for Income Tax Withholding

MARRIED Persons—**SEMIMONTHLY** Payroll Period

(For Wages Paid through December 2019)

And the wages are–		And the number of withholding allowances claimed is—										
At least	But less than	0	1	2	3	4	5	6	7	8	9	10
		The amount of income tax to be withheld is—										
$ 0	$492	$0	$0	$0	$0	$0	$0	$0	$0	$0	$0	$0
492	502	1	0	0	0	0	0	0	0	0	0	0
502	512	2	0	0	0	0	0	0	0	0	0	0
512	522	3	0	0	0	0	0	0	0	0	0	0
522	532	4	0	0	0	0	0	0	0	0	0	0
532	542	5	0	0	0	0	0	0	0	0	0	0
542	552	6	0	0	0	0	0	0	0	0	0	0
552	562	7	0	0	0	0	0	0	0	0	0	0
562	572	8	0	0	0	0	0	0	0	0	0	0
572	582	9	0	0	0	0	0	0	0	0	0	0
582	592	10	0	0	0	0	0	0	0	0	0	0
592	602	11	0	0	0	0	0	0	0	0	0	0
602	612	12	0	0	0	0	0	0	0	0	0	0
612	622	13	0	0	0	0	0	0	0	0	0	0
622	632	14	0	0	0	0	0	0	0	0	0	0
632	642	15	0	0	0	0	0	0	0	0	0	0
642	652	16	0	0	0	0	0	0	0	0	0	0
652	662	17	0	0	0	0	0	0	0	0	0	0
662	672	18	0	0	0	0	0	0	0	0	0	0
672	682	19	1	0	0	0	0	0	0	0	0	0
682	692	20	2	0	0	0	0	0	0	0	0	0
692	702	21	3	0	0	0	0	0	0	0	0	0
702	712	22	4	0	0	0	0	0	0	0	0	0
712	722	23	5	0	0	0	0	0	0	0	0	0
722	732	24	6	0	0	0	0	0	0	0	0	0
732	742	25	7	0	0	0	0	0	0	0	0	0
742	752	26	8	0	0	0	0	0	0	0	0	0
752	762	27	9	0	0	0	0	0	0	0	0	0
762	772	28	10	0	0	0	0	0	0	0	0	0
772	782	29	11	0	0	0	0	0	0	0	0	0
782	792	30	12	0	0	0	0	0	0	0	0	0
792	802	31	13	0	0	0	0	0	0	0	0	0
802	812	32	14	0	0	0	0	0	0	0	0	0
812	822	33	15	0	0	0	0	0	0	0	0	0
822	832	34	16	0	0	0	0	0	0	0	0	0
832	842	35	17	0	0	0	0	0	0	0	0	0
842	852	36	18	1	0	0	0	0	0	0	0	0
852	862	37	19	2	0	0	0	0	0	0	0	0
862	872	38	20	3	0	0	0	0	0	0	0	0
872	882	39	21	4	0	0	0	0	0	0	0	0
882	892	40	22	5	0	0	0	0	0	0	0	0
892	902	41	23	6	0	0	0	0	0	0	0	0
902	912	42	24	7	0	0	0	0	0	0	0	0
912	922	43	25	8	0	0	0	0	0	0	0	0
922	932	44	26	9	0	0	0	0	0	0	0	0
932	942	45	27	10	0	0	0	0	0	0	0	0
942	952	46	28	11	0	0	0	0	0	0	0	0
952	962	47	29	12	0	0	0	0	0	0	0	0
962	972	48	30	13	0	0	0	0	0	0	0	0
972	982	49	31	14	0	0	0	0	0	0	0	0
982	992	50	32	15	0	0	0	0	0	0	0	0
992	1,002	51	33	16	0	0	0	0	0	0	0	0
1,002	1,022	52	35	17	0	0	0	0	0	0	0	0
1,022	1,042	54	37	19	2	0	0	0	0	0	0	0
1,042	1,062	56	39	21	4	0	0	0	0	0	0	0
1,062	1,082	58	41	23	6	0	0	0	0	0	0	0
1,082	1,102	60	43	25	8	0	0	0	0	0	0	0
1,102	1,122	62	45	27	10	0	0	0	0	0	0	0
1,122	1,142	64	47	29	12	0	0	0	0	0	0	0
1,142	1,162	66	49	31	14	0	0	0	0	0	0	0
1,162	1,182	68	51	33	16	0	0	0	0	0	0	0
1,182	1,202	70	53	35	18	0	0	0	0	0	0	0
1,202	1,222	72	55	37	20	2	0	0	0	0	0	0
1,222	1,242	74	57	39	22	4	0	0	0	0	0	0
1,242	1,262	76	59	41	24	6	0	0	0	0	0	0
1,262	1,282	78	61	43	26	8	0	0	0	0	0	0
1,282	1,302	80	63	45	28	10	0	0	0	0	0	0
1,302	1,322	82	65	47	30	12	0	0	0	0	0	0
1,322	1,342	85	67	49	32	14	0	0	0	0	0	0
1,342	1,362	87	69	51	34	16	0	0	0	0	0	0

Internal Revenue Service

Wage Bracket Method Tables for Income Tax Withholding

MARRIED Persons—SEMIMONTHLY Payroll Period

(For Wages Paid through December 2019)

And the wages are–		And the number of withholding allowances claimed is—										
At least	But less than	0	1	2	3	4	5	6	7	8	9	10
		The amount of income tax to be withheld is—										
1,362	**1,382**	89	71	53	36	18	1	0	0	0	0	0
1,382	**1,402**	92	73	55	38	20	3	0	0	0	0	0
1,402	**1,422**	94	75	57	40	22	5	0	0	0	0	0
1,422	**1,442**	97	77	59	42	24	7	0	0	0	0	0
1,442	**1,462**	99	79	61	44	26	9	0	0	0	0	0
1,462	**1,482**	101	81	63	46	28	11	0	0	0	0	0
1,482	**1,502**	104	83	65	48	30	13	0	0	0	0	0
1,502	**1,522**	106	85	67	50	32	15	0	0	0	0	0
1,522	**1,542**	109	88	69	52	34	17	0	0	0	0	0
1,542	**1,562**	111	90	71	54	36	19	1	0	0	0	0
1,562	**1,582**	113	92	73	56	38	21	3	0	0	0	0
1,582	**1,602**	116	95	75	58	40	23	5	0	0	0	0
1,602	**1,622**	118	97	77	60	42	25	7	0	0	0	0
1,622	**1,642**	121	100	79	62	44	27	9	0	0	0	0
1,642	**1,662**	123	102	81	64	46	29	11	0	0	0	0
1,662	**1,682**	125	104	83	66	48	31	13	0	0	0	0
1,682	**1,702**	128	107	86	68	50	33	15	0	0	0	0
1,702	**1,722**	130	109	88	70	52	35	17	0	0	0	0
1,722	**1,742**	133	112	91	72	54	37	19	2	0	0	0
1,742	**1,762**	135	114	93	74	56	39	21	4	0	0	0
1,762	**1,782**	137	116	95	76	58	41	23	6	0	0	0
1,782	**1,802**	140	119	98	78	60	43	25	8	0	0	0
1,802	**1,822**	142	121	100	80	62	45	27	10	0	0	0
1,822	**1,842**	145	124	103	82	64	47	29	12	0	0	0
1,842	**1,862**	147	126	105	84	66	49	31	14	0	0	0
1,862	**1,882**	149	128	107	86	68	51	33	16	0	0	0
1,882	**1,902**	152	131	110	89	70	53	35	18	0	0	0
1,902	**1,922**	154	133	112	91	72	55	37	20	2	0	0
1,922	**1,942**	157	136	115	94	74	57	39	22	4	0	0
1,942	**1,962**	159	138	117	96	76	59	41	24	6	0	0
1,962	**1,982**	161	140	119	98	78	61	43	26	8	0	0
1,982	**2,002**	164	143	122	101	80	63	45	28	10	0	0
2,002	**2,022**	166	145	124	103	82	65	47	30	12	0	0
2,022	**2,042**	169	148	127	106	85	67	49	32	14	0	0
2,042	**2,062**	171	150	129	108	87	69	51	34	16	0	0
2,062	**2,082**	173	152	131	110	89	71	53	36	18	1	0
2,082	**2,102**	176	155	134	113	92	73	55	38	20	3	0
2,102	**2,122**	178	157	136	115	94	75	57	40	22	5	0
2,122	**2,142**	181	160	139	118	97	77	59	42	24	7	0
2,142	**2,162**	183	162	141	120	99	79	61	44	26	9	0
2,162	**2,182**	185	164	143	122	101	81	63	46	28	11	0
2,182	**2,202**	188	167	146	125	104	83	65	48	30	13	0
2,202	**2,222**	190	169	148	127	106	85	67	50	32	15	0
2,222	**2,242**	193	172	151	130	109	88	69	52	34	17	0
2,242	**2,262**	195	174	153	132	111	90	71	54	36	19	1
2,262	**2,282**	197	176	155	134	113	92	73	56	38	21	3
2,282	**2,302**	200	179	158	137	116	95	75	58	40	23	5
2,302	**2,322**	202	181	160	139	118	97	77	60	42	25	7
2,322	**2,342**	205	184	163	142	121	100	79	62	44	27	9
2,342	**2,362**	207	186	165	144	123	102	81	64	46	29	11
2,362	**2,382**	209	188	167	146	125	104	83	66	48	31	13
2,382	**2,402**	212	191	170	149	128	107	86	68	50	33	15
2,402	**2,422**	214	193	172	151	130	109	88	70	52	35	17
2,422	**2,442**	217	196	175	154	133	112	91	72	54	37	19
2,442	**2,462**	219	198	177	156	135	114	93	74	56	39	21
2,462	**2,482**	221	200	179	158	137	116	95	76	58	41	23
2,482	**2,502**	224	203	182	161	140	119	98	78	60	43	25
2,502	**2,522**	226	205	184	163	142	121	100	80	62	45	27
2,522	**2,542**	229	208	187	166	145	124	103	82	64	47	29
2,542	**2,562**	231	210	189	168	147	126	105	84	66	49	31
2,562	**2,582**	233	212	191	170	149	128	107	86	68	51	33
2,582	**2,602**	236	215	194	173	152	131	110	89	70	53	35
2,602	**2,622**	238	217	196	175	154	133	112	91	72	55	37
2,622	**2,642**	241	220	199	178	157	136	115	94	74	57	39
2,642	**2,662**	243	222	201	180	159	138	117	96	76	59	41
2,662	**2,682**	245	224	203	182	161	140	119	98	78	61	43
2,682 and over		Use Table 3(b) for a MARRIED person on page 46. Also see the instructions on page 44.										

Wage Bracket Method Tables for Income Tax Withholding

SINGLE Persons—MONTHLY Payroll Period

(For Wages Paid through December 2019)

And the wages are–		And the number of withholding allowances claimed is—										
At least	But less than	0	1	2	3	4	5	6	7	8	9	10
		The amount of income tax to be withheld is—										
$ 0	$317	$0	$0	$0	$0	$0	$0	$0	$0	$0	$0	$0
317	327	1	0	0	0	0	0	0	0	0	0	0
327	337	2	0	0	0	0	0	0	0	0	0	0
337	347	3	0	0	0	0	0	0	0	0	0	0
347	357	4	0	0	0	0	0	0	0	0	0	0
357	367	5	0	0	0	0	0	0	0	0	0	0
367	377	6	0	0	0	0	0	0	0	0	0	0
377	387	7	0	0	0	0	0	0	0	0	0	0
387	397	8	0	0	0	0	0	0	0	0	0	0
397	407	9	0	0	0	0	0	0	0	0	0	0
407	417	10	0	0	0	0	0	0	0	0	0	0
417	427	11	0	0	0	0	0	0	0	0	0	0
427	437	12	0	0	0	0	0	0	0	0	0	0
437	447	13	0	0	0	0	0	0	0	0	0	0
447	457	14	0	0	0	0	0	0	0	0	0	0
457	467	15	0	0	0	0	0	0	0	0	0	0
467	477	16	0	0	0	0	0	0	0	0	0	0
477	487	17	0	0	0	0	0	0	0	0	0	0
487	497	18	0	0	0	0	0	0	0	0	0	0
497	507	19	0	0	0	0	0	0	0	0	0	0
507	517	20	0	0	0	0	0	0	0	0	0	0
517	527	21	0	0	0	0	0	0	0	0	0	0
527	537	22	0	0	0	0	0	0	0	0	0	0
537	547	23	0	0	0	0	0	0	0	0	0	0
547	557	24	0	0	0	0	0	0	0	0	0	0
557	567	25	0	0	0	0	0	0	0	0	0	0
567	577	26	0	0	0	0	0	0	0	0	0	0
577	587	27	0	0	0	0	0	0	0	0	0	0
587	597	28	0	0	0	0	0	0	0	0	0	0
597	607	29	0	0	0	0	0	0	0	0	0	0
607	617	30	0	0	0	0	0	0	0	0	0	0
617	627	31	0	0	0	0	0	0	0	0	0	0
627	637	32	0	0	0	0	0	0	0	0	0	0
637	647	33	0	0	0	0	0	0	0	0	0	0
647	657	34	0	0	0	0	0	0	0	0	0	0
657	667	35	0	0	0	0	0	0	0	0	0	0
667	677	36	1	0	0	0	0	0	0	0	0	0
677	687	37	2	0	0	0	0	0	0	0	0	0
687	697	38	3	0	0	0	0	0	0	0	0	0
697	707	39	4	0	0	0	0	0	0	0	0	0
707	717	40	5	0	0	0	0	0	0	0	0	0
717	727	41	6	0	0	0	0	0	0	0	0	0
727	737	42	7	0	0	0	0	0	0	0	0	0
737	747	43	8	0	0	0	0	0	0	0	0	0
747	757	44	9	0	0	0	0	0	0	0	0	0
757	767	45	10	0	0	0	0	0	0	0	0	0
767	777	46	11	0	0	0	0	0	0	0	0	0
777	787	47	12	0	0	0	0	0	0	0	0	0
787	797	48	13	0	0	0	0	0	0	0	0	0
797	807	49	14	0	0	0	0	0	0	0	0	0
807	817	50	15	0	0	0	0	0	0	0	0	0
817	827	51	16	0	0	0	0	0	0	0	0	0
827	837	52	17	0	0	0	0	0	0	0	0	0
837	847	53	18	0	0	0	0	0	0	0	0	0
847	857	54	19	0	0	0	0	0	0	0	0	0
857	867	55	20	0	0	0	0	0	0	0	0	0
867	877	56	21	0	0	0	0	0	0	0	0	0
877	887	57	22	0	0	0	0	0	0	0	0	0
887	897	58	23	0	0	0	0	0	0	0	0	0
897	907	59	24	0	0	0	0	0	0	0	0	0
907	917	60	25	0	0	0	0	0	0	0	0	0
917	927	61	26	0	0	0	0	0	0	0	0	0
927	937	62	27	0	0	0	0	0	0	0	0	0
937	947	63	28	0	0	0	0	0	0	0	0	0
947	957	64	29	0	0	0	0	0	0	0	0	0
957	967	65	30	0	0	0	0	0	0	0	0	0
967	977	66	31	0	0	0	0	0	0	0	0	0
977	987	67	32	0	0	0	0	0	0	0	0	0
987	997	68	33	0	0	0	0	0	0	0	0	0
997	1,007	69	34	0	0	0	0	0	0	0	0	0

Internal Revenue Service

Wage Bracket Method Tables for Income Tax Withholding

SINGLE Persons—**MONTHLY** Payroll Period

(For Wages Paid through December 2019)

And the wages are–		And the number of withholding allowances claimed is—										
At least	But less than	0	1	2	3	4	5	6	7	8	9	10
		The amount of income tax to be withheld is—										
1,007	**1,027**	70	35	0	0	0	0	0	0	0	0	0
1,027	**1,047**	72	37	2	0	0	0	0	0	0	0	0
1,047	**1,067**	74	39	4	0	0	0	0	0	0	0	0
1,067	**1,087**	76	41	6	0	0	0	0	0	0	0	0
1,087	**1,107**	78	43	8	0	0	0	0	0	0	0	0
1,107	**1,127**	80	45	10	0	0	0	0	0	0	0	0
1,127	**1,147**	82	47	12	0	0	0	0	0	0	0	0
1,147	**1,167**	85	49	14	0	0	0	0	0	0	0	0
1,167	**1,187**	87	51	16	0	0	0	0	0	0	0	0
1,187	**1,207**	89	53	18	0	0	0	0	0	0	0	0
1,207	**1,227**	92	55	20	0	0	0	0	0	0	0	0
1,227	**1,247**	94	57	22	0	0	0	0	0	0	0	0
1,247	**1,267**	97	59	24	0	0	0	0	0	0	0	0
1,267	**1,287**	99	61	26	0	0	0	0	0	0	0	0
1,287	**1,307**	101	63	28	0	0	0	0	0	0	0	0
1,307	**1,327**	104	65	30	0	0	0	0	0	0	0	0
1,327	**1,347**	106	67	32	0	0	0	0	0	0	0	0
1,347	**1,367**	109	69	34	0	0	0	0	0	0	0	0
1,367	**1,387**	111	71	36	1	0	0	0	0	0	0	0
1,387	**1,407**	113	73	38	3	0	0	0	0	0	0	0
1,407	**1,427**	116	75	40	5	0	0	0	0	0	0	0
1,427	**1,447**	118	77	42	7	0	0	0	0	0	0	0
1,447	**1,467**	121	79	44	9	0	0	0	0	0	0	0
1,467	**1,487**	123	81	46	11	0	0	0	0	0	0	0
1,487	**1,507**	125	83	48	13	0	0	0	0	0	0	0
1,507	**1,527**	128	86	50	15	0	0	0	0	0	0	0
1,527	**1,547**	130	88	52	17	0	0	0	0	0	0	0
1,547	**1,567**	133	91	54	19	0	0	0	0	0	0	0
1,567	**1,587**	135	93	56	21	0	0	0	0	0	0	0
1,587	**1,607**	137	95	58	23	0	0	0	0	0	0	0
1,607	**1,627**	140	98	60	25	0	0	0	0	0	0	0
1,627	**1,647**	142	100	62	27	0	0	0	0	0	0	0
1,647	**1,667**	145	103	64	29	0	0	0	0	0	0	0
1,667	**1,687**	147	105	66	31	0	0	0	0	0	0	0
1,687	**1,707**	149	107	68	33	0	0	0	0	0	0	0
1,707	**1,727**	152	110	70	35	0	0	0	0	0	0	0
1,727	**1,747**	154	112	72	37	2	0	0	0	0	0	0
1,747	**1,767**	157	115	74	39	4	0	0	0	0	0	0
1,767	**1,787**	159	117	76	41	6	0	0	0	0	0	0
1,787	**1,807**	161	119	78	43	8	0	0	0	0	0	0
1,807	**1,827**	164	122	80	45	10	0	0	0	0	0	0
1,827	**1,847**	166	124	82	47	12	0	0	0	0	0	0
1,847	**1,867**	169	127	85	49	14	0	0	0	0	0	0
1,867	**1,887**	171	129	87	51	16	0	0	0	0	0	0
1,887	**1,907**	173	131	89	53	18	0	0	0	0	0	0
1,907	**1,927**	176	134	92	55	20	0	0	0	0	0	0
1,927	**1,947**	178	136	94	57	22	0	0	0	0	0	0
1,947	**1,967**	181	139	97	59	24	0	0	0	0	0	0
1,967	**1,987**	183	141	99	61	26	0	0	0	0	0	0
1,987	**2,007**	185	143	101	63	28	0	0	0	0	0	0
2,007	**2,047**	189	147	105	66	31	0	0	0	0	0	0
2,047	**2,087**	194	152	110	70	35	0	0	0	0	0	0
2,087	**2,127**	199	157	115	74	39	4	0	0	0	0	0
2,127	**2,167**	203	161	119	78	43	8	0	0	0	0	0
2,167	**2,207**	208	166	124	82	47	12	0	0	0	0	0
2,207	**2,247**	213	171	129	87	51	16	0	0	0	0	0
2,247	**2,287**	218	176	134	92	55	20	0	0	0	0	0
2,287	**2,327**	223	181	139	97	59	24	0	0	0	0	0
2,327	**2,367**	227	185	143	101	63	28	0	0	0	0	0
2,367	**2,407**	232	190	148	106	67	32	0	0	0	0	0
2,407	**2,447**	237	195	153	111	71	36	1	0	0	0	0
2,447	**2,487**	242	200	158	116	75	40	5	0	0	0	0
2,487	**2,527**	247	205	163	121	79	44	9	0	0	0	0
2,527	**2,567**	251	209	167	125	83	48	13	0	0	0	0
2,567	**2,607**	256	214	172	130	88	52	17	0	0	0	0
2,607	**2,647**	261	219	177	135	93	56	21	0	0	0	0
2,647 and over		Use Table 4(a) for a SINGLE person on page 46. Also see the instructions on page 44.										

Wage Bracket Method Tables for Income Tax Withholding

MARRIED Persons—**MONTHLY** Payroll Period

(For Wages Paid through December 2019)

And the wages are–		And the number of withholding allowances claimed is—										
At least	But less than	0	1	2	3	4	5	6	7	8	9	10
		The amount of income tax to be withheld is—										
$ 0	**$983**	$0	$0	$0	$0	$0	$0	$0	$0	$0	$0	$0
983	**994**	1	0	0	0	0	0	0	0	0	0	0
994	**1,005**	2	0	0	0	0	0	0	0	0	0	0
1,005	**1,016**	3	0	0	0	0	0	0	0	0	0	0
1,016	**1,027**	4	0	0	0	0	0	0	0	0	0	0
1,027	**1,038**	5	0	0	0	0	0	0	0	0	0	0
1,038	**1,049**	6	0	0	0	0	0	0	0	0	0	0
1,049	**1,060**	7	0	0	0	0	0	0	0	0	0	0
1,060	**1,071**	8	0	0	0	0	0	0	0	0	0	0
1,071	**1,082**	9	0	0	0	0	0	0	0	0	0	0
1,082	**1,093**	10	0	0	0	0	0	0	0	0	0	0
1,093	**1,104**	12	0	0	0	0	0	0	0	0	0	0
1,104	**1,115**	13	0	0	0	0	0	0	0	0	0	0
1,115	**1,126**	14	0	0	0	0	0	0	0	0	0	0
1,126	**1,137**	15	0	0	0	0	0	0	0	0	0	0
1,137	**1,148**	16	0	0	0	0	0	0	0	0	0	0
1,148	**1,159**	17	0	0	0	0	0	0	0	0	0	0
1,159	**1,170**	18	0	0	0	0	0	0	0	0	0	0
1,170	**1,181**	19	0	0	0	0	0	0	0	0	0	0
1,181	**1,192**	20	0	0	0	0	0	0	0	0	0	0
1,192	**1,203**	21	0	0	0	0	0	0	0	0	0	0
1,203	**1,214**	23	0	0	0	0	0	0	0	0	0	0
1,214	**1,225**	24	0	0	0	0	0	0	0	0	0	0
1,225	**1,236**	25	0	0	0	0	0	0	0	0	0	0
1,236	**1,247**	26	0	0	0	0	0	0	0	0	0	0
1,247	**1,258**	27	0	0	0	0	0	0	0	0	0	0
1,258	**1,269**	28	0	0	0	0	0	0	0	0	0	0
1,269	**1,280**	29	0	0	0	0	0	0	0	0	0	0
1,280	**1,291**	30	0	0	0	0	0	0	0	0	0	0
1,291	**1,302**	31	0	0	0	0	0	0	0	0	0	0
1,302	**1,313**	32	0	0	0	0	0	0	0	0	0	0
1,313	**1,324**	34	0	0	0	0	0	0	0	0	0	0
1,324	**1,335**	35	0	0	0	0	0	0	0	0	0	0
1,335	**1,346**	36	1	0	0	0	0	0	0	0	0	0
1,346	**1,357**	37	2	0	0	0	0	0	0	0	0	0
1,357	**1,368**	38	3	0	0	0	0	0	0	0	0	0
1,368	**1,379**	39	4	0	0	0	0	0	0	0	0	0
1,379	**1,390**	40	5	0	0	0	0	0	0	0	0	0
1,390	**1,401**	41	6	0	0	0	0	0	0	0	0	0
1,401	**1,412**	42	7	0	0	0	0	0	0	0	0	0
1,412	**1,423**	43	8	0	0	0	0	0	0	0	0	0
1,423	**1,434**	45	10	0	0	0	0	0	0	0	0	0
1,434	**1,445**	46	11	0	0	0	0	0	0	0	0	0
1,445	**1,456**	47	12	0	0	0	0	0	0	0	0	0
1,456	**1,467**	48	13	0	0	0	0	0	0	0	0	0
1,467	**1,478**	49	14	0	0	0	0	0	0	0	0	0
1,478	**1,489**	50	15	0	0	0	0	0	0	0	0	0
1,489	**1,500**	51	16	0	0	0	0	0	0	0	0	0
1,500	**1,511**	52	17	0	0	0	0	0	0	0	0	0
1,511	**1,522**	53	18	0	0	0	0	0	0	0	0	0
1,522	**1,533**	54	19	0	0	0	0	0	0	0	0	0
1,533	**1,544**	56	21	0	0	0	0	0	0	0	0	0
1,544	**1,555**	57	22	0	0	0	0	0	0	0	0	0
1,555	**1,566**	58	23	0	0	0	0	0	0	0	0	0
1,566	**1,577**	59	24	0	0	0	0	0	0	0	0	0
1,577	**1,588**	60	25	0	0	0	0	0	0	0	0	0
1,588	**1,599**	61	26	0	0	0	0	0	0	0	0	0
1,599	**1,610**	62	27	0	0	0	0	0	0	0	0	0
1,610	**1,621**	63	28	0	0	0	0	0	0	0	0	0
1,621	**1,632**	64	29	0	0	0	0	0	0	0	0	0
1,632	**1,643**	65	30	0	0	0	0	0	0	0	0	0
1,643	**1,654**	67	32	0	0	0	0	0	0	0	0	0
1,654	**1,665**	68	33	0	0	0	0	0	0	0	0	0
1,665	**1,676**	69	34	0	0	0	0	0	0	0	0	0
1,676	**1,687**	70	35	0	0	0	0	0	0	0	0	0
1,687	**1,698**	71	36	1	0	0	0	0	0	0	0	0
1,698	**1,709**	72	37	2	0	0	0	0	0	0	0	0
1,709	**1,720**	73	38	3	0	0	0	0	0	0	0	0
1,720	**1,731**	74	39	4	0	0	0	0	0	0	0	0
1,731	**1,742**	75	40	5	0	0	0	0	0	0	0	0

Wage Bracket Method Tables for Income Tax Withholding

MARRIED Persons—**MONTHLY** Payroll Period

(For Wages Paid through December 2019)

And the wages are–		And the number of withholding allowances claimed is—										
At least	But less than	0	1	2	3	4	5	6	7	8	9	10
		The amount of income tax to be withheld is—										
1,742	1,753	76	41	6	0	0	0	0	0	0	0	0
1,753	1,773	78	43	8	0	0	0	0	0	0	0	0
1,773	1,793	80	45	10	0	0	0	0	0	0	0	0
1,793	1,813	82	47	12	0	0	0	0	0	0	0	0
1,813	1,833	84	49	14	0	0	0	0	0	0	0	0
1,833	1,853	86	51	16	0	0	0	0	0	0	0	0
1,853	1,873	88	53	18	0	0	0	0	0	0	0	0
1,873	1,893	90	55	20	0	0	0	0	0	0	0	0
1,893	1,913	92	57	22	0	0	0	0	0	0	0	0
1,913	1,933	94	59	24	0	0	0	0	0	0	0	0
1,933	1,953	96	61	26	0	0	0	0	0	0	0	0
1,953	1,973	98	63	28	0	0	0	0	0	0	0	0
1,973	1,993	100	65	30	0	0	0	0	0	0	0	0
1,993	2,013	102	67	32	0	0	0	0	0	0	0	0
2,013	2,033	104	69	34	0	0	0	0	0	0	0	0
2,033	2,053	106	71	36	1	0	0	0	0	0	0	0
2,053	2,073	108	73	38	3	0	0	0	0	0	0	0
2,073	2,093	110	75	40	5	0	0	0	0	0	0	0
2,093	2,113	112	77	42	7	0	0	0	0	0	0	0
2,113	2,133	114	79	44	9	0	0	0	0	0	0	0
2,133	2,153	116	81	46	11	0	0	0	0	0	0	0
2,153	2,173	118	83	48	13	0	0	0	0	0	0	0
2,173	2,193	120	85	50	15	0	0	0	0	0	0	0
2,193	2,213	122	87	52	17	0	0	0	0	0	0	0
2,213	2,233	124	89	54	19	0	0	0	0	0	0	0
2,233	2,253	126	91	56	21	0	0	0	0	0	0	0
2,253	2,273	128	93	58	23	0	0	0	0	0	0	0
2,273	2,293	130	95	60	25	0	0	0	0	0	0	0
2,293	2,313	132	97	62	27	0	0	0	0	0	0	0
2,313	2,333	134	99	64	29	0	0	0	0	0	0	0
2,333	2,353	136	101	66	31	0	0	0	0	0	0	0
2,353	2,373	138	103	68	33	0	0	0	0	0	0	0
2,373	2,393	140	105	70	35	0	0	0	0	0	0	0
2,393	2,413	142	107	72	37	2	0	0	0	0	0	0
2,413	2,433	144	109	74	39	4	0	0	0	0	0	0
2,433	2,453	146	111	76	41	6	0	0	0	0	0	0
2,453	2,473	148	113	78	43	8	0	0	0	0	0	0
2,473	2,493	150	115	80	45	10	0	0	0	0	0	0
2,493	2,513	152	117	82	47	12	0	0	0	0	0	0
2,513	2,553	155	120	85	50	15	0	0	0	0	0	0
2,553	2,593	159	124	89	54	19	0	0	0	0	0	0
2,593	2,633	163	128	93	58	23	0	0	0	0	0	0
2,633	2,673	168	132	97	62	27	0	0	0	0	0	0
2,673	2,713	173	136	101	66	31	0	0	0	0	0	0
2,713	2,753	178	140	105	70	35	0	0	0	0	0	0
2,753	2,793	182	144	109	74	39	4	0	0	0	0	0
2,793	2,833	187	148	113	78	43	8	0	0	0	0	0
2,833	2,873	192	152	117	82	47	12	0	0	0	0	0
2,873	2,913	197	156	121	86	51	16	0	0	0	0	0
2,913	2,953	202	160	125	90	55	20	0	0	0	0	0
2,953	2,993	206	164	129	94	59	24	0	0	0	0	0
2,993	3,033	211	169	133	98	63	28	0	0	0	0	0
3,033	3,073	216	174	137	102	67	32	0	0	0	0	0
3,073	3,113	221	179	141	106	71	36	1	0	0	0	0
3,113	3,153	226	184	145	110	75	40	5	0	0	0	0
3,153	3,193	230	188	149	114	79	44	9	0	0	0	0
3,193	3,233	235	193	153	118	83	48	13	0	0	0	0
3,233	3,273	240	198	157	122	87	52	17	0	0	0	0
3,273	3,313	245	203	161	126	91	56	21	0	0	0	0
3,313	3,353	250	208	166	130	95	60	25	0	0	0	0
3,353	3,393	254	212	170	134	99	64	29	0	0	0	0
3,393	3,433	259	217	175	138	103	68	33	0	0	0	0
3,433	3,473	264	222	180	142	107	72	37	2	0	0	0
3,473	3,513	269	227	185	146	111	76	41	6	0	0	0
3,513	3,553	274	232	190	150	115	80	45	10	0	0	0
3,553	3,593	278	236	194	154	119	84	49	14	0	0	0
3,593 and over		Use Table 4(b) for a MARRIED person on page 46. Also see the instructions on page 44.										

Internal Revenue Service

Wage Bracket Method Tables for Income Tax Withholding

SINGLE Persons—DAILY Payroll Period

(For Wages Paid through December 2019)

And the wages are–		And the number of withholding allowances claimed is—										
At least	But less than	0	1	2	3	4	5	6	7	8	9	10
		The amount of income tax to be withheld is—										
$ 0	**$15**	$0	$0	$0	$0	$0	$0	$0	$0	$0	$0	$0
15	**25**	1	0	0	0	0	0	0	0	0	0	0
25	**35**	2	0	0	0	0	0	0	0	0	0	0
35	**45**	3	1	0	0	0	0	0	0	0	0	0
45	**55**	4	2	0	0	0	0	0	0	0	0	0
55	**65**	5	3	1	0	0	0	0	0	0	0	0
65	**75**	6	4	2	1	0	0	0	0	0	0	0
75	**85**	7	5	3	2	0	0	0	0	0	0	0
85	**95**	8	6	4	3	1	0	0	0	0	0	0
95	**105**	10	8	6	4	2	0	0	0	0	0	0
105	**115**	11	9	7	5	3	1	0	0	0	0	0
115	**125**	12	10	8	6	4	2	1	0	0	0	0
125	**135**	13	11	9	7	5	3	2	0	0	0	0
135	**145**	14	12	10	8	7	5	3	1	0	0	0
145	**155**	16	14	12	10	8	6	4	2	1	0	0
155	**165**	17	15	13	11	9	7	5	3	2	0	0
165	**175**	18	16	14	12	10	8	6	4	3	1	0
175	**185**	20	17	15	13	11	9	7	6	4	2	0
185	**195**	23	19	16	14	13	11	9	7	5	3	1
195	**205**	25	21	18	16	14	12	10	8	6	4	2
205	**215**	27	24	20	17	15	13	11	9	7	5	3
215	**225**	29	26	22	19	16	14	12	10	8	6	5
225	**235**	31	28	24	21	17	15	13	12	10	8	6
235	**245**	34	30	27	23	19	17	15	13	11	9	7
245	**255**	36	32	29	25	22	18	16	14	12	10	8
255	**265**	38	35	31	27	24	20	17	15	13	11	9
265	**275**	40	37	33	30	26	22	19	16	14	12	11
275	**285**	42	39	35	32	28	25	21	18	16	14	12
285	**295**	45	41	38	34	30	27	23	20	17	15	13
295	**305**	47	43	40	36	33	29	26	22	18	16	14
305	**315**	49	46	42	38	35	31	28	24	21	17	15
315	**325**	51	48	44	41	37	33	30	26	23	19	17
325	**335**	53	50	46	43	39	36	32	29	25	21	18
335	**345**	56	52	49	45	41	38	34	31	27	24	20
345	**360**	59	55	51	48	44	41	37	34	30	26	23
360	**375**	62	58	55	51	47	44	40	37	33	30	26
375	**390**	66	62	58	54	51	47	44	40	37	33	29
390	**405**	69	66	62	58	54	51	47	43	40	36	33
405	**420**	73	69	65	61	58	54	50	47	43	40	36
420	**435**	77	73	69	65	61	57	54	50	46	43	39
435	**450**	80	76	73	69	65	61	57	53	50	46	43
450	**465**	84	80	76	72	68	65	61	57	53	50	46
465	**480**	87	84	80	76	72	68	64	60	56	53	49
480	**495**	91	87	83	79	76	72	68	64	60	56	53
495	**510**	95	91	87	83	79	75	71	68	64	60	56
510	**525**	98	94	91	87	83	79	75	71	67	63	60
525	**540**	102	98	94	90	86	83	79	75	71	67	63
540	**555**	105	102	98	94	90	86	82	78	74	71	67
555	**570**	109	105	101	97	94	90	86	82	78	74	70
570	**585**	113	109	105	101	97	93	89	86	82	78	74
585	**600**	116	112	109	105	101	97	93	89	85	81	78
600	**615**	120	116	112	108	104	101	97	93	89	85	81
615	**630**	123	120	116	112	108	104	100	96	92	89	85
630	**645**	127	123	119	115	112	108	104	100	96	92	88
645	**660**	132	127	123	119	115	111	107	104	100	96	92
660	**675**	137	132	127	123	119	115	111	107	103	99	96
675	**690**	142	137	132	126	122	119	115	111	107	103	99
690	**705**	147	141	136	131	126	122	118	114	110	107	103
705	**720**	151	146	141	136	131	126	122	118	114	110	106
720	**735**	156	151	146	141	136	130	125	122	118	114	110
735	**750**	161	156	151	146	140	135	130	125	121	117	114
750	**765**	166	161	156	150	145	140	135	130	125	121	117
765	**780**	171	165	160	155	150	145	140	134	129	125	121
780	**795**	175	170	165	160	155	150	144	139	134	129	124
795	**810**	180	175	170	165	160	154	149	144	139	134	129
810	**825**	186	180	175	170	164	159	154	149	144	139	133
825	**840**	191	185	180	174	169	164	159	154	149	143	138
840	**855**	196	190	185	179	174	169	164	158	153	148	143
855	**870**	201	196	190	184	179	174	168	163	158	153	148
870	**885**	207	201	195	190	184	178	173	168	163	158	153

Internal Revenue Service

Wage Bracket Method Tables for Income Tax Withholding

SINGLE Persons—**DAILY** Payroll Period

(For Wages Paid through December 2019)

And the wages are–		And the number of withholding allowances claimed is—										
At least	But less than	0	1	2	3	4	5	6	7	8	9	10
		The amount of income tax to be withheld is—										
885	900	212	206	201	195	189	184	178	173	168	163	157
900	915	217	211	206	200	194	189	183	178	173	167	162
915	930	222	217	211	205	200	194	188	183	177	172	167
930	945	228	222	216	211	205	199	194	188	182	177	172
945	960	233	227	222	216	210	205	199	193	188	182	177
960	975	238	232	227	221	215	210	204	199	193	187	182
975	990	243	238	232	226	221	215	209	204	198	192	187
990	1,005	249	243	237	232	226	220	215	209	203	198	192
1,005	1,020	254	248	243	237	231	226	220	214	209	203	197
1,020	1,035	259	253	248	242	236	231	225	220	214	208	203
1,035	1,050	264	259	253	247	242	236	230	225	219	213	208
1,050	1,065	270	264	258	253	247	241	236	230	224	219	213
1,065	1,080	275	269	264	258	252	247	241	235	230	224	218
1,080	1,095	280	274	269	263	257	252	246	241	235	229	224
1,095	1,110	285	280	274	268	263	257	251	246	240	234	229
1,110	1,125	291	285	279	274	268	262	257	251	245	240	234
1,125	1,140	296	290	285	279	273	268	262	256	251	245	239
1,140	1,155	301	295	290	284	278	273	267	262	256	250	245
1,155	1,170	306	301	295	289	284	278	272	267	261	255	250
1,170	1,185	312	306	300	295	289	283	278	272	266	261	255
1,185	1,200	317	311	306	300	294	289	283	277	272	266	260
1,200	1,215	322	316	311	305	299	294	288	283	277	271	266
1,215	1,230	327	322	316	310	305	299	293	288	282	276	271
1,230	1,245	333	327	321	316	310	304	299	293	287	282	276
1,245	1,260	338	332	327	321	315	310	304	298	293	287	281
1,260	1,275	343	337	332	326	320	315	309	304	298	292	287
1,275	1,290	348	343	337	331	326	320	314	309	303	297	292
1,290	1,305	354	348	342	337	331	325	320	314	308	303	297
1,305	1,320	359	353	348	342	336	331	325	319	314	308	302
1,320	1,335	364	358	353	347	341	336	330	325	319	313	308
1,335	1,350	369	364	358	352	347	341	335	330	324	318	313
1,350	1,365	375	369	363	358	352	346	341	335	329	324	318
1,365	1,380	380	374	369	363	357	352	346	340	335	329	323
1,380	1,395	385	379	374	368	362	357	351	346	340	334	329
1,395	1,410	390	385	379	373	368	362	356	351	345	339	334
1,410	1,425	396	390	384	379	373	367	362	356	350	345	339
1,425	1,440	401	395	390	384	378	373	367	361	356	350	344
1,440	1,455	406	400	395	389	383	378	372	367	361	355	350
1,455	1,470	411	406	400	394	389	383	377	372	366	360	355
1,470	1,485	417	411	405	400	394	388	383	377	371	366	360
1,485	1,500	422	416	411	405	399	394	388	382	377	371	365
1,500	1,515	427	421	416	410	404	399	393	388	382	376	371
1,515	1,530	432	427	421	415	410	404	398	393	387	381	376
1,530	1,545	438	432	426	421	415	409	404	398	392	387	381
1,545	1,560	443	437	432	426	420	415	409	403	398	392	386
1,560	1,575	448	442	437	431	425	420	414	409	403	397	392
1,575	1,590	453	448	442	436	431	425	419	414	408	402	397
1,590	1,605	459	453	447	442	436	430	425	419	413	408	402
1,605	1,620	464	458	453	447	441	436	430	424	419	413	407
1,620	1,635	469	463	458	452	446	441	435	430	424	418	413
1,635	1,650	474	469	463	457	452	446	440	435	429	423	418
1,650	1,665	480	474	468	463	457	451	446	440	434	429	423
1,665	1,680	485	479	474	468	462	457	451	445	440	434	428
1,680	1,695	490	484	479	473	467	462	456	451	445	439	434
1,695	1,710	495	490	484	478	473	467	461	456	450	444	439
1,710	1,725	501	495	489	484	478	472	467	461	455	450	444
1,725	1,740	506	500	495	489	483	478	472	466	461	455	449
1,740	1,755	511	505	500	494	488	483	477	472	466	460	455
1,755	1,770	516	511	505	499	494	488	482	477	471	465	460
1,770	1,785	522	516	510	505	499	493	488	482	476	471	465
1,785	1,800	527	521	516	510	504	499	493	487	482	476	470
1,800	1,815	532	526	521	515	509	504	498	493	487	481	476
1,815	1,830	537	532	526	520	515	509	503	498	492	486	481
1,830	1,845	543	537	531	526	520	514	509	503	497	492	486
1,845	1,860	548	542	537	531	525	520	514	508	503	497	491
1,860	1,862	551	545	540	534	528	523	517	511	506	500	494

1,862 and over Use Table 8(a) for a SINGLE person on page 47. Also see the instructions on page 44.

Wage Bracket Method Tables for Income Tax Withholding

MARRIED Persons—DAILY Payroll Period

(For Wages Paid through December 2019)

And the wages are–		And the number of withholding allowances claimed is—										
At least	But less than	0	1	2	3	4	5	6	7	8	9	10
		The amount of income tax to be withheld is—										
$ 0	**$46**	$0	$0	$0	$0	$0	$0	$0	$0	$0	$0	$0
46	**56**	1	0	0	0	0	0	0	0	0	0	0
56	**66**	2	0	0	0	0	0	0	0	0	0	0
66	**76**	3	1	0	0	0	0	0	0	0	0	0
76	**86**	4	2	0	0	0	0	0	0	0	0	0
86	**96**	5	3	1	0	0	0	0	0	0	0	0
96	**106**	6	4	2	1	0	0	0	0	0	0	0
106	**116**	7	5	3	2	0	0	0	0	0	0	0
116	**126**	8	6	4	3	1	0	0	0	0	0	0
126	**136**	9	7	5	4	2	0	0	0	0	0	0
136	**146**	10	8	6	5	3	1	0	0	0	0	0
146	**156**	11	9	7	6	4	2	1	0	0	0	0
156	**166**	12	10	9	7	5	3	2	0	0	0	0
166	**176**	14	12	10	8	6	4	3	1	0	0	0
176	**186**	15	13	11	9	7	5	4	2	1	0	0
186	**196**	16	14	12	10	8	6	5	3	2	0	0
196	**206**	17	15	13	11	9	7	6	4	3	1	0
206	**216**	18	16	15	13	11	9	7	5	4	2	0
216	**226**	20	18	16	14	12	10	8	6	5	3	1
226	**236**	21	19	17	15	13	11	9	7	6	4	2
236	**246**	22	20	18	16	14	12	10	8	7	5	3
246	**256**	23	21	19	17	15	13	12	10	8	6	4
256	**266**	24	22	21	19	17	15	13	11	9	7	5
266	**276**	26	24	22	20	18	16	14	12	10	8	6
276	**286**	27	25	23	21	19	17	15	13	11	9	7
286	**296**	28	26	24	22	20	18	16	14	12	11	9
296	**306**	29	27	25	23	21	19	18	16	14	12	10
306	**316**	30	28	27	25	23	21	19	17	15	13	11
316	**326**	32	30	28	26	24	22	20	18	16	14	12
326	**336**	33	31	29	27	25	23	21	19	17	15	13
336	**346**	34	32	30	28	26	24	22	20	18	17	15
346	**361**	36	34	32	30	28	26	24	22	20	18	16
361	**376**	39	36	33	31	30	28	26	24	22	20	18
376	**391**	43	39	35	33	31	29	27	26	24	22	20
391	**406**	46	42	39	35	33	31	29	27	25	23	21
406	**421**	49	46	42	38	35	33	31	29	27	25	23
421	**436**	52	49	45	42	38	35	33	31	29	27	25
436	**451**	56	52	49	45	42	38	35	33	31	29	27
451	**466**	59	55	52	48	45	41	38	35	33	31	29
466	**481**	62	59	55	52	48	45	41	37	34	32	30
481	**496**	66	62	59	55	51	48	44	41	37	34	32
496	**511**	69	65	62	58	55	51	48	44	40	37	34
511	**526**	72	69	65	62	58	54	51	47	44	40	37
526	**541**	76	72	68	65	61	58	54	51	47	44	40
541	**556**	79	75	72	68	65	61	58	54	50	47	43
556	**571**	82	79	75	71	68	64	61	57	54	50	47
571	**586**	85	82	78	75	71	68	64	61	57	53	50
586	**601**	89	85	82	78	75	71	67	64	60	57	53
601	**616**	92	88	85	81	78	74	71	67	64	60	56
616	**631**	95	92	88	85	81	78	74	70	67	63	60
631	**646**	99	95	92	88	84	81	77	74	70	67	63
646	**661**	102	98	95	91	88	84	81	77	73	70	66
661	**676**	105	102	98	95	91	87	84	80	77	73	70
676	**691**	109	105	101	98	94	91	87	84	80	77	73
691	**706**	112	108	105	101	98	94	91	87	83	80	76
706	**721**	116	112	108	104	101	97	94	90	87	83	80
721	**736**	119	115	111	108	104	101	97	94	90	86	83
736	**751**	123	119	115	111	108	104	100	97	93	90	86
751	**766**	126	122	119	115	111	107	104	100	97	93	89
766	**781**	130	126	122	118	114	111	107	103	100	96	93
781	**796**	134	130	126	122	118	114	110	107	103	100	96
796	**811**	137	133	129	126	122	118	114	110	106	103	99
811	**826**	141	137	133	129	125	121	117	114	110	106	103
826	**841**	144	140	137	133	129	125	121	117	113	110	106
841	**856**	148	144	140	136	132	129	125	121	117	113	109
856	**871**	152	148	144	140	136	132	128	124	121	117	113
871	**886**	155	151	147	144	140	136	132	128	124	120	116
886	**901**	159	155	151	147	143	139	135	132	128	124	120
901	**916**	162	158	155	151	147	143	139	135	131	127	124
916	**931**	166	162	158	154	150	147	143	139	135	131	127

Internal Revenue Service

Wage Bracket Method Tables for Income Tax Withholding

MARRIED Persons—**DAILY** Payroll Period

(For Wages Paid through December 2019)

And the wages are–		And the number of withholding allowances claimed is—										
At least	But less than	0	1	2	3	4	5	6	7	8	9	10
		The amount of income tax to be withheld is—										
931	**946**	170	166	162	158	154	150	146	142	139	135	131
946	**961**	173	169	165	162	158	154	150	146	142	138	134
961	**976**	177	173	169	165	161	157	153	150	146	142	138
976	**991**	180	176	173	169	165	161	157	153	149	145	142
991	**1,006**	184	180	176	172	168	165	161	157	153	149	145
1,006	**1,021**	188	184	180	176	172	168	164	160	157	153	149
1,021	**1,036**	191	187	183	180	176	172	168	164	160	156	152
1,036	**1,051**	195	191	187	183	179	175	171	168	164	160	156
1,051	**1,066**	198	194	191	187	183	179	175	171	167	163	160
1,066	**1,081**	202	198	194	190	186	183	179	175	171	167	163
1,081	**1,096**	206	202	198	194	190	186	182	178	175	171	167
1,096	**1,111**	209	205	201	198	194	190	186	182	178	174	170
1,111	**1,126**	213	209	205	201	197	193	189	186	182	178	174
1,126	**1,141**	216	212	209	205	201	197	193	189	185	181	178
1,141	**1,156**	220	216	212	208	204	201	197	193	189	185	181
1,156	**1,171**	224	220	216	212	208	204	200	196	193	189	185
1,171	**1,186**	227	223	219	216	212	208	204	200	196	192	188
1,186	**1,201**	231	227	223	219	215	211	207	204	200	196	192
1,201	**1,216**	234	230	227	223	219	215	211	207	203	199	196
1,216	**1,231**	238	234	230	226	222	219	215	211	207	203	199
1,231	**1,246**	242	238	234	230	226	222	218	214	211	207	203
1,246	**1,261**	245	241	237	234	230	226	222	218	214	210	206
1,261	**1,276**	249	245	241	237	233	229	225	222	218	214	210
1,276	**1,291**	252	248	245	241	237	233	229	225	221	217	214
1,291	**1,306**	257	252	248	244	240	237	233	229	225	221	217
1,306	**1,321**	262	257	252	248	244	240	236	232	229	225	221
1,321	**1,336**	267	262	257	252	248	244	240	236	232	228	224
1,336	**1,351**	272	267	261	256	251	247	243	240	236	232	228
1,351	**1,366**	276	271	266	261	256	251	247	243	239	235	232
1,366	**1,381**	281	276	271	266	261	255	251	247	243	239	235
1,381	**1,396**	286	281	276	271	265	260	255	250	247	243	239
1,396	**1,411**	291	286	281	275	270	265	260	255	250	246	242
1,411	**1,426**	296	291	285	280	275	270	265	259	254	250	246
1,426	**1,441**	300	295	290	285	280	275	269	264	259	254	250
1,441	**1,456**	305	300	295	290	285	279	274	269	264	259	254
1,456	**1,471**	310	305	300	295	289	284	279	274	269	264	258
1,471	**1,486**	315	310	305	299	294	289	284	279	274	268	263
1,486	**1,501**	320	315	309	304	299	294	289	283	278	273	268
1,501	**1,516**	324	319	314	309	304	299	293	288	283	278	273
1,516	**1,531**	329	324	319	314	309	303	298	293	288	283	278
1,531	**1,546**	334	329	324	319	313	308	303	298	293	288	282
1,546	**1,561**	339	334	329	323	318	313	308	303	298	292	287
1,561	**1,576**	344	339	333	328	323	318	313	307	302	297	292
1,576	**1,591**	348	343	338	333	328	323	317	312	307	302	297
1,591	**1,606**	353	348	343	338	333	327	322	317	312	307	302
1,606	**1,621**	358	353	348	343	337	332	327	322	317	312	306
1,621	**1,636**	363	358	353	347	342	337	332	327	322	316	311
1,636	**1,651**	369	363	357	352	347	342	337	331	326	321	316
1,651	**1,666**	374	368	362	357	352	347	341	336	331	326	321
1,666	**1,681**	379	373	368	362	357	351	346	341	336	331	326
1,681	**1,696**	384	379	373	367	362	356	351	346	341	336	330
1,696	**1,711**	390	384	378	373	367	361	356	351	346	340	335
1,711	**1,726**	395	389	383	378	372	367	361	355	350	345	340
1,726	**1,741**	400	394	389	383	377	372	366	360	355	350	345
1,741	**1,756**	405	400	394	388	383	377	371	366	360	355	350
1,756	**1,771**	411	405	399	394	388	382	377	371	365	360	354
1,771	**1,786**	416	410	404	399	393	388	382	376	371	365	359
1,786	**1,801**	421	415	410	404	398	393	387	381	376	370	364
1,801	**1,816**	426	421	415	409	404	398	392	387	381	375	370
1,816	**1,831**	432	426	420	415	409	403	398	392	386	381	375
1,831	**1,846**	437	431	425	420	414	409	403	397	392	386	380
1,846	**1,861**	442	436	431	425	419	414	408	402	397	391	385
1,861	**1,876**	447	442	436	430	425	419	413	408	402	396	391
1,876	**1,891**	453	447	441	436	430	424	419	413	407	402	396
1,891	**1,906**	458	452	446	441	435	430	424	418	413	407	401
1,906	**1,908**	461	455	449	444	438	432	427	421	416	410	404
1,908 and over		Use Table 8(b) for a MARRIED person on page 47. Also see the instructions on page 44.										

D

Appendix D

State Income Tax Information

The employee income tax rates for each state for 2019 are presented below. *Tax Bracket* refers to the year-to-date earnings of the individual. *Marginal Tax Rate* refers to the amount of tax actually collected on each dollar the employee earns and is subject to change as the employee's earnings increase during the year. Note that the tax bracket, although generally pertaining to payroll-related income, also applies to other sources of personal revenue such as interest and dividends. (Source: Tax Foundation)

State	Tax Bracket (Single)	Tax Bracket (Married)	Marginal Tax Rate
Alabama	$0+	$0+	2.0%
	$500+	$1,000+	4.0%
	$3,000+	$6,000+	5.0%
Alaska	$0+	$0+	0%
Arizona	$0+	$0+	2.59%
	$11,047+	$22,092+	2.88%
	$27,614+	$55,226+	3.36%
	$55,226+	$110,450+	4.24%
	$165,674+	$331,347+	4.54%
Arkansas	$0+	$0+	0.9%
	$4,500+	$4,500+	2.5%
	$8,900+	$8,900+	3.5%
	$13,400+	$13,400+	4.5%
	$22,200+	$22,200+	6.0%
	$37,200+	$37,200+	6.9%
California	$0+	$0+	1.0%
	$8,544+	$17,088+	2.0%
	$20,255+	$40,510	4.0%
	$31,969+	$63,938+	6.0%
	$44,377+	$88,754+	8.0%
	$56,085+	$112,170+	9.3%

State	Tax Bracket (Single)	Tax Bracket (Married)	Marginal Tax Rate
	$286,492+	$572,984+	10.3%
	$343,788+	$687,576+	11.3%
	$572,980+	$1,000,000+	12.3%
	$1,000,000+	$1,145,960+	13.3%
Colorado	$0+	$0+	4.63%
Connecticut	$0+	$0+	3.0%
	$10,000+	$20,000+	5.0%
	$50,000+	$100,000+	5.50%
	$100,000+	$200,000+	6.0%
	$200,000+	$400,000+	6.50%
	$250,000+	$500,000+	6.90%
	$500,000+	$1,000,000+	6.99%
Delaware	$2,000+	$2,000+	2.20%
	$5,000+	$5,000+	3.90%
	$10,000+	$10,000+	4.80%
	$20,000+	$20,000+	5.20%
	$25,000+	$25,000+	5.55%
	$60,000+	$60,000+	6.60%
District of Columbia	$0+	$0+	4.0%
	$10,000+	$10,000+	6.0%
	$40,000+	$40,000+	6.50%
	$60,000+	$60,000+	8.50%
	$350,000+	$350,000+	8.75%
	$1,000,000+	$1,000,000+	8.95%
Florida	$0+	$0+	0%
Georgia	$0	$0+	1.0%
	$750+	$1,000+	2.0%
	$2,250+	$3,000+	3.0%
	$3,750+	$5,000+	4.0%
	$5,250+	$7,000+	5.0%
	$7,000+	$10,000+	6.0%
Hawaii	$0+	$0+	1.40%
	$2,400+	$4,800+	3.20%
	$4,800+	$9,600+	5.50%
	$9,600+	$19,200+	6.40%
	$14,400+	$28,800+	6.80%
	$19,200+	$38,400+	7.20%
	$24,000+	$48,000+	7.60%
	$36,000+	$72,000+	7.90%
	$48,000+	$96,000+	8.25%
	$150,000+	$300,000+	9.00%
	$175,000+	$350,000+	10.00%
	$200,000+	$400,000+	11.00%

State	Tax Bracket (Single)	Tax Bracket (Married)	Marginal Tax Rate
Idaho	$0+	$0+	1.125%
	$1,541+	$3,081+	3.125%
	$3,081+	$6,162+	3.625%
	$4,622+	$9,243+	4.625%
	$6,162+	$12,324+	5.625%
	$7,703+	$15,405+	6.625%
	$11,554+	$23,108+	6.925%
Illinois	$0+	$0+	4.95%
Indiana	$0+	$0+	3.23%
Iowa	$0+	$0+	0.33%
	$1,638+	$1,638+	0.67%
	$3,276+	$3,276+	2.25%
	$6,552+	$6,552+	4.14%
	$14,742+	$14,742+	5.63%
	$24,570+	$24,570+	5.96%
	$32,760+	$32,760+	6.25%
	$49,140+	$49,140+	7.44%
	$73,710+	$73,710+	8.53%
Kansas	$2,500+	$5,000+	3.10%
	$15,000+	$30,000+	5.25%
	$30,000+	$60,000+	5.70%
Kentucky	$0+	$0+	5.0%
Louisiana	$0+	$0+	2.0%
	$12,500+	$25,000+	4.0%
	$50,000+	$100,000+	6.0%
Maine	$0+	$0+	5.80%
	$21,850+	$43,700+	6.75%
	$51,700+	$103,400+	7.15%
Maryland	$0+	$0+	2.00%
	$1,000+	$1,000+	3.00%
	$2,000+	$2,000+	4.00%
	$3,000+	$3,000+	4.75%
	$100,000+	$150,000+	5.00%
	$125,000+	$175,000+	5.25%
	$150,000+	$225,000+	5.50%
	$250,000+	$300,000+	5.75%
Massachusetts	$0+	$0+	5.05%
Michigan	$0+	$0+	4.25%
Minnesota	$0+	$0+	5.35%
	$26,520+	$38,770+	7.05%
	$87,110+	$154,020+	7.85%
	$163,890+	$273,150+	9.85%

State	Tax Bracket (Single)	Tax Bracket (Married)	Marginal Tax Rate
Mississippi	$1,000+	$1,000+	3.0%
	$5,000+	$5,000+	4.0%
	$10,000+	$10,000+	5.0%
Missouri	$105+	$105+	1.5%
	$1,053+	$1,053+	2.0%
	$2,106+	$2,106+	2.5%
	$3,159+	$3,159+	3.0%
	$4,212+	$4,212+	3.5%
	$5,265+	$5,265+	4.0%
	$6,318+	$6,318+	4.5%
	$7,371+	$7,371+	5.0%
	$8,424+	$8,424+	5.5%
	$9,072+	$9,072+	5.9%
Montana	$0+	$0+	1.0%
	$3,100+	$3,100+	2.0%
	$5,400+	$5,400+	3.0%
	$8,200+	$8,200+	4.0%
	$11,100+	$11,100+	5.0%
	$14,300+	$14,300+	6.0%
	$18,400+	$18,400+	6.9%
Nebraska	$0+	$0+	2.46%
	$3,290+	$6,570+	3.51%
	$19,720+	$39,450+	5.01%
	$31,780+	$63,550+	6.84%
Nevada	$0+	$0+	0%
New Hampshire	$0+	$0+	0%
New Jersey	$0+	$0+	1.40%
	$20,000+	$20,000+	1.75%
	$35,000+	$50,000+	3.50%s/2.45%m
	$40,000+	$70,000+	5.525%s/3.50%m
	$75,000+	$80,000+	6.37%s/5.525%m
	$500,000+	$150,000+	8.97%s/6.37%m
	$5,000,000+	$500,000+	10.75%s/8.97%m
		$5,000,000+	10.75%
New Mexico	$0+	$0+	1.70%
	$5,500+	$8,000+	3.20%
	$11,000+	$16,000+	4.70%
	$16,000+	$24,000+	4.90%
New York	$0+	$0+	4.00%
	$8,500+	$17,150+	4.50%
	$11,700+	$23,600+	5.25%
	$13,900+	$27,900+	5.90%
	$21,400+	$43,000+	6.21%

State	Tax Bracket (Single)	Tax Bracket (Married)	Marginal Tax Rate
	$80,650+	$161,550+	6.49%
	$215,400+	$323,200+	6.85%
	$1,077,550+	$2,155,350+	8.82%
North Carolina	$0+	$0+	5.25%
North Dakota	$4,500+	$10,400+	1.10%
	$43,000+	$75,000+	2.04%
	$87,000+	$141,000+	2.27%
	$202,000+	$252,000+	2.64%
	$432,000+	$440,000+	2.90%
Ohio	$10,850+	$10.850+	1.980%
	$16,300+	$16,300+	2.476%s/2.746%m
	$21,750+	$21,750+	2.969%
	$43,450+	$43,450+	3.465%
	$86,900+	$86,900+	3.960%
	$108,700+	$108,700+	4.597%
	$217,400+	$217,400+	4.997%
Oklahoma	$6,350+	$12,700+	0.5%
	$7,350+	$14,700+	1.0%
	$8,850+	$17,700+	2.0%
	$10,100+	$20,200+	3.0%
	$11,250+	$22,500+	4.0%
	$13,550	$24,900+	5.0%
Oregon	$0+	$0+	5.0%
	$3,550+	$7,100+	7.0%
	$8,900+	$17,800+	9.0%
	$125,000+	$250,000+	9.9%
Pennsylvania	$0+	$0+	3.07%
Rhode Island	$0+	$0+	3.75%
	$64,050+	$64,050+	4.75%
	$145,600+	$146,000+	5.99%
South Carolina	$0+	$0+	1.1%
	$2,450+	$2,450+	3.0%
	$4,900+	$4,900+	4.0%
	$7,350+	$7,350+	5.0%
	$9,800+	$9,800+	6.0%
	$12,250+	$12,250+	7.0%
South Dakota	$0+	$0+	0%
Tennessee	$0+	$0+	0%
Texas	$0+	$0+	0%
Utah	$0+	$0+	4.95%

State	Tax Bracket (Single)	Tax Bracket (Married)	Marginal Tax Rate
Vermont	$0+	$0+	3.35%
	$39,600+	$66,150+	6.60%
	$95,900+	$159,850+	7.60%
	$200,100+	$243,650+	8.75%
	$416,650+	$416,650+	8.95%
Virginia	$0+	$0+	2.0%
	$3,000+	$3,000+	3.0%
	$5,000+	$5,000+	5.0%
	$17,000+	$17,000+	5.75%
Washington	$0+	$0+	0%
West Virginia	$0+	$0+	3.0%
	$10,000+	$10,000+	4.0%
	$25,000+	$25,000+	4.5%
	$40,000+	$40,000+	6.0%
	$60,000+	$60,000+	6.5%
Wisconsin	$0+	$0+	4.0%
	$11,760+	$15,680+	5.84%
	$23,520+	$31,360+	6.27%
	$258,950+	$345,270+	7.65%
Wyoming	$0+	$0+	0%

Appendix E

State Revenue Department Information

Alabama

Alabama Department of Revenue
50 North Ripley Street
Montgomery, AL 36104
334-242-1300
www.revenue.alabama.gov

Alaska

Juneau Commissioner's Office
P.O. Box 110400
Juneau, AK 99811-0400
907-465-2300
www.revenue.state.ak.us

Arizona

Arizona Department of Revenue
1600 West Monroe Street
Phoenix, AZ 85007
602-255-3381
www.azdor.gov

Arkansas

Department of Finance and Administration
1509 West 7th Street
P.O Box 8055
Little Rock, AR 72203-8055
501-682-7290
www.dfa.arkansas.gov

California

Employment Development Department
P.O. Box 826880
Sacramento, CA 94280-0001
888-745-3886
www.edd.ca.gov

Colorado

Colorado Department of Revenue
1375 Sherman Street
P.O. Box 17087
Denver, CO 8017-0087
303-238-7378
www.colorado.gov/revenue

Connecticut

Department of Revenue Services
450 Columbus Blvd., Suite 1
Hartford, CT 06103
860-297-5962
www.ct.gov/drs

Delaware

Delaware Department of Revenue
Carvel State Office Building
820 North French Street
Wilmington, DE 19801
302-577-8779
www.revenue.delaware.gov

District of Columbia

Office of Tax and Revenue
1101 4th Street SW, Suite 270
Washington, DC 20024
202-727-4829
otr.cfo.dc.gov

Florida

Florida Department of Revenue
5050 West Tennessee Street
Tallahassee, FL 32399
850-488-6800
floridarevenue.com

Georgia

Georgia Department of Revenue
1800 Century Blvd. NE, Suite 12000
Atlanta, GA 30345-3205
877-423-6711, option #1
dor.ga.gov/withholding-0

Hawaii

Department of Taxation (Oahu District)
Princess Ruth Keelikolani Building
830 Punchbowl Street
Honolulu, HI 96813-5094
808-587-4242
www.tax.hawaii.gov

Idaho

Idaho State Tax Commission
800 East Park Blvd., Plaza IV
Boise, ID 83712-7742
208-334-7660
www.tax.idaho.gov

Illinois

Illinois Department of Revenue
James R. Thompson Center—Concourse Level
100 West Randolph Street
Chicago, IL 60601-3274
800-732-8866
www2.illinois.gov/rev/Pages/default.aspx

Indiana

Indiana Department of Revenue
Indianapolis Taxpayer Services
100 North Senate IGCN Rm N105
Indianapolis, IN 46204
317-233-4016
www.in.gov/dor

Iowa

Iowa Department of Revenue
Hoover State Office Building, 4th Floor
1305 East Walnut
Des Moines, IA 50319
800-367-3388
tax.iowa.gov

Kansas

Kansas Department of Revenue
Docking State Office Building
915 SW Harrison Street
Topeka, KS 66612-1588
785-368-8222
www.ksrevenue.org

Kentucky

Kentucky Department of Revenue
501 High Street
Frankfort, KY 40601-2103
502-564-7287
www.revenue.ky.gov

Louisiana

Louisiana Department of Revenue
617 North Third Street
Baton Rouge, LA 70802
855-307-3893
revenue.louisiana.gov

Maine

Maine Revenue Services
51 Commerce Drive
P.O. Box 9107
Augusta, ME 04330
207-626-8475
www.maine.gov/revenue

Maryland

Comptroller of Maryland
80 Calvert Street
P.O. Box 466
Annapolis, MD 21404-0466
800-638-2937
www.comp.state.md.us

Massachusetts

Massachusetts Department of Revenue
P.O. Box 7010
100 Cambridge Avenue
Boston, MA 02204
800-392-6089
www.mass.gov/orgs/massachusetts-department-of-revenue

Michigan

Michigan Department of Treasury
Lansing, MI 48922
517-636-6925
www.michigan.gov/treasury

Minnesota

Minnesota Department of Revenue
600 North Robert Street
St. Paul, MN 55146
651-282-9999
www.revenue.state.mn.us

Mississippi

Mississippi Department of Revenue
500 Clinton Center Drive
Clinton, MS 39056
601-923-7700
www.dor.ms.gov

Missouri

Missouri Department of Revenue
Harry S. Truman State Office Building
301 West High Street
Jefferson City, MO 65101
573-751-3505
www.dor.mo.gov

Montana

Montana Department of Revenue
P.O. Box 5835
Helena, MT 59604-5835
406-444-6900
mtrevenue.gov

Nebraska

Nebraska Department of Revenue
Nebraska State Office Building
301 Centennial Mall South
Lincoln, NE 68508
402-472-5729
www.revenue.nebraska.gov

Nevada

Nevada Department of Taxation
1550 College Parkway, Suite 115
Carson City, NV 89706
775-684-2000
tax.nv.gov

New Hampshire

New Hampshire Department of Revenue Administration
Governor Hugh Gallen State Office Park
109 Pleasant Street (Medical & Surgical Building)
Concord, NH 03301
603-230-5000
www.revenue.nh.gov

New Jersey

New Jersey Division of Taxation
Trenton Taxation Building
50 Barrack Street, 1st Floor Lobby
Trenton, NJ 08695
609-292-6400
www.state.nj.us/treasury/taxation

New Mexico

Taxation & Revenue New Mexico
1100 South St. Francis Drive
Santa Fe, NM 87504
505-827-0700
www.tax.newmexico.gov

New York

New York State Department of Taxation and Finance
Building 9
W. A. Harriman Campus
Albany, NY 12227
518-485-6654
www.tax.ny.gov

North Carolina

North Carolina Department of Revenue
501 North Wilmington Street
Raleigh, NC 27604
877-252-3052
www.dornc.com

North Dakota

Office of State Tax Commissioner
600 East Boulevard Avenue, Department 127
Bismarck, ND 58505-0599
701-328-1248
www.nd.gov/tax

Ohio

Ohio Department of Taxation
4485 Northland Ridge Blvd.
Columbus, OH 43229
888-405-4039
www.tax.ohio.gov

Oklahoma

Oklahoma Tax Commission
Connors Building, Capitol Complex
2501 North Lincoln Blvd.
Oklahoma City, OK 73194
405-521-3160
www.ok.gov/tax

Oregon

Oregon Department of Revenue
955 Center Street NE
Salem, OR 97301-2555
503-378-4988
www.oregon.gov/dor

Pennsylvania

Pennsylvania Department of Revenue
Strawberry Square Lobby, First Floor
Fourth and Walnut Streets
Harrisburg, PA 17128
717-783-1405
www.revenue.pa.gov

Rhode Island

Rhode Island Division of Taxation
One Capitol Hill
Providence, RI 02908
401-574-8700
www.tax.ri.gov

South Carolina

South Carolina Department of Revenue
300A Outlet Pointe Blvd.
Columbia, SC 29210
803-898-5000
www.dor.sc.gov

South Dakota

South Dakota Department of Labor and Regulation
123 West Missouri Avenue
Pierre, SD 57501
605-773-3101
dlr.sd.gov

Tennessee

Tennessee Department of Labor and Workforce Development
220 French Landing Drive, 3-B
Nashville, TN 37243
844-224-5818
www.tn.gov/workforce

Texas

Texas Comptroller of Public Accounts
Lyndon B. Johnson State Office Building
111 East 17th Street
Austin, TX 78774
512-223-5400
comptroller.texas.gov/taxes/

Utah

Utah State Tax Commission
210 North 1950 West
Salt Lake City, UT 84134
801-297-2200
www.tax.utah.gov

Vermont

Vermont Department of Taxes
133 State Street
Montpelier, VT 05633
802-828-2505
tax.vermont.gov

Virginia

Virginia Tax
1957 Westmoreland Street
Richmond, VA 23230
804-367-8037
www.tax.virginia.gov

Washington

Washington State Employment Security Department
212 Maple Park Avenue SE
Olympia, WA 98501-2347
360-902-9500
www.esd.wa.gov

West Virginia

West Virginia Department of Revenue
Taxpayer Services
1124 Smith Street
Charleston, WV 25301
304-558-3333
revenue.wv.gov

Wisconsin

Wisconsin Department of Revenue
2135 Rimrock Road
Madison, WI 53713
608-266-2772
www.revenue.wi.gov

Wyoming

Wyoming Department of Workforce Services
1510 East Pershing Blvd.
Cheyenne, WY 82002
307-777-7261
www.wyomingworkforce.org/

Appendix F

Payroll Certification Information

Payroll certification examinations are available to document mastery of payroll accounting topics. The National Association of Certified Professional Bookkeepers (NACPB), the American Institute of Professional Bookkeepers (AIPB), and the American Payroll Association (APA) each offer certification exams. Contact details for each examination are at the end of this appendix.

Correlation of Certification Exam Topics and Specific Learning Objectives

The following table contains information about the topics covered by each payroll certification and the location of that information in this text.

Payroll Certification Exam Topics	Learning Objective
401(k) plans	4-2, 4-5
Account classification	7-2, 7-3
Accounting terminology	7-2
Additional Medicare tax—highly compensated employees	1-2, 5-3
Advances and overpayments	5-5
Affordable Care Act Form 1095	1-2
Benefits costs and benchmarking	6-6, 7-6
Bonuses and commissions	3-2, 3-6
Cafeteria (Section 125) plans	4-2
Calculation of FICA taxes (Social Security and Medicare): Employee	5-3
Calculation of FICA taxes (Social Security and Medicare): Employer	6-1, 6-3
Calculation of involuntary (mandated) deductions	4-5, 5-5
Communication with IRS and SSA	2-2, 4-6
Data privacy	1-4
Data retention	2-5
Deceased employee pay	3-7

Payroll Certification Exam Topics	Learning Objective
De minimis fringe benefits	4-1, 4-3
Deferred compensation	3-6
Docking exempt employee pay	3-2
Employee benefits	4-1, 4-2
Employee classification	1-6
Employee vs. independent contractor	1-2, 1-6, 2-2
Employer-provided benefits: Cafeteria plan, awards, personal use of company vehicle, group-term life insurance	4-2, 4-3, 4-4
Employment forms	2-2
Enterprise test	3-1
Exempt vs. nonexempt	1-6
Expatriate taxation	2-2
Fair Labor Standards Act	1-2
Federal forms	1-4, 6-3
Federal income tax calculation: Taxable wages, tax computation	5-2
Fiduciary responsibility	7-5
FLSA provisions	1-2
Form W-4: Additional withholding, employee changes	2-2
Form 843 treatment	6-3
Fringe benefits	4-1, 4-3, 4-4
FUTA, including credit reduction states	5-3
General Journal entries	7-3
General Ledger entries	7-4
Gross pay calculation	3-2, 3-3, 3-4, 3-5, 3-6
Gross-up of compensation	5-1
Identifying payroll job requirements	3-2, 3-4, 6-1, 6-2, 7-2
Internal controls	2-4
IRS regulations	5-2, 6-1, 6-2
Jury duty	3-7
Leased employees	2-3
Legislation affecting payroll, contract acts	1-1, 1-2
Multiple worksite reporting	1-4, 1-5, 2-2
Net pay calculations	5-1, 5-2, 5-3, 5-4, 5-5
New hire documentation	2-2
Nonproductive time	3-7
Nonqualified deferred compensation	3-7
Nonqualified plans	4-2, 4-3
Nontaxable benefits	4-3
On-premises benefits: Athletic facilities, child care, etc.	4-3
Overtime premium calculation: FLSA, weighted average, commission, salary, piece-rate	3-4
Pay calculation: Regular, tipped, time worked, other pay situations	3-2, 3-3, 3-5, 3-6
Payment methods: Cash, check, direct deposit, paycard	5-6
Payroll in the United States: Employee documentation	2-2

Payroll Certification Exam Topics	Learning Objective
Payroll practices, confidentiality	1-4, 1-5, 2-3
Payroll systems	1-4, 1-5, 7-5
Payroll: Process and challenges	1-4, 1-5, 7-5, 7-6
Payroll trending	7-6
Penalties	6-4
Pension payments and withholding	4-1, 4-6
Planning and organizing payroll operations	1-4, 1-5, 2-1
Qualified employee discounts	4-3, 4-4
Qualified moving expenses	4-3, 4-4
Reconciling wages and taxes	6-3
Recording accruals and reversals	7-4, 7-5
Recordkeeping requirements, including retention	2-3, 2-4, 2-5
Repaying employer loans	5-5
Resident nonalien	2-2
Retirement plans: Qualified	4-2
Retroactive pay	3-7
State wage and hour laws	3-1
State withholding certificates	2-2
Stock compensation	3-2, 3-6
Tax deposits: Requirements, lookback period, deposits	6-2, 6-3
Taxable tips	6-3
Temporary employees	2-3
Time management	1-4, 1-5
Trends: Technology	1-4, 1-5
Unemployment and disability taxes	6-1, 6-3
Voluntary deductions/other deductions calculations computation	4-5, 4-6
Withholding taxes, FICA taxes	5-2, 5-3, 5-4

Contact Information for Payroll Certifications

National Association of Certified Professional Bookkeepers

844-249-3551
http://certifiedpublicbookkeeper.org/certification.cfm

Requirement

- Successful completion of the NACPB Payroll Certification Exam.

American Institute of Professional Bookkeepers

800-622-0121
https://www.aipb.org/certification_program.htm

Requirements

- A minimum of 2 years' professional full-time (or part-time equivalent) experience, which may be obtained either before or after the exam.
- Successful completion of a two-part exam.
- Signed acknowledgement of the AIPB's Code of Ethics.

American Payroll Association

210-226-4600
http://www.americanpayroll.org/certification

Two levels of payroll certification are available from the American Payroll Association: Certified Payroll Professional (CPP) and Fundamental Payroll Certification (FPC). The following are the criteria for eligibility for each certification available from the APA.

Certified Payroll Professional

The Certification Board of the American Payroll Association (APA) requires that payroll professionals fulfill **ONE** of the following criteria before they take the Certified Payroll Professional Examination.

Criteria 1

The payroll professional has been practicing a total of three (3) years out of the five (5) years preceding the date of the examination. The practice of payroll is defined as direct or related involvement in at least one of the following:

- Payroll production, payroll reporting, payroll accounting.
- Payroll systems and payroll taxation.
- Payroll administration.
- Payroll education/consulting.

Criteria 2

Before a candidate takes the examination, the payroll professional has been employed in the practice of payroll as defined in Criteria 1 for at least the past 24 months *and* has completed within the last 24 months ALL of the following courses within **ONE** of the following three options offered by the APA:

Option 1

- Payroll Practice Essentials (three-day course: live or virtual) and
- Intermediate Payroll Concepts (two-day course: live or virtual) and
- Advanced Payroll Concepts (two-day course: live or virtual) and
- Strategic Payroll Practices (two-day course: live or virtual)

Option 2

- Payroll 101: Foundations of Payroll Certificate Program and
- Payroll 201: The Payroll Administration Certificate Program

Option 3

- Certified Payroll Professional Boot Camp

Criteria 3

Before a candidate takes the examination, the payroll professional has been employed in the practice of payroll as defined in Criteria 1 for at least the past 18 months, has **obtained** the **Fundamental Payroll Certification (FPC),** *and* has completed within the past 18 months ALL of the following courses within **ONE** of the following two options offered by the APA:

Option 1

- Intermediate Payroll Concepts (two-day course: live or virtual) and
- Advanced Payroll Concepts (two-day course: live or virtual) and
- Strategic Payroll Practices (two-day course: live or virtual)

Option 2

- Payroll 201: The Payroll Administration Certificate Program

Fundamental Payroll Certification (FPC)

The Fundamental Payroll Certification (FPC) is open to all those who wish to demonstrate a baseline of payroll competency. The FPC is designed for all of the following:

- Entry-level payroll professionals.
- Sales professionals/consultants serving the payroll industry.
- Systems analysts/engineers writing payroll programs.
- Payroll Service Bureau client representatives.

APA membership and payroll experience are not required to take the FPC examination.

Glossary

401(k): A defined contribution plan in which employees may contribute either a specific amount or a percentage of their gross pay on a pre-tax or post-tax basis through payroll deductions.

403(b): A retirement plan designed for employees of certain nonprofit organizations.

457 A retirement plan offered by governmental and certain non-governmental employers in which contributions are deducted on a pre-tax basis.

A

ACA: Affordable Care Act of 2010. Mandated health care coverage for all Americans regardless of employment status.

Accrual: An accounting method in which revenues and expenses are recorded when they occur, not necessarily when any cash is exchanged.

ADA: The Americans with Disabilities Act of 1990.

ADAAA: The Americans with Disabilities Act Amendments Act of 2008, which extended the definition of disabiities.

Additional Medicare tax: An additional 0.9% Medicare tax levied upon employees who earn in excess of $200,000 per year, as mandated by the Affordable Care Act.

ADEA: The Age Discrimination in Employment Act of 1967 that protects workers over age 40 from age-based discrimination.

Adjusting entries: Journal entries created at the end of an accounting period to allocate income and expenses to the proper accounts.

Allocation: The storing of costs in one account and then dividing the costs based on a quantifiable activity.

Annual schedule depositors: Employers who have an annual payroll tax liability of less than $1,000 during the lookback period and are notified in writing by the IRS that they submit Form 944 and remit taxes on an annual basis.

Annual total compensation report: A list of all compensation that an employee earns per year, including (but not limited to) salary, commissions, bonuses, and all fringe benefits; examples include health insurance, employer contributions to the employee's retirement plan, life insurance, and tuition reimbursement.

ARRA: The American Recovery and Reinvestment Act of 2009.

Asset: An item of value that a business uses in the course of its operations and from which it expects future economic benefit.

ATRA: The American Taxpayer Relief Act of 2012.

Automated Clearing House (ACH): The electronic network of financial institutions in the United States through which monetary transactions are transmitted in batches.

B

Balance sheet: A financial statement that lists the totals in the assets, liabilities, and owners' equity accounts of a firm for a specific date.

Benefit analysis: A calculation of the costs and benefits of a company, department, project, or employee.

Biweekly payroll: A pay frequency in which employees are paid 26 times per year.

Blockchain: A digital means of transferring electronic currency using small amounts of data transmitted via multiple computers.

C

Cafeteria plan: A benefit plan pursuant to Section 125 of the Internal Revenue Code that allows employees to designate specific amounts to be deducted from their payroll to pay for health and child care expenses on a pre-tax basis.

Cents-per-mile rule: A method use to determine the value of a company car fringe benefit based on a fixed amount times the number of miles driven for personal purposes.

Certified payroll: A report mandated for certain federal government contracts that verifies the accuracy of labor expenses incurred during completion of contract-related activities.

Charitable contribution: A payroll deduction in which an employee designates a specific amount of gross pay to be paid to community, religious, educational, or another IRS-designated charitable organization.

Circular E: See Publication 15.

Civil Rights Act of 1964: Federal legislation that protects employees from discrimination based on race, color, religion, sex, or national origin.

Civil Rights Act of 1991: Federal law that instituted monetary penalties for companies found guilty of discrimination as described under the Civil Rights Act of 1964.

COBRA: The Consolidated Omnibus Budget Reconciliation Act of 1985.

Combination pay: Employee compensation that reflects two or more discrete pay bases during the same pay period.

Commission: Employee compensation paid upon completion of a task, often pertaining to sales-based activities.

Commuting rule: A valuation method use to determine the personal use of a company vehicle based on the number of miles driven for commuting to and from work.

Compensation: The total amount of cash and noncash salary/wages and benefits that an employee receives in return for working for a company.

Compensatory (comp) time: Paid time off granted to employees instead of paid overtime.

Consolidated Appropriations Act of 2018: Signed into law in March 2018, this act increased the funding for the E-Verify program, which is an Internet-based system that offers employers instant verification of an employee's eligibility to work in the United States. It is important to note that the E-Verify program does not replace the need for the completion of Form I-9 upon employee hire because it is a voluntary service.

Consumer Credit Protection Act (CCPA): Federal law that pertains to the percentage of wage garnishment that may be withheld from employee pay to satisfy legal obligations.

Copeland Anti-Kickback Act: Federal legislation enacted in 1934 that prohibits a federal contractor or subcontractor from inducing an employee to forgo a portion of the wages guaranteed by the contract.

Credit: The right side of the T-account.

Cryptocurrency: A form of currency that is digitally encrypted and transmitted.

Current Tax Payment Act of 1943: Federal law enacted in 1943 that required employers to submit a timely remittance to the government of any taxes withheld from the employee pay.

D

Daily payroll: A pay frequency in which employees are paid each business day.

Davis–Bacon Act of 1931: Federal legislation enacted in 1931 that requires federal contractors to pay employees an amount commensurate with the prevailing local wage.

***De minimis*:** A benefit with a very small monetary value that is deemed impractical in terms of tracking using an accounting system.

Debit: The left side of the T-account.

Defined benefit: A company-sponsored pension plan that uses the employee's salary and length of service to compute the amount of the benefit.

Defined contribution: A retirement plan to which the employee, and sometimes the employer, makes a regular contribution.

Departmental classification: The division of payroll-related costs by employee function or organizational department.

Direct deposit: The electronic transmission of employee wages from the employer to the employee's account at a financial institution.

Disposable income: The amount of employee wages remaining after withholding federal, state, and local taxes.

Document destruction: The act of destroying documents that contain sensitive payroll and employee information.

DOMA: The Defense of Marriage Act of 1996, which was repealed in 2013.

Draw: A loan against future earnings that employees will repay from commissions.

Due care: The caution that a reasonable person would exercise to avoid being charged with negligence.

E

EEOC: The Equal Employment Opportunity Commission.

Eight and Eighty (8 and 80): A two-week, 80-hour pay period used to determine overtime for employees who work for hospitals and emergency providers.

Electronic Federal Tax Payment System (EFTPS): The Electronic Federal Tax Payment System, a free tax payment service provided for use for employers in the United States.

Equal Pay Act of 1963: Federal legislation mandating that males and females receive equal compensation for comparable work.

ERISA: The Employee Retirement Income Security Act of 1974.

Escheatment: The transfer of personal property to the employee's state of residence when no legal owner claims the property.

ESOP: Employee Stock Ownership Plan.

Ethics: An individual's definition of right and wrong.

Exempt: An employee who is not subject to the overtime provisions of the Fair Labor Standards Act.

Expense: The cost of doing business, which may contain both cash and noncash amounts.

F

Fair market value (FMV): The amount of money that a person would spend to obtain a good or service in an arm's-length transaction.

Federal income tax: A tax levied by the federal government on individuals.

FICA: The Federal Insurance Contributions Act of 1935.

FICA tax: The collective term for the combination of Social Security and Medicare taxes.

Fiduciary: A relationship, specifically financial, built on trust between a trustee and a beneficiary.

File maintenance: The application of all transactions, including any necessary modifications, to an employee's file.

File security: The protection of sensitive payroll information by restricting access and securely storing files.

Flexible spending arrangement (FSA): A tax-advantaged employee spending account as designated by the Internal Revenue Code.

FLSA: The Fair Labor Standards Act of 1935.

FMLA: The Family and Medical Leave Act.

Foreign Account Tax Compliance Act (FATCA): Federal law that regulates the income tax withholdings of foreign employees.

Form 940: The Employer's Annual Federal Unemployment Tax Return.

Form 941: The Employer's Quarterly Federal Tax Return.

Form 944: The Employer's Annual Federal Tax Return.

Form W-2: Wage and Tax Statement.

Form W-3: Transmittal of Wage and Tax Statements.

Fringe benefit: A company-sponsored benefit that supplements an employee's salary, usually on a noncash basis.

FUTA: Federal Unemployment Tax Act of 1939.

G

Garnishments: A legal procedure for the collection of money owed to a plaintiff through payroll deductions.

General Journal: A chronological record of a firm's financial transactions.

General Ledger: A record of a firm's financial transactions, grouped by account.

Generally Accepted Accounting Principles (GAAP): A framework relating to accounting practice including rules, procedures, and standards defined by industry professionals and used by U.S. companies.

General valuation rule (GVR): The method used to determine the value of most fringe benefits using fair market value.

Gross pay: The amount of wages paid to an employee based on work performed, prior to any deductions for mandatory or voluntary deductions.

H

Health savings account (HSA): A savings account that provides tax advantages for individuals with health plans that have high deductions via pre-tax payroll deductions.

High deductible health plan (HDHP): A health care plan with an annual deductible that is at least $1,350 for self-coverage and $2,700 for family coverage; annual out-of-pocket limits are $6,650 for self-coverage and $13,300 for family coverage.

HIPAA: The Health Insurance Portability and Accountability Act of 1996.

Hiring packet: A package of forms that a firm issues to new employees; examples are Form W-4, Form I-9, and health insurance enrollment.

Hourly: Wage determination based on the number of complete and partial hours during which an employee performs work-related tasks.

Hundredth-hour system: The division of an hour into 100 increments used to compute employee wages as accurately as possible.

I

I-9: The Employment Eligibility Verification.

Incentive stock options (ISOs): A type of employee compensation in which the employee receives a firm's stock on a tax-advantaged basis.

Income statement: A financial report used to determine a firm's net income by computing the difference between revenues and expenses for a period; also known as the profit and loss statement.

Independence: The ability of an accountant to act professionally without external pressures that would cause a third party to question the integrity of actions and decisions.

Independent contractor: An individual who contracts to do work for a firm using his or her own tools and processes without being subject to direction by a firm's management.

Integrity: Possessing honesty and high moral principles.

Internal control: A firm's process of maintaining efficiency and effectiveness, work quality, accurate and reliable financial reports, and legal compliance.

IRA: Individual Retirement Account.

IRCA: Immigration Reform and Control Act of 1986.

L

Labor distribution: The classification of a firm's labor by internally designated classifications.

Labor reports: Reports that contain details about the number of hours worked and the wages paid to employees.

Leased employee: A person who provides services for a company subject to the provisions of IRS code section 414(n).

Lease value rule: A method of determining the value of a company car as a fringe benefit using the fair market value and the annual lease as the basis.

Liability: A financial obligation of the firm arising from revenues received in advance of services or sales or expenses incurred but not paid.

Lilly Ledbetter Fair Pay Act of 2009: Federal law that removed the 180-day statute of limitations in allegations of unfair pay practices.

Local income taxes: Payroll taxes levied by a city or county government.

Lookback period: The time frame used by the IRS to determine the payroll tax deposit schedule for a firm.

M

Mandated deductions: Post-tax payroll deductions ordered by a court of law or otherwise nonvoluntary in nature.

Mandatory deductions: Payroll deductions over which the employee has no control; examples include taxes, garnishments, and certain retirement contributions.

Medicare tax: A payroll tax mandated to be paid by all employees of a firm to fund the Medicare program.

Minimum wage: The minimum hourly amount that employers may legally pay to employees.

Monthly depositor: A firm that must deposit its Federal Income Tax and FICA payroll withholdings and contributions on a monthly basis, based on the lookback period.

Monthly payroll: A pay frequency in which employees are paid 12 times per year.

N

Net pay: An employee's wages or salary less all mandatory and voluntary deductions.

New hire reporting: A process by which a firm notifies governmental authorities of any new hires shortly after the hire date.

Next business day depositor: A semiweekly schedule depositor whose payroll tax liabilities exceed $100,000 for any pay period.

Nonexempt: An employee who is subject to all overtime provisions of the Fair Labor Standards Act; generally, an hourly employee.

O

OASDI: Old-Age, Survivors, and Disability Insurance; synonymous with Social Security.

Objectivity: Making decisions that are free from bias or subjectivity.

On-call time: The nonwork time that an employee is expected to be available for workplace-related emergencies.

OSHA: The Occupational Safety and Health Act of 1970.

Outsourced vendor: A party external to a firm that provides goods or services.

Overtime: Time that an employee works beyond his or her normal working hours.

Owners' equity: The financial investment and any accumulated profits or losses of the owner of a firm.

P

Pay advice: A document detailing employee pay and deductions that either accompanies the paycheck or notifies the employee of the direct deposit of net pay.

Pay period: The recurring period during which a firm collects employee labor data and pays employees in accordance with wage or salary agreements.

Paycard: A debit card, issued to employees, that contains electronically transmitted wages.

Payroll audit: An examination of a firm's payroll records to determine legal compliance.

Payroll register: A payroll register is the payroll accountant's internal tool that helps ensure accuracy of employee compensation.

Payroll review: Verification of payroll accuracy for a period.

Payroll tax reports: Reports offering details of the period's tax liability that an employer must file with governmental authorities.

Percentage method: A method used to compute an employee's income tax liability that involves computations based on the employee's wages, marital status, pay frequency, and number of withholdings claimed on Form W-4.

Personal Responsibility, Work and Family Promotion Act of 2002: Act that reauthorized PRWOR when it expired

Piece rate: Employee compensation based on production of unit or completion of an action during a specified time period.

Post-tax deductions: Amounts deducted from employee pay after all income and FICA taxes have been deducted; amounts may be voluntary or court mandated.

Posting: Transferring the details of General Journal entries to the General Ledger accounts.

Premium only plan (POP): A form of cafeteria plan in which employee portions of employer-provided insurance plans may be deducted on a pre-tax basis.

Privacy Act of 1974: Protecting employees by removing personal identifiers from payroll records and restricting access to personnel records.

Professional competence: The continuing capability to perform professional duties with an agreed-upon standard of quality.

Professionalism: A process reflecting the transparency and public accountability of accounting records.

Protecting Americans from Tax Hikes (PATH) Act: An act to prevent tax fraud that extended the Work Opportunity Tax Credit.

Prove: Ensuring that the sum of the rows of the payroll register equals the sum of the columns.

PRWOR: Personal Responsibility and Work Opportunity Reconciliation Act of 1996.

Publication 15-b: The IRS Employer's Guide to Fringe Benefits.

Publication 15: The Employer's Tax Guide published by the Internal Revenue Service.

Q

Qualified plan: A written plan for the issuance of employee achievement awards that does not favor highly compensated employees.

Quarter-hour system: The division of an hour into 15-minute increments as a means of computing hourly work.

Quarterly depositors: Monthly schedule depositors who have a payroll tax liability of less than $2,500 during the preceding or current quarter may remit the payroll tax liability when filing Form 941.

R

Regulation E: Federal legislation protecting consumers who use electronic funds transfer to access their net pay.

Remit: To send money in payment of an obligation.

Resignation: Voluntary termination of employment.

Reversal: A general journal entry recorded at the start of the following month to undo the accruals recorded in the prior month.

Review process: Examination and analysis of accounting records to ensure accuracy and completeness.

Rule: The accounting practice in which the final totals of financial reports are double-underlined.

S

Salary: A fixed amount paid to an employee on a regular basis, often expressed in annual terms.

Schedule B: The report of tax liability for semiweekly depositors.

Semimonthly payroll: The payroll frequency in which employees are paid 24 times per year.

Semiweekly depositor: A firm that must deposit its federal income tax and FICA payroll withholdings and contributions within three days of the pay date, based on the lookback period.

SEP: A Simplified Employee Pension individual retirement account.

Separation of duties: An internal control method in which payroll duties are spread among two or more employees.

SIMPLE: The Savings Incentive Match Plan for Employees.

SIMPLE 401(k): A retirement plan for employees of companies that employ 100 or fewer workers. An annual investment limit of $11,500 exists for this type of retirement plan.

Sixteenth Amendment to the U.S. Constitution: Allowed the United States government to levy and collect income taxes on individuals.

Sleep time: Employees who are required to be on duty for 24 hours or more may be allowed up to 5 hours of sleep without a reduction in pay.

Social Security Act (SSA): An act that was passed to promote social welfare for old-age workers and surviving families of workers who had been disabled or deceased in the course of their employment.

Social Security tax: A tax paid by both employers and employees that is used to fund the Social Security program.

SOX: The Sarbanes–Oxley Act of 2002. Public law 107-204, concerning publicly owned companies and auditing firms to ensure appropriate internal controls and the integrity of financial statements.

Special accounting rule: Employers may elect to treat employee amounts for noncash fringe benefits used during November and December as not being paid until January of the following year; employees must be notified in writing by January 31 of the following year if the special accounting rule was used.

State income taxes: Income taxes levied by a state government on employee payroll.

Statutory deductions: Payroll deductions mandated by law.

Statutory employee: A special class of employees who run their own business but must be treated as employees for tax reasons.

SUTA: The State Unemployment Tax Act of 1939.

T

Tax Cuts and Jobs Act: An act to provide budget resolution that represented changes to individual and business tax rates.

Tax remittance: The payment of a firm's payroll tax liability.

Tax table: A set of precalculated tables issued by federal and state governments to facilitate income tax computations for employee payroll.

Temporary employee: A worker who is employed by a temporary staffing agency and works under the direction of the agency on a temporary basis for different companies.

Termination: Ceasing employment with a firm.

Time card: A record of the time worked during a period for an individual employee.

Tipped employee: An employee who engages in an occupation in which he or she customarily and regularly receives more than $30 per month in tips.

Tipped wage: The base wage paid to employees who earn the majority of their income through customer tips.

Total: Computing the sum of each row and each column of the payroll register.

Travel time: Time that an employee spends traveling for the employer's benefit.

Trial balance: An internal accounting statement in which the accountant determines that the debits equal the credits for the amounts in the General Ledger.

U

Union dues: Amounts paid on a regular basis by employees who are required to be part of a union as a condition of their employment.

USERRA: The Uniformed Services Employment and Reemployment Rights Act of 1994.

V

Voluntary deductions: Amounts that an employee elects to have deducted from his or her paycheck and remitted to a third party; examples include charitable contributions, savings bond purchases, and health club fees.

VPN: Virtual private network.

W

W-4: The Employee Withholding Allowance Certificate.

Wage base: The maximum annual salary that is subject to tax liability, commonly used for Social Security, FUTA, and SUTA taxes.

Wage-bracket method: The use of tax tables located in federal and state publications that facilitate the determination of employee income tax deductions for payroll.

Wait time: The time that an employee is paid to wait on the employer's premises for the benefit of the employer.

Walsh–Healey Public Contracts Act: Legislation enacted in 1936 that required employers working on federal contracts in excess of $10,000 to pay employees the federal minimum wage and follow the overtime provisions of the Fair Labor Standards Act.

Weekly payroll: The payroll frequency in which employees are paid 52 times per year.

Workers' compensation: A mandatory insurance policy paid by employers that provides wage replacement and medical benefits to employees who are injured in the course of their employment.

Index

A

Abbott, 5, 157
Accountants. *See also* Payroll accountants
- AICPA Code of Ethics for, 16, 18
- certification for, 441–445
- confidentiality of, 16
- document handling by, 40
- due care of, 17
- integrity of, 17
- math skills needed by, 120–123
- objectivity and independence of, 17
- organizations for, 16
- professionalism of, 16–17
- responsibilities of, 16, 331
- salaries for, 4
- sources of information for, 18

Accounting. *See also* Financial accounting concepts; Payroll accounting
- employment in, 4
- ethical guidelines for, 16–18
- trends in, 336

Accounting entries, 316
Accounting equation, 320–321
Accounting jobs, forecast for, 4
Accounting reports, payroll entries in, 332–335
Accounting software, 322–323
Accounting Today, 27
Accrual, in payroll, 326
Accuracy, in payroll, 43, 63
ACH (Automated Clearing House), 255
Achievement awards, 166
Acupuncture sessions, 158
ADA. *See* Americans with Disabilities Act of 1990 (ADA)
Additional Medicare tax, 208
Additional withholding, 47, 52
Adjusting entries, 326
Administrative exemption, 56, 112
Adobe Acrobat, 59, 66
ADP, 19, 24–25, 28, 129, 217
Advances, employee, 218
Affordable Care Act of 2010 (ACA)
- changes in, 14, 74
- coverage of children by, 173
- employee net pay and, 223
- employer contributions to, on Form W-2, 272
- explanation of, 14
- highly compensated employees, Medicare tax, and, 208–211
- lawsuit against, 3
- Medicare tax and, 208
- Minimum Essential Coverage of, 14, 173
- reporting requirements for, 14
- required reporting by employers, 272
- requirements of, 3
- Tax Cuts and Job Act of 2017 (TCJA) and, 3
- trends in, 223
- 2018 changes in, 14
- unconstitutionality of, 14

AFLAC (American Family Life Assurance Company of Columbus), 16, 174
Age
- employment restrictions and, 10
- to receive Medicare, 10

Age discrimination, 5
Age Discrimination in Employment Act of 1967 (ADEA), 5
Agricultural workers, 249
AICPA. *See* American Institute of Certified Public Accountants (AICPA)
AIDS, Civil Rights Act of 1964 and Executive Order 11478 protections, 5
Albuquerque, New Mexico, living wage ordinance, 11
Aliens, resident and nonresident, 249, 396
Alimony, 176
Allen Parish Office (Louisiana), 320
Allocations, overhead, 332
Alphabet (Google), 24
Alternating duties, of payroll professionals, 65–66
Amboy Bank, 19
Ambulance providers, 136
American Civil War, 9
American employers and American-controlled employers with internationally based operations, 6
American Family Life Assurance Company of Columbus (AFLAC), 16, 174
American Institute of Certified Public Accountants (AICPA)
- accountant integrity and, 17
- Code of Ethics guidelines of, 16, 17
- website of, 18

American Institute of Professional Bookkeepers (AIPB), 443
American Payroll Association (APA), 217, 444–445
- on breaches in accounting data software, 68
- certifications from, 444–445
- lump-sum distributions and employee garnishment, 217
- website of, 18

americanpayroll.org, 8
American Recovery and Reinvestment Act of 2009 (ARRA), 8
Americans with Disabilities Act Amendments Act of 2008 (ADAAA), 6
Americans with Disabilities Act of 1990 (ADA), 6, 7
American Taxpayer Relief Act of 2012 (ATRA), 8
Annual schedule depositors, 256, 257
Annual total compensation report, 284–285
App-based tax services, minimum hourly earnings (NYC), 111
Apple, 24
Apps
- Calculate Hours, 61
- ClockShark, 61
- ExacTime, 24
- iTookOff paid leave tracker, 61
- smartphone, 24
- TimeDock, 61
- TimeStation, 61
- for tracking employee attendance and productivity, 24
- WhenIWork, 24
- Zenefits, 65

Arizona, paid sick leave in, 12
Arm's-length transaction, 159, 168
ARRA (American Recovery and Reinvestment Act of 2009), 8
Artificial Intelligence (AI), 27, 323, 331, 335
Artificial Intelligence-based systems, 27
Asheville, North Carolina
- living age ordinance, 11
- working hours, 115

Assets, in financial accounting, 320–321
Assets = Liabilities + Owners' Equity, 320–321
ATRA (American Taxpayer Relief Act of 2012), 8
Audit
- agencies with right to audit payroll, 69
- defined, 21
- employer, increase in, 177
- of employers, reporting of fringe benefits and taxes due, 177
- example of, 320
- of payroll records, 68–69, 320

Automated Clearing House (ACH), 255
Automated payroll system, 55
Automobiles. *See* Company vehicle, personal use of
Average hours worked, 56–57
Awards, 166

B

Babysitters, 106
Back pay, 140, 217
Back wages, 47
Balance sheet, 332, 333, 334
Bank account reconciliation, 219
Banking
- direct deposit and, 221
- online, 219

Bank of America, 8
Banks, online, 19, 219
Base salary plus commission pay method, 132–133
Behavior control, 46
Ben and Jerry's, 21
Benefit analysis, as function of payroll, 282–285
Benefit analysis report, 283
Benefit errors, 179
Benefit reports, 179
Benefits. *See also* Fringe benefits
- customizing, 179
- depositing amounts related to, 178
- qualified insurance, 162
- reporting, rules for, 179
- second largest expense to employers, 282
- taxable withholdings and, 178
- trends in, 180
- withholding amounts related to, 177–178

Bereavement time, 30
Bermudez Vaquero v. Stoneledge Furniture LLC, 134
Billable vs. nonbillable report, 335
Biometric devices, 24
Bitcoin, 222–223
Biweekly payroll, 43, 45
Blockchain technology, 222–223, 335
Bonuses, discretionary and non-discretionary, 180
Borderless payroll accounts, 223
Brinker International, 17
Brinker International Payroll Company, L.P., 17
Business
- large, payroll processing in, 24–25
- legislation pertaining to, 4–9
- small, payroll processing in, 25–26, 28

Business expenses
- payroll in context of, 278–280
- pay-roll related entries and, 331–332

C

Cafeteria plans
- defined, 162
- exclusions in, 165
- explanation of, 162
- federal tax withholding and, 396
- flexible spending arrangement (FSA), 163
- health savings account (HSA), 163–165

IRS on, 162
premium only plan (POP), 162–163
qualified Section 125, exempt from FICA taxes, 209
CalculateHours app, 61
California
Assembly Bill (AB) 1513, 60
employers' contributions to retirement income, 5
Employment Training Tax (ETT) in, 253, 263
minimum wage and, 107
nonproductive time for piece-rate employees, 118
on-call breaks, 136
paid sick leave in, 12
personal income tax (PIT) in, 212
productive time and rest time for piece-rate employees, 60
Secure Choice Retirement Savings Program (SB-1234), 5
State Disability Insurance (SDI) in, 212, 263
state revenue department information, 433
Troester v. Starbucks Corp. (2018), 160
California Labor Code, 118
California Supreme Court, 160
CAPTCHA programs, 24
Carhartt, 157
Cash, as employee pay method, 219
Cash award, 166
Catch-up contributions, 164, 165, 175
CBL Data Shredder, 73
CCH Oncology of Buffalo, New York, 70
Cents-per-mile rule, 168, 170–171
Certification information, 441–445
Certified payroll, 28–29
Certified Payroll Professional (CPP), 444
Chapter 11 bankruptcy, 6
Charitable contributions, as post-tax deductions, 172, 175–176, 214–215
Chauffeurs, 106
Check fraud, 220–221
Checks, as employee pay method, 219–221
Child support
Census Bureau figures for, 52
court-mandated withholding for, 172, 176
court-ordered garnishment for, 215–216
enforcement problems in, 41
example of, 215–216
garnishments for, 42, 52, 176
independent contractors and, 41
legislation addressing, 7
new-hire database and, 52
new-hire reporting requirements and, 42
as post-tax deduction, 172, 176, 215–216
PRWOR and, 7
registry to monitor people owing, 47, 52
value of fringe benefits in calculating, 167
Chili's, 17
Chime Bank, 19
Circular E (Publication 15), 27, 59, 194
Civil Rights Act of 1964, 5, 6
Civil Rights Act of 1991, 6
Civil War, 9
Classification of workers, 41
Climate change, construction labor costs and, 245
ClockShark app, 61
Cloud-based computing, 28, 336
Cloud storage, 25
COBRA (Consolidated Omnibus Budget Reformation Act of 1985), 5–6
Code of Ethics, American Institute of Certified Public Accountants (AICPA), 16, 17
Code of ethics, basic guidelines of, 16
Collective bargaining unit, 217
Combination pay methods
base salary plus commission, 132–133
explanation of, 132
incentive stock options (ISOs), 135
payroll draw, 133–134
salary plus commission and draw, 134–135
Comerica, 222
Commission-based employees
compensation for, 60
explanation of, 116–117
gross pay for, 116–117
Commissions
base salary plus commission, 132–133
defined and example, 60, 104
explanation of, 116–117
minimum wage and, 117
tracking of, 117
Commission tracking sheet, 117
Commission work
defined, 115
employer variations, 117
types of, 115–116
Common-law employees, 58
Common Law Privacy Act, 22
Commuting rule, 168, 170
Company framework, employees and, 279–280
Company loans, repayment of, 172
Company profitability, labor expenses and, 280–282
Company vehicles, personal use of
about, 168
cents-per-mile rule and, 168, 170–171
commuting rule and, 168, 170
lease value rule and, 168–170
as nontaxable fringe benefit, 166–167
other transportation benefits and, 171
unsafe conditions and, 171
Compensation
fringe benefits as, 158
nonqualified deferred, 139–140
tracking of, with payroll register, 130–131
trends in, 141
Compensation structures, 60
Compensatory (comp) time, 136
Compliance Tools for HR Professionals, website of, 18
Computer-based systems, for payroll accounting processing, 26, 28
Computer Fraud and Abuse Act of 1986 (CFAA), 22
Computer glitches, 20, 331
Computer programs, 24–25
Computer-related employees, 112
Confidentiality
accountants and, 16
of payroll information, 62
Connecticut, paid sick leave in, 12
Consolidated Appropriations Act of 2018, 15
Consolidated Omnibus Budget Reformation Act of 1985 (COBRA), 5–6
Construction labor costs, climate change and, 245
Consumer credit
garnishment on employee's wages for repayment of, 176, 215–216
as post-tax deduction, 216–217
Consumer Credit Protection Act (CCPA), 176, 217
Consumer credit repayment, garnishments for, 176, 215–216
Consumer Financial Protection Bureau (CFPB), 65
Consumer Price Index (CPI), 11
Contribution-driven fund, 10
Conversion of minutes to decimals and fractions, 120
Copeland Anti-Kickback Act of 1934, 20
Corporate fraud, 64
Costco, 180
Cottage industry, 398
Countrywide Mortgage, 8
Court-mandated deductions, 172
Court-ordered garnishments, 176, 215–216
Creative professional, 56
Credit
in financial accounting, 321
on T-account, 321
Credit reduction, FUTA and, 250–251
Credit Union National Association (CUNA), 284
CR England, 105
Cross-training, of payroll professionals, 65–66
Crundwell, Rita, 317
Cryptocurrency, as employee pay method, 222–223
Culinary Institute of America, 70
Current Tax Payment Act of 1943 (CTPA), 12, 332
Custom benefits software, 179
Cybercrime, 22
Cybersecurity, 25

D

Daily payroll, 43, 45
Data adjusting entries, 326
Data breaches, 22
Data encryption programs, 66–67
Data privacy, 65
Data wiping tools, 73
Davis–Bacon Act of 1931, 9, 20, 28
DBAN, 73
Debit
in financial accounting, 321
on T-account, 321
Debit cards. *See* Paycards
Deceased employees, wages for, 140, 396
Decimals, conversion of minutes to, 120
Deductions. *See also* Net pay; Post-tax deductions; Pre-tax deductions
classes of, 172
mandated, 160, 172, 175, 198, 215–216
statutory, 246
voluntary, 172
Defense of Marriage Act of 1996 (DOMA), 6, 7, 7–8
Defined benefit retirement plan, 157, 174
Defined contribution retirement plan, 174
De minimis benefits, 160, 167
Denver, Colorado, head tax (Occupational Privilege Tax [OPT]), 196, 213, 263, 286
Departmental classification, 281–282
Department of Defense Data Wipe Method, 73. *See also* Employee earnings records
Department of Health and Human Services, U.S., 22
Department of Homeland Security, U.S., 52, 69
Department of Labor. *See* U.S. Department of Labor
Dependent care assistance programs, 396
Deposit frequencies, 256–257
Depositing amounts related to benefits, 178
Depositing taxes for noncash fringe benefits, 178
Determination of Worker Status for Purpose of Employment Taxes and Income Tax Withholding (IRS Form SS-8), 45, 47
Diane B. Allen Equal Pay Act (New Jersey), 16
Digital copies, 59
Direct deposit, as employee pay method, 221
Disability insurance, 174
Disabled persons
Civil Rights Act of 1964 and Executive Order 11478 protections, 5
sub-minimum wage situations and, 138–139
treatment under employment taxes, 397
Discretionary bonuses, 180
Discrimination
based on age, 5
Civil Rights Act of 1964 against, 5
Diane B. Allen Equal Pay Act and, 16
in employment, 4–5, 6, 92
Dismissal pay, 401
Disney, 158
Disposable income, 176, 216, 217

District of Columbia
Initiative 77 on increase of tipped wages, 108
minimum wage rate (2019), 107
Diversity, workplace, 6
Divorce, value of fringe benefits for determining defendant's income and, 167
Dixon, Illinois, 317
Documentation. *See also* Employee documentation; Employer earnings records
electronic, 66–67, 72
internal controls and record retention and, 62–70
for new employees, 47–54
pay records and employee file maintenance, 58–61
payroll, 45–55
preparing, 45–55
required, for payroll, 42–43, 44
technological advances and, 59
types of, 58
Documentation controls, 63
Document destruction, 72–73
Document retention
federal requirements, 69
payroll audits and, 68
payroll register and, 69
requirements for, 68–70
Document retention schedule, 68
Domestic service workers, 106, 399
Domino's Pizza, 36–37
Douglas O'Connor, et al. v. Uber Technologies, Inc. (2016), 47
Draw
payroll, 133–134
salary plus commission and, 134–135
Driver pay, 105
Due care, 17

E

Earnings records. *See* Employee earnings records
Ebola, 7
e-business, 22
Educational assistance, 160
Edwin de Luz Trucking and Gravel LLC, 128
EEOC. *See* Equal Employment Opportunity Commission (EEOC)
EFTPS (Electronic Federal Tax Payment System), 255, 258
e-Garnishments, 217
Eight and Eighty (8 and 80) rule, 125
e-IWOs (electronic income withholding orders), 217
Electronic accounting programs, 19–21
Electronic documentation, 72
Electronic Federal Tax Payment System (EFTPS), 255, 258, 286
Electronic Fund Transfer Act of 1978, 65
Electronic income withholding orders (e-IWOs), 217
Electronic money management, 219
Electronic paycards. *See* Paycards
Electronic payroll monitoring, 25
Electronic records. *See also* Employee earnings records
Department of Defense Data Wipe Method, 73
disposition/destruction of, 72–73
maintenance of, 66–67
purging from server, 72
Embezzlement, 17, 64
Emergency workers, 136
Employee advances, 218
Employee advances and overpayments, 218
Employee Benefits Security Administration (Department of Labor), 332
Employee business expense reimbursement, 397
Employee compensation
tracking, with payroll register, 130–131
trends in, 141
Employee database information (sample), 55
Employee discrimination, 4–5, 6, 92
Employee documentation. *See also* Documentation
destruction of, 72–73
electronic records and, 66–67
employee file maintenance, 66
employees vs. independent contractors and, 45–55
entering new employees into the database, 54–55
independent contractors vs., 45–47, 54
pay records and file maintenance, 58–61, 66
reporting new employees, 47–54
required information for, 42
retention requirements for, 68–69
Employee earnings records
defined, 319
example of, 318, 319–320
explanation of, 318–319
on Form 941, 320
function of, 318–319
General Journal and, 322
payroll register and, 318–320
periodic tax reports and, 320
summary of, 336
uses of, 320
for Wayland Custom Woodworking, 370–378
Employee file maintenance, 66
Employee Information Form, 42
Employee-paid taxes, 247
Employee pay-related General Journal entries, 324
Employee payroll tax requirements, 255–257
Employee PINs, 61
Employee portals, on company websites, 24, 25, 59
Employee Retirement Income Security Act (ERISA) of 1974, 5–6, 8, 174, 332
Employee rights and minimum wage, 44
Employees. *See also entries for specific types of employees;* Fair Labor Standards Act (FLSA) of 1938; Foreign workers; Overtime pay; Pay methods
average hours worked, 56–57
business expense reimbursement for, 397
classification for overtime pay, 11
classifications of, 106
common-law, 58
company framework and, 279–280
compensation trends, 141
computer-related, 112
deceased, wages for, 140, 396
determination of, criteria for, 46
disabled, 5, 397
disabled, sub-minimum wages and, 138–139
exempt, 104, 106
exempt vs. nonexempt, 55–58
expatriate workers, 54
family, 397
favorite fringe benefits, 157
file maintenance for, 66
foreign, 53–54
full-time equivalent (FTE), 14
full-time students and, 139
"ghost," 67
GPS location tagging of, 61
hospital and residential care, 125
hourly, 60, 104, 115
independent contractors vs., 41, 45–47, 54
leased, 57–58
morale of, 64
nonexempt, 60
nonexistent, 67
number with garnished wages, 217
part-time, 263
payroll as a non-solo effort and, 67–68
privacy issues and, 20, 21–22
resident alien, 249, 396
resignation of, 70–72
salaried exempt, 59–60, 104
salary basis of, 56–57
shared, 24
sick time, 61
statutory, 54
temporary, 57–58
terminated, fraud and, 67
termination of, 68, 70–72
tipped, 106, 108–111, 126, 272
underpayment of, 64
U.S. workers in foreign subsidiaries, 54
who work in two or more separate functions, 128
young, 138
Employee safety programs, 5
Employee Stock Ownership Plan (ESOP), 174, 175
Employee tax liabilities, underreporting of, 4
Employee termination
dismissal pay for, 401
employee resignation vs., 70–72
fraud and, 67
methods of, 70–72
retention of records after, 69
states' termination pay guidelines, 71–72
Employee Withholding Allowance Certificate (IRS Form W-4). *See* Form W-4 (Employee Withholding Allowance Certificate)
Employer data security procedures (FCC), 221
Employer deposit rules, related to benefits, 178
Employer Identification Number (EIN), 22, 42
Employer Identification Number Application (Form SS-4), 22, 23
Employer-paid taxes, 247
Employer payroll-related General Journal entries, 325
Employer payroll tax responsibilities. *See also entries for specific taxes*
benefit analysis, as a function of payroll, 282–285
federal unemployment taxes and, 248–251
labor expenses and company profitability, 280–282
local employer-only payroll taxes and, 253
mid-year and year-end tax reporting and deposits, 258–277
overview of, 244, 246
payroll as business expense and, 278–280
reporting periods and requirements for tax deposits and, 255–257
Social Security and Medicare taxes and, 246–248
state unemployment taxes and, 248, 251–253
summary of, 286
trends in, 286
workers' compensation insurance and, 253–254
Employer-provided pay advice, 219
Employer-provided snacks and meals, 167
Employers
fiduciary responsibility to remit withholdings from employee pay, 332
joint, 36–37
not required to offer fringe benefits, 156
payroll-related General Journal entries and, 323–327
penalty on, for misclassifying employees, 47
tax deposits by, 255–257
withholding taxes, 20–21
Employer's Annual Federal Unemployment (FUTA) Tax Return (Form 940), 22, 255, 263, 268–269, 270–271, 389–390
Employer-sponsored health care coverage, reporting, 272
Employer tax reporting and deposits, mid-year and year-end
explanation of, 258
Form 940 (Employer's Annual Federal Employment [FUTA] Tax Return, 258, 270–271

Form 941 (Employer's Quarterly Federal Tax Return), 258, 259–262
Form 944 (Employer's Annual Federal Tax Return), 263, 266–267
matching final annual pay to Form W-2, 269, 272–275
Schedule B, 258, 262
state tax remittance, 263, 264–265
unemployment tax reporting, 263, 268–269
Employment, growing level of, 335
Employment discrimination, 4–5, 6, 92
Employment Eligibility Verification (IRS Form I-9). *See* Form I-9 (Employee Eligibility Verification Form)
Employment legislation. *See entries for specific legislation;* Legal framework
Employment Standards Administration Wage and Hour Division of the U.S. Department of Labor, 10
Employment tax revenue remittances, 244
Employment Training Tax (ETT; California), 253, 263
Encryption, 24
Enron accounting scandal, 16
Entergy, 22
Enterprise Resource Planning (ERP), 26, 336
Entertainment park passes, 158
Equal Employment Opportunity Commission (EEOC)
on disability provisions of the ADA, 7
on privacy issues, 20
protection of employee rights, 43
Equal Pay Act of 1963, 4
Equifax, 22
ErAse, 73
ERISA (Employee Retirement Income Security Act of 1974), 5–6, 8, 174, 332
Escheatment, 220
ESOP plan (Employee Stock Ownership Plan), 174, 175
Estee Lauder, 157
Ethical guidelines
background of, 16
confidentiality, 16
due care, 17
integrity, 17
objectivity and independence, 17
professional competence, 17
professionalism, 16–17
Ethics, 16
Ethisphere, 16
European Union, 223
E-Verify program, 6, 15, 52
Excel (Microsoft), 28, 129
Excluded achievement award, 166
Exclusion rules (fringe benefits), 165–168
Executive exemption, 56
Executive Order 11478, 5
Executive Order 13765, 14
Executive salary, with ISO, 135
Exempt workers
defined, 11, 104, 106
explanation of, 55–56
FLSA and, 55–57
minimum salary for, 56
nonexempt workers vs., 55–58
salaried, 59–60, 104, 112
Expatriate workers, 54
Expense accounts, 324
Expenses, 326
External payroll providers, 28

F

Facebook, 180
Failure to deposit penalty, 278–279
Failure to file penalty, 278–279
Fair Labor Standards Act of 1938 (FLSA)
background of, 11–12
breaks and rest periods for piece-rate workers, 120
compensatory (comp) time and, 136
computer-related employees and, 112
on domestic workers, 106
employee exemption from certain jobs and, 112
employee files and, 42
employee hours worked, 20
on employee sick time, 61
enactment of, 11
exempt workers and, 55–56, 106
firms exempt from paying federal minimum wage, 106
guidelines for, 11–12
hourly employee protections of, 60
hours worked provisions, 20
information required in employee files, 42
inside and outside sales representatives and, 116
job descriptions for eligible exempt employees, 112–114
minimum wage/employee rights, 44
minimum wage provisions in, 106, 114
minimum wage regulation by, 11
modification of, 106
on overtime for tipped employees, 126
on overtime pay, 57, 60
overtime rules and, 124–125
piece-rate workers and, 118, 120
purpose of, 105, 106
on rest breaks, 134
on retroactive pay (back pay), 140
salaried workers eligible for overtime requirement, 114
sales representatives and, 116
on server tips, 11
on sleep, travel, and wait time, 137
state minimum wage and, 107–108
on student learners in vocational educational programs, 139
on sub-minimum wage situations, 138
on tips, 126
tracking piece-rate workers' hours, 118
on workers with disabilities, 138–139
on workers younger than 20, 138
Fair market value (FMV), 168
Fair scheduling legislation, 30
Fair v. Communications Unlimited Inc., 12
Family and Medical Leave Act of 1993 (FMLA), 6–7
Family employees, 397
"Family member," defined, 7
FASB (Financial Accounting Standards Board), 18, 286
Federal Bureau of Investigation (FBI), on hackers and ransomware, 67
Federal Communications Commission (FCC), guidelines for employer data security procedures, 221
Federal Deposit Insurance Corporation (FDIC), Regulation E of, 222
Federal Employment Compensation Act, 253
Federal government shutdown, partial (2019), 331
Federal income tax
computation examples for, 199
defined, 198
employer deposits for, 255–257
factors that determine, 198
historical background of, 9
institution of, 9
legislation addressing, 9–15
percentage method, 203–207
percentage method for wages paid in 2019, 360
Social Security and Medicare tax withholding, 207–211
special classes of withholding, 396–402
wage-bracket method for, 199–203, 406–425
withholding amounts, 198–207
Federal income tax tables, 403
married persons–biweekly payroll period, 412–413
married persons–daily payroll period, 424–425
married persons–monthly payroll period, 420–421
married persons–semimonthly payroll period, 416–417
married persons–weekly payroll period, 408–409
percentage method (2019), 404–405
single persons–biweekly payroll period, 410–411
single persons–daily payroll period, 422–423
single persons–monthly payroll period, 418–419
single persons–semimonthly payroll period, 414–415
single persons–weekly payroll period, 406–407
wage-bracket method (2019), 406–425
Federal income tax withholding, historical background of, 9
Federal Insurance Contributions Act (FICA), 10, 207, 211, 246–248. *See also* Social Security tax; Medicare tax
Federal privacy acts, 21–22
Federal tax withholding, special classes of, 396–402
Federal Unemployment Tax Act (FUTA), 196. *See also* Social Security Act of 1935 (SSA)
about, 10–11
credit reduction and, 250–251
employer responsibility for, 248–251
examples of, 249–250
explanation of, 10–11, 248–249
fringe benefits excluded from, 268
full 2019 rate, 249
professions exempt from, 249
U.S. citizens only, 249
Federation of Tax Administrators, 68
Fellowship grants, 401
FICA (Federal Insurance Contributions Act) taxes, 10, 207, 211, 246–248. *See also* Medicare tax; Social Security tax
Fictitious employees (fraud), 17
Fiduciary responsibility, of employers, 332
Fifth Amendment, 8
Filefax Inc., 8
File maintenance, 66
File security, 65. *See also* Privacy
Final hours calculations, 71
Final Regulations on the ADAAA, 6
Financial accounting concepts
categories of, 321
debits and credits, 321
example, 321
explanation of, 320–321
General Journal, 322
General Ledger, 322
Financial Accounting Standards Board (FASB), 18, 286
Financial business transactions, 321
Financial control, 46
Financial Executives International, 4
Fines
for employee payment errors, 64
for nonreporting of new hires, 53
Fingerprint readers, 24
Fire protection employees, 106, 136
Flexible spending arrangement (FSA), 163, 164
Florida Department of Transportation, 68
FLSA. *See* Fair Labor Standards Act (FLSA) of 1938
Fluctuating work week, 60
Food and Drug Administration, U.S., 67
Foreign Account Tax Compliance Act of 2010 (FATCA), 54
Foreign Earned Income Exclusion (IRS), 54
Foreign governments and international organizations, treatment under employment taxes, 397

Foreign service by U.S. citizens, 397
Foreign subsidiaries, U.S. workers in, 54
Foreign workers
acceptable documents for, 51
challenges of, 53
eligibility of, 52, 53
E-Verify program and, 52
Form 1042 and, 53
H-1B visas and, 54
as new employees, 52
Permanent Worker Visa Preference Categories and, 53
U.S. Citizen and Immigration Service (USCIS) changes regarding, 2017, 52
visas for, 54
Form 673 (IRS), 54
Form 940 (Employer's Annual Federal Employment [FUTA] Tax Return), 22, 255, 263, 268–269, 270–271, 389–390
Form 941 (Employer's Quarterly Federal Tax Return), 22, 255, 258, 259–262, 387–388
Form 944 (Employer's Annual Federal Tax Return), 263, 266–267
Form 1042, 53
Form 1095-A (IRS), 14
Form 1095-B (IRS), 14
Form 1095-C (IRS), 14
Form I-9 (Employee Eligibility Verification Form)
E-Verify program and, 6, 15
illustrated, 49–51
legal authority for employees to work in the United States, 6, 53
purpose of, 52
retention of, in employee's permanent file, 52
sample, 49–51
for Wayland Custom Woodworking, 379–381
Form SS-4 (Application for Employer Identification Number), 22, 23
Form SS-8 (Determination of Worker Status for Purposes of Employment Taxes and Income Tax Withholding), 45, 47
Form W-2 (Wage and Tax Statement). *See* W-2 Wage and Tax Form
Form W-3 (Transmittal of Wage and Tax Statements), 275–277, 395
Form W-4 (Employee Withholding Allowance Certificate)
highly compensated employees, Medicare tax, and, 208
purpose of, 47
retention of, in employee's permanent file, 52
sample, 48, 382–386
Form WH-347 (Certified Payroll), 28, 29
40-hour work week, 56–57, 61
401(k) retirement plan, 174
contributions, 5
description of, 175
number of participants and dollar contributions in, 332
popularity of, 157
purpose of, 157
student loan repayments and, 157
403(b) retirement plan, 174, 175
457 retirement plan, 174, 175
Fractions, conversion of minutes to, 120
Fraud
accounting, in small town, example, 317
check, 220–221
Computer Fraud and Abuse Act of 1986 (CFAA), 22
corporate, 64
detection of, in real time, 222
embezzlement, 17, 64
in employee termination, 67
fictitious employees, 17
"ghost" employees, 67
hacking and ransomware, 67
paycards to prevent, 65
payroll, 17, 68
payroll tampering, 64
preventing, 67–68
real-time detection of, 222
safeguarding of electronic records and, 67–68
using checks, 220–221
wire, 317
"Free" fringe benefits, 178
Fringe, 158
Fringe benefits. *See also* Cafeteria plans; Company vehicle, personal use of; Pre-tax deductions
change of tax calculations by, 159–161
defined, 156
employers not required to offer, 156
examples of, 156
excluded, not subject to FUTA taxes, 268
excluded from cafeteria plans, 268
exclusion rules and, 165–168
explanation of, 156, 158
"free," 178
hallmarks of, 158
as incentive, 156
including benefits in pay, 159
IRS on, 156, 160
most popular, for employees, 157
as negotiating tool for employees, 180
noncash, 180
payroll and business, 158–161
payroll taxes and, 159–161
payroll tax treatment and, 161
purpose of, 158
as significant amount of compensation, 158
state laws regarding, 159
summary of, 180
taxable, valuation of, 178
taxation and, 180
Tax Cuts and Job Act of 2017 (TCJA) and, 173
treatment under employment taxes, 397
trends in, 180
valuation rules and, 168–172
value of, 167
voluntary, 160
Full-time equivalent (FTE) employees, 14
Full-time students, as employees, 139
Full-time student wage, 139
Fundamental accounting equation, 320–321
Fundamental Payroll Certification (FPC), 444–445
Fund protection, 65
FUTA. *See* Federal Unemployment Tax Act (FUTA)

G

Gallup Work and Education poll (2017), 56–57
Garnishments, court-ordered/post-tax deductions
for consumer credit repayment, 216–217
lump-sum distributions and, 217
new-hire reporting and, 42
for new hires, 52
as post-tax deduction, 172, 175, 215–216
General Accounting Office (GAO), 22
General Data Protection Regulation (GDPR), 223
General Electric (GE), 24
General Journal
accounting conventions in, 322
completing payroll-related entries in, 323–327
defined, 322
employee pay-related entries in, 324
employer payroll-related entries in, 325
explanation of, 322
payroll accruals and reversals in, 326–327
payroll period, sample, 322
payroll register and, 324
payroll-related entries in, 325
transaction in, example, 322
in Wayland Custom Woodworking case study, 370–378
General Ledger
example of, 329–330
explanation of, 322, 328
payroll entries in, 329–330
posting example of, 322
posting practices for, 328
Generally Accepted Accounting Principles (GAAP), 316, 320
General valuation rule (GVR), 168
Georgia, administrative tax in, 253
"Ghost" employees, 67
Gift cards, 167
Gig economy, 41, 46, 65, 336
Gilroy (California) Federation of Paraeducators, 140
Glassdoor, 180
Goodyear Tire and Rubber Company, 4
Google, 6, 158, 180, 196
Government Against Misclassified Employees Operational Network (GAME ON) Task Force (Louisiana), 4
Governmental contracts, 9–10
Government employment, treatment under employment taxes, 398
GPS location tagging of employees, 61
Graziadio v. Culinary Institute of America (2016), 70
Great Depression (1930s), 9, 250
"Green" business, 221
Grossed-up net pay, 197–198. *See also* Minimum wage
Gross pay. *See also* Minimum wage; Overtime pay; Pay calculations
calculation of hours and fractions of hours, 120–123
combination pay methods to calculate, 132–135
commission-based employees and, 115–117
defined, 104, 141
FSA effect on, 163
for hourly workers, 115
for hourly workers in more than one job classification, 115
less 401(k) and insurance, 199
for piece-rate work, 118–120
pre-tax deductions withheld from, 172
for salaried workers, 112–114
special situations when calculating, 136–140
summary of computations for, 141
GrubHub, 46
Gusto, hosted payroll service, 25
Gym memberships, 166, 167, 172

H

Hacking/hackers, 67
Hasbro, 16
Head tax (Denver), 196, 213, 263, 286
Health insurance. *See also* Affordable Care Act of 2010 (ACA)
legislation addressing, 14
as pre-tax deduction, 162–165, 172–174
rising costs vs. pay raises, 195–196
subsidized, by employers, for employees, 172–174
supplemental, 174
Health Insurance Portability and Accountability Act of 1996 (HIPAA), 7, 8
Health savings account (HSA), 162, 163–165
High deductible health plan (HDHP), 163–165
Highly compensated employees
additional percent of Medicare tax on, 208–211
computation of net pay of, 209–211
Medicare taxes and, 248
Social Security taxes and, 247

HIPAA. *See* Health Insurance Portability and Accountability Act of 1996 (HIPAA)
Hiring packet, 52
Holiday time pay, 61, 113, 121, 282
Homeworkers, 398
H-1B visas, 54
Hospital employees, 125, 398
Hospitals, overtime for employees of, 125
Hosted payroll accounting software, 25
Hostile work environment, 7
Hosting services, 25
Hourly calculations of pay, 121
Hourly employees, 60. *See also* Overtime pay; Tipped employees
  calculating pay for, 115, 121–123
  defined, 104
  entering hours for, 60
  hourly pay with different rates, 115
  minimum wage provisions for, 106
  in more than one job classification, 115
  overtime pay and, 64, 115
  salary translation to hourly rates, 113–114
  time-and-a-half pay and, 64
Hourly rates, salary translation to, 113–114
Hourly vs. salary wages, 59–60, 104
Hours worked, 56–57
Household employees, 399
Hundred5, 279
Hundredth-hour system, 122–123

I

IBM, age discrimination by, 5
ICs. *See* Independent contractors (ICs)
Immigrants, legislation affecting, 6
Immigration, 6
Immigration Reform and Control Act of 1986 (IRCA), 6, 53
Incentive pay, 141
Incentive stock options (ISOs), 135
Income statement, 332–333
Income taxes. *See also* Federal income tax; Taxes
  historical background of, 9–10
  local, 213
  state, 196, 212–213
Income Tax Regulation §31.3301-1, 249
Income tax tables. *See* Federal income tax tables; State income tax tables
Independence, professional, 17
Independent contractors (ICs)
  classification of, 12, 46
  determination of, criteria for, 46
  employees vs., 41, 45–47, 54
  explanation of, 46–47
  lawsuits against employers permitted, 105
  not subject to the pay provisions of the FLSA, 12
Individual retirement account (IRA), 174, 175
Industrial Revolution, 9
Industrial workers, 398
Information safekeeping, 20
In-home companions, 106
Inside sales representative, 116
Institute of Management Accountants (IMA), 16
Insurance. *See also* Health insurance
  company-subsidized health insurance for employees, 172–174
  for employees, treatment under employment taxes, 399
  as pre-tax deduction, 162–165, 172–174
  supplemental health and disability, 174
Insurance agents or solicitors, 399
Integrity
  of accounting data, 65
  professional, 17
Interest loans with below-market interest rates, 399
Internal controls
  alternating duties and, 65–66
  authorized signers and, 63
  cross-training and, 65–66
  documentation controls and, 63
  document retention requirements and, 68–70
  electronic records and, 66–67
  employee file maintenance and, 66
  file security and, 65
  leave of absence and, 64–65
  need for, 62
  overtime approval and, 64
  overview of, 62–63
  payroll as a non-solo effort, 67–68
  review of time collected and, 64
  unpaid time off and, 64–65
Internal errors, 4
Internal Revenue Code
  on file maintenance, 66
  on nonqualified deferred compensation, 139–140
  payroll accounting defined by, 67
Internal Revenue Code 6056, 173
Internal Revenue Service (IRS)
  Affordable Care Act (ACA) of 2010 and, 173
  on benefits errors, 179
  on cafeteria plans, 162
  Circular E (Publication 15), 27, 59, 194
  on classification as American company, 249
  Code Section 414(n), 58
  common-law tests for employee vs. independent contractor, 46–47
  on *de minimis* benefits, 160
  on determining value of noncash benefits, 177
  on disability insurance, 174
  on document retention, 68
  on employee vs. independent contractor, 41, 46–47
  employer payroll tax deposit schedule, 255–257
  on failure to file returns, 70
  on file maintenance, 66
  financial records to be available for payroll audit, 68
  on flexible spending arrangements (FSAs), 163
  Foreign Earned Income Exclusion, 54
  Form 673, 54
  Forms 1095-A, B, and C, 14
  Form I-9 (Employee Eligibility Verification Form), 49–52
  Form SS-8 (Determination of Worker Status for Purposes of Employment Taxes and Income Tax Withholding), 45, 47
  Form W-4 (Employee Withholding Allowance Certificate), 47–48
  on fringe benefits, 156, 159
  health insurance pre-tax status guidelines, 172–173
  increase in number of employee audits and, 177
  investigations by, 317
  on leased and temporary employees, 58
  lien for failing to remit or file returns for income, 70
  on married same-sex couples, 8
  on Minimum Essential Coverage of Affordable Care Act, 14, 173
  on misclassification of workers, 45
  pay advice and, 159
  on payroll deposit frequencies, 256
  on payroll errors, 28
  preparation options and, 19
  Procedure 98-25, 1998-1 CB 689, 66
  Publication 15 (Circular E), 27, 59, 194
  Publication 15-b, 156, 160, 166, 168, 170, 171, 174
  Publication 502, 163
  Publication 535, 166
  Publication 1779, 47
  on qualified insurance benefits, 162
  Regulation 26 CFR 1.6001, 66, 68
  on retirement contributions, 5
  retirement plans and, 174
  Revenue Procedure 98-25, 1998-1 CB 689, 66
  Revision Ruling 2004-55, 174
  same-sex couples to be treated as married for tax purposes, 8
  §1.199A-2(b)(2)(ii), 58
  Section 125 plans, 162–165
  §6672, 280
  on the special accounting rule, 177
  spreadsheets and charts by, 19
  statutory employees defined by, 54
  Tax Cuts and Job Act of 2017 (TCJA) and, 15
  on tax treatment of short- and long-term disability insurance, 174
  on temporary employees, 58
  2019 cap on pre-tax retirement plan contributions, 175
  on voluntary fringe benefits, 160
  on wages earned prior to death of employee, 140
  waiving of penalties for failure to deposit and file, 278–279
  website of, 18
International Federation of Accountants (IFAC), 16
Internet, 22
Internet-based access to personnel files, 25
Internet-based accounting software, 26–27
Internet-based payroll systems and software, 26–27
Internet-based systems, for payroll processing, 26–27
Internet of Things (IoT), 335
Internet technology, cryptocurrency and, 222–223
Intuit, 19
Intuit Payroll, hosted payroll service, 25
Iowa, state income tax of, 214
IRA (individual retirement account), 174, 175
Iron Mountain, 72
IRS. *See* Internal Revenue Service (IRS)
IRS Circular E (Publication 15), 28, 59, 194
IRS Code 6056, 173
IRS Code for health insurance plans to qualify for pre-tax status, 172–173
IRS Code Sections 104(a)(3) and 105(a), 174
IRS forms. *See Forms entries*
IRS Letter 201833012, 157
IRS Notice 1036, 197–198
IRS Revision Ruling 2004-55, 174
iTookOff paid leave tracker app, 61

J

Jessie Chavez v. PVH Corporation (2013), 65
Job leveling, 112
Job swapping, 74
Joint employers, 36–37
Jury duty, 138

K

Kansas "paperless payroll law," 235–236
King County, Washington, 124
Kroc, Ray, 21
Kronos Inc., 331
Kronos system, 24

L

Labor distribution, 281
Labor distribution report, 281–282
Labor expenses, company profits and, 280–282
Labor planning. *See* Employer payroll tax responsibilities
Labor reports, 335
Labor trends, 335
Labor usage report, 335

Large companies, 24–25
Law enforcement employees, 60, 106, 136
Learned professional, 56
Leased employees, 57–58
Lease value rule, 168–170
Leave of absence, 64–65
Leave-sharing plans, 399
Ledbetter, Lilly, 4, 69, 92
Legal environment, trends in, 30
Legal framework. *See also entries for specific legislation;* Fair Labor Standards Act of 1938 (FSLA)
  background of, 9–15
  challenges in, 30
  E-Verify program and, 15
  federal income taxes and, 9, 12
  governmental contracts and, 9–10
  health care coverage and, 14
  independent contractors and, 12
  for information safekeeping, 20
  minimum wage and, 10, 11
  overtime provisions, 11–12
  privacy acts and, 22
  requirements of information safekeeping, 20
  social welfare system and, 9–15
  timeline of, 10
  trends in, 30
  worker protections and, 9–15
  workers' compensation and, 12–13
Legislation. *See also entries for specific legislation;* Fair Labor Standards Act of 1938
  common elements among privacy laws, 22
  payroll and business, 4–9
  payroll timeline, 10
  requirements of information safekeeping, 20
  on severance packages, 71
Liabilities
  in financial accounting, 320–321
  payroll-related, 332
Liability accounts, 324
Lien, for failing to remit or file returns for income, 70
Lilly Ledbetter Fair Pay Act of 2009, 4, 69, 92
Living wage
  defined, 11, 59
  minimum wage vs., 11
Local employer-only payroll taxes, 253
Local income tax, 213
Long-distance truck drivers, 105
Long-term disability insurance, 174
Lookback period, 255–256
Los Angeles Unified School District, 68
Louisiana Department of Revenue, 4
Lump-sum distributions, subject to garnishments, 217
Lyft, 111

M

Maggiano's Little Italy, 17
Maine, employer-paid Competitive Skills Scholarship Program tax, 253
Making Work Pay provisions, in ARRA, 8
Mandated deductions, 160, 175, 194, 215–216
Manual payroll systems, 25, 27–28, 54, 211
Maricopa County Community College, 218
Massachusetts
  MIT living wage calculator, 59
  overtime audit example, 69
  paid sick leave in, 12
MasterCard, 222
Material contribution, 46
Mazzant, Amos, 56
McDonald's Corporation, 12, 19, 21
McElrath v. Uber Technologies, 135
Meals and snacks, 167
Medicare tax
  about, 10
  Affordable Care Act (ACA) of 2010 and, 208–211
  computations for, 207–211
  employee and employer responsibilities, 246–248
  employer deposits for, 20
  explanation of, 207, 208
  no maximum wage base for, 208
  special classes of federal tax withholding and, 396–402
Mesa County, Colorado, 196
Microsoft, 24
Microsoft Dynamics GP, 26–27
Microsoft Excel, 28, 129
Mid-year employer tax reporting and deposits, 258–277
Military service members, 7
Minimum essential coverage requirement, of Affordable Care Act, 14, 173
Minimum salary, for exempt workers, 56
Minimum wage
  background of, 106–108
  commission-based pay vs., 116, 117
  conditions of, 11
  creation of, 10
  employee rights and (FLSA), 44
  example, 105
  Fair Labor Standards Act (FLSA) of 1938 and, 11, 105
  hourly rates (2019), 107
  legislation addressing, 106
  living wage vs., 11
  no maximum wage cap on, 11
  for nonexempt workers, 106–111
  overtime for, 124
  piece-rate work and, 118
  rates vary per state, 59
  regulation of, by the Fair Labor Standards Act, 11
  in restaurant industry, 107
  salaried wage compared to, 114
  state rates (2019), 107
  state variations in, 107–108
  state vs. federal, 108
  sub-minimum wage situations and, 138–139
  for tipped employees, 108–111
  for tipped employees, by state (2018), 109–110
  violations of, examples, 20
Misclassification of workers, 4, 12, 26, 47
MIT living wage calculator, 59
Mobile payments, 223
Monthly payroll, 43, 45
Monthly schedule depositors, 256
Mountain View, California, 196
Multistate Employer Notification Form for New Hire Reporting, 53
myPay Solutions, 19, 24–25

N

Nannies, 106
National Association of Certified Professional Bookkeepers (NACPB), 443
National Federation of Independent Business (NFIB), 221
National Labor Relations Board (NLRB), 54
Net pay. *See also* Federal income tax; Pay calculations; Pay methods; Post-tax deductions; Pre-tax deductions
  computing, 196–198
  defined, 104, 194, 196
  employee advances and overpayments and, 218
  explanation of, 196
  federal income tax withholding amounts and, 198–207
  grossed-up, 197–198
  local income taxes and, 213
  Medicare tax and, 207–211
  Social Security tax and, 207–211
  with state income tax, 212–213, 214
  state-specific taxes and, 212–213
  steps in computation, 196–198
  summary of, 224
  trends in, 223
New Hampshire, sick and vacation time, 159
New hire reporting
  classification of workers and, 41
  information required in employee files, 42
New hires. *See also* Employees
  database entry procedures for, 54–55
  documentation for, 47–54
  foreign workers, 53–54
  hiring packets contents for, 52
  notification to state offices for, 53
  reporting procedures for, 47–54
  statutory, 54
New Jersey, Diane B. Allen Equal Pay Act in, 16
Newspaper carriers and vendors, 399
New York, taxes in, 212
New York City Taxi and Limousine Commission, 111
New York State Comptroller, 220
Next business day schedule depositors, 256, 257
No maximum wage base, for Medicare taxes, 208
Non-Appropriated Fund Health Benefits Program (Department of Defense), 172
Noncash award, 166
Noncash compensation, 165
Noncash fringe benefits, 180
Noncash payments, treatment under employment taxes, 400
Non-discretionary bonuses, 180
Nonexempt salaried workers, 57
Nonexempt workers. *See also* Salaried nonexempt workers
  classification of, 60
  defined, 11, 104, 106
  exempt workers vs., 55–58
  explanation of, 60, 106
  FLSA and, 60
  fluctuating workweek for, 60
  40 hours per week standard for, 105
  hourly, 57
  minimum wage and, 106–111
  overtime calculation for, 124–125
  overtime pay for, 57, 60
  pay calculations for, 60
  salaried, 57, 60, 104, 112
  salaried, overtime pay for, 127–128
Nonexistent employees, 67
Nonprofit organizations, 400
Nonqualified deferred compensation, 139–140
Nonresident aliens, 396
Nontax debts owed to federal agencies, 176
Northwestern University, 54
Nurses, 60

O

Oakdale, Louisiana, 320
"Obamacare." *See* Affordable Care Act of 2010 (ACA)
Obergefell v. Hodges (2015), 5, 7
Objectivity, accounting, 17
Occupational Privilege Tax (OPT; head tax; Denver), 196, 213, 263, 286
Occupational Safety and Health Act of 1970 (OSHA), 5, 8, 254
Office of Civil Rights, 8
Office of Management and Budget (OMB), 53
Ohio, use of blockchain technology by, for payroll taxes, 223

Old-Age, Survivors, and Disability Insurance (OASDI), 10, 208. *See also* Social Security tax
On-call time, 136–137
Online banking, 219
Online banks, 19
Online privacy, 22. *See also* Privacy
OnPay, hosted payroll service, 25
On-site gourmet meals, 158
Oregon, paid sick leave in, 12
OSHA (Occupational Safety and Health Act of 1970), 5, 8, 254
Outside sales representatives, 112, 116
Outsourced payroll systems, 28, 129
Outsourcing, of payroll preparation, 19, 28
Overhead allocations, 332
Overpayment, of employee pay, 20, 64, 68, 218
Overtime pay, 104
  approval of, 64
  calculation of, 61, 123–128
  Eight and Eighty (8 and 80) rule, 125
  for employees of hospitals and residential care facilities, 125
  for employees who work in two or more separate functions, 128
  Fair Labor Standards Act (FLSA) of 1938 on, 11–12, 60, 114, 115
  for hospitals and residential care facilities, 125
  hourly workers and, 60, 115
  misclassification of employees and, 12
  nonexempt employees and, 57, 124–125
  for piece-rate employees, 119, 127
  requirements for, 60
  for salaried nonexempt workers, 127–128
  standard, 124–125
  for tipped employees, 126
  tracking of, 141
  violations of, examples, 20
Overtime reports, 335
Owners' equity, in financial accounting, 320–321

P

Paid leave provisions, 30
Paid sick leave, 12
Paid sick time. *See* Sick time
Paid time off, 11–12, 282
PAM Transport Inc., 105
"Paperless payroll law" (Kansas), 235–236
Paper shredders, 72
Parking subsidies, 171
Partners, 165, 400
Part-time employees, 263
Pay advice, 159, 219
Pay calculations. *See also* Gross pay; Net pay
  based on hours and fractions of hours, 120–123
  combination pay methods for, 132–135
  for hourly workers, 115
  hundredth-hour system for, 122–123
  overtime, for nonexempt employees, 124–125
  for piece-rate employees, 118–120
  quarter-hour system for, 122–123
  for salaried nonexempt workers, 127–128
  of weekly regular time and overtime, 61
Paycards
  as employee pay method, 221–222
  explanation of, 26
  popularity of, 222
  pros and cons of, 221–222
  security features of, 65
Paychex®, 16, 19, 28, 129, 282
Pay cycles/periods, 43, 45, 59
Pay methods, 218
  cash as, 219
  checks as, 219–221
  cryptocurrency as, 222–223
  direct deposit as, 221
  paycards as, 221–222
  summary of, 224
  trends in, 223
Pay period, 42
Pay period computation, 59
Pay raises, health insurance costs and, 195–196
Pay rate, 59–60
Pay records. *See also* Documentation
  calculations of weekly regular time and overtime in, 61
  documentation for, 58–61
  entering hours in, 60
  explanation of, 59
  file maintenance for, 66
  file security for, 65
  overtime calculation in, 61
  pay rate and, 59–60
  privacy and, 22, 65
  technological advances and, 59
Payroll
  access to, via smartphones, 19
  benefit analysis as function of, 282–285
  as business expense, 278–280
  certified, 28–29
  economic effects of, 331–332
  fringe benefits and, 158–161
  Kansas "paperless payroll law" and, 235–236
  legislation pertaining to, 4–9
  as non-solo effort, 67–68
Payroll accountants. *See also* Accountants
  certification for, 441–445
  confidentiality and, 16, 40, 62
  decision-making process of, 19
  due care by, 17
  integrity of, 17
  math skills needed by, 120–128
  new hires and, 41
  objectivity and independence of, 17
  responsibilities of, 40
  social obligations and objectivity of, 17
  sources of information for, 18
  vital role of, 19
Payroll accounting. *See also* Accounting
  cloud-based computing and, 28
  contemporary practices in, 18–23
  ethical guidelines for, 16–18
  function of, 4
  IRS definition of, 67
  legal framework for, 9–15
  trends in, 28
Payroll audit, 21, 68–69, 320
Payroll certification information, 441–445
Payroll changes, staying current with, 18
Payroll checks
  designated signatories for, 63
  use of, 219–221
Payroll-dedicated checking account, 219–220
Payroll disbursement. *See* Pay methods
Payroll documentation. *See* Documentation
Payroll draw method, 133–134
Payroll effects, on the accounting system, 331–332
Payroll entries, in accounting reports, 332–335
Payroll errors, 4, 28, 141
Payroll fraud, 17, 68. *See also* Fraud
Payroll legislation, timeline of, 10
Payroll practices, 30
  common mistakes in, 26
  integrated software packages for, 19
  in large businesses, 24–25
  modern tools of, 18
  overview of, 18–19
  preparation options and, 19–21
  privacy protection and, 21–22
  in small businesses, 25–26
  summary of, 29
Payroll preparation methods, 19–21
Payroll procedures. *See also* Internal controls
  cross-training of payroll professionals and, 65–66
  document destruction and, 72–73
  document retention requirements and, 68–70
  dual focus of, 40
  employee classification information and, 45–47
  employee documentation and, 45–55
  employee file maintenance, 58–61
  employee information requirements, 42–43
  employee termination and, 70–72
  entering new employees into the database, 54–55
  exempt vs. nonexempt workers and, 55–58
  identifying, 42–43, 44
  internal controls for, 62–70
  pay cycles/periods and, 43, 45
  pay records, 58–61
  record retention and, 68–70
  reporting new employees, 47–54
  summary of, 74
  trends in, 74
Payroll process flowchart, 337
Payroll processing
  certified payroll and, 28–29
  computer-based systems for, 26
  cross-training of payroll professionals and, 65–66
  documentation controls and, 63
  Internet-based systems and, 26–27
  in large businesses, 24–25
  manual systems in, 27–28
  options for, 24–29
  outsourced payroll systems for, 28
  in small businesses, 25–26
  trend in, 26
Payroll record maintenance, 66
Payroll records
  electronic records and, 66–67
  file maintenance for, 66–70
Payroll register
  data for, 129–130
  defined, 129
  employee earnings records and, 318–320
  explanation of, 129, 318–319
  function of, 318–319
  to General Journal entries, 324
  method to complete, 323–327
  retention of, 69
  sample, 130
  summary of, 336
  tracking employee compensation with, 130–131
Payroll regulations timeline, 10
Payroll-related business expenses, 331–332
Payroll-related General Journal entries. *See* General Journal
Payroll-related liabilities, 332
Payroll review process, 62–63
Payroll service vendors, 24–25
Payroll systems. *See also* Internal controls
  computer-based, 26
  document destruction in, 72–73
  Internet-based, 26–27
  manual, 27–28, 54, 211
  outsourced, 28, 129
  pay record maintenance in, 66
  planning for establishment of, 29
Payroll tampering, 64
Payroll taxes, fringe benefits and, 159–161
Payroll tax fraud, 317
Payroll tax reports, 284
Payroll tax treatment, fringe benefits and, 159–161
Payroll understatement, 4

Payroll verification process, 64
Penalties for failure to deposit and failure to file, 278–279
Pension payments, 140
Pension plans, 5, 400
Percentage method, of federal income tax computation
  examples of, 206–207
  explanation of, 203
  tables for, 204–205, 404–405
Periodic tax reports, 320
Period totals, 320
Permanent Worker Visa Preference Categories, 53
Personal identification number (PIN), 61
Personal income tax (PIT; California), 212
Personal Responsibility, Work and Family Promotion Act of 2002, 7
Personal Responsibility and Work Opportunity Reconciliation Act of 1996 (PRWOR), 7, 41
Personal use of company vehicle. *See* Company vehicle, personal use of
Personnel files, employee Internet-based access to, 25
Personnel records
  defined, 20
  Internet-based access to, 25
Pew Internet and American Life Project (2014), 219
Piece rate, 60
Piece-rate compensation, 60
Piece-rate employees
  breaks and rest periods for, 120
  calculation of compensation for, 118–120
  defined, 104
  overtime calculation for, 127
  overtime pay for, 119
  rest time for, 60
Piece-rate work
  calculation of compensation for, 118–120
  California Labor Code on, 118
  FLSA requirement for, 118
  gross pay for, 118–120
  types of occupations, 118–119
Pine Bluff, Arkansas, living wage ordinance, 11
Pittsburgh, Pennsylvania, living wage ordinance, 11
Point-of-sale (POS) purchases, 222
Police, 60, 106, 136
Portals, employee, on company websites, 24, 25, 59
Portland, Maine, living wage ordinance, 11
Post-closing trial balance, 332, 334
Posting practices, for General Ledger, 328
Post-tax deductions
  charitable contributions as, 175–176, 214–215
  consumer credit garnishment as, 216–217
  court-mandated, 172
  court-ordered garnishments as, 176
  defined, 172
  employee advances and overpayments and, 218
  explanation of, 172, 180, 214
  garnishments as, 215–216
  pre-tax deductions vs., 172–176
  union dues as, 176, 217
Predictive analytics, 222
Predictive software, 27
Pregnant workers, Civil Rights Act of 1964 and Executive Order 11478 protections, 5
Premium only plan (POP), 162–163
Prepaid commuter passes, 171
Preparation options, 19–21
Presidential memorandum M-17-16, 56
Pre-tax deductions. *See also* Cafeteria plans; Fringe benefits
  defined, 172
  explanation of, 172
  insurance as, 162–165
  post-tax deductions vs., 172–176
  purpose of, 156
  retirement plans and, 174–175
  Social Security and Medicare taxes computed with, 207–211
  supplemental health and disability insurance, 174
  as voluntary deduction, 172
Prevailing wage, 9
Prince George's County, Maryland, living wage ordinance, 11
Privacy
  company efforts to protect, 21–22
  of data, 65
  in information in payroll files, 22
  in large businesses, 24–25
  online, 22
  personnel, protection of, 20
Privacy Act of 1974, 20, 22
Privacy acts, 21–22
Privacy laws, federal, 73
Privacy protection, 21–22
Privilege taxes, 264, 286
Prizes, 166
Productive time, for piece rate employees, 60
Professional competence, 17
Professional Employer Organizations (PEOs), 58
Professional exemption, 56
Professionalism, accountants and, 16–17
Profit sharing, 174
Project labor agreements (PLAs), 189
Pro-Shred, 72
Protecting Americans from Tax Hikes Act of 2015 (PATH), 8
Prove, in payroll register, 130
PRWOR (Personal Responsibility and Work Opportunity Reconciliation Act of 1996), 7, 41
Publication 15 (Circular E), of the IRS, 27, 59, 194
Publication 15-b, 156, 160, 166, 168, 170, 171, 174
Publication 502 (IRS), 163
Publication 535 (IRS), 166
Publication 1779 (IRS), 47
Public Company Accounting Oversight Board (PCAOB), 17
Public employee compensatory time, 136
Public Law 115-97 (Tax Cuts and Jobs Act), 14–15
PULSE payroll software, 37
Punch clocks, 24

Q

Qualified insurance benefits, 162
Qualified plan, 166
Qualified Section 125 (cafeteria) plans, 209
Quarter-hour system, 121–122
Quarterly schedule depositors, 256
QuickBooks, 19, 26–27, 129, 219, 222
Quick-Read (QR) codes, 61

R

Radio frequency time cards, 25
Railroad Retirement Act, 400
Ransomware, 67
Real-time business analysis, 27
Real-time fraud detection, 222
Recession of 2007–2009, 5
Record identifiers, 67
Record logging, 67
Record retention requirements, federal, 69
Recovery breaks, 118
Regulation E (FDIC), 222
Relationship of parties, 47
Religious exemptions, 400
Remit, 325
Reporting periods, employer, 255–257
Resident aliens, 249, 396
Residential care facilities, overtime for employees of, 125
Resignation, employee, 70–72
Restaurant industry, wages in, 107. *See also* Tipped employees
Rest breaks, 118, 134
Rest time, 60
Retention schedule, 69
Retirement age, 10
Retirement plans
  contribution requirements for, 10
  defined benefit plans, 174
  defined contribution plans, 174
  employer contributions to, 5, 174, 263
  IRS on, 5
  Medicare and, 10
  treatment under employment taxes, 400
  types of, 174–175
Retroactive pay, 140, 217
Return on employee investment (ROEI), 353
Revenue Act of 1978, 157
Reversal, of General Journal entries, 327
Review process, 62–63. *See also* Internal controls
Richmond Living Wage Program (Virginia), 59
Right-to-work laws (2019), 8
Rotation of duties, 66
Rounding, 121–122, 360
Rule, in payroll register, 130

S

Sage, 19
Sage 100cloud, 19
Sage 100 Standard, 19, 26–27, 219
Salaried exempt employees, 59–60, 112–113
Salaried nonexempt employees, 60, 104, 112, 127–128
Salaried workers
  defined, 11
  exempt, 59–60, 104
  gross pay for, 112–114
  hourly wage computation for, 121
  minimum wage comparison and, 114
  nonexempt, 104
  salary translation to hourly rates, 113–114
  unpaid leave for, 113–114
Salary, 104
  determination of, 121
  for exempt workers, 56
  hourly wages vs., 59–60
  minimum wage vs., 114
  translation to hourly rates, 113–114
Salary basis, 56–57
salary.com, 4, 180
Salary plus commission and draw pay method, 134–135
Salespersons, 401
Sales representatives, 116
Same-sex marriage
  COBRA coverage for spouses in, 6
  couples treated as married for tax purposes, 8
  IRS on, 8
  legislation addressing, 5, 6, 7
  "spouse" defined in, by U.S. Department of Labor, 7
San Leandro, California, living wage ordinance, 11
Sarbanes–Oxley Act of 2002 (SOX)
  documentation of payroll and retirement plans, 20
  document retention and rotation of auditors' duties, 65
  protections of, 8, 16
Savings Incentive Match Plan for Employees (SIMPLE), 174, 175
Schedule B, for Form 941, 258, 262

Schedule deposit frequencies, 256–257
Scholars, 401–402
Scholarships, 401
S corporation, 165, 400
Scott v. Scott, 167
Seattle, Washington, commuter passes (2020), 171
Section 125 plans, 162–165, 396. *See also* Cafeteria plans
Secure Choice Retirement Savings Program (SB-1234; California), 5
Secure sockets layer (SSL) encryption, 24
Securities and Exchange Commission (SEC), 11
Security, 65. *See also* Privacy
Semimonthly payroll, 43, 45
Semiweekly schedule depositors, 256, 257, 258
SEP (Simplified Employee Pension), 174, 175
Separation of duties, 68
Severance packages, 71
Severance pay, 401
Sexual orientation, Civil Rights Act of 1964 and Executive Order 11478 protections, 5
Shared employees, 24
Shareholders, 165, 400
Shavertown, Pennsylvania, 312
Shield Packaging of Massachusetts, 20
Short-term disability insurance, 174
Sick leave, 12, 61, 113, 141, 180
Sick pay, 121, 401
Sick time, 30, 61, 71, 121, 159
Sign-on bonuses, 217
SIMPLE (Savings Incentive Match Plan for Employees), 174, 175
SIMPLE 401(k) plan, 174
Simplified Employee Pension (SEP), 174, 175
Sixteenth Amendment, 9
Slater, Lisa, 7
Sleep time, 105, 106, 137–138
Small businesses, 25–26, 28
Smartphone apps, 19, 24
Snacks and meals, 167
Social obligations, accountants and, 17
Social Security Act of 1935 (SSA), 10, 207
Social Security Administration (SSA), 207
Social Security tax
computations for, 207–211
deposit schedules for, 256–257
employee and employer responsibilities, 246–248
explanation of, 207, 208
highly compensated employees and, 247
special classes of federal tax withholding and, 396–402
2019 benefits payments, 11
withholding of, 207
Social welfare legislation, 9–12
Social welfare system, 9
Society for Human Resource Management (SHRM), Family and Medical Leave Act (FMLA) of 1993 and, 7
Software. *See also* Technology
for accounting, 26, 316, 322–323, 336
Artificial Intelligence (AI), 27, 323, 331, 335
Artificial Intelligence-based systems, 27
benefits to business owners, 19, 21
breaches in, 68
in computer-based payroll systems, 26, 67
for converting minutes into payable units, 120
for customizing benefits, 179
for data wiping tools, 73
for hosted payroll accounting, 25
increase in use of, 322–323
in Internet-based payroll systems, 26–27
outsourcing to external providers via, 19
password encryption, for paycards, 222
for paycards, 222
for pay records, 59
for payroll practices, 19
for payroll preparation, 19, 67
for payroll register, 129
predictive, 27
PULSE, 37
for sanitizing electronic records, 73
for small companies, 25
taxes submitted through, 20
Sole proprietors, 165
Sotheby's, 157
Special accounting rule, 177–178
Special pay situations, 136–140
"Specialty occupation," 54
"Spouse," defined, 7
Spreadsheet programs, for payroll registers, 129
SSL (secure sockets layer) encryption, 24
Stakeholders, 334
Starbucks, 160
State Comptroller of New York, 220
State Disability Insurance (SDI; California), 212, 263
State guidelines
for minimum wage, 106–108
for reporting new hires, 53
for termination pay, 69
State income taxes, 196, 212–213
State income tax information and tax tables, 426–431
State revenue department addresses, telephone numbers, and URLs, 432–440
State-specific taxes, 212–213
State tax remittance, 263
State Unemployment Tax Act (SUTA)
determination of, criteria for, 252
employer deposits to, 20–21
examples of, 252–253
explanation of, 10–11, 248, 251, 252
purpose of, 248
requirements of, 250
state variations in, 248, 251–252
wage base and rates of (2019), 251–252
wage base of, 250
Statutory deductions, 246. *See also* Employer payroll tax responsibilities
Statutory employees, 54
Student loan repayments, 180
Student loan repayments, 401(k) contributions and, 157
Student loans, 176
Students
full-time, as employees, 139
full-time, wages of, 139
treatment under employment taxes, 402
in vocational education program, 139
Sub-minimum wage situations, 138–139
Subsidized health insurance coverage, 172–174
Supplemental health and disability insurance, 174
Supplemental Unemployment Compensation Plan Benefits, 402
Supreme Court. *See* U.S. Supreme Court
Supreme Court of Georgia, 167
SurePayroll, hosted payroll service, 25
SUTA. *See* State Unemployment Tax Act (SUTA)

T

T-accounts, 321
Take-home pay, 194. *See also* Net pay
TALX (Equifax), 22
Taxable benefit withholdings, 177–178
Tax Cuts and Job Act of 2017 (TCJA)
ACA minimum essential coverage and, 173
Affordable Care Act (ACA) and, 3
employers, FMLA, and, 7
enactment of, 14–15
leased employees and profit deduction and, 58
Tax deposits, employer
deposit frequencies, 256–257
lookback period, 255–256
Taxes. *See also entries for specific types of taxes;* Income taxes
employee- and employer-paid, 247
historical background of, 9
overview of, 20–21
Tax remittance, 263
Tax reports, periodic, 320
Tax withholding, 20–21
Taylor, Frederick, 118
Teachers, 401–402
Technology. *See also* Software
access to payroll via smartphones, 19
Artificial Intelligence (AI), 27, 323, 331, 335
blockchain, 222–223, 335
changes due to, 336
cryptocurrency and, 222–223
digital documentation, 58
electronic accounting programs, 19
integrated software packages, 19
password encryption, for paycards, 222
for paycard protection, 222
privacy issues and, 22
for tracking employee attendance and calculating pay, 61
Visa Advanced Authorization technology, 222
vulnerability of company data caused by, 62
Temporary employees, 57–58
Termination. *See* Employee termination
Termination pay, 217
Time-and-a-half overtime pay, 64
Time cards, 64, 114
Time clocks, 24
Time collection, 64
Time-collection devices, 24
TimeDock app, 61
Timekeeping, 25
Time-measurement systems, 25
Time off, 11–12, 64, 282
Time reported, 64
Time sheets, 24
TimeStation app, 61
Tip credit, 108
Tipped employee minimum wage vs. federal minimum wage, 108
Tipped employees
Employer penalties for inappropriate withholding of tips, 15
examples of, 108
exempt from minimum wage standards under FLSA, 11
explanation of, 108
Form W-2 for, 272
lower wages for, 106
minimum hourly wages for, by state (2018), 109–110
minimum wage for, 108–111
overtime calculation for, 126
state information for (2019), 107
2019 minimum hourly wage, 106
wages for, 106
Tipped wages, 106, 108
Tips, 402
Toll roads, 171
Tom's of Maine, 21
Total, in payroll register, 130
Total compensation report, 179, 284–285
Tracking
of employee compensation, with payroll register, 130–131
of employee payroll expenses, 280
Trainees, 401–402

Transaction analysis, using T-accounts, 321
Transit pass, 171
Transparency, 17, 62, 74, 286
Transportation benefits, 171
Travel time, 137
Trend reports, 335
Trial balance, 332, 334
Troester v. Starbucks Corp. (2018), 160
Truck drivers, 105
Trump, Donald J., 15
26 IRC Section 3306, 263
29 CFR 2510, 332
Twitter, 158

U

Uber
  drivers as independent contractors, 47
  lawsuit over incentive stock options, 135
  New York City per-minute, per-mile formula for, 111
Underpayment, of employee pay, 64
Unemployment taxes. *See* Federal Unemployment Tax Act (FUTA); State Unemployment Tax Act (SUTA)
Unemployment tax reporting, 263, 268–269
Uniformed Services Employment and Reemployment Rights Act of 1994 (USERRA), 7
Unilever Corporation, 21
Union dues, as post-tax deduction, 172, 175, 176, 217
Unpaid leave, 113–114
Unpaid time off, 64–65
Unsafe conditions, company provided vehicles and, 171
U.S. Bureau of Labor Statistics
  accounting jobs forecast, 4
  average number of hours worked per week, 57
  average number of weekly overtime hours (2019), 124
  on fringe benefits, 158
  growing level of employment figures, 335
  overtime statistics, 124
  wage determination by, 10
U.S. Census Bureau, 2015 child support figures by, 52
U.S. Citizenship and Immigration Service (USCIS), 52, 53
U.S. Department of Defense, Non-Appropriated Fund Health Benefits Program, 172
U.S. Department of Health and Human Services Privacy Act 09-40-0006, 22
U.S. Department of Homeland Security, 52, 69
U.S. Department of Labor
  on back pay to former employees, 71
  on benefits errors, 179
  common types of employees, 56
  on discretionary and non-discretionary bonuses, 180
  Employee Benefits Security Administration, 332
  employee classification, FLSA stipulations and, 112
  on employee tips, 15
  on employee vs. independent contractor, 41
  employers exempt from paying federal minimum wage, 106
  Employment Standards Administration Wage and Hour Division of, 10
  on exempt and nonexempt employees, 106
  exempt classification and, 56
  guidelines for exempt employees, 106
  independent contractor classification and, 12
  information required in employee files, 42
  investigations of employee classifications, 112
  investigations of service members' rights by, 7
  minimum wage exemptions and, 114
  on misclassification of employees, 12
  OCFP-1, 21
  on overtime pay, 12
  privacy and, 22
  on service members' rights, 7
  sleep-time requirement of, 106
  "spouse" defined by, 7
  Wage and Hour Division of, 10, 47, 140, 217
  website of, 10, 18
  on whistle-blowers, 8
"Use it or lose it" provision, 163
U.S. Food and Drug Administration, 67
U.S. statute 20 CFR § 655.700, 54
U.S. Supreme Court
  definitions of "spouse" updated, 7
  employment discrimination and, 4–5
  independent contractors may sue employers, 105
  Lilly Ledbetter and, 4
  on male/female pay rates, 4
  Obergefell v. Hodges (2015), 5, 7
  repeal of Defense of Marriage Act (DOMA), 7–8
  on same-sex marriage, 5, 7
  U.S. v. Windsor (2013), 7–8
U.S. v. Windsor (2013), 7–8
U.S. workers in foreign subsidiaries, 54
Utah Employer Quarterly Wage List and Contribution Report, 392

V

Vacation days, 71
Vacation time, 61, 113, 159
Valuation of taxable fringe benefits, 178
Valuation rules, fringe benefits and, 168–172
Vanderbilt University, 282
Vermont, paid sick leave in, 12
Veterans Opportunity to Work Act of 2011, 7
Virginia, Richmond Living Wage Program, 59
Virtual marketplace, 74
Visa Advanced Authorization technology, 222
Visa Inc., 222
Visas, for foreign workers, 54
Voluntary deductions, 172, 180, 364
Voluntary fringe benefits, 160
VPN (virtual private network), 24

W

W-2 Wage and Tax Form
  electronic delivery of, 26
  example of, 274–275
  examples of, 27
  explanation of, 269, 272, 273
  forms, 393–395
  gift cards as compensation on, 167
  insurance coverage by employer on, 173–174
  matching final annual pay to, 269, 272–275
  purpose of, 179
  Social Security and Medicare wages on, 272
  for tipped employees, 272
W-4 Form. *See* Form W-4 (Employee Withholding Allowance Certificate)
Wage and Hour Division (U.S. Department of Labor), 10, 47, 140, 217
Wage base, 208
Wage-bracket method, for federal income tax, 199–203, 406–425
Wages
  back wages, 47
  for deceased employees, 140
  salary vs. hourly, 59
Wait time, 137
Walsh–Healey Public Contracts Act of 1936, 10
Washington
  minimum wage and, 107
  paid sick leave in, 12
Wave, 27
Wayland Custom Woodworking (continuing payroll project)
  forms used for, 379–395
  general information about, 360–369
  General Journal entries, 370–378
Weather changes, 245
Web-based applications, 61
Web-based portals, 24
Weekly payroll, 43, 45
Wellness programs, 336
Western District Court of Arkansas, 105
Whistle-blower provision, 8
Wilkes-Barre Bookkeeping LLC, 312
Wire fraud, 317
Wire transfers, 255
Withholding
  additional, 47, 52
  amounts, related to benefits, 177
  taxable benefits, treatment of, 177–178
Withholding taxes, 9, 12, 14–15, 20–21, 198–207
Work direction, 46
Worker classification, 4, 12, 26, 41, 46, 47, 59–60
Workers' compensation (workers' comp)
  categories of injuries for, 254
  defined, 12
  employer requirements for, 12–13, 253–254
  explanation of, 12
  laws, by state, 13
  premium computation for, 254
  when required, 12
Work Opportunity Tax Credit, 8
Workplace diversity, 6
Workplace prizes, 166

X

Xero, 27

Y

Year-end employer tax reporting and deposits, 258–277
Young employees, 10, 138

Z

Zenefits app, 65